CHILDREN AND CHILDHOOD IN THE OTTOMAN EMPIRE

Edinburgh Studies on the Ottoman Empire
Series Editor: Kent F. Schull

Published and forthcoming titles

Migrating Texts: Circulating Translations around the Ottoman Mediterranean
Edited by Marilyn Booth

Ottoman Sunnism: New Perspectives
Edited by Vefa Erginbaş

Jews and Palestinians in the Late Ottoman Era, 1908–1914: Claiming the Homeland
Louis A. Fishman

Spiritual Vernacular of the Early Ottoman Frontier: The Yazıcıoğlu Family
Carlos Grenier

Armenians in the Late Ottoman Empire: Migration, Mobility Control and Sovereignty, 1885–1915
David Gutman

The Kizilbash-Alevis in Ottoman Anatolia: Sufism, Politics and Community
Ayfer Karakaya-Stump

Çemberlitaş Hamami in Istanbul: The Biographical Memoir of a Turkish Bath
Nina Macaraig

Nineteenth-Century Local Governance in Ottoman Bulgaria: Politics in Provincial Councils
Safa Saraçoğlu

Prisons in the Late Ottoman Empire: Microcosms of Modernity
Kent F. Schull

Ruler Visibility and Popular Belonging in the Ottoman Empire
Darin Stephanov

Children and Childhood in the Ottoman Empire: From the 15th to the 20th Century
Edited by Gülay Yılmaz and Fruma Zachs

euppublishing.com/series/esoe

CHILDREN AND CHILDHOOD IN THE OTTOMAN EMPIRE

FROM THE 15TH TO THE 20TH CENTURY

Edited by Gülay Yılmaz and Fruma Zachs

Consultant Editor: Colin Heywood

EDINBURGH
University Press

Edinburgh University Press is one of the leading university presses in the UK. We publish academic books and journals in our selected subject areas across the humanities and social sciences, combining cutting-edge scholarship with high editorial and production values to produce academic works of lasting importance. For more information visit our website: edinburghuniversitypress.com

© editorial matter and organisation Gülay Yılmaz and Fruma Zachs, 2021, 2023
© the chapters their several authors, 2021, 2023

Edinburgh University Press Ltd
The Tun – Holyrood Road
12 (2f) Jackson's Entry
Edinburgh EH8 8PJ

First published in hardback by Edinburgh University Press 2021

Typeset in Jaghbuni by
Servis Filmsetting Ltd, Stockport, Cheshire

A CIP record for this book is available from the British Library

ISBN 978 1 4744 5538 1 (hardback)
ISBN 978 1 4744 5539 8 (paperback)
ISBN 978 1 4744 5541 1 (webready PDF)
ISBN 978 1 4744 5540 4 (epub)

The right of the contributors to be identified as authors of this work has been asserted in accordance with the Copyright, Designs and Patents Act 1988 and the Copyright and Related Rights Regulations 2003 (SI No. 2498).

Contents

Illustrations	viii
Acknowledgements	x
Notes on Transliteration and Pronunciation	xii
Foreword by Suraiya Faroqhi	xv

    Introduction   1
    Gülay Yılmaz and Fruma Zachs

1. Ottoman Childhoods in Comparative Perspective   31
   Colin Heywood

PART I   CONCEPTS OF CHILDHOOD

2. Childhood in the Peasant Militia Registers and the Age Boundaries of Adolescence   57
   Cahit Telci

3. An Ottoman Boyhood: Child Life in the Late Eighteenth Century through the Lens of Panayis Skouzes' Autobiography   77
   Eleni Gara

PART II   FAMILY INTERRELATIONSHIPS

4. Preliminary Observations on the Demographic Roots of Modern Childhood in the Ottoman Empire: Wealth, Children and Status in Ruse, Vidin and Sofia, 1670–1855   103
   İrfan Kokdaş

5. The Emotional Bond between Early Modern Ottoman Children and Parents: A Case Study of Sünbülzade Vehbi's 'Ideal' Child (1700–1800)   129
Leyla Kayhan Elbirlik

6. A World of Conflicts: Youth and Violence towards Parents in the Family in Rural Wallachia, 1716–1859   151
Nicoleta Roman

PART III   CHILDREN OUTSIDE FAMILY CIRCLES

7. Born and Bred in Seventeenth-century Crimea: Child Slavery, Social Reality and Cultural Identity   177
Fırat Yaşa

8. Rural Girls as Domestic Servants in Late Ottoman Istanbul   196
Yahya Araz

9. Muslim Orphans and the *Shari'ah* in Nineteenth-century Palestine: Cases from Nablus   220
Mahmoud Yazbak

PART IV   CHILDREN'S BODIES

10. Body Politics and the *Devşirme*s in the Early Modern Ottoman Empire: The Conscripted Children of Herzegovina   239
Gülay Yılmaz

11. Pastimes for the Child Breadwinners: The Sanitisation and Recreation Facilities of the Hereke Factory Campus   264
Didem Yavuz Velipaşaoğlu

12. Beating is Heaven-sent: Corporal Punishment of Children in the Late Ottoman and Early Republican Era   289
Nazan Çiçek

PART V   CHILDREN AND EDUCATION

13. Childhood and Education in Ottoman Bosnia during the Early Modern Period (Mid-fifteenth to Late Eighteenth Century)   315
Elma Korić

Contents

14. Children's Education in Ottoman Jewish Society (Sixteenth to
    Eighteenth Centuries)   336
    Ruth Lamdan

15. Women as Educators towards the End of the *Nahda* Period:
    Labiba Hashim and Children's Upbringing   363
    Fruma Zachs

Glossary   387
Notes on Contributors   390
Index   395

Illustrations

Tables

2.1	Ages of children in different peasant militia (*yaya-müsellem*) registers	64
4.1	Number of surviving children for wealth groups, 1670–1800	108
4.2	Number of surviving children for wealth groups, 1801–55	109
4.3	Number of surviving children for civilian and title-holding couples, 1670–1800	115
4.4	Number of surviving children for civilian and title-holding couples, 1801–55	116
4.5	Wealth distribution by social groups, 1670–1800	118
4.6	Wealth distribution by social groups, 1801–55	119
6.1	Minors arrested or sentenced in 1853	158

Graphs

10.1	The ages of the boys conscripted from Herzegovina in 1493–4	249
10.2	The eye colours of the boys conscripted from Herzegovina in 1493–4	249
10.3	The colouration of the boys conscripted from Herzegovina in 1493–4	250
10.4	The ages of the boys conscripted from Herzegovina in 1604	250
10.5	The eye colours of the boys conscripted from Herzegovina in 1604	251
10.6	The colouration of the boys conscripted from Herzegovina in 1604	251
10.7	Comparison of the ages of the boys conscripted from Herzegovina in 1493–4 and 1604	252

10.8   Comparison of the religions of the levied boys from
       Herzegovina in 1493–4 and 1604   253

Figures

10.1   Circumcision ceremony of Muslim and *Devşirme* boys
       together, 1582   257
11.1   Workers at the Hereke factory with a Gördes-style carpet in
       the background   271
11.2   The dormitories for the single workers at the waterfront, and
       the row houses for the technical staff behind the dormitories   273
11.3   Girls on the carpet loom   275
11.4   Hereke Imperial Factory   277
11.5   Hypothetical plan showing the functions of the buildings   278
11.6   Young girls having lunch in the gardens of the factory
       campus, c. 1900   279
15.1   'The fashion'   376
15.2   'Fashions of the month'   377

Acknowledgements

It is always a pleasure to thank those who have supported and encouraged our work. The process of editing a book is not an easy one, yet it is a great learning experience and is never completed alone.

This project began in May 2016 at an international symposium on 'the History of Children and Childhood in the Ottoman Empire' in Antalya, organised by Gülay. Five of the fifteen contributors to this book participated in the conference, although the chapters now are quite different from the papers that they presented back then. We would like to thank the participants from this conference. Their enthusiasm and fresh ideas spurred on this project and made us realise that there is an enormous need for a comprehensive book on the topic in this field. Encouraged by Colin Heywood, a participant at the conference, and his wife Olena Heywood, we embarked on this journey together. We thank Olena for her meticulous editing, Colin for being the consultant editor and both for their encouragement. The book has their refined touch throughout. We also want to thank Esther Singer for her knowledgeable editing of some of the chapters.

Special thanks go to the book contributors who came on board after the conference and made the project a richer one. All of them patiently bore with us during the process of endless editions. In addition, we would like to mention Yahya Araz and İrfan Kokdaş for reading chapters from the book, stepping in at critical times and contributing their insightful remarks.

We deeply appreciate the support of Suraiya Faroqhi for finding interest in the volume and being willing to write its foreword.

We would also like to thank Kent Schull, editor of the 'Edinburgh Studies on the Ottoman Empire' series, who believed in the project from its outset. We also greatly appreciate the team at Edinburgh University Press. In particular, we thank Head of Editorial, Nicola Ramsey, for her

Acknowledgements

continuous support, assistant editor Kirsty Woods for her helpfulness along the way and Elizabeth Welsh for her painstaking final touches. We also thank Abdullah Zararsız and Diren Çakılcı for their support in technical editing.

We are thankful to grant-givers and other sponsors, universities and organisations who engaged with us in different parts of this project. EXPO 2016, which took place in Antalya with the theme of 'Flowers and Children', and the Society for the History of Children and Youth (SHCY) generously sponsored the conference. Our affiliated institutions, Akdeniz University and the University of Haifa, also supported us at different stages of this journey. Both the conference and the book were supported by the Scientific and Technological Research Council of Turkey (TÜBİTAK) as part of a research project titled 'The Devshirme System and the Levied-Children of the Ottoman Empire (1460–1650)', no 115K354.

Finally, we want to thank our beloved husbands who tolerated us through the ups and downs, long hours of work and many Skype conversations. It would have been impossible without their understanding and patience. Last but not least, we thank our children, who are our inspiration, and whom we hope live in a better world than that of the Ottoman children we describe in the following chapters.

It was also the start of a fruitful friendship and a harmonious working partnership for us, as editors. Of course, any errors in the volume are ours.

Notes on Transliteration and Pronunciation

Ottoman–Turkish words have been written according to the conventions of modern Turkish spelling, except for the fact that we have maintained the final voiced consonant that corresponds to the Ottoman spelling: 'Mehmed' instead of 'Mehmet' and 'İzmid' rather than 'İzmit'. Place names and words that are more familiar to English-language speakers, such as 'Istanbul', 'Beirut', 'qadi', 'pasha' are spelled according to common English usage. We have chosen not to use transliteration markings, except for the occasional apostrophe to signify both the *'ayn* and the *hamza*.

The editors of this volume have left individual authors to make their own choices between transliterating names and terms from Arabic or Ottoman Turkish, Hebrew and Balkan languages.

We look at the world once, in childhood.
The rest is memory.

Louise Glück

To my dear son Eren.
G.Y.

To my dear daughters, Offir and Inbar, from whom I draw inspiration.
F.Z.

Foreword

Suraiya Faroqhi

Today, at least some historians accept that we can write a coherent history of Ottoman society, although – as is true of any historical field – certain aspects probably will remain unknowable. Put differently, we now can study groups of people who lived lives of their own, apart from the sultans' commands ordering them to do certain things and refrain from doing others. Admittedly, private archives are few and often not very rich; by contrast, the documentation in the central archives in Istanbul and in the registers of local judges is overwhelming, both in quantity and in quality. Therefore, it is not astonishing that the process of conceptualising Ottoman society apart from the governmental apparatus is slow and difficult. After all, in today's Istanbul, Izmir or Ankara, many readers of newspapers and watchers of television shows may believe that 'the state' is a superhuman entity, which imposes values next to which all others are irrelevant. Positing, as subjects worthy of study, categories of people without any share in the operation of the state thus may seem a futile exercise. It takes a certain stubbornness to insist that women, slaves and children were part of Ottoman society; and if we want to figure out how this society functioned, some historians at least will need to focus on children, by definition human beings with very limited contact to the state apparatus.

With respect to boys and girls, the task of the social historian is especially difficult. For as Yahya Araz has said in an important article, children were (and are) unable to speak for themselves and in any official procedure, they needed (and need) a representative to speak on their behalf (*kendi adına konuşamaz*).[1] If we want to establish the history of children as a viable part of Ottoman social history, it thus makes sense to focus on cases where children's lives as reconstructed by twentieth- and twenty-first-century historians intersect with problems that have occupied these scholars for some time already. Among other questions, the present volume highlights the transition from childhood to the life of a peasant-soldier and furthermore, the question whether recruits levied for service to the sultans and never manumitted (*devşirme*) were slaves or freemen. Even more difficult is the question whether workers in state factories and private households had sold their labour voluntarily, as the capitalist model assumes that they had done. Furthermore, a chapter in this volume refers to the demographic transition, which during the 1800s and 1900s resulted in the wealthier part of society having fewer children and investing money and effort in their upbringing. As for the poor, with no money to invest, they had no alternative but to continue producing offspring in large numbers. Finally, the articles in this volume encourage us to discuss the integration of pre-*Tanzimat* and post-*Tanzimat* social history, which is a recent phenomenon. Older readers remember that throughout the twentieth century, scholars were often specialists of one or the other period, with a tendency to treat the years on which the relevant historian had not done much work as a *quantité négligeable*.[2] While this attitude has not completely disappeared, it is now less pervasive, and compared to earlier studies of Ottoman childhoods, the present collection innovates by bringing together specialists on the early modern period and others whose main interest is in the later Ottoman Empire.

From Children's Fates to Debates in Historiography: The Beginnings of a Soldier's Life

Given space limitation, we can only introduce a few historiographical debates with linkages to the reconstruction of children's lives. Cahit Telci revisits the vexed question of when adolescence began, when it ended and when a youngster with a hereditary obligation to serve the Ottoman ruler needed to join the sultan's armies. Certainly, the *Shari'ah* posits puberty as the time when a boy became a man, when he might found a family and represent himself in court. However, what other obligations, including military service, did physical maturity entail in the 1400s and 1500s?

To answer this question, at least where the Ottoman authorities are at issue, Telci has used registers listing the members of peasant militias and containing references to the ages of the youngsters on record. These lists show that boys between ages twelve and sixteen, who often had passed the upsets of puberty, were available for inclusion into the army and thus formed a separate category of juveniles, which perhaps we can describe as 'young men'. Military needs thus overdetermined the stages of youth as ordinary people viewed them.

Foreword

From Children's Fates to Debates in Historiography: The Freedom or Slavery of Devşirme *Boys*

Another difficult historiographical question tackled in this volume concerns the personal status of boys levied for the sultan's service. Were they slave or free? While Islamic law recognises only the two absolutes of slavery and freedom, *devşirme* boys must have been somewhere 'in between'.[3] After all, the sultan never sold these draftees, while the same thing was not true of ordinary slaves, including the girls serving in the sultan's palace, whom the queen mother might send to the slave market in her capacity as the head of the sultan's harem. Moreover, a slave could not marry a free woman; but a vizier of *devşirme* origin, while never emancipated, might marry a princess or a descendant of the Prophet Muhammad, to the great scandal of certain members of the Egyptian and Iranian elites.

Given these difficulties, Gülay Yılmaz has analysed the status of the boys, whom in the late 1400s and early 1600s the sultan's officials levied for service in the army. The author focuses on the physical characteristics of these youngsters, recorded in the relevant registers. These descriptions allow her to 'place' the boys on the continuum between 'slave and free' – apparently, they were much closer to slavery than to freedom.[4]

Therefore, we should not be too optimistic when evaluating the levying process. Certainly, some of these youths might aspire to a future that was more brilliant than that awaiting them in their villages. Even so, perhaps many Muslims of Bosnia and Herzegovina did not send their sons voluntarily, as twentieth-century scholars often have assumed. It is quite possible that the administration had placed this obligation on them when they were still Christians and had not released them after their conversion to Islam. This argument coheres with Yusuf Hakan Erdem's assumption that Balkan subjects of the Ottoman sultans had not necessarily received protected (*zımmi*) status, but given the right of conquest, they were – at least in principle – slaves. For this reason, the sultan could take away their sons and have these youngsters serve him in a status that was – at the very least – slave-like.[5]

From Children's Fates to Debates in Historiography: Voluntary as Opposed to Forced Labour

Is it possible to differentiate between voluntary and forced labour when children are at issue? If we admit that such a differentiation is indeed possible – I have some doubts on this issue – we need to delineate the borders between forced labour and labour provided (more or less) voluntarily. Adults normally accord only limited importance to the wishes of children, at least once the latter have passed the age of five to seven. For once arrived at this stage of their lives, they can no longer use fits of screaming to persuade their parents to do their bidding. It is thus a matter of argument whether the efforts of children employed in workshops are freely given.

In his memoir of a childhood in Istanbul during and immediately after World War I, Irfan Orga has provided a lively account of the feelings of a boy from a once wealthy family, when apprenticed to a barber.[6] As Orga tells us, he was a complete failure, and his relatives discontinued the exercise in short order. We may take this fact as an indication of abiding privilege, for a boy from a lower-class background simply might have suffered a bad beating. After that, he would have had no alternative but to satisfy his master to the best of his ability.

Legally speaking, children who laboured in households and factories might be slaves or free, but regardless of their exact status, they worked because their owners or parents had concluded contracts obliging them to provide service to third parties. Alternatively, the state apparatus needed the children as workpeople and forcibly employed them in workshops and factories.

Didem Yavuz Velipaşaoğlu has studied the latter phenomenon, discussing the textile and carpet factory of Hereke on the Gulf of İzmid, where from the mid-1800s onward, Muslim and non-Muslim children worked for eleven hours a day, six days a week. Given the paternalism of Abdülhamid II (r. 1876–1909) however, the factory campus contained some provisions for the entertainment of these young workers, which they might use if after sixty-six hours of unremitting labour, they still had the energy to do so. Hygienic conditions were often deplorable: in this sense, this was a classic case of the exploitation of cheap labour, known from all industrialising countries.

Among household servants, conditions varied: some of these children had responsible employers and others lived lives of misery. Court records give us a sampling of the worst cases, as the compassionate employers of juvenile household servants did not usually end up in court. However, even if the worst cases, with which the work of Yahya Araz has familiarised us, were a minority – and perhaps even a small one – the problem was the lack of outside supervision. As the girls were often under-age, they could not turn to the courts to complain of mistreatment or exploitation. Furthermore, even if they were old enough to do so, current standards of proof usually prevented the courts from providing any relief. Some of these young women may have felt that they were worse off than slaves were; for at least in the late 1800s, the latter might invoke a foreign consul, a governor or a judge and obtain manumission.[7] Parents and relatives were often unable to help as they had lost touch with the girls that they had placed in service: after all, the feminist writer Fatma Aliye, when hiring a young household help for a lengthy period, made it quite clear that she would not welcome any visits of the girl's relatives to her home.[8] As the servant and her family likely were illiterate, the girl could thus not count on any outside protection, any more than a slave could do.

Child slaves in Crimea must have suffered from similar loneliness and lack of protection. As Fırat Yaşa has shown, Crimea was exceptional in the sense that many children born into slavery lived there, a situation uncommon in the central Ottoman lands due to frequent manumissions. Even after liberation, integration into Crimean society was difficult, as ex-slaves often lived together in separate town quarters. However, for many liberated former child slaves returning home was impossible too, as they had been born in Crimea, raised as Muslims and spoke no language but that of the Crimean Tatars.

Moreover, these people had no connection with their villages of origin – if they even knew from where they had come. As Yaşa recounts in a telling anecdote, in 1675 Ukrainian Cossacks raided a Tatar settlement, taking away some seven thousand Christians in addition to their Tatar captives. After the band had left Crimea, the Cossack leader asked the Christians whether any one of them wished to return, and nearly half the 'liberated' captives expressed this wish, explaining that they had made their home in Crimea. While the Cossack commander first consented to let them go, he then sent soldiers after the returnees to kill them all. Probably, some of those who did return 'home' found integration difficult as well, and they may have wondered whether there was much to choose between serfdom in Ukraine and slavery in Crimea.

From Children's Fates to Debates in Historiography: Wealthier Couples having Fewer Children

Historians with an interest in demography working on European societies have long known that in wealthy milieus, people had fewer children, a tendency that in the Netherlands and in Geneva/Switzerland was apparent already in the seventeenth century. For a long time, historians of South Eastern Europe have asked themselves what happened in the Balkan provinces of the Ottoman Empire, with Maria Todorova's analysis of the nineteenth-century church registers of Bulgaria's Catholic minority a major contribution.[9] However, nobody will claim that the demographic behaviour of a small minority of Christian villagers can tell us anything about the wealthy sections of Muslim urban society.

Admittedly, the evidence on Muslim families in three Bulgarian towns is of limited use because post-mortem inventories, the only source for this kind of study, only record children who were alive at the time when their parent died. Given the large number of diseases that might end the lives of children, many others must have predeceased their parents, but these youngsters remain inaccessible to the historian. Despite this limitation, the study of Irfan Kokdaş has shown that in Sofia, Vidin and Ruse the tendency of wealthy people to have fewer (surviving) children is observable from the nineteenth century onward. Therefore, the tendencies observed in early modern Catholic and Protestant Europe appear among the wealthy Muslim populations of present-day Bulgaria as well. Unfortunately, the patchy survival of sources does not allow us to discern whether there were any centres in the Ottoman world, from which this tendency originated and diffused. We might hypothesise that Istanbul was such a place. Alternatively, the limited integration of markets in the Ottoman world may have meant that social customs changed in different towns quite independently of one another.

Farewell to 'Traditional Society'

Before the 1970s, the tendency to separate pre- and post-*Tanzimat* historiographies had an intellectual underpinning, namely the assumption that before the 1850s, subjects of the sultan had lived in a 'traditional society', established in the second half of the fifteenth century and which changed very little until the challenges of the 1800s. In terms of method, this assumption had negative consequences: as researchers assumed that society was static over several centuries, it was acceptable to 'mix' data from different periods, a proceeding, which in turn rendered changes nearly invisible.

However, increasing numbers of archival documents becoming available to researchers induced more and more people to doubt the existence of a nearly unchanging 'traditional society'. When scholars examined the implications of the texts that they studied, they often came to very different conclusions. Legal historians made us aware that in the 1700s, Ottoman sultans and their officials instituted de facto appellate courts, a practice not foreseen by the *Shari'ah*.[10] A historian of education pointed out that in the late 1700s and an early 1800s, a sizeable number of Istanbul girls, perhaps some twenty per cent, had a few years of elementary schooling, and female teachers of young boys and girls were active as well.[11] In Orthodox communities, embroidering textiles for church use, long a specialty of monks and nuns, from the late 1500s became an activity of lay professionals, among whom women were prominent.[12] Moreover, historians of crafts and guilds have traced changes in practices and organisational structures.

Taken together, all these changes have made historians realise that in the late 1800s and early 1900s, dramatic changes certainly occurred, but the latter were no 'rootless imports' but often had roots in changes that had occurred during the 1600s and 1700s. We can assume that what was true of women or artisans was true of children as well, and slow but long-term changes preceded the more dramatic mutations of the late 1800s and early 1900s. Containing a balanced overview over the different childhoods experienced by Ottoman subjects, the present collection invites us to rethink questions of continuity and change, between the early modern period and the years about and after 1850.

Notes

1. Araz, 'Osmanlı İstanbul'unda Çocukluk, Çocuk Evlilikleri ve Cinsellik Yaşı üzerine bir Değerlendirme', pp. 42–9.
2. Exceptions did however exist, for example Halil İnalcık and particularly Mübahat Kütükoğlu.
3. Toledano, 'The Concept of Slavery in Ottoman and Other Muslim Societies: Dichotomy or Continuum?', pp. 159–76.
4. Nur Sobers-Khan has focused on the possible implications of describing the physical appearances of liberated slaves: *Slaves without Shackles: Forced Labour and Manumission in the Galata Court Records*, pp. 219–78.
5. Erdem, *Slavery in the Ottoman Empire and its Demise*, p. 3.
6. Orga, *Portrait of a Turkish Family*, pp. 179–83.
7. Toledano, *As if Silent As if Silent and Absent*, pp. 92–3.
8. Araz, *16. Yüzyıldan 19. Yüzyıl Başlarına Osmanlı İstanbul'unda Çocuk Emeği 1750–1920*, p. 240.
9. Todorova, *Balkan Family Structure and the European Pattern: Demographic Developments in Ottoman Bulgaria*.
10. Tuğ, *Politics of Honour in Ottoman Anatolia*.
11. Akiba, '"Girls Are Also People of the Holy Qur'an": Girls' Schools and Female Teachers in Pre-Tanzimat Istanbul'.
12. Ballian (ed.), *Relics of the Past: Treasures of the Greek Orthodox Church and the Population Exchange*, pp. 48, 154–6.

Bibliography

Akiba, Jun, '"Girls Are Also People of the Holy Qur'an": Girls' Schools and Female Teachers in Pre-Tanzimat Istanbul', *Havva: Journal of Women of the Middle East and the Islamic World*, 17 (2019), pp. 21–54.

Araz, Yahya, 'Osmanlı İstanbul'unda Çocukluk, Çocuk Evlilikleri ve Cinsellik Yaşı üzerine bir Değerlendirme (19. yüzyılın başlarından imparatorluğun sonuna): Cinsel İlişkiye Uygundur Lakin Kendi Adına Konuşamaz!' *Toplumsal Tarih*, 274 (2016), pp. 42–9.

_____, *16. Yüzyıldan 19. Yüzyıl Başlarına Osmanlı İstanbul'unda Çocuk Emeği 1750–1920* (Istanbul: Kitap Yayınevi, 2020).

Ballian, Anna (ed.), *Relics of the Past: Treasures of the Greek Orthodox Church and the Population Exchange: The Benaki Museum Collection* (Athens: The Benaki Museum and 5 Continents, 2011).

Erdem, Hakan Y., *Slavery in the Ottoman Empire and its Demise 1800–1909* (London: Palgrave Macmillan, 1996).

Orga, Irfan, *Portrait of a Turkish Family*, ed. Ateş d'Arcy Orga (London: Eland, 2011).

Sobers-Khan, Nur, *Slaves without Shackles: Forced Labour and Manumission in the Galata Court Records, 1560–1572* (Berlin: Klaus Schwarz Verlag, 2014).

Todorova, Maria N., *Balkan Family Structure and the European Pattern: Demographic Developments in Ottoman Bulgaria* (Washington, DC: The American University Press, 1993).

Toledano, Ehud, 'The Concept of Slavery in Ottoman and Other Muslim Societies: Dichotomy or Continuum?', in Miura Toru and John Edward Philips (ed.), *Slave Elites in the Middle East and Africa: A Comparative Study* (London: Kegan Paul International, 2000), pp. 159–76.

_____, *As if Silent As if Silent and Absent: Bonds of Enslavement in the Islamic Middle East* (New Haven and London: Yale University Press, 2007).

Tuğ, Başak, *Politics of Honor in Ottoman Anatolia: Sexual Violence and Socio-Legal Surveillance in the Eighteenth Century* (Leiden: Brill, 2017).

Introduction

Gülay Yılmaz and Fruma Zachs

In the last three decades, child-centred history has attracted increased research attention and has become a separate field of inquiry in which children are perceived as active agents in the historical narrative. For decades, historians of childhood have focused predominantly on Europe and North America; however, in recent years a growing number of scholars has begun to explore histories of childhood in a range of non-Western societies.[1] This work has brought to light parallel and overlapping, but at times radically different, histories/narratives. Importantly, this literature clearly indicates that no general definition of childhood can cover early modern to modern times. This volume, by focusing on Ottoman culture and society, shows that the history of childhood and children is not a simplistic framework that originated in the 'West' and then influenced other parts of the world, but rather is also specific to Ottoman lands and even varied within Ottoman society itself.

The Ottoman Empire was a multicultural and multicommunal entity covering a vast geographic area that incorporated a range of societies and cultures. This volume reflects this complexity by exploring the evolution of social, cultural and political attitudes towards children and childhood over five centuries in extremely different regions of the Ottoman Empire, by covering Christian, Jewish and Muslim children in Ottoman Romania, Bulgaria, Rumelia, Greece, Bosnia, Crimea, Syria, Palestine and Istanbul. It depicts the fluidity and flexibility of the perceptions and experiences of childhood in the Empire. It also sheds light on the differences and commonalities in perceptions of childhood over a lengthy period, from the fifteenth to the twentieth century. Its aim is to implement an interdisciplinary approach by presenting and analysing forms and conceptions of childhood, attitudes towards children in Ottoman societies, the experiences of children themselves, and how these changed over time in different geographic locations. The premise is that the study of children is indispensable to a better understanding of Ottoman society at large and its transformations.

From Constructed Childhood to Voices of Children

Western research on children, which was primarily guided by psychological and educational perspectives,[2] began to view childhood as a social, cultural and historical construct[3] as of the 1960s, prompted by Philippe Ariès'[4] influential book *Centuries of Childhood: A Social History of Family Life*. Western historical research in the decades that followed treated the emergence of childhood as a monolithic concept across a large number of geographic regions and cultures, primarily during the Middle Ages, but also in terms of the evolution of the notion of childhood at the beginning of the modern period.

However, since the 1980s, research on children has been considered a branch of social and cultural history and sees children as active social actors and agents in society. This approach has prompted childhood historians to revisit their methodology and analyse new materials, such as ego documents (personal memoirs) written by children, teenagers and young adults, as a way to identify the representational features of childhood at different periods of time across societies and cultures, thus forming a 'bottom-up' history of children. This has contributed to a better understanding of how children perceived themselves, rather than how they were constructed by adults or through the voices of adults.

In the 1990s, work by the sociologists Alan Prout and Allison James underscored the role of children as agents and social participants who were not only shaped by, but also shaped society themselves, rather than being purely the products of their social environment.[5] Prout also stressed that 'children's agency' was inadequately theorised and that agency should be decentred.[6] This became known as the field of 'new childhood studies' that encouraged, for example, the study of children's bodies as 'hybrid entities' to apprehend 'both material and representational entities'.[7] This approach treats children's bodies as entities affected by society and actively moulded in their daily lives by their social context and their place in social relations.[8] Children's material relations or corporeal contact is thus seen as reflective of nurture, social solidarity or transmission of authority. Another contribution to theorising the agency of children was developed by Peter Stearns. He argued that the study of emotions was not the exclusive domain of scientists, but fair game for historians as well. His reasoning had considerable influence on studies of the history of children and childhood because it drew attention to the importance of children's emotions.[9] In the last twenty years there has been such an intensification of historical work on emotions that some have referred to it as an 'emotional turn',[10] which is likely to impact future research on children and childhood in regions such as the Ottoman Empire, and may thus broaden the 'bottom-up' approach.

The agency of children is prioritised in this volume.[11] The vast majority of children in the Ottoman Empire, however, (as elsewhere in the world) left very few written accounts. Self-representative accounts were even scarcer in the pre-modern era. One of the key innovations of this volume is to show that exploring children's history also means creatively using existing sources – state archives, institutional records, data collected from adults – to address the fundamental question of the most efficient way to study the history of Ottoman children and childhood when personal accounts are rare. Since the task of the historian is to recapture history from the evidence that remains, it behoves historians to search for new sources and devise new ways/tools/theories to examine the available sources. As Tobias Hecht notes, 'even the silence about children in certain contexts is telling', and suggests that more can be discovered when the historian asks the right questions.[12]

The chapters in this volume all implement innovative approaches to sources, which prompt new questions that endeavour to turn the history of children into a reflection of Ottoman societies. Attitudes toward children, the public and private conditions in which children grew up, the responsibilities assigned to them and the very definition of childhood itself can inform historians about the society in which these children lived. This type of research can delineate the power structures and trace the development of institutions such as slavery and the family. The military organisation of the Empire, the institutions that controlled the labour force, and pious endowments, which were all crucial to Ottoman society, cannot be fully grasped without examining the role and agency of children. More generally, studying the changes or preservation of societal attitudes toward children over time can reveal differences in perceptions/attitudes of this society toward itself.

A Multigeographic Long-term Perspective

In the introduction to her watershed collective volume on *Childhood, Youth and Emotions in Modern History*, Stephanie Olsen pointed out that historians of childhood interpret the duality between childhood and children as artificial.[13] Instead of thinking of them as two separate categories, historians have treated them as mutually interdependent. However, one is meaningless in the absence of the other.[14] She writes that 'childhood is a historically and geographically contingent category'[15] which is perceived differently in different times and places. In this sense, Ottoman childhood needs to be historicised in diverse spatial settings and time periods to enable a continuous and meaningful analysis of the experiences of children that were shaped around historically changing concepts – in particular, since there are almost no comprehensive studies covering the early modern and modern periods of the Empire.[16]

Avner Giladi's pioneering *Children of Islam: Concepts of Childhood in Medieval Muslim Society* and his other publications laid the groundwork for concepts of childhood in Muslim societies, but do not cover modern times or the Ottoman Empire.[17] Amira El Azhary Sonbol's important edited volume on women and the family devoted a section to children and family law that has become one of the most frequently consulted sources in the field.[18] To date, most research has consisted of articles on the familial and legal aspects of early modern childhood in the Empire. Child marriages, child custody and criminal liability are some of the most prominent issues examined, based on court records and Islamic legal texts.[19] Another set of studies has examined child-rearing manuals and medical texts.[20] Hülya Tezcan's study on the upbringing and education of sultans' sons and daughters provides another important perspective on the history of education.[21]

Although the history of childhood is a relatively new field in Ottoman history, the modern era has been examined in a number of key publications. Most earlier works on the late Ottoman and early Republican history of childhood were based on Ariès' definition of childhood, and accepted it as a developmental phase in becoming an adult.[22] Bekir Onur made important contributions to the development of the history of childhood, but interprets it as a part of the modernisation process in the late Ottoman Empire and the early Republican era.[23] Nazan Maksudyan's 2008 work on vocational orphanages (*ıslahhanes*) in the 1860s stressed the methodological importance of focusing on the experiences of children as valid historical actors, and thus helped lay the methodological groundwork for an Ottoman history of children and childhood. Her work paved the way for more complex questions and has sparked numerous publications.[24] Kent Schull, for example, examined the transformation of these vocational orphanages into reformatories for juvenile delinquents under the age of fourteen.[25] Benjamin Fortna edited a volume entitled *Childhood in the Late Ottoman Empire and After* that concentrates on concepts of childhood, the effects of war and nationalism on the experiences of children, and analyses how childhood is recollected through ego documents.[26] Eyal Ginio's work on the Balkan Wars provides an in-depth exploration of the patriotic education of children, who were seen as the future generation of soldier–citizens and as active agents of change.[27] Several other publications have dealt with modernity, proto-nationalism and nationalism, consumerism, military mobilisation, law, charity/philanthropy, the household, the family, and education and are indicative of the surge in economic and cultural encounters in the nineteenth century between the Middle East and the West. These studies reflect the acknowledgment in Ottoman societies of the needs of children (with respect to education, hygiene, leisure time, dress and emotions) and the increasing centrality of children in the Ottoman family and the nation, which had implications for child-rearing. They chart the ways in which these issues became central to the Ottoman public sphere among the local middle and upper classes and point to changes in the concept of childhood from the early modern to the modern era.[28]

This change, as stressed in some of the works mentioned above, was triggered in part by the introduction and influence of Western values and notions about children and ideas of what childhood meant. However, modernity was not simply imported from the West and was not merely the outcome of imperialism or the encounter with Western culture.[29] An evolution was also taking place within Ottoman society, in some cases even in the early modern period. Thus, the complex unfolding of the modernisation of Ottoman societies not only involved processes of change, but also the responses to these changes that resulted in the adoption of new ideas/concepts, literary genres and technologies.

One way to capture internal/local notions of Ottoman modernity that has been neglected in scholarship is to compare perceptions of childhood in the early modern Empire – which was less exposed to Western influence – to periods in which industrialisation, modernisation, nationalism, globalisation and other influences left their mark on daily life and the lives of children. For example, Chapter 4 of this volume shows that wealthier families at times chose to have fewer children as early as the eighteenth century, as also noted by Duben and Behar in their work on Istanbul. This may imply that the concept of the modern family – in other words, the perception that children are the core of the family and society, and the notion that smaller families would lead to more investment in the children raised within them – was also fed by local and internal process in the Ottoman Balkans. Hence, historicising the discourse on fertility decisions of Muslim Balkan families shows how the history of children intersects with studying modernisation in Ottoman society.[30]

By juxtaposing the pre-modern era against the modern era, this volume underscores two other dimensions in the history of children: the dynamic nature of the Ottoman Empire throughout the centuries, and the prolongation of some early modern patterns into the modern period. The literature tends to concentrate on how modern childhood came into being, which presupposes that prior to modernity the Ottoman Empire did not undergo changes. However, the dynamism of the Empire was not restricted to modern times, and children's experiences, as well as attitudes toward them, changed in concert. This is because as of its inception, the Empire expanded its territory, incorporated new populations and had flourishing slave markets. This continuously transformed institutions such as the military, education and pious endowments, which became increasingly more bureaucratised.

Exploring the ways the state recruited adolescents and young men for the military helps sheds light on the changing and/or preserved structures and perceptions within this institution over time. In the modern period, defining children as future citizens not only glorified childhood, but also placed them under the stricter discipline of such modern institutions as armies, factories, state schools, orphanages and reformatories.[31] The enrolment of adolescents into military institutions was couched in terms of the new pre-national and national societies/countries. Adolescents were also an important component of the military in the early modern period in peasant militia armies (*yaya* and *müsellem* army) and the janissary army. The state recruited children, adolescents and young men under the *devşirme* system and used early modern mechanisms of surveillance, discipline and indoctrination. The context and methods of recruitment, indoctrination and disciplining the cadets differed tremendously, yet adolescent boys were traditionally the primary pool for the military. Analysing recruitment patterns in different contexts and observing the differences and similarities in the mechanisms of discipline and indoctrination contributes to a better understanding of the changing structure of the state apparatus and its definitions of children, adolescents and young people.

One of the shortcomings of Ottoman studies, and Arab and Balkan studies more generally, is that most concentrate on one specific geographic region, and predominately the perspective of Istanbul. By shifting our gaze away from the centre of the Empire, attitudes toward children become more visible and diverse. Specifically, examining educational institutions in the Ottoman Empire through a multigeographic long-term lens helps identify the variety of education systems in the early modern Empire, but also preservation of local cultural attitudes towards children in a range of societies into modern times. This perspective reveals that the survival and

Introduction

perpetuation of different communities was sometimes highly dependent on the future generation and their education. For example, Chapter 14 shows the extent to which the Jewish community was intent on maintaining its educational institutions and structures during the early modern period. Chapter 13, which deals with Ottoman Bosnia, makes it clear that even when a community was not powerful enough to generate institutional structures to sustain its language and culture, it did everything in its power to achieve this end. In this instance, language and culture were transmitted to the next generation by Bosnian mothers, who taught their children the Bosnian language at home.

Early modern models of education were more centred on the survival and perpetuation of local culture under an imperial structure. Education in the modern era became a way to modernise Ottoman/Arab/Balkan societies and to reshape diverse communities to develop stronger loyalties to the new modern state. Many works have described changes in the Ottoman educational system (as well as the missionary network) for children, adolescents and young adults (boys and girls).[32] Education had previously been limited to *waqf*-endowed schools and private endowments and initiatives that focused on religious education, which was mainly for boys. The Ottoman Public Education Regulation of 1869 mandated the founding of a comprehensive and secular public school system throughout the Ottoman Empire for both boys and girls.[33]

The education systems of local communities were threatened by the emergence of nationalism. The Ottoman educational policy included teaching Turkish in the public schools, which kindled fierce reactions from the non-Turkish areas of the Empire. For example, the Albanians resisted by opening secret schools to provide primary education in the Albanian language.[34] However, merely focusing on early modern education suggests that the reactions were fed by centuries-old perceptions of child education, rather than solely by modern nationalist aspirations. Nevertheless, just as it is impossible to understand changes in children's education without examining the emergence of the nation-state, it is not enough to study the emergence of the modern state without investigating how it was affected by earlier approaches to children and their education.

Finally, tracing the changing and persistent patterns in child labour from early modern to modern times is also illuminating. There were many types of labourers in the early modern world, including slaves, serfs, convicts, prisoners of war, debtors, contract workers and apprentices.[35] Children were part of many of these categories in early modern Ottoman society. Children were engaged in domestic slave labour, *devşirme* coerced labour, and they were given away by their parents to pay off their debts, were apprenticed to masters in guilds in large cities and worked with their fathers to acquire vocational skills at a young age in a society that lacked education systems for the masses.[36] One of the key issues in relation to industrialisation is the transformation of slave labour into coerced labour, since the corveé was often made obligatory for women and children in the Armenian and Greek communities during the modern era.[37] It would be difficult to fully understand the emergence of forms of new economic dependencies, such as servants, convicts, corveés or contract labourers, without analysing the economic effects of the disappearance of the ideological and cultural justifications for slavery in modern times, just as it is impossible to fully grasp slavery without examining its relationship to labour. Therefore, these studies on women and children forced into coerced labour provide a useful framework for observing the transformation of unfree labour to other forms of labour arrangements in the markets of the Ottoman Empire.

This transformation involved the perpetuation of earlier definitions and expectations of the labour force as much as it signifies a shift away from slavery. In addition to industrial coerced labour that replaced older forms of forced labour, Donald Quataert also highlights the excessive use of female and child labour from all ethnic origins, both by private and state structures, dominated by the poor and orphans.[38] Yahya Araz, in Chapter 8, discusses the relationship between the abolishment of slave labour to the internal developmental dynamics of the domestic child labour market in Istanbul.[39] Araz's sound analysis, in his latest publication with İrfan Kokdaş, makes an important contribution to the field in the sense that it shows that Islamic law and early modern legal structures were highly influential in the formation of contractual agreements and the monetarisation of the domestic labour market.[40]

Thus, the broad chronological approach adopted in this volume helps present a more fine-grained Ottoman history of children and childhood. It points to the continuous (but constantly evolving) development of Ottoman attitudes toward children and childhood in a dynamic Empire. This long-term perspective grouped in one volume further reveals recurrent issues, such as the stratification of age groups and categories of childhood and adolescence. Identifying and defining early modern perceptions of childhood and adolescence constitute the first steps toward grasping this historic category, which makes it possible to trace the ways in which this category changed in the nineteenth and twentieth centuries and what it preserved from the early modern structures. This approach also shows that emotional bonds and violence were a central part of the history of children in both time periods and were related to how patriarchy was experienced.

Introduction

OTTOMAN CHILDHOOD AND ADOLESCENCE AS SEPARATE CATEGORIES

Western historians today note that adolescence as a transitional stage only emerged as a separate social category during the nineteenth century among the middle classes. The acknowledgment of this period of time when enormous physiological and physical changes take place translated into new, more intense and lengthier familial relationships on the one hand, and extended involvement in educational institutions on the other.[41] Although adolescence only came into its more clearly defined form in the modern period, Ariès' depiction of an 'ageless' early modern society that lacked 'generational differences' has been widely criticised.[42] However, this issue has not been examined in depth in Middle Eastern and North African Studies (MENA) in general, or Ottoman studies in particular. Several Ottoman historians have suggested that child age categories traditionally existed in Ottoman society and have shown that they were defined in terms of mental capacity and sexual puberty, according to religious, juridical and administrative concepts. These studies show that the social and legal category of adolescence existed in Muslim and Ottoman societies in pre-modern times.[43] Adolescence in early modern Ottoman history was thus perceived in many ways and was defined through different systems.

Shari'ah law on child custody itself makes a distinction between 'tender ages' and the 'ages of discernment', which differ according to the gender and the legal stances of the four Islamic schools in the early modern era.[44] The different age categories and the fact that the corresponding ages varied according to Islamic schools suggests that pre-modern Islamic societies did not have a simplistic attitude towards children or notions as to how childhood should unfold at different ages. Generally, the ages of seven to eight were defined as the age of discernment, signalling the end of the tender years, and ages thirteen to fifteen marked the beginning of adolescence. These flexible age categories were highly gendered, since they were based on physical maturity and the socio-sexual perceptions of the society. Children were generally defined as *sagir/e* (young child), while *sabi, oğlancık* or *uşak* were used to refer to the tender ages of childhood. The onset of puberty (*ergenlik* or *buluğ*) was the main determinant of adolescence. Terms such as *murahık/a* (a child on the verge of puberty, but still not having shown the physical signs of puberty) and *mümeyyiz/e* (a child who has reached puberty, the age of discernment) were used for defining pubescent teens (*ergen*), among many others.[45] Young boys were called *emred, şabb-ı emred* or *oğlan* – these also meaning beardless youth. For girls, the usage was limited to *kız* (girl), indicating an unmarried female past puberty, a virgin past puberty. This term also meant 'daughter', which gives it a sense of continuity, just as *oğul*, a variation of *oğlan*, means 'son'.[46]

Islamic law defines children who have reached puberty as 'adult enough' to get married, and puberty is widely treated as the transition to adulthood in works concentrating on familial relations, marriage or children in MENA studies. These early marriages curtailed the period of youth in the Ottoman world and resulted in a rapid transition to adulthood, especially for girls. A marriage contract could be agreed to between families even before adolescence and began when the girl reached physical maturity with her first menstrual cycle. This was the case not only for the Muslim community, but also for Christians and Jews.[47] Adolescent marriage was also part of early modern Mediterranean culture,[48] which hints that these marriages should be interpreted more in relation to economic factors and a cultural interpretation of marriage as an institution, rather than solely in terms of religion.[49] Studies on family and marriage relations in the early modern MENA conclude that marrying before eighteen was widespread.[50] The sources from pre-modern periods, however, cannot be subjected to statistical analyses that would clarify the ages of females and males at marriage in Ottoman society. The lack of data and the prevalence of concepts such as *kız* suggest that not all families married off their daughters as soon as they reached adolescence.[51]

Ilana Krausman Ben-Amos stressed that the issue of adolescence should be examined from different biological, cognitive, psychological, social, economic and cultural perspectives. This encourages a more complex interpretation of early modern Ottoman childhood, and further complicates the transformation of these changing perceptions of childhood in modern times.[52] There was no clear definition of adolescence in Islamic law; however, society had a grasp of the notion. This was particularly true for boys. Adolescents were defined as individuals who did not have the maturity, for example, to control their finances or to make economic decisions; therefore, the control of their finances was given to the father, including the selection of their work setting. Nevertheless, as seen in Skouzes' biography in Chapter 3, boys worked in jobs found by their fathers during their teen years and supported their families.[53] Physical maturity and rebellion were considered the defining parameters of adolescence. According to Skouzes, Athenian women were aware that a fifteen-year-old boy should no longer be allowed to enter the women's public bath. Sources in Lamdan's Chapter 14 indicate that Jewish communities in the sixteenth century were aware of a stage in the life of teenage boys when they tended to behave wildly, show disrespect for adults and rebel against their parents. They recognised that young men were expected to reject their elders and perceive their advice as silliness.

In the early modern military institutions of the Ottoman Empire there were categories corresponding to adolescence. Both in the earlier forms of the Ottoman peasant militia army (*yaya-müsellem*) and in the janissary army there had always been an in-between category of adolescence, between childhood and young men who were eligible for combat. Adolescence was regularly targeted as an age group that would produce cadets, those who would be prepared to join the army when they became young men. The age thresholds including or excluding adolescents varied, but always existed.[54]

The definition of adolescence and its corresponding age category remained vague during the early modern era. This ambiguity and flexibility of the age range persisted into the nineteenth century. The cultural and moral codes of *Shari'ah* continued into the modern period and formed the basis for change, as can be seen in examples where the court set age thresholds for juvenile delinquents and child marriages. In Chapter 6, Nicoleta Roman's comparison of the 1852 Criminal Code of Romania to the 1858 Ottoman Penal Code reveals that whereas the Ottoman Penal Code had a vague age threshold related to sexual maturity and ranged from the age of nine to fifteen and differed according to gender, in the Romanian Code it was set at twenty-five. Schull shows that the 1858 Ottoman Penal Code also preserved an ambiguous age category for juvenile delinquents, because the lawmakers adopted Islamic legal concepts. The Ottoman Parliament only revised Article 40 of 1858 and changed the age threshold for juvenile delinquents to fourteen regardless of puberty in 1911.[55] Nevertheless, child marriages were problematised and discussed widely in the nineteenth century. However, legislators did not forbid it, since they believed quashing this practice would go against 'personal freedom'. It was only in 1917 that the age of marriage was raised to eighteen for boys and seventeen for girls, but if the girl declared that she wanted to marry earlier, this was permitted if she could prove having reached puberty.[56] However, public consensus seems to have changed earlier than reflected in the legal reforms. According to the 1885 census, 93.2 per cent of all girls in Istanbul between the ages of ten and fourteen were single. In the 1907 Istanbul census, the rate was 91.2 per cent. For single girls aged fifteen to nineteen, the percentages were 57.3 and 60.7, respectively.[57] Notions of adolescence thus changed over time, but evolved into a more clearly defined age category when the legal age thresholds shifted away from a strictly Islamic legal interpretation towards more secular definitions during the CUP (Committee of Union and Progress) era. The CUP's other policies, such as establishing scout organisations and the spread of public education, contributed to this new perception and definition of childhood in the Empire.[58]

PATRIARCHY, EMOTIONAL BONDS AND VIOLENCE

There were certain commonalities in the perception of childhood in early modern Ottoman communities that shaped children's experiences. The chapters devoted to the early modern period show that children took on a range of active roles in Ottoman society during this period. Religion, gender and economic status were important determinants in defining these roles within this strictly patriarchal society.

In Christian, Jewish and Muslim communities, children were predominantly given a religious education. This was also vital for the preservation of these communities within the imperial structure. Children were expected to follow rules, and community traditions were key features of children's education. The patriarchal structure was particularly apparent in terms of the dominance of fathers in the lives of their children. Boys, especially in urban environments, were generally sent to learn trades exercised by their fathers, whereas girls were brought up to adhere to the codes of decorum of their community and prepare for marriage.[59] Child labour was widespread, and few children received schooling.

Another important dimension of the patriarchal and gender- and age-based hierarchical structure of the society was institutional violence. One of the early modern institutions that left many children vulnerable to structural violence was slavery. Fırat Yaşa's examination of enslaved children and children who were born to slave parents in early modern Crimea shows that there were several forms of child slavery. Physical and sexual abuse of female slaves was common.[60] State-controlled enslavement (the *devşirme*), which involved conscription of the young sons of Christian subjects living in the Balkans and Anatolia, continued until the eighteenth century.[61]

All the above dovetail into the issue of whether there was an emotional bond between children and their parents in pre-modern Ottoman society, where age was one of the criteria of status. Ariès claimed that childhood was an invention of modern society. He emphasised that parents during the medieval period did not love their offspring, and that during that period children were treated as 'miniature adults'.[62] However, researchers have shown that in the medieval period, both in Europe[63] and also in Muslim[64] cultures, parents had emotional ties to their children. Nicolas Vatin's examination of inscriptions in Istanbul cemeteries reveals the attachment

Introduction

of parents to their children. He reported that 249 of 1,176 gravestones in the cemeteries of Eyüp, Merdivenköy, Sinope and Karacaköy belong to children, adolescents and young people.[65] In forty-eight of these, the parents' pain and sorrow is expressed through terms of abandonment and suffering, such as falling apart (*fırak*), mournful separation (*iftirak*), to be separated (*ayırmak*), abandon (*terk eylemek*) and leaving (*bırakmak*). Many contain expressions such as longing (*hasret*), wound (*yara*) and devastated (*harab*). The loss of a child was described as a fire of loss (*ateş-i fırkat*) that burned (*yakdı*) and had no cure (*yokdur çaresi*).[66]

The chapters here also suggest that the general tendency in ethics manuals, but also in the behaviour of adults in early modern Ottoman society, favoured treating children gently and kindly, and that there was an attempt to educate children with love and care. In the pre-modern era, emotional bonding with the child was believed to lead to a better upbringing. Chapter 5 discusses the Ottoman society's attitudes toward childhood as reflected in a late eighteenth-century manual which explored the emotional bond between father and son. However, these manuals (and sometimes autobiographies) also hint that corporal punishment was administered whenever it was found necessary. This punishment was not interpreted as violence, but as a natural and much needed educational gesture. Chapter 3 shows that toward the end of the eighteenth century in Ottoman Athens, very young children were subjected to corporal punishment at school. Gara emphasises that for centuries it was the preferred method for disciplining boys and adolescents in Europe and continued to be a socially accepted practice until well into the nineteenth century in the Ottoman Empire. This included flogging, standing on one leg, sometimes with a bag of stones hanging from the child's neck, and foot whipping. In Chapter 12, Nazan Çiçek indicates that physical punishment of children was widespread as recently as the modern period, both in the Ottoman Empire and the Republican era. In fact, corporal punishment was not seen as a form of violence until modern times.

Patriarchy was still a powerful component of modern conceptions of childhood, but was replaced with 'state patriarchy' as the state became more involved in controlling and disciplining the domestic realm from the eighteenth century onwards. Compulsory state education with its new regularised curricula that emphasised obedience and respect for the state, the founding of vocational orphanages, reformatories or orphanages (*darüleytam*s), attempts to improve child safety and welfare, the promotion of companionate marriage at older ages or defining the age of accountability for juvenile delinquents created a new form of 'state patriarchy'.[67] The family did not lose its exalted status, but the state took on increasing responsibility for protecting familial values and structures by controlling children, adolescents and young single men.[68]

Overview of this Volume

This volume brings together an impressive number of innovative studies of Ottoman sources. The quantity in itself is significant, but even more crucially it suggests new ways of utilising existing sources to derive information about children living under imperial rule. Each chapter presents the author's own research and interpretations. Nevertheless, this volume constitutes a coherent whole that makes a novel contribution to the field through the thematic organisation of each of its parts, which enables the elaboration of certain topics from a long-term perspective. It introduces new perspectives in the history of children and Ottoman historiography, which explains why it is organised thematically rather than chronologically. This also reflects a critical stance towards the classical periodisation of Ottoman history. Each part groups chapters dealing with the early modern and modern periods to encourage comparison of features of childhood and experiences of children over time.

This volume sheds light on Ottoman childhood in five main sections: concepts of childhood, family interrelationships, children living outside family circles (slaves, child labourers and orphans), children's bodies, and education from the fifteenth century to the early twentieth century. Evidently, there are many other crucial topics and regions that could not be covered in a single volume, all of which clearly deserve to be studied. Topics such as children at war, child marriages and child custody, for example, which have received more attention in scholarship, are not included. Geographically speaking, we were not able to include the African lands of the Empire, since the region is extremely understudied by Ottomanists. Data from urban centres outweigh data on rural areas. Nomads, due to lack of written sources or completed research, are not represented, and neither are some other groups. Thus, this book should be seen as a first attempt at a comparative volume, an introduction to a nascent field that is gradually emerging in Ottoman studies, especially as concerns the pre-modern period.

Chapter 1, by Colin Heywood, a prominent historian of children and childhood in Europe, who took part in the workshop that forms the basis for this volume, emphasises the key content and characteristics of Ottoman societies and the global history of children and childhood. Professor Heywood kindly accepted the difficult task of providing an overview. He situates the life of Ottoman children, adolescents and young people in

Introduction

a wider perspective pertinent to historians studying the Empire, and the Middle East, as well as scholars from other disciplines. By placing the Ottoman case within a global perspective, he presents the Ottomans as part of global developments regarding children and childhood, to prompt new historiographical questions and ways of thinking on Ottoman children and the history of childhood.

The first section focuses on the concepts of childhood, based on state archives and autobiographies that help better define attitudes toward children. The two chapters in this section explore, in Chapter 2, the determination of the appropriate age for conscription in the Ottoman state documents and, in Chapter 3, personal memoirs, by providing examples of how childhood was perceived at the state and personal levels. They examine methodological issues and discuss their advantages and shortcomings. In Chapter 2, Cahit Telci deals with childhood and unmarried adolescents (*mücerred*) as reflected in the peasant militia registers (*yaya* and *müsellem* registers) in the fifteenth and sixteenth centuries. He investigates how the age thresholds between these two categories varied across different regions. Telci innovates by studying the registers of the army as a source of social history. His chapter problematises the age differences in conscripted children from different regions, shows the transformation of the conscription process throughout the fifteenth and sixteenth centuries and discusses the nature of these registers and how they can be used as a valuable source of childhood history.

In Chapter 3, Eleni Gara examines Ottoman boyhood and children's lives in late eighteenth-century Athens through the lens of Panagis Skouzes' childhood memoirs. She shows that these memoirs, which were written in the aftermath of the Greek War of Independence (1821–30), offer a rare glimpse into the lives of children in this time of crisis. She explores the issues of recall and subjectivity when using memoirs as a source of childhood history and discusses in what ways Skouzes' autobiography belongs to a world that had ceased to exist; namely, the Ottoman regime overthrown by the Greek Revolution. Gara examines the various factors that impacted Skouzes' lived experience, brings to light experiences of childhood that demonstrate agency and enterprising spirit, meaning the active side of children, and discusses the broader implications for concepts of childhood in the late eighteenth-century Aegean world.

The second section discusses family interrelationships. It deals with the family – the primary social unit. It includes topics such as the history of demographic trends among families to have fewer children in the early modern to the modern Ottoman Balkan world, the emotional bond between parents and children in early modern Ottoman families in Istanbul and parent–child relationships in terms of familial violence in Ottoman Wallachia. In Chapter 4, İrfan Kokdaş concentrates on the historical roots of the nineteenth century demographic transition in the Ottoman lands, with a special emphasis on the associations between wealth and the surviving numbers of children in Ruse, Sofia and Vidin (currently Bulgaria) from 1660 to 1850. He examines the relationship between wealth and social status of couples by using over 7,000 inheritance records (*tereke defter*s) and argues that low fertility rates in these towns appeared at the beginning of the nineteenth century, at least among wealthy couples.

The issue of whether children and parents had an emotional bond in pre-modern societies has been discussed at great length in childhood studies. In Chapter 5, Leyla Kayhan Elbirlik deals with the emotional bond between early modern children and their parents through the case study of Sünbülzade's 'ideal' child in *Lütfiyye*, which was a conduct manual written by Sünbülzade Vehbi for his son *Lütfullah*. The author, who became a father one last time at fifty-one, composed this manual to guide his son, then a young adult, in his moral, ethical, religious and intellectual undertakings. The manual provides insights into the imagined 'ideal' relationship between a child and a father in early modern Istanbul. *Lütfiyye* takes a gender-segregated attitude, particularly with respect to the shared and separate roles of the mother and the father in accordance with *Shari'ah* law. In comparing the definition prescribed by this conduct manual to what could be deduced from several divorce and child custody cases in contemporaneous court records, Kayhan Elbirlik taps into the nature of the emotional bond between parents and children in early modern Ottoman families.

In Chapter 6, Nicoleta Roman describes conflicts between parents and their offspring resulting in violent acts, including parricide in Wallachia (1716–1859). Roman examines the roots and reasons for violence, how families dealt with violence and how and when the state and the community intervened. It also discusses the development of criminal legislation concerning punishment for juvenile delinquents under Romanian law by contrast to the 1858 Ottoman Penal Code and explores the different age thresholds for a person to be considered a minor in court. Roman underscores the divergence between two legal interpretations: *Shari'ah*, which accepts the physical signs of puberty as the age of discernment, differing according to gender; and the 1652 Romanian Law and Customs statute, which treats any person below twenty-five as a minor.

The third section deals with children outside family circles. In Chapter 7, Fırat Yaşa concentrates on children who were inborn slaves in seventeenth-century Crimea. Yaşa examines the Crimean court records and cases

Introduction

related to inborn slaves or children who became slaves at a young age. By comparing the cases, the chapter elaborates on the issues of cultural belonging and cultural awareness in relation to these two different modes of childhood slavery. In his analysis of the terminology related to child slaves, Yaşa shows that in the seventeenth-century Crimean court records, male-enslaved children from birth to the age of six or seven were recorded as *dogma*s, as *çora*s from seven until they reached maturity, and that female child slaves were referred to as *devke*s until they reached to the age when they could have sexual relations. In Chapter 8, Yahya Araz concentrates on the lives of the girls who worked in domestic service in Istanbul in the late Ottoman Empire. Araz argues that the domestic service sector was an important vector of labour mobility between the provinces and Istanbul. He examines this market by tracing the lives of children who were brought from northern and north-western Anatolia to work in Istanbul households. Araz notes that these girls were active agents in the marketplace and were at times successful in manipulating the fate that modern society had reserved for them. This chapter delves into court records from Istanbul, Ordu and Safranbolu, newspapers of the period and other archival sources.

In Chapter 9, Mahmoud Yazbak focuses on Muslim orphans and the *Shari'ah* in nineteenth-century Ottoman Palestine, especially cases from Nablus. Yazbak traces the experiences of Muslim orphans by examining the *Shari'ah* court records. He describes the social status of Muslim orphans according to *Shari'ah*, which considered children as orphans only after their father passed away, but not so when they lost their mothers. The chapter draws attention to the patrimonial approach of the court, society and family towards orphans, which lasted at least until 1874, when the first orphanage in Ottoman Palestine was founded. He concludes that the state's approach to orphan children preserved the early modern Islamic approach, in that it adhered to the regulations of *Shari'ah* law.

The fourth section examines the ways in which children's bodies were perceived in Ottoman society in various contexts. In Chapter 10, Gülay Yılmaz concentrates on how the Ottoman government transformed the bodies of non-Muslim children into *devşirme* bodies and enslaved these children by imposing its authority on them. Yılmaz uses regulations of the janissary army (*Kavanin-i Yeniçeriyan*) and unique levy registers from the 1490s and 1603–4 to compare how the Ottoman state developed certain physical criteria for *devşirme* candidates and to what extent these criteria were applied by examining the depictions of levied children from Herzegovina. She examines whether there was a transformation in the application of the selection criteria and terms this selection process the 'body politics' (or biopolitics) of the *devşirme* system.

In Chapter 11, Didem Yavuz Velipaşaoğlu examines the physical and sanitary conditions of child labourers in the nineteenth-century Hereke factory, which was organised as a campus with its own hospital, communal gardens, orchards and recreational areas that served as control mechanisms over social cohesion and the physical health of the child labourers. The author also looks at the spatial transformation of the factory over this time period and the possible associations between the building of a sewage system and recreational gardens and the implementation of social institutions that created social cohesion as well as social control. She shows that the creation of new industrial spaces could offer girls a rather pleasant experience of labour and economic independence. In Chapter 12, Nazan Çiçek examines corporal punishment as a method of upbringing, and how it was perceived and experienced by children through an in-depth analysis of memoirs, biographies, autobiographies, personal letters, newspaper columns, magazine articles, as well as child-rearing manuals and news reports published during the late Ottoman and early Republican times. Based on the Foucauldian framework of biopolitics Çiçek argues that corporal punishment of children in modern times was an anachronism. Although forms of punishment shifted from physical torture to surveillance and confinement from the eighteenth century onwards, corporal punishment of children never disappeared. However, she also highlights the fading of this practice in the last quarter of the nineteenth century, at least in some circles, with the introduction of the modern notion of children as angelically innocent beings.

The fifth section discusses the ways in which education was implemented to turn children into mature adults in Ottoman society. It elaborates on the attitudes of religious institutions toward children's education in the minority communities of the Ottoman Empire between the fifteenth and eighteenth centuries. It also examines how, as a result of the encounter with the West during the nineteenth century and the process of modernisation, children's education took on greater importance. In Chapter 13, Elma Korić examines data from several pious endowment deeds (*vakfiyes*) from the Bosnian province during the sixteenth and seventeenth centuries, and shows how the education of children was organised, from the hiring of a teacher to enrolment criteria. Some documents also mention the supplies required for school and the acquisition of modern textbooks, all of which provide a glimpse into everyday life.

In Chapter 14, Ruth Lamdan deals with children and child-rearing in Ottoman Jewish society. The subject of childhood is rarely dealt with in Jewish sources, and there is scant material on children. Lamdan elaborates on Jewish attitudes toward raising children and children's education in

Introduction

Jewish sources from the sixteenth through to the eighteenth centuries, such as Jewish law (*halakha*) and the ethical literature (*musar* books). She examines what was expected of children, the moral instruction they received, where they studied and class content and how long children were dependent on their families. In the last chapter, Fruma Zachs shows how during the end of the nineteenth century and the beginning of the twentieth century, when processes of modernisation, pre-national aspirations and gender transformations took place, there was growing awareness of the importance of children's education in the regions of Greater Syria and Egypt among male educators, but more importantly among women educators, such as Labiba Hashim (1882–1952). The chapter argues that whereas men educators were in favour of children's education because it benefitted the family, society and the nation, women educators challenged and broadened the scope of children's education in general and girls' education in particular to turn them (and themselves) not only into educated mothers, but also into educated women. Via children's education, women transformed attitudes toward themselves and redefined their place and their children's place in the patriarchal family and society.

This volume raises, as well as leaves, many questions unanswered. Can childhood as described through personal experiences respond to larger questions concerning the Ottoman Empire? What is the best way to produce a micro history of children; in other words, the existence of the story of one individual child? What methodologies should historians implement to pave the way for new directions in researching the history of children and childhood in the Ottoman Empire? Last but not least, should Ottoman, Arab and Balkan historians harness comparisons and perspective-taking to reassess children's lives elsewhere and at different periods? Future research is likely to lead to a more global/universal approach to the history of children and childhood and provide a better understanding of how cultures and societies differ in their attitudes towards children.

Notes

1. See, for example, for the Ottoman Empire: Maksudyan, *Ottoman Children and Youth during World War I*; Maksudyan, *Orphans and Destitute Children in the Late Ottoman Empire*; Fortna, *Childhood in the Late Ottoman Empire and After*; İnanç, 'The Formation of Children in the Late Ottoman Empire'; Ibrahim, *Child Custody in Islamic Law*. For the Middle East in general, see Fernea, *Children in the Muslim Middle East*; Fernea, *Remembering Childhood in the Middle East*; Giladi, 'Concepts of Childhood and Attitudes towards Children in Medieval Islam'; Giladi, *Children of Islam*; Baron, *The Orphan Scandal*; Morrison, *Global History of Childhood Reader*; Morrison,

Childhood and Colonial Modernity in Egypt; Zachs, 'Growing Consciousness of the Child in Ottoman Syria in the 19th Century'.
2. See, for example, Zuckerman, *Beyond the Century of the Child*; DeMause, *The History of Childhood*.
3. See, for example, Boswell, *The Kindness of Strangers*; Hanawalt, *Growing Up in Medieval London*; Krausman Ben-Amos, *Adolescence and Youth in Early Modern England*.
4. Ariès, *Centuries of Childhood*. Ariès' depiction was highly criticised. See, for example, Krausman Ben-Amos, 'Adolescence as a Cultural Invention', pp. 74–5; Burton, 'Looking Forward from Ariès?', pp. 207, 210; Wilson, 'The Infancy of the History of Childhood', pp. 140, 145.
5. James and Prout, pp. 1–5.
6. Prout, p. 16.
7. Ibid., p. 2.
8. Ibid., pp. 3–6.
9. Olsen and Boddice, 'Styling Emotions History', p. 476; Stearns and Haggerty, 'The Role of Fear', pp. 63–94; Stearns, *Childhood in World History*; Stearns and Stearns, 'Emotionology: Clarifying the History of Emotions and Emotional Standards', pp. 813–36.
10. See, for example, Reddy, *The Navigation of Feeling*; Rosenwein, *Generations of Feeling*.
11. For example, as discussed in Chapters 8 and 11, and the entire section on Children's Bodies, children (both girls and boys) were active agents in the market and were at times successful in manipulating the circumstances that modern society reserved for them.
12. Hecht, *Minor Omissions*, p. 7.
13. Olsen, *Childhood, Youth and Emotions in Modern History*, p. 3.
14. Ibid., p. 3.
15. Ibid.
16. The only comprehensive work on Ottoman children is Yahya Araz's book that covers the sixteenth century to the early nineteenth century. Araz discusses some important issues related to Ottoman childhood, such as age categories, the transmission of family property through children, childhood diseases, accidents and death, gender inequalities, education and upbringing and child labour within Muslim (mostly Anatolian) society. For more details, see Araz, *Osmanlı Toplumunda Çocuk Olmak*. Another important work that covers the history of childhood from medieval to modern times is an edited volume on childhood by Georgeon and Kreisers. This collection of articles does not clearly define which 'Mediterranean countries' reflect the Muslim World. It is a compilation of individual articles that are not organised thematically or chronologically. Yet, the volume is an important one that reflects a broad spectrum of topics, including eighteen articles, eleven of which deal with the period from the Ottoman Empire to the Republic of Turkey. For details, see Georgeon and Kreisers, *Enfance*

Introduction

  et jeunesse dans le monde musulman (Childhood and Youth in the Muslim World).
17. Giladi, *Children of Islam*; Giladi, *Infants, Parents, and Wet Nurses* and several other articles, including 'Concepts of Childhood and Attitudes towards Children in Medieval Islam: A Preliminary Study with Special Reference to Infant and Child Mortality'.
18. Meriwether, 'The Rights of Children and the Responsibilities of Women: Women as Wasis in Ottoman Aleppo, 1770–1840'; Sonbol, 'Adults and Minors in Ottoman Shari'a Courts and Modern Law'.
19. For example, see Lamdan, 'Child Marriage in Jewish Society in the Eastern Mediterranean during the Sixteenth Century'; Motzki, 'Child Marriages in Seventeenth-Century Palestine'; Yazbak, 'Minor Marriages and Khıyar al-Bulugh in Ottoman Palestine'; Ginio, 'Childhood, Mental Capacity and Conversion to Islam in the Ottoman State'; Tucker, *In the House of the Law*; Kermeli, 'Children Treated as Commodity in Ottoman Crete'; Araz, '17. ve 18. Yüzyılda İstanbul ve Anadolu'da çocuk evlilikleri ve erişkinlik olgusu üzerine bir değerlendirme'; Araz, 'Cinsel ilişkiye Uygundur Lakin Kendi Adına Konuşamaz!'.
20. Necdet Sakaoğlu, *Osmanlı'dan Günümüze Eğitim Tarihi*; Necmettin Şafak, 'İlk dönem (14. ve 15. yüzyıl) Türkçe Tıp Yazmalarında çocuk Sağlığı Hastalıkları ve Tedavileri'.
21. Hülya Tezcan, *Osmanlı Sarayının Çocukları*.
22. Okay, *Osmanlı Çocuk Hayatında Yenileşmeler*; Tan et al., *Cumhuriyet'te Çocuktular*.
23. Onur, *Türkiye'de Çocukluğun Tarihi*.
24. Nazan Maksudyan's dissertation on orphanages was one of the first works to examine Ottoman children by giving them agency. She has published extensively on this subject since then. Maksudyan, 'Hearing the Voiceless – Seeing the Invisible'.
25. Schull, *Prisons in the Late Ottoman Empire*, Chapter 6.
26. Fortna, *Childhood in the Late Ottoman Empire and After*.
27. Ginio, *The Ottoman Culture of Defeat*, Chapter 4.
28. See, for example, Baron, *The Orphan Scandal*; Morrison, *Childhood and Colonial Modernity in Egypt*; Morrison, *Global History of Childhood Reader*; Fernea, *Children in the Muslim Middle East*; Zachs, 'Growing Consciousness of the Child in Ottoman Syria in the 19th Century'; Zachs, 'The Private World of Women and Children'; Doumani, *Family Life in the Ottoman Mediterranean*; İnanç, 'The Formation of Children in the Late Ottoman Empire'; Agmon, *Family and Court*; Meriwether, *The Kin Who Count*; Somel, *The Modernization of Public Education*.
29. Notions such as 'modernism', 'modern society' or 'the modern concept of childhood' are framed in this volume in terms of Eisenstadt's 'multiple modernities', which challenge certain Western narratives of modernity by showing that in non-Western societies modernisation did not necessarily

imply Westernisation, but rather included some of its pluralistic features. Eisenstadt, 'Multiple Modernities', pp. 1–29; Lal, 'Does Modernization Require Westernization?', pp. 5–24. For research on this topic on the Ottoman Empire, see Blumi, *Reinstating the Ottomans*; Worringer, *Ottomans Imagining Japan*; Amzi-Erdogdular, 'Alternative Muslim Modernities'.
30. Duben and Behar, *Istanbul Households*.
31. Kabadayı, 'Working in a Fez Factory in Istanbul in the Late Nineteenth Century'; Kabadayı, 'Working for the State in a Factory in Istanbul'; Maksudyan, 'Foster-Daughter or Servant, Charity or Abuse', pp. 488–512.
32. For example, see Fortna, *Imperial Classroom*; Fortna, 'Education and Autobiography at the End of the Ottoman Empire'; Somel, *The Modernization of Public Education*.
33. Deringil, *The Well Protected Domains*.
34. Somel, *The Modernization of Public Education*, pp. 205–41, esp. p. 206.
35. David Eltis and Stanley L. Engerman provide a good framework for the range of dependencies around labour production in a chapter in the Cambridge World History of Slavery series. Eltis and Engerman, 'Dependence, Servility, and Coerced Labor in Time and Space', pp. 1–21.
36. Zilfi, 'Muslim Women in the Early Modern Era', pp. 233–5; Veinstein, *Les Esclaves du Sultan chez les Ottomans*; Kermeli, 'Children Treated as Commodity in Ottoman Crete'; Araz, *Osmanlı Toplumunda Çocuk Olmak*, pp. 142–75.
37. Kabadayı, 'Working in a Fez Factory in Istanbul in the Late Nineteenth Century'; Kabadayı, 'Working for the State in a Factory in Istanbul'; Maksudyan, 'Foster-Daughter or Servant, Charity or Abuse', pp. 488–512; Emre Dölen, 'İplikhane-i Amire'; see Yavuz Velipaşaoğlu's Chapter 11 in this volume.
38. Quataert, *Ottoman Manufacturing*, pp. 33–4, 86, 156.
39. His latest book is a more detailed analysis of child labour based on domestic female labourers: Araz, *Çocuk Emeği*.
40. Araz and Kokdaş, 'The Changing Nature of the Domestic Service Sector in Nineteenth Century', pp. 103–4.
41. Demos and Demos, 'Adolescence in Historical Perspective', pp. 632–8; Habermas and Bluck, 'Getting a Life: The Emergence of the Life Story in Adolescence', pp. 748–69; Kett, 'Reflections on the History of Adolescence in America', pp. 355–73; Koops and Zuckerman, 'Introduction: A Historical Developmental Approach to Adolescence', pp. 345–54.
42. Burton, 'Looking Forward from Ariès?', pp. 207, 210; Wilson, 'The Infancy of the History of Childhood', pp. 140, 145.
43. Ze'evi, for example, who deals with sexuality in the Ottoman Empire, refers to young Ottoman and Arab boys as a specific administrative category called 'beardless youth'. He claims that they were the object of desire of certain male adults, but 'with encroachment of European values and norms the Arab and Turkish elite began to develop a hetero-normalized sexual discourse'.

Introduction

Ginio's work on the eighteenth century in the Ottoman Empire also shows that adolescents lived in a grey zone between childhood and adulthood and were not perceived as full adults. See Ze'evi, *Producing Desire: Changing Sexual Discourse in the Ottoman Middle East*, p. 96; Ginio, 'Childhood, Mental Capacity and Conversion to Islam in the Ottoman State', p. 110.

44. According to Maliki, at the end of the 'tender years', boys reach puberty and girls get married. In Hanafi legal discourse, the custody of boys was transferred from the mother to patrilineal relatives at the age of seven, but the father's agnatic line had custody of girls after they reached physical maturity (*buluğ*) and was determined by the start of menstruation. The Hanbali School gave the custody of girls to the male line of relatives around the age of seven to nine. *Shafi'i* legal discourse differed, since both boys and girls were given the opportunity to choose their own custodian at the age of discernment; in other words, at the age of seven or eight. Ibrahim, *Child Custody in Islamic Law*, pp. 65–9.
45. Araz, *Çocuk Olmak*, p. 88.
46. Peirce, 'Seniority, Sexuality, and Social Order', pp. 176–7.
47. For a detailed analysis of child marriages in different communities within the Empire, see Araz, '17. ve 18. Yüzyılda İstanbul ve Anadolu'da çocuk evlilikleri ve erişkinlik olgusu üzerine bir değerlendirme'; Araz, 'Cinsel ilişkiye Uygundur Lakin Kendi Adına Konuşamaz!'; Motzki, 'Child Marriages in Seventeenth-Century Palestine'; Yazbak, 'Minor Marriages and Khıyar al-Bulugh in Ottoman Palestine'; Ginio, 'Childhood'; Lamdan, 'Child Marriage in Jewish Society in the Eastern Mediterranean during the Sixteenth Century'; Ze'evi, *An Ottoman Century*, p. 180; Rozen, *A History of Jewish Community in Istanbul*, pp. 114–20.
48. Physical maturity was considered the decisive factor in setting the legal age for marriage in early modern cultures and societies. Canon law in line with Roman law allowed boys to get married at the age of fourteen at the earliest, but was set at twelve for girls. Aristocratic families in the Roman and Byzantine Empires married off girls at a very young age. This was also the case for medieval European nobility. Italian men married in their twenties or early thirties, whereas women usually married in their teens, earlier than in north-western Europe. The average age of female marriage did not rise until the fifteenth century, but teenage marriage still existed, even in the eighteenth century, since 15 per cent of all girls in Venice married between the ages of fourteen to twenty. Therefore, some early modern societies were most likely aware that these were child marriages. Rozen, *A History of Jewish Community in Istanbul*, p. 115; Nick Davidson, *Response* to '"Under-age" Sexual Activity in Reformation Genova'; Daniela Hacke, *Women, Sex and Marriage in Early Modern Venice*, pp. 116–17.
49. For a comparative analysis of early modern European marriage patterns with those prevalent in Ottoman society, see Rozen, A *History of Jewish Community in Istanbul*, pp. 117–20.

50. Araz, '17. ve 18. Yüzyılda İstanbul ve Anadolu'da çocuk evlilikleri ve erişkinlik olgusu üzerine bir değerlendirme', p. 106; Marcus, *The Middle East on the Eve of Modernity Aleppo in the Eighteenth Century*; Rapoport, *Marriage, Money and Divorce in Medieval Islamic Society*, pp. 38–9; Todorova, *Balkan Family Structure and the European Pattern Demographic Developments in Ottoman Bulgaria*, pp. 38–44.
51. Duben and Behar's work on nineteenth-century Istanbul households shows that actual age at marriage and the rates of polygamy differed from what is typically assumed in the literature. Specifically, the age of marriage was higher, and the rate of polygamy was lower, according to the data derived from the 1885 and 1907 censuses. Similarly, making predictions for the early modern period can be misleading. See Duben and Behar, *Istanbul Households*, pp. 123–4.
52. Krausman Ben-Amos, 'Adolescence as a Cultural Invention', pp. 74–5.
53. Gara also compares this to a study of customary law in pre-revolutionary Greece, which gave full legal responsibility to children at the age of thirteen, but still stipulated that the child should be under parental authority. See Gara's Chapter 3 in this volume; Maurer, *Das Griechische Volk*, vol. 1, p. 151.
54. The standard age for puberty in the registers for enrolment in the early peasant militia army (*yaya* and *müsellem* army) of the Empire was defined as twelve years for boys during the early years of Sultan Mehmed II (r. 1444–6). However, it gradually rose to fourteen in the sixteenth century. See Telci's Chapter 2 in this volume. During the classical application of the early modern recruitment method of the janissary army (the well-known *devşirme* system), the age category for conscription was from twelve to fifteen. See Yılmaz's Chapter 10 in this volume.
55. Schull, *Prisons in the Late Ottoman Empire*, pp. 171–3.
56. Araz, 'Cinsel ilişkiye Uygundur Lakin Kendi Adına Konuşamaz!', p. 48.
57. Duben and Behar, *Istanbul Households*, p. 123.
58. Schull, *Prisons in the Late Ottoman Empire*, pp. 176–9.
59. For a detailed analysis of the role of apprenticeships at young ages in transforming vocational skills in the guilds, see Araz, *Osmanlı Toplumunda Çocuk Olmak*, pp. 146–75. See Lamdan's Chapter 14 in this volume.
60. Ehud Toledano, *As if Silent and Absent*, pp. 19, 84.
61. See Yaşa's Chapter 7 and Yılmaz's Chapter 10 in this volume for a detailed analysis.
62. Heywood, *A History of Childhood*, pp. 11–19; Shahar, *Childhood in the Middle Ages*.
63. Krausman Ben-Amos, *Adolescence and Youth in Early Modern England*.
64. See, for example, Giladi, 'Concepts of Childhood and Attitudes Towards Children in Medieval Islam'; Giladi, *Children of Islam*.
65. Vatin, 'Réaction de la société Ottomane à la mort de ses "jeunes"', p. 176.
66. Ibid., pp. 182–3.

67. Fortna, 'Emphasizing the Islamic: Modifying the Curriculum of Late Ottoman State Schools'; Somel, 'Regulations for Raising Children during the Hamidian Period'; Okay, 'War and Child in the Second Constitutional Period'; Schull, *Prisons in the Late Ottoman Empire*, p. 176; Maksudyan, 'Orphans, Cities, and the State', pp. 493–5; Maksudyan, *Ottoman Children and Youth*, pp. 16–47; Zachs, 'Children in War Time'; Araz, 'Cinsel ilişkiye Uygundur Lakin Kendi Adına Konuşamaz!'.
68. Başaran, *Selim III, Social Control and Policing in Istanbul at the End of the Eighteenth Century*; Schull, *Prisons in the Late Ottoman Empire*, p. 176.

Bibliography

Agmon, Iris, *Family and Court: Legal Culture and Modernity in Late Ottoman Palestine* (New York: Syracuse University Press, 2006).

Amzi-Erdogdular, Leila, 'Alternative Muslim Modernities: Bosnian Intellectuals in the Ottoman and Habsburg Empires, Comparative Studies', *Comparative Studies in Society and History*, 59/4 (2017), pp. 912–43.

Araz, Yahya, '17. ve 18. Yüzyılda İstanbul ve Anadolu'da çocuk evlilikleri ve erişkinlik olgusu üzerine bir değerlendirme', *Kadın/Woman 2000*, 13/2 (2012), pp. 99–121.

―――, *Osmanlı İstanbul'unda Çocuk Emeği, Ev İçi Hizmetlerde İstihdam Edilen Çocuklar (1750–1920)* (Istanbul: Kitapyayınevi, 2020).

―――, 'Osmanlı İstanbul'unda Çocukluk, Çocuk Evlilikleri ve Cinsellik Yaşı üzerine bir Değerlendirme (19. Yüzyılın Başlarından İmparatorluğun Sonuna) Cinsel ilişkiye Uygundur Lakin Kendi Adına Konuşamaz!', *Toplumsal Tarih*, 274 (October 2016), pp. 42–9.

―――, *Osmanlı Toplumunda Çocuk Olmak* (Istanbul: Kitap Yayınevi, 2013).

Araz, Yahya, and Irfan Kokdaş, 'The Changing Nature of the Domestic Service Sector in Nineteenth Century', *International Labor and Working-Class History*, 97 (2020), pp. 81–108.

Ariès, Philippe, *Centuries of Childhood*, trans. Robert Baldick (New York: Vintage Books, 1966).

Baron, Beth, *The Orphan Scandal: Christian Missionaries and the Rise of the Muslim Brotherhood* (Palo Alto: Stanford University Press, 2014).

Başaran, Betül, *Selim III, Social Control and Policing in Istanbul at the End of the Eighteenth Century: Between Crisis and Order* (Leiden and Boston: Brill, 2014).

Blumi, Isa, *Reinstating the Ottomans: Alternative Balkan Modernities, 1800–1912* (New York: Palgrave Macmillan, 2011).

Boswell, John, *The Kindness of Strangers: The Abandonment of Children in Western Europe of the Late Antiquity to the Renaissance* (Chicago: University of Chicago Press, 1988).

Burton, Anthony, 'Looking Forward from Ariès? Pictorial and Material Evidence for the History of Childhood and Family Life', *Continuity and Change*, 4 (1989), pp. 203–29.

Büssow, Johann, 'Children of the Revolution: Youth in Palestine Public Life, 1908–14', in Yuval Ben Bassat and Eyal Ginio (eds), *Late Ottoman Palestine: The Period of Young Turk Rule* (London: I. B. Tauris, 2011), pp. 55–78.

Davidson, Nick, *Response* to '"Under-age" Sexual Activity in Reformation Genova', in George Rousseau (ed.), *Children and Sexuality from the Greeks to the Great War* (New York: Palgrave Macmillan, 2007), pp. 134–41.

DeMause, Lloyd (ed.), *The History of Childhood* (Maryland: The Rowman and Littlefield Publishing Group, 2006).

Demos, John, and Virginia Demos, 'Adolescence in Historical Perspective', *Journal of Marriage and Family*, 31/4 (1969), pp. 632–8.

Deringil, Selim, *The Well Protected Domains: Ideology and the Legitimation of Power in the Ottoman Power, 1876–1909* (London: I. B. Tauris, 2009).

Doumani, Beshara, *Family Life in the Ottoman Mediterranean: A Social History* (Cambridge: Cambridge University Press, 2017).

Dölen, Emre, 'İplikhane-i Amire', *İstanbul Ansiklopedisi*, vol. 4 (Istanbul: Kültür Bakanlığı ve Tarih Vakfı Yayınları, 1994), pp. 184–5.

Duben, Alan, and Cem Behar, *Istanbul Households: Marriage, Family and Fertility, 1880–1940* (Cambridge: Cambridge University Press, 1991).

Eisenstadt, Shmuel N., 'Multiple Modernities', *Daedalus*, 129/1 (2000), pp. 1–29.

Eltis, David, and Stanley Engerman, 'Dependence, Servility, and Coerced Labor in Time and Space', in David Eltis and Stanley Engerman (eds), *The Cambridge World History of Slavery*, vol. 3 (Cambridge: Cambridge University Press, 2011), pp. 1–21.

Fernea, Elizabeth Warnock (ed.), *Children in the Muslim Middle East* (Austin: University of Texas Press, 1987).

_____, *Remembering Childhood in the Middle East: Memoirs from a Century of Change* (Austin: University of Texas Press, 2002).

Fortna, Benjamin C. (ed.), *Childhood in the Late Ottoman Empire and After* (Leiden, Boston: Brill, 2016).

_____, 'Education and Autobiography at the End of the Ottoman Empire', *Die Welt des Islams*, 41/1 (2001), pp. 1–31.

_____, 'Emphasizing the Islamic: Modifying the Curriculum of Late Ottoman State Schools', in François Georgeon and Klaus Kreiser (eds), *Enfance et jeunesse dans le monde musulman/Childhood and Youth in the Muslim World* (Paris: Maisonneuve and Larose, 2007), pp. 193–210.

_____, *Imperial Classroom: Islam, the State, and Education in the Late Ottoman Empire* (Oxford: Oxford University Press, 2002).

Georgeon, François, and Klaus Kreisers, *Enfance et jeunesse dans le monde musulman/Childhood and Youth in the Muslim World* (Paris: Maisonneuve & Larose, 2007).

Giladi, Avner, *Children of Islam: Concepts of Childhood in Medieval Muslim Society* (London: Macmillan/St Antony's College Series, 1992).

_____, 'Concepts of Childhood and Attitudes Towards Children in Medieval

Introduction

Islam: A Preliminary Study with Special Reference to Reaction to Infant and Child Morality', *Journal of the Economic and Social History of the Orient*, 32/2 (1989), pp. 121–52.

_____, *Infants, Parents and Wet Nurses* (Leiden: Brill, 1999).

Ginio, Eyal, 'Childhood, Mental Capacity and Conversion to Islam in the Ottoman State', *Byzantine and Modern Greek Studies*, 25 (2001), pp. 90–119.

_____, *The Ottoman Culture of Defeat: The Balkan Wars and their Aftermath* (New York: Oxford University Press, 2016).

Habermas, T., and S. Bluck, 'Getting a Life: The Emergence of the Life Story in Adolescence', *Psychological Bulletin*, 126/5 (2000), pp. 748–69.

Hacke, Daniela, *Women, Sex and Marriage in Early Modern Venice* (Aldershot: Ashgate, 2004).

Hanawalt, Barbara A., *Growing Up in Medieval London: The Experience of Childhood in History* (New York, Oxford: Oxford University Press, 1992).

Hecht, Tobias, *Minor Omissions: Children in Latin American History and Society* (Madison: University of Wisconsin Press, 2002).

Heywood, Colin, *A History of Childhood: Children and Childhood in the West from Medieval to Modern Times* (Cambridge: Polity Press with Blackwell Publishing Ltd, 2001).

Ibrahim, Ahmed Fekry, *Child Custody in Islamic Law: Theory and Practice in Egypt since the Sixteenth Century* (Cambridge: Cambridge University Press, 2018).

İnanç Özekmekçi, Mehmet, 'The Formation of Children in the Late Ottoman Empire: An Analysis through the Periodicals for Children (1869–1914)', MA thesis, Boğaziçi University, 2005.

James, Allison, and Alan Prout (eds), *Constructing and Reconstructing Childhood: Contemporary Issues in the Sociological Study of Childhood* (New York: Routledge, 2015).

Kabadayı, Erdem, 'Working for the State in a Factory in Istanbul: The Role of Factory Workers' Ethno-Religious and Gender Characteristics in State-Subject Interaction in the Late Ottoman Empire', PhD dissertation, Munich University, 2008.

_____, 'Working in a Fez Factory in Istanbul in the Late Nineteenth Century: Division of Labour and Networks of Migration Formed Along Ethno-Religious Lines', *International Review of Social History*, 54 (2009), pp. 69–90.

Kermeli, Eugenia, 'Children Treated as Commodity in Ottoman Crete', in Eugenia Carmeli and Oktay Özel (eds), *The Ottoman Empire: Myths, Realities and 'Black Holes'* (Istanbul: Isis Press, 2006), pp. 269–82.

Kett, Joseph F., 'Reflections on the History of Adolescence in America', *The History of the Family*, 8/3 (2003), pp. 355–73.

Koops, Willem, and Michael Zuckerman, 'Introduction: A Historical Developmental Approach to Adolescence', *The History of the Family*, 8/3 (2003), pp. 345–54.

Krausman Ben-Amos, Ilana, 'Adolescence as a Cultural Invention: Philippe Ariés and the Sociology of Youth', *History of the Human Sciences*, 8/2 (1995), pp. 69–89.

———, *Adolescence and Youth in Early Modern England* (New Haven and London: Yale University Press, 1994).

Lal, Deepak, 'Does Modernization Require Westernization?', *Independent Review*, 5 (2000), pp. 5–24.

Lamdan, Ruth, 'Child Marriage in Jewish Society in the Eastern Mediterranean during the Sixteenth Century', *Mediterranean Historical Review*, 2/1 (1996), pp. 37–59.

Maksudyan, Nazan, 'Foster-Daughter or Servant, Charity or Abuse: *Beslemes* in the Late Ottoman Empire', *Journal of Historical Sociology*, 21/4 (2008), pp. 488–512.

———, 'Hearing the Voiceless – Seeing the Invisible: Orphans and Destitute Children as Actors of Social, Economic, and Political History in the late Ottoman Empire', PhD dissertation, Sabancı University, 2008.

———, 'Orphans, Cities, and the State: Vocational Orphanages (*Islahhanes*) and Reform in the Late Ottoman Urban Space', *International Journal of Middle East Studies*, 43 (2011), pp. 493–511.

———, *Orphans and Destitute Children in the Late Ottoman Empire* (New York: Syracuse University Press, 2014).

———, *Ottoman Children and Youth during World War I* (New York: Syracuse University Press, 2019).

Marcus Abraham, *The Middle East on the Eve of Modernity Aleppo in the Eighteenth Century* (New York: Columbia University Press, 1989).

Maurer, Georg Ludwig, *Das griechische Volk in öffentlicher, kirchlicher und privatrechtlicher Beziehungvor und nachdem Freiheitskampfe bis zum 31 Juli 1834*, 2 vols (Heidelberg: J. C. B. Mohr, 1835).

Meriwether, Margaret L., *The Kin Who Count: Family and Society in Aleppo, 1770–1840* (Austin: Texas University Press, 1999).

———, 'The Rights of Children and the Responsibilities of Women: Women as Wasis in Ottoman Aleppo, 1770–1840', in Amira El Azhary Sonbol, *Women, the Family, and Divorce Laws in Islamic History* (Syracuse: Syracuse University Press, 1996), pp. 219–35.

Morrison, Heidi, *Childhood and Colonial Modernity in Egypt* (London: Palgrave, 2015).

———, (comp. and ed.), *Global History of Childhood Reader* (New York: Routledge, 2012).

Motzki, Harald, 'Child Marriages in Seventeenth-Century Palestine', in Khalid Masud, Brinkley Messick, and David Powers (eds), *Legal Interpretation Muftis and their Fatwas* (Cambridge, MA: Harvard University Press, 1996), pp. 129–40.

Okay, Cüneyd, *Osmanlı Çocuk Hayatında Yenileşmeler 1850–1900* (Istanbul: Kırkambar Yayınları, 1998).

———, 'War and Child in the Second Constitutional Period', in François Georgeon and Klaus Kreiser (eds), *Enfance et jeunesse dans le monde musul-*

Introduction

man/Childhood and Youth in the Muslim World (Paris: Maisonneuve & Larose, 2007), pp. 219–32.

Olsen, Stephanie (ed.), *Childhood, Youth and Emotions in Modern History: National, Colonial and Global Perspective* (New York: Palgrave Macmillan, 2015).

Olsen, Stephanie, and Rob Boddice, 'Styling Emotions History', *Journal of Social History*, 51/3 (2018), pp. 476–87.

Onur, Bekir, *Türkiye'de Çocukluğun Tarihi* (Ankara: İmge Kitabevi, 2005).

Peirce, Leslie, 'Seniority, Sexuality, and Social Order: The Vocabulary of Gender in Early Modern Ottoman Society', in Madeline C. Zilfi (ed.), *Women in the Ottoman Empire, Middle Eastern Women in the Early Modern Era* (Leiden: Brill, 1997), pp. 169–96.

Prout, Alan, *The Body, Childhood and Society* (London: Palgrave Macmillan, 2000).

Quataert, Donald, *Ottoman Manufacturing in the Age of the Industrial Revolution* (Cambridge: Cambridge University Press, 1993).

Rapoport, Yossef, *Marriage, Money and Divorce in Medieval Islamic Society* (Cambridge: Cambridge University Press, 2005).

Reddy, William M., *The Navigation of Feeling: A Framework for the History of Emotions* (New York: Cambridge University, 2001).

Rosenwein, Barbara H., *Generations of Feeling* (Cambridge: Cambridge University, 2016).

Rozen, Minna, *A History of the Jewish Community in Istanbul Formative Years, 1453–1566* (Leiden, Boston: Brill, 2010).

Schull, Kent, *Prisons in the Late Ottoman Empire* (Edinburgh: Edinburgh University Press, 2014).

Shahar, Shulamith, *Childhood in the Middle Ages* (London: Routledge, 2005).

Somel, Selçuk Akşin, *The Modernization of Public Education in the Ottoman Empire 1839–1908* (Leiden: Brill, 2001).

_____, 'Regulations for Raising Children During the Hamidian Period', in François Georgeon and Klaus Kreiser (eds), *Enfance et jeunesse dans le monde musulman/Childhood and Youth in the Muslim World* (Paris: Maisonneuve and Larose, 2007), pp. 211–18.

Sonbol, Amira El Azhary, 'Adults and Minors in Ottoman Shariᶜa Courts and Modern Law', in Amira El Azhary Sonbol (ed.), *Women, the Family, and Divorce Laws in Islamic History* (Syracuse and New York: Syracuse University Press, 1996), pp. 236–56.

Stearns, Peter N., *Childhood in World History* (Abingdon: Routledge, 2011).

Stearns, Peter N., and Timothy Haggerty, 'The Role of Fear: Transitions in Emotion Standards for Children 1850–1950', *The American Historical Review*, 96 (1991), pp. 63–94.

Stearns, Peter N., and Carol Z. Stearns, 'Emotionology: Clarifying the History of Emotions and Emotional Standards', *The American Historical Review*, 90/4 (1985), pp. 813–36.

Şafak, Necmettin, 'İlk Dönem (14. ve 15. Yüzyıl) Türkçe Tıp Yazmalarında Çocuk Sağlığı Hastalıkları ve Tedavileri', *Yeni Tıp Tarihi Araştırmaları* 12–15 (Istanbul, 2006–9), pp. 227–313.

Tan, Mine Göğüş, Özlem Şahin, Mustafa Sever, and Aksu Bora, *Cumhuriyet'te Çocuktular* (Istanbul: Boğaziçi Üniversitesi Yayınevi, 2007).

Tezcan, Hülya, *Osmanlı Sarayının Çocukları* (Istanbul: Aygaz, 2006).

Todorova, Maria, *Balkan Family Structure and the European Pattern Demographic Developments in Ottoman Bulgaria* (Budapest: Central European University Press, 2006).

Toledano, Ehud, *As if Silent and Absent: Bonds of Enslavement in the Islamic Middle East* (New Haven and London: Yale University Press, 2007).

Tucker, Judith, *In the House of the Law: Gender and Islamic Law in Ottoman Syria and Palestine* (Berkeley: University of California Press, 1998).

Veinstein, Gilles, *Les Esclaves du Sultan chez les Ottomans, Des mamelouks aux janissaires (xive–xviie siècles)* (Paris: Les Belles Lettres, 2020).

Wilson, Adrian, 'The Infancy of the History of Childhood: An Appraisal of Philippe Ariès', *History and Theory*, 19 (1980), pp. 132–53.

Worringer, Ranée, *Ottomans Imagining Japan: East, Middle East, and non-Western Modernity at the Turn of the Twentieth Century* (New York: Palgrave and Macmillan, 2014).

Yazbak, Mahmoud, 'Minor Marriages and Khıyar al-Bulugh in Ottoman Palestine: A Note on Women's Strategies in a Patriarchal Society', *Islamic Law and Society*, 9/3 (2002), pp. 386–409.

Zachs, Fruma, 'Children in War Time: The First Pupils of the Syrian (Schneller) Orphanage in Jerusalem 1860–1863', *Middle Eastern Studies*, 55 (2019), pp. 1–16.

———, 'Growing Consciousness of the Child in Ottoman Syria in the 19th Century: New Modes of Parenting and Education in the Middle Class', in Eyal Ginio and Eli Podeh (eds), *Researching Ottoman History: Studies in Honour of Amnon Cohen* (Leiden: Brill, 2013), pp. 113–28.

———, 'The Private World of Women and Children: Lullabies and Nursery Rhymes in 19th Century Greater Syria', in Hoda Mahmoudi and Steven Mintz (eds), *Children and Youth in an Interconnected World: Multidisciplinary Perspective* (London: Routledge, 2019), pp. 77–99.

Ze'evi, Dror, *An Ottoman Century, The District of Jerusalem in the 1600s* (New York: State University of New York Press, 1996).

———, *Producing Desire: Changing Sexual Discourse in the Ottoman Middle East* (Berkeley: University of California Press, 2006).

Zilfi, Madeline, 'Muslim Women in the Early Modern Era', in Suraiya N. Faroqhi (ed.), *The Cambridge History of Turkey*, vol. 3, The Later Ottoman Empire, 1603–1839 (Cambridge: Cambridge University Press, 2006), pp. 226–55.

Zuckerman, Michael, *Beyond the Century of the Child: Cultural History and Developmental Psychology* (Philadelphia: Pennsylvania Press, 2003).

Chapter 1

Ottoman Childhoods in Comparative Perspective

Colin Heywood

The notion that childhood could have a history, that conceptions of this stage of life varied over time and that the experiences of children in the past were worthy of scholarly attention came relatively late in the day. The conventional starting point has been the publication of *L'Enfant et la vie familiale sous l'ancien régime* by the French historian Philippe Ariès in 1960, with research in this area rapidly gaining momentum in Europe and North America during the late twentieth century.[1] Interest in studying the history of childhood on a global scale came later, and even now remains at an early stage.[2] The upshot is that at present the West is the most intensively studied area, although an increasing volume of material is becoming available on Latin America, Africa and Asia.[3] This collection of essays, besides adding to a still meagre literature on the history of childhood in the Ottoman Empire, helps historians interested in making international comparisons. An empire that lasted for approximately 600 years, from the early fourteenth century to 1922, ruled over diverse ethnic, cultural and religious groups, and at its peak straddled Asia, Europe and Africa, is an excellent vehicle for comparisons and contrasts with other parts of the world. This opening chapter will set the context of the existing historiography on childhood and children for the detailed studies that follow, beginning with conceptions of childhood (the cultural history of childhood), and moving on to children with and without a family, and the trade-off between work and education (the related social history of children).

Conceptions of Childhood

Ping-chen Hsiung suggests that '[i]f Philippe Ariès had known Chinese and the world of China, he probably would have hesitated before making his assertion that until relatively recent times people had little notion of children or childhood'.[4] The same might be said of the Ottoman world, where there is ample evidence of an awareness of the particular nature of the child during the medieval period. Even in western Europe, historians have long since moved on from the Ariès' thesis, with a mass of textual and visual evidence from the Middle Ages countering its principal claims.[5] For most of the Ottoman era, ideas on childhood were inspired by a combination of religious beliefs and legal texts. From the very beginning, Judaism, Christianity and (from the seventh century) Islam taught that children were a blessing for their parents, rejecting the Greek and Roman practices of limiting family size by means of abortion, exposure and infanticide. Islamic ethics were strongly pro-natalist, with the theologian and jurist Al-Ghazali (1058–1111) encouraging the faithful to 'marry and multiply'.[6] Likewise, in the Old Testament Jewish tradition, children were a divine gift: in the Creation story, God created male and female, and then commanded them to 'Be fruitful, and multiply, and replenish the earth' (Genesis 1: 27–8).

This is not to say that the population followed these exhortations to the letter. Certainly, women in the Ottoman lands and in the early modern world in general had large numbers of births, for children were a form of wealth in rural society, supplying labour and carers for old age. Yet in some circumstances, children could be a burden rather than a blessing for a family. Doubtless, the old methods of disposing of them lingered on, though they are not always easy to document. The abandonment of infants, while present in the Ottoman Empire, was nowhere near the scale found in parts of southern, 'Catholic' Europe. In the latter case it peaked during the nineteenth century: in Milan, until mid-century 30 to 40 per cent of all babies born in the city were abandoned.[7] It should be added that, typical of agrarian societies everywhere, people in the villages and towns of the Ottoman Empire (see Elbirlik's Chapter 5), as in Japan and the West, welcomed the birth of a boy more than a girl. A pastor in the Ariège (France), for example, reported that the birth of a boy was signalled with the firing of guns and celebrations, a girl with 'cruel disappointment'.[8]

THE EXTENT OF CHILDHOOD

Boundaries between childhood, youth and adulthood in the Ottoman Empire were, as everywhere else, vague and fluid before the efficient registration of births and the age-grading of classes in modern schools began to take effect during the nineteenth century.[9] Biological influences, such as puberty, provided possible turning points in the life cycle in all societies.

However, boundaries were also affected by differing legal, educational and employment systems. Telci's Chapter 2 gives a striking example of varying age limits for adolescence within the Ottoman Empire during the fifteenth and sixteenth centuries in registers for fiscal and military recruitment purposes.

For Muslim, Jewish and Christian communities of the Empire, there was an early turning point around the age of seven, bringing the age of reason or discernment, when children could start their education or their work on a farm or in a workshop.[10] The onset of puberty marked a further transition – in this case, in gendered form.[11] Following Islamic law, the legal age of majority in the Empire came with puberty and sexual maturity, which could set in as early as the age of nine or as late as fifteen. According to *Shari'ah*, it generally arrived between the ages of twelve and fourteen among girls, and at around fifteen among boys.[12] For boys in particular, the phase of pubescence (or 'beardless youth') was followed by a further transitional stage as a *mücerred*, a young bachelor, who was sexually mature, but still not considered to be fully socialised.[13] As Eleni Gara shows in her case study here of an eighteenth-century Ottoman boyhood, even after puberty Panayis Skouzes continued for a few years to perceive himself as a minor, a 'semi-adult' still subject to his father's authority. Similarly, in Europe and North America, before the twentieth century, First Communion (for Roman Catholics) or Confirmation (for Protestants) could be regarded as a marker of maturity, ushering in a start to work. This was taken as early as ten or eleven in some cases, or later during the mid-teens. Puberty was less significant, or rather as the ethnologist Arnold Van Gennep argued during the nineteenth century, less so than a later 'social puberty' around the age of sixteen. At this point, a boy or girl was likely to be sufficiently mature to join the society of local youth.[14]

Marriage, and the birth of a first child, secured the final achievement of adulthood in the pre-modern world. During the late twentieth century, historians generally followed the historical demographer John Hajnal in asserting that there was a stark difference between north-western and south-eastern Europe concerning the age at which people married. In the former, Hajnal assumed that couples married late, towards the end of their twenties. In the latter, and in Africa and Asia also, he assumed early marriage was the rule, before the age of twenty-four for women.[15] However, it soon became clear that this model rested on very few studies from the south and east. Specialists in eastern European demography accused their counterparts in the West of persisting with old-established stereotypes of an exotic but 'backward' civilisation in the Slav lands, countering with evidence of a diversity of marriage patterns in south-eastern Europe.

Since then, historians have either adopted a modified version of the Hajnal schema or preferred to emphasise complexity right across the continent.[16] Thus, for the former, early marriage appears common in Russia, as in the Slav lands of the Empire: Savva Dmitrievich Purlevskii, a former serf from Central Russia, helpfully observed that: 'According to our local customs, marriage at the age of eighteen was nothing unusual'. For the latter, there is the assertion that even during the nineteenth century 'the differences within countries were stronger than those between countries'.[17] The Italian peninsula was notable for its pronounced regional variations during the eighteenth and nineteenth centuries. In the Veneto, for example, the average age at marriage was thirty to thirty-one for men and twenty-nine for women, while in parts of the south the average was twenty-three for men and twenty for women.[18] A hint of such diversity is also to be found in the Ottoman Empire. In Istanbul, during the late nineteenth and early twentieth centuries, men, on average, married at the age of thirty, women at the age of twenty, whilst in Bulgaria (part of its southern European territory) during the period 1834–86 in the Catholic village of Baltadzhi the respective averages were 20.1 and 18.8.[19] Leslie Peirce, discussing gender in the Empire during the early modern period, observes that where there was a significant gap in the preferred age of marriage for men and women, '[f]emales were married upon physical maturation so that the awakening of sexual desire occurred within marriage, while the marriage of males might be delayed beyond the awakening of desire'.[20] By contrast, where late marriage was the norm, the result was an exceptionally long period of youth, lasting for ten to fifteen years.

THE NATURE OF THE CHILD

A tendency to ambivalence was common to many religions when they discussed the nature of the child. Islamic scriptures noted the purity and innocence of children, but also their ignorance and weakness of spirit. Similarly, Jesus Christ himself was reported to have highlighted children as models of humility for adults to follow, but later, St Augustine (354–430) was influential in arguing that children were born with the taint of original sin.[21] This latter was a notion entirely absent from Jewish and Islamic teaching, but it weighed heavily on Christians' attitude to children, particularly as it was taken up by Protestants after the Reformation. The American Calvinist Jonathan Edwards (1703–58), for example, stood out for his emphasis on the depravity of children before they converted, describing them as 'young vipers' – though he also granted that they could be filled with grace as well as sin.[22] Whatever religious leaders had to say, it seems that ordinary people in the towns and villages everywhere had a more down-to-earth view of their young, considering them as 'little animals' that needed to be tamed and civilised.

The eighteenth-century Enlightenment in Europe brought a more secular attitude to childhood, and a generally more positive image of children. *Emile, or On Education* (1762), by the Swiss-born Jean-Jacques Rousseau, was an influential text, opposing the doctrine of original sin with his 'incontestable maxim' that 'the first movements of nature are invariably right'. He invited his readers to 'love childhood, promote its games, its pleasures, its amiable instinct'.[23] This work was widely read in literate circles, including by intellectuals in the Ottoman Empire. With the Romantic movement that followed, such luminaries as William Wordsworth (1770–1850) and Jean Paul Richter (1763–1825) were even more effusive on the outstanding spiritual sensibility of children. Older views on depravity continued to challenge such a vision, as in the case of the Evangelicals in England, but they gradually faded from the scene. The new ideas encouraged greater attention to the welfare of children, leading eventually to the modern, protected childhood. They also struck a chord in non-Western societies, including the Ottoman Empire, where they predominantly took root among the elite in Istanbul during the *Tanzimat* period of reform (1839–76). Alan Duben and Cem Behar assert that: 'Nineteenth-century Ottomans began to make connections between child-rearing, education and social reform and turned to the betterment of children's health, character and knowledge as the road to the betterment of society at large'. They also note the defence of Islamic and Turkish traditions in newspapers and popular magazines, and the way ideas, values and meanings were 'transmitted, absorbed, adapted and often distorted in their movement from the West to Ottoman Istanbul'.[24] Thus, the emergence of the concept of the modern child in the Ottoman Empire was not simply due to the import of Western ideas, but to an internal process with its own characteristics and development. As Benjamin Fortna puts it, although Western ideas about childhood were important, 'they were unevenly absorbed, and always mediated through indigenous institutions, individuals, traditions and desires'.[25] For example, Kokdaş' Chapter 4 reveals that the wealthier families in the towns of Ruse, Sofia and Vidin (now in Bulgaria) leaned towards having fewer children during the first half of the nineteenth century. This may indicate that the modern perception of children as the core of the family and society was partly an indigenous development and not solely the result of the encounter with Western ideas.

Children and Family Life

The family was the bedrock of society for much of the Ottoman period, as the state (like the Empire's counterparts in Europe) relied on it to fulfil many functions, including responsibility for the health, education, entertainment and disciplining of its members. As a preliminary, what can be said about the size and structure of households in the Empire compared with its neighbours? Research on the history of the family has in the Ottoman Empire been hampered by a scarcity of sources; one is bound to agree with Donald Quataert that: 'On this issue, much research is needed'.[26] What does emerge is that small, nuclear families were the most common form in the Empire, though complex families were rather more common than in north-western Europe. Studies of the Muslim household in nineteenth-century rural Anatolia produced an average size of between 5.3 and 6.5 persons.[27] This may be compared to a sample of English parishes running from the late sixteenth to the early twentieth century that had a mean size of 4.75.[28] There were, of course, more complex family forms apparent in both the Empire and the rest of the world. In Istanbul, an estimated 16 per cent of households had an extended form; in rural Anatolia, no more than 30 per cent. In Japan, by contrast, the basic household (the *ie*) was a form of stem family, in which one child married and lived with the parents, while the others either set up families elsewhere or remained unmarried at home. Similar forms were found in Europe, including parts of Austria, France and Norway.[29] Later, during the late nineteenth and early twentieth centuries, there was a move towards even smaller families in much of western Europe and parts of the Empire, notably Istanbul. This was the setting for the modern, child-centred family: as Michael Anderson observes in the case of England and Wales, married women born during the 1880s 'had only half as many children to care for, entertain, clothe and feed as their parents had had'.[30]

PARENT–CHILD RELATIONSHIPS

Early historians of childhood, taking a lead from Philippe Ariès, devoted a good deal of attention to the question of whether parents in the past loved their children. Ariès himself had very little to say about the early years of childhood before the age of seven, but in so far as he did, generally conveyed an impression of parental indifference and even callousness towards their offspring before the supposed 'discovery' of childhood during the early modern period.[31] Influential historians from the 1970s, including Lawrence Stone and Edward Shorter, adopted a similar pattern, with remote parent–child relations, followed by more affection between the two sides from the eighteenth century onwards. A later generation of historians in the West has reacted against such claims, emphasising long-term continuities, rather than a turning point during the eighteenth century. Citing evidence from as far back as the Middle Ages, they argue that the vast majority of parents had always loved their children as best they could.[32] Historians of the Ottoman Empire have generally agreed; Margaret Meriwether asserts that: 'There is no reason to doubt that strong emotional attachments between parents and children were the norm'.[33]

This is not to say that all was sweetness and light in family life, in the past as in the present. Family history in the West has revealed a number of issues that cast a shadow over affectionate relations between the generations. In the first place, the employment of 'mercenary' wet nurses was not unknown in the Ottoman Empire, though it was largely restricted to upper-class families, while in parts of Europe the practice was far more widespread. It might appear the height of callousness to hand over a newborn baby for a year or two to a nurse who would be paid to breastfeed it. Critics, notably Rousseau in *Emile*, urged women to breastfeed their own offspring, and the vast majority of mothers probably did so.[34] Outstanding exceptions were often aristocrats or wealthy bourgeois, who felt entitled to spare themselves the disruption to their social life. In France and Italy in particular, the custom spread well down the social scale to shopkeepers and artisans in the towns.[35] The harsh reality for many families was that the need for mothers to help run a family business made wet-nursing, in the words of George Sussman, 'a necessity, but not a very attractive one'.[36]

A second custom with the potential to sour relations between parents and their children was the resort to harsh punishments. Çiçek's Chapter 12 gives a disturbing account of violence towards children within the family as well as in schools among the Ottoman–Turkish population during the late Empire period. Likewise in Europe, there was a widespread custom of 'beating, whipping, abusing and scolding children and holding them in great fear and subjection', as Pierre Charron observed in France at the beginning of the seventeenth century.[37] Advice manuals, ranging from those from sixteenth-century Germany to others from modern Britain and the United States, recommended moderation in the infliction of punishments, and, from the nineteenth century onwards, they began to turn against corporal punishment and the practice of terrorising children with threats of assorted bogeymen or eternal damnation.[38] There was always an awareness of the difference between normal and excessive or abusive application of these punishments, with the result that most children appeared to take them in their stride. However, some childhood reminiscences reveal a fierce reaction against the parent involved. Edmund Gosse (1849–1928) remembered from his London childhood that 'I went about the house for some days with a murderous hatred of my father locked in my bosom' after a caning at the age of six.[39]

ORPHANED, ABANDONED AND DESTITUTE CHILDREN

In the global context, children without a family to support them were in a precarious position, until the establishment of welfare states during the twentieth century. Such children were numerous: estimates from French, Spanish and English villages during the seventeenth and eighteenth centuries suggest that a third of the children would lose a parent while growing up.[40] Yet there is evidence that the old regime states and charities in Europe during the early modern period lacked the resources to cope. Many children in need of care and protection did not live for long. In the foundling hospitals of the European nations the high mortality rates were a scandal for contemporaries. In Florence's famous *Ospedale degli Innocenti*, during the 1770s, around three quarters of the infants died within a year of being deposited.[41] Children who did survive had to rely on kin and neighbours for support or hope for some assistance from locally organised public and private institutions. Sadly, these vulnerable children were often despised rather than pitied, treated callously rather than with compassion. Their fate in the modern world was to be seen as a threat to the social order, as the very antithesis of the ideal of the pure and innocent child. In the case of the Ottoman Empire, as Nazan Maksudyan puts it, orphans and destitute children were perceived to be endangered by the modernising world around them, but at the same time were themselves a new danger created by that world.[42]

Boarding out children with a local family was a cost-effective solution for those without friends or relatives to support them. In the Ottoman Empire, young girls who might be orphans or abandoned children, or more often those whose families who could not afford to keep them, were fostered by well-off families. Less affluent families could participate with subsidies from the government. Typically, in Istanbul, girls were taken on when they were somewhere between the ages of seven and thirteen. In principle, this was a charitable act – feeding, clothing and lodging these foster daughters (*beslemes*) – but in practice the unfortunate girls were often treated as servants, rather than as daughters. During the first half of the nineteenth century, it was common for all (or nearly all) of their wages to be spent on their subsistence, with gifts in kind given at the discretion of the employer when they left. Their education was also neglected, and it was expected that they were to be available for sexual relations with males in the household. However, change came during the second half of the century, as the girls became 'free wage labour', with standardised wage contracts and cash payments when they left becoming the norm in Istanbul.[43] Similar customs applied in much of Europe. Scotland stood out for its policy of boarding out both boys and girls wherever possible, in contrast to the English preference after the Poor Law Amendment Act of 1834 for the harsh rigours of the workhouse. In Scandinavia, it was common practice to auction impoverished children, with the very young going to childless couples, and older ones again providing cheap labour.[44] All of these children risked abuse in the form of beatings and sexual harassment.

Various specialised institutions were also available to care for destitute children. In Europe there were numerous hospitals, orphanages, asylums, refuges and free schools run by religious charities or civil associations throughout the early modern and modern periods.[45] Nearly all made an attempt to provide the children with some form of vocational training as well as food and shelter, hoping to prepare them for their working life: usually a trade envisaged for the boys, domestic service for the girls. The English workhouses were notoriously hard on children after 1834. There was a policy of separating them from their parents, and keeping boys and girls apart. Their food and clothing were barely adequate, as Charles Dickens made clear in *Oliver Twist* (1838), and the discipline they faced was brutal. It is possible that this austere regime left the unfortunate children 'permanently wounded', rather than set up for adulthood.[46]

During the second half of the nineteenth century the Ottoman state set up a number of vocational orphanages (*ıslahhane*s) in their bid to protect and educate impoverished street children, boys in particular. This included the large numbers of refugees, such as those from the Russo-Ottoman War of 1877–8. The emphasis was always on learning a trade rather than formal schooling, and on encouraging loyalty to the Ottoman state among Muslims and non-Muslims alike. Where poverty caused children to slide into criminality, attracting attention as vagrants, beggars, thieves or prostitutes (in the case of girls), reformers in the West experimented during the nineteenth century with various ways of removing them from the corrupting influence of adult prisons. These included dispatching them to start a new life in Canada (in the British case), or sending them off to agricultural colonies, such as Mettray in France, to experience the supposedly moralising influence of work on the land.[47] The Ottomans turned to the ready-made solution of the *ıslahhane*s during the final years of their Empire.[48]

Work and Education

In the long run, children everywhere in the world have tended to move towards the 'modern' childhood pattern of spending most of their time in school rather than at work, though it has been invariably adapted to local circumstances.[49] In the contemporary world the shift has been by no means achieved in some low-income societies, and even in Europe and North America it is not possible to talk of mass education taking hold until the nineteenth century. In the West, and in the Ottoman lands, work on the land or in a workshop loomed large in the childhood of all but a small, privileged group. Yet there were schools of various types to be found in these areas during the medieval and early modern periods, dominated by religious authorities. The balance between work and education at any particular point has been a complex matter, influenced by class, gender, ethnic background and location.

CHILDREN AT WORK IN AGRICULTURE AND HANDICRAFT TRADES

The large majority of children during all periods under the Ottomans doubtless worked on small family farms and in the associated rural industries. In 1859, smallholdings occupied no less than 82 per cent of land under cultivation in the Empire. Such farms relied on the labour of all family members, avoiding the resort to outside help as far as possible.[50] In Europe, there was more large-scale farming and manufacture in various regions, but peasant farms and domestic workshops were still numerous across the continent during the nineteenth and early twentieth centuries. Unfortunately for historians of all societies, children's experiences at this type of work remain largely buried in the depths of the countryside. 'Invisible hands' was the apt description by Beverly Grier of this type of labour, in her study of child labour in colonial Zimbabwe.[51] Contemporary opinion regarded farm work as healthy and a matter for parents rather than government, so that there was no investigation of conditions to match those concerning factories and mines. In the West, historians can rely on numerous peasant and working-class autobiographies to give a hint of the child's perspective: a recent study of childhood during the Industrial Revolution period by Jane Humphries was based on no less than 600 of such works.[52] On a family farm, there was the satisfaction of helping with the workload, picking up little tasks such as childminding and bird scaring and acquiring new skills working beside their parents. But there were also the long hours, insecurity in the face of harvest failures and, particularly in the north, bitterly cold weather conditions. In France, Jeanne Bouvier

(1865–1964) recalled that during her childhood in the Isère: 'I would help my mother do all the little farm chores: hoeing, gleaning, and gathering grass for the animals. But my main job was tending the cows'. This latter task involved the 'torment' of getting up before daybreak, but at least out in the pastures she could play with other children occupied in the same way.[53]

As recent scholarship on the Ottoman Empire has emphasised, entrepreneurs in the Ottoman Empire concentrated their resources in the handicraft trades, rather than large-scale industry. This played to their strengths – notably, the abundance of workers willing to work long hours for low wages. Indeed, the success of those trades that were most successful on the international market rested on the widespread exploitation of young women and children in the workshops. 'Oriental' carpets from Anatolia were the outstanding example, with part of their allure for consumers in Europe and the United States being the assumption that they were an individual work of art produced by a skilled artisan. The sad reality was that they were increasingly mass produced during the nineteenth century by a vast army of largely female and youthful carpet knotters. Household production predominated, though in the newer centres centralised workshops were established by merchants from Izmir and Istanbul. Here it was possible to 'sweat' the trade with low wages, deskilled workers and an increasing pace of work.[54] In modern Europe as well, most children continued to work in traditional settings, using hand technologies and employing both skilled workers and 'a plentiful supply of drudges'. This mirrored the organisation of labour in the Empire in industries such as silk reeling and tobacco, as well as in others such as glass and paper.[55]

CHILD LABOUR IN INDUSTRY

The late nineteenth and early twentieth centuries witnessed a few initiatives to introduce the factory system in the Ottoman lands, but they were tentative. This was only to be expected, given that the factor endowment was unsuited to this form of production. On the eve of the First World War, mechanised cotton spindles in the Empire, confined to a small area in Macedonia, amounted to 0.02 per cent of the British total.[56] This meant that Ottoman children were spared the grim conditions of the coal mines, mills and slums: the latter, a case of modernisation, in the form of industrial capitalism, producing in the short term a distinctly non-modern childhood.[57] However, the Hereke factory campus studied in Velipaşaoğlu's Chapter 11 reveals an Ottoman version of some of the recruitment strategies familiar from European and Japanese experiences in the textile industry. Its labour force was decidedly youthful, employing large numbers of girls between the ages of four and fifteen. Similarly, early British factories during the late eighteenth century relied heavily on children. Those under thirteen accounted for 40 per cent of the workers at Robert Owen's famous cotton mill at New Lanark during the 1790s. Likewise, in the Osaka cotton mills in Japan, a survey undertaken in 1898 found that around two-thirds of the largely female labour force were under twenty.[58] The Hereke mill also made use of forced labour. In Europe it took the form of 'apprentices' from the poor houses, rather than slave children and conscripted Christian girls (as well as orphans). Finally, the Hereke mill provided dormitories that helped it to recruit girls from outlying villages, with the reassurance for their families that their daughters were in safe hands. This mirrored the example of the dormitories established by silk mill owners in southern France, the 'Waltham system' deployed by cotton manufacturers in the northern part of Massachusetts and the hostels for girls in Osaka.

This brings us to the young people working in the service sector of the economy. If child labour in the textile mills and other large-scale enterprises was quite rare in the Empire, the employment of young girls as domestic servants in the towns was much in evidence. Yahya Araz (in this volume) and others have highlighted the common experience of village girls from certain provinces of the Empire moving to Istanbul to spend a few years before marriage as live-in servants. They note the many parallels with the labour market in Europe. Everywhere, girls worked long hours for low pay, risked corporal punishments and were vulnerable to sexual abuse by male members of the household, as mentioned above. At the same time, their board and lodging in the house provided some security. They might accumulate savings and useful skills, and they usually had some family or village contacts to support them.[59] In Britain, the 1881 census revealed that a little under half of girls below the age of fifteen listed with an occupation were in domestic service. Worst off amongst them were the child-servants, aged around thirteen or fourteen, working all hours as the only hired help for a lower middle-class family. During the 1870s, a contemporary observed that, besides routine tasks in the scullery and around meals, these maids-of-all-work had to 'take up the carpets, scrub the stairs, wash the babies, wait on the boarders, carry the children out for an airing, make the beds, black the grates, and run messages'.[60] The combination of drudgery and isolation was, as the social reformer Charles Booth noted in 1896, keenly felt by any fifteen-year-old, accustomed to living in a crowd. In the suburbs of Paris, Jeanne Bouvier recalled working as a maid for the owners of a hardware store as crushingly dull: 'I spent my days working alone, always alone, between a kitchen that resembled a tomb and a bedroom that was a real dungeon'.[61]

PRIMARY AND SECONDARY SCHOOLING

Across the globe in the modern world the school system has played a key role in separating children from the world of adults, and hence in moving towards a protected childhood. Early schools, before the eighteenth century, were more in evidence in the towns than the villages globally, and as already noted, were largely the responsibility of religious authorities. Among the Muslim population of the Empire, there was a long tradition of sending young children to a Qur'an school. As Korić's Chapter 13 on education in Bosnia illustrates, schools were usually located in or near a mosque, and run by a member of the lower *ulema* (a learned Muslim teacher). The main aim was to teach the rudiments of religious knowledge, notably by reciting Quranic verses, though this might also involve learning to read and write. Schooling was often an unpleasant experience for the pupils, with much rote learning and frequent resort to corporal punishments, such as the notorious bastinado (*falaka*). Note that these Qur'an schools were very different from our current conception of the institution. The students sat on cushions on the floor around the teacher. Children of all ages were taught together in a single room. Some of the students might go on to a *madrasa* (institute of higher education), with a more varied curriculum, though a similarly informal arrangement of the classes.[62] There was a tendency to favour boys' education over that of girls, but there is evidence that already by the late eighteenth and early nineteenth centuries around one-fifth of girls in Istanbul, mainly from elite Muslim families, were receiving some elementary education, often with a female teacher in a private house.[63]

Many of the schools in early modern Europe were not so very different, with makeshift classrooms, children sitting on benches rather than at desks, a mixing of ages and a focus on teaching religion and morality. A child's education might amount to no more than catechism classes with the parish priest in preparation for First Communion, or a short spell in school that left him or her with some rudimentary religious knowledge and a very basic literacy. Teaching was by the 'individual method', whereby each pupil spent a few minutes with the teacher three or four times a day for individual instruction, and the rest of the time was left to his or her own devices. This usually required the use of the rod to keep some sort of order. As in the Ottoman Empire, the population in Europe was more interested in supporting the education of boys than girls. School attendance and literacy rates varied considerably across the European nations, but the gender gap was substantial during the early modern period. Overall, by the late eighteenth century, in a few countries in the north and north-west of Europe, the bulk of the population could at least read. At the other extreme, in parts of the countryside in southern and eastern Europe, the written word was largely unknown, and literacy rates could be in single figures.

It was during the eighteenth and nineteenth centuries that a major transformation of schooling in Europe occurred, as the various states set out to establish national systems of education. The religious orientation of the early schools was modified to serve secular and national aims. This movement can be linked to state-building and the drawing of lines on citizenship among the newly emerging nations on the continent.[64] State policy was therefore, sooner or later, to make elementary education compulsory, and to separate elementary schools for the masses from secondary schools and universities for a tiny elite drawn from the middle and upper classes. Prussia was an early starter during the early nineteenth century. Wilhelm von Humbold and other reforming ministers instituted the elementary *Volksschule*, declared the secular nature of education and in 1810 made attendance compulsory for three years. In 1812 they reformed the Gymnasium as a state institution, involving a classical curriculum lasting for nine years, which in turn, with an *Abitur* certificate, could lead to a place in the reformed university system. France was also an early starter, notably with the launch under Napoleon Bonaparte of the *lycée* as an elite secondary school for boys.[65] By 1910, several northern European states had high primary enrolment rates, including 85.7 per cent of children aged five to fourteen in France, and 72.5 per cent in Germany, while in southern Europe, Spain, for example, had only 35.3 per cent.[66] Beyond Europe, the Japanese Meiji regime was outstanding for its commitment to the establishment of compulsory universal education, with 82 per cent of the age group attending primary school by 1900. Colonial regimes in Africa and Asia stood at the opposite extreme. During the 1920s, in the settler colony of Kenya, the state allocated a disproportionate share of the education budget to the tiny white and Indian minorities, leaving the African majority – 98 per cent of the population – with only 49 per cent of the funds, and so obliged to rely largely on missionary schools.[67]

Reformers in Istanbul were also interested in encouraging mass education, partly on European lines. Promoting 'Ottomanism' in the schools had the potential to hold together the multiethnic empire through the process of modernisation. At the same time, as noted above, they made certain that Western institutions such as the *lycée* were adapted to local conditions, insisting that state schools continued to teach Islamic and Ottoman morality to their pupils.[68] Until the 1860s, the regime continued the traditional strategy of using the Qur'an schools to control and discipline the population. With the Regulation of Public Education in 1869, it began to provide all villages and urban neighbourhoods with an elementary school, and to make attendance compulsory for boys aged seven to eleven and for girls aged six to ten. The pupils sat at desks, continued with their religious instruction as well as learning to read, write and do their arithmetic and faced strict discipline. In this way, combined with reforms in governance and other welfare measures, the Ottomans took their own path to modernity.[69]

However, there were obvious difficulties with using Turkish and Islam as the glue in the multiethnic Empire. The state schools of the late nineteenth and early twentieth centuries also faced a host of competing institutions. There were the faith schools of other religions, such as those of the Armenian Christians that the Ottomans had themselves encouraged during earlier periods. There were the numerous missionary schools, the foreign schools such as those set up by the French, British and Americans, and the local private schools. Moreover, many parents among conservative Muslim families preferred the Qur'an schools to those run by the government, while children from poorer families often skipped school and went straight into an apprenticeship. Şevket Süreyya Aydemir recalled that in his hometown of Edirne hardly any of the children in his neighbourhood attended a school.[70]

No less importantly, Ottoman schools often provoked much the same hostility among some of their pupils as their Western counterparts. The elementary schools in both cases were notorious for long hours of tedious rote learning, as well as for their brutal corporal punishments. At the secondary level, a study of childhood reminiscences asserts that '[t]here are no children in the world who appear to loathe their schools and to despise their teachers as much as the inmates of the typical French *lycée*'. Not surprisingly, the Ottoman version in its turn was open to the criticism, as one memoir put it, of a mechanical approach to its teaching, a lack of creativity and harsh discipline.[71] In these circumstances, there is the argument from Emine Evered that: 'Educational policies aimed at building citizenship and loyalty instead heightened ethnolinguistic and religious identities, thus contributing to – rather than inhibiting – the empire's demise'. Under it all, the appeal of Ottomanism failed to match the fervour aroused by rival ethnic and nationalist ideologies.[72]

In addition, the Ottomans, like the Europeans, began to take the education of girls more seriously, beginning with those from the upper and middle classes, as Zachs' Chapter 15 exemplifies. The general assumption among ruling elites in both cases was that girls needed education to make them better wives and mothers, rather than career women – though this was contested by a feminist line that they should have equality with males in this sphere. In France, typically enough, the Camille Sée law of 1880 permitted girls to attend a *lycée* for the first time, with a broad humanities curriculum. Yet it also insisted on courses in domestic science and hygiene, and it denied them the opportunity to take the *baccalauréat* examination and its path to a career (the latter decision was only reversed, following opposition, in 1924).[73]

Conclusion

During the final years of the Ottoman Empire, as the reforms of the *Tanzimat* period gradually took shape, childhood was increasingly dominated by that 'quintessentially modernizing novel institution' – the state school.[74] Historians are generally agreed that it was the rise of mass education that, sooner or later in the various nations, ensured that children were separated from the world of adults. Before the nineteenth century, in the West no less than in the Empire, the young often worked and relaxed in the company of adults, and apart from a minority among the social elite, acquired their skills and their values in the rough-and-tumble world of the farm and the workshop. But once children began to be thought of as innocent, vulnerable creatures, there were campaigns to 'quarantine' them in the schools. Everywhere this involved a protracted struggle to persuade parents to make sacrifices for the schooling of their offspring. This was relatively straightforward in the urbanised areas of western Europe and in Istanbul and other towns in the Empire. Conversely, it was challenging in the case of agrarian societies, where there was poor communication and the reliance of farming communities on the work of their children, evident in nations such as Spain, Russia and Italy, as well as the Empire. Campaigns to establish a state system of education were often driven by members of the social elite, rather than pressure from below.

The officials of the Ottoman regime joined the ranks of reformers elsewhere – notably, those in Prussia in the wake of the Napoleonic invasions and in Meiji Japan after contact with the West in 1868. At the same time, as Benjamin Fortna notes, change in the Empire was also attributable to shifts in society, such as the spread of companionate marriage and changing fertility rates, indicating 'shared dynamics of childhood', rather than one-way borrowing from the West. Moreover, despite the efforts of the state schools to impose the culture and values of the Ottomans, the variety of childhoods was as much in evidence in their territories as in the West. The chapters in this volume provide ample illustration of such differences, and of the assumption that childhood is a cultural construction, as well as a biological phenomenon. The chapters also touch on differences between middle-class childhoods in towns such as Istanbul or Athens and those of their servants or of the rural population, for example, or those of Muslims, Christians and Jews, or of child workers in a model factory such as Hereke and those in the dispersed 'sweatshops'. Finally, the history of childhood on a global scale requires more attention to the Ottoman Empire, which had a centuries-long history and a vast geography, as well as to multidimensional comparisons with the new research becoming available on Latin America, Africa and Asia.

Notes

1. The English translation is *Centuries of Childhood*.
2. Stearns, *Childhood in World History*, pp. 1–16.
3. Surveys of the West include Cunningham, *Children and Childhood*; Foyster and Marten, *A Cultural History*; Fass, *The Routledge History of Childhood*; Heywood, *A History of Childhood*.
4. Hsuing, *A Tender Voyage*, p. 220.
5. Giladi, 'Concepts', pp. 122–3; Heywood, 'Centuries of Childhood: An Anniversary – and an Epitaph'.
6. As cited in Gundry-Volf, 'The Least and the Greatest: Children in the New Testament', p. 35; Giladi, 'Islam', pp. 155, 164–5.
7. Maksudyan, *Orphans*, pp. 18, 31–2; Hunecke, 'Intensità e fluttuazioni'; Levene, 'Infant Abandonment', pp. 75–9.
8. As cited in Weber, *Peasants into Frenchmen*, p. 172.
9. Fortna, 'Preface', p. IX.
10. Ginio, 'Childhood', pp. 100–4.
11. See Kozma, 'Girls', pp. 346–9.
12. Meriwether, 'The Rights of Children', p. 225; Giladi, 'Islam', p. 155.
13. Peirce, 'Seniority', pp. 173–81.
14. Van Gennep, *The Rites of Passage*, p. 67.
15. Hajnal, 'European Marriage Patterns', pp. 101–20.
16. Sovič, 'European Family History', pp. 141–63; Szołtysek and Zuber-Goldstein, 'Historical Family Systems', pp. 5–10.
17. Purlevskii, *A Life*, p. 73; Ehmer, 'Marriage', p. 305.
18. Barbagli, 'Marriage and the Family', pp. 107–8.
19. Quataert, 'The Age of Reforms', p. 786; Todorova, *Balkan Family*, pp. 39–40.
20. Peirce, 'Seniority', p. 181.
21. Giladi, 'Islam', p. 156; Bunge and Wall, 'Christianity', pp. 85–6.

22. Brekus, 'Children of Wrath', pp. 300–28.
23. Rousseau, *Emile*, pp. 79, 92.
24. Duben and Behar, *Istanbul Households*, pp. 13, 21 and 230.
25. Fortna, 'Preface', p. vii.
26. Quataert, 'The Age of Reforms', p. 785.
27. Duben, 'Turkish Families', p. 88; see also Meriwether, *The Kin Who Count*.
28. Laslett, 'Mean Household Size', pp. 125–58.
29. Quataert, 'The Age of Reforms', pp. 784–6; Uno, 'Child-Rearing', p. 410; Fauve-Chamoux and Ochiai, *The Stem Family*, passim.
30. Anderson, 'The Social Implications of Demographic Change', p. 39.
31. Ariès, *Centuries of Childhood*, p. 37.
32. Bailey, 'Family Relationships', pp. 15–31.
33. Merriwether, 'The Rights of Children', p. 223.
34. Fildes, *Breasts, Bottles*, Chapter 3.
35. Sussman, *Selling Mother's Milk*, passim.
36. Sussman, 'Parisian Infants', p. 652.
37. As cited in Hunt, *Parents and Children*, p. 134.
38. Stearns, 'Childhood Emotions', pp. 160–6.
39. Gosse, *Father and Son*, p. 65.
40. Brunet, 'Orphans', p. 641.
41. Viazzo et al., 'Five Centuries', p. 84.
42. Maksudyan, *Orphans*, p. 11.
43. Maksudyan, 'Foster-Daughter', pp. 488–512; Araz and Kokdas, 'In Between Market and Charity', pp. 85–108. I am grateful to the authors of the latter for showing me this work before publication.
44. Abrams, *The Orphan Country*, Chapter 2; Engberg, 'Boarded Out', pp. 431–57.
45. Innes, 'State, Church', p. 23.
46. Humphries, 'Care and Cruelty'.
47. Ipsen, *Italy*, Chapter 4.
48. Maksudyan, 'State "Parenthood"'; Schull, *Prisons*, pp. 179–84.
49. Fass, 'Is There a Story?', pp. 2–3.
50. Quataert, 'The Age of Reforms', p. 861, and Quataert, *Ottoman Manufacturing*, p. 165.
51. Grier, *Invisible Hands*.
52. Kelly, *The German Worker*; Burnett, *Destiny Obscure*; Maynes, *Hard Road*; and Traugott, *The French Worker*; Humphries, *Childhood and Child Labour*.
53. Bouvier, 'My Memoirs', p. 340.
54. Quataert, *Ottoman Manufacturing*, Chapter 5.
55. Samuel, 'Workshop', passim.
56. Ibid., pp. 16–17, 162.
57. Milanich, 'Latin American Childhoods', pp. 493, 495–7.
58. Bolin-Hort, *Work, Family*, p. 35; Tsurumi, *Factory Girls*, p. 130.
59. Hufton, *The Prospect Before Her*, pp. 77–86.

60. Davin, *Growing Up Poor*, pp. 159–60.
61. Burnett, *Useful Toil*, p. 170; Bouvier, 'My Memoirs', p. 359.
62. Somel, *The Modernization of Public Education*, Introduction and Chapter 1; Hanna, 'Literacy', pp. 179–82.
63. Akiba, 'Girls Are Also People', pp. 24–7.
64. Green, *Education*, p. 80.
65. Ibid., passim.
66. Benavot and Riddle, 'The Expansion of Primary Education', pp. 205–7.
67. Weiner, *The Child*, p. 150; Natsoulas and Natsoulas, 'Racism', p. 117.
68. This section relies on Somel, *The Modernization of Public Education*; Fortna, *Imperial Classroom*; and Evered, *Empire and Education*.
69. See Eisenstadt, 'Modernities'.
70. Somel, *The Modernization of Public Education*, Chapter 1 and p. 253.
71. Coe, *Autobiography*, p. 233; Sommel, *The Modernization of Public Education*, p. 268.
72. Evered, *Empire and Education*, pp. XIV and 3.
73. Offen, 'The Second Sex', pp. 252–86.
74. Fortna, 'Preface', p. viii.

Bibliography

Abrams, Lynn, *The Orphan Country: Children of Scotland's Broken Homes from 1845 to the Present* (Edinburgh: John Donald, 1998).

Akiba, Jun, '"Girls Are Also People of the Holy Qur'an": Girls' Schools and Female Teachers in Pre-Tanzimat Istanbul', *Journal of the Women of the Middle East and the Islamic World*, 17 (2019), pp. 21–54.

Anderson, Michael, 'The Social Implications of Demographic Change', in F. M. L. Thompson (ed.), *Cambridge Social History of Britain, 1750–1950*, 3 vols (Cambridge: Cambridge University Press, 1990), vol. 2, pp. 1–70.

Araz, Yahya, and Irfan Kokdaş, 'In Between Market and Charity: Child Domestic Work and Changing Labor Relations in Nineteenth-Century Ottoman Istanbul', *International Labor and Working-Class History*, 97 (2020), pp. 81–108.

Ariès, Philippe, *Centuries of Childhood*, trans. Robert Baldick (London: Jonathan Cape, 1962).

Bailey, Joanne, 'Family Relationships', in Elizabeth Foyster and James Marten (eds), *A Cultural History of Childhood and Family in the Age of Enlightenment* (Oxford: Berg, 2010), pp. 15–31.

Barbagli, Marzio, 'Marriage and the Family in Italy', in John Davis and Paul Ginsborg (eds), *Society and Politics in the Age of the Risorgimento* (Cambridge: Cambridge University Press, 1991), pp. 92–127.

Benavot, Aaron, and Phyllis Riddle, 'The Expansion of Primary Education, 1870–1940: Trends and Issues', *Sociology of Education*, 61/3 (1988), pp. 191–210.

Bolin-Hort, Per, *Work, Family and the State: Child Labour and the Organization* of Production in the British Cotton Industry, 1780–1920 (Lund: Lund University Press, 1989).

Bouvier, Jeanne, 'My Memoirs', in Mark Traugott (ed.), *The French Worker: Autobiographies from the Early Industrial Era* (Berkeley: University of California Press, 1993), pp. 336–82.

Brekus, Catherine A., 'Children of Wrath, Children of Grace: Jonathan Edwards and the Puritan Culture of Child Rearing', in Marcia Bunge (ed.), *The Child in Christian Thought* (Grand Rapids, MI: William B. Erdmans, 2001), pp. 300–28.

Brunet, Guy, 'Orphans', in Paula Fass (ed.), *Encyclopedia of Children and Childhood in History and Society*, 3 vols (New York: Macmillan Reference, 2004), vol. 2, pp. 640–3.

Bunge, Marcia J., and John Wall, 'Christianity', in Don M. Browning and Marcia J. Bunge (eds), *Children and Childhood in World Religions* (New Brunswick, NJ: Rutgers University Press, 2009), pp. 83–150.

Burnett, John (ed.), *Destiny Obscure: Autobiographies of Childhood, Education and Family from the 1820s to the 1920s* (London: Routledge, 1994).

_____, *Useful Toil: Autobiographies of Working People from the 1820s to the 1920s* (London and New York: Routledge, 1994).

Coe, Richard N., *When the Grass was Taller: Autobiography and the Experience of Childhood* (New Haven: Yale University Press, 1984).

Cunningham, Hugh, *Children and Childhood in Western Society Since 1500*, 2nd edn (Harlow: Pearson Education, 2005).

Davin, Anna, *Growing Up Poor: Home, School, and Street in London, 1870–1914* (London: Rivers Oram Press, 1996).

Duben, Alan, 'Turkish Families and Households in Historical Perspective', *Journal of Family History*, 10/1 (1985), pp. 75–97.

Duben, Alan, and Cem Behar, *Istanbul Households: Marriage, Family and Fertility, 1880–1940* (Cambridge: Cambridge University Press, 1991).

Ehmer, Josef, 'Marriage', in David Kertzer and Marzio Barbagli (eds), *The History of the European Family*, 3 vols (New Haven: Yale University Press, 2001–3), vol. 2, pp. 282–321.

Eisenstadt, S. N., 'Multiple Modernities', *Daedalus*, 129/1 (2000), pp. 1–29.

Engberg, Elisabeth, 'Boarded Out by Auction: Poor Children and their Families in Nineteenth-Century Northern Sweden', *Continuity and Change*, 19 (2004), pp. 431–57.

Engel, Barbara Alpern, 'Mothers and Daughters: Family Patterns and the Female Intelligentsia', in David L. Ransel (ed.), *The Family in Imperial Russia* (Urbana: University of Illinois Press, 1978), pp. 44–59.

Evered, Emine, *Empire and Education under the Ottomans: Politics, Reform and Resistance from the Tanzimat to the Young Turks* (London: I. B. Tauris, 2012).

Fass, Paula, 'Is There a Story in the History of Childhood?', in Paula Fass (ed.), *The Routledge History of Childhood in the Western World* (Abingdon: Routledge, 2013), pp. 1–14.

Fass, Paula (ed.), *The Routledge History of Childhood in the Western World* (Abingdon: Routledge, 2013).
Fauve-Chamoux, Antoinette, and Emiko Ochiai (eds), *The Stem Family in Eurasian Perspective* (Bern: Peter Lang, 2009).
Fildes, Valerie A., *Breasts, Bottles and Babies* (Edinburgh: Edinburgh University Press, 1986).
Fortna, Benjamin C., *Imperial Classroom: Islam, the State, and Education in the Late Ottoman Empire* (Oxford: Oxford University Press, 2002).
Fortna, Benjamin C. (ed.), 'Preface', in *Childhood in the Late Ottoman Empire and After* (Leiden: Brill, 2016), pp. vii–xvii.
Frijhoff, Willem, 'Gymnasium Schooling', and 'Latin School', in Paula Fass (ed.), *Encyclopedia of Children and Childhood in History and Society*, 3 vols (New York: Thomson-Gale, 2004), vol. 2, pp. 410–11, 536–8.
Giladi, Avner, 'Concepts of Childhood and Attitudes towards Children in Medieval Islam: A Preliminary Study with Special Reference to Reaction to Infant and Child Mortality', *Journal of the Economic and Social History of the Orient*, 32/2 (1989), pp. 121–52.
_____, 'Islam', in Don M. Browning and Marcia J. Bunge (eds), *Children and Childhood in World Religions* (New Brunswick, NJ: Rutgers University Press, 2009), pp. 151–216.
Ginio, Eyal, 'Childhood, Mental Capacity and Conversion to Islam in the Ottoman State', *Byzantine and Modern Greek Studies*, 25 (2001), pp. 90–119.
Gosse, Edmund, *Father and Son: A Study of Two Temperaments* (London: Penguin, 1983).
Green, Andy, *Education and State Formation: The Rise of Education Systems in England, France and the USA* (Basingstoke: Macmillan, 1990).
Grier, Beverly, *Invisible Hands: Child Labor and the State in Colonial Zimbabwe* (Portsmouth, NH: Heinemann, 2006).
Gundry-Volf, Judith M., 'The Least and the Greatest: Children in the New Testament', in Marcia J. Bunge (ed.), *The Child in Christian Thought* (Grand Rapids, MI: William B. Eerdmans Publishing, 2001), pp. 29–60.
Hajnal, John, 'European Marriage Patterns in Perspective', in D. V. Glass and D. E. C. Eversley (eds), *Population in History: Essays in Historical Demography* (London: Edward Arnold, 1965), pp. 101–43.
Hanna, Nelly, 'Literacy and the "Great Divide" in the Islamic World, 1300–1800', *Journal of Global History*, 2 (2007), pp. 175–93.
Heywood, Colin, 'Centuries of Childhood: An Anniversary – and an Epitaph', *Journal of the History of Childhood and Youth*, 3/3 (2010), pp. 343–65.
_____, *A History of Childhood: Children and Childhood in the West from Medieval to Modern Times*, 2nd edn (Cambridge: Polity, 2018).
Hsuing, Ping-chen, *A Tender Voyage: Children and Childhood in Late Imperial China* (Stanford: Stanford University Press, 2005).
Hufton, Olwen, *The Prospect Before Her: A History of Women in Western Europe*, vol. 1, '1500–1800' (London: Fontana, 1997).

Humphries, Jane, 'Care and Cruelty in the Workhouse: Children's Experiences of Residential Poor Relief in Eighteenth and Nineteenth-Century England', in Nigel Goose and Katrina Honeyman (eds), *Childhood and Child Labour in Industrial England: Diversity and Agency, 1750–1914* (Farnham: Ashgate, 2013), pp. 115–34.

———, *Childhood and Child Labour in the British Industrial Revolution* (Cambridge: Cambridge University Press, 2010).

Hunecke, Volker, 'Intensità e fluttuazioni degli abbandoni dal XV al XIX secolo', in *Enfance abandonné et société en Europe, XIVe-XXe siècle* (Rome: Ecole Française de Rome, 1991), pp. 27–72.

Hunt, David, *Parents and Children in History: The Psychology of Family Life in Early Modern France* (New York: Harper Torchbooks, 1972).

Innes, Joanna, 'State, Church and Voluntarism in European Welfare, 1690–1850', in Hugh Cunningham and Joanna Innes (eds), *Charity, Philanthropy and Reform: From the 1690s to 1850* (Basingstoke: Palgrave, 1998), pp. 15–65.

Ipsen, Carl, *Italy in the Age of Pinocchio: Children and Danger in the Liberal Era* (New York: Palgrave Macmillan, 2006).

Kelly, David, *The German Worker: Working-Class Autobiographies from the Age of Industrialization* (Berkeley, CA: University of California Press, 1987).

Kozma, Liat, 'Girls Labor, and Sex in Precolonial Egypt, 1850–1882', in Jennifer Helgran and Colleen Vasconcellos (eds), *Girlhood: A Global History* (New Brunswick, NJ: Rutgers University Press, 2010), pp. 344–62.

Laslett, Peter, 'Mean Household Size in England Since the Sixteenth Century', in Peter Laslett and Richard Wall (eds), *Household and Family in Past Time* (Cambridge: Cambridge University Press, 1972), pp. 125–58.

Levene, Alysa, 'Infant Abandonment in Europe 1700–1850', in Laurence Brockliss and Heather Montgomery (eds), *Childhood and Violence* (Oxford: Oxbow Books, 2010), pp. 75–9.

Lundh, Christer, 'The Social Mobility of Servants in Rural Sweden, 1740–1894', *Continuity and Change*, 14/1 (1999), pp. 57–89.

Maksudyan, Nazan, 'Foster-Daughter or Servant, Charity or Abuse: *Beslemes* in the Late Ottoman Empire', *Journal of Historical Sociology*, 21/4 (2008), pp. 488–512.

———, *Orphans and Destitute Children in the Late Ottoman Empire* (Syracuse, NY: Syracuse University Press, 2014).

———, 'State "Parenthood" and Vocational Orphanages (*Islâhhanes*): Transformation of Urbanity and Family Life', *The History of the Family*, 16 (2011), pp. 172–81.

Maynes, Mary Jo, *Taking the Hard Road: Life Course in German and French Workers' Autobiographies in the Era of Industrialization* (Chapel Hill, NC: University of North Carolina Press, 1995).

Meriwether, Margaret L., *The Kin Who Count: Family and Society in Ottoman Aleppo, 1770-1840* (Austin: University of Texas Press, 1999).

_____, 'The Rights of Children and the Responsibilities of Women: Women as *Wasis* in Ottoman Aleppo, 1770–1840', in Amira El Azhary Sonbol (ed.), *Women, the Family, and Divorce Laws in Islamic History* (Syracuse NY: Syracuse University Press, 1998), pp. 219–35.

Milanich, Nara, 'Latin American Childhoods and the Concept of Modernity', in Paula Fass (ed.), *The Routledge History of Childhood in the Western World* (Abingdon: Routledge, 2013), pp. 491–508.

Natsoulas, Anthula, and Theodore Natsoulas, 'Racism, the Schools and African Education in Colonial Kenya', in J. A. Mangan (ed.), *The Imperial Curriculum: Racial Images and Education in British Colonial Experience* (London: Routledge, 1993), pp. 108–34.

Offen, Karen, 'The Second Sex and the Baccalauréat in Republican France, 1880–1924', *French Historical Studies*, 13/2 (1983), pp. 252–86.

Peirce, Leslie P., 'Seniority, Sexuality, and Social Order: The Vocabulary of Gender in Early Modern Ottoman Society', in Madeline C. Zilfi (ed.), *Women in the Ottoman Empire: Middle Eastern Women in the Early Modern Era* (Leiden: Brill, 1997), pp. 169–96.

Purlevskii, Savva Dmitrievich, *A Life under Russian Serfdom: The Memoirs of Savva Dmitrievich Purlevskii, 1800–1868*, trans. and ed. Boris Gorshkov (Budapest: Central European University Press, 2005).

Quataert, Donald, *Miners and the State in the Ottoman Empire: The Zonguldak Coalfield, 1822–1920* (New York and Oxford: Berghahn Books, 2006).

_____, 'Ottoman History Writing and Changing Attitudes Towards the Notion of "Decline"', *History Compass*, 1 (2003), pp. 1–9.

_____, *Ottoman Manufacturing in the Age of the Industrial Revolution* (Cambridge: Cambridge University Press, 1993).

_____, 'Part IV, The Age of Reforms, 1812–1914', in Halil Inalcik and Donald Quataert (eds), *An Economic and Social History of the Ottoman Empire, 1300–1914* (Cambridge: Cambridge University Press, 1994), pp. 759–933.

Rahikainen, Marjatta, *Centuries of Child Labour: European Experiences from the Seventeenth to the Twentieth Century* (Aldershot: Ashgate, 2004).

Rousseau, Jean-Jacques, *Emile, or On Education*, trans. Allan Bloom (London: Penguin, 1991).

Samuel, Raphael, 'Workshop of the World: Steam Power and Hand Technology in mid-Victorian Britain', *History Workshop Journal*, 3 (1977), pp. 6–72.

Schull, Kent F., *Prisons in the Late Ottoman Empire: Microcosms of Modernity* (Edinburgh: Edinburgh University Press, 2014).

Somel, Selçuk Akşin, *The Modernization of Public Education in the Ottoman Empire, 1839–1908* (Leiden: Brill, 2001).

Sovič, Silvia, 'European Family History: Moving Beyond Stereotypes of "East" and "West"', *Cultural and Social History*, 5 (2008), pp. 141–63.

Stearns, Peter N., 'Childhood Emotions in Modern Western History', in Paula Fass (ed.), *The Routledge History of Childhood in the Western World* (London and New York: Routledge, 2013), pp. 158–73.

_____, *Childhood in World History*, 3rd edn (New York and London: Routledge, 2017).

Sussman, George D., 'Parisian Infants and Norman Wet Nurses in the Early Nineteenth Century: A Statistical Survey', *Journal of Interdisciplinary History*, 7/4 (1977), pp. 637–53.

_____, *Selling Mother's Milk: The Wet-Nursing Business in France, 1715–1914* (Urbana: University of Illinois Press, 1982).

Szołtysek, Mikołaj, and Barbara Zuber-Goldstein, 'Historical Family Systems and the Great European Divide: The Invention of the Slavic East', *Demográfia*, 52 (2009), pp. 5–47.

Tilly, Louise, Rachel Fuchs, David Kertzer, and David Ransel, 'Child Abandonment in European History: A Symposium', *Journal of Family History*, 17/1 (1992), pp. 1–23.

Todorova, Maria, *Balkan Family Structure and the European Pattern: Demographic Developments in Ottoman Bulgaria*, 2nd edn (New York: Central European University Press, 2006).

Traugott, Mark (ed.), *The French Worker: Autobiographies from the Early Industrial Era* (Berkeley: University of California Press, 1993).

Tucker, Judith E., *In the House of the Law: Gender and Islamic Law in Ottoman Syria and Palestine* (Berkeley: University of California Press, 1998).

Uno, Kathleen, 'Child-Rearing in the Nineteenth Century', in Heide Morrison (ed.), *The Global History of Childhood Reader* (London: Routledge, 2012), pp. 408–29.

Van Gennep, Arnold, *The Rites of Passage* [1909], trans. Monika B. Vizedom and Gabrielle L. Caffee (London: Routledge and Kegan Paul, 1960).

Viazzo, Pier Paolo, Maria Bortolotto, and Andrea Zanotto, 'Five Centuries of Foundling History in Florence: Changing Patterns of Abandonment, Care and Mortality', in Catherine Panter-Brick and Malcolm T. Smith (eds), *Abandoned Children* (Cambridge: Cambridge University Press, 2000), pp. 70–91.

Wall, Richard, 'The Social and Economic Significance of Servant Migration', in Antoinette Fauve-Chamoux (ed.), *Domestic Service and the Formation of European Identity* (Bern: Peter Lang, 2004), pp. 19–42.

Weber, Eugen, *Peasants into Frenchmen: The Modernization of Rural France, 1870–1914* (London: Chatto and Windus, 1979).

Weiner, Myron, *The Child and the State in India: Child Labor and Education Policy in Comparative Perspective* (Princeton: Princeton University Press, 1991).

Wilson, Adrian, 'The Infancy of the History of Childhood: An Appraisal of Philippe Ariès', *History and Theory*, 19 (1980), pp. 132–53.

Worobec, Christine, *Peasant Russia: Family and Community in the Post-Emancipation Period* (DeKalb: Northern Illinois University Press, 1995).

PART I
CONCEPTS OF CHILDHOOD

Chapter 2

Childhood in the Peasant Militia Registers and the Age Boundaries of Adolescence

Cahit Telci

Almost forty years ago, in his pioneering work on the land registers (*tahrir defterleri*), Geza David put a special emphasis on the ages of unmarried adolescents (*mücerred*s).[1] According to him, the registration of children's ages in surveys had to do with the different workings of the fiscal apparatus in the various localities. Reflecting on the sixteenth-century surveys of the Hungarian territories, he also wrote that it would be a mistake to use a standard population multiplier for listed persons in all cases, because the age of inscribed unmarried males and particularly that of children could not be characterised by one definite value. Despite his valuable observations, the ages of children in Ottoman surveys have so far attracted little scholarly attention. One of the main reasons behind this lack of interest is that until the nineteenth century, Ottoman land registers were mainly kept for fiscal purposes. As a standard tax assessment procedure, the Ottoman officials often, if not always, divided the *timar* zones into basic tax units in accordance with the traditional system of peasant family farms (*çift-hane*) and were not interested in specifying the ages of taxpayers. Together with the land possessors of full holdings (*tam çift*) and half holdings (*nim çift*), the producers with less than a half *çift* (*bennak*s) and unmarried males, still living under their father's roof (*mücerred*s), were entered into the cadastral surveys without any reference to their ages.

However, a boy born in a typical peasant militia region rather than in a *timar* zone was meticulously listed with his age in other registers – namely, peasant militia registers. Unlike individuals in the *timar* zones, those in these peasant militia areas were considered to be part of the recruitment pools to be used in military and service works. These registers with their age entries constitute a very important, and perhaps the only source that allows us to examine the early modern demographic structure in the fifteenth and sixteenth centuries across the various provinces. It also gives the official perception(s) of childhood in the early modern empire during the period of centralisation during the reigns of Mehmed II, Bayezid II and Süleyman I.

Dwelling upon these valuable registers, this study aims not only to problematise the ages of unmarried males within the Ottoman concept of childhood, but also to contextualise the constructed notions of childhood, as well as adulthood, in the early modern Ottoman official parlance. It contends that rather than formalising the already existing vague perceptions of childhood, the Ottoman state apparatus systematised a relatively well-defined category of adolescence (*mücerredlik*) to characterise the period of young people's transition from childhood to adulthood. Although in the late fifteenth and early sixteenth centuries, the identification of children was mainly influenced by the personal interpretations of clerks and social perceptions, it came to be systematised throughout the sixteenth century by designating specific lower and upper age limits for categories such as children, adolescents and adults. In this respect, this study argues that the notion of childhood in the early modern era did not simply emerge out of the existing social repertoire, as the state formation process, to a large extent, set the contours of childhood and adulthood according to the needs of the centralising state apparatus to finance its armies.

Starting with the mid-fifteenth century, Ottoman clerks compiled the peasant militia registers – a practice which continued well into the official end of this system in the late sixteenth century. With the exception of the fifteenth-century registers of Aydın and Manisa,[2] Kızılca,[3] Kaş, Karahisar, Çirmen (Chernomen), Zağra Yenicesi (Nova Zagora),[4] Akçakızanlık and other Balkan districts,[5] most of the peasant militia registers list the ages of the children. The effort of Ottoman officials to update the ages of juveniles leads one to think that these statistics formed an important dimension of the peasant militia system. In this respect, one must first answer the question of why the peasant militia registers, rather than other contemporary surveys, contain detailed information on the ages of children.

Different record-keeping practices in the peasant militia registers reflected the strategy of the Ottomans to separate individuals within the peasant militia system such as auxiliaries (*yamak*s) and adolescents (*mücerred*s) from *timariot*s, ordinary peasants as well as townsmen. In other words, to determine whether an individual was the child of an ordinary peasant or the offspring of an auxiliary, Ottoman authorities usually registered the offspring of auxiliaries above the age of one. For this reason, the recording of peasant children in the militia system with their ages in separate charts had to do with the Ottoman authorities' deep concern to prevent any future problems arising from the ambiguity over the fiscal and legal status of these children.

The Peasant Militia System and its Registers

From the time of Sultan Orhan, the Ottoman polity had set up a distinct military organisation under the name of the peasant militia system. The core of the peasant militia institution was the formation of foot corps paid for by the assignment of agricultural holdings. Some non-Muslims, albeit a small number, were integrated into the system, but on the whole these troops consisted mainly of Turcoman groups from earlier times. These military units were established mainly around the sub-provinces of Aydın, Menteşe, Kütahya, Hüdavendigar, Saruhan Karahisar, Karesi, Bolu, Ankara, Sultanönü, Kocaeli, Hamid and Biga in Anatolia; Gelibolu (Gallipoli), Tekirdağ (eastern Thrace), as well as Çirmen (Chernomen) in the Rumelia. It means that the peasant militia system was not implemented throughout the whole Ottoman territory.[6]

Coexisting with the *timar* system, the peasant militia structures were organised in some sub-provinces called peasant militia areas (*yaya-san-cak*s). The fiscal boundaries of these two systems in each sub-province were so interchangeable that the geographical boundaries of the peasant militia and *timar* systems became a perennial problem for authorities from the fifteenth century onwards. For example, in several petitions sent to the Ottoman Imperial Chamber many individuals claimed that they were not the offspring of the peasant militia. The authorities were aware of the possible fraudulent claims of auxiliaries, who frequently attempted to escape from the service obligation of the system. However, not all of these claims were false. In several cases the centre had to admit to claims of inhabitants who appeared to have been already expelled from the peasant militia system. In such cases the new status of these claimants was added into the rolls with explanations, such as being excluded from service or freed of service obligation. Due not only to these changes but also to the rising number of competing claims over the status of auxiliaries, the peasant militia gradually lost their military nature in the sixteenth century and came to be recruited as reserve units in service works, such as bridge repairing and construction (*köprücülük*), protecting mountain passes (*derbendcilik*),[7] maintaining water supplies (*su yolculuk*)[8] and salt working (*tuzculuk*).[9]

One of the earliest peasant militia registers dating back to 19–29 April of 1455 had a well-defined recording system which was repeated with minor variations in the following period.[10] Therefore, probing into this early survey of the Karahisar sub-province gives us a clue as to the process of standardisation in peasant militia censuses. This register starts with the names of foot soldiers acting under the authority of a headman for the peasant militia areas. In this introductory section, foot soldiers of a sub-province were listed for each sub-district. After writing the name of each sub-district – such as 'Nahiye-i Sandıklı' – in this section, censors then inserted the name of the holder of the existing foot soldiers with expressions such as 'under the reign of Hüdavendigar, the headman of the foot soldiers was Hamza, now it is under the control of his son Rüstem'. In the next part, the names of villages were put as units of sub-districts, followed by the enumeration of farms. Under the heading of farms, scribes put the names of all auxiliaries, adolescents and children. The structure of this one register attests to the fact that farms were the fundamental and smallest units of the peasant militia system, whose integrity was put under the close scrutiny of the Ottoman centre.

A typical soldier–farm consisted of adult auxiliaries and their offspring as the labour force who were categorised as children and adolescents. Shaped by the military duties of auxiliaries, the system fundamentally rested on maintaining a volatile balance between the optimum number of labour force and military personnel in the designated agricultural units. As long as the auxiliaries left numerous descendants behind, the centre could continue to recruit the functionaries of farms as military personnel without dividing the assigned farms into unproductive smaller agricultural units. For this reason, the Ottoman centre tried to prevent the escape of auxiliaries and their offspring from the system, whose harsh military obligations limited the flow of new labour into the militia farms.

Although the Ottoman authorities devised several measures to protect the integrity of each agricultural unit, the delicate balance between agricultural production and military obligations was threatened as early as the late fifteenth century in various localities. Not surprisingly, the Ottoman authorities insisted on attributing the deterioration of the system to the declining population on the farms. As can be seen in entries of registers, such as those from Sayi and Ismail, foot soldiers were transferred by the Imperial centre from Turcoman groups and *timar* villages into the farms, once the population decline had reached alarming levels. Under-populated agricultural units were also filled with cultivators from other militia farms, who were officially described as separated foot soldiers (*ayırma yaya*). In certain farms, some transfers were observed as being excessive, such as the Hüseyin farm in Umurlu.

It seems that there were some villages and farms which were designated by the Ottoman authorities as the potential pool of reserve manpower for militia farms. In cases of the repopulation of farms, newly arriving inhabitants were mostly entered into records under their original residences. In addition to these repopulating strategies from other villages and farms, the Ottoman authorities frequently consolidated two deserted farms into the larger one.[11] The fact that the strategy to increase the labour force of farms through consolidation became quite common clearly shows the difficulty in maintaining the active military and labour force in the production areas. Perhaps, from the very beginning, the obligatory military service brought about a high burden on auxiliaries, while inhabitants of other villages were also hesitant to settle in militia farms. But it is also possible that for the Ottoman centre the strategy of repopulation became less attractive as the high number of geographically scattered farms reduced the efficient central control over the system. Be that as it may, the average number of functionaries per farm dramatically increased throughout the sixteenth century.

The number of auxiliaries in each farm was around three or four in the fifteenth century, while throughout the first quarter and particularly the second quarter of the following century the farms with three or four auxiliaries almost disappeared in records. In a register of the sub-province of Hamid dated 1545, scribes added that in one farm with twenty residents there were an extra eleven auxiliaries.[12] It is understood from this marginal note that a standard militia farm contained a maximum of nine auxiliaries. But in many cases, fifteen to forty auxiliaries and several adolescents aged between fourteen and fifteen, together with their leaders, settled on farms.[13] At first glance, the rise of the farm population seems to have stemmed from the well-known demographic upswing in the sixteenth century. But the repeated complaints on the workings of farms in this period indicate that the rise of the average number of auxiliaries in each farm seems to have resulted from the policy of consolidation.[14] This policy, however, did not solve the problems in the peasant militia system in the second half of the sixteenth century, which would explain why the system was abolished in the 1570s and finally integrated into the existing *timar* organisation with the preparation of the new *timar* registers of the old peasant militia units (*mensuhat* registers).

Ages of Children in the Peasant Militia Registers: Problems and Trends

On the organisational structure of the peasant militia system, the most detailed studies have been carried out by Muzaffer Arıkan and Halime Doğru.[15] Although in several studies on the administration scheme of the sixteenth-century sub-provinces and districts the peasant militia system has been analysed as a secondary theme, the ages of children have only attracted the attention of a few scholars, such as Eugenie Elifoğlu[16] and Fikret Yılmaz.[17] In parallel to their observations regarding the scribal terminology of age groups, findings of this study suggest that the census enumerators used several age categories for children, such as minors (*sagir*), adolescents (*mücerred*) and infants (*masum*, lit. innocent), while in some cases children were also listed with vague identity markers, such as a person called so and so. Such markers were usually used for the identification of the handicapped. In fact, a relatively high number of the handicapped and sick at the point of maturity in the peasant militia system makes us suspect the accuracy of age entries in registers. Since the handicapped were exempted from service, some of the sons of auxiliaries tried to escape the obligatory service by registering themselves in this way. Therefore, a caveat here is in order before beginning the analysis of the ages enumerated in the peasant militia registers. Like other early modern and modern censuses, the peasant militia surveys, influenced by all sorts of social relations and state policies, might not perfectly reflect the demographic realities.

Looking at the reasons behind the pattern of recording ages in the peasant militia system, Arıkan has speculated that the strategy of auxiliaries to keep others out of their farms would explain their willingness to register their descendants as auxiliaries.[18] As exemplified by several examples, Arıkan's argument rests on the hypothesis that in order to keep the farms under their control, some auxiliaries did not want the registration of extra auxiliaries on their depopulated farms. True, in some cases, when farms suffered from labour shortage for agricultural production and obligatory service requirements, the state populated the farms by designating the adolescent sons of auxiliaries as additional auxiliaries, 'those from among auxiliaries' sons who reached their puberty'.[19]

But considering the fact that in times of labour shortage adults rather than children must have been inserted into the system, Arıkan's argument on the linkage between age recording and the strategies of auxiliaries does not hold true for understanding the registration process. Moreover, Arıkan's argument is built upon the hypotheses that rural notables and prominent villagers tried to acquire the lands of the auxiliaries due to the attractive tax exemptions offered in the system. As a response to the rising encroachment upon the militia farms, auxiliaries attempted to consolidate their presence in farms by registering their offspring. Yet this argument, again, does not answer the question of why auxiliaries encouraged the census officers to list both the names and ages of their boys. By adding the ages of descendants of auxiliaries, the centre indeed aimed to calculate the obligatory service entrance year for each child and to prevent children in the following years from making a false claim that they were not the sons of militia.

As a result of these fiscal and administrative concerns, Ottoman authorities were not interested in developing a coherent and homogenous census system for the registration of militia. Although personal decisions made by the compilers as to what to enter gradually disappeared in the rosters, they continued to manifest themselves in identification of some boys, even in the sixteenth century. For instance, 'Çalış son of Mehmed who was the son of Ramazan' (*Çalış veled-i Mehmed b. Ramazan*), a nine-year-old child, was added into files with a second name 'Haydar'.[20] There was even an identity marker for a five-year-old child[21] together with an entry for a child aged two or three years without a name.[22] It is not known how these infants could be entered at such an early age. Furthermore, in the militia farms of one sub-province, the ages of children registered were concentrated in the range of eight to ten years, whereas in most of the other sub-provinces the minors entered were aged between three and five years of age. In some entries the enumerators listed the ages in a suspiciously sequential series, such as two, four, six and eight or eight, seven, six, five, four and three, which suggests that children were not always enumerated with the inspection of farms.[23] It is almost impossible to know whether the enumerators visited the site to inspect the farms or not, since we have no precise information on the registration process of auxiliaries. Another possibility is that they made a rough estimate of the ages of children at the first glance.

Table 2.1, based on the ten peasant militia registers of Karahisar-ı Sahib, Aydın, İznik, Kütahya, Sultanönü, Biga and Hüdavendigar, reveals the ages of listed children in the fifteenth and sixteenth centuries. There are three important trends that can be observed in this table. The first trend is that Ottoman officials usually enrolled children aged between three and seventeen during the period under study.[24] With an exception of the İznik survey, the fifteenth-century registers did not list minors below three years of age, while none of the surveys utilised in this study contain information about adolescents above seventeen years of age. A small number of children aged two without their classification as minors (*sagir*s) also appeared in the peasant militia registers from the 1520s, but those aged between three and fifteen years always constituted the majority of listed children.

The second trend displayed in Table 2.1 is that from the 1540s onwards the age range seems to have expanded and started to include children aged between one and fifteen. Since it was forbidden to use the term *sagir*

Table 2.1 Ages of children in different peasant militia (*yaya-müsellem*) registers.

Age	859/1455 (MAD 4) Karahisar-ı Sahib	871/1466 (MAD 8) Hüdavendigar	XV. Century (MAD17) Hüdavendigar	XV. Century (TD43) İznik	927/1521 (MAD64) Sultanönü	927/1521 (TD104) Aydın	937/1530 (TD158) Sultanönü	959/1551 (TD278) Biga	968/1560 (TD328) Kütahya	969/1561 (TD334) Biga
1	–	–	–	–	–	–	–	1	109	3
2	–	–	–	3	–	–	1	7	114	25
3	1	1	1	6	271	–	119	24	131	15
4	2	–	8	28	223	1	54	27	111	19
5	6	5	60	40	178	1	34	25	113	48
6	21	1	40	42	84	3	17	24	62	32
7	12	4	31	17	95	2	21	15	59	17
8	57	12	48	94	118	7	4	11	33	24
9	3	2	2	8	80	–	1	20	2	4
10	67	65	66	113	98	33	–	13	18	68
11	8	–	–	1	16	–	3	7	–	–
12	10	27	33	95	77	9	30	11	11	20
13	–	7	7	32	37	1	139	4	3	1
14	–	2	–	–	15	6	168	4	6	1
15	–	–	5	–	1	–	140	6	–	–
16	–	3	–	–	–	–	–	3	–	–
17	–	–	–	–	–	–	13	–	2	–
18	–	–	–	–	–	–	–	–	–	–
19	–	1	–	–	–	–	–	–	–	–
Total Number of Registered Children/Adolescents	187	130	301	479	1,293	63	744	201	774	278

Source MAD 4, 8, 17, 64, TD 104, 158, 278, 328, 334.

as a specific category in surveys during the reign of Sultan Süleyman I, one- to two-year-old infants began to be enumerated in the peasant militia registers with their ages. Interestingly, nine- and eleven-year-olds were rarely listed, while five- to ten-year-olds frequently appeared in rosters, particularly boys aged eight and ten. For instance, in the early register of Karahisar-ı Sahib, there were fifty-seven aged eight, as well as sixty-seven ten-year-olds. But the number of nine-year-old children was only three in the same chart.

The third trend observed in Table 2.1 is that children in the age range from three to seven years started to be entered into census files more frequently in the sixteenth century, when the census officers also paid special attention to the listing of twelve-year-old children. The age range between thirteen and fifteen became more visible in the post-1530 period; and youths aged fifteen were increasingly entered into files, particularly after the 1540s.

As discussed before, the small number of minors under the age of three in the fifteenth-century registers does not reflect the demographic realities in the Ottoman provinces. Given the high infant mortality rate in the Ottoman lands,[25] at first glance one might think that the authorities did not feel it necessary to give details of this highly vulnerable age group. At the same time, one could also assert that the small number of listed persons above thirteen years of age was the by-product of Ottoman perceptions of childhood, which conceived of these persons as adolescents, rather than as children. But these hypotheses do not sufficiently explain why the upper and lower age bounds, as well as the terms for boys, significantly changed, especially after the 1520s. In the fifteenth-century recording system, sons listed with their ages were often considered as minors. For instance, in a register of foot soldiers in Biga, prepared in 1490, the individuals with ages for each leader were enumerated under the heading of minors (*küçük*s).[26] In the following century this heading, however, changed into 'those below puberty' (*na-reşide*) and was used in different registers. This type of recording suggests that from the late fifteenth century onwards individuals aged between one and fourteen were officially considered to be children.

In the peasant militia registers from the early years of the reign of Sultan Mehmed II, the standard age for adolescence was ascribed as twelve years for boys, below the age of maturity or puberty under Islamic law. However, this age gradually rose to fourteen years during the reign of the Sultan Mehmed II. In her study of detailed *timar* registers (*derdest defter*s), Özünlü notes that clerks added the approximate ages of *timariots*' offspring into files at a time when the *timar* lands were transferred to heirs after the death of a *timariot*.[27] Such a finding again raises the question of how the clerks of the peasant militia were able to determine the exact ages of children, while other clerks within the Ottoman state apparatus either ignored them or could give only give the approximate ages of the listed. Perhaps the ages listed in the peasant militia charts largely reflected the interpretations of clerks. In fact, the identification of a person as a child within the peasant militia system in the fifteenth and early sixteenth centuries was based on the fluid construction of age categories, rather than on static formulations. In this respect, the second and third trends displayed in Table 2.1 suggest that the age range for listed children dramatically expanded in the sixteenth century, probably due to the rising efforts of the Ottoman centre to increase its control over the system. Having formulated the offspring of auxiliaries in farms as potential soldiers, the centre endeavoured to register as many children as possible, while the farm desertions became a headache for the officials. Thus, the expansion of age range in survey files seems to have arisen from the need of the Ottoman centre to maintain a delicate balance between the number of agricultural labourers and military men in the farms.

Adolescence in Ottoman Registers

The adolescents (*mücerred*s), one of the integral parts of the peasant farm system in the Ottoman land-fiscal regime, have been considered as bachelors by recent studies.[28] Almost twenty-five years ago Huricihan İslamoğlu-İnan put forward the argument that the *mücerred* was not a well-defined category that could simply be reduced to that of bachelorhood.[29] For instance, a provincial code of Aydın in 1528 determined the relationship between the adolescents and married men as follows: if an individual identified as adolescent gets married or is an adult with an independent means of income, he shall pay the land tax for peasants having small plots (*bennak*). But a bachelor still living under his father's roof at the age of thirty cannot be designated simply as an unmarried 'young' male, so there must have been lower and upper age boundaries for adolescence. By pointing out the upper and lower limits in this category, M. A. Cook rightly argues that mature bachelors, rather than all bachelors, were characterised as adolescents by the Ottoman officials.[30] Even though land registers did not include the ages of adolescents, several provisional codes set varying upper age bounds for adolescence, ranging from seventeen to nineteen years.

According to one description in the code of Turcomans for the Tanrıdağı region dated 1584, adolescents were defined 'as bachelors with an ability to get the income'.[31] This description clearly points to the fact that minor and beardless youth aged fourteen to fifteen years (*emred*) were not recorded as adolescents. Compatible with this description, as well as with the modern Ottoman usage of the term puberty, the nineteenth-century revenue censuses (*temettü'at defter*s) defined adolescents as bachelor youth who had just reached maturity and were able to contribute to the household income.[32] Influenced by geographical conditions and the physical characteristics of individuals, Ottoman authorities appear to have codified children in the post-puberty period as adolescents who were mostly twelve- to nineteen-year-old boys. Such a codification, particularly in revenue registers, is quite revealing, because it points to the clear connection between the categorisation of boys as adolescents and their economic capacity. In the eyes of the Ottoman authorities, the period in which a boy could contribute to household income started roughly at the age of fourteen.

There are also some documents which set an upper boundary for adolescence. For instance, one entry in Aydın's tax surveys (*mufassal defter*s) defined a fiscally responsible person as an individual at age twenty who was no longer an adolescent and paid *resm-i kara*, which was collected from those without sheep.[33] Another entry of the land register of Aydın dated 1573–4 set the taxes imposed on Turcomans and indicates that when individuals reached seventeen or eighteen years of age, they became non-adolescents.[34] However, the code of oil-makers (*yağcılar*), studied by Halil İnalcık, put an ambiguous upper limit for the adolescence – the youth pay eight *akçe*s as tax on adolescents (*resm-i mücerred*) from puberty up to the age of twenty, after which they have to pay three *vukiyye*s (equivalent to 3.8 kg) of oil.[35] The vague use of the age of twenty in this code also suggests that a youth aged around twenty seems to have been deemed an adolescent. Although it is impossible to determine an exact age range of adolescence, provincial codes of Aydın and oil-makers designated three different ages (seventeen, eighteen and nineteen) for its upper boundary.

Adolescents in Peasant Militia Registers

The legal–fiscal term 'adolescent', defined by provincial codes, was indeed an integral part of the peasant farm system. Influenced by the classical peasant farm system, the peasant militia organisation similarly defined adolescence as a period beginning at twelve to fourteen years of age, after the end of childhood. As in the peasant farm system, which established the end of the adolescence period as the beginning of full fiscal responsibility for taxpayers, in the peasant militia system the onset of military service obligations was conceived as the termination of the adolescence period.

Scholars such as Feridun Emecen, Turan Gökçe and Fikret Yılmaz have therefore highlighted the close relationship between the age of potential auxiliaries and the lower age boundary for service obligations in the peasant militia organisation. For instance, in his study on the auxiliaries of the Nif region, Gökçe points to the lower age limit for entering service at fourteen.[36] The same age has been observed for other districts by Emecen and Doğru.[37] According to Yılmaz, the fourteen- and fifteen-year-olds, however, were considered not simply as possible recruits, but as potential candidates suitable for obligatory service (*işe yarayan*).[38] Our findings from the fifteenth-century peasant militia registers corroborate his observation. Rosters under study indicate that the minimum age for potential candidates for obligatory service was set at twelve, thirteen or fourteen, even though there were also exceptional cases in some regions, where the minimum age of sixteen years was specified. Notwithstanding register-specific regional differences, various inspections held after the 1530s did not point to the direct transition from childhood to service age. Adolescence was thus perceived as a preparatory period just before entering service.

Perhaps nothing illustrates the interim term between childhood and the period of auxiliary services better than adolescent auxiliaries (*mücerred yamak*s). In compliance with Islamic law, in some surveys the age of boys from one to thirteen was recorded, while those over thirteen-years-old were marked simply as adolescent auxiliaries. In fact, two marginal notes found in registers explained clearly the relationship between adolescent auxiliaries and those younger than thirteen. The first note clarified the status of adolescent auxiliaries within the system by stating: '[T]hey were put into service after five years'.[39] The second note included the description for the twelve- to fourteen-year-olds as 'persons suitable for the service'.[40] All these notes suggested that they could be put into service when it was believed that they were useful.[41] Interestingly enough, the censuses of foot soldiers (*piyade defter*s) of Sultanönü and Hamid dated 1530–1 do not contain any entry for the adolescents who were instead classified as auxiliaries. In the preparation of these rolls, the clerks made the distinction between auxiliaries and adolescents clear: '[S]ome of the auxiliaries will be put into service when they become mature enough for the service (*işe yarayınca*)'.[42] In the 1531 register of Bolu, the adolescents were also described as those who were to enter into the service after five years.[43] Some of the auxiliaries in the survey of Bolu were indeed adolescents in the eyes of the Ottoman clerks, who identified the adolescents with the Arabic letter '*mim*'.[44]

As understood from the two standardised marginal notes, the adolescent auxiliaries must have been individuals older than the twelve- and fourteen-year-old age range and usually entered into service at the ages of seventeen to nineteen years. This definition is consistent with the entries in the two detailed land registers of Aydın dated 1528–9 and 1573–4, which set the upper age limits for the end of adolescence at seventeen, eighteen and nineteen.[45] Considering the fact that boys older than twelve to fourteen years were labelled as adolescents or adolescent auxiliaries, they therefore became auxiliaries with full responsibility at the age of seventeen to nineteen years, as indicated by the marginal notes.

Minors in Peasant Militia Registers

In the code for the sons of cavalry in İçel, some individuals marked with the Arabic letter 'sad' were classified as *sagir* (minors), who entered into service at age eighteen.[46] This type of entry does not exist in the cadastral surveys, whereas the peasant militia registers like those of Saruhan and Aydın designate the *sagir* status as a specific period of childhood.[47] A relatively high number of entries of minors in a number of censuses raises the question of whether the category 'minor' was a legally formulated concept, and whether it reflected the scribal conceptions based on social perceptions.

In fact, the term 'minor', introduced into censuses by the initiatives of censors, was widespread until the early years of the reign of Süleyman I when it fell into disuse and was replaced with the actual ages of boys.[48] For instance, in the Kütahya roster of 1520–1, which included the entries for children ranging in age from three to thirteen, clerks did not use the term minor,[49] nor did they identify one- to two-year-old children. There were also a few fourteen- and fifteen-year-olds in this register. The prohibition of the use of the term 'minor' in surveys during the reign of Sultan Süleyman I stopped clerks from enumerating one- to two-year-olds who had been perceived as minors until then. Thus, it is not a coincidence that in several rolls, compiled just after this prohibition, there was no entry of infants aged up to two years. When the registration of the ages of the boys became an established practice, even one- to two-year-olds began to be enumerated in the post-1540 period. Nonetheless, although age recording for boys became a widespread practice within the peasant militia system during the reign of Sultan Süleyman I, some minors, albeit a very small number, continued to appear in the surveys. In the peasant militia register of Karahisar-ı Sahib dated 1559, children ranging in age from one to fourteen years were listed with their ages, while there were only eleven minors with unknown ages.[50] In the Kütahya register of 1571, scribes listed two minors in Yaya Şamlu Çiftlik of Homa after the entry of three children ranging from one to five years of age.[51]

Besides the term minor, there is also another ambiguous term – *masum* (infant, lit. innocent) – used in the peasant militia registers. With a reference to the term *sabi* (infant), Ferit Devellioğlu has concluded that an innocent was a breastfed infant aged up to three years.[52] For instance, in the early auxiliary census of Biga, most of the listed boys were between three and twelve years of age, while there were two thirteen-year-olds together with sixteen innocents. These innocents were between one and three years of age, yet clerks also added five one- to two-year-old infants into the Biga surveys without using this term.[53]

Despite the vagueness of some terms in the various registers, one may argue that the sixteenth-century Ottoman clerks and officials seem to have perceived childhood in the peasant militia system as a period consisting of two stages, from birth to puberty. Infants of the first stage, called innocents, were usually between one and three years of age, while minors were pre-pubescent boys. Since the age of puberty to a large extent determined the lower age bound of adolescence, boys older than twelve years were designated young adolescents.

Conclusion

Recording the ages of children in the registers emerged as a result of the policies of the Ottoman central administration separating the peasant militia system from the classical *timar* organisation. Unlike what has been usually proposed by several studies, the registration of boys with their ages did not fully reflect the strategies to populate the militia farms. In fact, the policies regarding the repopulation of the farms involved the transfer of adult auxiliaries from other farms and did not require the listing of the children's or infants' ages.

Unique among the Ottoman surveys, the peasant militia registers give information about the ages of children. Although those registering a high number of the handicapped contain some vague qualifiers attached to boys like unknown and person called so and so, they provide us with a valuable glimpse into the Ottoman perceptions of childhood. Highly sensitive to regional varieties in the Ottoman lands, the system of recording in these registers underwent a significant change throughout the fifteenth and sixteenth centuries, which also makes them a valuable source for comparative studies on fertility and the demographic structure, as well as the categorisations of childhood.

The practice of recording children's ages went through three distinct stages in the peasant militia system until its abolition around 1575. In the early surveys, children ranging in age from three to thirteen were recorded in the files, while one- to two-year-old infants were designated as minors. By defining the age of puberty as the lower age limit for adolescence, Ottoman officials in the late fifteenth and early sixteenth century defined the adolescents ranging in age from twelve to twenty years as boys in their pre-service period. In the early years of the reign of Sultan Süleyman I, one- to two-year-old infants, and with them the term minor, disappeared from the rosters. From the 1540s onwards, census officers tended to enumerate boys ranging from one to fifteen years old, without the use of the term minor. Since the peasant militia system was shaped by the age of puberty, the changes in scribal practices give us clues as to the conception of the age of puberty in the Ottoman world. With a special emphasis on legal opinions (*fetva*s), Ottoman scholarship has usually analysed the age of puberty within the context of marriage and marital responsibilities.[54] But the peasant militia rosters show us that the legally defined concept of puberty also involved non-marital responsibilities of a youngster. The lower and upper age limits of the pubertal period formulated by Ebussuud Efendi resemble the age range for adolescence in the peasant militia organisation. For instance, as in the legal codes of Ebussuud Efendi, the fifteenth-century censuses set the lower age limit for adolescence at twelve years of age. The sixteenth-century surveys include several entries of children aged up to sixteen without any reference to the eighteen-year-olds. It means that twelve- to fourteen-year-old children began to be added to the files as adolescents to be recruited into the system as legally responsible auxiliaries at the end of the five-year adolescent period.

Undoubtedly, this formulation involved three age groups in the definition of both children and youth. The first category consisted of the one- to three-year-old minors, while the second category of boys constituted those recorded with their approximate ages until twelve years of age. As individuals of the third category, the adolescents were between twelve and nineteen years of age before entering service. 'Infants' (*masum*) and 'minors' (*sagir*) were the terms used by Ottoman officials to signify that these particular children were not legally responsible. The emergence of multiple terms for designating the different stages of childhood and adolescence in the sixteenth-century registers gradually replaced the use of more vague social terms in the identification of children. Such systematisation for different stages of childhood resulted from the ongoing early state formation process in the sixteenth century, which not only formalised the age categories of childhood, but also informed the official discourses on the transition from childhood to adulthood.[55] In this respect, scrutinising children's ages in peasant militia registers provides us with a glimpse of the relationship between the dominant perceptions of childhood and state formation in the Ottoman Empire. As Krausman Ben-Amos rightly claims, both in modern and pre-modern societies the transition from childhood to adulthood in perceptions and social practices involved a set of transformations shaped by biological, cognitive, psychological, social, economic and cultural factors which varied from place to place and did not necessarily appear synchronically or even gradually.[56] Reflecting on these transformations, she also adds that political circumstances appeared as one of the factors that set the patterns for this transformation. In this regard, this study reveals how the early modern state centralisation in the Ottoman Empire during the late fifteenth and sixteenth centuries determined the definitions of adolescence, as well as the transition from childhood to adulthood in conformity with the state's financial and military needs. However, the extent to which the formal attempts to set clear boundaries for this transition overlapped with social practices and perceptions remains unknown and awaits further investigation.

Notes

1. David, 'The Age of Unmarried Children in the Tahrir-Defters (Notes on the Coefficient)', pp. 347–57.
2. The age of children began to be recorded in the Saruhan Sancak after 1575. Emecen, *XVI. Asırda Manisa Kazası*, p. 144.
3. BOA, MAD 251 (951/1544–5).
4. BOA, MAD 35, p. 549 (Reign of Mehmed II – before Evail-i Cemaziyelahir 869/January–February 1465).
5. BOA, MAD 342 (Reign of Bayezid II).
6. Emecen, *XVI. Asırda Manisa Kazası*, p. 355.
7. '... Ayende ve revendeyi gözettükleri sebebden yamaklarınun ziyadesi ayrılmadı'. *Muallim Cevdet Yazmaları*, O.93, p. 138b.
8. BOA, TD 591, pp. 13–15 (988/1580).
9. For the Menteşe *müsellem*s in the service of salt works around İstanköy, see BOA, MD 24, p. 103, no. 282 (981/1574); BOA, TD 573, pp. 96–7 (986/1578–9).
10. BOA, MAD 4 (859/1455–6).
11. For example, *Muallim Cevdet Yazmaları*, O.93, p. 11.
12. BOA, TD 244, p. 166 (952/1545–6); Arıkan, 'Yaya Müsellemlerde Toprak Tasarrufu', pp. 46–7. See also Süleymaniye, Esad Efendi, 2362, p. 18b (981/1573–4). These compilations were produced in the period when the peasant militia system was abolished. The code utilised in this study was recorded in 981/1573–4.

13. BOA, TD 159, p. 117–18, 124–6 (937/1530–1); BOA, TD 206, p. 29 (947/1540–1); BOA, TD 238, p. 80 (952/1545–6); BOA, TD 328, p. 47 (968/1560–1); BOA, TD 349, pp. 9–10 (971/1563–4).
14. However, one must note that while the state tried to consolidate some farms in the late fifteenth and sixteenth centuries, it also devised some measures to limit the number of residents in each farm.
15. Arıkan, 'Yaya Müsellemlerde Toprak Tasarrufu', pp. 175–201; Doğru, *Osmanlı İmparatorluğu'nda Yaya-Müsellem-Taycı Teşkilatı (XV ve XVI. Yüzyılda Sultanönü Sancağı)*.
16. Elifoğlu, 'Ottoman Defters Containing Ages of Children', pp. 321–9.
17. Yılmaz, 'Edremit Yayaları ve Yaya Teşkilâtının Kaldırılması Hakkında Bilgiler', pp. 149–80.
18. Arıkan, 'XV. Asırda Yaya Müsellem Ocakları (Toprak Tasarrufu Vergi Muafiyetleri ve Hizmet', pp. 15–18.
19. '*Hadd-i buluğa erişmiş oğullarından*'. Akgündüz, *Osmanlı Kanunnâmeleri ve Hukuki Tahlilleri*, vol. 5, p. 30.
20. BOA, TD 328, p. 32 (968/1560–1).
21. BOA, TD 347, pp. 122, 145, 158 (971/1563).
22. BOA, TD 347, p. 125 (971/1563).
23. The repetitive ages in the sequence are 8–6–5–4–3 or 10–9–7–6. BOA, MAD 64, p. 64a (927/1521). BOA, MAD 64, p. 93a (927/1521); BOA, MAD 64, p. 106a (927/1521).
24. In some exceptional cases, the scribes recorded a different age structure for children. In the register of foot soldiers in Biga Sancak dated 1490 there are many two-year-old infants. BOA, MAD 3, p. 3b (895/1490–1).
25. Todorova, *Balkan Family*, pp. 18–45.
26. BOA, MAD 3, pp. 8b, 16a, 18b (895/1490–1).
27. Özünlü, 'Osmanlı Dönemi Balkan Tarihine Dair Önemli Bir Kaynak: Derdest Defterleri', p. 198.
28. Doğru, *XVI. Yüzyılda Eskişehir ve Sultanönü Sancağı*, p. 117; Solak, *XVI. Asırda Maraş Kazası*, p. 45; Yörük, *XVI. Asırda Aksaray Sancağı (1500–1584)*, p. 51; Gündüz, 'XVI. Yüzyılın İkinci Yarısında Amik Nahiyesi', p. 243.
29. İslamoğlu, *Osmanlı İmparatorluğu'nda Devlet ve Köylü*, p. 61.
30. Cook, *Population Pressure in Rural Anatolia 1450–1600*, p. 64.
31. '*ve maişetleri babaları yanından olan sagir ü emred oğlanlarından maada müstakil kar u kisbe kadir olanlardan ki evlü olmayub mücerred olalar.*' BOA, TD 631, p. 8 (999/1591).
32. In many codes, it was stated that: '[P]eople with no independent means of income were exempted from taxation' (... *Ehl-i kisb olmayan mücerredden nesne alınmaz.*). Barkan, *Kanunlar*, p. 10.
33. Ibid, p. 10; TKGM.KK, TD 129, p. 4 (981/1573–4).
34. TKGM.KK, TD 144, p. 318a (981/1573–4).
35. Barkan, *Kanunlar*, p. 245.

36. Gökçe, 'XV–XVI. 'Yüzyıllarda Nif Kazâsı Piyade Teşkilâtı ve Yaya Çiftlikleri', pp. 147–8.
37. Emecen, *XVI. Asırda Manisa Kazası*, p. 144; Doğru, *Yaya Müsellem ve Taycı Teşkilatı*, p. 65.
38. Yılmaz, 'Edremit Yayaları ve Yaya Teşkilâtının Kaldırılması Hakkında Bilgiler', p. 156.
39. BOA, TD 587, pp. 16, 32, 36, 37, 41, 61, 85 (987/1580). '. . . *Beş yıldan sonra hizmet eyleye.*'.
40. '. . . *Yarayınca eşdireler, yarayınca eşe, yamaklığa yarar idüğü zahir olup, yamaklığa yarar.*'.
41. BOA, TD 158, p. 16 (937/1530–1); BOA, TD 277, pp. 35, 36, 44, 56, 60 (959/1551–2); BOA, TD 320, p. 212 (977/1569–70); BOA, TD 328, pp. 14, 27, 50, 66, 72, 73, 75, 96, 99, 105, 136, 148 (968/1560–1); BOA, TD 447, p. 52 (938/1532); BOA, TD 510, p. 32 (979/1571).
42. BOA, TD 158, pp. 34, 51, 55, 63, 76, 77, 79, 83, 88, 96, 97, 100, 107, 111, 118, 120, 122 127, 143, 145, 147, 154, 155, 161, 166 (937/1530–1); BOA, TD 159, pp. 7, 8, 9–11, 13, 14, 19, 24, 27–9, 34–6, 53, 55, 79, 164 (937/1530–1).
43. BOA, TD 587, p. 41 (987/1580).
44. BOA, TD 587, pp. 26–9 (987/1580).
45. TKGM.KK, TD 144 (981/1573–4); TKGM.KK, TD 129 (981/1573–4). Although these two registers are catalogued with the date 981/1573–4, they must have been compiled after 982/1574–5, given the monogram (*tuğra*) in the registers designed for the Sultan Murad II (r.1574–95). Considering the compilation of other contemporary registers, the recording date of these two must have been 983/1575–6.
46. Barkan, *Kanunlar*, p. 55.
47. In a register of Aydın Sancak dated 1477, numerous children were identified by the term minor (*sagir*). See also Bizbirlik and Çiçek, 'XV. Yüzyıl Sonlarında Saruhan Sancağı'nda Piyâde Teşkilatı', p. 18.
48. BOA, TD 591, p. 106 (988/1580); Akgündüz, *Osmanlı Kanunnâmeleri ve Hukuki Tahlilleri*, vol. 5, p. 42.
49. BOA, TD 103 (927/1520–1).
50. BOA, TD 320, p. 216 (977/1569–70). See also BOA, TD 237, pp. 51, 53, 60, 72, 73, 75, 76, 77, 78, 119, 159, 186, 205, 210, 227, 231, 238–9 (952/1545–6).
51. BOA, TD 510, p. 107 (979/1571).
52. Devellioğlu, *Osmanlıca-Türkçe*, p. 1085.
53. BOA, MAD 13, pp. 6b, 7 (Reign of Mehmed II). This register also covers militia farms around Bursa.
54. Araz, '17. ve 18. Yüzyıllarda İstanbul ve Anadolu'da Çocuk Evlilikleri ve Erişkinlik Olgusu Üzerine Bir Değerlendirme', pp. 101–2.
55. For the impact of state formation on the emergence of modern childhood, see Pollard, 'Learning Gendered Modernity', pp. 249–69.
56. Krausman Ben-Amos, 'Adolescence', pp. 81–5.

Bibliography

Archival Sources
Atatürk Library
Muallim Cevdet Yazmaları, O.93.
Cumhurbaşkanlığı Devlet Arşivleri (Presidency Ottoman Archives) (BOA)
Maliyeden Müdevver Defterler (MAD) 3 (895/1490–1); 4 (859/1455–6); 13 (Reign of Mehmed II); 35 (869/1465); 64 (927/1521); 251 (951/1544–5); 342 (888/1483–4).
Mühimme Defteri (MD) 24 (981/1574).
Tahrir Defteri (Cadastre Registers) (TD) 103 (927/1520–1); 158 (937/1530–1); 159 (937/1530–1); 206 (947/1540–1); 237 (952/1545–6); 238 (952/1545–6); 244 (952/1545–6); 277 (959/1551–2); 320 (977/1569–70); 328 (968/1560–1); 347 (971/1563); 349 (971/1563–4); 447 (938/1532); 510 (979/1571); 573 (986/1578–9); 587 (987/1580); 591 (988/1580); 631 (999/1591).
Tapu ve Kadastro Genel Müdürlüğü, Kuyud-ı Kadime Arşivi (General Directorate of Land Registry and Cadastre, Archives of Historic Records) (TKGM.KK)
Tahrir Defteri (TD) 129 (981/1573–4); 144 (981/1573–4).
Süleymaniye Library
Esad Efendi 2362 (981/1573–4).

Secondary Sources
Akgündüz, Ahmet, *Osmanlı Kanunnâmeleri ve Hukuki Tahlilleri Cilt V* (Istanbul: Osmanlı Araştırmaları Vakfı, 1992).
Araz, Yahya, '17. ve 18. Yüzyıllarda İstanbul ve Anadolu'da Çocuk Evlilikleri ve Erişkinlik Olgusu Üzerine Bir Değerlendirme', *Kadın/Woman*, 13/2 (2000), pp. 99–121.
Arıkan, Muzaffer, 'XV. Asırda Yaya Müsellem Ocakları (Toprak Tasarrufu Vergi Muafiyetleri ve Hizmet)', unpublished thesis, Ankara, 1966.
———, 'Yaya Müsellemlerde Toprak Tasarrufu', *Atatürk Konferansları*, 8 (1975–6), pp. 175–201.
Barkan, Ö. Lütfi, *XV-XVI. Asırlarda Osmanlı İmparatorluğunda Zirai Ekonominin Hukuki ve Mali Esasları I, Kânunlar* (Istanbul: İstanbul Üniversitesi Yayınları, 1943).
Bizbirlik, Alpay, and Yusuf Çiçek, 'XV. Yüzyıl Sonlarında Saruhan Sancağı'nda Piyâde Teşkilatı, Yaya çiftlikleri ve Demografik Yapı', *Türkiyat Mecmuası*, 23 (Bahar, 2013), pp. 1–26.
Cook, Michael A., *Population Pressure in Rural Anatolia 1450–1600* (London: Oxford University Press, 1972).
Devellioğlu, Ferit, *Osmanlıca-Türkçe Ansiklopedik Lügat* (Ankara: Aydın Kitabevi, 1986).
Doğru, Halime, *Osmanlı İmparatorluğu'nda Yaya-Müsellem-Taycı Teşkilatı (XV ve XVI. Yüzyılda Sultanönü Sancağı)* (Istanbul: Eren Yayıncılık, 1990).

_____, *XVI. Yüzyılda Eskişehir ve Sultanönü Sancağı* (Ankara: AFA, 1992).
Elifoğlu, Eugenie, 'Ottoman Defters Containing Ages of Children: A New Source for Demographic Research', *Archivum Ottomanicum*, 9 (1984), pp. 321–9.
Emecen, Feridun, *XVI. Asırda Manisa Kazası* (Ankara: TTK, 1989).
Erdoğan Özünlü, Emine, 'Osmanlı Dönemi Balkan Tarihine Dair önemli Bir Kaynak: Derdest Defterleri', *Gazi Akademik Bakış*, 4/7 (2010), pp. 193–200.
Géza, Dávid, 'The Age of Unmarried Children in the Tahrir-Defters (Notes on the Coefficient)', *Acta Orientalia Academiae Scientiarum Hungaricae*, 31/3 (1977), pp. 347–57.
Gökçe, Turan, 'XV–XVI. Yüzyıllarda Nif Kazâsı Piyade Teşkilâtı ve Yaya Çiftlikleri', *Tarih İncelemeleri Dergisi*, 15 (2000), pp. 137–53.
Gündüz, Ahmet, 'XVI. Yüzyılın Ikinci Yarısında Amik Nahiyesi', *MKÜ Sosyal Bilimler Enstitüsü Dergisi*, 5–10 (2008), pp. 233–56.
İslamoğlu, Huricihan, *Osmanlı İmparatorluğu'nda Devlet ve Köylü* (İstanbul: İletişim, 1991).
Krausman Ben-Amos, Ilana, 'Adolescence as a Cultural Invention: Philippe Ariès and the Sociology of Youth', *History of the Human Sciences*, 8/2 (1995), pp. 69–89.
Pollard, Lisa, 'Learning Gendered Modernity: The Home, the Family, and the Schoolroom in the Construction of Egyptian National Identity (1885–1919)', in Amira El Azhary Sonbol (ed.), *Women, the Family, and Divorce Laws in Islamic History* (New York: Syracuse University Press, 1996), pp. 249–69.
Todorova, Maria, *Balkan Family Structure and the European Pattern: Demographic Developments in Ottoman Bulgaria* (Budapest and New York: Central European University Press, 2006).
Yılmaz, Fikret, 'Edremit Yayaları ve Yaya Teşkilâtının Kaldırılması Hakkında Bilgiler', *Osmanlı Araştırmaları*, 19 (1999), pp. 149–80.

Chapter 3

An Ottoman Boyhood: Child Life in the Late Eighteenth Century through the Lens of Panayis Skouzes' Autobiography

Eleni Gara

In 1841 the sixty-four-year-old Panayis Skouzes (1777–1847), a rich merchant, ship-owner and banker, and a native of Athens, started writing his autobiography. Skouzes had lived as a boy through a time of trouble caused by political factionalism, internal strife and the ruthlessness and greed of the tax farmer *cum* governor (*voyvoda*) of Athens, Hacı Ali.[1] The loss of his mother at the age of ten and the rapid impoverishment of his father turned his life upside down, brought him misery and deprivation and left lasting memories. His account, which follows his life in Athens and Euboea (Eğriboz) from his tenth to his seventeenth year, as well as his passage to Izmir and the first months of his life there, is one of the earliest autobiographies of childhood concerning the Ottoman lands and a rare source for the experience of growing up as a Christian urban boy in the late eighteenth century.

Critical reflection on autobiography's nature, its performative and identity-fashioning aspects and its relation to lived experience has sufficiently demonstrated the discursive mediation of the past it entails.[2] The use of autobiography in history becomes even more complicated when there is considerable distance between the world of the author and that of his or her younger self, like in the present case. Skouzes' autobiography relates to a political, socio-economic and cultural order that was completely demolished by the eruption of the Greek Revolution in 1821, the ensuing anti-Ottoman and civil wars and the establishment of a nation-state. In the 1840s, the time of his writing, there were neither Muslim neighbours and Ottoman officials anymore, nor Christian notables and roving Albanian irregulars such as those who had haunted his childhood; Athens was no longer a provincial town of the Ottoman Empire, but the capital of the Greek Kingdom. Skouzes' autobiography is an invaluable source that offers a window into the life of Ottoman children, but this window is veiled by an intricate interplay between past and present, and between personal and social memory.

This chapter engages in an analysis of Skouzes' autobiography that focuses on the lived experience of the author's childhood, while taking into consideration the role of memory and authorial purpose in its textual representation. Autobiographies have been widely used for discovering subaltern and 'muted' voices and are arguably the most important sources for looking into the lived experience of childhood.[3] Following this understanding, I argue that delving into a biography of childhood – in the present case, that of Skouzes – helps in bringing to light experiences of childhood that demonstrate agency and enterprising spirit, that is the active side of children. Exploring Skouzes' autobiography will help in looking into the many different factors that impacted his lived experience and also in discussing the broader implications for concepts of childhood, while building on the premise that the author's personal experience was not isolated, but reflective of the socio-cultural milieu to which he belonged.

From Memory to Life Narrative

Skouzes started working on his autobiography in 1841. He was not used to writing, therefore he wrote slowly and in instalments, and at some point he stopped altogether. In February 1845 he began afresh, including in his account more details than before, but did not manage to get far. He died in 1847, leaving his autobiography unfinished.[4]

Both times, Skouzes stated in the introduction of his text that he was able to remember 'in good order' 'all that had happened to him' since he was about seven years old,[5] evidently implying that, because of his fine memory, he had written a truthful and comprehensive account. Remembering personal events, however, and telling ourselves or others about them, is a complex process of reinterpreting past experiences that cannot be reduced to the mere retrieval of stored memories. First of all, autobiographical memories are shaped by the present as well as the past, and are defined by the social and cultural contexts within which remembering takes place.[6] Secondly, they are often inaccurate in detail and sometimes outright false. Distortions can occur at the time a memory is formed, or later, when it is recalled. The passage of time, the frequency of retrieval and/or rehearsal, the need for maintaining a sense of personal coherence, the emotional content and the social or cultural significance of the memory are all factors that have been found to affect the veridicality of autobiographical memories.[7]

Truthfulness, however, is not identical with accuracy. As Ulric Neisser has argued in his notable analysis of John Dean's testimony during the Watergate hearings, personal memories can be correct representations of experiences even if particular episodes did not unfold in exactly the way one remembers them.[8] Furthermore, autobiographical memory[9] is not merely the aggregate of – more or less truthful – personal memories, but the construction of a coherent narrative out of them that is intertwined with a person's sense of identity.[10] Life narratives are socially embedded and integrate cultural interpretative frameworks. Representations of how a life is supposed to unfold form life scripts that provide scaffolding for the organisation and retrieval of autobiographical memories, while values, norms and notions of what constitutes a meaningful life create master narratives that define the way personal lives are remembered and narrated.[11] Narrative forms and conventions dominant in a particular society, together with identity-forming factors such as gender, class, ethnicity and religion, shape autobiographical memory further by defining what is appropriate to tell and how to tell it.[12]

Narrations about our lives, whether written or oral, are stories that articulate who we are and how we relate to others and the world. They do not recall but re-enact the past through a selective use of memories, reworked so as to produce a coherent and culturally acceptable narrative about the self; therefore, they are informed by the worldviews, concerns and priorities of the self in the present, and are co-shaped by collective memory.[13] Moreover, they do not remain static. Written accounts capture and perpetuate in time only one from among the many versions of the life story their author has (or will have had) created in the course of his or her life.

An Autobiography of Sorts

Autobiography, according to Philippe Lejeune, is 'the retrospective narrative in prose that someone makes of their own existence when he puts the accent upon his life, especially upon the story of his own personality'.[14] This careful formulation encapsulates the most salient features of what Sidonie Smith and Julie Watson call 'the traditional Western mode of the retrospective life narrative'[15] and has justly found wide acceptance. It is, however, a normative conceptualisation of autobiography to which the life narrative of Panayis Skouzes does not fully conform. For, in order to write about his life, Skouzes had first to write about his hometown:

> 1841: In the name of the Lord, I will relate my *vita*, I, myself. But first I will start with the cause of the misfortune of the Athenians, and also of my father, that happened and Athens was devastated; and three-fifths of the Athenians fled

and went to Anatolia, to the Islands and other adjacent areas, because of the great tyranny of Hacı Ali, called the Haseki.[16]

At first glance Skouzes' narrative appears to be a crossover between an autobiography, a chronicle, a memoir and a testimony.[17] It is, however, more accurate to describe it as a hybrid piece of life writing, consisting of two distinct parts: an autobiography and a chronicle. Skouzes set out to write his autobiography or, in his own words, 'the *vita* of his life'.[18] He regarded his account of Hacı Ali's era as an indispensable part of his life narrative, but he took pains to keep the two parts separate. The chronicle is there to set the stage for the real drama: the life of the author as a child.

Skouzes' autobiography also falls short of Lejeune's definition in another way: it does not concern his personality. Skouzes does not even give an appreciation of how he felt about the course his life had taken or about his many achievements.[19] It is doubtful that he ever thought about such matters; neither his education nor his social background was conducive to that kind of reflection. Judging from his writing, Skouzes was a rather modest and reticent person, prone neither to self-glorification nor to self-pity. In his boyhood he was not afraid to act out his feelings, at least those of discontent, or to take his life into his own hands.[20] In his old age, however, he chose not to talk about his thoughts and feelings, only about his actions. Skouzes considered his life story worth telling; but he set out to relate his experiences and adventures, not to engage in introspection.

The close reading of his text reveals, however, deep emotions. Evidently, he was very attached to his mother, whom he presents as a paragon of womanly virtue: an intelligent and literate woman, a capable housewife and a hard worker.[21] He was bitter toward his father, who 'became very fainthearted' after the death of his wife, and blamed him in part for the family's misfortunes, because of his second marriage to an 'unworthy' woman.[22] He clearly despised his stepmother, a woman from an 'inferior family' and of 'small fortune', whom his father married despite his relatives' vehement opposition. Not only does he not mention her name, but he also repeats malicious gossip about how her family may have poisoned his mother so that this woman could marry his father.[23] Skouzes does not talk about his feelings; but they permeate his narrative and subvert his otherwise detached tone.

The Present in the Past

Panayis Skouzes wrote with an audience in mind, probably people of his generation who were circulating their own versions of life under the rule of Hacı Ali, or younger persons eager to learn about the past. An obvious target was his immediate family, especially his children and grandchildren, who had no memories of Ottoman Athens.[24] His insistence on the hardships and deprivations of his childhood indicates that he conceived his narrative as a moral tale. His autobiography tells the story of an impoverished boy who, thanks to his wit, managed to overcome misfortune and find his way in the world.

In this respect, Skouzes' narrative resonates unexpectedly with current trends in autobiography. In the last decades of the twentieth century, the autobiography of childhood emerged as a distinct subgenre with a focus on the representation of traumatic childhoods. As Kate Douglas argues, such writings are closely associated with current debates about trauma and childhood and have the capacity to function both as instruments of cultural memory and as weapons of counter-memory.[25]

There is no doubt that Skouzes' childhood was hard and that the loss of his mother, the imprisonment of his father and of himself, and his family's flight from Athens were traumatic events. His writing, however, does not share the preoccupation with the plight of childhood that is the hallmark of the subgenre. There is no conceptual antithesis between the world of children and that of adults, nor any exploration of the self and one's feelings that are so characteristic in autobiographies of childhood. Quite tellingly, Skouzes' narration becomes emotional only when he speaks of the misdeeds of Hacı Ali and his allies, the ultimate culprits for his and his family's misfortune. His writing is an autobiography of childhood *avant la lettre*, the unintentional consequence of his preoccupation with the troubled era of Hacı Ali (1772–96), which roughly coincided with his childhood years (1777–95).

Like his contemporaries in post-Ottoman Greece, Skouzes was not so much concerned with personal passages to adulthood, but rather with the nation's transition to independence. In recording his life, Skouzes was following the tide of autobiographical narration that was sweeping through his generation. After the end of the war against the Ottomans and the creation of the Greek state, many military and political figures, simple fighters or other persons involved in any one capacity in the struggle for independence wrote or dictated memoirs and accounts of their exploits. Skouzes had a sterling example among his own relatives: General Yannis Makriyannis (1797–1864), who had been writing an extensive memoir for many years, was married to his niece.

Skouzes did not write a freedom fighter's narrative, even though he had taken part in the war. His resolve to focus on the era of Hacı Ali, his childhood years, may have been formed in the course of discussions about the 'old times' or 'old Athens' and on comparisons with the current situation. Two sections in the autobiographical part of the text – on school punishments[26] and on his life as a Sinaite monk's acolyte in Euboea during the plague epidemic of 1791[27] – are quite elaborate, probably through reflection or retelling. Though at first glance innocuous, they both relate to two of the most controversial issues in Greek public discourse during Skouzes' lifetime: education and the Church.[28] Skouzes does not directly engage in these debates, but the way he presents his memories shows that he had thought extensively about such matters and wanted to offer his own insights on the brutality of the teachers, especially of the 'wild-monks' (*agriokalogeroi*) who taught at the elementary schools, and of the hypocrisy and dishonesty of the monks who took advantage of the villagers' credulity and faith in holy relics.

The connection between present concerns and past remembrances is easier to substantiate in the part of the text that chronicles Hacı Ali's rule of Athens. The clash between the archons or notables (*archontes*, *kocabaşıs*) and the burgesses (*noikokyraioi*),[29] which had played a crucial role in the events of that period, had not abated after Hacı Ali's deposition and execution, but continued to simmer.[30] Political infighting among the Greeks reached new heights during the War of Independence (1821–30);[31] and the impassioned debates about the role of the notables in Ottoman times continued to be part of the public discourse throughout the nineteenth century and much of the twentieth. In the 1840s, at the time of Skouzes' writing, political life in Athens was again in turmoil. The state was on the verge of bankruptcy, dissatisfaction was widespread and King Otho (1832–62), who continued to refuse a constitution, was dismissing civil servants and cutting down salaries and pensions. The struggle against Otho's authoritarian rule, and for a constitutional monarchy that would allow the nation to have a say in government, culminated in the so-called Revolution of the 3rd of September 1843, in which Makriyannis, Skouzes' nephew-in-law, had a leading part.[32]

Whether it was his involvement in the ongoing debates about history and politics that reminded Skouzes of his childhood years, also a time of authoritarian rule and economic difficulties, or, conversely, his vivid memory of his life as a boy that triggered his recollection of the turbulent time of Hacı Ali's 'tyranny', is a matter of speculation. What is certain is that Skouzes construed his writing as a record of both a personal and a collective past, and composed a chronicle so as to provide a context for his autobiography. By using in parallel the public voice of the chronicler and the private voice of the autobiographer, Skouzes transformed his individual experience into a general one and created a narrative that could be integrated into the history of the nation.

Between Childhood and Adulthood

From our point of view, given that we define children as those below the age of eighteen, Panayis was certainly a child; but was he considered one according to the notions of his society and/or his socio-cultural milieu? Historical and socio-anthropological research on child life and childhood has shown that contemporary 'Western' conceptualisations do not necessarily apply to the past or to other societies. Notions of childhood, like those of adulthood, are historical constructs, embedded in particular social and cultural discourses.[33] The rule of thumb is that human societies designate as children those from among their younger members who have not yet reached sexual maturity; the transition to adolescence, marked by the onset of puberty, often entails entrance into adulthood. Many societies, however, including our present 'Western' one, connect childhood not so much with sexual but rather with socio-emotional immaturity and with the lack of specific cognitive skills, and regard adolescents as children.

As the sultan's subject and a Greek Orthodox by religion, Skouzes grew up in a society in which formal discourses on childhood and adulthood were shaped by two religio-legal traditions: that of the Hanafi school of Islamic law, the official *madhab* of Ottoman judicial institutions, and that of Eastern Roman (Byzantine) law, upheld by the ecclesiastical courts.[34] Local custom also had a bearing in whether a young person would be perceived either as a child or an adult, and defined norms about what was expected from them and how they related to the adult world. Thus, even though legal majority was attained upon puberty, in accordance with the stipulations of Islamic law, paternal authority was not necessarily discontinued.[35] More often than not, emancipation took place at a later age, at marriage or after the father's death.[36]

For most of the period covered by the autobiography, which corresponds to the last years of his middle childhood and most of those of his early adolescence, Panayis was in the grey zone of the 'semi-adult'.[37] On the one hand, at eleven he was considered old enough to be put into prison as a surety until his father paid his tax arrears. However, he had not yet attained legal majority, since it was the father who sold, on behalf of his children, some pieces of land they had inherited from their mother.[38] On the other hand, Panayis may have already been liable to the payment of the non-Muslim poll-tax (*cizye*, commonly referred to as *haraç*). Youths started paying upon entering puberty, and the authorities applied a practical method to find out a boy's physical maturity by measuring the analogies between the circumference of the head and that of the neck.[39]

In any case, the formal attainment of legal majority did not entail independence from paternal authority. As long as his father was alive, it was he who took all major decisions about Panayis' life and made the necessary arrangements for his employment. At the time of his father's death, seventeen-year-old Panayis was still considered a minor by his relatives and compatriots – and also thought of himself as one.[40] Even though he was legally an adult as far as the Ottoman authorities were concerned, he had not yet attained legal majority according to the stipulations of Byzantine law;[41] he passed thus under the authority of his paternal uncle, the monk Ierotheos, and went to live with him on the island of Hydra.

A Hard Life

The narrative thread of Skouzes' autobiography is hardship, mostly manifested as violence and deprivation, sometimes also as misfortune. Violence was present from early on in his life in the form of corporal punishment at school. Thrashing had been for centuries the preferred method for disciplining boys and adolescents in Europe and the Middle East, and continued to be a socially accepted practice well into the nineteenth century.[42] Skouzes asserts that he 'had suffered all the tortures of the "wild-teachers" and head boys of the time', which included flogging, standing on one leg, sometimes with a sack full of stones hanging from the child's neck, and also foot whipping (bastinado).[43] His discussion of corporal punishment at school shows that he clearly condemned it as a form of discipline. His younger self, however, must have regarded such 'tortures' as a fact of life, since they were ubiquitous.

Beatings, sometimes even bastinado, were a regular experience also during the early years of his apprenticeship. Skouzes reports that at his first position he was thrashed when he became insolent or neglected his duties, and that his second master, who was a drunkard, beat him every day.[44] He does not mention any beatings from subsequent masters. Panayis was fourteen years old when he entered his third position and probably knew by then how to handle situations so as to avoid corporal punishment. Surprisingly, there is no mention of any thrashings by his father, which is indeed noteworthy and rather suspicious. Perhaps Skouzes, who had never been reconciled with his father's imprudent second marriage to an – in his view – inferior woman, preferred to remember him only as a 'fainthearted' and 'melancholic' man[45] and not as a cruel person.

The other hardships of his life he often talks about are poverty and hunger. Skouzes had been born into a prosperous household. The way he talks about the wealth of his grandparents and the rich dowry of his mother, in contrast to subsequent deprivations, indicates that he could not easily be reconciled with his father's impoverishment and the social degradation it entailed. Becoming poor must have come as a shock to the eleven-year-old Panayis and was still heartily felt by his older self. Imprisonment was a watershed experience in this respect:

> I stayed in prison a whole week. My father came each dawn and brought me some bread and a few olives. I was telling him: – Father, when are you going to get me out of prison? He was saying to me: – My child, I cannot raise money; I also do not know what to do. At the time I was only 11 years old; the prison was crowded, I was being tramped over by people. My father says to me: – My child, the only thing I reckon is to sell the olive trees, 60, of your mother, those in Hryssavyiotissa. What else can I do? I told him: – Do it so that I can get out of prison.[46]

Panayis had now to learn what it meant to live in poverty and hunger:

> Until then he had me [studying] at the so-called Greek school ... But my father, because of [his] misfortune, took me out [of school], telling me that 'our circumstances are dreadful' and that he must find me a placement so as to receive something to pay my poll-tax. Thus, he took me out of school ... and made an arrangement for me [to get apprenticed] ... Hacı Ali's tyranny was on the rise; I was asking my stepmother to give me bread and there wasn't any. My father was in prison.[47]
>
> My father was in a wretched condition of misery. He went to the soap-makers [to work] for a weekly wage; he produced a kettleful of soap and was given five *guruş*. They did this because he was a master craftsman and as a form of charity.[48]

As a master soap-maker, Panayis' father was entitled to the charity of his fellow guildsmen; his children, however, could not expect much from them or from the family's relatives. As an apprentice to his mother's brother, Panayis was not spared either hard work or beatings. And when, after the death of their father, his sister was taken up by this same uncle, the arrangement was that Panayis and his brother would pay him sixty *para* a year for their sister's upkeep and would buy her cotton and other materials for her to weave her own clothes.[49] Skouzes seems to resent both his father's degradation to receiver of charity and his relatives' ungenerous behaviour, but it is not clear whether he believed that they should have acted otherwise. His writing reveals a society that conceived charity in terms of reciprocity, did not give anything for free and in general avoided acts of generosity that would create obligation and dependency. To receive only limited charity meant to maintain a greater degree of independence.

Panayis was not really destitute. He still had his paternal uncle in Hydra, who took him in after his father's death, and some income from real property.[50] Strangers sympathised with him and were ready to help and give him credit once they knew who he was. His account of how he managed to reach Izmir and find a position there demonstrates how crucial family connections and local networks were. Panayis had entered the service of an Armenian Catholic commercial agent who was staying at his uncle's monastery in Hydra and needed a person to nurse him through his illness. After his recovery, they left together for Izmir; but during a stopover in Tinos, his master, whose mother (a Greek Catholic) was from the island, took on as a servant one of his young relatives there and dismissed Panayis.[51] The boy had the good fortune to meet a fellow Athenian in Tinos, who gave him a letter of introduction to his brother in Izmir. In the course of his journey, when he ran out of money, Panayis claimed this person as an uncle in order to receive credit and to be able to travel to his destination. The so-called uncle, in his turn, as soon as he was informed about Panayis' family and learned his story, paid the outstanding fare and expenses, took him in and eventually found him a position as a servant in a rich household.[52]

Had Panayis been a penniless lad from an insignificant family without relations, he would not have been met with such kindness from strangers. Nowhere in his text does Skouzes mention any gratuitous offer. Whatever he received, including food during his time as a monk's acolyte, when he was able to 'fill his belly' for the first time in many months, was either payment for his services or credit that had to be repaid. Only his paternal uncle appears not to have demanded anything from Panayis or his siblings.

A Working Boy

Urban boys from families of craftsmen or traders who did not attend school were, as a rule, expected to learn a trade, starting as apprentices between nine and twelve years of age, either in their father's or in another guildsman's workshop.[53] Panayis' first position, at eleven, was as an apprentice to his mother's brother and his two companions. For a meagre wage of five *guruş* per year, the boy was expected to do the housework at his master's place until noon (he took turns between the three houses) and in the afternoon go to the workshop to make galloons.[54] In addition, he had to gather olives, and on Sundays, after market hours, he had to sell kerchiefs around the neighbourhoods.[55]

His second master, a poor shoemaker from Athens who had settled in the village of Vassilikon in Euboea, woke him up to work in the middle of the night and beat him cruelly. The arrangement was for Panayis to be apprenticed without wages, but to sleep and eat at his master's house.[56] It was his first position with a shoemaker, and his father was in dire circumstances; this probably explains the unfavourable conditions of his employment. His next position, at the age of fourteen, was substantially better. Panayis was placed with a Muslim shoemaker in the town of Chalkis (Eğriboz) for a wage of one *guruş* per month plus food. He did not have to endure long hours or hard work at the workshop, but his master expected him to do the household chores. The family did not have a servant and so Panayis doubled as one: he shopped, cooked, carried water, helped his mistress and also carried around on his back the family's older child, a five-year-old boy who could not walk.[57]

By the time of his fourth position, back in Athens this time, Panayis was sixteen years old and an experienced hand as a shoemaker's apprentice. His father was able to arrange a yearly wage of twenty-four *guruş* for him. At the end of the year he placed him with a new master, who was willing to pay the boy a wage of thirty-five *guruş*.[58] Skouzes does not mention how much he earned at his first position as a servant in Izmir. It is probable that he did not receive any money; his wages may have gone directly to the so-called uncle who had taken him in and paid his travel debt when he arrived penniless in Izmir. At seventeen, when he entered his second position as a servant, this time to keep the household of a merchant who lived alone with only one secretary, he was able to claim fifty *guruş* per year.[59]

As long as Panayis remained under his father's authority, he did not receive any money for his work. His wages were given to his father, who had negotiated with the various masters and concluded the agreements. Skouzes does not imply anywhere that there was anything uncommon or unjust in this arrangement. Since Panayis lived under his father's roof, he was expected to contribute to the family income. The boy did have some money of his own: the meagre earnings from some personal work as a shoemaker. In the course of two years he had been able to save about five *guruş*. But he did not have the opportunity to spend the money on himself; he was forced to use it for his father's funeral and the qadi's fee.[60]

Except for the master (*usta*) Mehmed in Chalkis, with whom he stayed almost two years, Panayis did not stay with his masters longer than twelve months. Given that a usual contract of apprenticeship ran to three years or 1,001 days,[61] the boy's constant change of employment must be rather attributed to his father's efforts to find him positions with better wages. Had his father not lost his capital and his workshop, Panayis would have had a more settled apprenticeship. The same is true about his leaving his hometown. Both his father's and mother's families were long-established in Athens; they were 'indigenous Athenians', Skouzes proudly writes.[62] Only one uncle lived elsewhere, the monk Ierotheos, who had also taken under his care Panayis' older brother.

For Panayis and his family, and for many other Athenians at the time, mobility was a corollary of poverty, indebtedness and the father's inability to make a living under Hacı Ali's regime. Panayis' family were neither seamen nor long-distance merchants (although he eventually became one), had no diasporic tradition, nor expected its scions to migrate as part of their life cycles. In the few years following his father's impoverishment, however, Panayis found himself travelling first to the island of Euboea, then back to Athens and, after his father's death, first to Hydra and finally to Izmir, after an eventful passage through the Aegean.

A Christian among Muslims

A most interesting and at first glance surprising feature of Skouzes' autobiography is that the author, a veteran of the War of Independence, displays no animosity toward Ottoman Muslims. He is, of course, disparaging of the 'tyrant' Hacı Ali. But the real villains of his story – and equally culprits of Athens' ruin – are the Christian notables of the town, the 'aristocratic archons *kocabaşı* knavish tyrants' who had sided with Hacı Ali against 'the people'.[63] It is true that he mentions a couple of Muslim rogues: a neighbour who allegedly emptied his family house during their absence, and the poll-tax collector (*haraççı*) of Chios who extorted money from him although his papers were in order.[64] But there is no generalised negative image of the Muslim or Turkish other.

In fact, Skouzes had more positive memories from his two Muslim masters than from his Christian ones, given that the payment was better and the workload lighter. He remembers with particular respect Zülfikar Softa, his second Muslim master, a 'worthy man' who had praised him for his work and foretold his future success.[65] He also distinguishes between the situation in Athens, where 'the Turks lived peacefully with the Christians', and in Chalkis, where the 'Turks' were 'of the worst sort', 'wild and lewd', 'killed Christians for insignificant reasons and did other vile things to the boys'.[66]

It was because of the bad reputation of the local Muslims that his father had hesitated to place him with a Muslim master when they had first arrived in Chalkis. Some months later, however, after the debacle with the drunkard master in Vassilikon, who used to beat Panayis, and a failed negotiation with the Sinaite monk, who would not offer him any wages, his father found him a position with a Muslim guildsman. His employer, Usta Mehmed, was a young master shoemaker from among the descendants of the Prophet. Such persons, Skouzes says, were 'well-respected in matters of religion', hence trustworthy.[67] A young Christian boy at the time had less to fear in a Muslim household that scrupulously observed the tenets of religion than among people who took a more relaxed view of the matter.

There is, of course, nothing particularly unusual in finding a Christian boy working at the workshop of a Muslim guildsman in the mixed towns of the Ottoman Empire. Living in a Muslim household, however, was less common. It also might create unforeseen complications.[68] Skouzes relates an episode from his life at the house of Usta Mehmed that is equally unexpected and thought-provoking for what it reveals about the intricate interplay of age, gender and religion in everyday life and in personal relationships. His master, Skouzes says, used to go to Athens rather frequently, ostensibly to buy raw material for his workshop, but mostly to have a good time with his Athenian friends and drink wine in the company of other Muslim shoemakers, which he did not dare to do in Chalkis. During his absence, that could last over a month at a time, Panayis stayed at home with his mistress and the children.

> I was at his home with his wife, Ayşe, and the two young children; to shop whatever was necessary for the house, for the mistress to have me cook and so on; every evening to take me to the inner rooms of the *harem* and let me sing for her. She was young and she took me to the inner part of the house so that my voice would not be heard [outside]. . . . One day, the mistress prepared to go to the [public] bath. I always went with her, with the bath clothes, and entered the bathhouse. That time the naked Turkish women told me to get out. My mistress objected to them. Then the others answered her that 'if you want the Rum *gavur*, the infidel, you can have him in your house like you [already] do and put him beside you every night to sing for you; but bring him no more to the bathhouse'. I was up to 15 years old at the time, good-looking and with a nice voice; my age, however, was still far away from such things. But she also was not that kind of woman.[69]

Prepubescent boys were not banned from the presence of women who were not their relatives. A young servant was therefore allowed to stay in his mistress' quarters and serve her in the public bath, going about his chores among naked women. It is, however, surprising to find a fifteen-year-old in such a position. All the more so since Hanafi legal discourse considered boys as capable of sexual arousal already at ten,[70] and gender segregation was perceived as essential for safeguarding the virtue of married women.[71] Ayşe's attitude toward Panayis and her surprise at the demand of the other women to oust him from the bathhouse is certainly unexpected. Can it be that she considered Panayis as too young for sexual desire? It is rather early for such a conceptualisation of childhood, but it is not unthinkable. After all, Panayis entered Ayşe's life after an agreement between his father and her husband. Neither of the two men considered his living in close proximity to Ayşe as a breach of propriety or as a potential threat to her honour.

Judging from the scolding she received from the other women at the *hammam*, Ayşe's behaviour during her husband's absence must have been a subject of much gossip in the neighbourhood. Panayis was a grown-up boy and an infidel to boot. His presence at the *hammam* was a cause of embarrassment and could not be tolerated any more. As to the boy's emotions and thoughts, we can only speculate. Skouzes' denial of any romantic feelings toward Ayşe is probably more telling about his ideas regarding morality and propriety in old age than about his emotions as a young person.

Conclusion

Panayis' story unfolds in the complex social environment of the Ottoman Aegean world, with its particular tinge of religious, linguistic and social multiplicity and of intersecting religious and class divisions. This was a world in which Muslims were a numerical minority, but a social majority, thanks to the institutionalised primacy of Islam, and home to three high cultures – the Ottoman Muslim, the Greek Orthodox and the Roman Catholic – and their respective religious and educational institutions. The low level of societal cohesion was offset, up to a point, by family, work and local networks that often cut through religious lines and did not allow religious separation to take the form of full-fledged segregation. Panayis had Muslim neighbours and Muslim masters in Athens, lived in a Muslim household in Chalkis and was fluent in Turkish; and for a while he became a servant to a sick Armenian Catholic man whose mother was Greek Catholic and who had found lodging and care in a Greek Orthodox monastery. Cross-religious alliances were also manifested in the composition of the two factions that were vying for the control of the communal affairs of Athens when Panayis was growing up; and the victims of Hacı Ali's unscrupulous and ruthless policies not only included Christians, but also Muslims.[72]

In the autobiography of Panayis Skouzes, a boy's childhood emerges as a time of dependency, obedience and harsh beatings. There is nothing

Child Life in Skouzes' Autobiography

positive in the image of child-life he conveys. In fact, his choice of words in the few places in which he refers to his young age indicates that he conceived childhood as an age of deficiency, a time of 'not yets', as a consequence of both minority and immaturity. In the urban world of the late eighteenth century, in which Skouzes grew up, the state of childhood did not end with the onset of puberty, but continued for as long as a boy remained under the authority of his father or uncle. It is perhaps for that reason that the adolescent Panayis enjoyed such unexpected freedom in Usta Mehmed's household in Chalkis. Even though he was a grown boy, his master and mistress treated him as a child: Mehmed did not hesitate to leave him for long periods alone with his wife, whereas Ayşe did not deem it inappropriate to take him with her to the public bathhouse. I would argue that Panayis' self-perception as a 'quasi-child' until seventeen had more to do with this social practice of prolonged minority than with any legal stipulations (at that age he was an adult by Ottoman law) or with physical growth (the ladies in the bath had had a better understanding of the matter). Panayis was still a child when he left Hydra with the consent of his uncle to accompany his new master; he stopped being one less than a month later, when he decided on his own not to return to his uncle, but to seek his fortune in Izmir.

This brings to the fore the issue of agency. Skouzes' biography reveals what recent research on childhood indicates – namely, that working children were not so much passive recipients or victims, but rather agents in their own experiences.[73] The travel to Izmir was not the first occasion on which young Panayis had made his own decisions. At the age of fourteen, after a particularly harsh beating by his drunken master, he had left his position and joined an elderly Sinaite monk who was touring the country performing blessings and purification rituals against the plague. Panayis followed the monk and another manservant in their peregrinations among the plague-ridden villages of Euboea and lived for a while with a family of villagers, reaping grain and grazing sheep. It was only after the end of the epidemic six months later that his father was able to locate him.[74] It is evident from this and other instances that Panayis was assertive and enterprising, ready to make his own decisions if necessary. His father, on the contrary, was – or is presented as – a rather passive person who sought the opinion and consent of his young son and did not punish him for his transgressions. In short, there is a discrepancy in the autobiography between a concept of childhood as an age of absolute submissiveness to paternal authority and a lived experience characterised by a rather significant degree of self-determination.

Skouzes' emphasis on the negative experiences of his childhood must be attributed to a certain extent to his priorities as an author. It is not by chance that the childhood memories he considered worth relating and chose to include in his autobiography are connected to episodes that could have had a grown man as their protagonist. His imprisonment, the stealthy flight from Athens with his father, his life with the Sinaite monk, the arrangement with his brother of their father's funeral, his nursing of a bedridden man in a monastery on the island of Hydra, his passage to Izmir in search of work; there is nothing particularly child-related in any of the above. Only his experiences as a schoolboy and as an apprentice are inextricably connected to the age of childhood. A boy's life, of course, did not unfold only within the confines of the house, the schoolroom or the workshop. Panayis must have had friends, pastimes and playgrounds. Skouzes, however, chose not to talk about such matters.

This choice of his is closely related to how the autobiography came into being. Skouzes turned to his childhood not through reminiscing or self-exploration, but by following the current of memoir writing that had engulfed the nation after Independence. Given that the focus of his writing is not the experience of childhood or the perplexities of growing up, but the troubled times of Hacı Ali's tenure as governor of Athens, it is not surprising that his account is not particularly self-reflective. In many respects, Skouzes is more of a chronicler of his own life than a full-fledged autobiographer. Yet, when he describes his adventures, he displays a distinct personal voice that is at the same time reticent and revealing.

Skouzes' boyhood was an individual experience, but not a singular one; there were innumerable Ottoman children and adolescents all over the Empire whose lives were comparable to that of Panayis in at least some respects.[75] If we forget Hacı Ali for a moment and the particular circumstances that brought Skouzes' family into misfortune, the story of his childhood years reads like the Ottoman version of a rather common experience throughout eighteenth-century Europe: growing up as the son of an impoverished and indebted craftsman who struggled to make a living. Hardship and deprivation similar to what Skouzes, a rich old man, had found memorable and worth relating in the 1840s was still in the everyday order for the poorer part of the population, and children continued to be expected to contribute to the family income.

Perceptions of childhood, however, were fast changing in the nineteenth century, and Skouzes' writing also reflects the transition from pre-modern to modern conceptualisations. Thus, although he does not question the propriety of child labour, at least when necessary for survival, he makes clear that he disapproves of corporal punishment. And, even though he does not project an image of childhood as a time of innocence, he does present his younger self as devoid of romantic feelings. The autobiography of Panayis Skouzes, reflective of both his Ottoman boyhood and his Greek old age, stands at the threshold of modernity in more ways than one.

Notes

1. For a brief account of the events, based on Skouzes, see Strauss, 'Ottoman Rule Experienced and Remembered'; Vryonis, 'The Ghost of Athens'. For a chronology, based on the account of Ioannes Benizelos, see Gara, 'Patterns of Collective Action', pp. 424–33.
2. For a comprehensive overview, see Smith and Watson, *Reading Autobiography*, Chapters 7 and 8.
3. See, for example, Burnett, *Destiny Obscure*; Humphries, 'Care and Cruelty in the Workhouse'.
4. Skouzes left three manuscripts. The first one is the lengthiest and most complete; the second includes more details about the history and topography of Athens, but covers a shorter period of his life; whereas the third is just a fragment. The best publication is by Thanases Papadopoulos: Skouzes, *Apomnemoneumata*, pp. 63–106 (first MS), 109–25 (second MS) and 129–39 (third MS).
5. Ibid., pp. 63–4. The second time he claimed that he could remember since he was 'five six years old'. Ibid., p. 109.
6. There is a burgeoning bibliography on the subject. For an overview and further bibliography, see Conway and Jobson, 'On the Nature of Autobiographical Memory', pp. 58–65.
7. Bluck and Levine, 'Reminiscence as Autobiographical Memory', pp. 189–93.
8. Neisser compared Dean's testimony with the actual transcripts of his conversations with Richard Nixon and found out that, while Dean was often wrong in terms of the particular episodes he was describing, he was fundamentally right about what had been happening. His account was truthful, Neisser concluded, because very often the subjective belief about having a clear memory of an episode is due to that the memory's 'real basis' is 'a set of repeated experiences, a sequence of related events that the single recollection merely typifies or represents'. Neisser, 'John Dean's Memory', p. 20.
9. There are various understandings of autobiographical memory and different approaches to its study. A good introduction is Berntsen and Rubin (eds), *Understanding Autobiographical Memory*, which brings together contributions on the neural, cognitive, psychological and socio-cultural aspects of autobiographical memory, and on its relation to personality and the self.
10. On this aspect, see especially, Fivush, 'Subjective Perspective'; McAdams, 'Identity and the Life Story'.
11. For an overview and further bibliography, see Berntsen and Bohn, 'Cultural Life Scripts'; Fivush and Merrill, 'The Personal Past'.

12. See, for example, Fivush, 'The Silenced Self'; Wang and Ross, 'What We Remember and What we Tell'.
13. For a thoughtful discussion and further bibliography, see Bruner, 'Self-Making Narratives'; Freeman and Brockmeier, 'Narrative Integrity'.
14. As quoted in Smith and Watson, *Reading Autobiography*, p. 1.
15. Ibid., p. 4.
16. Skouzes, *Apomnemoneumata*, p. 63.
17. On the various genres of life writing, see Smith and Watson, *Reading Autobiography*, pp. 253–86.
18. 'I was taken by a whim to write the *vita* of my life (*ton vion tes zoes mou*) in order to pass the time . . .'. Skouzes, *Apomnemoneumata*, p. 109.
19. Skouzes became a seaman and later a merchant ship-owner, and acquired considerable wealth. After the eruption of the Greek Revolution he fought against the Ottomans and became a major landowner and a banker in post-Ottoman Athens.
20. At thirteen he ran away from his abusive master, and at seventeen he left on his own to seek his fortune in Izmir.
21. Skouzes, *Apomnemoneumata*, pp. 84, 112, 132.
22. Ibid., pp. 85, 89, 113.
23. Ibid., pp. 85, 113.
24. Skouzes had one son and two daughters from his first marriage and another son from his second. The children were born between 1811 and 1821.
25. Douglas, *Contesting Childhood*, p. 171.
26. Skouzes, *Apomnemoneumata*, pp. 99, 111–12.
27. Ibid., pp. 94–7.
28. On the relevant debates, see Clogg, 'Anti-Clericalism'; Kitromilides, *Enlightenment and Revolution*, especially Chapter 8; Makrides, 'The Enlightenment', pp. 33–45.
29. According to Kampouroglou, *Istoria ton Athenaion*, vol. 3, pp. 175–8, the Christians of Athens were divided into four classes (*taxeis*). The 'first class' or *archontes* consisted of twelve 'aristocratic' families of landowners with a hereditary monopoly in the running of communal affairs, the 'second class' or *noikokyraioi* consisted of twenty-four families of propertied and respected burgesses, the 'third class' or *pazarites* included guildsmen, craftsmen and traders working at the market of Athens, while the 'fourth class' or *xotaredes* consisted of persons living outside the core area of the town and mostly working at gardens and farms on the outskirts of Athens.
30. See the discussion of Thanases Papadopoulos in Skouzes, *Apomnemoneumata*, pp. 23–6.
31. See, especially, Stamatopoulos, *O esoterikos agonas*; Rotzokos, *Epanastase kai emphylios*. For an English-speaking account, see Dakin, *The Greek Struggle*, especially pp. 218–20, 301–10.
32. Petropulos, *Politics and Statecraft*, pp. 408–52.
33. For an overview, see Jenks, *Childhood*, especially Chapter 3; Montgomery,

An Introduction to Childhood, especially Chapter 2; Gittins, 'The Historical Construction of Childhood'; Fass, 'Introduction'.

34. Church authorities retained the right to regulate and adjudicate matters of family and inheritance law. For a discussion of the parallel functioning of qadi, ecclesiastical and communal courts, see Kermeli, 'The Right to Choice'.
35. Motzki, 'Child Marriage', pp. 129–30; Tucker, *In the House of the Law*, pp. 119–20. Compare also a report on customary law in pre-revolutionary Greece, included in Maurer, *Das griechische Volk*, vol. 1, p. 151, according to which the 'Turkish law' acknowledged full legal capacity and responsibility upon completion of thirteen years, but without dismissing children from paternal authority.
36. For variations in the age of emancipation in the Islands and the Peloponnese, see Maurer, *Das griechische Volk*, vol. 1, pp. 151–2.
37. According to Ginio, 'Childhood', p. 110, in the eighteenth-century Ottoman Empire adolescents 'lived on the borderline between adulthood and childhood. They were not perceived as full adults; the scribes designated particular adjectives that emphasized their young age and categorized them as different from adults'.
38. Skouzes, *Apomnemoneumata*, pp. 89–90.
39. Ibid., p. 134.
40. 'We, the three siblings, were thus left on our own, with arms crossed, under-age'. Ibid., p. 101.
41. It sets the age of majority at twenty-five. Patlagean, 'L'entrée dans l'âge adulte', pp. 264–5.
42. For a discussion and further bibliography, see Kennell et al., 'Physical Cruelty and Socialization'. See also Çiçek's Chapter 12 in this volume.
43. Skouzes, *Apomnemoneumata*, pp. 91, 111–12.
44. Ibid., pp. 91, 93.
45. Ibid., p. 113.
46. Ibid., pp. 89–90.
47. Ibid., pp. 90–2.
48. Ibid., p. 100.
49. Ibid., p. 100.
50. Ibid., pp. 100–1.
51. Ibid., pp. 102–3.
52. Ibid., pp. 103–5.
53. Papageorgiou, 'L'apprentissage', pp. 313–14, 318.
54. Galloon: a narrow trimming (as of lace or braid with metallic threads) having both edges scalloped.
55. Skouzes, *Apomnemoneumata*, pp. 90–1. Five *guruş* was a small amount of money. In 1789, Panayotakis Kodrikas, a well-off but not wealthy person, agreed to pay one *guruş* per day for board during a sea voyage. Kodrikas, *Ephemerides*, p. 5.

56. Ibid., p. 93.
57. Ibid., p. 98.
58. Ibid., p. 100.
59. Ibid., pp. 105–6.
60. Ibid., p. 101.
61. Papageorgiou, 'L'apprentissage', p. 314.
62. Skouzes, *Apomnemoneumata*, p. 64.
63. Ibid., p. 122.
64. Ibid., pp. 89, 104. Non-Muslims travelling outside their hometowns had to carry on them the so-called '*haraç* paper', a receipt testifying to their having paid the poll-tax.
65. Skouzes, *Apomnemoneumata*, p. 100.
66. Ibid., pp. 122, 92–3.
67. Ibid., p. 98. About the Ottoman *eşraf* (Skouzes calls them *emir*s), see Canbakal, 'On the "Nobility" of Provincial Notables'.
68. Compare also with Ginio, 'Childhood', pp. 105–6.
69. Skouzes, *Apomnemoneumata*, p. 99.
70. Tucker, *In the House of the Law*, p. 155.
71. Peirce, 'Seniority, Sexuality, and Social Order', p. 184.
72. Gara, 'Patterns of Collective Action', pp. 414–17.
73. See the relevant chapters in Goose and Honeyman (eds), *Childhood and Child Labour*, and the editors' discussion in Chapter 1 (Introduction), pp. 8–12.
74. Skouzes, *Apomnemoneumata*, pp. 93–8.
75. Compare with Araz, *Osmanlı Toplumunda Çocuk Olmak*.

Bibliography

Primary Sources

Kodrikas, Panagiotes, *Ephemerides*, ed. Alkes Angelou (Athens: Ermes, 1991).
Maurer, Georg Ludwig, *Das griechische Volk in öffentlicher, kirchlicher und privatrechtlicher Beziehung vor und nach dem Freiheitskampfe bis zum 31 Juli 1834*, 2 vols (Heidelberg: J. C. B. Mohr, 1835).
Skouzes, Panages, *Apomnemoneumata: E tyrannia tou Chatze Ale Chaseke sten tourkokratoumene Athena (1772–1796)*, ed. Thanases Ch. Papadopoulos (Athens: Kedros, 1975).

Secondary Sources

Araz, Yahya, *16. Yüzyıldan 19. Yüzyıl Başlarına Osmanlı Toplumunda Çocuk Olmak* (Istanbul: Kitap Yayınevi, 2013).
Berntsen, Dorthe, and Annette Bohn, 'Cultural Life Scripts and Individual Life Stories', in Pascal Boyer and James V. Wertsch (eds), *Memory in Mind and Culture* (Cambridge: Cambridge University Press, 2009), pp. 62–82.
Berntsen, Dorthe, and David C. Rubin (eds), *Understanding Autobiographical*

Memory: Theories and Approaches (Cambridge: Cambridge University Press, 2012).

Bluck, Susan, and Linda J. Levine, 'Reminiscence as Autobiographical Memory: A Catalyst for Reminiscence Theory Development', *Ageing and Society*, 18 (1998), pp. 185–208.

Bruner, Jerome, 'Self-Making Narratives', in Robyn Fivush and Catherine A. Haden (eds), *Autobiographical Memory and the Construction of a Narrative Self: Developmental and Cultural Perspectives* (Hillsdale, NJ: Erlbaum, 2003), pp. 209–25.

Burnett, John (ed.), *Destiny Obscure: Autobiographies of Childhood, Education and Family from the 1820s to the 1920s* (London and New York: Routledge, 1982).

Canbakal, Hülya, 'On the "Nobility" of Provincial Notables', in Antonis Anastasopoulos (ed.), *Provincial Elites in the Ottoman Empire* (Rethymno: Crete University Press, 2005), pp. 39–50.

Clogg, Richard, 'Anti-Clericalism in Pre-Independence Greece c. 1750–1821', *Studies in Church History*, 13 (1976), pp. 257–76.

Conway, Martin A., and Laura Jobson, 'On the Nature of Autobiographical Memory', in Dorthe Berntsen and David C. Rubin (eds), *Understanding Autobiographical Memory: Theories and Approaches* (Cambridge: Cambridge University Press, 2012), pp. 54–69.

Dakin, Douglas, *The Greek Struggle for Independence 1821–1833* (Berkeley and Los Angeles: University of California Press, 1973).

Douglas, Kate, *Contesting Childhood: Autobiography, Trauma, and Memory* (New Brunswick, NJ, and London: Rutgers University Press, 2010).

Fass, Paula S., 'Introduction: Is There a Story in the History of Childhood?', in Paula S. Fass (ed.), *The Routledge History of Childhood in the Western World* (London and New York: Routledge, 2013), pp. 1–14.

Fivush, Robyn, 'The Silenced Self: Constructing Self from Memories Spoken and Unspoken', in Denise R. Beike, James M. Lampinen and Douglas A. Behrend (eds), *The Self and Memory* (New York: Psychology Press, 2004), pp. 75–93.

_____, 'Subjective Perspective and Personal Timeline in the Development of Autobiographical Memory', in Dorthe Berntsen and David C. Rubin (eds), *Understanding Autobiographical Memory: Theories and Approaches* (Cambridge: Cambridge University Press, 2012), pp. 226–45.

Fivush, Robyn, and Natalie Merrill, 'The Personal Past as Historically, Culturally and Socially Constructed', *Applied Cognitive Psychology*, 28 (2014), pp. 301–3.

Freeman, Mark, and Jens Brockmeier, 'Narrative Integrity: Autobiographical Identity and the Meaning of the "Good Life"', in Jens Brockmeier and Donal Carbaugh (eds), *Narrative and Identity: Studies in Autobiography, Self and Culture* (Amsterdam and Philadelphia: John Benjamins, 2001), pp. 75–102.

Gara, Eleni, 'Patterns of Collective Action and Political Participation in the Early

Modern Balkans', in Antonis Anastasopoulos (ed.), *Political Initiatives 'From the Bottom Up' in the Ottoman Empire* (Rethymno: Crete University Press, 2012), pp. 399–433.

Ginio, Eyal, 'Childhood, Mental Capacity and Conversion to Islam in the Ottoman State', *Byzantine and Modern Greek Studies*, 25 (2001), pp. 90–119.

Gittins, Diana, 'The Historical Construction of Childhood', in Mary Jane Kehily, *Introduction to Childhood Studies*, 2nd edn (Maidenhead: McGraw-Hill and Open University Press, 2008), pp. 35–49.

Goose, Nigel, and Katrina Honeyman (eds), *Childhood and Child Labour in Industrial England: Diversity and Agency, 1750–1914* (Farnham: Ashgate, 2013).

Humphries, Jane, 'Care and Cruelty in the Workhouse: Children's Experiences of Residential Poor Relief in Eighteenth- and Nineteenth-Century England', in Nigel Goose and Katrina Honeyman (eds), *Childhood and Child Labour in Industrial England: Diversity and Agency, 1750–1914* (Farnham: Ashgate, 2013), pp. 115–34.

Jenks, Chris, *Childhood*, 2nd edn (London and New York: Routledge, 2005).

Kampouroglou, Demetrios, *Istoria ton Athenaion*, 3 vols (Athens, 1889–96).

Kennell, Nigel, Henrietta Leyser, Laurence Brockliss, Anja Müller, Jane Humphries, Heather Ellis, and Stephen Cretney, 'Physical Cruelty and Socialization', in Laurence Brockliss and Heather Montgomery (eds), *Childhood and Violence in the Western Tradition* (Oxford: Oxbow Books, 2010), pp. 105–58.

Kermeli, Eugenia, 'The Right to Choice: Ottoman Justice *vis-à-vis* Ecclesiastical and Communal Justice in the Balkans, Seventeenth-Nineteenth Centuries', in Andreas Christmann and Robert Gleave (eds), *Studies in Islamic Law: A Festschrift for Colin Imber* (Oxford: Oxford University Press, 2007), pp. 165–210.

Kitromilides, Paschalis M., *Enlightenment and Revolution: The Making of Modern Greece* (Cambridge, MA, and London: Harvard University Press, 2013).

Makrides, Vasilios N., 'The Enlightenment in the Greek Orthodox East: Appropriation, Dilemmas, Ambiguities', in Paschalis M. Kitromilides (ed.), *Enlightenment and Religion in the Orthodox World* (Oxford: Voltaire Foundation, 2016), pp. 17–47.

McAdams, Dan P., 'Identity and the Life Story', in Robyn Fivush and Catherine A. Haden (eds), *Autobiographical Memory and the Construction of a Narrative Self: Developmental and Cultural Perspectives* (Hillsdale: Erlbaum, 2003), pp. 187–207.

Montgomery, Heather, *An Introduction to Childhood: Anthropological Perspectives on Children's Lives* (Oxford: Wiley-Blackwell, 2008).

Motzki, Harald, 'Child Marriage in Seventeenth-Century Palestine', in Muhammad Khalid Masud, Brinkley Messick, and David S. Powers (eds), *Islamic Legal Interpretation: Muftis and Their Fatwas* (Cambridge, MA: Harvard University Press, 1996), pp. 129–40.

Neisser, Ulric, 'John Dean's Memory: A Case Study', *Cognition*, 9 (1981), pp. 1–22.
Papageorgiou, G., 'L'apprentissage dans les corporations pendant la domination Turque', in *Historicité de l'enfance et de la jeunesse* (Athens: Archives Historiques de la Jeunesse Greque, 1986), pp. 313–22.
Patlagean, Evelyne, 'L'entrée dans l'âge adulte à Byzance aux XIIIe-XIVe siècles', in *Historicité de l'enfance et de la jeunesse* (Athens: Archives Historiques de la Jeunesse Greque, 1986), pp. 263–70.
Peirce, Leslie P., 'Seniority, Sexuality, and Social Order: The Vocabulary of Gender in Early Modern Ottoman Society', in Madeline C. Zilfi (ed.), *Women in the Ottoman Empire: Middle Eastern Women in the Early Modern Era* (Leiden, New York and Köln: Brill, 1997), pp. 169–96.
Petropulos, John Anthony, *Politics and Statecraft in the Kingdom of Greece 1833–1843* (Princeton: Princeton University Press, 1968).
Rotzokos, Nikos V., *Epanastase kai emphylios sto Eikosiena* (Athens: Plethron, 1997).
Smith, Sidonie, and Julia Watson, *Reading Autobiography: A Guide for Interpreting Life Narratives*, 2nd edn (Minneapolis and London: University of Minnesota Press, 2010).
Stamatopoulos, Takes, *O esoterikos agonas prin kai kata ten Epanastase tou 1821*, 4 vols, 3rd edn (Athens: Kalvos, 1979).
Strauss, Joseph, 'Ottoman Rule Experienced and Remembered: Remarks on Some Local Greek Chronicles of the Tourkokratia', in Fikret Adanır and Suraiya Faroqhi (eds), *The Ottomans and the Balkans: A Discussion of Historiography* (Leiden, Boston and Köln: Brill, 2002), pp. 193–221.
Tucker, Judith E., *In the House of the Law: Gender and Islamic Law in Ottoman Syria and Palestine* (Berkeley, Los Angeles and London: University of California Press, 1998).
Vryonis, Speros, 'The Ghost of Athens in Byzantine and Ottoman Times', *Balkan Studies*, 43/1 (2002), pp. 5–115.
Wang, Qi, and Michael Ross, 'What We Remember and What We Tell: The Effects of Culture and Self-Priming on Memory Representations and Narratives', *Memory*, 13/6 (2005), pp. 594–606.

PART II
FAMILY INTERRELATIONSHIPS

Chapter 4

Preliminary Observations on the Demographic Roots of Modern Childhood in the Ottoman Empire: Wealth, Children and Status in Ruse, Vidin and Sofia, 1670–1855

İrfan Kokdaş

The pioneering study of Alan Duben and Cem Behar on households in the Ottoman capital shows that the low fertility pattern was already established in the late nineteenth century, while the emerging discourses on the importance of a protected and carefree childhood for a civilised society put a special emphasis on the quality rather than the quantity of children (the quantity–quality trade-off).[1] Parallel to the spreading family planning practices among all sectors of the society, intellectual and bureaucratic circles eagerly idealised Ottoman parents who preferred to have fewer, well-educated and healthy children, rather than a large number of children with little investment in each. At the heart of this idealisation lay the demographic tendency among families to have fewer children, which was accompanied by the promotion of 'socially defined childcare'.

As in other parts of Eurasia and America,[2] the change in parental decisions on fertility through a combination of birth stopping, birth spacing and older ages at marriage thus constituted one of the core elements of modern childhood in the Ottoman world, as the term childhood came to acquire its modern meaning in the late nineteenth century, referring to a stage of life distinguished by dependence, vulnerability and emotional care.[3] While the demographic transition brought fertility decline and birth control, it led families to invest more in food, clothing, housing, schooling and health care for a child. In other words, the notion of modern childhood emerged as a socially constructed idea in the context of declining fertility that not only affected children themselves, but also began to determine the social roles, values and responsibilities for couples and society, as well as state apparatus. Reflecting on the relationship between the appearance of modern discourses about the importance of children for society at large and the ongoing demographic transition in Ottoman Istanbul, Duben and Behar rightly claim that nineteenth-century Ottomans also interpreted the strategy of the child quantity–quality trade-off as a means for the betterment of society at large.[4]

Although during the early modern era the socio-demographic transformation set the contours of new family ideology, centred on the social importance of the declining number of offspring per married couple, it has received little scholarly attention so far in Ottoman historiography. In the dominant narrative of Middle Eastern scholarship, there seems to be a consensus that the emerging modernist discourses on childbearing and parental fertility choice appeared in the late nineteenth century as a result of the diffusion of European family ideals into the Ottoman world together with ambitious centralisation policies of the Ottoman state.[5] In Balkan scholarship, with the remarkable exception of Maria Todorova's study, the static conceptualisation of Ottoman society also overlooks the interaction between socio-economic status and changing perceptions of childhood before and during the demographic transition.[6] Although the studies of Todorova and Duben and Behar challenge the static description of Ottoman or Islamic demographic structures and provide valuable insights into the discourses on the child-centred family, they do not analyse the historical origins of the nineteenth-century demographic metamorphosis and the socio-economic bases of modern childhood in Ottoman society. As these studies rely exclusively upon the nineteenth-century sources, they confine the scope of their study to the late Ottoman period and do not include the breaks and continuities between the early modern period and the world of the nineteenth century.

In this respect, examining the demographic transformation of three Ottoman provincial towns – that is, Sofia (Sofya), Ruse (Rusçuk) and Vidin (Vidin) – in the 1670–1855 period, in other words prior to the nineteenth century, this study investigates the historical roots of the nineteenth-century demographic transition in the Ottoman lands with a special emphasis on the correlation between wealth and the surviving number of children. The study suggests that there was a Malthusian relationship between the total number of surviving children and wealth in all three Ottoman towns during the period under study. However, as far as the couples with at least one mature child were concerned, such a relationship existed strongly in the eighteenth century, whereas it became weaker after 1800. The civilian middle wealth groups gradually tended to have more children in the post-1800 period, while there was a remarkable decline in the number of surviving children on the part of the wealthiest group, particularly title-holding couples (*askeri* groups. *Askeri* are state elite, lit. military). The study thus considers the wealthiest group as the forerunners of the demographic transition in the Ottoman Balkans at the dawn of the modern age, as it attempts to explain the socio-demographic bases of modern discourses, as well as practices regarding the ideal size of family and childhood in the late Ottoman Empire.

Methodological Problems and Sources

The upper age boundary for childhood is a major point of controversy among different schools of Islamic jurisprudence (*fiqh*). In their attempt to define the transition from childhood, Islamic jurists and officials in the early modern Ottoman world usually characterised puberty as a convenient marker for the onset of adolescence. But the age of puberty varied greatly across Ottoman regions, as it ranged between thirteen and twenty years of age.[7] Therefore, most Ottoman registers and censuses list children without any reference to their ages and do not specify the age of puberty. Probate inventories utilised in this study, for instance, indicate the number of surviving children a deceased person had, as well as whether the surviving children were young (*sagir*) or mature (*kebir*).

The study is based on the data set consisting of fifty-eight court registers for Vidin, twenty-five registers for Ruse and twenty-eight registers for Sofia. It involves a total of 4,113 probate inventories belonging to Muslims and non-Muslims from urban centres and the countryside. Of these 4,113 inventories, 981 are derived from Ruse, 726 from Sofia and, finally, 2,406 from the Vidin region. The probate inventories are, for the most part, not evenly distributed across court records. As probate inventories are irregularly scattered across records in all three towns under study, individual periodisation is compulsory for each town. Such periodisation attempt is made in order to sift significant samples out of the bulk of the inventories in the light of the critical events impacting upon the socio-economic making of the towns. For the case of Vidin, the first period is fixed between 1700 and 1800, followed by the 1801–40 period. For Ruse, the data is organised into two periods, the first between 1685 and 1800, and the second from 1801 to 1855. The data pertaining to Sofia is considered for the periods of 1670–1800 and 1801–33. The year 1800 is taken as a turning point for all towns, as it represents the transition period, involving the struggle among the local notables (*ayans*), Kardzhali revolts and Ottoman centralisation attempts. As the study deals with the relationship between wealth, social status and surviving children, the inventories in our sample are organised under three main sections, as per the inheritance of the deceased. The highest and lowest wealth categories each consist of twenty-five percentiles of the entire sample, while the middle wealth level in between the two constitutes 50 per cent.

Together with the lists of heirs, Ottoman probate records include lists and estimated value of movable property and other assets owned by the deceased. Despite the richness of information provided by these sources, they do have serious limitations.[8] In fact, the Ottoman court's compulsory law of probate registration generates biases in a data based on probate inventories. In the Ottoman Empire probate registration was compulsory if the deceased was a member of the state elite (*askeri*). Keeping inheritance records was also compulsory when there were juveniles, individuals without legal capacity and missing persons among the heirs of the deceased. Moreover, the Ottoman courts got involved in the division of a deceased's estate when there were either no heirs other than a spouse or no heirs at all. Since Islamic courts charged a fraction of the estate's overall value as inheritance tax, many individuals from the lower wealth groups who had at least one adult son or daughter frequently avoided the court's involvement in the division of estates.[9]

Even a cursory look into probate inventories drawn up by an Ottoman court shows that the number of couples with only a child or children who were still minors was very high. In fact, as Fatih Bozkurt rightly argues, as a result of the nature of probate registration in the Ottoman lands, probate inventories overrepresented the couples who only had minors.[10] It seems that the early death of one of the parents ended their reproduction period, which left only underage children. The number of children resulting from the premature death was therefore below the natural fertility capacity of the family. This phenomenon led many researchers to misleadingly assume that the average number of surviving children per household was very low in the Ottoman world.

In order to address this issue, this study focusing on Sofia, Ruse and Vidin differentiates between the couples with at least one child who reached maturity and those who had only young children.[11] To this end, a data set involving a list of heirs (hereditament) and the children in the 'mature' (*kebir/kebire*) and 'young' (*sagir/sagire*) categories was created based on probate inventories, which are extracted through a reading of court records of the three cities for the 1670–1855 period.[12] The study focuses specifically on the reproduction capacity of the couples with at least one mature child who were relatively close to reaching the end of their fertility. Thus, the number of surviving children recorded in probate inventories of these couples reflects better the long-term equilibrium between mortality and fertility rates within the family than does the number of surviving children of young couples.[13]

Demographic Trends and Wealth

As far as the total number of surviving mature children was concerned, the wealthiest group in the eighteenth and early parts of the nineteenth centuries was better off than the lower wealth groups. As shown in Tables 4.1 and 4.2, the lowest wealth group in Vidin, Ruse and Sofia certainly had fewer surviving children than other wealth groups during the period under study. In all three regions, the wealthiest group with at least one mature child also had more surviving children in absolute terms between 1670 and 1855. It was only in nineteenth-century Vidin that the middle wealth groups with at least one mature child had more children than the wealthiest group. In this sense, one might argue that the high number of surviving children was closely associated with social stratification, with material wealth forming its backbone. In this regard, the demographic patterns in Vidin, Ruse and Sofia seem to fit in with Clark's idea of the 'survival of richest'.[14] Yet, this strong correlation between wealth and the number of children is less manifest in the case of couples with only children of minor age (*sagir*). For instance, considering the couples with only minor child/children, middle wealth groups were more productive than the wealthiest in Ruse during the pre-1800 period. Similarly, the poorest families were found to have considerably more children than the middle-wealth category in Vidin during the first half of the nineteenth century.

More interestingly, the relationship between wealth and the number of surviving children for couples who were relatively close to reaching the end of their fertility became weaker in the first half of the nineteenth century. Couples with at least one mature child belonging to the wealthiest group tended to have fewer children after the 1800s in Sofia, Vidin and Ruse. During the first half of the nineteenth century the middle-wealth category, however, experienced an upward trend in all three regions. Our dataset shows that these differences in demographic trends across wealth groups were paralleled by changes in the socio-economic profile of the expectant couples with at least one *kebir* child throughout the eighteenth and early nineteenth centuries.

Expectant Couples and Wealth

Among the existing probate inventories that are used as part of this study to analyse the wealth and desired number of children for couples, records pertaining to the deceased leaving behind their pregnant wives with mature children are of particular importance. The registration of expectant couples in probate inventories who had only young offspring or no children at

Table 4.1 Number of surviving children for wealth groups, 1670–1800.

		Childless Couples	Couples With Only Young Child/Children			Couples With at Least One Mature Child		
		Number of Observations	Number of Observations	Total Number of Children	Average Number of Children	Number of Observations	Total Number of Children	Average Number of Children
Ruse	Poorest 25%	14 (30%)	21 (46%)	38	1.80	11 (24%)	31	2.82
(1685–1800)	Middle Wealth Group	21 (22.5%)	38 (41%)	69	1.82	34 (36.5%)	100	2.94
Base Year: 1680	Richest 25%	11 (24%)	18 (39%)	32	1.77	17 (37%)	69	4.05
Sofia	Poorest 25%	48 (43%)	51 (45%)	70	1.37	14 (12%)	31	2.21
(1670–1800)	Middle Wealth Group	65 (29%)	114 (50%)	190	1.66	48 (21%)	121	2.52
Base Year: 1670	Richest 25%	19 (17%)	54 (48%)	103	1.91	40 (35%)	133	3.32
Vidin	Poorest 25%	166 (42%)	168 (43%)	276	1.64	61 (15%)	149	2.44
(1700–1800)	Middle Wealth Group	206 (26%)	437 (55%)	825	1.88	148 (19%)	460	3.10
Base Year: 1700	Richest 25%	67 (17%)	208 (53%)	405	1.94	120 (30%)	430	3.58

Note The percentages in parentheses represent the distribution of couples falling under the same wealth category.
Source Court Records of Ruse, Sofia and Vidin.

Table 4.2 Number of surviving children for wealth groups, 1801–55.

		Childless Couples	Couples With Only Young Child/Children			Couples With at Least One Mature Child		
		Number of Observations	Number of Observations	Total Number of Children	Average Number of Children	Number of Observations	Total Number of Children	Average Number of Children
Ruse	Poorest 25%	56 (28%)	90 (45%)	152	1.68	53 (27%)	144	2.71
(1801–55)	Middle Wealth Group	82 (21%)	181 (45%)	331	1.82	135 (34%)	412	3.05
	Richest 25%	28 (14%)	100 (50%)	194	1.94	71 (36%)	238	3.35
Sofia	Poorest 25%	20 (29.5%)	30 (44%)	50	1.66	18 (26.5%)	44	2.44
(1801–33)	Middle Wealth Group	28 (20.5%)	76 (55.5%)	146	1.92	33 (24%)	100	3.03
	Richest 25%	10 (15%)	39 (57%)	82	2.10	19 (28%)	59	3.11
Vidin	Poorest 25%	36 (17%)	140 (68%)	234	1.67	30 (15%)	76	2.53
(1801–40)	Middle Wealth Group	64 (15%)	256 (62%)	420	1.64	93 (23%)	298	3.20
	Richest 25%	34 (17%)	124 (60%)	234	1.88	48 (23%)	147	3.06

Source Court Records of Ruse, Sofia and Vidin.

the time of the father's death does not provide clear information as to whether the couples resorted to the birth spacing or parity-specific stopping methods as part of birth control. It is also possible that since these couples may have been in the early stages of their marriage, they could only have young children as a result of their limited reproduction period. Moreover, although probate inventories involving pregnant women and families with young children only provide information about the couples' social standing, real estate, loans and assets, they do not allow us to conceptualise the linkages between the status of couples and their surviving number of children. In fact, as young adults could accumulate wealth only after a considerable period, they were poorer than middle-aged or older adults in any economic class. That is why it is difficult to make any observation regarding the relationship between demographic decisions and the status of couples with young children only.

Probate inventories involving at least one grown-up child pose similar methodological problems. This type of inventory does not offer us exact data in understanding the number of children who died before the demise of one of the partners. But despite this limitation, probate inventories with at least one mature child allow us to make some preliminary observations on the long-term capacity of the couples regarding the surviving number of children. For example, in the case of a couple with two children of full age but also expecting a new baby, we cannot know with any certainty whether the couple practised parity-specific birth spacing and whether they had lost any children before this. What we know for certain is the fact that a period of at least fifteen to seventeen years had elapsed since the first birth, with the existing two children keeping the couple far from their 'ideal' number. Entering the stage of maturity in their marriage, such couples wished to extend their family beyond the two children. Considering altogether the actual number of children for all couples in the society, this offers us a valuable insight into the eagerness and capacity on the part of social groups to attain their 'desired number' of children, as well as varying tendencies across periods concerning the 'desired number' in question.

An examination of the inventories of the deceased leaving behind a pregnant wife and at least one mature child reveals that the overwhelming majority of decedents in the period before 1800 were among the wealthiest in our sample of all three towns. In the sample of the three towns, there was a total of seventeen decedents before 1800, twelve of whom were from the wealthiest stratum. However, in the post-1800 period only 30 per cent of expectant couples with at least one mature child belonged to the wealthiest quartile. Discussing the implications of this finding in the context of the relationship between wealth and the number of surviving children, it is possible to conclude that while the pre-1800 period was characterised by a strong relationship between wealth, producing babies and their survival, this relationship became apparently less visible after the 1800s, with the middle-wealth categories also developing such a capacity.

Socio-economic Dynamics and Demographic Structures

The decline in the number of surviving children among the wealthiest segments of the society attracted the attention of Ottoman bureaucrats and intellectuals mainly in the late Ottoman period. But the main demographic problem in the eyes of Ottoman bureaucrats was, indeed, the small number of children among the poor throughout the nineteenth and early twentieth centuries. For instance, Besim Ömer, a well-known medical man in the late Ottoman period, saw a strong relationship between infant mortality and wealth.[15] For Besim Ömer, since women of poor families were obliged to work, mothers could not effectively breastfeed their babies, thus depriving them of breast milk. In his view, this was the reason why the infant mortality rate was much higher among families in need. He also added that poor housing and environmental conditions caused notably higher infant mortality rates among poor families. Population statistics of the nineteenth-century district of Karahisar-ı Sahib reveal that the local Armenian community had an infant mortality rate of 311 per 1,000, a figure which tended to be significantly lower in the better-off neighbourhoods of the town.[16]

The positive correlation between infant mortality rate and poverty is also corroborated by the population statistics published by the Principality of Bulgaria in 1891. Pertaining to the vital statistics for the year 1888, these data also contained death and birth figures for occupational groups in Vidin and Ruse.[17] Accordingly, the natural demographic increase rate (excess of births over deaths) was much lower for people (both under and over the age of fifteen) working in casual labour and low-paid domestic service, as well as the clothing and weaving industries with a high proportion of female employment. Economically relying on casual labour or low wages, these sectors had apparently lower birth/mortality rates than all other economic sectors.

Poor families also resorted to abortion due to economic hardships, which could eventually curb the increase in the average number of children for the group in question. In the early nineteenth century when the Ottoman central bureaucracy began to show interest in the demographic tendencies of the society, the authorities considered the issue of fertility in the same context with the cases of miscarriage and abortion (*ıskat-ı cenin*), attributing the increase in the latter to financial difficulties of families.[18] In a similar vein, when the Ottoman authorities in the mid-nineteenth century began to consider marriage as a means to boost the Empire's population, they interpreted the low rate of marriages within the context of social stratification and considered economic problems as the main reason behind such a low rate.[19]

Economic conditions not only caused the low rate of marriages, but also played an important role in the increase of the average age at first marriage for men and women. As Todorova has observed for nineteenth-century Ottoman Bulgaria, in non-agricultural sectors of the local economy, a considerable period was needed for a man to become established, to pass through a number of preparatory stages, such as apprentice and journeyman, and to accumulate certain means.[20] As a result of these socio-economic conditions, the average marriage age rose across several areas in Ottoman Bulgaria, whose provincial economies were commercially oriented.

Particularly poor male members of the working class might have been more intensively affected by this situation. Any rise in the marriage age in turn shortened the reproductive period for couples, which brought about a decline in the number of their children. Yet, an upward trend in the age-at-marriage might not have necessarily reduced the reproductive period in all cases. For instance, when individuals married for a second time after divorce or loss of a spouse, they brought their children to the new marriage and extended the reproduction period with their new partners. Indeed, the available data pertaining to Ruse and Vidin indicate that the number of children for remarried individuals (at least for a second time) was higher than the average. In our Ruse data for the 1801–55 period, the average number of surviving children for the deceased was around 1.8. But for individuals who married at least twice, this ratio was around 2.2. During the 1801–40 period in Vidin, while the rate of average surviving children for the deceased was 1.7, it was 2.5 for those who entered a second marriage.

In her study on eighteenth- and nineteenth-century Nablus, Judith Tucker suggests that it was the poor who tended to remarry more frequently than the rich.[21] However, the cases of remarriage were almost evenly distributed across the poor and the rich in the towns under study. As revealed by our sample for Vidin belonging to the 1801–40 period, 139 individuals had been married more than once. Of these, forty fell under the wealthiest 25 percentile, while thirty-five belonged to the poorest category. Likewise, during the period between 1801 and 1855 in Ruse, there were a total of thirty-eight remarried individuals, nine of whom belonged to the wealthiest and eight to the poorest quartile. Thus, the relatively lower number of children for poor individuals cannot be completely explained by their slim chances of remarrying. The presence of polygyny is generally considered to be the key factor impacting on the number of children for men in the Ottoman society. However, as Svetlana Ivanova shows, Muslim marriage in the eighteenth century, as well as in the preceding century, was monogamous in the overwhelming majority of cases.[22] It is an obvious fact that poor families had fewer surviving children than wealthy couples. This could be because young couples at the early stages of their marital life were poor or because the poor brought down birth rates due to economic reasons, or were affected by high mortality rates and poor living conditions or even because they married at a later age (thereby shortening the reproduction period).

Socio-economic Status and Demographic Transformation in the Ottoman Balkans

In the scholarship on demographic history a number of writers have generally assumed that the association between social status and reproductive behaviour changed in conjunction with the demographic transition, particularly in the nineteenth century.[23] According to this common assumption, there was a positive correlation between status and fertility in the pre-modern period, while from the nineteenth century onwards higher status came to be correlated with low fertility. Although in the Ottoman lands, like in other parts of the world, the socio-economic status of an individual was determined by a complex web of societal relations, honorifics were, indeed, the indicators of the individual's position within the community.[24] Probate inventories include titles with the names, which allows us to distinguish the social standing of individuals and their affiliation with the Ottoman state apparatus.

However, the use of titles as indicators of the individuals' affiliation with the military, administrative and religious establishment generates methodological problems. Recent studies have shown that the early modern socio-economic metamorphosis in the Ottoman lands transformed the composition of *askeri* groups, as well as their status and titles in the social fabric. In fact, the titles of individuals belonging to the *askeri* class and rank-and-file soldiers – i.e., janissaries – underwent changes over time, becoming more and more intertwined with titles granted for reasons associated with the market economy.[25]

Individuals appearing with military, religious and administrative titles in court records, but later coming to be known by their professions, such as *ekmekçi* (baker) *ağa*, *nalband* (farrier) *beşe*, *attar* (herbalist) *ağa* and so on, apparently availed themselves of their status in the market. Consequently, it is extremely difficult to consider them as either title-holders or civilians. For this reason, this study has considered as civilians those individuals enjoying *askeri* status, but appearing in court registers with titles other than those associated with their official duties.[26] For example, Mehmed Beşe as one of the janissaries in the city was engaged in the tannery business, and scribes at the Vidin court recorded both his profession and military title *beşe*.[27] In such cases, individuals are categorised as civilians. According to this classification, if a groom, the groom's father and the bride's father did not bear honorific titles indicating their position in the state mechanism, the family would be considered a civilian household. If the groom, his father and/or the bride's father held a military or religious title, then such couples were defined as title-holders.

Janissaries with the honorific *beşe* constituted one component of the military elite. Religious dignitaries possessed titles such as *şerif*, *şerife*, *seyyid*, *seyyide*, *imam*, *efendi*, *hafız* and *hoca*. And titles like *ağa*, *bey*, *alemdar*, *paşa*, *bölükbaşı*, *kethüda*, *sekban*, *sipahi* and *odabaşı* (including the suffix-*zade*) belonged to the military–administrative elite. If the groom, his father and the bride's father bore double honorifics, then the couple was classified as part of both military and administrative elites.[28]

Tables 4.3 and 4.4 represent title holdership in relation to the number of children for couples at the death of either of the spouses. If we are to take a closer look at Tables 4.3 and 4.4, there appear to be three trends. The first trend attracting attention is that the downward tendency in the number of surviving children for couples with at least one mature child is observable for the wealthiest couples with titles and for those without. The second trend displayed by Tables 4.3 and 4.4 is that civilian couples with at least one mature child belonging to groups of middle wealth were comparably much more successful than their counterparts with titles in boosting or stabilising the number of surviving children in the post-1800 period.

This civilian group with at least one grown-up child (*kebir*) in Vidin, Ruse and Sofia had clearly succeeded in increasing the number of their children, whereas there was not a consistent trend for title-holding couples who had at least one grown-up child and fell under the same wealth category. As far as couples with at least one mature child were concerned, in the pre-1800 period, the number of surviving children for civilian and title-holding couples in the wealthiest category was always higher than their counterparts in the middle wealth groups. But after 1800, civilian couples in the middle wealth groups exceeded the wealthiest title-holding

Table 4.3 Number of surviving children for civilian and title-holding couples, 1670–1800.

		Childless Couples	Couples with Only Young Child/Children			Couples with at Least One Mature Child		
		Number of Observations	Number of Observations	Total Number of Children	Average Number of Children	Number of Observations	Total Number of Children	Average Number of Children
Ruse (1685–1800)								
Poorest 25%	Civilian	8 (17%)	12 (26%)	22	1.83	6 (13%)	14	2.33
	Title-Holders	6 (13%)	9 (20%)	16	1.77	5 (11%)	17	3.40
Middle Wealth Group	Civilian	11 (12%)	19 (20%)	41	2.15	22 (24%)	68	3.09
	Title-Holders	10 (11%)	19 (20%)	28	1.47	12 (13%)	32	2.66
Richest 25%	Civilian	5 (11%)	7 (15%)	9	1.28	6 (13%)	29	4.83
	Title-Holders	6 (13%)	11 (24%)	23	2.09	11 (24%)	40	3.63
Sofia (1670–1800)								
Poorest 25%	Civilian	39 (35%)	45 (40%)	63	1.40	13 (11%)	30	2.31
	Title-Holders	9 (8%)	6 (5%)	7	1.17	1 (1%)	1	1
Middle Wealth Group	Civilian	46 (20%)	91 (40%)	145	1.59	35 (16%)	85	2.43
	Title-Holders	19 (8%)	23 (10%)	45	1.95	13 (6%)	36	2.77
Richest 25%	Civilian	7 (6%)	29 (26%)	69	2.38	19 (17%)	63	3.31
	Title-Holders	12 (11%)	25 (22%)	34	1.36	21 (18%)	70	3.33
Vidin (1700–1800)								
Poorest 25%	Civilian	50 (13%)	59 (15%)	94	1.59	21 (5%)	49	2.33
	Title-Holders	116 (29%)	109 (28%)	182	1.66	40 (10%)	100	2.5
Middle Wealth Group	Civilian	47 (6%)	106 (14%)	206	1.94	48 (6%)	140	2.91
	Title-Holders	159 (20%)	331 (41%)	619	1.87	100 (13%)	320	3.2
Richest 25%	Civilian	14 (4%)	25 (7%)	53	2.12	22 (5%)	76	3.45
	Title-Holders	53 (13%)	183 (46%)	352	1.92	98 (25%)	354	3.61

Source Court Records of Ruse, Sofia and Vidin.

Table 4.4 Number of surviving children for civilian and title-holding couples, 1801–55.

			Childless Couples	Couples with Only Young Child/Children			Couples with at Least One Mature Child		
			Number of Observations	Number of Observations	Total Number of Children	Average Number of Children	Number of Observations	Total Number of Children	Average Number of Children
Ruse (1801–55)	**Poorest 25%**	Civilian	44 (22%)	73 (36%)	122	1.67	44 (22%)	122	2.77
		Title-Holders	12 (6%)	17 (8%)	30	1.76	9 (6%)	22	2.44
	Middle Wealth Group	Civilian	55 (14%)	113 (28%)	204	1.80	84 (21%)	273	3.25
		Title-Holders	27 (7%)	68 (17%)	127	1.86	51 (13%)	139	2.72
	Richest 25%	Civilian	13 (6.5%)	42 (21%)	79	1.88	28 (14%)	100	3.57
		Title-Holders	15 (7.5%)	58 (29%)	115	1.98	43 (22%)	138	3.20
Sofia (1801–33)	**Poorest 25%**	Civilian	17 (25%)	26 (38%)	43	1.65	12 (18%)	31	2.58
		Title-Holders	3 (4%)	4 (6%)	7	1.75	6 (9%)	13	2.17
	Middle Wealth Group	Civilian	21 (16%)	47 (34%)	98	2.09	23 (17%)	73	3.17
		Title-Holders	7 (5%)	29 (21%)	48	1.66	10 (7%)	27	2.7
	Richest 25%	Civilian	6 (9%)	21 (31%)	47	2.24	10 (15%)	31	3.10
		Title-Holders	4 (6%)	18 (26%)	35	1.94	9 (13%)	28	3.11
Vidin (1801–40)	**Poorest 25%**	Civilian	24 (12%)	81 (39%)	143	1.76	21 (10%)	50	2.38
		Title-Holders	12 (6%)	59 (29%)	91	1.54	9 (4%)	26	2.88
	Middle Wealth Group	Civilian	35 (8%)	143 (35%)	231	1.61	57 (14%)	184	3.22
		Title-Holders	29 (7%)	113 (27%)	189	1.67	36 (9%)	114	3.16
	Richest 25%	Civilian	14 (7%)	43 (21%)	89	2.06	16 (8%)	55	3.43
		Title-Holders	20 (10%)	81 (39%)	145	1.79	32 (15%)	92	2.87

Source Court Records of Ruse, Sofia and Vidin.

couples in terms of the average number of surviving children in all three regions.

The third important trend is the existence of the strong positive relationship between status and the number of surviving children for mature couples – that is, couples with at least one grown-up child – in Sofia and Vidin until 1800, while in the first half of the nineteenth century this status effect diminished in strength. In other words, the average number of surviving children for the title-holders lagged behind civilians until 1800 only in Ruse. Yet this process saw the wealthiest with the larger number of surviving children before 1800 reversed in the next century, with civilians tending to have more children compared to title-holders in all three regions.

One can propose three hypotheses as to why and how such trends happened. The first could be that throughout the eighteenth and nineteenth centuries a change took place in the impact of mortality rates upon social groups. Vidin, Ruse and Sofia went through serious political and military turmoil in the last quarter of the eighteenth century and in the early nineteenth century.[29] No doubt, this produced economic winners and losers across all segments of the society.[30] However, there has so far been very little analysis of how different social groups were affected by the turmoil and the subsequent Ottoman centralisation efforts. One might assume that rather than civilians, it might be the military groups who were mostly affected by the military struggle among the local elites, as well as their concomitant strife against the Ottoman central authority in the last quarter of the eighteenth century and early nineteenth century.[31] Based on this presumption, the first hypothesis suggests that prolonged military conflicts might have increased the mortality rate of this group, which in turn brought about a decline in the number of children.

As Tables 4.5 and 4.6[32] show, the share of administrative–military elites and rank-and-file soldiers declined in Vidin and Ruse samples after 1800, while increasing in Sofia.[33]

As the Ottoman courts became directly involved in the division of estates belonging to the Ottoman state functionaries due to Ottoman inheritance law, one might thus speculate that the declining shares of military groups in probate samples reflected the declining mortality rates among these groups. However, the decrease in the share of the military title-holders among the probate records may also be related to their decline in the real population, due to military conflicts at the turn of the nineteenth century. Even though one might accept the upswing of mortality rates among military and administrative elites in the first half of the nineteenth century suggested by the first hypothesis, this way of thinking does not

Table 4.5 Wealth distribution by social groups, 1670–1800.

		Administrative and Military Elites	Rank-and-File Soldiers	Religious Functionaries	Civilians
Ruse (1685–1800) Base Year: 1680	Poorest 25% Number of Observations	4 (9%)	9 (19.5%)	7 (15%)	26 (56.5%)
	Average Real Wealth (*Guruş*)	108.5	85.7	82	74
	Middle Wealth Group Number of Observations	15 (16%)	11 (12%)	15 (16%)	52 (56%)
	Average Real Wealth (*Guruş*)	258.3	271	309.3	287.5
	Richest 25% Number of Observations	19 (41%)	2 (5%)	7 (15%)	18 (39%)
	Average Real Wealth (*Guruş*)	2,660.2	804	1,473	1,464.1
Sofia (1670–1800) Base Year: 1670	Poorest 25% Number of Observations	1 (1%)	8 (7%)	7 (6%)	97 (86%)
	Average Real Wealth (*Guruş*)	25	22.8	32.5	25.7
	Middle Wealth Group Number of Observations	20 (9%)	16 (7%)	19 (8%)	172 (76%)
	Average Real Wealth (*Guruş*)	184	122	169.4	138
	Richest 25% Number of Observations	29 (25%)	11 (10%)	18 (16%)	55 (49%)
	Average Real Wealth (*Guruş*)	1,963	1,051	1,150.2	859.7
Vidin (1700–1800) Base Year: 1700	Poorest 25% Number of Observations	60 (15%)	188 (48%)	17 (4%)	130 (33%)
	Average Real Wealth (*Guruş*)	38.6	35.5	43	31.9
	Middle Wealth Group Number of Observations	166 (21%)	388 (49%)	36 (5%)	201 (25%)
	Average Real Wealth (*Guruş*)	196.7	188.8	179	181.2
	Richest 25% Number of Observations	145 (37%)	171 (43%)	18 (5%)	61 (15%)
	Average Real Wealth (*Guruş*)	2,022	1,115	1,795	964.8

Source Court Records of Ruse, Sofia and Vidin.

Table 4.6 Wealth distribution by social groups, 1801–55.

			Administrative and Military Elites	Rank-and-File Soldiers	Religious Functionaries	Civilians
Ruse	**Poorest 25%**	Number of Observations	23 (11.5%)	3 (1.5%)	12 (6%)	161 (81%)
(1801–55)		Average Real Wealth (*Guruş*)	160.2	141.3	170.5	158.7
Base Year: 1800	**Middle Wealth Group**	Number of Observations	92 (23%)	2 (1%)	52 (13%)	252 (63%)
		Average Real Wealth (*Guruş*)	782.4	836.4	690.7	688.2
	Richest 25%	Number of Observations	93 (47%)	0	23 (11%)	83 (42%)
		Average Real Wealth (*Guruş*)	8,733.7	0	4,731.6	3,793.2
Sofia	**Poorest 25%**	Number of Observations	7 (10%)	0 (0%)	6 (9%)	55 (81%)
(1801–33)		Average Real Wealth (*Guruş*)	182.7	0	168	150.4
Base Year: 1800	**Middle Wealth Group**	Number of Observations	29 (21%)	2 (1%)	15 (11%)	91 (67%)
		Average Real Wealth (*Guruş*)	853.3	670.5	796.1	879.1
	Richest 25%	Number of Observations	26 (38%)	0	5 (7%)	37 (55%)
		Average Real Wealth (*Guruş*)	14,848	0	4,688.1	5,242.6
Vidin	**Poorest 25%**	Number of Observations	15 (7%)	58 (28%)	7 (4%)	126 (61%)
(1801–40)		Average Real Wealth (*Guruş*)	152.9	160	137.2	171.4
Base Year: 1800	**Middle Wealth Group**	Number of Observations	71 (17%)	87 (21%)	20 (5%)	235 (57%)
		Average Real Wealth (*Guruş*)	797.5	683.3	656.9	701
	Richest 25%	Number of Observations	102 (50%)	14 (7%)	17 (8%)	73 (35%)
		Average Real Wealth (*Guruş*)	4,558.8	2,375	4,406.3	3,821

Source Court Records of Ruse, Sofia and Vidin.

explain the difference in mortality rates between the wealthiest civilians and their counterparts in the middle wealth groups throughout the same period. It seems that there is no clear evidence to support the first hypothesis regarding the variation in mortality rates across different social groups in Vidin, Ruse and Sofia during the late eighteenth and early nineteenth centuries.

The second hypothesis also suggests that from the mid-eighteenth century onwards, couples without titles who rose to prominence in terms of wealth might have adopted a pattern of increase in the number of children. In his analysis of the social structures of the cities of Vidin, Ruse and Sofia in the early eighteenth century, Todorov demonstrates that prospering thanks to commerce and craftsmanship, the new rich and middle wealth groups came to transform the social hierarchy that had been dominated by the Ottoman ruling class, particularly in the early decades of the century.[34]

According to Todorov, the middle wealth groups came to enjoy a different social position from the mid-eighteenth century onwards in the Ottoman Balkans. The commercial and artisanal activities of members of this group had brought them sufficient material prosperity to be independent and to support a standard of living equal to that of the rich subjects of the Empire. In his view, with their clothing as well as furniture, this new rich and middle wealth group imitated the earlier local Ottoman elites in cultural matters. One might postulate the idea that these newly rising civilian groups possibly perceived that a greater number of children helped to increase their social status.[35] However, as shown in Tables 4.5 and 4.6, there was no direct relationship between social mobility and demographic trends in the three regions under study. True, in Vidin the share of titleless population increased among middle wealth groups after 1800, while at the same time there was a rise in the number of surviving children among civilian middle wealth couples with at least one mature child. But in Ruse and Sofia the number of surviving children among the wealthiest civilian group with at least one mature child dramatically declined after 1800, whereas the wealth share of the same group rose in our sample.

A third possible hypothesis about the trends is that social groups started to make different fertility decisions. To put it another way, the fact that middle wealth civilians had a relative increase in the number of children and there was a drop in the surviving number of children of the wealthiest group might have to do with the decisions made by these groups about fertility. At least in these three towns of the Ottoman world, the wealthiest couples (title-holders and civilians) appear, after 1800, to have fewer surviving children. It is no coincidence that the tendency on the part of the wealthiest group to reduce the number of children was also a major topic of debate among late Ottoman intellectuals. In his work *Mesail-i Mühimme*, Avanzade Süleyman, for instance, mentioned that in Ottoman society, it was usually the poor who gave birth to the larger number of children, and the wealthier and affluent families tended to have the smaller number of children.[36] Concerned with the 'demographic quality of population', Avanzade was indeed a sharp observer of the demographic structures in the late Ottoman period and insisted that Ottoman families should arrange their ideal number of children according to their socio-economic status. Therefore, he did not hesitate to express his anxiety over the lower fertility rates of the rich compared to those of the poor. In other words, the tendency among the wealthiest to have fewer children started in the early nineteenth century, but appears to have been more and more visible toward the end of the century, a process that did not escape the Avanzade's attention.

Conclusion

Writing on the nineteenth-century demographic patterns in Bulgaria, Todorova argues that a very high fertility rate and only moderately high mortality rate resulted in the growth of population in Ottoman Bulgaria.[37] It seems that the civilian middle wealth groups, rather than wealthiest civilians and title-holders, were the main force behind the nineteenth-century population growth, at least in three Ottoman towns across the Balkans. In their study on household formation in Istanbul, Duben and Behar observe that the relatively low fertility rates in the second half of the nineteenth century were very likely not a new phenomenon, but most probably extended further back in time.[38] Findings of this study corroborate the observation that this process was visible already in the early nineteenth century.

The wealthiest mature couples, especially title-holders, compared to all other social groups, quite clearly had fewer children after 1800, at least in three Ottoman regions across the Balkans. In fact, the tendency to have fewer children gradually became an established pattern after the 1880s in some regions of the Ottoman Empire going hand-in-hand with a greater social emphasis placed on the nuclear family unit. As Kenneth Cuno rightly claims, in earlier times a family was almost an extended kinship group with servants in Ottoman lands, whereas the ideal of child-centred conjugal family began to undermine the underpinnings of 'old family ideology'.[39] Not surprisingly, in this period the child-centred family was promoted by wealthy circles, intellectuals and bureaucrats, who also began to advocate child quality by reducing the number of children and investing more resources in each child.[40] Considering the fact that the 'modernist' discourses and practices revolving around the nuclear family and higher human capital investment per child diffused into the middle classes, becoming widespread across all social sectors in the late Ottoman period particularly in large cities, one might argue that the wealthiest groups, particularly title-holders, possibly led the way in the three analysed Ottoman towns as far as the decline in the surviving children rate was concerned. In the words of Livi-Bacci, this group could be considered in some way as the avant-garde of the Ottoman demographic system in the three towns in question.[41] Whether cultural attitudes and practices of the wealthy segments of the Ottoman society related to child-rearing beliefs and the importance of children for families went hand-in-hand with the changing demographic behaviour of couples remains unknown, since very little research has been conducted on the transformation of family values in the early modern period. In this regard, the findings of this study call for further research on this issue.

Notes

1. Duben and Behar, *İstanbul Haneleri*.
2. Clark, *A Farewell to Alms*, pp. 1–19; Cummins, 'Why Did Fertility Decline?', pp. 11–38; Dribe and Scalone, 'Social Class and Net Fertility', pp. 429–64; Tsuya et al., *Prudence and Pressure*, pp. 3–24. For recent debates on the appearance of the 'modern family' in the Middle East, see Kenneth Cuno, *Modernizing Marriage*, pp. 78–9.
3. This argument, however, does not mean that in the early modern age the concept of childhood did not exist in Ottoman society. See Yahya Araz, *16. Yüzyıldan 19. Yüzyıl Başlarına Osmanlı Toplumunda Çocuk Olmak*.
4. Duben and Behar, *İstanbul Haneleri*, pp. 188–255.
5. Kenneth Cuno, *Modernizing Marriage*, pp. 1–56; Hakkı Dursun Yıldız (ed.), *Sosyo-Kültürel Değişme Sürecinde Türk Ailesi*. For recent revisionist studies and debates on the Ottoman family as well marriage patterns, see also Meriwether, *The Kin*, pp. 73–101; Schilcher, 'The Lore and Reality', pp. 504–9; Hanna, 'Marriage', pp. 149–54; Hatem, '19. Yüzyıl Mısır'ında Sağlık', pp. 66–73.
6. Todorova, *Balkan Family*; Kaser, *Household and Family in the Balkans*.
7. See David, 'The Age of Unmarried Male Children', pp. 347–57; Ginio, 'Childhood, Mental Capacity', pp. 90–119; Kiel, 'Population, Settlement', pp. 213–30.
8. See, for instance, Coşgel and Ergene, 'Inequality of Wealth', pp. 312–13.
9. As in other parts of the world, the optional nature of probate registration in

the early modern Ottoman world caused the underrepresentation of rural populations, women, non-Muslims and poor segments of society. In Sofia in the early nineteenth century, non-Muslims constituted 90 per cent of the population, whereas the percentage of non-Muslims in our Sofia sample is only 11 per cent. In Vidin and Ruse, with 78 and 30 per cent of the non-Muslim population respectively, their percentage of probate inventories is around 10 per cent. In the 1870s, rural inhabitants made up 78 per cent of the whole population in Vidin, Ruse and Sofia. But in our Ruse sample, only 10 per cent are related to rural groups; 5 per cent in Vidin and 14 per cent in Sofia.
10. Bozkurt, 'Tereke Defterleri', pp. 104–5.
11. The idea has been put forward earlier by Fatih Bozkurt. See Bozkurt, 'Tereke Defterleri', pp. 91–120.
12. Another age category under the name of *murahık/murahıka* (novices on the verge of puberty) became common in probate inventories towards the late eighteenth century. In this study, however, these *murahık/murahıka* children are categorised as young children.
13. Probate inventories contain information only about the numbers of surviving offspring and a simple dual classification (*kebir/sagir*) for their ages. In fact, these numbers depend on (a) past fertility and (b) past mortality rates, on which probate inventories do not provide any information. In other words, the existing number of children for couples recorded in probate inventories does not represent the overall birth rates, for the registers did not keep the number of other children who had succumbed between two childbirths.
14. Clark and Hamilton, 'Survival of the Richest', pp. 1–30.
15. Ömer, *Nüfus Meselesi*, pp. 57–61.
16. Polat, 'Osmanlı Devleti'nde Ermenilerin Sosyo-Ekonomik Yapısından Kentsel Kesitler', p. 5.
17. Движение на населението в Българското княжество през 1888 година/ Mouvement de la population dans la principauté de Bulgarie pendant l'année 1888/Bureau statistique de la principauté de Bulgarie, pp. 70–90, 388–403.
18. Somel, 'Osmanlı Son Döneminde', pp. 66–79; Balsoy, 'Gender and the Politics of the Female Body', pp. 124–8.
19. Ercoşkun, 'Osmanlı İmparatorluğu'nda 19. Yüzyılda Evlilik', pp. 75–103.
20. Todorova, *Balkan Family Structure*, p. 44.
21. Tucker, 'Marriage and Family in Nablus', pp. 175–6.
22. Ivanova, 'Muslim and Christian Women', pp. 165–6.
23. Dribe et al., 'Socioeconomic Status and Fertility', pp. 162–6.
24. Coşgel and Ergene, 'Inequality of Wealth', pp. 311–18.
25. Başaran, *Selim III*, pp. 117–51; Tülüveli, 'Honorific Titles', pp. 17–27; Yilmaz, 'The Economic and Social Roles', pp. 175–222.
26. For similar observations on the activities of title-holders in the commercial markets, see Yılmaz Diko, 'Blurred Boundaries', pp. 182–8.
27. VCR 78, p. 41, no. 2 (1178/1764).

28. Inflation adjustment and the categorisation of social groups based on the titles of couples have a significant impact on the socio-economic composition of samples. For a comparison between adjusted values and raw data, see Kokdaş, 'Land Ownership', pp. 1–25. The analysis takes into account the titles of the couples' families rather than those of individuals, which has a significant impact upon the sampling. In a previous study on the land and credit markets in the Balkans, I categorised women as a separate social group. However, the present study focusing on the demographic decisions of couples highlights the titles that women inherited from their fathers, as well as the status of their husbands. This choice has a considerable influence upon the share of two social categories in particular – that is, elites and military groups – within the sampling as a whole.
29. Georgieva, 'Administrative Structure', pp. 8–18; Zens, 'The Ayanlik', pp. 99–150.
30. Davidova, *Balkan Transitions*, pp. 12–16.
31. For a similar presumption on seventeenth-century Karaferye, see Gara, 'Moneylenders', p. 145.
32. All monetary values presented in Tables 4.5 and 4.6 are real values adjusted for inflation using the Istanbul Consumer Price Index. Pamuk, 'The Price Revolution', pp. 76–8.
33. Vidin was the eighteenth-century fortified military town, which was the most affected by the winds of change blowing in the first half of the nineteenth century. Because janissaries were deprived of their privilege as part of the Ottoman central army after the abolition of the janissary corps in 1826, the town's former status-holding wealthy members of janissary origin were replaced at this point by the civilian rich groups. Without doubt, this transformation became an important factor determining the demographic structure of families in the Vidin area during the first half of the nineteenth century.
34. Todorov, *The Balkan City*, pp. 161–84.
35. Ibid., pp. 182–4.
36. Balsoy, 'Geç Osmanlı', p. 60.
37. Todorova, *Balkan Family Structure*, pp. 76–122.
38. Duben and Behar, *İstanbul Haneleri*, pp. 18–26.
39. Cuno, *Modernizing Marriage*, pp. 3–86.
40. Duben and Behar, *İstanbul Haneleri*, pp. 186–8, 193–240. For the nineteenth-century discourses revolving around the new family ideology, see also Baron, 'The Making and Breaking', pp. 277–84; Russell, 'The Use of Textbooks', pp. 284–88; Pollard, 'Learning Gendered Modernity', pp. 255–68; Schilcher, 'The Lore and Reality of Middle Eastern Patriarchy', pp. 496–512.
41. Livi-Bacci, 'Social Group Forerunners', pp. 182–200.

Bibliography

Archival Sources

Ruscuk Şer'iyye Sicilleri – Ruse Court Records (RCR): 2; 3; 4; 7; 8; 9; 10; 12; 13; 14; 15; 16; 18; 19; 20; 21; 22; 23; 25; 36; 37; 38; 51; 52; 53 (1096/1685–1270/1855)

* Note: The numbers above represent registers. Also, years are not indicated per register due to discrepancies between the catalogue and the documents included in it.

Sofya Şer'iyye Sicilleri – Sofia Court Records (SCR): 12; 16; 17; 20; 21; 22; 23; 25; 26; 27; 29; 30; 31; 32; 161; 164; 173; 309; 309–2; 309–4; 309–5; 311–2; 312–3; 312–5; 311–6; 311–7; 312–8; 312–9 (1080/1670–1248/1833).

Vidin Şer'iyye Sicilleri – Vidin Court Records (VCR): 8; 11; 18; 19; 25–a; 34; 35; 36; 37; 38; 39; 40; 41; 42; 43; 47; 48; 49; 50; 52; 53; 54; 55; 56; 57; 59; 60; 61; 62; 63; 64; 65; 66; 67; 68; 69; 70; 71; 74; 78; 80; 82; 84; 159–a; 160; 160–a; 161–a; 163; 167; 168; 169; 305; 307; 309; 310; 311–a; 311–b; 346 (1111/1700–1255/1840).

Published Primary Sources

Ömer, Besim, *Nüfus Meselesi ve Küçük Çocuklarda Vefiyat* (Istanbul: Kanaat Matbaası, 1339).

Движение на населението в Българското княжество през 1888 година/ Mouvement de la population dans la principaute de Bulgarie pendant l'annee 1888/Bureau statistique de la principaute de Bulgarie, 1891, Sofia.

Secondary Sources

Araz, Yahya, *16. Yüzyıldan 19. Yüzyıl Başlarına Osmanlı Toplumunda Çocuk Olmak* (Istanbul: Kitap Yayınevi, 2013).

Balsoy, Gülhan, 'Gender and the Politics of the Female Body: Midwifery, Abortion, and Pregnancy in Ottoman Society (1838–1890s)', unpublished PhD dissertation, Binghamton University, 2009.

_____, 'Geç Osmanlı Öğüt Kitaplarında Kısırlık', *OTAM*, 35 (2014), pp. 41–64.

Baron, Beth, 'The Making and Breaking of Marital Bonds in Modern Egypt', in Nikki Keddie and Beth Baron (eds), *Women in Middle Eastern History* (New Haven and London: Yale University Press, 1981), pp. 275–91.

Başaran, Betül, *Selim III, Social Control and Policing in Istanbul at the End of the Eighteenth Century Between Crisis and Order* (Leiden: Brill, 2014).

Bozkurt, Fatih, 'Tereke Defterleri ve Osmanlı Demografi Araştırmaları', *Tarih Dergisi*, 54 (2011/12), pp. 91–120.

Clark, Gregory, *A Farewell to Alms: A Brief Economic History of the World* (Princeton, NJ: Princeton University Press, 2007).

Clark, Gregory, and Gillian Hamilton, 'Survival of the Richest: The Malthusian Mechanism in Pre-Industrial England', *The Journal of Economic History*, 66/3 (2006), pp. 1–30.

Coşgel, Metin, and Boğaç Ergene, 'Inequality of Wealth in the Ottoman Empire: War, Weather, and Long-Term Trends in Eighteenth-Century Kastamonu', *The Journal of Economic History*, 72/2 (2012), pp. 308–31.

Cummins, Neil, 'Why Did Fertility Decline? An Analysis of the Individual Level Economic Correlates of the Nineteenth Century Fertility Transition in England and France', PhD dissertation, London School of Economics and Political Science, 2009.

Cuno, Kenneth, *Modernizing Marriage: Family, Ideology, and Law in Nineteenth- and Early Twentieth-Century Egypt* (Syracuse: Syracuse University Press, 2015).

David, Geza, 'The Age of Unmarried Male Children in the Tahrir Defters (Notes on the Coefficient)', *Acta Orientalia Academiae Scientiarum Hungaricae*, 31/3 (1977), pp. 347–57.

Davidova, Evguenia, *Balkan Transitions to Modernity and Nation-States: Through the Eyes of Three Generations of Merchants (1780s–1890s)* (Leiden: Brill, 2013).

Dribe, Martin, and Francesco Scalone, 'Social Class and Net Fertility Before, During and After the Demographic Transition: A Micro-level Analysis of Sweden 1880–1970', *Demographic Research*, 30 (2014), pp. 429–64.

Dribe, Martin, Michel Oris, and Lucia Pozzi, 'Socioeconomic Status and Fertility Before, During, and After the Demographic Transition: An Introduction', *Demographic Research*, 31 (2014), pp. 161–82.

Duben, Alan, and Cem Behar, *İstanbul Haneleri: Evlilik, Aile ve Doğurganlık, 1880–1940* (Istanbul: Boğaziçi Üniversitesi Yayınları, 2013).

Ercoşkun, Tülay, 'Osmanlı İmparatorluğu'nda 19. Yüzyılda Evlilik ve Nikâha Dair Düzenlemeler', PhD dissertation, Ankara Üniversitesi, 2010.

Gara, Eleni, 'Moneylenders and Landowners: In Search of Urban Muslim Elites in the Early Modern Balkans', in Antonis Anastasopoulos (ed.), *Provincial Elites in the Ottoman Empire* (Rethymno: University of Crete Press, 2003), pp. 135–47.

Georgieva, Gergana, 'Administrative Structure and Government of Rumelia in the Late Eighteenth and Early Nineteenth Centuries: The Functions and Activities of the Vali of Rumelia', in Antonis Anastasopoulos and Elias Kolovos (eds), *The Ottoman Rule and the Balkans, 1760-1850: Conflict, Transformation, Adaptation* (Rethymno: University of Crete Press, 2007), pp. 3–19.

Ginio, Eyal, 'Childhood, Mental Capacity and Conversion to Islam in the Ottoman State, *Byzantine and Modern Greek Studies*, 25 (2001), pp. 90–119.

Gradeva, Rossitsa, 'Between Hinterland and Frontier: Ottoman Vidin, Fifteenth to Eighteenth Centuries', *Proceedings of the British Academy*, 156 (2012), pp. 331–51.

Hanna, Nelly, 'Marriage among Merchant Families in Seventeenth-Century Cairo', in Amira El Azhary Sonbol (ed.), *Women, the Family, and Divorce Laws in Islamic History* (New York: Syracuse University Press, 1996), pp. 143–54.

Hatem, Mervat, '19. Yüzyıl Mısır'ında Sağlık Mesleği ve Kadın Bedeninin Denetlenmesi', in Madeline Zilfi (ed.), *Modernleşmenin Eşiğinde Osmanlı Kadınları* (Istanbul: Tarih Vakfı Yurt Yayınları, 1997), pp. 63–76.

Ivanova, Svetlana, 'Muslim and Christian Women before the Kadi Court in Eighteenth Century Rumeli: Marriage Problems', *Oriente Moderno*, 18/79 (1999), pp. 161–76.

Kaser, Karl, 'The Balkan Joint Family: Redefining a Problem', in Karl Kaser (ed.), *Household and Family in the Balkans: Two Decades of Historical Family Research at University of Graz* (Vienna: LIT Verlag, 2012), pp. 89–108.

Kiel, Machiel, 'Population, Settlement and Economy of Serres from the Late-Byzantine Period to the 19th Century According to Little-Known or Unused Ottoman Administrative Records', *Οι Σέρρες και η περιοχή τους από την οθωμανική κατάκτηση μέχρι τη σύγχρονη εποχή* (Δήμος Σερρών, 2013), pp. 213–30.

Kokdaş, İrfan, 'Land Ownership, Tax Farming and the Social Structure of Local Credit Markets in the Ottoman Balkans, 1685–1855', *Financial History Review*, 24/1 (2017), pp. 53–81.

Livi-Bacci, Massimo, 'Social Group Forerunners of Fertility Control in Europe', in Ansley J. Coale and Susan Cotts Watkins (eds), *The Decline of Fertility in Europe* (Princeton, NJ: Princeton University Press, 1986), pp. 182–200.

Meriwether, Margaret, *The Kin Who Count: Family and Society in Ottoman Aleppo, 1770-1840* (Austin: University of Texas Press, 2010).

Pamuk, Şevket, 'The Price Revolution in the Ottoman Empire Reconsidered', *International Journal of Middle East Studies*, 33/1 (2001), pp. 69–89.

Polat, Zelkif, 'Osmanlı Devleti'nde Ermenilerin Sosyo-Ekonomik Yapısından Kentsel Kesitler', *Yeni Türkiye*, 60 (2014), pp. 1–18.

Pollard, Lisa, 'Learning Gendered Modernity: The Home, the Family, and the Schoolroom in the Construction of Egyptian National Identity (1885–1919)', in Amira El Azhary Sonbol (ed.), *Beyond the Exotic: Women's Histories in Islamic Societies* (Cairo: The American University in Cairo Press, 2006), pp. 249–69.

Russell, Mona, 'The Use of Textbooks as a Source of History for Women: The Case of Turn-of-the-Century Egypt', in Amira El Azhary Sonbol, *Beyond the Exotic: Women's Histories in Islamic Societies* (Cairo: The American University in Cairo Press, 2006), pp. 270–94.

Schilcher, Linda Schatkowski, 'The Lore and Reality of Middle Eastern Patriarchy', *Die Welt des Islams*, 28/1–4 (1988), pp. 496–512.

Somel, Selçuk A., 'Osmanlı Son Döneminde Iskat-ı Cenin Meselesi', *Kebikeç*, 13 (2002), pp. 65–88.

Todorov, Nikolai, *The Balkan City, 1400–1900* (Seattle and London: University of Washington Press, 1983).

Todorova, Maria, *Balkan Family Structure and the European Pattern: Demographic Developments in Ottoman Bulgaria* (Budapest and New York: CEU Press, 2006).

Tsuya, Noriko O., Wang Feng, George Alter, James Z. Lee, et al., *Prudence and Pressure: Reproduction and Human Agency in Europe and Asia, 1700–1900* (Cambridge, MA: MIT Press, 2010).

Tucker, Judith, 'Marriage and Family in Nablus, 1720-1856: Toward a History of Arab Marriage', *Journal of Family History*, 13/2 (1988), pp. 165–79.

Tülüveli, Güçlü, 'Honorific Titles in Ottoman Parlance: A Reevaluation', *International Journal of Turkish Studies*, 11/1–2 (2005), pp. 17–27.

Yıldız, Hakkı Dursun (ed.), *Sosyo-Kültürel Değişme Sürecinde Türk Ailesi-I* (Ankara: Başbakanlık Aile Araştırmaları Kurumu Yayınları, 1992).

Yılmaz Diko, Gulay, 'Blurred Boundaries between Soldiers and Civilians: Artisan Janissaries in Seventeenth-Century Istanbul', in Suraiya Faroqhi (ed.), *Bread from the Lion's Mouth: Artisans Struggling for a Livelihood in Ottoman Cities* (New York and Oxford: Berghahn Books, 2015), pp. 175–93.

Yilmaz, Gulay, 'The Economic and Social Roles of Janissaries in a 17th Century Ottoman City: The Case of Istanbul', PhD dissertation, McGill University, 2011.

Zens, Robert, 'The Ayanlik and Pasvanoğlu Osman Paşa of Vidin in the Age of Ottoman Social Change, 1791–1815', PhD dissertation, University of Wisconsin-Madison, 2004.

Chapter 5

The Emotional Bond between Early Modern Ottoman Children and Parents: A Case Study of Sünbülzade Vehbi's 'Ideal' Child (1700–1800)

Leyla Kayhan Elbirlik

Who would have thought it possible a century ago that the first hesitant words of infants or the blushes of adolescents—or the shape of houses—could become the objects of serious scientific study?

Henri Lefebvre[1]

Studies focusing on the history of childhood in the Ottoman world have maintained that the extant sources allow for a limited view of how the idea of childhood was perceived in the early modern period. Compared to the sources of European history, historical accounts on Ottoman children and biographical narratives focusing on children's lives are rare in the Ottoman context. Nevertheless the *Shariʻah* court records and fatwa collections that reflect the daily concerns of the populace are primary documents that inform on children's lives and attitudes toward childhood. These normative–theoretical sources offer only a partial view of children's relationship to their surroundings, as well as their reception by society at large. Recent works have linked the reticence of such sources on the subject of children to their assumption of them as 'fragile', 'passive receptors' lacking agency, and therefore not being historically meaningful actors.[2]

While the field of Ottoman childhood study is developing to call this perspective into question, the need for furthering our knowledge on the relationship between parents and children is even more pertinent, as well as similar source-related concerns with respect to child-rearing and nurturing practices. Views on parenthood not only bring into consideration a variety of sensibilities and tension points vis-à-vis children, but also allow for a discussion of how childhood is perceived in a particular time and culture. Any effort in reconstructing child life through the court records and fatwa collections is inevitably restricted, given the 'canonised' language and formulaic recording of cases. They do not provide a comprehensive understanding of the details of an incident. Elements that are likely the most intriguing for the historian are commonly left out of the narrative of the court cases and *fatwa*s, since they are not legally relevant.[3] Consequently, it is with these methodological concerns that the literature of conduct, and advice manuals in particular, are used for the purposes of a more insightful depiction of parenthood.

Although advice manuals do not necessarily diverge from the traditionally accepted conventions of conduct writing, they manifest the personal inclinations and principles of the author beyond the prescriptive nature of the source. In order to determine the significance of advice literature and its influence on attitudes toward the raising and educating of children, one first needs to identify the underlying purpose of its conception, as well as its intended reception. Historians have often considered advice literature as a genre that should be used alongside other primary sources, since the legitimacy of such ideological treatises has been contested for understanding 'life as it was lived'.[4] Identifying the nature and significance of a given advice manual is crucial to the evaluation of its possible function. For a more cognisant assessment, it is essential to differentiate between an advice manual conceived as a source reflecting current practice or one that has a prescriptive agenda of how things ought to be. The example of child-rearing advice manuals popular in Europe in the early modern period illustrates this point. Jay Mechling, in a study that problematised the use of this genre as historical evidence, stresses the strong possibility of there being no direct relationship between child-rearing advice and actual child-rearing practice in a given culture.[5] Mechling suggests that 'child-rearing manuals are the consequents not of child-rearing values but of child-rearing manual-writing values', concluding that it is much more probable that parents learned about parenting through identification, imitation, instruction and invention.[6] That said, given the social invisibility of children's lives, advice literature must be an influential source representing certain values regarding the expected role of parents in the life of children. Advice manuals, with a target audience ranging from young children to adults, may be studied as educatory treatises setting behavioural and moral standards with the anticipation of contributing to the wellbeing of society.

In his examination of different approaches in early modern European family history, Michael Anderson categorises the method of those studies examining the socio-cultural factors affecting the emergence of the modern nuclear family without the use of demographic and other quantitative data as the 'sentiments approach'. Although scholars such as Philippe Ariès and Edward Shorter have been contested for constructing their theses of the family on sources that were considered atypical, irregular and unstandardised, their contribution in bringing into view features of family life that were mostly overlooked by family history cannot be disputed. Ariès, among others, was one of the first historians to draw attention to the changes in aspects of socio-cultural life, such as religious practices and educational vision, generating new attitudes towards the history of children and private life.

The initial appeal in the history of emotions owed much to a particular interest in searching for changing patterns in emotionality to explain the circumstances that contributed to the birth of the modern family, and its more sophisticated interpersonal relationships.[7] Acknowledging that emotions are period- and context-specific, and hence vary over time, this chapter attempts to contextualise the theory that emotions are 'socially constructed and enacted on the basis of "scripts", or "schemas"'.[8] My assessment interprets the narrative of the advice manual as a script-world that reflects the emotional standards and attitudes of the society that enabled its expression. This chapter will, on the one hand, focus on the Ottoman society's attitudes toward childhood as reflected in the late eighteenth-century advice manual, *Lütfiyye* of Sünbülzade Vehbi, and on the other, explore the nature of the emotional bond between a father and his son.

Sünbülzade Vehbi's Life and Career

Situating Vehbi's intellectual, emotional and career-related guidelines informed by his own personal history provides a comprehensive framework. Vehbi was born to a prominent *ulema* (men of religion) family in Maraş circa 1719.[9] After acquiring his principal education in Maraş, he left for Istanbul to start his career as a teacher (*müderris*) in a *madrasa*. His poetic rigour earned him a promotion among the palace elite, and he soon acquired a place in Ottoman bureaucracy as a scribe. Sünbülzade Vehbi's competence in the Persian language led to his being dispatched as the envoy of Abdülhamid I to report on the Zand dynasty in Iran. Unfortunately, his close liaisons with members of the the Iranian court caused him to fall from favour in the Ottoman court. Due to an execution decree being issued against him, Vehbi returned to Istanbul in disguise, and was unable to find a post for seven years. But thanks to his verse, Vehbi regained the favour of the palace and was given his initial post as *qadi* by the Grand Vizier Halil Hamid Pasha. Vehbi's turbulent career serving as *qadi* in Rhodes, Manisa, Siroz, Manastır, Zağra and Bolu during the reign of Selim III was laced with stories about political intrigue and conspiracies.

Much of what is known about Sünbülzade Vehbi's life and personality was recorded by his close friend and chamberlain in Zağra – the poet, Sururi. In his *Hezeliyyat*, a literary genre that uses dark humour and criticism, Sururi's portrayal of Vehbi is less than sympathetic. Ali Canip Yöntem has commented that Sururi's slanderous comments about Vehbi having a bad reputation, being cruel, living off orphan property, hurting those that are innocent and not 'having any virtuous woman or man under his safekeeping in Eski Zağra (Stara Zagora in Southern Bulgaria)' should not be taken as his genuine opinion, since this sardonic stance is Sururi's usual unremitting habit towards his friend.[10] Sururi goes as far as to suggest Vehbi's blindness and deafness caused him to remain ignorant of his faults and fail to listen to others' advice. Sururi emphasised Vehbi's drunkenness and excessive foolish talking, as inappropriate characteristics for his position.[11] Historical accounts such as Sururi's depict Vehbi's controversial personality; however, this side of his character is not readily displayed in the advice manual for Lütfullah, in that he intends to set an example for his son.

As a writer, Vehbi is considered to be among those eighteenth-century poets whose reformed approach to Ottoman verse brought about radical transformations in the linguistic structure and content of their compositions. Already by the second half of the seventeenth century, the localisation movement that promoted a departure from the canonical aesthetics of divan poetry had generated such new trends as the use of *lisan-ı Osmani* Turkish in syntax, the incorporation of the colloquial language of Istanbul neighbourhoods and the inclusion of themes pertinent to Turkish folk song in poetry.[12] Sünbülzade Vehbi was influenced by popular poets of his time, such as Sabit and Nedim, also partaking in the breaking of conventions that were formerly assumed essential to the aesthetics of *divan* poetry.

Vehbi's choice of material, related to his own experiences and examples from everyday life in Istanbul, demonstrated his vision on the proper instruction of children and young adults. Vehbi was writing for an audience, namely his son Lütfullah, who had already lived through his early childhood years, and was at an age at which he could appreciate proper guidance with regard to the personal choices that were to shape the rest of his life. It was perhaps for this reason that the author did not hesitate to include issues that might be considered controversial in a treatise of this kind. The Ottoman state did not develop any policies regarding the fostering and education of children until the nineteenth century. In the absence of such social regulation, it could be argued that children were not perceived as empowered beings whose presence impinged on the future of the state affecting society at large. Consequently, the colloquial and intimate narrative style of the *Lütfiyye* distinguishes it from other works that situated parenthood within the context of a sacred realm. This 'secular' stance was possibly an attempt to construct a future determined by the prospective candidates to which Vehbi was attempting to reach out. Similar to Rousseau, who will be dealt with further on in the chapter, Vehbi regarded his role in giving advice as a service to the general populace, as well as a father's legacy.

Sünbülzade Vehbi's **Lütfiyye**

Vehbi composed *Lütfiyye* in 1790 when he was a seventy-one-year-old father. In writing this narrative his intention was to guide his son Lütfullah in his moral, ethical, religious and intellectual undertakings during his early adulthood. In the introduction Vehbi states that he completed writing the advice manual (*nasihatname*) in a week, while he was ill, perhaps to stress the intimateness of this work in contrast to the rest of his literary oeuvre. Although we do not have extensive information about his son, we can estimate that Lütfullah was a young adult in his early twenties at the time of the composition of the advice manual.[13] *Lütfiyye* is conceived in the manner of a handbook comprising ninety-one chapters, incorporating topics ranging from what constitutes a proper education and vocation, to what it means to have good conduct, as well as addressing the moral and practical principles of marriage, family and the raising of children. *Lütfiyye* was a popular text that was widely used in schools for educational purposes.

Vehbi's advice writing is not unique. It, in fact, harks back to earlier forms of Ottoman advice manuals and bears many similarities to an earlier treatise written by the Ottoman poet Nabi (1642–1712). Like Vehbi, he wrote his *nasihatname* at a later age, at sixty-one, for his seven-year-old son, Ebu'l-Hayr Mehmed Çelebi, in 1701. The tone and content of the two treatises, written almost a hundred years apart and both composed in their authors' mature age, display similarities. In the case of Vehbi, the text is written for a much older male offspring who is perhaps at a more suitable phase in his life to appreciate the significance of the advice given by his father. According to Sururi, Lütfullah was a *müderris* when he died prematurely at the age of twenty-six in 1795.[14] Curiously not mentioned in *Lütfiyye*, Vehbi also had an older son, Hayrullah Efendi, who, a poet like his father, served as *qadi* and died in 1853.[15]

Sünbülzade Vehbi's work addresses the kind of child who will decidedly submit himself to the vision of the didactic, authoritative and yet affectionate voice of the father. While the – advice manual reflects the sensibilities particular to the learned milieu to which Vehbi belongs, it provides insight into the relationship between a young adult and his aging father in the early modern period. Peter Stearns and Carol Stearns, in a seminal contribution to the field of emotions in history, have stressed the importance of differentiating between 'the collective emotional standards of a society' and the 'emotional experiences of individuals and groups'. This distinction facilitates the study of emotions within the scope of the values and principles that produce and enable their expression.[16] The present study bases the conclusions it draws on the representation of affect by the author as 'father' on Stearns' definition of the term 'emotionology'.[17]

The advice manual of Sünbülzade is representative of the social conditions and delimitations of a certain milieu's mentality with regard to fatherhood and parenthood in general. The treatise depicts how the responsibilities of a parent shape the kind of emotion felt for the child. Consequently, what emerges from *Lütfiyye* is an 'ideal' child that is the project of a suggestively gender-segregated order. The work portrays a society in which parental roles are distinctly delineated according to prescribed gendered functions, rather than being mutually shared and cohesive within the family.[18] In addition, the separation of parental duties is also articulated as a division between the different phases in a child's life, with the expectation of the mother's more exclusive involvement in the early infant years, and the father's in the puberty years. It could be argued that this division possibly created an emotional separation between the mother and the child in the later stages of the child's life.

In the case of Sünbülzade's narrative, a clear divide is likewise discernible in the relationship between the father and the mother, since the author barely makes reference to the mother of Lütfullah.[19] The apparent separation of parental roles potentially affected the conjugal pair that had a child in common. In the emotionology of this particular society it could be suggested that the changing child-rearing patterns and the transformation of the responsibilities of the mother and the father possibly initiated a change in the relationship of the parents with each other. The emergence of a more private and companionate conjugal relationship could perhaps be the result of the gradual shift in mentality from exclusively conducted parental duties to mutually shared familial responsibilities. The changing of the emotional composition of the family may be seen more clearly in the nineteenth and early twentieth centuries when the educational reforms and new personal status laws regulating the family were more effectively imposed than before.

In 1762, Jean Jacques Rousseau, a contemporary of Vehbi, published his popular treatise on child-rearing in France, *Émile*, proposing his novel educational philosophy on raising the 'ideal' male child. The scope and intention of the two projects were similar, both assumed a literate audience, and both were interested in producing a compendium of principles for raising an 'ideal' male child that would benefit the society. It seems that Vehbi and Rousseau's writing relied more on their observations than on 'lived' experiences of parenthood. Their narratives were not necessarily intended as instructions for practical child-rearing methods. Instead, they were both more focused on establishing an overarching philosophy of proper conduct. While Rousseau's text begins with the birth of *Émile*, the fictional character to which he addresses his advice manual, and ends with him finding a suitable female partner in life, Sophie, Vehbi's account begins with the period of Lütfullah's initiation into adulthood. Although one major difference between Rousseau and Vehbi is that unlike the latter, the former had not raised his own children, they are both writing about, and writing for, an imagined relationship between the father and his son.

Parental Love and Divided Roles

Sünbülzade's attitude toward the education of children and the separate roles that parents should have during different stages of their life cycle endorses that of the *Shari'ah*, which assigns distinctive roles to the mother and father, differentiating between their responsibilities in childcare, nurture and education. However, a closer analysis of the court cases illustrate that parents tended to be involved in their children's emotional and intellectual upbringing beyond the advised phases in children's lives. The underlying perception of the *Shari'ah* demotes the mother's level of influence on her child to a merely domestic function, bestowing on her the provision of such primary necessities as nursing, food, dress and hygiene.[20] Thus, the mother is designated as a temporary custodian until the child is able to independently perform these chores. The father, on the other hand, is defined in terms of his obligations in the child's moral and emotional upbringing, performing the part of a mentor and permanent custodian that is to prepare the child intellectually and emotionally for future adult life. Sünbülzade's tone and attitude toward parents' duties with regard to their children's education is aimed at the construction of the 'ideal' child. The narrative of the court cases provides a contrasting view to this approach.

Sources are generally silent about the idea of motherhood, and about how women experienced motherly love in Ottoman society.[21] Colin Heywood, in his comparative analysis of early modern European sources on childhood, suggests that since most of what we know about motherhood has been mediated by men, the muteness regarding mothers' relationship to children is not coincidental.[22] Divorce and parents' attitudes toward the issue of child support and custody provide information on the actual division of parental responsibilities in Ottoman culture. The numerous suits and appeals to court concerning child custody demonstrate that the role of the mother and the father in children's lives were not as black and white as instructed by the jurists, and many individuals adhered to strategies to subvert the commonly accepted rules based on their realities and sentiments. For instance, Hanafi law upheld that it was more favourable for children to be either in the care of their mother, or a close female relative of the mother, until they reached a certain age: seven for boys, and nine for girls. Women's prescribed involvement in the early phases of infancy was due to the common supposition of them being more tender and compassionate in terms of child-rearing.[23] The mother, regardless of the kind of divorce, was given priority in the supervision and nurturing of children during the early phases of childhood.

In cases when the mother was remarried after a divorce, the father of the child was not bound by law to pay for the child's maintenance. A fatwa recorded in the *Behcetü'l-Fetava*, which states that a woman would lose the guardianship of her child if she married another man, better explains the issue of parental roles during and after divorce.[24] The case of Hanife, registered in Davudpaşa's court regarding the maintenance allowance of her five-year-old daughter, Emine, demonstrates that a mother could remain as her children's guardian even after her remarriage to another man.[25] Accordingly, Hanife, after her second marriage, insisted in court that she be allowed to continue caring for her daughter Emine. She even managed to obtain child support from Emine's father, so that she could attend to the needs of her daughter.

There is also the case of Hadice, who was previously married and divorced from es-Seyyid Mehmed Celaleddin Efendi, the *sheikh* of the tekke of el-Hac Evhadeddin and had a daughter named Şerife Aliye, illustrates the norms regarding a mother's childcare responsibilities.[26] Hadice received from Mehmed Celaleddin Efendi a total of 273 *qurush*es for the care of her daughter. When Şerife Aliye was nine years of age, Hadice released Mehmed Celaleddin Efendi from the obligation of paying for her allowance. The record does not mention whether Şerife Aliye continued to live with her mother or her father, but it shows that children could stay with their mothers for a longer period than normally prescribed by the *Shari'ah*.

In relation to child custody, Ottoman officials prioritised the wellbeing of the child. Naile, from the Veled-i Karabaş neighbourhood, presented her case in court regarding her former husband Mehmed Beşe and their two-year-old son, previously in her care.[27] The little child was taken from

Naile by his father when she married another man, but Mustafa wanted to continue living with his mother. Consequently, the court decided that Mustafa would be cared for by his mother Naile until he was seven.

There were also circumstances in which fathers were the primary caretakers, though this was not that common. For instance, the case of İsmail Çelebi demonstrates how a single male parent could, at times, find the responsibility of caring for their children in the early stages of life difficult.[28] İsmail Çelebi ended up placing his little daughter Hamide (who was present in court) into the care of Hace Ayşe and commanding Ayşe to spend twenty-three *para*s as part of the child's allowance. It appears from this record that Hace Ayşe was not the mother of this child, nor was she a close relative of İsmail Çelebi's. He simply was not capable of taking care of the child himself.

If a father divorced his wife after having taken her and their child to a different town, the mother was free to take the child back to the child's birthplace, since she was considered to be the primary caretaker.[29] Hence, the *fatwa*s delineate the roles of the mother as the caretaker and the father as the legal custodian. The use of two different terminologies for the mother and father, who both acted as primary protectors of the children in different stages of their lives, suggests that the mother's role was seen as more essential during the period that the children needed her nurturing physically, while the father's became more prominent later, since he was designated to take over from the mother and provide the children's education later in life.

Philippe Ariès, in his contested interpretation of attitudes toward childhood in medieval European society, argued that the notion of childhood as a separate category in the life cycle of humans did not exist until after the seventeenth century.[30] Ariès legitimised this argument by stating that before then, as soon as children were separated from their mothers, they were treated as young adults. Accordingly, he stated that children that were seen as too 'delicate' to be able to participate in this adult existence simply 'did not count'.[31] Ariès assessed the changes in the educational system to be one of the major turning points altering attitudes toward children. As the spatial focus of children shifted from the home to the school, it created possibilities for socialisation of children, separating them from the sphere of adults. For Ariès, this separation was one of the reasons for perceiving children as beings in need of proper safeguarding and guidance of adults so that they could distinguish between good and evil. Ariès' main thesis on the discovery of childhood has been widely criticised for being a teleological narrative deliberately progressing toward the birth of the modern family in Europe.[32]

In the Ottoman case, children occur as figures that are part of a narrative that submits them to the authoritarian voice of a dominant patriarchy. This narrative of deference is also perceivable in the structural organisation and style of address in Sünbülzade Vehbi's advice manual. For instance, Vehbi regards himself as the sole model for his son's moral and intellectual development. In this disciplinary and didactic framework Lütfullah is given guidance on the creation of the 'self', which is in the service of the society at large. Vehbi's advice on spouse selection, forewarnings against the expression of individual autonomy and decisions, as well as criticism regarding social change are manifest in the way he perceives the idea of fatherhood in a society that contested the outward expression of sentiments. However, his use of endearing terms to describe his emotions of gratitude and appreciation for his son prompts the question of whether parental sentiments surpassed the well-defined contours of a discursive order founded on a gender- and age-segregated parent–child relationship.

Vehbi's 'ideal' child is envisioned in the image of the father. His lyrical prelude begins with an endearing address to his son: '[M]y dearest Lütfullah, my son who is foresighted; O my son, the apple of my eye, the joy of my heart, the source of peace in me, and the reason for my existence'.[33] He continues expressing his admiration by comparing his son's youthfulness and good morals to a budding sapling and a fresh rose 'in the midst of the garden of hope', stating that he has been nurtured with eternal prosperity. In his interpretation of the Ottoman garden as an image depicting an emotional system, Walter Andrews states that the idealised gardens represented an overarching cultural ecosystem for the expression and acting-out of emotional life, suggesting that 'emotions (were) mapped onto nature'.[34] Hence, each element in the garden becomes a signifier for a 'weighty burden of meaning'. For instance, the garden motif exposes a formal social structure in which the budding and flourishing youth will ultimately find his praiseworthy place in the real world.[35] In discussing the emotional ecology of the garden as an integrating symbolic sphere, Andrews suggests a merely political reading. He states: '[T]his formal structure reflects a holistic (ecological) integration of nature, social structure, interpersonal relations, relations to power and patron, an economy of gifting, love, spirituality and emotion which is also expressed (or implied)'.[36] Similar to Rousseau, in Sünbülzade's narrative the dynamics of the relationship between the father and son find a setting in nature. However, the garden that is described is hardly a natural space that allows for uncultivated wild flora to grow in their natural habitat. Instead, Vehbi's garden is crafted according to the rules of etiquette of the Ottoman learned milieu. Just like the carefully groomed rose, the son has to grow according to the rules of this controlled environment. This garden resembles a microcosm in which the power of the father over his son reproduces and regenerates others like him. This construction is achieved through the father's recognition of the naïveté of the youth, who needs to avoid standing out in any obtrusive manner in this observed sphere.

The garden serves as a demarcated and protected space in which the youth is surrounded by the ones that also have good morals like him. He is receptive to his father's advice in this impenetrable place that hinders evils and protects him from the perils of humanity. What instigates the advice giving is the premise that society degenerates and corrupts human's innately good nature. If raised conscientiously, with the right kind of advice, the innocence and good nature of the boy will necessarily be protected. Hence, the advice given by the father is his ultimate gift to the son. Although the statement that 'God makes all things good; man meddles with them and they become evil', which prompted Rousseau's *Émile*, might at first seem to be congenial with Sünbülzade's educational vision, significant differences exist between the two contemporaries. While Rousseau emphasises the aim of education as an enabler of the conditions for 'nature to reassert itself', I will argue that Sünbülzade constructs a safe haven within nature, namely the metaphorical garden, in which the crafting and nurturing of the 'ideal' man is made possible. This 'ideal' man is an imagined outcome of Vehbi's concerns about gender, social and class relationships. Consequently, the future manifestation of the son delineates the success of the 'good father'.

In this emotional landscape, Lütfullah's existence is a cause of joy for Vehbi in his old age. He takes pride in his son's already exemplary character and noble principles. Vehbi links the desirable attributes to Lütfullah's lineage, emphasising that he comes from a family that is renowned for being pure of heart. Our knowledge is limited to his father, Reşid Efendi, being a scholar and poet, and his grandfather, Mehmed Efendi, being a well-respected *mufti* in Maraş and an author of *fiqh* commentaries.[37] Lütfullah is expected to exert great effort to live up to the reputation of the Sünbülzade family. Vehbi desires his son to be compliant and hardworking so that he will gain acceptance from society, and God will be content with him.[38]

The father's love is the type that is compassionate and endearing, yet it is not unconditional. Vehbi's expression of his son's good manners comes with a warning that Lütfullah needs to work to gain and maintain his love. The only love that one should aspire to obtain is that of the father. Attaining the father's love is rendered as an advancement in the journey to attaining that of God's. It is for this reason that the experienced father shares his sentiments by way of advice. He clearly states that even though his son, who naturally has a noble and virtuous spirit, does not need this kind of guidance, his true sentiments force him to deliver the necessary tools to transform him into a highly revered person in society. Vehbi's apprehension about Lütfullah's future is wrought by an overemphasis on the opinion of others. This concern of Vehbi's is possibly due to the socially dominant models of masculinity and imagined roles of fatherhood.[39] He ends this introductory section with the hope that Lütfullah will eventually take pride in what his father composed for him and pass on his advice to future generations.

The Advice to Lütfullah

In the section following his prologue, Vehbi introduces the significance of possessing good qualities, and explains why it will add to one's true value in life. Much of the vocational advice given by Vehbi relies on his own personal experience. He deems only certain professions to be worthy of respect, while counselling his son to steer away from careers that will make him suffer in the future. According to him, Lütfullah should not rely on his father's fame and status when building his own career. He cautions him that even if people refer to him as 'the son of Vehbi', this connection will not have the expected advantages for him. His suggestion, thus, is for Lütfullah to establish his own name by way of his profession, education and wisdom. For Vehbi, wisdom is the one quality that may not be passed on from father to son, while virtue and good morals are transmitted from one's ancestors.[40] He stresses that knowledge is the most important source of power. He cautions Lütfullah to distinguish between the significance of property and knowledge, advising him not to equate these two concepts. For Vehbi, owning property may only be a temporal attribute, since one may easily lose their possessions, while having knowledge is permanent, and therefore cannot be lost. He suggests: '[F]illing your bosom with wisdom will benefit you under all circumstances.'.[41] Evidently, Vehbi prioritises the importance of studying and education, stating that those who denigrate its role in one's life are foolish. For him, scholars are the most venerated in society. It is for this reason that he first directs Lütfullah to science, because he believes that knowledge is the foundation of good conduct and nature.[42] Vehbi's educational recommendations also include reading works such as those of al-Ghazzali and Fahruddin al-Razi, especially focusing on the Qur'anic commentary and theological treatises of the latter.

Vehbi's discussion of the sciences (*ilm*) becomes more meaningful as he distinguishes between those sciences that he finds rewarding and those that he deems as 'untruthful'. While it is not possible to list all the scientific fields that he addresses in terms of his son's training, I will be focusing on a selection of these categories to depict better Vehbi's authoritatively didactic role as the parent who is responsible for initiating in his son the possession of a world view. For Vehbi, among the most worthwhile of these sciences are the Qur'anic exegesis, the study of Hadith and the principles of Islamic jurisprudence. He urges his son to become learned in these sciences so that he will be considered worthy in the eyes of God. Vehbi's second important category is the science of human anatomy. However, he cautions his son against becoming a doctor.[43] Vehbi's reluctance is linked to his criticism that doctors of his day are no longer trustworthy or conscientious about their profession. In fact, he counsels Lütfullah to take good care of his health so that he will not have to rely on them. Vehbi's discussion on yet another scientific category, that of philosophy, focuses on a comparison of God's word to the teachings of the Greek philosophers on metaphysics and the natural sciences. In comparing God's teachings to those of the philosophers, he states that the profundity of God is hidden in his word, while the words of philosophers may at best be illusory and invented. He legitimises this point by suggesting that even though at first philosophers' ideas might seem plausible, the fact that they diverge from Hadith and the Qur'an is troublesome. Hence, Vehbi's stance against the philosophical treatises is possibly a result of the traditional education that he himself received and therefore that he advocates. Vehbi then gives the example of himself having been interested in, and curious about, the cosmos, natural sciences and philosophy. When he denounces these sciences as deceptive, the basis for this argument is that the believers may not know the profoundness of God. He names thinkers such as Avicenna, Aristotle and Plato among those who do not truly understand God and his virtue, and discredits Aristotle's natural philosophy with regard to his views on human perception.[44] Ultimately, among the sciences that he approves of studying are *Sufism* (*tasavvuf*) and the teachings of Muhiddin Arabi. He argues that the study of the human mind enables one to come closer to God, since all his virtue and qualifications are encompassed in humans, as well as in history, literature and poetry.

Vehbi's advice regarding the pastimes and interests that he views as appropriate for his son is informed by his sense of what is suitable for males. For instance, although he defines music as having a calming and enriching effect on the soul, he discourages his son from singing, since it would not be considered suitable for a man of his lineage and status.[45] Vehbi also cautions his son to stay away from playing such instruments as the *saz*, a string instrument, and a *ney*, the reed-flute. He postulates that his son's becoming proficient in playing these instruments would lead to a drastic change in his lifestyle. Vehbi warns him against such a possibility, claiming that those who are made to play the *saz*, or those who spend time with *saz* players, would be committing a mistake. He clearly sees the music-loving and instrument-playing assemblies as hubs of idleness and mischief. Vehbi emphasises his disapproval by stating that 'the violin only looks good on the chest of a Georgian', further illustrating that being involved with these groups would be considered disgraceful, costing Lütfullah his reputation.

Other pastimes which the author criticises are backgammon and chess.[46] Vehbi believes that entertainment and play is part of everyday life, so much so that one should not feel the necessity for diversions. He claims that both women and men are fooled by all the play that is extant in the world. After this general complaint, he reverts to a more authoritative voice, stating that it is not appropriate for a homeowner to turn his house into a playground. His overall opinion about games and toys is that they are illusory and evasive. Hence, if one succumbs to backgammon or chess, these pastimes will ultimately overtake him, and make him lose sense of reality.[47] In other words, games and toys serve the purpose of deceiving a child, ultimately disguising what is real and imaginary. Since Vehbi perceives Lütfullah to be stepping into early adulthood, his advice is supposed to awaken him to the serious realm of adults. Consequently, it may be suggested that Vehbi's attitude toward toys and games displays an observable variance with the late nineteenth century, during which a shift in the approach to toys can be explained by the growing number of shops, which in hindsight reflected society's acknowledgement of these objects and spaces as exclusive to children.

In another section, Vehbi professes his views about proper attire, as to how one should dress according to etiquette, advising his son never to surpass the dress of his peers.[48] In this instance, he illustrates his argument by suggesting that gold, jewels and ornaments are only suitable for women, and that a man should always dress like a man. Vehbi adds to this that one should always try to be humble, even if one has much to feel proud about. In this section, while Vehbi is building an argument about attire being modest and 'manly', he also links the idea of dressing properly to belief in Islam, suggesting that it is a sign of spiritual 'cleanliness' and practice of 'good conduct'. Vehbi's comment on the issue reveals his concerns about how one ought to carry oneself in a society that produces and accommodates strictly delineated gendered identities. Thus, within this patriarchal order, one's choice of interests and their self-expression ought to be manifested precisely through the prescribed terms. In the three instances discussed above, Vehbi's suggestions indirectly reflect his categorisation of women and children's place in society. An adult male's interest in music should solely be restricted to the classical theory of music, as opposed to enjoying and partaking in musical assemblies. Therefore, it is not surprising to see that for him, the ideal leading figure in society is the adult male. In contrast to the nineteenth century, when there was a growing emphasis on the involvement of women in the education of their children; Vehbi's view deliberately subjects women to their appropriate position as being more suitable than men for ornamentation and luxury items. Finally, Vehbi situates games and play firmly in the world of children, for he views them as immature and credulous beings that can be positively persuaded by these pastimes. Vehbi's advice manual functions as a script in which he voices his emotions of disapproval about the changing dynamics and trends in society. The advice manual for his son inevitably serves as an instrument for public education.

A typical feature of the *nasihatname* is instruction on how to treat one's mother and father. Vehbi warns his son to respect both his mother and father, and to honour each of them. He states that those who oppose the will of their parents are equated with sinners.[49] According to him, children need to seek the approval and consent of their parents in their decisions. In other words, the ideal child is one that is submissive and subservient to their parents. Thus, Vehbi's perspective conditions the child to avoid exercising free will, and to feel an indefinite indebtedness toward his parents. In a recent study, Yahya Araz has argued that this kind of gratitude and appreciation is a lifelong debt that is expected to be repaid by unconditional servitude.[50] According to this argument, the child is immediately reminded of the mutual loyalty that exists between parents and children, and advised not to search for this kind of trust elsewhere. As in the *Hayriyye* of Nabi (1642–1712), a prevalent example of advice literature genre, Vehbi creates a natural link between religion and parenthood, demarcating the figures of the mother and father as sacrosanct by referencing such popular expressions as: '[I]n this world, paradise is under the foot of mothers'. Hence, all the present and future actions of the child are geared toward obtaining the favour and prayers of his parents, a virtue equated to the procurement of an approval from the messenger of God, the Prophet.

The importance of a functional household and family life is depicted as one of the most central aspects of one's future goals. In that respect, Vehbi's advice to his son outlines how much control he should be exerting in the management of his household.[51] According to this narrative, it is thought that if as a man he is unable to exercise full authority in his dominion, then he would be unable to assert it in other areas of life. He compares a man's hegemony over his household to a poet's command over his verse. Vehbi's suggestions concerning household economics designate the male as the main provider. He warns Lütfullah against living in a house which surpasses his ability to support and protect. It is significant to note that his advice regarding the father's role in caring for his children concerns both the physical and the emotional bond. He counsels Lütfullah never to let his children go hungry or destitute or need the help of others, since no one can provide for them what a father can deliver. Vehbi emphasises his point about the distinctive role of the father in the child's life precisely to address the importance of working toward the building of a sentimental connection with one's children. Therefore, he cautions Lütfullah to deter from flaunting his good deeds to his children. Most importantly, he advises him to treat them with compassion and affection, and to think of them highly. According to Vehbi, being on good terms with one's offspring is what enriches one's life, and makes the household stand on strong foundations. Vehbi's philosophy of child-raising is concerned more with instilling moral standards that would weigh heavily on the conscience,[52] rather than heralding physical punishment.[53]

In Vehbi's idea of household, the concept of marriage and the choice of wife are subordinate to establishing domination over that space. To that effect, he views marriage as a difficult task that might cause future setbacks.[54] It is for this reason that he states that those that are intelligent take on a slave concubine (*cariye*) instead of a free woman as wife. For Vehbi, the choice of wife is a relative one, and it would not be appropriate to make any suggestions on such a decision that relies heavily on one's taste and personality. That said, he claims to personally prefer women that are soft-spoken as wives. He also states that soft-spoken and easy-natured women make better caretakers of children. Vehbi informs his son that 'docile' women are befitting nannies when nurturing children. On the issue of bearing children, he clearly differentiates between having sons and daughters, stating that having a boy is God's blessing, whereas having girls and therefore contributing to the increase in the number of women is a worthless act.[55] Sünbülzade Vehbi's narrative ends with his final remarks on staying away from mood-altering substances such as alcohol and other opiates.[56] He finishes by stating that he has written this advice over the course of one week, during which he was resting in bed due to an illness, informing his audience that his main purpose in writing this book was for his main requests to be heard. For that reason, rather than resorting to sophisticated poetic conventions, he states that he consciously chose to write in a manner that would satisfy the general populace.

Conclusion

Lütfiyye, as a script-world, is a space where an imagined relationship between a father and son is shaped. The text serves as an instrument of relating the decidedly inhibited emotions of its author toward his son. Vehbi distances himself from his narrative in that the space he establishes between himself as the father and as the one composing the advice manual allows him to control the emotional bond that is otherwise uncontrollable. Sünbülzade Vehbi's reality is perhaps constructed by the fraction of society in which he finds a voice. In this chapter, I have shown by way of examples from court cases and *fatwa*s that the separation of the roles of the mother and the father at different stages in children's lives was not as clearly defined in reality. While fathers had the full custody and legal responsibility of children according to the *Shari'ah*, under certain circumstances they allowed their children to continue living with their mother beyond the prescribed age limits. The significance of such shifts from the predominant view is that they show how parents, in caring for the emotional wellbeing of their children, prioritised the children's needs over theirs. For instance, we find men consenting to their children's living with their mother irrespective of her remarriage. In contrast to the court cases, which offer the possibility of viewing 'life as it was lived', the advice manual *Lütfiyye* allows a glimpse into the emotional landscape of an imagined fatherhood. In analysing this narrative that does not speculate on principles, but rather subtly imposes them, one is simultaneously exposed to the haughty figure of the father weighed down by emotions of disapproval, compassion and love. Vehbi's disapproving emotions are never directed at Lütfullah, instead they are pointed at the society which he has lived in and which in return has produced his sentiments.

Notes

1. Lefebvre, *Critique of Everyday Life*, p. 136.
2. Maksudyan, 'A New Angle of Observation: History of Children and Youth for Ottoman Studies', pp. 120–1.
3. For example, in cases about child victims of domestic accidents, it is next to impossible to know more about the aftermath of a child's death due to a parent's neglect. See Araz, 'Ölmek için Çok Erken!', pp. 25–54.
4. Lees-Maffei, 'Introduction Studying Advice', p. 3.
5. Mechling, 'Advice to Historians on Advice to Mothers', p. 46.

6. Ibid., pp. 46–7.
7. Flandrin's study of the seventeenth- and eighteenth-century family focused on the changes in the familial expression of emotion and changing practices in child-rearing; Jean-Louis Flandrin, *Families in Former Times*, 1979. See also Rosenwein, 'Theories of Change in the History of Emotions', pp. 7–21.
8. In his essay on Ottoman love and its textual and artistic expression, Walter Andrews argues that emotions are 'constructed and enacted on the basis of "scripts"', underlining the connection between the 'notion of scripting', social psychology and cultural ecology; Andrews, 'Ottoman Love: Preface to a Theory of Emotional Ecology', pp. 22–3.
9. For biographical information on Sünbülzade Vehbi, see Beyzâdeoğlu, *Sünbülzâde Vehbî*, 2000; Kuru, 'Sünbülzâde Vehbî', pp. 140–1; Yöntem, 'Sünbülzade Vehbi', pp. 81–104; Björkman – [Burrill], 'Sünbülzade Wehbi', pp. 876–7; Muallim Nâci, *Osmanlı Şâirleri*, pp. 86–91.
10. Yöntem, 'Sünbülzade Vehbi', p. 92.
11. Ibid.
12. Sılay, 'Follower and Critic of the New Discourse', pp. 109–11.
13. Lütfullah's age is only mentioned by one biographical source as twenty-four years old: Gürgendereli, 'Sünbülzâde Vehbî Mehmed Efendi'. The age of his son is not stated in the *Lütfiyye*. See: <http://www.turkedebiyatiisimlersozlugu.com/index.php?sayfa=detay&detay=2123>.
14. Mehmed Süreyya, *Sicill-i Osmani*, vol. 3, p. 904. Sururi composed a eulogy for Lütfullah: '*Lütfullah Molla 'azm-i sahra-ı beka / Ruh-ı Vehbi-zade rahmetle ide kesb-i safa*' (Lütfullah Molla has begun his eternal journey / May the soul of Vehbi's son have mercy in eternal peace).
15. Mehmed Süreyya, *Sicill-i Osmani*, vol. 2, p. 665.
16. Stearns and Stearns, 'Emotionology', p. 813.
17. Emotionology is defined as: '[T]he attitudes or standards that a society, or a definable group within a society, maintains toward basic emotions and their appropriate expression; ways that institutions reflect and encourage these attitudes in human conduct . . .'; Stearns and Stearns, 'Emotionology', p. 813.
18. See Heywood's discussion of the emergence of a more moderate and courteous type of parenting of the evangelists in eighteenth-century Europe; Heywood, *A History of Childhood*, p. 44.
19. Sünbülzade only acknowledges the existence of mothers when he discusses the respect that a child should have for both parents.
20. For instance, in a related fatwa a jurist is asked: 'Zeyd demands the return of his child to his custody claiming that he has matured completing seven years of age. Until then, the child has been in the care of his mother, Hind. If Hind denies Zeyd's claim by stating that the child is only six and a half years old, what would be the ruling?'. To which, he replied that 'if the child was mature enough to eat, drink and dress on his own, then he could be given to his father, if not, then he should remain with his mother'; Yenişehirli Ebü'l-Fazl Abdullah, *Behcetü'l-Fetava*, p. 117.

21. On the growing awareness about the importance of women's involvement in the education of children, and the shift from male to female educators in late nineteenth- and early twentieth-century Egypt, see Zachs' Chapter 15 in this volume.
22. Heywood, *A History of Childhood*, p. 44.
23. Bilmen, *Hukuk-i İslamiyye ve Istılahat-ı Fıkhiyye*, vol. 2, p. 470.
24. Translated it reads: '*Question*: Hind has a two-year-old daughter, Zeyneb, from her previous marriage to Zeyd. Hind married a stranger, Bekir, while her daughter was still in her care, and Zeyneb was left without a female caretaker. Would Hind be able to prohibit Zeyd from taking his daughter to his hometown, while Hind is still the wife of Bekir? *Response*: No, she would not'. Yenişehirli Ebü'l-Fazl Abdullah, *Behcetü'l-Fetava*, p. 118.
25. DCR 2, p. 25, no. 2 (1197–8/1782–3).
26. DCR 2, p. 25, no. 3 (1197–8/1782–3).
27. DCR 2, p. 18, no. 1 (1197–8/1782–3).
28. ACR 206, p. 3, no. 1 (1169–70/1756–7).
29. This is stated clearly in a fatwa by Yenişehirli Abdullah Efendi: '*Question*: If Zeyd marries Hind in a certain town and after the birth of their daughter, Zeyneb, he takes both of them to another town and divorces Hind, given that the entitled guardian of the little child is Hind, would it be lawful for Hind to take Zeyneb to the previous town and raise her there? *Response*: Yes, it would'. *Behcetü'l-Fetava*, p. 118.
30. Ariès, *Centuries of Childhood*, pp. 33–50.
31. Ibid. See also Anderson, *Approaches to the History of the Western Family*, p. 44.
32. Ibid.
33. Beyzâdeoğlu, *Lütfiyye*, pp. 21–2.
34. Andrews, 'Ottoman Love', p. 28.
35. Ibid., pp. 40–1.
36. Ibid., p. 40.
37. Beyzâdeoğlu, *Sünbülzâde Vehbî*, p. 13.
38. Beyzâdeoğlu, *Lütfiyye*, p. 25.
39. In an article on imagined fatherhood(s) in the Georgian Era, Joanne Bailey links the construction of the 'affectionate and sensitized' father in the social imaginary to both class and gender relationships and to the 'Christian ideals' predating the evangelical revival; Bailey, 'A Very Sensible Man', pp. 267–92.
40. Beyzâdeoğlu, *Lütfiyye*, p. 24.
41. Ibid.
42. Ibid., p. 28.
43. Ibid., p. 29.
44. Ibid., p. 30.
45. Ibid., p. 51.
46. Ibid., p. 63.
47. Ibid.

48. Ibid., p. 81.
49. Ibid., p. 30. See Roman's Chapter 6 in this volume.
50. Araz, 'Osmanlı Ahlak ve Terbiye Kitaplarında Ebeveynlere Hürmeti Teşvik Etmeye Yönelik Hikâyeler', pp. 103–4.
51. Beyzâdeoğlu, *Lütfiyye*, pp. 141–2.
52. Norbert Elias argues that parents' habits and impulses condition those of their children, explaining that 'the interrelation of the habits of parents and children, through which the instinctive life of the child is slowly moulded, is thus determined by nothing less than by "reason" ... in this way the social standard of shame and repugnance is gradually reproduced in the children'; *The Civilizing Process*, p. 155.
53. See Çiçek's Chapter 12 in this volume.
54. Ibid., p. 143.
55. Ibid., p. 145.
56. Ibid., pp. 156–66. In this section, Vehbi also discusses the new regulations against those occupations which he finds to be pointless. The first of these is the acculturation of birds, and the second, the banished profession of selling flowers.

Bibliography

Archival Sources
Ahi Çelebi Şer'iyye Sicilleri – Ahi Çelebi Court Records (ACR) 206, p. 3, no. 1 (1169–70/1756–7).
Davudpaşa Şer'iyye Sicilleri – Davudpaşa Court Records (DCR) 2, p. 25, no. 2 (1197–8/1782–3); 25, p. 8, no. 1 (1209–10/1794–5).

Primary Sources
Mehmed Süreyya, Seyit Ali Kahraman (trans.), *Sicill-i Osmanî*, vols 2, 3 (Istanbul: Kültür Bakanlığı ve Türkiye Ekonomik Toplumsal Tarih Vakfı, 1996).
Sünbül-zâde Mehmed Vehbî, *Lütfiyye-i Vehbî*, Süleymaniye Kütüphanesi, Esat Efendi Bölümü, 3695 (folios 69–99), 1205/1790–1.
Yenişehirli Ebü'l-Fazl Abdullah, Mehmed Fıkhi el-ᶜAyni (compiler), *Behcetü'l-feteva*, (Istanbul: Darü't-Tıbaᶜati'l-Amire, 1266/1849).

Secondary Sources
Akün, Ömer Faruk, 'Sünbülzâde Vehbî', *İslam Ansiklopedisi*, vol. 11 (Istanbul: MEB Yayınları, 1950–88), pp. 238–42.
_____, 'Sürûrî', *İslam Ansiklopedisi*, vol. 11 (Istanbul: MEB Yayınları, 1950–88), pp. 250–2.
Alıcı Tanıdır, Gülcan, *Lutfiyye-i Vehbî* (Kahramanmaraş: Ukde Yayınları, 2011).
Ambros, Edith G., 'Sururi', *EI²*, vol. 9, p. 896, available at: <https://referenceworks.brillonline.com/search?s.f.s2_parent=s.f.book.encyclopaedia-of-islam-2&search-go=&s.q=sururi>.

Anderson, Michael, *Approaches to the History of the Western Family, 1500–1914* (Cambridge: Cambridge University Press, 1995).

Andrews, Walter, and Jonas Liliequist (eds), 'Ottoman Love: Preface to a Theory of Emotional Ecology', *A History of Emotions, 1200–1800* (London and New York: Routledge, 2012), pp. 21–49.

Araz, Yahya, 'Osmanlı Ahlak ve Terbiye Kitaplarında Ebeveynlere Hürmeti Teşvik Etmeye Yönelik Hikâyeler', *Milli Folklor*, 25/100 (2013), pp. 99–109.

_____, '"Ölmek için Çok Erken!" 17. ve 18. Yüzyılda Anadolu'da Kazaların Sebep Olduğu Çocuk Ölümleri ve Yaralanmaları Üzerine bir Değerlendirme', *Tarih Dergisi*, 56 (2012–13), pp. 25–54.

Ariès, Philippe, *Centuries of Childhood: A Social History of Family*, trans. Robert Baldick (New York: Alfred A. Knoph, 1962).

Ayan, Elif, 'Sürûrî ve Hezeliyyat'ı: İnceleme-Tenkitli Metin-Sözlük', MA thesis, Hacettepe Üniversitesi Sosyal Bilimler Enstitüsü, 2002.

Bailey, Joanne, '"A Very Sensible Man": Imagining Fatherhood in England c.1750–1830', *History*, 95/3 (319) (2010), pp. 267–92.

Beyzâdeoğlu, Süreyya, 'Sünbülzâde Vehbî: Hayatı, Edebî Şahsiyeti, Dîvanı'nın Tenkitli Metni ve İncelemesi', PhD dissertation, İstanbul Üniversitesi (no. 1838), 1985.

_____, *Lütfiyye* (Istanbul: Bedir Yayınevi, 1994).

_____, *Sünbülzâde Vehbî* (Istanbul: Şule Yayınları, 2000).

Bilmen, Ömer Nasuhi, *Hukuk-i İslamiyye ve Istılahat-ı Fıkhiyye*, vol. 2 (Istanbul: Bilmen Basım ve Yayınevi, 1967–9).

Björkman, W., and Kathleen R. F. Burrill, 'Sünbülzade Wehbi', *EI²*, vol. 9, pp. 876–7, available at: <https://referenceworks.brillonline.com/browse/encyclopaedia-of-islam-2>.

Elias, Norbert, *The Civilizing Process: The History of Manners and State Formation and Civilization*, trans. Edmund Jephcott (Oxford: Blackwell, 1994).

Erbay, Nazire, 'Hayriyye-i Nâbi, Lutfiyye ve Telemak Aynı Yüzyılların Farklı Kültürlerinden Çocuklara Ortak Nasihatler', *A.Ü. Türkiyat Araştırmaları Enstitüsü Dergisi*, vol. 51 (2014), pp. 171–85.

Flandrin, Jean-Louis, *Families in Former Times: Kinship, Household and Sexuality*, trans. Richard Southern (Cambridge: Cambridge University Press, 1979).

Güdek, Meral, 'Modernleşme Döneminde Osmanlı'da Çocuk Eğitimi ve Literatürü', unpublished MA thesis, Ankara Üniversitesi, 2012.

Gürgendereli, Müberra, 'Sünbülzâde Vehbî Mehmed Efendi', *Türk Edebiyatı İsimler Sözlüğü*, available at: <http://www.turkedebiyatiisimlersozlugu.com>.

Heywood, Colin, *A History of Childhood: Children and Childhood in the West from Medieval to Modern Times* (Malden, MA: Polity Press, 2009).

Kaplan, Mahmut, *Hayriyye-i Nâbî (İnceleme-Metin)* (Ankara: Atatürk Kültür Merkezi Yayınevi, 2008).

Kuru, Selim Sırrı, 'Sünbülzâde Vehbî', *TDV İslam Ansiklopedisi*, vol. 38 (2010), pp. 140–1.

Lees-Maffei, Grace, 'Introduction Studying Advice: Historiography, Methodology, Commentary, Bibliography', *Journal of Design History*, 16/1 (2003), pp. 1–14.

Lefebvre, Henri, *Critique of Everyday Life*, vol. 1, trans. John Moore (London: Verso, 1991).

Levend, Agah Sırrı, 'Ümmet Çağında Ahlak Kitaplarımız', *Türk Dili Araştırmaları Yıllığı Belleten*, 234 (1963–5), pp. 89–115.

Maksudyan, Nazan, 'A New Angle of Observation: History of Children and Youth for Ottoman Studies', *Journal of the Ottoman and Turkish Studies Association*, 3/1 (2016), pp. 119–22.

Mechling, Jay, 'Advice to Historians on Advice to Mothers', *Journal of Social History*, 9 (1975), pp. 44–63.

Muallim Nâci, *Osmanlı Şâirleri*, compiled by Cemâl Kurnaz (Ankara: Kurgan Edebiyat, 1986), pp. 86–91.

Onur, Bekir, *Cumhuriyet ve Çocuk 2. Ulusal Çocuk Kültürü Kongresi Bildirileri 4–6 Kasım 1998* (Ankara: Ankara Üniversitesi Çocuk Kültürü Araştırma ve Uygulama Merkezi Yayınları, 1999).

Rosenwein, Barbara H., 'Theories of Change in the History of Emotions', in Jonas Liliequist (ed.), *A History of Emotions, 1200–1800* (London and New York: Routledge, 2012), pp. 7–21.

Sather, Kathryn, 'Sixteenth and Seventeenth Century Child-Rearing: A Matter of Discipline', *Journal of Social History*, 22/4 (1989), pp. 735–43.

Sılay, Kemal, 'Follower and Critic of the New Discourse: Sünbülzade Vehbi and the Eighteenth-Century Reformers of Ottoman Poetry', *Turkish Studies Association Bulletin*, 18/1 (1994), pp. 109–11.

Stearns, Peter N., and Carol Z. Stearns, 'Emotionology: Clarifying the History of Emotions and Emotional Standards', *The American Historical Review*, 90/4 (1985), pp. 813–36.

Şahin, Haşim, and Nurdan Şafak (eds), *Osmanlı Dünyasında Çocuk Olmak* (Istanbul: Değerler Eğitimi Merkezi Yayınları, 2012).

Yenikale, Ahmet, *Sünbülzâde Vehbî Divânı* (Kültür Bakanlığı, 2012, available at: <https://archive.org/stream/DivanESunbul-ZadeVehbiTurki/10651%2Csunbul-zade-vehbipdf_djvu.txt>).

Yöntem, Ali Canip, 'Sünbülzade Vehbi', *Türk Dili ve Edebiyatı Dergisi*, 1/2 (1946), pp. 81–104.

Chapter 6

A World of Conflicts: Youth and Violence towards Parents in the Family in Rural Wallachia, 1716–1859

Nicoleta Roman

It has rightly been said that the family is a place of paradox,[1] a space of protection and affection, but also of conflict and brutality, and knowledge of the relations between the members of a family can only be achieved by entering into its intimacy.

In modern times, although the bourgeois ideal that 'built upon, rather than overturned, their fathers' manhood ideals'[2] still dominates, the economic and family pressures on children and youth have lessened to some extent. During the nineteenth century, when paternal authority diminished and familial conflicts declined as a result of the increasing penetration of state institutions,[3] the level of delinquency and criminality also dropped in urban society. By contrast, in agrarian regions and among peasants, this shift came about more slowly. With the advent of the Industrial Revolution, young people left home to work, gathered in groups in urban areas and created new forms of sociability. They, at times, became a threat to the prevailing social order and forced the state to intervene through specific legislation.[4] Nevertheless, especially in rural areas, the family remained the last bastion when it came to reining in violence.[5] Manifestations of family violence continued to be tolerated throughout the nineteenth century, especially in rural areas, where the state had little influence. These rural areas evolved at their own pace and with their specific customs.[6] In this sense, the medieval model of parenthood and family structures was transformed and/or continued to exist in modern times, especially in the nineteenth century, when state intervention became stronger and more visible. Regardless, the rural family still exerted pressure on individuals whose violent impulses were unleashed during events such as a conflict over inheritance rights, or constraints in marriage. This type of violent situation has not been explored in reference to the Balkans. This chapter examines the issue of violence committed by children and youth against their parents in the nineteenth-century Romanian space. In so doing, it constitutes an exploratory attempt that may lead to new research directions in the future.

The first part of this chapter discusses the role of the Romanian province of Wallachia in Ottoman history, followed by the emergence of the Romanian Criminal Code. It provides a comparative analysis of how legalisation concerning juvenile delinquents evolved as a function of changing attitudes toward children/youth and childhood from the mid-seventeenth century to the mid-nineteenth century in Wallachia. It shows that changes in legislation were influenced by the Ottoman and French criminal codes, but also by Byzantine tradition. This was one of the factors that resulted in the emergence of 'Romanian modernity', which was one of many coexisting modernities in these territories.

The next section concentrates on juvenile delinquents in 1853 with an analysis of the nature of their crimes, as well as the statistical surveys of crimes published by the Romanian Department of Justice regularly after 1859. The 1869 survey, when the data became more reliable, indicates that homicide (including parricide, assassination, poisoning, violent death) was one of the most common types of crime in general (248 cases alone in that year). The final section presents some specific cases of violence, committed especially by young men below the age of twenty-five, who were still considered minors by the Romanian Criminal Code, toward their parents in rural regions in the mid-nineteenth century. It discusses the ways in which these cases were treated differently than other adult crimes by the authorities and society, in order to maintain an equilibrium within family dynamics.

Overall, the present study focuses on changes in legislation with regard to juvenile delinquents to better understand criminal law and the relevance of these changes in the case of acts of violence against parents in the countryside. Violence by young people toward their parents reveals a great deal about family life and the perceptions of children in rural Romanian society. Parricide is especially understudied in Ottoman studies and can shed further light on the agency of these youth in dealing with family problems.

Wallachia, an Ottoman Province in South-eastern Europe: An Overview

Romania has had a tumultuous history in which its territories belonged to the Ottoman Empire (the Danubian Principalities of Moldavia and Wallachia), the Russian (Bessarabia) or the Austrian (Transylvania,

Bukovina), and thus acquired a specific cultural heritage from each. In 1859 the Danubian Principalities united into a single state known as Romania, which obtained its independence from Ottoman rule in 1878 after the Treaty of Berlin. The new state became a kingdom in 1881 under the German prince Carol I of Hohenzollern-Sigmaringen and was recognised as such by the European powers.

The Ottoman governance system was not uniform throughout the Empire, with provinces retaining their specific internal administration. Until 1878, both Wallachia and Moldavia were provinces of the Ottoman Empire and switched from the status of 'tributary-protected principalities' to 'protected Christian provinces'.[7] They, however, were not alone. Ragusa, Transylvania (between 1541 and 1699) and the islands of Chios and Naxos were also Christian provinces. Despite paying tribute and other obligations, in both principalities the boyars were free to choose their own rulers and to administer the territory according to local customs and characteristics. Given that these principalities were on the border with European powers, the ruling princes sometimes pursued an anti-Ottoman policy, but they could not do so with impunity. The Ottoman Empire became aware that these buffer provinces could no longer be successfully controlled by the Romanian elite, and in 1711 and 1716 it introduced the Phanariot regime as a solution in Moldavia and Wallachia respectively. The ruling princes were now appointed from among the Greek dignitaries of the Phanar district of Constantinople, and they came with an entire entourage representing a cultural synthesis between East and West.[8] The successive wars between the Ottoman Empire and its neighbours Russia and Austria during the eighteenth and early nineteenth centuries caused the Romanian space to become a battleground. The principalities of Wallachia and Moldavia were obligated to contribute money and produce regularly, and to provide shelter and provisions to the Ottomans. A continuous participation in the Ottoman war effort combined with political instability, rising taxes and concomitant numerous natural disasters and epidemics made the population despise the Phanariots, although the regime undoubtedly supported culture and education.

The Revolution of 1821 and its ties with the Greek Filiki Eteria prompted the Ottoman Empire to return to its previous tactic of naming the ruling princes from among the indigenous boyars. By now, Russia was a political power in the area and had been a secondary actor in the revolution. The Treaty of Adrianople (1829) marked a turning point that brought the Danubian Principalities under Russian protection until the Crimean War (1853–6), while maintaining Ottoman suzerainty. Through the Russians, French culture and ideas were introduced to these territories, and the first

Romanian constitution, the Organic Regulation, was established (1831). On the fringes of two competing empires, it was clear that the West was silently becoming the winner. The existence of semi-autonomous provincial power-holders was indisputable, but this was a situation created and accepted by the Ottoman Empire, which oscillated between a policy of accommodation and suppression of local elites in a way that could be observed in other territories as well, such as Bosnia, Egypt and Tunis.[9] Decentralisation thus appeared as a form of government that fit into a pluralist Ottoman society, as a conscious policy pursued by the centre, which took the provinces perception of it into account.[10]

Romanian Sources on Delinquency and Criminality

Current historiography on the Ottoman Empire has favoured certain territories and cities in Turkey, the Middle East and Greece, particularly Istanbul, Anatolia, Egypt, Salonica and, more recently, Bulgaria. It has dealt less with other parts of the Empire, including Romania.[11] Regarding the history of the family within the Empire, the most important sources are the court registers (*sicill*s), which were kept in the larger cities of the Empire,[12] followed by parish registers and the judicial records of the local and central courts (for non-Muslims). The records of Romanian criminal trials were housed in local and central archives, in collections dedicated to the bodies responsible for cases of crime and delinquency (the police, courts, prisons), with two main centres: the Criminal Court in Craiova and the Criminal Section of the Bucharest Court. Two other institutions are also important, the High Court (*Înaltul Divan*) and the Chancery of Justice (*Logofeția Dreptății*), which had the capacity to present cases to the ruling prince.

The nineteenth century is also a good source of useful statistical data, since the Organic Regulation (1831), the Romanian constitution drawn up during the Russian protectorate, made it obligatory to maintain precise information about the population. Lists of people arrested during the period of the Organic Regulation (1831–56) are preserved in the archives.[13] The data consists of the names of the people who were condemned, their date of birth, where they were arrested and prosecuted, the crime committed and the sentence. These lists were drawn up annually until 1859, when the administration was reorganised after the union of the two principalities of Moldavia and Wallachia. However, there are also lacunae in the lists which impede research. These include the absence of data such as the age of the arrestee/convict and the date of the offence. Full details of the offence are likewise not provided. For example, Nicolae Digoreanu, from

Targoviște, was convicted in 1853 of 'wounding' somebody,[14] but no details are provided as to whom he wounded, whether it was a member of his family, somebody with whom he had contractual relations (an employer or a servant) or a stranger. For this reason, the lists only reveal the ratio of serious crimes to lesser offences and between the sexes of the perpetrators, as well as their frequency within particular regions of the principality and over the course of the period under study. It was the first working method used by the authorities, which, however, was inferior to the one that existed in France since 1825[15] or the *Criminal Statistics* for the same period in England.[16] In order to obtain all the information, the court records themselves need to be examined,[17] as was undertaken in the present study.

What the Law Said

The *Guide to the Law* (Îndreptarea Legii) (1652), which is regarded as a major reference work because of its dual canonical and lay provisions, was often called the *Pravilă* (rulebook). In the Balkan Peninsula, Byzantine Law was the point of reference, including in Ottoman provinces such as Serbia and Bulgaria, where the Church had considerable influence in domestic matters.[18] According to the *Guide to the Law*, a minor was a person under twenty-five years of age,[19] and there were three degrees of culpability and punishment (not responsible: before seven years of age; responsible to a certain degree: between ten and fourteen;[20] and with a reduced penalty: until twenty-five). There is an age gap for seven- to ten-year-olds. Another article in the same law specifies that a person can discern right from wrong as early as twelve years of age.[21]

There are a few examples in Wallachia where violence against parents was punished by death. As a form of parricide, the term 'parent' was understood in the wider sense of kinship and included grandparents and siblings. Adoption did not in any way reduce guilt, since it was still a legitimate filial bond.[22] Self-defence, drunkenness and rage were not accepted as mitigating factors. Canon 55 of St Basil states that he who kills with premeditation and is forgiven 'shall not take communion for twenty years', and for ten years if the killing is accidental.[23] Age could be a factor in reducing the punishment, but could also be ignored, because the judges decided to take in to account how 'evil' the individual was. In other words, if the criminal showed no remorse, a minor was treated as an adult and punished accordingly.[24]

Much later, in 1818, the Caragea Laws (Legiuirea Caragea) brought about significant changes, which related to the gradation of punishments and the social status of the murderer.[25] Although it remained on the statute books, the death penalty was rarely applied, and in the early nineteenth century there were few death sentences. A more common crime was that of dishonouring one's parents verbally (curses, calumny) or physically (assault), which were punished corporally and by seclusion in specially designated monasteries.

Under a new act passed in Wallachia in 1831, *The Organic Regulation*, it was accepted that the death penalty should be maintained for murder, but it was recognised that the ruler was free to alter, reduce or annul this punishment (article 298). In practice, this article was frequently applied at the recommendation of the Department of Justice, which took factors such as age, family circumstances and the nature of the crime into account.[26]

In 1852, ruling Prince Barbu Știrbey issued the *Criminal Code and Procedures*. Minor children were now defined as being fifteen years of age or less, a significant change compared to the only definition in force at the time in the *Guide to the Law*. The law acknowledged that the roots of vice began in childhood and adolescence. Responsibility in the case of minors lay with the family, and those found guilty were not punished, but rather placed 'under the closest supervision of their parents'.[27] If they did not have parents and were 'nobody's', then 'in order to rein them in through the taking of appropriate measures for their moral education and correction', they were imprisoned in a monastery for a period of between three months and three years, depending on the gravity of the offence.[28] In theory, murder remained punishable by death (article 234), but it was clearly stated that only premeditated killing was to be punished in this way. Anything that could be labelled accidental killing was subject to a reduction in the sentence, often to six months. Bodily harm, whether causing infirmity or not, was punishable by either imprisonment or a fine or corporal punishment. Compounded punishments were no longer handed down in such cases.

When Barbu Dimitrie Știrbei[29] published the *Criminal Code* in 1852, it was after the initiative by the Ottoman government in 1840 with respect to its Muslim subjects and after the establishment of the Russian Penal Code (1845). The Romanian authorities began translating the French code in the 1840s,[30] even though they did not adopt it *ad litteram*.

Alexandru Ioan Cuza's[31] *Penal Code* of 1865 standardised the laws of Wallachia and Moldavia, which had some similarities with the 1858 Ottoman Penal Code and other types of European penal legislation. Based on the French model (1810), both these penal codes classified crimes in three categories (delicts, misdemeanours and contraventions), with a clear tendency to reduce the penalty to imprisonment and to place minors in the care of their family; if no family existed, they were put under the temporary supervision of the police in the Ottoman case or, in the Romanian case, of a specially designated monastery/correctional institution,[32] which by the end of the century was at Mislea. Other differences arise when we compare the two codes with their common French source of inspiration. First, there is the problem of defining childhood for judicial purposes. It is associated with references to puberty and adolescence in the Ottoman case, whereas for the Romanians there is a clear distinction based on age.

Following Byzantine tradition, the Romanians retained the idea of non-responsibility for minors until eight years of age.[33] This issue also arose in the Ottoman case, where in the pre-modern period the law differentiated between the undiscerning child (up to seven or eight years of age), the child whose discernment must be verified (between seven and ten) and the adolescent who has acquired the capacity to distinguish right from wrong.[34] Guilt is connected to awareness of one's actions, which is possible only from the onset of puberty, depending on gender: between twelve and fifteen for boys, and between nine and fifteen for girls.[35] Puberty in relation to punishment is not discussed in the Romanian *Guide to the Law* (1652) or later on. It should be emphasised that in the eyes of the Romanian law, a minor encompassed two chronological phases: childhood, which in the 1852 code was defined as under fifteen, and the transitional phase of youth, defined as under twenty-five. The category of 'minor youth' would only be redefined as all those under twenty-one years of age in 1865.

The Ottoman Penal Code of 1840 was initially aligned with the French model, but incorporated the tradition of the *Shari'ah* courts.[36] Important changes came about in 1858, when, as Kent Schull showed, corporal punishment was replaced by prison and fines, while maintaining puberty as a delimitating factor in terms of the age of discernment for minors.[37] The Ottoman Empire's civil law of *Mecelle* (1877) ruled that discernment emerged as late as the age of fifteen, but was dropped to the age of fourteen in the 1911 revisions to the penal code.[38] Thus, both legal codes (with or without the puberty factor) tended to use the age of fifteen to define criminal accountability in children. However, in Wallachia, individuals between the ages of fifteen to twenty-five (twenty-one after 1865) were also considered minors and were entitled to lighter sentences. In addition, both penal codes maintained parts of previous laws: in Wallachia, a person was still a minor until the age of twenty-five as in the *Guide to the Law*, whereas the 1911 revised article of the Ottoman code preserved the 'Islamic interpretations of accountability as the oldest possible age prior to the manifestation of puberty'.[39]

Thus, although there was a clear spread of the legal model, its integration depended on local specifics and customs. Besides the French influence, the Romanians relied on their Byzantine heritage and their contacts with the neighbouring examples of Russia and Austria. Both Schull and Avi Rubin suggest that with regard to legislation, there were different adaptations of Western modernity in terms of criminal law.[40] A recent analysis of its application shows that this overlap between religious and secular frameworks meant that 'the Ottoman legal system became increasingly both more modern and more authoritarian'.[41] Western ideas became a mark of civilisation for different imperial systems,[42] and were gradually introduced even on the margins of Europe. Although it is not always possible to trace the same pattern, there was a process of 'adoption and adaptation, continuity and change'[43] that was visible throughout the Ottoman Empire.

THE LIST OF MINORS CONDEMNED IN 1853

The available Romanian lists of arrestees show that the number of those found guilty of theft and verbal dishonour was higher among minors aged fifteen.

The statistics show that dishonour was far more frequent than murder, including involuntary manslaughter. However, there are gaps in the sources, and it is difficult to know what percentage of cases of dishonour involved parents, but what is certain is that violence of this type was far more frequent. The term 'dishonour' covered anything from verbal aggression to murder and only came to light when the repeated action became unbearable. Fear of a violent son, the victim's early death or silence motivated by shame caused some cases to remain unreported. For comparison, according to Schull's analysis, during 1911–12, in the prisons of the Ottoman Empire, there were 241 children under fourteen, most of

Table 6.1 Minors arrested or sentenced in 1853.

Guilt	Arrested	Condemned
Theft	471	52
Brigandage	–	51
Homicide	15	11
Other	49	8
Dishonour	53	5
Forgery	17	4
Assault	68	2
Accomplice	16	1

Source ANIC, *Ministerul Justiției. Penale*, 8/1854.[44]

whom (234) were boys; in 1917, there were 1,676 young people up to the age of nineteen arrested, who were also mostly male.[45] This points to a rise in juvenile criminality with age, which became visible to the authorities with the reform of the criminal justice system that began in the *Tanzimat* period.

Statistical surveys made by the Romanian Department of Justice were published regularly after the Union of the Romanian Principalities (1859) and the issuance of the Romanian Penal Code (1865). Until 1869 the data are problematic, but thereafter become more reliable. In that year, homicide (248 cases) appears as the most frequent violent act related to the family, followed by adultery and bigamy (thirty-two), manslaughter, rape and corporal wounds (thirty-one) and so on. Parricide was put in the same category as poisoning and murder, thus making it difficult to assess the actual number of cases. However, it is known that out of 1,798 people brought to trial, twenty-four were under the age of sixteen, while 193 were between sixteen and twenty-one, but all were considered as minors in criminal law. This makes parricide as an exceptional crime in this age group. Undoubtedly, parricide is predominantly a masculine violent act, while the single crime that is characteristically feminine remains infanticide;[46] there is evidence of parricide by a small number of minors. The state authorised the granting of reduced sentences to these minors on the grounds of good behaviour, the length of time served and age. For poor families, especially in the countryside, the detention of a young person had economic consequences.

How Murder Came About in the Family

In Romanian society, as in other societies, children were regarded as the greatest wealth to be had, all the more so for people living in villages, where children had greater economic significance. As a proverb recorded by the *vornic*[47] Iordache Golescu (1768–1848) aptly puts it: 'The more children the man who works the land has, the more he works it.'[48] The parent–child relationship thus took on other meanings than love and affection, because each member of the family had value for the prosperity of the household: children were desired and raised to provide assistance and support in their parents' old age, while parents represented power and a model for their children's upbringing. The house and areas of cohabitation and interaction (the farmstead, the land owned and worked by the family, etc.) were not only areas where the daily activities required for survival unfolded, but were also areas of conflict.[49] Insinuating itself into everyday life, conflict gave rise to interpersonal violence, where every dispute made matters worse, escalating from words to aggression, to the point where, smouldering beneath more or less peaceful appearances, things degenerated, culminating in bodily harm, which was sometimes fatal. The familial structure, which was based on children's contribution to the family's economic support, had an impact on approaches towards guilty adult children on the part of the family, as well as the authorities.

When accusations of bodily harm were made, the authorities sought not only testimony to support them, but also physical evidence. Tudora Zgaba was subjected to this examination after she was no longer able to endure the insults and beatings she received from her son Marin. Speaking as the injured party, she described how it all started: an argument 'about the partition and ownership of property left by her husband'. Before developing the thread of the story, it should be mentioned that it is always the injured party who must provide the motive for the conflict, rather than the offender, even if the latter is interrogated on a number of occasions. In Tudora's case, in addition to the testimony of her other son, Tudorache ('who claims that the defendant Marin always beats his mother and dishonours her with curses'); the judges also saw the 'injuries' on her body. There could be no more conclusive proof than this, and so they ruled: 'Let the aforementioned Marin be beaten at the scene with fifty corrective lashes on the back and also be imprisoned in the gaol for three months, to restrain him and to set an example.'[50]

However, this punishment was never administered, since the woman was unexpectedly reconciled with the son who had dishonoured her, and both parties put the reconciliation in writing. And so her story fades into the background together with so many other similar stories, demonstrating how common such violence was and perhaps suggesting the pressures that existed to keep such offences hidden, to prevent them from being aired to the authorities.

The penal files, which record the largest number of family disputes, can also shed light on power relations between family members.[51] Premeditation was not the only route leading to a crime where a child might go from dishonouring a parent to murdering him/her. Spontaneous acts also took place, caused by rage or drunkenness, when the child seemed to find the courage to confront the head of the family. Various weapons such as knives, pitchforks and sickles, characteristic of the rural environment, were commonly used. Alcohol abuse among Romanians was also mentioned by foreign travellers such as Anatol Demidov, who estimated in 1837 that the high murder rate – fifty-six in 1835 and sixty-six in 1836 – could be attributed to alcohol.[52] These figures are debatable, however, since they need to be compared to the official statistics[53] and viewed over the longer term to detect fluctuations. In the period for which official lists of arrestees and convictions are available, dishonouring, bodily harm and murder are listed as the causes of interpersonal violence, in that order.

From a historiographical point of view there is a general consensus that the recorded number of offences was lower than the actual one,[54] but at the same time the number of murders recorded is likely to be more accurate than the number of cases of theft, for example.[55] Even before the Organic Regulation era, when the police had not yet developed into a modern institution with a much greater territorial range, murder could not be ignored: the authorities had to be informed, the body had to be given to the family for burial, an enquiry had to be carried out in order to discover the guilty party, who was viewed as a danger to the community as a whole. Theft, whatever its nature, could be overlooked and forgiven, as a kind of delinquency to which children were also prone. The fact that these statistics are not fully accurate, but only represent tendencies is illustrated in the case of Ion, a young man of twenty from the village of Gumești, Muscel County, who attacked and killed his father in 1853 and was sentenced in July 1854 to exile in the Snagov Monastery prison for three years. After his release, he was supposed to be placed under police supervision for one-and-a-half years. But strangely, his name cannot be found in either of the two existing types of lists (the lists of arrestees for 1853 and the lists of convicts sent to monasteries in 1854). This story is worth telling because it reveals a pattern as regards to violence within the home.

According to the young man's confession, it all started after he came back from a wedding in March 1853. He would not have returned home if he had not wanted to eat and rest a little before going back to the party; in fact, he was a little drunk. While he was sitting at the table eating, and slicing a piece of meat with a knife, his father entered the room, also having returned from the wedding party and also a little drunk. He looked at Ion for a brief moment and began to scold and revile him, but Ion did not report the words he used. The young man expressed himself vaguely, without revealing the real reason for the quarrel. Things then became heated, the young man answered his father back, and his father became so enraged that he rushed at him, ready to grab his hair and beat him. Ion defended himself and without thinking took the knife and threw it at his father. In front of the judges, he said that that Niță was only 'pricked'. Being angry, he did not look back to see what had happened. He left his father in the room and went back to the wedding.[56]

The moments that followed were reconstructed from witness testimonies, because Niță, who was wounded, cried out for help, and the people in the immediate vicinity came running and then went to fetch Ion. The father survived for another four days, and then died. After the councillors (*aleșii satului*) of Gumești had informed the local authority (*subocîrmuire*) of what had happened, a physician was sent to examine the body. He declared that the wound would not have been fatal if Niță had not been old and sick.[57] Subsequently, the physician's declaration was used as evidence in reducing the young man's sentence. Taking into account all the circumstances, the criminal court decided:

> It remains proven that no premeditation impelled the defendant Ion to kill his father and consequently he cannot be labelled a deliberate killer or guilty of parricide, and his deed remains merely a crime of deliberate bodily harm without intent to kill.[58]

As a result, the court sentenced him, based on the *Criminal Register and Its Procedure* (1852), to five years' reclusion in Snagov Monastery. The sentence took into account Ion's age, since for any crime of this kind adults were usually sentenced to ten years in the salt mines, but, for minors, the law stipulated a reduction of this sentence by half.[59] The case was sent to the High Court (*Înaltul Divan*), where it was decided that it was more appropriate to sentence him to three years in a monastery and one-and-a-half years under police supervision. The reason for the reduction was his age, the doctor's statement and the fact that the act had been provoked by drunkenness.[60] In fact, Ion did not survive even one year in the monastery, since he died in May 1855.

This case shows that family quarrels could be hotbeds of violence, and the people involved did not always admit to the causes. Analysis of the sources suggests that there was a difference in decision-making between county and central courts. The former was inclined to inflict the maximum sentence, while the latter were inclined to reduce it. Thus, what might initially appear to be murder and is described as such, might later be reduced to manslaughter.

Even earlier than this period, before the issuance of the *Criminal Register and Its Procedures* (1852), there are similar cases, which suggests there was continuity in the application of the law in accordance with the mentality/norms of the time. A good example is the case in 1838 of Dumitru, an agricultural labourer of twenty-five from Olt County. While drunk, he struck his father, without premeditation, also during a family quarrel. In fact, he had been talking with his wife, this had deteriorated into a quarrel, and after mocking her he had begun to beat her. As his house was not far from that of his parents, his brother, Trașcă, went to get their father, who was the only person with enough authority to settle the argument. Before the father arrived, another brother, Radu, tried to step in between the husband and wife, but ended up being beaten himself. Then the father, Stancu, arrived. He too had been drinking wine and raki and was in no better mood than his son, so he only made matters worse. Dumitru was unable to stop himself and struck his father on the back of the neck with a cudgel. He then left. Stancu staggered through the village, drunk and wounded, and collapsed at the gate of his house. Unlike in the case mentioned above, a medical examination was not asked for, but there were other significant testimonies: that of Trașcă, who stated that both Dumitru and Stancu were drunk, but that he did not see his brother striking their father with the cudgel; nine villagers, including two priests, stated that they knew about the quarrels in the family, and that they had heard the uproar, but had arrived on the scene when it was too late. Like so many other defendants brought before the courts, when asked to explain the reason for the quarrel and how it had degenerated into such violence, Dumitru merely denied everything.[61]

It was decided that because 'the act stemmed from drunkenness, because the dead man and the perpetrator were both in the same state',[62] since there were no witnesses able to give more details and since it was not a case of premeditation, Dumitru should remain free. Such cases, in which the guilty party was exonerated, were frequent. However, the case also reveals family solidarity with the man who survived the conflict. He had to be defended to ensure the financial survival of his household, but also because of a change in attitude towards authority. The decision-makers become those who were outside the conflict, because only they could restore a minimum of familial and economic equilibrium.

This is perhaps most clearly seen in the case of Dumitrache Cocargea, also known as Mirea, a resident of the Precupeții Noi district of Bucharest, who in 1851 mortally wounded his father. The two, along with other residents of the district, were working in the fields near the capital, when the young man, aged nineteen, struck his father with a knife during an argument. Before this, the father had tried to discipline his son violently, using the utensil at hand – in this case, a scythe. What shocked the authorities was the description of the older man's body, left to bleed to death in the field. However, the perpetrator, Dumitrache, described the event as follows:

> I did not have any quarrel with my father except that when I was at work in the field I lay down in some hay because I had grown weary and when my father went by and saw me lying down he started to curse me in the name of the devil for not working, and half an hour later, feeling thirsty I went to where he was, next to the water jug, so that I could drink and my father again began to curse me for strolling about rather than working, he raised his scythe to strike me

and I raised my hand to defend myself, my father hit me and wounded my left arm with the scythe. In my right hand I had a knife I had been using to sharpen a pitchfork and when my father hit me I dropped the knife in pain, thinking that I was throwing it on the ground but I hit my father without realising it and straight away I ran away as if driven by madness, to go home, where I found my stepmother without knowing what had happened after I threw the knife. The event happened around noon after we ate, and after I returned home around the time for vespers my uncle, my father's brother came to the house to inform me that I had killed him and then straight away the commissioner came to take me to the commission.[63]

From other eyewitness accounts, it emerged that the son had no longer wanted to help his father with the reaping and that this had been a long-standing quarrel between them. After Dumitrache's arrest, his stepmother circulated a petition, signed by a significant number of relatives (including his sister Maria and his uncles Sandu Ulier and Gheorghe Cocargea), as well as by neighbours. Drawing on biblical teachings, they begged forgiveness for the young man, due first of all to:

> The sins of the fathers (as in the Holy Scriptures that determine what kind of death a man will endure); secondly, it has been almost three months since the crime took place caused by diabolical urge to be with his father in the field and they fell out with each other, first of all his father, namely Ion Cocargea who insanely raised his scythe to strike his son and his son lifted his arm and he struck his arm, his son took fright when he saw he had been hurt, and hurled a small knife and struck his father in a vein on his leg, but because there was nobody to apply a tourniquet the boy fled, not realising that harm had been done, but only a mistake. Because his father was old and frail he bled out and died.[64]

A bloody crime, in which the body of the parent seems to have been forgotten, could have no other explanation in people's minds than a momentary lapse of reason, caused by evil thoughts instilled by the Devil ('diabolical urge'). In this way, the long-standing sins and youthful errors of the slain man were avenged. Obviously, the petition mirrors the beliefs and mentality of the villagers when faced with violence and death, but what matters here is the motivation behind the request that the young Dumitrache be forgiven. It counteracts the cruelty of an act that affected the family at its very heart; for this reason, only members of the same family could initiate it if it were to have any weight with the authorities. The petition was unsuccessful, and in late 1850 the young man was imprisoned in Snagov Monastery for six years. Just three months after the ruling, his stepmother, Safta, submitted another petition, insisting that he be released, restating her previous argument, but this time giving priority to economic motives.

The conviction and imprisonment of the young man meant she had lost the only support that she had, an elderly woman and mother caring for his younger sisters:

> Today I am the most unfortunate and wretched woman in the whole world, a widow with three small girls, one of whom has been ill for three years, and I roam the streets seeking comfort and support because a nineteen-year-old lad in whom I placed my hope of support is today unfortunately sentenced to prison for an accident.[65]

Dumitrache is described as the only person who could take on the role of head of the family, and this was reinforced by the fact that his father had forgiven him before he died.[66] In reducing the sentence, the authorities could have taken into account his new status, despite his youth. It was a status that his father did not deny him, but reconfirmed, despite his son's act. Other, weaker people depended on Dumitrache, and his stepmother, although she herself could have become the head of the family or could have delegated one of the uncles, was prepared to yield to preserve the direct line of family authority. Family solidarity remained a factor that influenced judicial decisions. In society it was known that a reduction in a sentence could be obtained for the head of a family who accidentally killed his father, and this was what was being argued here.

Conclusion

The Ottoman Empire ruled over Christians and Muslims alike, and although there was a political unity that came from the centre, the imperial authorities decided to preserve the local administrative, judicial and religious laws and customs in some of their border provinces. For the Romanian principality of Wallachia this meant continuing the Byzantine tradition and being receptive to Western ideas, although these were transmitted through intermediaries such as the Phanariot Greeks or the Russian occupants. The legislative transformations started with the French code (1810), and were adopted throughout the Ottoman Empire, with adjustments to certain local specificities. This legal adaptation was accepted by the centre (1840, 1851, 1858) and afterwards by Wallachia (1852, 1865), but was part of a global movement to civilise and modernise 'customs' with regard to violence.[67] The gradation of punishments was introduced, and compound punishments were no longer handed down. The circumstances of the crime were considered, and a clear distinction was made as to the age at which an individual might be regarded as a minor from the penal standpoint.

Whereas the Ottoman centre raised the age of 'vague puberty' from roughly the ages of nine to fifteen to a clearly defined norm of fifteen in 1911, Romanian legislation lowered the definition of a minor from twenty-five to twenty-one in 1865. Legal differences between the Ottoman centre and its Romanian province persisted, since there was no common ground in terms of religion, language or even culture, thus enabling the coexistence of multiple and distinct modernities within the same territory. Nevertheless, this process created a better adapted local legislative footing and a different Romanian legislative interpretation of children's and young men's violence, which was particularly important in cases of parricide and other forms of familial violence.

Co-residence, age and socio-economic status of family members were highly important in cases of violence committed by young people (between the ages of fifteen to twenty-five) in rural areas with extended households. The conflict between generations was inherent to this struggle for power and household control. Typically, problems related to the father's status as an authority figure, and economic issues, such as not receiving a fair share from an inheritance, brought about ruptures and violent acts. The family tended to deal with these situations internally, mainly for economic reasons and in solidarity with the young survivor of the conflict. At the same time, the authorities reduced the sentences of parricidal young men to preserve pre-modern rural patriarchal familial customs and enforced relaxed age definitions of a minor in an attempt to protect young offenders.

Notes

1. Author's note: I would like to thank Alistair Ian Blyth and James Christian Brown for translating and revising the text. Chesnais, *Histoire de la violence en Occident*, p. 78.
2. Romesburg, 'Making Adolescence More or Less Modern', p. 233.
3. Heywood, *A History of Childhood*, pp. 106–8; Stearns, *Childhood in World History*, pp. 74–5; Lapalus, *La mort du vieux*, p. 15.
4. For Europe, see Hess and Clement, *A History of Juvenile Delinquency*; Brockliss and Montgomery, *Childhood and Violence in the Western Tradition*; Ellis (ed.), *Juvenile Delinquency and the Limits of Western Influence, 1850–2000*. For the Ottoman Empire, please see Başaran, *Selim III, Social Control and Policing in Istanbul at the End of the Eighteenth Century*; Schull, *Prisons in the Late Ottoman Empire*, p. 176.
5. Lapalus, *La mort du vieux*, p. 15.
6. For example, in cases of infanticide, when the child's body was buried within the boundaries of the home, according to folk customs and beliefs relating to the body, this practice was described by representatives of the state as being

'wholly inhuman'; cf. Roman, 'L'infanticide en Valachie: lois, discours et réponse sociale (1831–1860)', p. 111.
7. Panaite, *Război, pace și comerț în Islam*, pp. 440, 451.
8. Göçek, *East Encounters West*, p. 125.
9. Khoury, 'The Ottoman Centre versus Provincial Power-Holders', p. 137.
10. Faroqhi, 'Introduction', p. 17.
11. Faroqhi, *Approaching Ottoman History*, p. 20.
12. Ibid., p. 58.
13. From my preliminary investigations, I know that there was an initial interest on the part of the authorities. Subsequently, matters become confused, and the initiative was taken up once more in 1852. The year is by no means accidental, since this was when the *Criminal Register and Its Procedures* was published, a legislative act initiated by Ruling Prince Barbu Știrbey (1849–53; 1854–6), which was enacted two years earlier.
14. ANIC, *Ministerul Justiției. Penale*, 8/1854, f. 7.
15. *Compte général de l'administration de la justice criminelle*. The series continued until 1932.
16. Radzinowicz and Hood, *The Emergence of Penal Policy*, pp. 94–5; Emsley, *Crime, Police and Penal Policy, 1750–1940*, pp. 57–8.
17. Sharpe, 'Histoire de la violence en Angleterre', p. 235.
18. Pantazopoulos, *Church and Law in the Balkan Peninsula*, pp. 52–3.
19. *Îndreptarea Legii (1652)*, gl. 354, zac. 4, p. 334.
20. *Îndreptarea Legii (1652)*, gl. 353, zac. 3, p. 333. There was also a gender difference in punishment according to age: boyhood was defined as ten to fourteen, girlhood from nine to twelve. This definition indirectly acknowledges puberty as a transitional period from childhood to young adulthood.
21. *Îndreptarea Legii (1652)*, gl. 324, p. 299.
22. *Îndreptarea Legii (1652)*, gl. 244, zac. 1, zac. 6, pp. 238, 239; Teodorescu, *Minoritatea în fața legei penale*, pp. 67–8, who also mentions the case of a boy punished by death in the seventeenth century for cutting his father's head off, p. 77; for a discussion on how childhood was defined in modern Wallachia, see Roman, 'Copilul și familia în Valahia primei jumătăți a veacului al XIX-lea', pp. 91–100.
23. Ibid., gl. 335, p. 306.
24. Ibid., gl. 354, zac. 3, p. 333.
25. Compounded punishments sought to rectify the murderer's moral turpitude, as well as provide justice to the victim's family, but this was often hampered by social differences. Unlike the poor, boyars, merchants and the rich in general were not subjected to corporal punishment. Their honour could not be stained by having their bodies subjected to lashes before the eyes of the populace. The individual could be compromised, and his deed recorded, but public exposure would have affected the family name.
26. Toivo, 'Violence between Parents and Children', p. 342; Roman 'A Dimension of Private Life in Wallachia', pp. 182–201.

27. *Condica criminalicească cu procedura ei* 1852, art. 55.
28. Ibid.
29. Barbu Dimitrie Știrbei (1799–1869), Reigning Prince of Wallachia (1848–53; 1854–6).
30. Herlea, *Aspects de l'histoire du statut juridique de l'enfant en Roumanie; étapes de l'histoire de la délinquance juvénile en Roumanie; sur l'histoire du droit à l'éducation de l'enfant en Roumanie*, p. 339.
31. Alexandru Ioan Cuza (1820–73), Reigning Prince of the United Principalities of Moldavia and Wallachia (1859–66).
32. *Codice penale și de procedura criminale* 1865, 17, art. 62; 18, art. 64; Young, *Corps de droit ottoman. recueil des codes, lois, reglements, ordonnances et actes les plus importants du droit interieur, et d'études sur le droit coutumier de l'Empire Ottoman*, p. 8, Chapter 4, art. 66–7.
33. Teodorescu, *Minoritatea în fața legei penale. studiu statistic și de legislație comparată*, p. 84; Herlea, *Aspects de l'histoire du statut juridique de l'enfant en Roumanie*, p. 341.
34. Ginio, 'Childhood, Mental Capacity and Conversion to Islam in the Ottoman State', pp. 98–110.
35. Schull, *Prisons in the Late Ottoman Empire*, p. 171.
36. Schull, 'Criminal Codes, Crime, and the Transformation of Punishment', pp. 158–9; Aykut, 'Toxic Murder, Female Prisoners, and the Question of Agency at the Late Ottoman Law Courts', p. 116.
37. Schull, 'Criminal Codes, Crime, and the Transformation of Punishment', p. 160.
38. Schull, *Prisons in the Late Ottoman Empire*, pp. 172, 175.
39. Ibid., p. 175.
40. Rubin, *Ottoman Nizamiye Court: Law and Modernity*, p. 5; Schull, *Prisons in the Late Ottoman Empire*, p. 175.
41. Miller, 'Apostates and Bandits: Religious and Secular Interactions in the Administration of Late Ottoman Criminal Law', p. 156; Rubin, *Ottoman Nizamiye Court: Law and Modernity*, p. 24.
42. Ellis, 'Constructing Juvenile Delinquency in a Global Context', pp. 3, 5–6 when speaking about the East–West division from a juvenile delinquency perspective.
43. Schull, 'Criminal Codes, Crime, and the Transformation of Punishment', p. 157.
44. The documents analysed to date indicate a total of 691 arrests and 140 condemnations for 1853. This ongoing study will cover the era of the Organic Regulation (1831–59), although for the first two decades there are many gaps. Of those arrested, the records show that minor boys were charged with forgery (12 per cent), theft (5 per cent), assault (1 per cent) and minor girls only for theft (1 per cent).
45. Schull, *Prisons in the Late Ottoman Empire*, p. 183.
46. For a comparison with the Ottoman case, see Balsoy, 'Infanticide', pp. 976–7.

47. The title of *Vornic* denotes a Romanian boyar who had administrative and judicial responsibilities in provincial cities.
48. In this respect, see also the proverb recorded by Vasile Alecsandri and published in 1897 in *Poesii populare*: 'Many children, a man's wealth', and the original proverb from France: 'Enfants sont richesses de pauvres gens'; cf. Zanne, *Proverbele românilor din România, Basarabia, Bucovina, Ungaria, Istria și Macedonia*, p. 77.
49. Walker, *Crime, Gender and Social Order*, p. 9, who includes cohabitants (servants, apprentices). Emsley, *Hard Men: The English and Violence since 1750*, p. 59, believes that domestic violence was common and caused by drink, quarrels over money and disputes over the duties of different family members.
50. ANIC, *Ministerul Justiției. Penale*, 55/1840, f. 3.
51. Walker, *Crime, Gender and Social Order*, pp. 11–12.
52. *Călători străini*, p. 635. In 1837, Anatoli Demidov (1812–70) launched a campaign to learn more about Russia and the surrounding regions and contacted experts in various fields. The result of this expedition was the work *Esquisse d'un voyage dans la Rusie méridionale et la Crimée, par la Hongrie, la Valachie et la Moldavie*, Paris, 1838.
53. Nevertheless, we should grant a certain degree of credence to what Demidov says, since he worked with representatives of the authorities during his journey.
54. Radzinowicz and Hood, *The Emergence of Penal Policy in Victorian and Edwardian England*, p. 107.
55. Emsley, *Hard Men: The English and Violence since 1750*, p. 73.
56. ANIC, *Ministerul Justiției. Penale*, 97/1854, f. 4.
57. In such cases, the physician appeared as an expert witness, whereas in cases of infanticide in the same period, there was concurrent expert testimony from both physicians and, more importantly, midwives.
58. Ibid., f. 3.
59. Ibid., f. 3v.
60. Ibid., f. 14–14v.
61. ANIC, *Ministerul Justiției. Penale*, 58/1838, f. 2
62. Ibid.
63. ANIC, *Ministerul Justiției. Penale*, 4/1851, f. 4.
64. Ibid.
65. Ibid., f. 12–12v.
66. Ibid.
67. Wood, *Violence and Crime in Nineteenth Century England. The Shadow of Refinement*, p. 14.

Bibliography

Archival Sources

Arhivele Naționale Istorice Centrale (Department of Central Historical Archives of Romania)
Fond Ministerul Justiției. Penal (Ministry of Justice Fund), files 58 (1838), 179 (1838), 55 (1840), 4 (1851), 8 (1854), 97 (1854).

Primary Sources

Călători străini despre țările române în secolul al XIX-lea, new series, Paul Cernovodeanu and Daniela Bușă (eds) (Bucharest: Editura Academiei Romane, 2006).
Codice penale și de procedura criminale, edițiune oficiale (Bucharest: Imprimeria Statului, 1865).
Compte général de l'administration de la justice criminelle en France pendant l'année 1825 (Paris: L'Impremerie Royale, 1827).
Condica criminalicească cu procedura ei, ed. Clucer Ștefan Burke (Bucharest: Tipografia lui Iosef Copainig, 1852).
Îndreptarea Legii (1652), critical edition (Bucharest: Editura Academiei R.P.R., 1952).
Legiuirea Caragea (1818), critical edition (Bucharest: Editura Academiei R. P. R., 1955).
Regulamentul organic întrupat cu legiuirile din anii 1831, 1832 și 1833, și adăogat la sfârșit cu legiuirile de la anul 1834 până acum, împărțite pe fiecare an, precum și o scară deslușită a materiilor (Bucharest: Tipărit la Pitarul Z. Carcaleki, 1847).
Statistica din România. Statistica judiciară pe anu(l) 1870 (Bucharest: Tipografia Statului, 1875).
Young, George, Corps de droit ottoman. Recueil des codes, lois, règlements, ordonnances et actes les plus importants du droit intérieur, et d'études sur le droit coutumier de l'Empire Ottoman, vol. 7 (Oxford: Clarendon Press, 1906).
Zanne, Iuliu, Proverbele românilor din România, Basarabia, Bucovina, Ungaria, Istria și Macedonia. Proverbe, dicetori, povatuiri, cuvinte adeverate, asemenari, idiotisme si cimilituri: cu un glosar romano-frances, vol. 2 (Bucharest: Editura Socec, 1897).

Secondary Literature

Amussen, Susan Dwyer, 'Punishment, Discipline, and Power: The Social Meanings of Violence in Early Modern England', Journal of British Studies, 34/1 (1995), pp. 1–34.
Aykut, Ebru, 'Toxic Murder, Female Prisoners, and the Question of Agency at the Late Ottoman Law Courts, 1840–1908', Journal of Women's History, 28/3 (2016), pp. 114–37.
Balsoy, Gülhan, 'Infanticide in Nineteenth Century Ottoman Society', Middle Eastern Studies, 50/6 (2014), pp. 976–7.

Başaran, Betül, *Selim III, Social Control and Policing in Istanbul at the End of the Eighteenth Century: Between Crisis and Order* (Leiden and Boston: Brill, 2014).

Brockliss, Laurence, and Heather Montgomery, *Childhood and Violence in the Western Tradition* (Oxford: Oxbow Books, 2010).

Cavallo, Sandra, 'Family Relationships', in Sandra Cavallo and Silvia Evangelisti (eds), *A Cultural History of Childhood in the Early Modern Age* (London and New York: Bloomsbury Academic, 2014), pp. 15–32.

Chesnais, Jean-Claude, *Histoire de la violence en Occident de 1800 à nos jours* (Paris: Editions Robert Laffont, 1981).

Elias, Norbert, *La civilisation des mœurs*, trans. Pierre Kamnitzer (Paris: Calmann-Lévy, 1973).

Ellis, Heather, 'Constructing Juvenile Delinquency in a Global Context', in Heather Ellis (ed.), *Juvenile Delinquency and the Limits of Western Influence, 1850–2000* (London and New York: Palgrave Macmillan, 2014), pp. 1–16.

Emsley, Clive, *Hard Men: The English and Violence since 1750* (London: Hambledon, 2005).

———, *Crime, Police and Penal Policy: European Experiences, 1750–1940* (Oxford: Oxford University Press, 2007).

Faroqhi, Suraiya N., *Approaching Ottoman History: An Introduction to the Sources* (Cambridge: Cambridge University Press, 2004).

———, 'Introduction', in Suraiya N. Faroqhi (ed.), *The Cambridge History of Turkey*, vol. 3, The Later Ottoman Empire, 1603–1839 (Cambridge: Cambridge University Press, 2006), pp. 3–17.

Ginio, Eyal, 'Childhood, Mental Capacity and Conversion to Islam in the Ottoman State', *Byzantine and Modern Greek Studies*, 25 (2001), pp. 90–119.

Goldberg, P. J. P., 'Family Relationships', in Louise J. Wilkinson (ed.), *A Cultural History of Childhood and Family in the Middle Ages* (London and New York: Bloomsbury Academic, 2014), pp. 21–39.

Göçek, Fatma Müge, *East Encounters West: France and the Ottoman Empire in the Eighteenth Century* (New York, Oxford: Oxford University Press, 1987).

Herlea, Alexandru, *Aspects de l'histoire du statut juridique de l'enfant en Roumanie; étapes de l'histoire de la délinquance juvénile en Roumanie; sur l'histoire du droit a l'éducation de l'enfant en Roumanie* (Bruxelles: Société Jean Bodin, 1977).

Hess, Albert G., and Priscilla F. Clement, *History of Juvenile Delinquency: A Collection of Essays on Crime Committed by Young Offenders, in History and in Selected Countries*, 2 vols (Aalen: Scientia Verlag, 1990–3).

Heywood, Colin, *A History of Childhood: Children and Childhood in the West from Medieval to Modern Times* (Cambridge: Polity, 2001).

Lapalus, Sylvie, *La mort du vieux: Une histoire du parricide au XIXe siècle* (Paris: Tallandier, 2004).

Miller, Ruth A., 'Apostates and Bandits: Religious and Secular Interactions in the Administration of Late Ottoman Criminal Law', *Studia Islamica*, 97 (2003), pp. 155–78.

Muravyeva, Marianna, and Raisa Maria Toivo, 'Conclusion', in Marianna Muravyeva and Raisa Maria Toivo (eds), *Parricide and Violence Against Parents throughout History. (De)Constructing Family and Authority* (London: Palgrave Macmillan, 2017), pp. 243-61.

Panaite, Viorel, *Război, pace și comerț în Islam: țările române în dreptul otoman al popoarelor*, 2nd edn (Iași: Polirom, 2013).

Pantazopoulos, N. J., *Church and Law in the Balkan Peninsula during the Ottoman Rule* (Amsterdam: Adolf M. Hakkert Publisher, 1984).

Radzinowicz, Leon, and Roger Hood, *The Emergence of Penal Policy in Victorian and Edwardian England* (Oxford: Clarendon Press, 1990).

Rizk Khoury, Dina, 'The Ottoman Centre Versus Provincial Power-Holders: An Analysis of the Historiography', in Suraiya N. Faroqhi (ed.), *The Cambridge History of Turkey*, vol. 3, The Later Ottoman Empire, 1603–1839 (Cambridge: Cambridge University Press, 2006), pp. 135–56.

Roman, Nicoleta, 'Copilul și familia în Valahia primei jumătăți a veacului al XIX-lea', in Luminița Dumănescu (ed.), *9 Ipostaze ale copilăriei românești: istorii cu și despre copiii de altădată* (Cluj-Napoca: International Book Access, 2008), pp. 91–113.

———, 'A Dimension of Private Life in Wallachia: Violence between Parents and Children (1830–1860)', *The History of the Family*, 19/2 (2014), pp. 182–201.

———, 'L'infanticide en Valachie: lois, discours et réponse sociale (1831–1860)', *Annales de Démographie Historique*, 130 (2015), pp. 103–31.

Romesburg, Don, 'Making Adolescence More or Less Modern', in Paula Fass (ed.), *The Routledge History of Childhood in the Western World* (New York: Routledge, 2013), pp. 229–48.

Rubin, Avi, *Ottoman Nizamiye Court, Law and Modernity* (New York: Palgrave Macmillan, 2011).

Schull, Kent F., *Prisons in the Late Ottoman Empire: Microcosms of Modernity* (Edinburgh: Edinburgh University Press, 2014).

———, 'Criminal Codes, Crime, and the Transformation of Punishment in the Late Ottoman Empire', in M. Safa Saraçoğlu and Robert F. Zens (eds), *Law and Legality in the Ottoman Empire and Republic of Turkey* (Bloomington: Indiana University Press, 2016), pp. 156–78.

Sharpe, James, 'Histoire de la violence en Angleterre (XIIIe–XXe siècles)', in Laurent Mucchielli and Pieter Spierenburg (eds), *Histoire de l'homicide en Europe: De la fin du Moyen Âge à nos jours* (Paris: La Découverte, 2009), pp. 233–50.

Stearns, Peter N., *Childhood in World History*, 2nd edn (New York: Routledge, 2011).

Teodorescu, Iulian, *Minoritatea în fața legei penale. studiu statistic și de legislație comparată* (Bucharest: Alex Th. Doicescu, 1928).

Toivo, Raisa Maria, 'Violence between Parents and Children: Courts of Law in Early Modern Finland', *The History of the Family*, 18/3 (2013), pp. 331–48.

Vintilă-Ghițulescu, Constanța, '"You Would Have Them Lock Me Up and Sell

Me As Slave": Parents and Children in Long Eighteenth-Century Wallachia', in Marianna Muravyeva and Raisa Maria Toivo (eds), *Parricide and Violence Against Parents throughout History. (De)Constructing Family and Authority?* (London: Palgrave Macmillan, 2017), pp. 81–96.

Walker, Garthrine, *Crime, Gender and Social Order in Early Modern England* (Cambridge: Cambridge University Press, 2003).

Wood, Carter J., *Violence and Crime in Nineteenth Century England. The Shadow of Refinement* (London and New York: Routledge, 2004).

PART III
CHILDREN OUTSIDE FAMILY CIRCLES

Chapter 7

Born and Bred in Seventeenth-century Crimea: Child Slavery, Social Reality and Cultural Identity

Fırat Yaşa

A poor captive sent his greetings
From the Turkish land, from the infidel faith,
To the Christian cities, to his father and mother.
He could not greet them himself,
But sent his greetings by grey dove:
O grey dove!
You fly far, you see distant lands
Fly to the Christian cities,
Alight in my parents' yard,
Coo mournfully,
Tell them about my Cossack misfortune.[1]

Folk songs, which are one way people convey their love, feelings of separation, hopes, expectations and longings, provide certain clues to researchers about the social realities of the period in which they were composed. The song quoted above tells the story of a young man forced to live as a slave in sixteenth- or seventeenth-century Crimea, and reveals his longing for the life he was torn away from in his native Ukraine. In the story, the slave is addressing a grey dove, begging it to carry the news of his misfortune to those he left behind in his homeland, to which he will probably never return. The slave's cultural background, in a society where he is unfamiliar with the language, religion and lifestyle, not only leads to his inability to tolerate the burdens generated from being the lowest in status, but also increases the slave's sense of longing. For most of the time, the imposition of slave status on a free person also entails experiencing, adapting to or accepting the traumatic effects of the differences of language, religion and culture. One possible course of action was to try to escape. In the seventeenth century, there were many fugitive slaves in the Crimean Khanate who would sooner or later try to flee for their original homelands.² Although this meant travelling a considerable distance across the steppe frontier back to south-eastern Poland–Lithuania (especially the Ukraine), southern Muscovy, the Danubian Principalities of Moldavia and Wallachia or the Circassian polities in the North Caucasus, they were certainly not an ocean away from home, as was the case for the African slaves in the New World. When emotions of oppression, entrapment, helplessness or longing became unbearable, slaves took a chance and made a break for home.³ However, since capturing fugitive slaves and returning them to their owners became a significant source of income for some, most of the time such escape attempts ended in failure.⁴ Slaves who had seized the opportunity to run away only to be recaptured realised they would not obtain their liberty in this way, and either accepted their situation and continued to live as slaves, or put an end to their enslavement by killing themselves.⁵

The song in question is about the misfortune of individuals who became slaves later in life. But children were also enslaved. These children, captured during slaving raids, are termed *çora* in the sources. There is also historical evidence from the *Shari'ah* court records of child slaves known as *dogma*, who were born to slave mothers and slave fathers in seventeenth-century Crimea. When children born into slavery grew up, their designations changed as a function of their gender and age categories. It is evident from the court records that the compound term *dogma–çora* was used for male slaves who had been born in Crimea, but were older children, rather than infants. *Devke* was a term commonly used for young female slaves. These girls, with their maidenhood, beauty and youth, were the most popular of all slaves in the slave market. However, it is difficult to ascertain the exact age when slave children were eligible to be called *dogma–çora* (or simply *çora*) or *devke*. In a good number of court cases, male enslaved children were recorded as *dogma* from birth until the age of six to seven, and *çora* from the age of seven until they reached maturity. Young girls, like the *çora*, were called *devke* from the age of seven years until they reached the age when they could have sexual relations. When female slaves lost their virginity, they were known as *cariye* rather than *devke*. Throughout this study, I address the status of these children from various viewpoints based on the designations given to slaves.

As they adapted to the society in which they grew up, these slaves were brought up and detached from the religion and culture of their families. These offspring of a Christian slave parent were raised as Muslim in seventeenth-century Ottoman or Crimean society, which was doubtless fraught with difficulty, especially if they were living in the same house as their master and his family.

Child Slavery, Social Reality and Cultural Identity

Many slaves converted, possibly because they assumed that religion would provide a common cultural denominator, which in turn would make it easier for them to adapt to the environment in which they lived. Most of the slaves in Crimean society who were originally from the Christian countries located to the north of the Khanate took Muslim names. Religious conversion among these slaves was widespread during that period, and in addition to those who had recently been enslaved, the majority of these slaves also became Muslim.[6]

This chapter deals with the seventeenth-century Crimean *Shari'ah* court records, which are housed today in St. Petersburg, Russia.[7] In these documents, child slaves are easy to identify, since the scribes registered them as *dogma*, *çora* and *devke*. I suggest that slaves born into Crimean society felt less like strangers than those brought in from outside. In many ways, they lived and sometimes even thought like other inhabitants of Crimea.[8]

This chapter also examines the ways in which slavery affected children born into this condition; that is, boys and girls who were the offspring of parents who were slaves. These children experienced their parents as human beings forced to obey the dictates of a master or mistress, and grew up knowing that a similar fate awaited them. For purposes of comparison, I also trace the social status and emotions of slaves captured during raids at a young age. It is fortunate that there are accounts that reveal the longing of these slaves for the lives the slave raiders and traders had abducted them from. This allows me to compare the cultural identity, cultural awareness and social reality of slave-born children to those who became slaves after abduction at a young age.

Slaves condense almost three lives into their lifetimes: their life as young free children prior to slavery when they shared the same language, faith, culture and space with their family and friends, their life as a slave when they lose their freedom and, in some cases, their new status as ex-slaves after manumission, which often involved a new name, religion and language.

To the best of my knowledge, there are no studies on the lives of child slaves in seventeenth-century Crimean society. Attempting to respond to the issues raised above is in itself a new approach to the documentation of Ottoman children's history. It is almost impossible to specify the feelings of disappointment and other emotions of children born to Christian slave families when they learned that they themselves were slaves. Nevertheless, this chapter attempts to present aspects of boys' and girls' experiences of slavery. Clearly, gender also affected children's and adults' experiences as slaves. In patriarchal seventeenth-century Crimea, men worked outside the home, whereas the interior was associated with women and privacy. Thus, male slaves spent more of their time outside from the moment they were able to perform physical work. Most boy slaves worked in mills, vineyards, gardens and fields and were thus exposed to a whole host of dangers, including violence, not only by their master. Because children are more vulnerable and lack self-confidence, they are likely to be more obedient. The experience of female slaves was significantly different. They were considered sexual objects as of an early age and could become their master's concubines. Some were forced into prostitution, which resulted in deep trauma. This makes it difficult to understand why some of them, after being abducted from the Ukraine, Muscovy, Poland, Georgia, Wallachia or Circassia, chose to remain in Crimea, instead of returning to their respective home countries. As the Crimean archival materials show, some of these child slaves lived miserable lives both before and after manumission, and were exposed to plague, hunger and thirst, and occasionally even committed suicide. This chapter endeavours to explain why some remained, while addressing the issue of the cultural identity of these child slaves more broadly.

Social Realities and Children

In almost every age, rulers defend their power, the lives and property of their inhabitants and ensure peace. Most of the time, this sense of peace and security is associated with large, protective structures. This is also confirmed in the historical sources on the Ottoman Empire and Crimean Khanate. In court records, 'registers of important affairs' (*mühimme defter*s) and various other sources, the term well-protected (*mahrusa*) appeared immediately before the names of cities. Thus, even in the registration documents the city was declared a protected, peaceful place.[9] In other words, the inhabitants of the city were able to pursue their social and economic affairs with ease and, when travelling to distant lands, would not have to worry about the family members they had left behind. Cities also encompassed various public spaces, not only for adults, but also for children, such as schools (*maktab*s and *madrasa*s) where children received basic religious education.[10]

Nevertheless, when considering the Crimean Peninsula as a geographical entity, it must also be viewed as a region bordered from the north by Christian countries. Just as the Muslim Crimean Tatars organised raids on non-Muslim territories, seized their property and took their people as captives, raids were also carried out from these regions on Crimean lands.[11] Hence, irrespective of how well a city was protected, the people of Crimea doubtless internalised the fear of pillage and being themselves enslaved at any moment. Raids on Crimea from the Polish–Lithuanian Commonwealth took a substantial number of Crimean Tatar women, men and children captive. There is evidence that some of these captives were released in exchange for ransom.[12] These raids are an indication that the Crimean cities were less secure than their Anatolian counterparts.

Reciprocal raids were memorialised in folk songs and judicial court records. The Ukrainian folk song below, for example, describes slaves who were forced to leave their homelands, and separated from their mothers, fathers and siblings:

On the Black Sea,
Slaves cursed the Turkish land, the infidel faith.
'O Turkish land, O infidel faith,
O separation from fellow Christians!
You have separated many in the seven years of war:
Husbands from their wives, brothers from their sisters,
Little children from their fathers and mothers'.[13]

Kołodziejczyk notes that in raids carried out by the Crimean Tatars in the first half of the seventeenth century mostly on south-eastern Poland–Lithuania, mainly young adult males and females were captured and eventually enslaved. The raiders preferred to capture horses and cattle rather than small children, as child slaves were almost valueless in terms of resale price.[14] Walking such a long distance to reach Crimea was extremely difficult for children, and because they were still young the price of these slaves was very low. For example, Hüseyin bin el-Hac Mehmed purchased a young slave from Hüseyin Beşe ibn Hasan. He paid seven *esedi guruş* and a dagger for the slave. As the sale was concluded without any problem, Hüseyin bin el-Hac Mehmed left with the slave. But when the master realised that the child slave, who was still very young, was wetting himself he appealed to the court to be allowed to return him.[15] However, when female slaves were brought to Crimea they could be trained and sold for a higher price, although this often involved an extremely gruelling process.

Like Christians captured during the raids, Muslim Crimean Tatars were also enslaved and taken to foreign lands. Like the songs that conveyed emotions of despair, anger and longing of those who lived as slaves in Crimea, the emotions of the enslaved children of local Crimean residents were at times preserved in the court records. A court record dated 1674 shows, for instance, that a Crimean Muslim, Abdurrahman, son of Uzun İvaz bin Murad, was captured in a place not specified in the court record.

He was simply described as being captured by infidels (*kafir eli*). His distraught father vowed that 'if my son is released I will free Devletgeldi, my *kazak* slave of medium height, blond beard and Ukrainian origin'.[16] Somehow Abdurrahman managed to escape enslavement and returned to his Crimean homeland. Devletgeldi obtained his freedom with the help of witnesses who were present when Murad made his vow.[17]

Crimea was the centre of the Black Sea slave trade. Christians were not the only peoples enslaved during slaving raids. Crimean Tatars were also exposed to pillage, raids and capture. Although local rulers enabled inhabitants to live in comparative safety, the fact that they could be exposed to slaving raids in Crimea at any moment was a social reality. Inevitably, children had to cope with this reality from the moment they were cognisant of their environment.

Cultural Belonging and Children

Cultural identity and the feeling of belonging are considered societal universals. Since life isolated from society is virtually impossible, individuals naturally become part of the society in which they live. This is the reason why the first or second generations of those who are forced to live in a foreign country adapt to the places in which they live.[18] This argument also applies to seventeenth-century Crimean society. Since the non-Muslim captives could no longer maintain their own cultures and customs, the surrounding social establishment absorbed these small communities and assimilated them into society.

In seventeenth-century Crimean society, most of which was Muslim, a lack of social status could have a deleterious effect on the lives of individuals. Slaves were at the bottom of the social ladder that adhered strictly to a hierarchical order. Prestige, wealth and affiliation with a military or religious group meant a restricted life in many respects. This was also true for education. No child slaves, not even males, attended *maktab*s and *madrasa*s. It was virtually impossible for children of slave status to get an education.

The term *dogma*, defining those who were born into the slave status, was added immediately after their names in legal records. Examples include Kenan bin Abdullah nam *dogma*,[19] Kutlu Kız ibnet-i Abdullah nam *dogma*,[20] Mehmed Ali bin Abdullah nam *dogma*,[21] Maliş bin Abdullah nam mid-height, blond, blue-eyed *dogma*.[22] As it is seen in these examples, all the children whose names indicate they were born into slavery in Crimean society had Muslim names. In an inheritance record dated September 1608, it is stated that three *kazak* slaves, one *cariye* and two *dogma–çora* were inherited by the Crimean khan chief treasurer (*hazinedarbaşı*) Halil Aga from his sister Hatice.[23]

Court records of this period indicate that slave children worked in orchards and as shepherds or as apprentices in shops and learned certain crafts.[24] It was extremely rare for these children to run away. Although many slaves who were captured when older tried to escape, *dogma* and *çora* fugitives were exceptionally rare. Even if they did escape, they had nowhere to go. These slaves grew up in Crimean society and became individuals who were strangers to other cultures. In fact, there were *çora*s who even took part in slaving raids.[25]

Slaves who adapted culturally to the regions and conditions where they lived are not limited to the examples given above. The Ukrainian Cossack chronicler Samijlo Velyčko wrote that in 1675 the commander of the Zaporozhian Sich (*košovyj otaman*) Ivan Sirko organised a raid on Crimea. In addition to the Crimean Tatars he captured during the raid, he also rescued 7,000 native Christians from captivity. After travelling approximately 20 km to 30 km from Crimea, Sirko assembled the captives he rescued and asked if any of them wanted to return to Crimea. Of these, 3,000 Christians said they wanted to return. When he asked why they chose to return to Crimea, they responded by saying they had settled in Crimea and were established there, so he allowed them to return. He watched them at first as they went, but when they were out of sight, he ordered the soldiers under his command to attack and kill all of them. Thus, the soldiers killed their brethren and co-religionists.[26]

There are a number of reasons why such a large number of people preferred not to return to their ancestral homeland, but the inability to earn a livelihood on their return was probably the prime reason. In addition, slaves born in Crimea or taken there as children would feel like strangers in other societies, since they spoke Crimean Tatar language as fluently as the Crimean Tatars themselves, and the majority adhered to Muslim culture and customs.[27] Records show that even when they were manumitted and were able to leave, they remained in Crimea.[28] It is believed that a great majority of those who did not want to remain in Crimea were individuals who had become slaves as adults.

Child Slaves and Violence

Children of the slaves, who were termed *mal-i natık* (lit. speaking property), blended in with the society from a young age. Because slaves were regarded as the property of their masters by law, violence committed against them by others was legally considered as damage to the master's property, rather than to the person of the slave. In such situations, the perpetrator simply paid the master a sum to cover the damage. For example, in one court record, a woman named Tokay Bikeç appealed to the court, claiming that her child slave (*çora*) named Akbaş had been murdered. According to her, the child slave she owned was beaten on the head seven times with a piece of wood and brutally murdered. Tokay Bikeç found out that a man called Hasan Atalık had buried her slave in a field, and she filed a claim against him for monetary compensation.[29]

Child slaves were exposed to violence in various ways. They spent most of their time fulfilling their assigned tasks. Freeborn children were also exposed to violence. For example, in June 1685 the youngest son of Musa Sufi from the Karadal district in Crimea was strangled to death. Claiming that Halim and Bayram Gazi murdered his son, Musa Sufi demanded that the individuals in question pay him compensation. However, the case was dismissed, as there was no evidence to prove they had murdered his son.[30]

The court records provide few details as to who and why a child was killed. This was not the only freeborn child murder case in Crimea that year. In Bakhchysarai (Bahçesaray), İbrahim, son of cook (*aşçı*) Esin Bolat, was beaten with a piece of wood by a man called Kablan from the Orta Congar district and died as a result of his injuries.[31] When the victim was a slave, the affair was only brought to court if someone harmed a slave owned by another person. In other words, when a master inflicted violence on his own slave, this was not reflected in the court records. Therefore, cases of injury and murder of slaves usually appeared in court records in connection with damage to a master's property. Because the visibility of female slave children in society was more restricted, they are rarely mentioned in court records in the context of violence.

'If Only I Owned a Devke*': Sexuality and Female Children*

> My Sultan! If you gave me a horse and ordered a raid (*çapul*) on this city and we captured some of these tall/thin girls and devke and returned to Crimea, we would have no regrets when we die.[32]

While Evliya Çelebi was with the Crimean khan, Polat Agha, the commander (*Kırım serdarı*) came up to them and expressed his desire to the khan as quoted above. This suggests that tall, beautiful, young northern girls were much in demand in Crimea. There was a huge interest in these white-skinned northern girls not only in Crimea, but also in Ottoman society in general. In Crimea, girls that were captured in slaving raids were called *devke*. The same term was used for these young girls in Evliya Çelebi's *Seyahatname* and in the Crimean court records. *Devke*s, who were still virgins, were in great demand in the slave market and commanded the highest prices. The price of *devke*s was relatively high in comparison to that of the black female slaves from Africa.[33]

Whereas the average price of a strong male slave was fifty gold coins, the price of *devke*s could be two, three and sometimes even four times higher. The value of *devke*s depended on their beauty, height, their ability to display certain skills or being a member of a noble family.

These female slaves, who were for the most part pre-adolescents, were classified as sexual objects. According to Evliya Çelebi, the Mehmed Giray Khan Hamam in Bakhchysarai was the finest public bath (*hammam*) in Crimea, since girls with henna-dyed hands between the age of ten to fifteen from Circassia, Abkhazia, Georgia, Ukraine, Poland and Muscovy worked there. Although there were girls providing similar services in other *hammam*s, this was the most popular. The *Seyahatname* makes it clear that the girls served the males there and satisfied their sexual desires.[34] Thus, these girls were no longer virgins, but were now classified as *cariye*s; slave girls that were forced into prostitution.

As slaves were classified as property, the slaves known as *devke* were generally mentioned in sale agreements or inheritance cases in the Crimean court records. Although the sale of slaves created no problem among the Crimean Tatars or local non-Muslim inhabitants, if the purchasers were foreigners, permission from the Crimean khan was sometimes necessary. For example, Moşe, son of David, a Jew from Chufut Kale, sold a Ukrainian *devke* named Marina to the ambassador of Wallachia (Kara Ulah) with the permission of the Crimean khan.[35] By contrast, permission was not required when Musa bin Ali from the Şehreküstü district of Bakhchysarai purchased a *devke* for ninety-five *guruş*.[36]

If sales were finalised without any problem, they were not mentioned in the court records. Nevertheless, problems did occur if a 'defective' slave was sold by deception. Any deformation of the bodies of these commodities that had a high market value led to the termination of the sale agreement. If a customer/purchaser appealed to the court and proved that the defect had existed before the slave was purchased, the slave could be returned and the money spent recovered.

On 7 April 1674, a trader named İsmail Beşe purchased a *devke* in return for 215 *vukiye* of tobacco (*duhan*). Later, when he realised there was pus exuding from her ear, he appealed to the court and demanded to be able to return the slave.[37] In another court record, a man named Esad Çelebi asked for an expert to examine a *devke* he had purchased for 108 gold coins to prove that the slave was defective.[38] However, the document does not state the nature of the defect.

Young female slaves were made to perform domestic chores and were not very involved in social life. As a female slave was a valuable commodity to the master, injuring, beating or maiming the slave led to a decrease in her value. This suggests that the majority of the slaves subjected to violence were male slaves, a category that can be classified as less valuable. A female slave's value remained high for as long as she was a virgin, which suggests that their expected duties went beyond simply performing domestic chores. According to a court record, a man named Hacı Mustafa owned a *devke*. She lived in a room adjacent to the house called 'Cossack chambers' (*kazak odaları*) and allowed three *kazak* male slaves named Yusuf, Kaytas and Gazanfer into her room where she drank raki and wine with them. Hacı Mustafa was concerned because the virginity of his *devke* was at stake. He asked the court to have her examined by an expert to determine whether she was still a virgin.[39]

The *devkes*' beauty was also reflected in their names. In records, some of the *devkes* are referred to as Şekerpare (Sugar Blossom),[40] Gülperi (Rose Fairy),[41] Mahidevran (Moon of Fortune)[42] and Abıhayat (Water of Life).[43] This suggests that the slave girls' names were changed by their masters to correspond to their beauty. The majority of these slaves clearly became Muslims over a period of time, since their fathers' names were recorded as Abdullah. In all likelihood, they continued to live in Crimea after they were manumitted.

Changes in Status, Unchanging Realities

Because they were still juveniles, children were unable to defend themselves in seventeenth-century Crimean courts, and a guardian had to be appointed to represent them in court. Being a free and rational person is also equivalent to having free will. Regardless of whether he was an adult or rational, when the individual in question was a slave he was classified as not having free will, and thus most of the time the testimonies of slaves were not recognised in court. In the Crimean court records, on the few occasions when slave testimonies were accepted, the court records emphasise the slave identity of the person testifying. Recall that if a slave was born in Crimea, the term *dogma* was used after his name; if he was still a child, he was identified as *çora*; and in the case of a mature male slave irrespective of his ethnic background, the term *kazak* was added after his name. As long as they remained in bondage, these titles haunted slaves in their daily lives as a whole. When slaves who were born in Crimea grew up, they were identified as *dogma–çora*.

If a slave child did not die at a young age, he would not necessarily continue to live as a slave until his death. In the court records, masters freed children at a young age in various ways. An individual who was issued a manumission certificate (*ıtkname/itakname*) became an ordinary, free person in society. Freedom also meant recognition of their free will. Freed slaves could testify in court, and their statements were considered admissible. In the court records it is clear that like adult slaves, in addition to voluntary manumission, child slaves were also freed through different manumission contracts (*tedbir* or *mükatebe*). In these manumission contracts a master could make an agreement with the slave to liberate him or her either unconditionally, or under certain conditions. A slave whose freedom was promised was more likely to work efficiently and not consider escaping.[44]

When slave children were not old enough to work to fulfil the conditions of their manumission contract (*mükatebe*), their parents worked in their stead. For example, a *kazak* slave named Keyvan was owned by Mehmed Aga, the Crimean khan's butler (*kilercibaşı*). A *mükatebe* agreement he made with his slave required the slave to plant and produce grapes on barren land. According to the agreement, when the master ate grapes from the produce of that land, Keyvan was to be freed. Keyvan fulfilled his duty and was later freed. However, Keyvan had two daughters named Eftade and Mehtab. A separate *mükatebe* agreement he made for his daughters stipulated the construction of a mosque in the neighbourhood where they lived. When he had fulfilled this duty, he also rescued his daughters from enslavement.[45]

*Çora*s and *dogma–çora*s who were ten to eleven years of age and intellectually capable could personally fulfil the obligations of the *mükatebe* agreement. A woman named Melek from Harami, a village in the vicinity of Bakhchysarai, declared that she and her sister Ümmü Gülsüm had inherited a *dogma–çora* named Mehmed Ali bin Abdullah from their father. Ümmü Gülsüm emancipated her share of the slave, whereas Melek chose to make a *mükatebe* agreement. According to the agreement, she gave fifty sheep to Mehmed Ali; he was to graze and breed the sheep, and when he had bred 200 sheep, he was to be freed. Although it is not known when the agreement was contracted, Mehmed Ali delivered 200 sheep in mid-March of 1650 and was manumitted.[46]

By making a *mükatebe* agreement, the owner ensured that the slave would work diligently and productively for a certain length of time, thus producing significant profits in the process. Furthermore, depending on the attitude of the master at the time, utterances pledged in public could also lead to the slave's freedom. In this respect, the most interesting court record encountered is dated 22 June 1676. In the record, Güher Han Bikeç, who lived in the Atalık village of the Alma River district of Crimea, said: 'If Islam Giray Sultan, son of Gazi Giray Sultan from Yanbol comes to my village and I see him with my own eyes I will free my beloved devke (*devkeciğim*) named Gülperi'.[47] The court record in question provides certain clues to historians. It is clear from the title *bikeç* used immediately after her name that the woman, Güher Han, was a wealthy woman and a member of the noble class. Otherwise, she would not have owned such a presumably valuable young slave girl. We can assume that the child slave named Gülperi was still very young. In fact, Güher Han used the phrase 'my beloved *devke*' (rather than *devke*) in the document. Thus, affection on the part of the owner could generate opportunities that worked in favour of the slaves.

Some slaves were voluntarily freed by their masters unconditionally. Young slave girls who gave birth to a child as a result of sexual relations with their master could be granted the status of mother of a child (*ümm-i veled*).[48] However, these girls were called *cariye*, rather than the virginal *devke*. Young girls who were slaves of common people might also become wives of free individuals. For example, Hasan Bölükbaşı bin Ali, who lived in the Bakhchysarai mosque (*cami-i kebir*) neighbourhood, freed his female slave called Naz; he gave her fifty gold coins as a dowry and married her.[49]

In the examples above, once liberated, these young slave girls married and settled in Crimea. Furthermore, when *çora* and *dogma*s acquired the status of a free person, they became Crimean Tatars, both socially and culturally. After slaves were freed, they could continue to use the term *çora* after their names. The Crimean court records document this trend. For example, on 5 June 1674, Kul Çora from the village of Mehmed Şah apprenticed his son Ali İvaz to the tailor (*terzi*) Ali from the Hüseyin Bölükbaşı neighbourhood. In return for the work performed by his son, he agreed that Terzi Ali would pay him three *akçe*s a day.[50] This case shows that although status might change, there were certain unchanging realities. Even though the slave was freed, the term *çora* remained a part of his name. Because the *çora*'s son was given the name Ali İvaz, this would erase all traces distinguishing him from a free person later on in life. A few generations later, a person like Ali İvaz could appear in the documents as a native Crimean, a property owner, a member of a military or religious group or as a merchant. A good example is the case of a free person named Devin Çora from the Sarı Hafız village. In mid-March 1674, Devin Çora's son donated the property he owned to a pious endowment (*waqf*).[51]

During their childhood and the period that followed, social and cultural ties made slaves dependent on Crimea. Shedding the status of slavery and engaging more actively in social life, purchasing and selling property, donating their wealth and becoming skilled in various trades are all indications that these individuals adapted to a more normal existence in Crimea.[52]

An exploration of the Rus/Urus, a quarter founded in Bakhchysarai by manumitted slaves, can shed light on issues of cultural identity and help identify the feelings of ex-slaves, a topic which has not has been examined in Ottoman research. These slaves, who constantly experienced changes in status and identity crises, were in uncharted waters in their host society after being freed. The ambiguity of their status and identity may have prompted them to settle in areas separate from the Crimean Tatars. This uncertainty was manifested by the inhabitants of the Rus/Urus district of Bakhchysarai, and suggests that at least in Crimean society, the addition of terms such as *çora* and *dogma* to names of children of the majority of freed slaves reflects this phenomenon. It is thought that some freed Ukrainian slaves settled in this district rather than in the Armenian, Jewish or Gypsy neighbourhoods where specific ethnic groups lived.[53] In the court records there are indications that manumitted *çora*s lived in this neighbourhood. For example, a property sale agreement from 1650 involved Devin Çora, who lived in the Rus/Urus district, as did his sister.[54] Since they were free people, they could engage in trade, own, sell or donate their property.

Conclusion

Childhood and children still tend to be ignored by historians dealing with the early modern period of the Crimean Khanate. Slaves are often classified as a trade commodity and regarded chiefly in economic terms. This chapter examined child slaves in seventeenth-century Crimea, and in particular the differences between enslaved children and children born to slave mothers.

The findings suggest that over time, the majority of Christian slaves who were unable to maintain their own culture and customs converted and adapted to the customs of Crimean society. Those who became slaves later in life often tried to flee, out of longing for their former lives and their desire to escape slavery. However, those born into slavery did not experience the same degree of longing for the Christian past of their ancestors and had less of an incentive to escape slavery and live elsewhere. The Jewish, Armenian and Gypsy communities of Crimea did not undergo major changes over the course of time because they maintained their own cultures and customs. Slaves who converted forgot their Christian past and even spoke the Crimean Tatar language as proficiently as the Crimean Tatars themselves, and settled in Crimea when they were liberated.

These depictions of the lives of child slaves in Crimea thus lend weight to the view that societal structures and pressures tended to marginalise the customs and practices the slaves were unable to maintain, and constituted the basis for their adaptation to their new environment. It is clear that over the years, the *dogma*s, *çora*s and *devke*s in Crimea gradually took on the mentality, traditions and lifestyle of Crimean Tatars; in brief, these slaves became part of the Crimean Tatar culture.

Notes

1. *Ukrainian Dumy*, p. 27.
2. For detailed information about runaway slaves, see CCR 8, f. 25 (1073/1663); CCR 10, f. 12 (1078/1668); CCR 11, f. 11, 32, 33, 41, 51, 55, 82 (1077–8/1667–8); CCR 13, f. 30, 31 (1078/1668); CCR 14, f. 128 (1080/1669); CCR 15, f. 2 (1086/1675); CCR 17, f. 54 (1085/1674); CCR 18, f. 20, 24 (1084/1673).
3. Peçevi, *Peçevi Tarihi*, p. 354; Kaysunî-zade, *Tarih-i Sahib Giray Han*, p. 31; Davies, *Warfare, State and Society*, p. 20; Ostapchuk, 'The Ottoman Black Sea', p. 3; Matsuki, 'The Crimean Tatars', p. 172.
4. Yvonne, 'Fugitives and Factotums', pp. 136–69; Faroqhi, 'Mostly Fugitives', pp. 129–42; Yaşa, 'Yavuz Sultan Selim Dönemi İstanbul'unda Kuzeyli Firariler ve Düşündürdükleri', pp. 539–54.
5. Yaşa, 'Desperation, Hopelessness, and Suicide', pp. 198–211.
6. Yaşa, 'Bahçesaray (1650–1675)', p. 164.
7. The collection of 121 Crimean court records books is preserved in fond 917 of the Manuscript Division of the Russian National Library (Otdel Rukopisey Rossiyskoy Natsional´noy Biblioteki) in St Petersburg, Russia. The records that have been brought to Turkey are copies of a collection of old photographs made from the originals and consisting of sixty volumes preserved at the İsmail Gaspıralı Library in Simferopol, Crimea. One such set is available at the Bilkent University Library and the other one is housed at the Islamic Research Centre (ISAM). I used the ISAM set. For reference purposes, Crimean court record is abbreviated as CCR. See İnalcık, 'Kırım Hanlığı Kadı Sicilleri', pp. 165–91; Cihan and Yılmaz, 'Kırım Kadı Sicilleri', pp. 131–76.
8. Kizilov, 'Slave Trade', p. 7.
9. For further information on *mahrusa*, see Öztürk, 'Mahrusa ve Mahmiye', pp. 331–42; there are similar usages elsewhere, not only in Ottoman and Crimean historical sources. For example, in Mamluk sources, Cairo was called Kahire al-mahrusa. Muhammed Ahmed Dehman, *El-Irak beyne el-Memalik*, p. 95; in archival records, the phrase *la Serenissima* (most peaceful city) is used frequently for Venice. See Pedani, *Relazioni*.
10. Schools and *madrasa*s were where free children received basic religious education. Generally, religious education was given to male children between

four to five years of age by the *imam*s in their neighbourhood as soon as they were capable of understanding a normal conversation. For the case of early modern Bosnia, see Korić's Chapter 13 in this volume; in Crimea's capital city of Bakhchysarai alone there were seventeen primary schools where Muslim boys were educated, if we are to take the numbers given by Evliya as correct. Evliya Çelebi, *Evliya Çelebi Seyahatnamesi*, vol. 7, p. 226. Children who completed their education in primary schools continued their education at the Zincirli Madrasa. This was the most prestigious *madrasa* in Crimea. Kançal-Ferrari, 'Zincirli Medrese', p. 445.

11. Just as a Muslim could not enslave another Muslim in Islamic law, a Christian could not enslave another Christian. Öztürk, 'XIII. ve XVII. Yüzyıllarda Karadeniz Ticareti', p. 131.
12. Another example pertains to Tatar Mehmed Ali Hafız and his family. According to the records, his two wives, two daughters and young son were abducted, whereupon he paid a ransom for their release. See Archiwum Glówne Akt Dawnych w Warszawie (AGAD, Central Archives of Historical Records in Warsaw), Dział turecki, teczka 96, no. 198, p. 11. However, although he paid the ransom, we do not have information as to whether they were released or not.
13. *Ukrainian Dumy*, p. 29.
14. Kołodziejczyk, 'Slave Hunting', p. 150.
15. CCR 21, f. 73 (1083/1672).
16. For the most part, the Crimean *Shar'iah* court records differentiated between Ukrainians (usually recorded as 'Rus' or 'Rusi') and Russians (normally called 'Moskof' or 'Moskov'). See Yaşa, 'Desperation, Hopelessness, and Suicide', p. 201, note 13.
17. CCR 22, f. 49 (1088/1677). The word *kazak* was used in Crimea for adult male slaves irrespective of their ethnic background. Yaşa, 'Desperation, Hopelessness, and Suicide', p. 201; Yaşa, 'Köleliğin Sosyal ve Mali Boyutları', p. 659.
18. Alba and Nee, 'Rethinking Assimilation Theory', pp. 826–74.
19. CCR 3b, f. 16 (1060/1650).
20. CCR 3b, f. 22 (1060/1650).
21. CCR 3b, f. 27 (1060/1650).
22. CCR 22, f. 51 (1088/1677).
23. CCR 1, f. 43 (1020/1611).
24. *Çora*s were put to work as shepherds CCR 1, f. 91 (1018/1609); CCR 4, f. 72 (1061/1651); CCR 15, f. 48 (1086/1675); CCR 22, f. 71 (1088/1677); in mills CCR 3b, f. 14 (1060/1650); or apprenticed to learn various crafts such as barbers, shoemakers or bakers (*habbaz*) CCR 22, f. 71 (1088/1677); CCR 23a, f. 37 (1094/1683).
25. CCR 8, f. 24–5 (1073/1663).
26. Velička, *Letopis' sobytiy*, pp. 375–7. I would like to thank Oles Kulchynskyi for drawing my attention to this source and information.

27. Kizilov, 'Slave Trade', p. 7.
28. CCR 3b, f. 9 (1060/1650).
29. CCR 13, f. 63 (1078/1668); Yaşa, 'Efendi Köle İlişkisi', p. 223.
30. CCR 26, f. 9 (1096/1685); see also Yaşa, 'Between Life and Death', pp. 433–43.
31. CCR 26, f. 44 (1096/1685). Another child was murdered in the Orta Çongar district in a similar way. CCR 26, f. 87 (1095/1684). For similar child murders, see CCR 26, f. 34 (1096/1685); CCR 22, f. 97 (1083/1673); CCR 23a, f. 62 (1093/1682).
32. '*Sultanım bir bargir verseniz şu şehre bir çapul civerüp şu şılga kızlardan ve devkelerden alub Kırım'a doyum varsak ölyüdüğümüzge gam yemezdik*'. Evliya Çelebi, *Evliya Çelebi Seyahatnamesi*, vol. 6, p. 32.
33. Jennings, 'Black Slaves', p. 296.
34. Evliya Çelebi, *Evliya Çelebi Seyahatnamesi*, vol. 7, p. 227.
35. CCR 13, f. 41 (1078/1668).
36. CCR 11, f. 73 (1077/1667).
37. CCR 17, f. 47 (1084/1674).
38. CCR 18, f. 6 (1084/1673). For similar court records, see CCR 18, f. 26 (1084/1674); CCR 20, f. 22 (1085/1675).
39. CCR 18, f. 22 (1084/1674).
40. CCR 17, f. 11 (1084/1674).
41. CCR 21, f. 31 (1087/1676).
42. CCR 23a, f. 80 (1093/1682).
43. CCR 9, f. 29 (1076/1666).
44. Some slave owners, such as daughters and wives of the Crimean khans, freed their female slaves after the latter had given birth. In this case, both the mothers and their children were manumitted if acknowledged by their Muslim fathers. Their former owners gave them the means to maintain themselves in Crimea. Compare the standard provision of Islamic law pertaining to a male slave owner whose recognised child by his *ümm-i veled* was free, whereas the mother could not be sold and became free upon her master's death, unless he had manumitted her earlier. For various manumission records, see CCR 9, f. 29 (1076/1666); CCR 10, f. 133 (1077–1666); CCR 11, f. 48, 69 (1077–8/1667–8); CCR 17, f. 22, 38 (1085/1674); CCR 21, f. 31 (1087/1676); CCR 22, f. 51, 73 (1088/1677); CCR 24, f. 3, 39, 73 (1088–90/1677–9); CCR 26, f. 58 (1096/1685). Sahillioğlu, 'Slaves in the Social and Economic Life', pp. 53–4.
45. CCR 1, f. 10 (1021/1612).
46. CCR 3b, f. 27 (1060/1650).
47. CCR 21, f. 31 (1087/1676).
48. Manumission of a *cariye* who had a baby by her master is prescribed by Islamic law upon the master's death. Erdem, *Slavery in the Ottoman Empire*, p. 152; Toledano, *As If Silent*, p. 85.
49. CCR 13, f. 63 (1078/1668).

50. CCR 17, f. 19 (1085/1674).
51. CCR 20, f. 88 (1084/1674).
52. CCR 3b, f. 7 (1060/1650); CCR 19, f. 42 (1086/1675); CCR 20, f. 83, 84 (1084/1674).
53. Yaşa, 'Mahalle ve Konut', p. 395.
54. CCR 3b, f. 9 (1060/1650).

Bibliography

Archival Sources

Archiwum Główne Akt Dawnych w Warszawie – Central Archives of Historical Records in Warsaw (AGAD), Dział turecki, teczka 96, no. 198.

Manuscript Division of the Russian National Library (Otdel Rukopisey Rossiyskoy Natsional´noy Biblioteki), Fond 917, Crimean Court Records, CCR 1 (1017–22/1608–13); 3b (1057–61/1647–50); 4 (1061–3/1650–3); 8 (1070–4/1659–64); 9 (1075–6/1666); 10 (1077–9/1666–7); 11 (1077–8/1667–8); 13 (1078–9/1668–9); 14 (1079–82/1669–72); 15 (1083–7/1672–7); 17 (1084–5/1673–5); 18 (1083–4/1672–3); 19 (1082–3/1672–3); 20 (1084–6/1673–6); 21 (1086–7/1675–7); 22 (1087–9/1677–8); 23a (1090–5/1679–84); 24 (1088–90/1677–8); 26 (1095–6/1684–5).

Primary Sources

Evliya Çelebi, *Evliya Çelebi Seyahatnamesi Topkapı Sarayı Kütüphanesi Revan 1457 Numaralı Yazmanın Transkripsiyonu-Dizini*, eds Y. Dağlı and S. A. Kahraman, vol. 6 (Istanbul: Yapı Kredi Yayınları, 2002).

_____, *Evliya Çelebi Seyahatnamesi Topkapı Sarayı Kütüphanesi Bağdat 308 Numaralı Yazmanın Transkripsiyonu-Dizini*, eds Y. Dağlı and R. Dankoff, vol. 7 (Istanbul: Yapı Kredi Yayınları, 2003).

Kaysunî-zade Nidaî Remmal Hoca, *Tarih-i Sahib Giray Han*, ed. Özalp Gökbilgin (Ankara: 1973).

Muhammed Ahmed Dehman, *El-Irak beyne el-Memalik ve el-Osmaniyyîn el-Etrak ma'a Rıhle Emîr Yeşbek min Mehdî ed-Devadar li-Muhammed b. Mahmud el-Halebî el-Mulakkab bi-İbn Eca* (Damascus: 1986).

Peçevi İbrahim Efendi, *Peçevi Tarihi, I*, ed. Bekir Sıtkı Baykal (Ankara: Kültür Bakanlığı Yayınları, 1981).

Relazioni di ambasciatori veneti al Senato, vol. 14, *Relazioni inedite. Costantinopoli (1508–1789)*, ed. Maria Pia Pedani (Padova: Bottega d'Erasmo, 1996).

Ukrainian Dumy, trans. George Tarnawsky and Patricia Kilina (Toronto and Cambridge, MA: Canadian Institute of Ukrainian Studies and Harvard Ukrainian Research Institute, 1979).

Veličko, Samoil, *Letopiś sobytiy v Yugozapadnoy Rossii v XVII-m veke*, vol. 2 (Kiev: Vremennaya Komissiya dlya Razbora Drevnikh Aktov, 1851).

Secondary Sources

Alba, Richard, and Victor Nee, 'Rethinking Assimilation Theory for a New Era of Immigration', *International Migration Review*, 31/4 (1997), pp. 826–74.

Cihan, Ahmet, and Fehmi Yılmaz, 'Kırım Kadı Sicilleri', *İslam Araştırmaları Dergisi*, 11 (2004), pp. 131–76.

Davies, Brian L., *Warfare, State and Society on the Black Sea Steppe, 1500–1700* (London and New York: Routledge, 2007).

Erdem, Y. Hakan, *Slavery in the Ottoman Empire and its Demise, 1800–1909* (Basingstoke: Macmillian Press, 1996).

Faroqhi, Suraiya, 'Mostly Fugitives: Slaves and their Trials and Tribulations in Sixteenth-Century Üsküdar', in Suraiya Faroqhi (ed.), *Travel and Artisans in the Ottoman Empire: Employment and Mobility in the Early Modern Era* (London: I. B. Tauris, 2014), pp. 129–42.

İnalcık, Halil, 'Kırım Hanlığı Kadı Sicilleri Bulundu', *Belleten*, 60/227 (1996), pp. 165–91.

Jennings, Ronald C., 'Black Slaves and Free Blacks in the Ottoman Cyprus, 1590–1640', *Journal of the Economic and Social History of the Orient*, 30 (1987), pp. 286–302.

Kançal-Ferrari, Nicole, 'Zincirli Medrese', *Diyanet İslam Ansiklopedisi*, 44 (2013), pp. 445–6.

Kizilov, Mikhail, 'Slave Trade in the Early Modern Crimea from the Perspective of Christian, Muslim and Jewish Sources', *Journal of Early Modern History*, 11 (2007), pp. 1–31.

Kołodziejczyk, Dariusz, 'Slave Hunting and Slave Redemption as a Business Enterprise: The Northern Black Sea Region in the Sixteenth to Seventeenth Century', *Oriente Moderno Nuova Serie*, 25/86 (2006), pp. 149–59.

Matsuki, Eizo, 'The Crimean Tatars and their Russian-Captive Slaves: An Aspect of Muscovite-Crimean Relations in the 16th and 17th Centuries', *Mediterranean World*, 18/3 (2006), pp. 171–82.

Ostapchuk, Victor, 'The Ottoman Black Sea Frontier and the Relations of the Porte with the Polish-Lithuanian Commonwealth and Muscovy, 1622–1628', unpublished PhD dissertation, Harvard University, 1989.

Öztürk, Mustafa, 'Osmanlı Devlet Anlayışında "Mahrusa" ve "Mahmiye" Terimlerinin Mana ve Meftumu', in Selda Kılıç, Bekir Koç and Tülay Ercoşkun (eds), *Musa Çadırcı'ya Armağan Yazılar* (Ankara: Bilgin Kültür Sanat Yayınları, 2011), pp. 331–42.

Öztürk, Yücel, 'XIII. ve XVII. Yüzyıllarda Karadeniz Ticareti', *Türk Dünyası Araştırmaları*, 97 (1995), pp. 113–36.

Peirce, Leslie, *Morality Tales: Law and Gender in the Ottoman Court of Aintab* (Berkeley, Los Angeles and London: University of California Press, 2013).

Sahillioğlu, Halil, 'Slaves in the Social and Economic Life of Bursa in the Late 15th and Early 16th Centuries', *Turcica*, 17 (1985), pp. 43–112.

Seng, Yvonne J., 'Fugitives and Factotums: Slaves in Early Sixteenth-Century

Istanbul', *Journal of the Economic and Social History of the Orient*, 39/2 (1996), pp. 136–69.

Toledano, Ehud R., *As If Silent and Absent: Bonds of Enslavement in the Islamic Middle East* (New Haven and London: Yale University Press, 2007).

Yaşa, Fırat, 'Kırım Hanlığı'nda Köleliğin Sosyal ve Mali Boyutları', *Gaziantep University Journal of Social Sciences*, 13/3 (2014), pp. 657–69.

_____, 'Bahçesaray (1650–1675)', unpublished PhD dissertation, Sakarya University, 2017.

_____, 'Efendi Köle İlişkisi Bağlamında Şeyhülislam Fetvaları', in Zübeyde Güneş Yağcı, Fırat Yaşa and Dilek İnan (eds), *Osmanlı Devleti'nde Kölelik, Ticaret, Esaret, Yaşam* (Istanbul: Çamlıca Yayınları, 2017), pp. 209–26.

_____, 'Desperation, Hopelessness, and Suicide: An Initial Consideration of Self-Murder by Slaves in Seventeenth-Century Crimean Society', *Turkish Historical Review*, 9/2 (2018), pp. 198–211.

_____, 'Mahalle ve Konut Tipolojisi Açısından Bahçesaray (1650–1675)', *Selçuk Üniversitesi Edebiyat Fakültesi Dergisi (SEFAD)*, 39 (2018), pp. 389–402.

_____, 'Yavuz Sultan Selim Dönemi İstanbul'unda Kuzeyli Firariler ve Düşündürdükleri', in Nilüfer Alkan Günay (ed.), *Yavuz Sultan Selim Dönemi ve Bursa* (Bursa: Gaye Kitabevi, 2018), pp. 539–54.

_____, 'Between Life and Death: Slaves and Violence in Crimean Society in the Last Quarter of 17th Century', *Selçuk Üniversitesi Türkiyat Araştırmaları Dergisi (SUTAD)*, 47 (2019), pp. 433–43.

Chapter 8

Rural Girls as Domestic Servants in Late Ottoman Istanbul[1]

Yahya Araz

'My childhood is what I'd like to forget the most in my life.'[2]

Domestic service was the key area of employment for girls (*çocuk hizmetçi*) in late Ottoman Istanbul. Mostly of rural origins, these children played an indispensable role for middle- and particularly upper-class Istanbulites. Recruited under various conditions,[3] these girls were replaced by newcomer novices after completing a few years of service.[4] As the late nineteenth-century newspapers and novels indicate, Istanbul would continue to increasingly attract cheap female child labour, with growing discussions about their status. One of the key themes of late Ottoman and early Republican novels is children and young girls who were brought from the countryside for employment in domestic services, but were later somehow 'dragged astray' by their misfortune.[5]

The rising employment of young girls in domestic service in Istanbul had to do with the large-scale socio-economic changes in the second half of the nineteenth century. Despite the revival of slaveholding in the late 1850s and 1860s due to the rising Circassian inflow into the Ottoman lands, the employment of slaves in domestic service and the slave trade itself gradually declined in this period.[6] As the intellectual and political climate turned against slavery, Istanbulites began to prefer servants to bound laborers, and domestic work began to be performed mainly by recruited girls.[7] As several studies suggest, one must, however, be cautious not to overemphasise the link between the decline of slaveholding and the rising employment of young girls in the domestic service sector. In fact, slaves and free labour continued to exist side by side in late Ottoman Istanbul.[8]

The ever-growing population of Istanbul, which soared to almost a million in the late nineteenth century,[9] accompanied by the expanding class of civil servants following the reorganisation of the bureaucracy[10] and the tendency to have housemaids on the part of families with even modest means, resulted in a greater demand for provincial girls. Between 1865 and 1875, at a time when the Circassian slave trade was still active, Circassian slave children were sold in Istanbul at a rate of 4,000 to 5,000 *guruş* on average. However, most Istanbulites could not afford slaves at such prices. If we do not take into account spending on food and clothing, the average monthly cost of hiring a provincial girl in domestic services was estimated to be only ten *guruş* in this period.[11] Such a low cost meant that with the rising number of provincial girls in domestic service, a large portion of Istanbul society was able to afford the luxury of employing domestic servants.

In late Ottoman Istanbul, a significant number of girls employed in domestic services were of Anatolian origin. Circassian children arrived in the 1860s, and Rumelian refugee children in the aftermath of the Russo-Turkish War of 1877–8. The government encouraged Istanbulites to protect destitute emigrant children in need, and ultimately employ them in domestic service. This eased the burden on the government, which, with the limited means at hand, tried to tackle the problem of destitute and poor children caused by famines, wars and mass migrations. In doing so, its aim was to keep poor orphan girls from wandering out in the streets and going astray, thereby securing their future.[12]

Rather than focusing on refugee children from Circassia or Rumelia, this chapter is a preliminary attempt to explore the issue of the status of girls from central and north-western Anatolia who came or were brought to Istanbul for employment in domestic service. It underlines three key questions. First, what was the socio-economic background of girls employed in domestic service; second, how did they find their way to Istanbul; and third, what was the relationship of these girls with their host families, and how did this shape their future lives? This chapter suggests that in the late Ottoman world, the domestic service sector was an integral component of labour mobility between the provinces and Istanbul. Contary to the two-way traffic of male workers, the mobility of girls was usually one-way migration, since a very small number of girls returned permanently to their native villages. Sending their children to Istanbul enabled families not only to benefit financially, but also to transfer the heavy financial burden of the wedding trousseau to their own daughters and their employers. In fact, the employment of girls in the domestic service sector of the Ottoman capital during the late nineteenth century served the interests of both their biological families and Istanbulites. This clarifies why the volume of migration of young girls increased dramatically, despite the rising concerns over abused girls in the same period. It also explains why most government efforts in the late nineteenth century were aimed at controlling and standardising the mobility of young girls, rather than preventing it. These government policies were likely designed to reconcile the interests of the parties involved; namely, the girls, their families and Istanbulite households.

Despite its importance, studies on labour and migration in Ottoman historiography have paid very little attention to girls employed in domestic service. Rather, they focus on the mobility of men, which increasingly became a source of concern for the central government in the eighteenth and nineteenth centuries.[13] Immigrant men in workshops, coffeehouses, bachelors' rooms and *han*s who were usually associated with the mischief were even placed under police surveillance in this period.[14] But it was not only men who migrated into the Ottoman capital, it was also provincial girls. However, since family–child relations in domestic service were considered part of the private domain, they became visible only when the issues involving tensions between girls and Istanbulite households were carried into the legal domain. It is exactly for this reason that documents prepared by state authorities and kept at the Prime Ministerial Ottoman Archives usually only treated the working of girls at Istanbulite homes through an examination of these tensions.

Though this chapter draws upon these documents left behind by Ottoman bureaucrats and periodicals of the period, it mainly relies on court records belonging to Istanbul and a number of Anatolian towns and cities. The records in question contain copious data that would allow for an understanding and interpretation of the evolution and transformation of the relations established between Anatolia and Istanbul through the recruited children.[15] However, it should be noted that in regard to Istanbul, these records have so far not been used.[16] The practice of placing children with host families to employ them in domestic service was mentioned by late Ottoman courts commonly with reference to a contract termed as *icar-ı sagir/e* (hiring of child labour). Still, it is difficult to estimate to what extent these labour-hiring contracts were included in court records. As in other parts of the Empire, most of the agreements were probably made verbally in Istanbul, while fewer agreements were committed to writing.

Poverty in Anatolia

On his way from Bursa to Ankara during his travels in Anatolia in 1878, British traveller Henry C. Barkley (1837–1903) came upon a series of isolated, distant settlements where poverty held sway, and which one would hardly call villages.[17] Barkley's visit came directly after the famine of 1873–5, which swept across central Anatolia and its vicinity. His remarks describe a landscape devastated by the famine. However, those who visited Anatolia before as well as after spoke about a wretched land with very limited means of transportation, inhabited by destitute people struggling against disease.

In the early 1860s, the Ottoman government dispatched to Anatolia inspectors vested with broad authorities to monitor on site the local implementation of *Tanzimat* reforms, as well as to identify and remedy the problems in provincial settings. In their reports sent to Istanbul from the inspected cities and towns, the inspectors provided exhaustive descriptions of peasants suffering at the hands of usurers, poor road infrastructure, as well as ruined bridges, places of worship and buildings in disrepair.[18] In a similar vein, on one of his visits to Anatolia following the proclamation of the Second Constitution in 1908, Ahmed Şerif, a columnist for the newspaper *Tanin*, wrote: 'Moving inland from the coast into the Anatolian heartland, one sees more of dilapidation and misery'.[19] Hiring out their children to Istanbulites, Anatolian families stated that they were in extreme poverty and in desperate need of a single loaf of bread. While some families used overstatement to describe their situation, such as '*afkar-ı fukaradan ve muhtac-ı nan*' (the poorest of the poor and in need of bread), poverty was a widespread phenomenon in Anatolia. Starting from the second half of the 1850s, this was further complicated by the burden of the incoming Caucasian and then Rumelian refugees.

Studies on the socio-economic status of Anatolia have thus far tended to focus on the implementation of reforms at the provincial level and institutions as a byproduct of bureaucratic expansion in the provinces.[20] One cannot deny the significance and revolutionary impact of new developments upon the provinces that brought about a convergence between the capital and the provinces, such as the *Tanzimat* reforms, bureaucratic expansion in the provinces, tax regulations and road works. Still, the countryside of the period cannot be simply reduced to such developments. As portrayed by Şerafeddin Mağmumi (1860–1931), a young Ottoman physician; in Anatolia of the 1890s people were suffering from epidemics such as cholera, typhoid and dysentery, drinking water was contaminated by sewage and villages lost contact with urban centres, particularly in winter.[21] It seems that the available literature fails to pay due attention to disasters, epidemics and other hardships mentioned by Mağmumi, all of which eventually touched the lives of people and ultimately redefined social relations.

One fundamental problem that challenged the people of Anatolia in the late Ottoman period involved a variety of disasters caused by climatic fluctuations and concomitant famines.²² Accompanied by human incapacity to respond, bad harvests resulting from locust infestations, excessive rain or drought further widened the impact area of famines, prolonging their effects. Finding their way into folklore in the form of folk songs and stories, famines put people through painful experiences that would live in their memories for decades to come, exacerbating poverty in a perpetual state.²³ The famine of 1845, which had swept through most of central and north-western Anatolia, and the famine of 1873–5, with more or less the same impact areas as the former, went down in history as the most severe natural disasters of Anatolia during the period in question.²⁴

People living in famine-stricken regions tended to develop similar reactions. They made do with what they had, boiling various herbs and plant roots as meal and sometimes having to eat animal carcasses.²⁵ The fight against starvation manifested itself in various forms from writing petitions begging for help to looting provision stores and bakeries.²⁶ Still, the most common reaction was emigration. Mobility could extend from rural areas to the closest town, and further to large cities.²⁷ Indeed, right after the famine of 1845, some rural emigrants took refuge in the closest towns and cities with available food, while others made their way to Bursa and Istanbul. Those emigrating to find food to survive lived on the streets as beggars and strived to keep death at a distance by consuming whatever they could find. Contemporary sources relate similar scenes of misery after every Anatolian famine in the late Ottoman Empire.²⁸

Famine took its toll on everyone. However, as they were dependent on adults, it was children who were the most vulnerable to such disasters. In those difficult times, children were abandoned on the streets, forced into beggary and were even left to die. It was also a common practice for famine-stricken families to give up their children to other families as foster children or domestic servants. Yet, this option was only possible so long as they could find a family to adopt them. During the famine of 1873–5, Colonel Ahmed Hilmi Bey reported to the capital on the impact of the disaster in Yozgat and the nearby vicinity, stating that the famine victims in despair were at a loss about what to do and eager to give up their sons and daughters for adoption; yet, no one was willing help 'as everyone was obviously in dire straits' (*herkesin müzayakaları meydanda olduğundan*).²⁹ As related in a folk story on the famine of 1873–5, no one even hired 'servants to work for food and lodging' (*boğaz tokluğuna hizmetkar*) in those times of scarcity.³⁰ Thus, the victims were forced to make their way towards less impacted regions and large cities, such as Istanbul in particular.

The famine of 1845 took its greatest toll on central and north-western

Anatolian cities and towns, such as Çankırı, Gerede, Dörtdivan and Yabanabad (Kızılcahamam). The crops failed, livestock perished and, consequently, people fled to areas where food was available. Some of the emigrants went as far as Istanbul, never to return. Escalating famine resulted in a serious increase in the number of children from central and north-western Anatolia to be employed in Istanbulite households for domestic services. A recent study on the impact of the 1845 famine upon labour relations demonstrates that the famine led to labour transfer from agriculture to other sectors.[31] This finding is corroborated by the results of the present chapter, at least as far as children are concerned. Famine-stricken and impoverished families from central and north-western Anatolia would hire their children to work as domestic servants for Istanbulite households in return for certain fees. It was the first time that the presence of Anatolian children was so strongly felt in the Ottoman capital.[32]

The famine of 1845 swept through the cities and towns in central Anatolia and the vicinity. Yet, among the children struck by famine, those who found their way to Istanbul to work in domestic services were mostly from cities and towns located to the north and north-west of Ankara. Cities and towns to the south of Ankara were also affected by famine, yet sent very few children to the capital.[33] There are various factors to account for such a contrast. In the aftermath of the famine, one of these factors probably being geographical proximity that made it easier to establish communication and relations with Istanbul for cities and towns to the north and north-west of Ankara. This region had relatively easier overland and maritime access to the capital. Nevertheless, geographical proximity and other transport-related advantages still fail to adequately explain how these girls from the towns and cities to the north and northwest of Ankara came to take up residence in Istanbulite households at such a surprising speed right after the famine and subsequent years. A more satisfactory explanation considers how exactly these girls found their way to Istanbul.

Reaching Istanbul

In the years following the famine of 1845, many provincial girls succeeded in making their way to Istanbulite households, mostly owing to assistance from their relatives and fellow countrymen (*hemşehri*), who either lived in Istanbul or enjoyed close relations with the city. It would, indeed, be the mediation of those networking relatives which facilitated the migration of girls from central and north-western Anatolia. Rural families, willing to hire out their children on the one hand, and Istanbulites keen on benefitting from their labour on the other, would continue to take advantage of the intermediary role of relatives and countrymen, which inspired trust in both parties, up until the end of the Empire. However, during the last quarter of the nineteenth century, the increasing demand for girls on the part of Istanbulites would also include two formerly less visible groups – that is, civil servants and professional intermediaries, notoriously dubbed trustees (*emanetçi*), brokers (*dellal*) or muleteers (*katırcı*).[34]

In the aftermath of the 1845 famine, immigrants who left famine-stricken areas for Istanbul and the vicinity had lost all they had, struggling to survive under harsh circumstances. In the eyes of the authorities, these immigrating famine victims were simply guests (*misafir*) who would soon return to their hometowns. Yet, it is difficult to ascertain how many of them moved back. Some did return, but left their children in Istanbul. For instance, a certain Hasan and his family, originally hailing from Haslar village of Ayaş district in Ankara, were among the famine victims who fled to the Üsküdar and Kadıköy districts. Hasan was the head of a family of six who took to the road and reached Istanbul. Containing the names of famine victims coming from Ankara and the vicinity to Üsküdar and Kadıköy, a list mentions his wife as '*kadın*' (some woman). But the same document refers to his four children (three daughters and a son) with their proper names – namely, the girls, Fatma, Ümmühan and Havva, and the boy, Mehmed. Appearing before Istanbul Mahmudpaşa Court on 24 May 1846, Hasan hired out his twelve-year-old daughter Fatma as a domestic servant to Şerife Rukiye Hanım in return for a monthly fee of thirty *guruş*. As per the agreement, twenty-five *guruş* of Fatma's fee was to be spent on her subsistence and other needs, while the remaining five *guruş* was to be saved for the girl. About twenty days later, on 14 June 1846, Havva, the second daughter of the family, entered into the records of the same court. Although she was a fifteen-year-old girl of full age who was entitled to make her own decisions, she was accompanied by her mother at the court. Havva concluded a labour-hiring (*icar*) contract with another Rukiye, in return for a monthly fee of thirty *guruş*.[35] It is plausible to assume that the remaining two children of Hasan – namely, Ümmühan and Mehmed – must have shared the same fate as their siblings.

Hasan managed to save his family from starvation, but failed to keep them together. During the same period, some central and north-western Anatolian immigrants in Istanbul who were recorded as guests lost this temporary status over time, turning into permanent residents of the capital. In one such case, a certain Mehmed Durmuş, a father from Dörtdivan, hired out his nine-year-old daughter Rukiye on 27 February 1846, and although records implied his temporary residence in Istanbul, he was designated as a resident in the caretaker's house (*kayyumhane*) of Nuruosmaniye Mosque.

About a month later, on 1 April 1846, as he appeared before the same court to hire out his other daughter, eight-year-old Hatice, he was now recorded as a resident of the Koğacı Dede neighbourhood (*mahalle*), near Çarşamba Pazarı (Wednesday Market).[36] There are two likely possibilities to account for his elevation in status from a temporary provincial dweller in the house of a mosque caretaker to an ordinary neighbourhood resident within only a month's time. First, countrymen such as Mehmed Durmuş from central and north-western Anatolia must have also known Istanbul prior to the famine, which made it easier and faster to permanently settle in the city. Well before the famine, adult males from central and north-western Anatolia also played a crucial role in meeting the labour needs of Istanbul.[37] It is highly likely that, in the years following the famine of 1845, such men, already settled in Istanbul for work, began to move their families from the countryside to join them in the city. Later on, during the famine of 1873–5, Basiretçi Ali Efendi remarked that many women moved to Istanbul to join their husbands, along with their children.[38] Second, early settlers in Istanbul offered assistance to their relatives and fellow countrymen who arrived in the aftermath of the famine, willing to settle permanently. Had he not previously been to the capital, Mehmed Durmuş would have definitely received assistance from his fellow countrymen already familiar with the city. In any case, for individuals such as Mehmed Durmuş, there was already a strong web of relations which would make them feel at home in Istanbul.

Fellow countrymen, either resident or working in Istanbul, played a vital role in establishing connections between rural people eager to hire out their children and Istanbulites willing to employ them in return, as well as in building relations of mutual trust between these two parties. It was mostly these fellow countrymen who not only fulfilled the wishes of Istanbulites, but also convinced their relatives and friends in the countryside that there was a better future ahead for their children. Those arriving from the provinces temporarily stayed in the workplaces of their fellow countrymen. From coffee houses to confectioneries, the facilities of all such enterprises run by rural immigrants were available to those coming to Istanbul to hire out their daughters.[39] A great majority of these rural newcomers had no worries about where to stay in Istanbul. Places such as coffeehouses in particular were a venue for people from the same towns and cities, helping these fresh immigrants connect with their fellow countrymen in order to sell the labour of their daughters. As a sign of their function as a sort of hometown association, some of the coffee houses were known by names such as the coffee house of the Safranbolulu, Çerkeşli, Çankırılı and so on.[40]

After assisting with the process of hiring provincial girls, relatives and acquaintances living in Istanbul also continued to look after them. For instance, a certain Fatma of Gerede was eight years old when she was placed under the care of her namesake, a woman named Fatma, who was a resident of the *mahalle* of Atik İbrahim Pasha. Her father Ali hired her out to Fatma as a domestic servant with a monthly fee of ten *guruş* on 28 May 1846. Three *guruş* of her monthly fee was to be kept for her, while the remaining seven would be spent for her subsistence and other needs. Ali returned to his hometown after securing the employment of his daughter. However, things were not going well for Fatma, who took the girl into her service, and soon enough she realised that she could not pay the fee. This being the case, what were the chances for a provincial girl who was not even ten years old? In such circumstances, the acquaintances and relatives of girls would step in, either taking them under their wings or finding them new families who could afford their services. The nine-year-old Fatma also had relatives in Istanbul to watch over her. Her older sister, the wife of Seyyid Salih Efendi, who was the *imam* of Molla Hüsrev Mosque, lived in Istanbul. Ayşe took her sister Fatma in, doing her best to make her feel that she was not all alone in Istanbul.[41]

Without taking into account the 'voluntary' mediation of provincials either settled or temporarily living in Istanbul for work, it is impossible to understand the mobility of young girls between the provinces and Istanbul during the late Ottoman Empire. *Tanzimat* reforms paved the way for the rise of new institutions in provincial cities and towns, and concomitantly resulted in the restructuring of the bureaucracy and its expansion from the capital to the provinces. Government departments now diversified and expanded in provincial cities and towns and boosted the provincial visibility of civil servants who were raised or educated in Istanbul.[42] Civil servants in many ways helped the process whereby provincial girls made their way to Istanbul. In this context, one of the first things they did upon arrival in their places of duty was to find girls to help with the housework for their own families. The only difference among civil servants in this respect was the number of girls they could afford to hire. Families of low-ranking civil servants had to make do with a single girl, while high-ranking officials such as district governors (*kaimmakam*) and governors (*vali*) could afford to employ two or more girls under their roof. Civil servants also acted as intermediaries for their relatives, acquaintances and colleagues residing in the capital, thus contributing to the mobility of girls between the provinces and Istanbul.

From the late nineteenth century onwards, rural girls received greater coverage in the Istanbul press, as well as in bureaucratic correspondence. News about girls running away from their host families, who were later sold to beggary and prostitution, finally committing suicide alarmed the authorities and consequently the Istanbul press, both of whom now turned greater attention towards juvenile mobility between rural areas and Istanbul. In the eyes of the authorities, the issue also had to do with social morality, as well as law and order in the capital.[43] In fact, such concerns about girls who, with various false promises such as marriage or domestic employment, were lured from the countryside to large cities and ended up in beggary or prostitution were not limited to the Ottomans and Istanbul. European cities such as London, which acted as centres of attraction for girls from the countryside, also had similar problems and concerns.[44] Western media coverage must have been another factor that raised greater concerns among Ottomans for rural girls. An untitled article published in *Hanımlara Mahsus Gazete* (Gazette for Women) on 4 May 1899 discussed the issue of girls who were enticed away from their families with false promises and dragged into prostitution, underlining the fact that the problem was already escalating 'in the large cities of Europe day after day'. The article also announced an upcoming congress to be held in London in June of the same year, intended to curb such illegal trade.[45]

The challenges that life in the capital posed for rural girls were mostly attributed to the intermediaries who played a part in their arrival. Notoriously dubbed as *emanetçi*, *katırcı* and *dellal* in the contemporary press, these intermediaries were defined as individuals who lured the provincial girls with promises of domestic employment, but had the hidden agenda of abusing them.[46] On 23 July 1903, the newspaper *Sabah* cautioned its readers against trusting individuals offering mediation for taking provincial girls to Istanbul. The newspaper argued that such individuals should be kept under strict government surveillance.[47] In fact, long before such warnings by *Sabah*, the government had already attempted to regulate child mobility between the capital and provinces. During the second half of the 1880s, problems facing provincial girls in the capital prompted authorities to pay closer attention to the question. In 1887, an official correspondence addressed by the Ministry of the Interior (*Dahiliye Nezareti*) to the *vilayet* of Kastamonu[48] alerted the local authorities against malevolent (*hamiyyetsiz*) individuals who lured poor and destitute children to Istanbul and elsewhere, with the aim of selling them, condemning them to misery.[49] However, the government did not seek to prohibit the mobility of girls to the capital. Istanbulites needed the labour of these girls for domestic tasks. They were particularly in high demand among civil servants.

Instead, the aim was to check and record child mobility originating from the countryside. In doing so, the government planned to obviate potential problems for girls in the capital. Orders issued to local authorities required them to record all details pertaining to girls dispatched to the capital, and deny travel permits to anyone travelling with girls but lacking the necessary documents. Accordingly, documents to be issued by local authorities had to indicate various details, such as the name of the girl and her custodian, the name of the prospective employer, the place(s) of origin and residence, the girl's age and agreed fee, including the portion to be spent on her subsistence and other needs, as well as the portion to be saved for herself or her custodian.[50]

Evidence suggests that the years following the regulations of the 1880s witnessed increased surveillance of the trips taken by provincial girls to the capital for domestic employment or other purposes.[51] In the aftermath of the regulations, information pertaining to girls taken to Istanbul began to appear with greater frequency in local court records. Nevertheless, one cannot assume that these regulations succeeded in removing the grievances of girls in Istanbul. The basic fallacy of the contemporary bureaucracy and press lies in their tendency to insist on solely accusing the intermediaries for such grievances. Indeed, certain individuals did abuse the girls they brought from the provinces, in order to derive undeserved profits out of their labour. Becoming all the more visible during the last quarter of the nineteenth century, these intermediaries earned commissions for their efforts and just like the girls they helped to find jobs in Istanbul, they mostly originated from the provinces. What distinguished them from the above-mentioned relatives and fellow countrymen who also served the same purpose was the success of the former in turning what they did into a profession, out of which they earned money. These professional middlemen acted on demand to travel to the farthest rural villages, cities and towns, to find appropriate girls, who they brought to the capital.[52] For these girls, life in the capital was largely shaped by their experiences there, rather than who brought them and how. For it was almost impossible to regulate working conditions, relationships and life in general for the girls in their host households.

Living in Istanbul, Working in Domestic Service

Wage contracts for the girls hired for domestic service only spanned their childhood years. In late Ottoman Istanbul, girls reached puberty at the age of thirteen or fourteen, when they stepped into adulthood. Hence, the service period lasted for several years from the employment age of seven to ten until the time when they were old enough to make their own decisions. Throughout this period, there were many different factors shaping their lives, including their socio-economic background, adaptation skills, their relations with their families, if any, and how they were treated by the host families. It was due to their cheap labour that they could be hired by all echelons of the Istanbulite population. While they all shared the same fate of being hired for domestic service, household duties and lives were different for girls employed in seaside villas (*sahilhane*) and mansions of wealthy families (*konak*), who also had slaves and other servants, and for those who worked for modest Istanbulite households.

When deciding to hire provincial girls, Istanbulite families often relied on a series of inquiries and recommendations. They did so, consistently use the same sources, which indicates that Istanbul households shared amongst each other their experiences with such girls. Provincial girls would arrive in Istanbul after an arduous journey. Apart from novels and stories, there is a scarcity of accounts on how these girls felt upon arrival in the capital and in the houses of their employers. They were probably quite astonished, as they had been born into a world of poverty where people lived in single-room cottages and could barely make ends meet. Most would get over their astonishment in time by observing, getting to know and understanding. On the other side of the picture, the case was different for host families who were accustomed to having provincial girls as maidservants. In nineteenth-century Britain, some families tested their maidservants by leaving some cash out in the open. A decent girl was expected to inform her master right away upon discovering the money.[53] Likewise, Istanbulites probably tested servant girls in a similar manner, and admonished them, if need be, on how to behave properly. It appears that some sort of 'probation period' was already in place for girls hired for domestic service, though it was not explicitly specified in wage contracts. It was not uncommon for parties to fall into conflict and terminate the wage contract (*fesh-i icar*) as a result. However, in such circumstances, there was no need to worry for either party. Late Ottoman Istanbul was a buoyant market for girls employed in domestic service. So, in case of contract termination, it was not hard to find new host families for them. The same applied to unsatisfied families, who could easily terminate contracts, as they enjoyed the networks and means by which to swiftly replace a former employee with a new one.[54]

Young maidservants were faced with greater expectations over time. They would perform all sorts of chores in Istanbulite households as a single servant: they were set to various tasks, such as washing the dishes, drawing water from the well, lighting the brazier, cleaning the windows, looking after younger children of the family, running errands and even cooking after gaining some experience. Accidents could occur where the young, inexperienced maidservants were concerned. In November 1910, a certain Halime, a nine-year-old maidservant from Cide/Kastamonu working in a mansion house in Üsküdar, accidentally caught her dress on fire as she lit the brazier in the morning and got her hands burnt as she was trying to extinguish the fire.[55] In large mansions of the upper classes (*kübera*), where a certain hierarchy existed among the servants, young maidservants could either be expected to fulfil only specific tasks, or were treated more patiently until they became competent enough to help with different chores.[56]

Still, domestic service did not take up all of the girls' time. Apart from serving the families, some girls learned various arts and professions, as well as how to read and write. Women engaging in crafts such as needlework and embroidery often passed their experiences on to young girls in their service. Girls with such an opportunity were considered lucky to learn a handicraft by which they could make a living in the future. Besides, different occupations also brought a sense of relaxation for girls who spent most of their time on domestic tasks. It should also be remembered that these children, mostly under the age of ten, were very enthusiastic about playing and amusing themselves. It would be reasonable to presume that they, at odd times, played with the children of their host families. Yet, this was not necessarily an activity allowed by all families, as some believed that it would not be proper for their children to fraternise with servant girls.[57] These domestic servants had other, albeit limited, options to play and socialise with peers. It was not uncommon for them to find female peers among the children of neighbours on the same street, or even children working under the same roof. As time and opportunity allowed, these girls sharing the same street would evidently come together to play and dream of the future.

Many girls were able to make their dreams come true, but there were also those who found that Istanbul fell short of their expectations. So long as they lived under a roof with a job, girls were provided with a relatively secure environment. Indeed, a great majority of domestic servant girls enjoyed such comfort.[58] However, close contact with people living within the same four walls posed its own risks and problems. For the most part, it was practically impossible for girls to stand up to violence, pressure and charges directed against them.[59] Consequently, some ran away from their host families. Some of these fleeing girls were lucky enough to return to their own families, come under the protection of other families or take refuge with the police (*zaptiye*); others were never heard of again.

Intervention in the problems of domestic servant girls was, to a certain degree, possible only when they went beyond the confines of the households they were serving. Until then, they had to endure all sorts of oppression and maltreatment. To illustrate this, a certain Emine, a girl from the town of Ordu, was staying in Çorlu for a 'change of air' (*tebdil-i hava*) along with her host family when she ran away from the house to take refuge in the residence of the *kaimmakam* of Lüleburgaz. This was followed by an intriguing dialogue between the *kaimmakam* and the head of the host family, İbrahim Hakkı, who was the President of the Court of First Instance (*Bidayet Mahkemesi Reisi*) of İskeçe (Xanthi). Protesting against the argument that Emine had run away as she had been battered, İbrahim Hakkı responded: 'A girl may be admonished reprimanded, and may even be beaten at times in case of recurrence [of her wrongdoing], which is undeniably common for every named Mustafa Efendi head of household'.[60] In the middle- and upper-class Istanbulite households, it was probably domestic servant girls of rural origins who were often beaten 'for the sake of discipline'. Apparently in this case, Emine was often beaten for 'disciplinary' reasons. For the problem to become public, she would have to run away, thereby taking the problem beyond the confines of the family.[61]

The problems these girls experienced in Istanbul call for particular attention to their relations with the host family. And this is open to all sorts of interpretation. Records on the provincial girls tell tragic stories of solitude and helplessness. A certain Mihri of Erzurum, who was just fifteen, had arrived in Istanbul at the age of ten accompanied by İhsan Bey, but later ended up having serious problems with her host family and had lost her virginity. She was then forced to leave the house and take refuge in a washerwoman's house, where she was proposed to and married a retired civil servant named Mustafa Efendi. Throughout this ordeal she was all alone, without family or relatives.[62] For provincial girls, losing their virginity, which they preferred to spare for their future husbands, destroyed both their future in Istanbul and their hopes of securing a good marriage. This was a constant source of fear for girls employed in domestic service. In Mihri's case, as she had lost her virginity, she was forced to agree to a marriage with a much older man. Nevertheless, such emphasis on the tragic stories of girls like Mihri with apparently severed family ties, who had unfavourable experiences in the capital, should not rule out the existence of parents and relatives who strived to maintain their connections with children in any way they could. A large majority of provincial girls came from a relatively more accessible part of the Empire, such as central and north-western Anatolia, which enjoyed close links with the capital. Parents hiring out their daughters would receive news of their children through their relatives and acquaintances in Istanbul.

It would contribute to a better understanding of the issue at hand to underline three factors that influenced and shaped the relations of provincial girls with their families. The first factor has to do with the obligations that the wage contract imposed on both parties. Such contracts usually did not specify the exact service duration for the girls. Yet, if everything worked out smoothly, they would serve at least until they reached puberty. Nevertheless, there were certain contracts that required a designated term of employment for the girls. For instance, Fatma Aliye Hanım, daughter of Ahmed Cevdet Pasha, hired a twelve-year-old girl for a period of ten years. The girl's mother was forced to agree that she would reimburse the fee of three *liras*, along with all other expenses incurred for her daughter, if she ever reclaimed or attempted to reclaim her daughter before the expiry of the ten-year period.[63] And this was not an exceptional wage contract. On the contrary, many Istanbulites employed provincial girls on similar terms.[64] They did not like seeing their young female employees maintain close bonds with their families and visitors from the countryside, and therefore did not welcome them into their houses.[65]

The second factor concerns the financial state of families hiring out their daughters. Istanbulite families would often bear the travel expenses for the provincial children they employed, as well as for the accompanying persons, if any. Such expenses, *harcırah* or *masarıf-ı rahiyye* (travel pay), consisted of the round trip costs to Istanbul for the family members accompanying the girls.[66] In most cases, families of the girls could not afford the trips if the expenses were left uncovered. For example, Hatipoğlu Ali of Araç had hired out her nine-year-old daughter to a civil servant in Kastamonu, but had to track her down in Istanbul. He could embark on his twenty-eight day land journey only by selling his black beef cattle (*kara sığır*), which was the main source of livelihood for his family. However, he was left penniless in Istanbul by the time he found his daughter, who he called my beloved one (*ciğerparem*). When he asked his daughter's employers for some money, they dismissed him in disdain by telling him to 'beg for money at the nearest bridge'.[67] It was not always possible for provincial families to be in contact with their daughters any time they wished to be. By keeping these families away from their daughters, employers left the girls in a vulnerable position, rendering them open to abuse.

The third factor is related to those who hired out the girls. In their petitions to the authorities, family members wishing to contact the girls often expressed strong sentiments of longing and affection. However, there is strong evidence that expressions such as 'my beloved child' (*ciğerparem*) used in the petitions were nothing more than exaggerated euphemisms.

Still, the use of such phrases point to the existence of emotional ties. Those who enquired after the girls were usually parents, but could also include close relatives, such as siblings and grandparents. It was not easy for orphan girls hired out by their close relatives to maintain their contact with their home and the relatives they left behind. Many girls were hired out by relatives such as uncles and aunts, but few looked out for the girls when needed, or even enquired after them. Narrating the story of a provincial girl called Fatma, the novel *Besleme* (Foster Servant) written by Edhem Veysi in the early 1920s[68] makes no mention of the relatives of the protagonist who had been brought from a village. After all, with her mother passing away and her father being conscripted into the army, Fatma was a girl considered as a useless burden. Her aunt and uncle, under whose protection she was living, were eager to get rid of her. So, in this case, was it really possible for Fatma to maintain ties with her relatives after being adopted or hired by another family?

Aftermath: Becoming Istanbulites!

The unfortunate circumstances suffered by some of the provincial domestic servants in Istanbul must have spread through word-of-mouth by relatives, fellow countrymen and those travelling back and forth between Istanbul and the provinces. Despite such news, there was an ongoing influx of domestic servant girls to Istanbul from the same villages, towns and cities. For instance, the Arıcık village of Safranbolu sent four domestic servant girls to Istanbul from 20 July to 24 October 1887.[69] Other girls from the same village continued to go in subsequent years.[70] Many villages in central and north-western Anatolia could easily compete with Arıcık as sources of servant girls bound for Istanbul. Istanbul's glamour always prevailed, continuously attracting provincial girls. Deprivation in the provinces converged with the needs of Istanbul, prompting more girls to set out for the capital.

The case of provincial girls sent to Istanbul for employment in domestic service was an example of one-way mobility. In this sense, it is distinguished from the seasonal/temporary mobility of adult males to Istanbul. Some of the rural men frequenting Istanbul for work and earning livelihoods finally settled in the city. Yet, others returned to their hometowns, where they invested the money they earned. In contrast, save for short visits, a large majority of provincial girls never saw their family homes again, due to various reasons. After so many years, neither they nor their family homes were the same as they had been before. Furthermore, those willing to return might not even have family left. But more importantly, the girls had undergone a transformation during their stay in Istanbul. Although they worked as servants, these girls acquired certain cultural patterns and a new lifestyle in the houses of middle- and upper-class Istanbulite families. Thus, over time they became estranged to their homes and the families they had left behind.[71]

Also, the hometowns did not promise the girls a better future than Istanbul. Domestic servant girls ultimately wished to get married after serving for several years. They reached puberty at the age of thirteen or fourteen, thus stepping into adulthood and gaining the right to decide for themselves. However, it would be misleading to assume that reaching adulthood diversified their alternatives in the capital. Most of these girls continued to work in domestic service until marriage, for they had nothing else to do. Some of them were lucky enough to marry soon after reaching puberty, while others had to wait for longer periods. Their employers played an important part in preparing their dowries and finding them proper suitors. Saving penny by penny in return for their services for long years, the wages of many girls were spent on their dowries. If they enjoyed good relations, host families also contributed to their trousseaux.

Getting married and having children in due time, provincial girls built their futures in Istanbul. In fact, all that happened to provincial girls is nothing more than a bitter story of becoming Istanbulites, due to tragic events such as famine. A complete and elaborate history of migration and labour mobility between Istanbul and the provinces in the late Ottoman Empire therefore requires not only focusing on male adults who easily capture the attention of researchers, but also taking a closer look into the stories of provincial children, young girls and women, who were employed in domestic service and led relatively quieter lives within the private confines of households.

Notes

Author's note: I would like to thank Olena Heywood, Colin Heywood, İrfan Kokdaş, Mahmut Tat and Semih Çelik for their helpful comments and suggestions.

1. This study is part of a research project (Child Labour in Ottoman Istanbul: A Research on Children Working in Domestic Services 1800–1920, no: 114K862) funded by the *Scientific and Technological Research Council of Turkey (TÜBİTAK)*.
2. 'Çocukluğum, ömrümün en çok unutmak istediğim dönemidir'. Neyzi, *Evlatlık Bir Kızın Gizli Güncesi: "Pafe"*, p. 13.
3. These girls were hired and settled down with the families in various capacities, such as *besleme*, *evlatlık* (foster child) or *manevi evlat*. All these changing

statuses carried different nuances and meanings, and they change throughout time, especially from the late-eighteenth century to the beginning of the twentieth century. For a more detailed description and analysis, see Araz and Kokdaş: 'In Between Market and Charity', pp. 81–108.
4. Duben and Behar, *Istanbul Households*, pp. 62–9.
5. See Karakışla, *Osmanlı Hanımları ve Hizmetçi Kadınlar (1869–1927)*; Özbay, *Turkish Female Child Labor in Domestic Work*.
6. See Erdem, *Slavery in the Ottoman Empire and its Demise, 1800–1909*; Toledano, *Slavery and Abolition in the Ottoman Middle East*.
7. Toledano, *Slavery and Abolition in the Ottoman Middle East*, pp. 112; Parlatır, *Tanzimat Edebiyatında Kölelik*, pp. 58–67.
8. See Maksudyan, 'Foster-Daughter or Servant, Charity or Abuse', p. 493; Özbay, *Turkish Female Child Labor in Domestic Work*.
9. On the evolution of Istanbul's population, see Behar, *Osmanlı İmparatorluğu'nun ve Türkiye'nin Nüfusu 1500–1927*, pp. 69–83; Karpat, *Ottoman Population 1830–1914*, pp. 86–105.
10. Findley, *Ottoman Civil Officialdom*, pp. 22–8.
11. Araz, 'Kölelik ve Özgürlük Arasında', p. 306.
12. See BOA, Y.PRK.KOM. 3/68 (1299/1882); BOA, DH.MKT. 2704/97 (1326/1908); BOA, ŞD. 2554/19 (1303/1886); BOA, ZB. 329/106 (1326/1909); BOA, İ.MVL. 584/26270 (1284/1867); BOA, MV. 220/85 (1338/1920); BOA, DH.MKT. 1061/5 (1324/1906); BOA, DH.İD. 161–1/6 (1331/1913); BOA, ZB. 490/101 (1326/1908). Also see Özbek, *Osmanlı İmparatorluğu'nda Sosyal Devlet*, pp. 195–253; Maksudyan, *Orphans and Destitute Children in the Late Ottoman Empire*.
13. See Başaran, *Selim III*; Nacar, 'İstanbul Gurbetinde Çalışmak ve Yaşamak', pp. 30–4; Kırlı, 'İstanbul'da Hemşehrilik Tabanlı Tabakalar/Yoğunlaşmalar', pp. 72–9; Lévy-Aksu, *Osmanlı İstanbulu'nda Asayiş 1879–1909*, pp. 77–84.
14. Başaran, *Selim III*, pp. 106–67.
15. Kokdaş and Araz, 'İstanbul'da Ev İçi Hizmetlerinde İstihdam Edilen Anadolulu Kız Çocuklarının Göç Ağları Üzerine Bir Değerlendirme (1845–1911)', pp. 41–68.
16. For a study drawing upon court records, yet not pertaining to Istanbul, see Kurt, *Bursa Sicillerine Göre Osmanlı Ailesi (1839–1876)*, pp. 91–106.
17. Barkley, *A Ride Through Asia Minor and Armenia*, pp. 49, 64–5.
18. See Öntuğ, *Ahmed Vefik Paşa'nın Anadolu Sağ Kol Müfettişliği*; Serbestoğlu, *Bir Taşra Şehrinde Tanzimat ve Modernleşme Canik Sancağı 1863–1865*.
19. Ahmet Şerif, *Anadolu'da Tanin*, p. 15.
20. For examples on the subject, see Çadırcı, *Tanzimat Döneminde Anadolu Kentlerinin Sosyal ve Ekonomik Yapısı*; Ortaylı, *Tanzimat Devrinde Osmanlı Mahallî İdareleri (1840–1880)*; Avcı, *Osmanlı Hükümet Konakları*; Kırmızı, *Abdülhamid'in Valileri*.
21. Şerafeddin Mağmumi, *Yüzyıl Önce Anadolu ve Suriye*.

22. For famines and other disasters in Anatolia, see Erler, *Osmanlı Devleti'nde Kuraklık ve Kıtlık Olayları (1800–1880)*; Ertem, 'Eating the Last Seed'.
23. Öztelli, *Uyan Padişahım*, pp. 609–25.
24. Erler, *Osmanlı Devleti'nde Kuraklık ve Kıtlık Olayları*; Ertem, 'Eating the Last Seed'.
25. BOA, DH.MUİ. 1–6/55 (1327/1909) and various dates; Şaşmaz, 'Niğde ve Çevresinde Kıtlık (1887–1892)', p. 184; Bayar, '1873–1875 Orta Anadolu Kıtlığı', p. 163. For the non-Turkish areas of the Empire, see Çiçek, *War and State Formation in Syria*, p. 244; Al-Qattan, 'When Mothers Ate Their Children', p. 720.
26. For a number of examples, see BOA, A.DVN.MHM. 2–A/75 (1262/1846); BOA, A.DVN. 16/56 (1262/1846); BOA, A.MKT. 46/87 (1262/1846); BOA, ŞD. 1642/19 (1290/1874); BOA, Y.PRK.UM. 11/8 (1305/1888).
27. Özkan, 'Unification of the Market, Fragmentation of the People', pp. 217–45.
28. BOA, İ.MVL. 78/1519 (1262/1846) and various dates; BOA, İ.MVL. 79/1545 (1262/1846) and various dates; BOA, A.MKT.MHM. 2/19 (1262/1846).
29. Bayar, '1873–1875 Orta Anadolu Kıtlığı', pp. 162–4.
30. Öztelli, *Uyan Padişahım*, p. 618.
31. Çelik, 'No Work for Anyone in this Country of Misery', pp. 148–73.
32. Kokdaş and Araz, 'İstanbul'da Ev İçi Hizmetlerinde İstihdam Edilen Anadolulu Kız Çocuklarının Göç Ağları Üzerine Bir Değerlendirme (1845–1911)', pp. 41–68.
33. Ibid. Unless otherwise stated, the term 'central and northwestern Anatolia' refers throughout the article to towns and cities falling to the north and northwest of Ankara.
34. Kokdaş and Araz, 'İstanbul'da Ev İçi Hizmetlerinde İstihdam Edilen Anadolulu Kız Çocuklarının Göç Ağları Üzerine Bir Değerlendirme (1845–1911)', pp. 41–68.
35. For the family, see BOA, İ.MVL. 79/1545 (1262/1846) and various dates. For the hired sisters, see MCR 62, p. 63a, no. 1 (1262/1846); MCR 62, p. 68b, no. 4 (1262/1846).
36. MCR 62, p. 29b, no. 6 (1262/1846); MCR 62, p. 40b, no. 6 (1262/1846).
37. Kırlı, 'İstanbul'da Hemşehrilik Tabanlı Tabakalar/Yoğunlaşmalar', p. 74; Başaran, *Selim III, Social Control and Policing*, pp. 133–48, particularly the map on p. 138.
38. Basiretçi Ali Efendi, *İstanbul Mektupları*, p. 327.
39. See ACR 425, p. 83a, no. 2 (1263/1847); MCR 62, p. 16a, no. 4 (1262/1846); MCR 62, p. 18b, no. 5 (1262/1846); DCR 111, p. 29a, no. 3 (1262/1846); DCR 111, p. 60b, no. 4 (1262/ 1846).
40. DCR 147, p. 83, no. 37 (1308/1891); DCR 165, p. 82, no. 142–3 (1321/1904).
41. BCR 421, p. 70b, no. 6 (1263/1847); BCR 421, p. 76a, no. 2 (1263/1847).
42. Ortaylı, *Tanzimat Devrinde Osmanlı Mahallî İdareleri*; Findley, *Ottoman Civil Officialdom*, pp. 22–8; Aydın et al., *Küçük Asya'nın Bin Yüzü: Ankara*, p. 201.

43. Özbek, 'The Regulation of Prostitution in Beyoğlu (1875–1915)', pp. 555–68; Maksudyan, 'Foster-Daughter or Servant, Charity or Abuse', pp. 500–1.
44. Bartley, *Prostitution Prevention and Reform in England 1860–1914*, p. 103.
45. *Hanımlara Mahsus Gazete*, no. 7–209, p. 8. This trade also had its repercussions in the Ottoman Empire. See Biancani, 'International Migration and Sex Work in Early Twentieth-Century Cairo', pp. 109–33.
46. Rana Hanım bint Safvet, 'Ahretlik', *Hanımlara Mahsus Gazete*, no. 56, pp. 4–5; no. 57, pp. 2–4; no. 58, pp. 4–5.
47. 'Hıdmetci Kızlar', *Sabah*, no. 4935, p. 1.
48. As far as the regulation of juvenile female mobility between the capital and provinces is concerned, it was quite natural for the authorities to address the *vilayet* of Kastamonu in the provinces. As a large administrative unit consisting of the four *sancak*s of Çankırı, Bolu, Sinop and Kastamonu, the *vilayet* was the main source of domestic servant girls sent to Istanbul. For a general view and administrative structure of the *vilayet* in the late nineteenth century, see Gömeç et al., *Kastamonu Salnamesi*.
49. BOA, DH.MKT. 1417/14 (1304/1887).
50. SCR 2147, p. 55b/56a; BOA, DH.MKT. 1417/14 (1304/1887).
51. BOA, DH.MKT. 1785/68 (1308/1890); BOA, DH.MKT. 1799/3 (1308/1891); BOA, Y.PRK.ASK. 154/70 (1317/1899); BOA, ZB. 415/65 (1322/1905).
52. Kokdaş and Araz, 'İstanbul'da Ev İçi Hizmetlerinde İstihdam Edilen Anadolulu Kız Çocuklarının Göç Ağları Üzerine Bir Değerlendirme (1845–1911)', pp. 41–68.
53. Horn, *The Rise and Fall of the Victorian Servant*, p. 76.
54. Araz and Kokdaş, 'In Between Market and Charity', pp. 81–108.
55. BOA, DH.EUM.KADL. 01/39 (1326/1910).
56. Zilfi, 'Servants, Slaves, and the Domestic Order in the Ottoman Middle East', pp. 17–18.
57. Doktor Kerim, 'Çocuğunuzun Bir Kapıda Besleme Olmasını İster Misiniz?', pp. 33–5.
58. Araz and Kokdaş, 'In Between Market and Charity', pp. 81–108.
59. See BOA, DH.EUM.AYŞ. 12/43 (1335/1919); BOA, DH.EUM.KADL. 3/13 (1328/1910); BOA, DH.EUM.THR. 48/3 (1312/1894).
60. 'terbiye için bir kız tekdir ve tevbih edilir tekerrür halinde bazen dövüldüğü de olur bu hal her hane sahibinde görülür bu hal kabil-i inkar değildir'.
61. BOA, TFR.I.ED. 4/346 (1321/1903). Also see BOA, DH.MKT. 224/79 (1310/1893).
62. DCR 160, p. 6, no. 7 (1318/1900).
63. IMM Atatürk Library, FA. EVR. 12/12, undated. Also see BOA, DH.H. 26/8 (1329/1911).
64. See OCR 1476 (1323–30/1905–12).
65. BOA, DH.MUİ. 41-2/20 (1327/1909); BOA, DH.EUM.VRK. 21/50 (1329/1911).

66. BOA, DH.EUM.VRK. 21/50 (1329/1911).
67. BOA, DH.MUİ. 41–2/20 (1327/1909). Also see BOA, DH.EUM.THR. 49/31 (1328/1910).
68. Veysi, *Besleme*.
69. SCR 2147, p. 5a, no. 23 (1304/1887); SCR 2147, p. 5b, no. 26 (1304/1887); SCR 2147, p. 9b, no. 50 (1305/1887); SCR 2147, p. 9b, no. 51 (1305/1887).
70. SCR 2156/1, p. 219, no. 225 (1324/1906).
71. 'Hıdmetci Kızlar', *Sabah*, no. 4935, p. 1.

Bibliography

Archival Sources

Cumhurbaşkanlığı Devlet Arşivleri (Presidency Ottoman Archives) (BOA)
Bab-ı Asafi Divan-ı Hümayun Kalemi (A.DVN.) 16/56 (1262–1846).
Bab-ı Asafi Divan-ı Hümayun Mühimme Kalemi (A.DVN.MHM.) 2–A/75 (1262–1846).
Bab-ı Asafi Mektubi Kalemi (A.MKT.) 46/87 (1262–1846).
Dahiliye Nezareti Emniyet-i Umumiye Kısm-ı Adli Kalemi Evrakı (DH.EUM. KADL.) 1/39 (1326/1910), 3/13 (1328/1910).
Dahiliye Nezareti Emniyet-i Umumiye Tahrirat Kalemi Evrakı (DH.EUM.THR.) 48/3 (1312/1894), 49/31 (1328/1910).
Dahiliye Nezareti Emniyet-i Umumiye Evrak Odası Kalemi Evrakı (DH.EUM. VRK.) 21/50 (1329–1911).
Dahiliye Nezareti Emniyet-i Umumiye Asayiş Kalemi Evrakı (DH.EUM.AYŞ.) 12/43 (1335/1919).
Dahiliye Nezareti Hukuk Evrakı (DH.H.) 26/8 (1329/1911).
Dahiliye Nezareti İdare Evrakı (DH.İD.) 161–1/6 (1331/1913).
Dahiliye Nezareti Mektubi Kalemi Evrakı (DH.MKT.) 224/79 (1310/1893), 1061/5 (1324/1906), 1417/14 (1304/1887), 1785/68 (1308/1890), 1799/3 (1308/1891), 2704/97 (1326/1908).
Dahiliye Nezareti Muhaberat-ı Umumiye İdaresi Evrakı (DH.MUİ.) 1–6/55 (1327/1909), 41–2/20 (1327/1909).
İrade Meclis-i Vala (İ.MVL.) 78/1519 (1262/1846), 79/1545 (1262/1846), 584/26270 (1284/1867).
Meclis-i Vükela Mazbataları (MV.) 220/85 (1338/1920).
Ordu Şer'iyye Sicilleri-Ordu Court Records (OCR) 1476 (1323–30/1905–12).
Rumeli Müfettişliği Edirne Evrakı (TFR.I.ED.) 4/346 (1321/1903).
Sadaret Mektubi Mühimme Kalemi Evrakı (A.MKT.MHM.) 2/19 (1262/1846).
Safranbolu Şer'iyye Sicilleri-Safranbolu Court Records (SCR) Reg. 2147; Reg. 2156/1.
Şura-yı Devlet Evrakı (ŞD.) 1642/19 (1290/1874), 2554/19 (1303/1886).
Yıldız Perakende Evrakı Askerî Maruzat (Y.PRK.ASK.) 154/70 (1317/1899).
Yıldız Perakende Evrakı Komisyonlar Maruzatı (Y.PRK.KOM.) 3/68 (1299/1882).
Yıldız Perakende Evrakı Umumi (Y.PRK.UM.) 11/8 (1305/1888).

Zabtiye Nezareti Evrakı (ZB.) 329/106 (1326/1909), 415/65 (1322/1905), 490/101 (1326/1908).
Atatürk Library (Istanbul)
Fatma Aliye Evrakı (FA.EVR.) 12/12.
İstanbul Müftülüğü Şer'iyye Sicilleri Arşivi (Archives of Istanbul Religious Courts)
Ahi Çelebi Şer'iyye Sicilleri – Ahi Çelebi Court Records (ACR) 425.
Bab Şer'iyye Sicilleri – Bab Court Records (BCR) 421.
Davudpaşa Şer'iyye Sicilleri – Davudpaşa Court Records (DCR) 111; 147; 160; 165.
Mahmudpaşa Şer'iyye Sicilleri – Mahmudpaşa Court Records (MCR) 62.
Journals and Newspapers
Doktor Kerim, 'Çocuğunuzun Bir Kapıda Besleme Olmasını İster Misiniz?', *Resimli Ay*, no. 10, Teşrinisani 1341/November 1925.
Hanımlara Mahsus Gazete, no. 7–209, 22 Nisan 1315/4 May 1899.
'Hıdmetci Kızlar', *Sabah*, no. 4935, 10 Temmuz 1319/23 July 1903.
Rana Hanım bint Safvet, 'Ahretlik', *Hanımlara Mahsus Gazete*, no. 56, 21 Mart 1312/2 April 1896; no. 57, 28 Mart 1312/9 April 1896; no. 58, 4 Nisan 1312/16 April 1896.

Secondary Sources
Ahmet Şerif, *Anadolu'da Tanin*, vol. 1, ed. Mehmed Çetin Börekçi (Ankara: Türk Tarih Kurumu Yayınları, 1999).
Al-Qattan, Najwa, 'When Mothers Ate Their Children: Wartime Memory and the Language of Food in Syria and Lebanon', *International Journal of Middle East Studies*, 46/1, (2014), pp. 719–36.
Araz, Yahya, 'Kölelik ve Özgürlük Arasında: 19. Yüzyılın Ortalarında İstanbul'da Çerkes Çocuklar', in Kerim İlker Bulunur, Fatih Bozkurt and Mahmut Cihat İzgi (eds), *Osmanlı'da Şehir, Vakıf ve Sosyal Hayat* (Istanbul: Mahya Yayınları, 2017), pp. 29–308.
Araz, Yahya, and İrfan Kokdaş, 'In Between Market and Charity: Child Domestic Work and Changing Labor Relations in Nineteenth-Century Ottoman Istanbul', *International Labor and Working-Class History*, 97 (2020), pp. 81–108.
Avcı, Yasemin, *Osmanlı Hükümet Konakları Tanzimat Döneminde Kent Mekanında Devletin Erki ve Temsili* (Istanbul: Tarih Vakfı Yurt Yayınları, 2017).
Aydın, Suavi, Ömer Türkoğlu, Kudret Emiroğlu, and E. Deniz Özsoy, *Küçük Asya'nın Bin Yüzü: Ankara* (Ankara: Dost Kitabevi, 2005).
Barkley, Henry C., *A Ride Through Asia Minor and Armenia* (London: Murray, 1891).
Bartley, Paula, *Prostitution Prevention and Reform in England 1860–1914* (London and New York: Routledge, 2000).
Basiretçi Ali Efendi, *İstanbul Mektupları*, ed. Nuri Sağlam (Istanbul: Kitabevi, 2001).

Başaran, Betül, *Selim III, Social Control and Policing in Istanbul at the End of the Eighteenth Century, Between Crisis and Order* (Leiden: Brill, 2014).

Bayar, Yener, '1873–1875 Orta Anadolu Kıtlığı', unpublished MA thesis, Marmara Üniversitesi, 2013.

Behar, Cem, *Osmanlı İmparatorluğu'nun ve Türkiye'nin Nüfusu 1500–1927* (Ankara: T. C. Başbakanlık Devlet İstatistik Enstitüsü, 2003).

Biancani, Francesca, 'International Migration and Sex Work in Early Twentieth-Century Cairo', in Cyrus Schayech, Avner Wishnitzer and Liat Kozma (eds), *A Global Middle East Mobility, Materiality and Culture in the Modern Age, 1880–1940* (London–New York: I. B. Tauris, 2015), pp. 109–33.

Çadırcı, Musa, *Tanzimat Döneminde Anadolu Kentlerinin Sosyal ve Ekonomik Yapısı*, 3rd edn (Ankara: Türk Tarih Kurumu Yayınları, 2013).

Çelik, Semih, '"No Work for Anyone in this Country of Misery": Famine and Labour Relations in Mid-Nineteenth Century Anatolia', in Leda Papastefanaki and Erdem Kabadayı (eds), *Working in Greece and Turkey: A Comparative Labour History from Empires to Nation-States, 1840–1940* (New York: Berghahn Books, 2020), pp. 148–73.

Çiçek, M. Talha, *War and State Formation in Syria: Cemal Pasha's Governorate during the World War I, 1914–1917* (London: Routledge, 2014).

Duben, Alan, and Cem Behar, *Istanbul Households Marriage, Family and Fertility 1880–1940* (Cambridge: Cambridge University Press, 1991).

Edhem Veysi, *Besleme* (Samsun: Şems Matbaası, 1339).

Erdem, Y. Hakan, *Slavery in the Ottoman Empire and its Demise, 1800–1909* (London: Macmillan Press Ltd, 1996).

Erler, Mehmet Yavuz, *Osmanlı Devleti'nde Kuraklık ve Kıtlık Olayları (1800–1880)* (Istanbul: Libra Yayıncılık ve Kitapçılık, 2010).

Ertem, Özge, 'Eating the Last Seed: Famine, Empire, Survival and Order in Ottoman Anatolia in the Late Nineteenth Century', unpublished PhD dissertation, European University Institute, 2012.

Findley, Carter Vaughn, *Ottoman Civil Officialdom: A Social History* (Princeton: Princeton University Press, 1989).

Gömeç, Saadettin Yağmur, Hamiyet Sezer Feyzioğlu and Tülay Ercoşkun, *Kastamonu Salnamesi* (Ankara: Berikan Yayınevi, 2016).

Horn, Pamela, *The Rise and Fall of the Victorian Servant* (Stroud: Sutton Publishing, 1997).

Karakışla, Yavuz Selim, *Osmanlı Hanımları ve Hizmetçi Kadınlar (1869–1927)* (Istanbul: Akıl Fikir Yayınları, 2014).

Karpat, Kemal H., *Ottoman Population 1830–1914* (Madison: University of Wisconsin Press, 1985).

Kırlı, Cengiz, 'İstanbul'da Hemşehrilik Tabanlı Tabakalar/Yoğunlaşmalar', in Arif Bilgin (ed.), *Antikçağ'dan XXI. Yüzyıla Büyük İstanbul Tarihi: Toplum*, vol. 4 (Istanbul: İslam Araştırmaları Merkezi-İBB Kültür AŞ., 2015), pp. 72–9.

Kırmızı, Abdülhamit, *Abdülhamid'in Valileri Osmanlı Vilayet İdaresi 1895–1908*, 4th edn (Istanbul: Klasik Yayınları, 2016).

Kokdaş, İrfan, and Yahya Araz, 'İstanbul'da Ev İçi Hizmetlerinde İstihdam Edilen Anadolulu Kız Çocuklarının Göç Ağları Üzerine Bir Değerlendirme (1845–1911)', *Tarih İncelemeleri Dergisi*, 33/1 (2018), pp. 41–68.

Kurt, Abdurrahman, *Bursa Sicillerine Göre Osmanlı Ailesi (183–1876)* (Ankara: Sentez Yayıncılık, 2013).

Lévy-Aksu, Noémi, *Osmanlı İstanbul'unda Asayiş 1879–1909*, trans. Serra Akyüz (Istanbul: İletişim Yayınları, 2017).

Maksudyan, Nazan, 'Foster-Daughter or Servant, Charity or Abuse: Beslemes in the Late Ottoman Empire', *Journal of Historical Sociology*, 21/4 (2008), pp. 488–512.

——, *Orphans and Destitute Children in the Late Ottoman Empire* (New York: Syracuse University Press, 2014).

Nacar, Can, 'İstanbul Gurbetinde Çalışmak ve Yaşamak', *Toplumsal Tarih*, 245 (2014), pp. 30–4.

Neyzi, Ali H., *Evlatlık Bir Kızın Gizli Güncesi: "Pafe"* (Istanbul: Cem Yayınevi, 2005).

Ortaylı, İlber, *Tanzimat Devrinde Osmanlı Mahallî İdareleri (1840–1880)* (Ankara: Türk Tarih Kurumu Yayınları, 2011).

Öntuğ, M. Murat, *Ahmed Vefik Paşa'nın Anadolu Sağ Kol Müfettişliği* (Konya: Palet Yayınları, 2009).

Özbay, Ferhunde, *Turkish Female Child Labor in Domestic Work: Past and Present* (Istanbul: ILO/IPEC, 1999).

Özbek, Müge, 'The Regulation of Prostitution in Beyoğlu (1875–1915)', *Middle Eastern Studies*, 46/4 (2010), pp. 555–68.

Özbek, Nadir, *Osmanlı İmparatorluğu'nda Sosyal Devlet Siyaset, İktidar ve Meşruiyet 1876–1914* (Istanbul: İletişim Yayınları, 2002).

Özkan, Fulya, 'Unification of the Market, Fragmentation of the People: Famine and Migration on the Tabzon-Bayezid Road in the Late Ottoman Empire', in Selim Karahasanoğlu and Deniz Cenk Demir (eds), *History from Below: A Tribute in Memory of Donald Quataert* (Istanbul: Bilgi University Press, 2016), pp. 217–45.

Öztelli, Cahit, *Uyan Padişahım* (Istanbul: Milliyet Yayınları, 1976).

Parlatır, İsmail, *Tanzimat Edebiyatında Kölelik* (Ankara: Yargı Yayınevi, 2012).

Serbestoğlu, İbrahim, *Bir Taşra Şehrinde Tanzimat ve Modernleşme Canik Sancağı 1863–1865* (Malatya: Mengüceli Yayınları, 2015).

Şaşmaz, Musa, 'Niğde ve Çevresinde Kıtlık (1887–1892)', in Musa Şaşmaz (ed.), *Niğde Tarihi Üzerine* (Istanbul: Kitabevi, 2005), pp. 181–209.

Şerafeddin Mağmumi, *Bir Osmanlı Doktorunun Seyahat Anıları Yüzyıl Önce Anadolu ve Suriye*, trans. Cahit Kayra (Istanbul: Boyut Kitapları, 2008).

Toledano, Ehud R., *Slavery and Abolition in the Ottoman Middle East* (Seattle and London: University of Washington Press, 1998).

Zilfi, Madeline C., 'Servants, Slaves, and the Domestic Order in the Ottoman Middle East', *Hawwa*, 2/1 (2004), pp. 1–33.

Chapter 9

Muslim Orphans and the *Shari'ah* in Nineteenth-century Palestine: Cases from Nablus

Mahmoud Yazbak

Bringing Up Orphans

A document from the court records (*sijill*)[1] of the *Shari'ah* court of Nablus from 1881 stated that:

> Upon the death of Hajj Hamdan son of Hajj Khalil Darwaza from the Qaysariyya quarter of Nablus, his legal inheritance passed to his wife Amina . . . and to his [two] adult sons, Yusuf and Salih, and to his . . . [other sex] minor children.
>
> Before the enlightened and honorable *Shari'ah* court of Nablus came Hajj Yusuf, the eldest of the deceased's sons. He claimed that his father, before his death, had lent twenty-five *qurush* to al-Sayyid 'Umar al-Khmmash from the al-Habala quarter . . . [Hajj Yusuf continued that] in the second of Shawwal 1298 AH (28 August 1881), his father, before his death, while being compos mentis (*rashid*), had nominated him as his chosen guardian (*wasiyy mukhtar*) over his minor children. . . . [Hajj Yusuf] accepted the duty at the time of the nomination and continued to accept it after the death of the father, who had died in the eighteenth century of *Dhi-al-Qi'da* of that year (12 October 1881) after reiterating his choice. Since the father had died without getting back the aforementioned loan, and because his properties were divided among the legal legatees, the loan had become their property through the inheritance laws. At this point, the 'alleged' *wasiyy* became the plaintiff and asked the court on behalf of himself and on behalf of the orphans whose guardian he was, to order the borrower (now the defendant) to pay him his legal share in the inheritance and the shares of the orphans, for a male twice as much as a female according to the *Shari'ah* law. Questioned by the *qadi* (judge) about the loan, the defendant acknowledged that he had borrowed the money, but denied that Yusuf Darwaza was *wasiyy mukhtar* with the right to collect the debt and to administer the orphans' wealth. At this stage the *qadi* asked the plaintiff to prove before the court that he was indeed the *wasiyy mukhtar* of his father. The plaintiff thereupon brought to the court two witnesses who attested to his position.

Muslim Orphans: Cases from Nablus

The *qadi* then judged that Yusuf Darwazah was the *wasiyy mukhtar* of the orphans and of their inherited property, and ordered the defendant to pay to the *wasiyy mukhtar* the orphans' legal portion of their inherited debt.[2]

Until the 1860s, and mainly under the *Tanzimat* reforms, no state orphanages existed in the Ottoman Empire. The first orphanage was founded by the Ottomans in 1867 in the *vilayet* (province) of Danube. In 1874 the Ottoman state established an orphanage in Jerusalem, which was the only Ottoman orphanage in Palestine up to the end of Ottoman rule.[3] The establishment of Ottoman orphanages was a renovation in the wake of Christian missionary institutions acting throughout the Ottoman Empire, including Palestine.[4] In 1851, the Ottomans set up an Administration of Orphans' Funds (*Nizarit Amwal al-Aytam*). This constituted a form of modernisation specific to the Ottoman case, where the state was responsible for orphans in the Empire. Up to then, the Ottoman state reforms and laws concerning orphans' rights had been entirely based on Islamic jurisprudence, a topic that will be covered in detail in this chapter. Although the *Tanzimat* reforms transformed the state's approach to orphan children, this was not a departure from the early modern attitude. Rather, it maintained a certain degree of continuity with the early modern Islamic approach in that it adhered strictly to *Shari'ah* law.

In the absence of orphanages or other public institutions to look after orphans in pre-modern Islamic societies but also in Ottoman culture, the above case raises many questions concerning the bringing up of orphans in Islamic society. How did Islam define an orphan? Who was to bring them up? What institutions looked after them? What were their sources of living? How did Islam see the relationships between them and their extended families? What responsibilities had a family over its orphans? The answers to these questions are tackled in this chapter in detail. Before dealing with them, it is worth briefly examining how Islam considered orphans in general.

Islam and Orphans

In Islamic jurisprudence minor children became orphans upon the death of their father, not their mother. This, of course, had much to do with the social construction of gender in Muslim societies. That is, it was the father who had the full responsibility for the material well-being and maintenance (*nafaqa*) of his family, and he, not the mother, was the natural guardian of his children.[5] Automatically, when a father died, the guardianship of the persons (*wilayat al-nafs*) and the property (*wilayat al-mal*) passed to the paternal grandfather.[6] The grandfather took over the father's duties toward the orphans, including the overall responsibility for their physical care, socialisation and education. At the same time, the grandfather had the right to choose someone else as guardian instead of him.[7] Not surprisingly, we find rich merchants who, wanting to safeguard the future of their wealth and that of their minor children, appointing a guardian during their lifetime, someone whom they could trust to look after the interests of their minor children and their wealth.[8] When a minor became an orphan with no living grandfather, it was always the main duty of their relatives to look after them.

Although such a chosen guardian took up his duties automatically after the father's death, the above document shows that he needed official recognition and appointment from the *qadi*, which would only follow after the court had been presented with convincing evidence that the father, when he chose the *wasiyy*, had been compos mentis (*rashid*). As the court case shows, this involved a trial initiated by the 'alleged' *wasiyy*, in which he had to refute claims to the contrary brought by a second party.[9]

It is important to recall that the Prophet himself was an orphan. Born after his father's death, Muhammad was placed under the guardianship of his paternal grandfather and, when the latter died, that of his uncle. With the many casualties among his followers during the early wars (especially the battle of *Uhud*), Muhammad was confronted with increasing numbers of orphans in his camp.[10] Being aware of the difficulties that orphans might face, the Qur'an called upon believers in twenty-three different verses (*aya*s) to treat them justly and with kindness.

The Qur'an and the Hadith stress the believer's responsibility towards the poor, especially orphans. It was said that during the Prophet's era, if there happened to be no relatives for a certain orphan, or if they did not or could not take care of their orphans, the Prophet himself, as the leader of the community, took the responsibility upon himself. Later this was then transferred to the *qadi* as the representative of the Muslim community, whose task it became to appoint someone trustworthy as guardian.[11]

When it institutionalised the community's responsibility towards orphans in general, the *Shari'ah* also put in place a system that would adequately guarantee lonely and poor orphans a minimum livelihood. This was the *zakat*, the obligatory alms that are one of the five pillars of the Islamic faith, which aimed among other things to raise money for social aid, and orphans were allotted a share in this aid.[12] Charity (*sadaqa*) to the poor in Islam was portrayed as the true gateway to paradise.

Evidence from medieval Cairo, Damascus, Baghdad and Jerusalem shows that governors, as well as ordinary people, endowed properties to establish elementary schools for orphans,[13] frequently located near a mosque or adjoining a *madrasa*. Orphans studying in these schools received daily stipends and sustenance and were also given winter and summer garments.[14] The kitchens affiliated to mosques and other holy places (*simat*), such as al-Haram al-Ibrahimi in Hebron, Sidna 'Ali near Jaffa, and al-Khadir in Nablus, from the Middle Ages until the late Ottoman period, distributed food to the poor in general and, of course, to needy orphans. The Ottomans also established large public soup kitchens (*'imaret*) adjoining the imperial mosques in Ottoman Turkey and Jerusalem.[15] For example, by the end of the eighteenth century, up to 30,000 people a day were fed at the 'Imarets of Constantinople alone.[16]

The Orphan's **Kafil** *or Guardian*

In his efforts to encourage Muslims to look after orphans, Muhammad promised those who took on the duty a place in Heaven by saying: 'I and the *kafil* (guardian or sponsor) will be together in heaven like this: and the Prophet crossed his two fingers'.[17] The *Shari'ah* was quite specific regarding the role of guardians and the protection of orphan's rights.[18] It allowed guardians to invest their ward's money, setting aside for themselves some form of remuneration if necessary.[19] That is to say that wealthy orphans were viewed as an asset, because of the financial benefits they could bring their guardians.[20] As there was also the reward of the Hereafter, it was never too difficult to find guardians for them.

It is when we come to the Ottoman period that we begin to find a good deal of information on many aspects of the daily lives of orphans in the court records (*sijillat*). Usually, after the death of a minor's father, whether the division of his inheritance had come to court or not, someone from among the orphan's relatives appeared in court and asked to be nominated as guardian. Often this would be someone chosen by the other members of the extended family. Cases such as this read as follows:

> In the honourable *Shari'ah* court session held in Nablus, our respected lord, the *qadi* . . . nominated the holder of this legal document of nomination, Hafiz *efendi* son of the great dynasty of the . . . 'Abd al-Hadi respected *umara'*, as the lawful guardian, to legally act and speak on behalf of Dhib *efendi*, Muhammad *efendi*, Fahim *efendi*, and Sa'da, the minor children of his deceased cousin Husayn *efendi* . . . to deal with all matters concerning the minors in the minors' interest. Our lord the *qadi*, allowed the guardian, in accordance with his guardianship, to lay his hand on the minors' inherited property and funds. [He was allowed too] to rent, cultivate and administer its products and incomes on behalf of the minors. At the same time, he was requested to support all that

they needed for their living in terms of food and garments. [The guardian] was allowed too to legally invest all funds, belonging to the minors, after deducting annual expenses. Our lord, the aforementioned *qadi* prohibited him to sell any of the minors' [inherited] property. The aforementioned guardian committed himself to carry over the duty without any payment to do God's pleasing. When the guardian's reliability, suitability, religiousness and integrity was attested by Rif'atlu 'Abd al-Hadi Zade and by Makrimatlu Shaykh Sayf al-Din *efendi*, our lord the *qadi* recited for his sake the Qur'anic verse: 'those who unjustly devour the property of orphans, they do but eat a fire into their own bodies, and will soon be enduring a blazing fire'.[21]

Looking closely at this nomination document, we realise that it belonged to orphans of the 'Abd al-Hadi family, one of the most powerful and wealthiest families of Nablus. Though the document does not specify how large the orphans' inheritance was, it points out that they inherited a significant number of movable and immovable assets. It is also obvious that administering such large assets would need much energy and effort. The guardian, a family relative, himself of the wealthiest Nabulsi elite, was chosen by other family members to take on the duty with no remuneration. Of course, the family's interest in preserving its assets stood behind its readiness to guard its orphans and their material belongings. What is interesting here is that the *qadi* permitted the guardian to enhance the orphans' inherited assets. He was encouraged to cultivate their lands and to develop the principal, by either lending money for interest (*murabaha*) or by commercialisation. While care for orphans in general was subsumed within the emphasis the Qur'an placed on the well-being of the weak and destitute in society, orphans who inherited property were singled out in the Qur'an and later prophetic traditions for two main reasons. One is that the fact that they had funds or real estate to their name made it attractive for people to seek guardianship over them. This widened the choice for the *qadi*, who was thus more likely to find the right person, that is, someone trustworthy. Not only was it important to ensure that the orphans could make a good start in life once they reached adulthood, but wise investment of the orphan's funds contributed to the economy of the town or region. The second reason has to do with the other side of the coin: as I already indicated, there was always the danger that a guardian might abuse his stewardship, if not completely cheat the orphan out of his wealth. Thus, the Qur'an, time and again, admonished the believers to act faithfully when accepting guardianship of orphans. For example: 'Do not interfere with the property of orphans except with the best of motives, until they reach maturity. Keep your promises; you are accountable for all that you promise.'[22] In another verse, the Qur'an says:

[T]hey question you concerning orphans, say: to deal justly with them is best. If you mix their affairs with yours, remember they are your brothers. God knows the just from the unjust. They ask thee concerning orphans, say: the best thing to do is what is for their good.[23]

Prophetic traditions, *fiqh* (jurisprudence) and *fatawa* books encouraged guardians not to freeze the orphan's money, and they went into great detail as to how a guardian should invest the property of his ward, again stressing this as his duty. It is believed that the Prophet encouraged guardians not to let an orphan's property sit idle: 'Beware! Whoever is the guardian of an orphan who has property, should trade with it, and should not leave it [undeveloped], so that the *zakat* should consume it'.[24] Al-Astrushni's book, *Ahkam al-Sighar* (Childrens' Bylaws), which summarises the Hanafi's attitude towards orphans, deals in detail with the large spectrum of matters relating to the investment of orphans' assets.[25] The same goes for al-Ramli, the famous seventeenth-century Palestinian *mufti*. In one case, al-Ramli was asked, for example, '... whether the chosen guardian does or does not have the right to trade with his ward's money, lend it with interest (*ribh*) of twenty percent for example?'. The response he gave was: 'Yes, the guardian is allowed to do that'.[26] To encourage guardians to invest the assets and to trade with them, al-Astrushni made it clear that if the guardian lost some or all of the orphan's assets in the process of legally trading with it, he could not be held personally responsible.[27] The Hanafi *Fiqh*, of course, allowed a guardian trading with an orphan's assets to set aside part of the earnings for himself.[28]

If we look at Palestinian society, we find that guardians were keen not to freeze an orphan's properties. This was because the way they dealt with an orphan's assets was supervised by the *qadi*, and the orphan's money in their trust had to be returned to its owner at some future date. Guardians on the whole used safe, but profitable ways to develop the funds. Lending an orphan's funds against a 20 per cent annual profit was most common. In fact, the lending system made it possible for the orphan's funds to be safely invested in the local economy, and merchants in particular made much use of this opportunity. Loans from guardians of orphans were registered routinely and in Nablus, for example, appear in every court records volume from 1655 (the first volume still existing). In such cases the creditor (the guardian) and the borrower came to the court and registered the amount of the loan, the interest and the surety that was to be put up, ways of payment and maturity. A typical case of this kind reads as follows:

X borrowed from Y the guardian of the orphan ... from the orphan's money 100 *qurush* (the fund: Ras al-Mal), and the legal profit for this (*ribh dhalika bilmuʿamalati al-sharʿiyya*) is twenty *qurush* which will be paid against a watch, for example, bought by the borrower from the creditor. The two sums, the capital and its profit will be returned a year from today.

As a surety for such loans, borrowers generally deposited some property that was to be sold if the money was not returned in time.[29] In some cases, borrowers were asked to bring before the *qadi* people who could be guarantors to back up the loan and its profits. Part of the profits was used by the guardian for the orphan's patrimony and to develop his capital.

In fact, the *Shariʿah* encouraged guardians of wealthy orphans to try to make as much profit as possible. Besides benefiting the orphan, this would help the local economy and the poor because of the obligatory donation (*zakat*) imposed on capital and profit. The more profitable a guardian succeeded in making an orphan's capital, the more he could expect God's mercy. Materially, if he so wished, a guardian could ask a fixed wage for his service, according to the Qur'an: 'Let not the rich guardian touch the property of his orphan ward; and let him who is poor use no more than a fair portion for his own advantage'.[30] When asked about the amount that should be fixed as remuneration, al-Ramli allowed the *qadi* to set it in relation to the size of the assets and the period they were to be invested.[31] Guardians had the right too, if they wished, to share with the orphan in the profits accrued from his capital.

When funds belonging to a rich orphan were exceptionally large, the guardian was asked to keep a detailed account (*muhasaba*) of the orphan's fund, which was to be examined yearly by the court. Such an account had to include full registration of the profits, ways of investment and the amount of expended patrimony.[32] When one checks these account books, it appears that in most cases brought before the court, guardians, indeed, did their best to make the fund profitable. Of course, from one orphan to another, there could be large differences in patrimony, which was not always relative to the size of the orphan's fund. For example, one guardian declared that annually he had expended 1,000 *qurush* on his ward, who had inherited 39,000 *qurush*.[33] In another case, which involved an orphan with a similarly large inheritance, the guardian declared that he had spent 3,000 *qurush* yearly.[34] Of course, needs could differ from one orphan to another, but in this case one suspects that the declared expenditures were not really put towards the orphan's needs. Also, the only evidence needed by the *qadi* to sign the account register was the guardian's declaration concerning the expenditures.[35] Orphans who had reason to be suspicious about the behaviour of their guardians could only bring a complaint after they had reached maturity.[36]

Muslim Orphans: Cases from Nablus

When cases of clear misappropriation led to an official complaint, it was the *qadi*'s duty to carry out a thorough investigation. A member of the famous Nabulsi merchant family, al-Kharuf, brought such a complaint before the *qadi* against a relative who had been handling the property of one of the family's orphans. The orphan had inherited from his father the not insubstantial amount of half a million *qurush*, but after six years the fund was found to contain only 280,000 *qurush*. The *qadi* then ordered this particular person to relinquish the guardianship, in favour of the orphan's mother.[37]

Obviously, the level of expenditures differed from one orphan to another, as it was a function of the orphan's economic capacity and social status, according to which the *qadi* fixed his patrimony (*nafaqa*). The amount of *nafaqa* was suggested by the guardian, who brought two witnesses that confirmed before the *qadi* that the guardian's suggestion was just and reflected the economic capacity of the orphan. Once it had been fixed, the guardian needed permission from the *qadi* to change it, whether because prices had gone up or the orphan's needs had become greater.[38]

In case of orphans who inherited cash, guardians were usually directed not to touch the inherited principal, but to take *nafaqa* only from the principal's earnings.[39] At the same time, guardians who were nominated over less fortunate orphans, whose capital earnings did not suffice for their living, were allowed to consume the inherited capital for the orphan's patrimony.[40] If there was a need, the *qadi* even allowed them to sell the orphan's inherited properties – houses, lands, etc. – to cover the patrimony expenses. One case read as follows:

> Before the honourable session of *Shari'ah* court held in Nablus, appeared Hasan Batbut from the Qaysariyya quarter. Earlier he was nominated by our lord the respected *qadi* as a guardian over the minor Amin Jamus. He stated before the *qadi* that the aforementioned minor possessed through legal inheritance from his deceased father two *Qirat*s and one third of a *Qirat* of two houses located in the al-Gharb quarter ... [He continued by saying] that the minor legally needed an allowance and clothing, but he possessed no other assets that could be sold to provide his livelihood. The guardian asked the court to allow him to sell the aforementioned assets to the brothers 'Abd al-Khaliq and Muhammad Hashhush [who want to buy it] for 400 *qurush*. The suggested price was twice the value of its real price. He asked the court to allow him to receive the money from the buyers to be used for providing a source of living for the aforementioned minor. When our lord, the *qadi*, was fully convinced of the credibility of the guardian after hearing the statements of ... those who attested that the guardian was reliable and that the suggested price was double the real price, and that the minor needed an allowance and clothing but possessed no other source to provide his livelihood, our lord the *qadi* then permitted him to sell the

aforementioned portion and to receive the money for providing his ward with his necessary livelihood.[41]

As no official system was in place that took care of the material needs of poor orphans, the court records, as well as other sources prior to the 1870s, tell us nothing about how poor orphans survived or how their guardians were supposed to behave. When checking the correlation between family names of orphans and those of nominated guardians, we find that, for the most part, no familial relationship existed when the orphan was alone or poor. This may point to volunteer guardians chosen by the *qadi* from among the local community and thus shows how the community acted in such situations. Given the priority that charity is given in Islam, it may well be that local communities decided to support orphans by insuring guardianship for lonely and very poor orphans.

We may equally assume that poor orphans belonging to poor families with poor guardians could count on the community's help, through the charity (*sadaqat*), pious endowments (*waqf*) and obligatory donations (*zakat*). The *zakat* ensured that the rich supported the poor. *Sadaqat* and the wills of the wealthy were supposed to afford help for the poor in general and poor orphans in particular with minimal subsistence.[42]

From the 1870s onward, and with the establishment of municipalities, the state began increasingly to concern itself with the problem of poor orphans. The municipality, as a local institution serving the local community, had relief of the poor as part of its task. For example, in the budget of the municipality of Nablus from 1870 we can find an item called 'poor relief', with names of poor orphans among those who were entitled to monthly stipends from this budget.[43] True, the municipality's budget relied only on local income,[44] but it institutionalised a new system for aiding poor orphans. That is, it entailed the shift from communal charity to state help.

Ottoman Reform

In 1851, as part of their overall efforts at reforming the Empire's institutions during the second half of the nineteenth century, the Ottomans set up an 'Administration of Orphans' Funds' (*Nizarit Amwal al-Aytam*),[45] with bureaus in the centres of provinces (*wilaya*s), districts (*sanjaq*s), sub-districts (*qada*s) and villages (*nahiya*s). The new regulations effectively meant that supervision over an orphan's assets from inheritance moved from the *Shari'ah* court and the *qadi* to the Orphans' Administration.

As with other reforms, undoubtedly the new regulations were intended to limit the spheres of action of the *Shari'ah* court. Moreover, under the old system, in cases of inheritance in which outstanding debts had to be collected for orphaned legatees, the *qadi* had not always transferred the collected portions to the orphans or their guardians at once. His office would often hold on to them until all debts had been collected. Obviously, the procedure could take a long time, and one assumes that it could have been tempting for the *qadi* or other court's functionaries to use the assets in their control to their own advantage. Under the new regulations, collected portions of inherited debts had to be transferred immediately to the treasury of the Orphans' Administration to serve the orphan's benefit.

Also, from this point on, all loans spent from an orphan's fund had to be put through the newly founded Orphans' Treasury (*sunduq al-aytam*), and no longer through the court (*mahkama*).[46] The new regulation clearly stipulated that:

> Orphans' inherited money, after being registered in the *sijill*, must be transferred to the treasury of the Orphans' Administration. Each orphan will have a detailed account which will contain his fund's investments and accrued profits ... the Administration has to do its utmost to invest the orphans' money by lending it against valuable mortgage and guarantors. An annual customary *ribh* (profit) [interest] of eleven and a half percent must be paid against the money lent.[47]

But if large sums had accumulated in the Orphans' Treasury, these could be lent to exchange bureaus with 10 per cent interest or less, depending on the economic situation. Furthermore, if no borrowers could be found, the Orphans' Treasury was allowed to exchange the cash for government bonds.[48]

Regarding orphans who had no 'chosen guardian', the new regulations authorised the newly founded councils in towns, such as the consultative council, to choose and recommend someone they considered suitable.[49]

Orphans' Treasuries were soon found in the major Palestinian towns, and the court records of Haifa, Nablus and Jerusalem give us some idea about who filled the job of Orphans' Treasurer (*Mudir Sunduq al-Aytam*).[50] Nominated from among the rich local merchants, a candidate had to present the local authorities and the *Mahkama* with letters of recommendation from the local commerce bureau and from the town's administrative council. He also had to be vouchsafed by three persons, who had to agree to stand as sureties for the treasurer.[51]

The treasurer was responsible for the cash deposited in the Orphans' Treasury and had to keep individual accounts for each orphan until they came of age. The treasurer was expected to invest these funds in the most profitable manner. Part of the profits was transferred to the guardian to cover the orphan's expenses, while the remainder was added to the fund.[52]

As *qadi*s had done through the centuries, the Orphans' Treasurer had instructions from the central government to invest the orphans' funds by lending them out. Borrowers paid 12 per cent annual interest and were required to mortgage against the loan assets assessed at twice the amount of the loan. The Orphans' Treasury also asked for two guarantors. Interest was paid using the traditional *shar'i* device: the borrower supposedly 'bought' a book, a watch or some other item from the lender, which became a new loan added to the actual borrowed capital, making up the sum that had to be paid back.[53] If a borrower or his guarantors at the end of the agreed upon period defaulted in part or on all of their payments, the *qadi* could have them jailed at the request of the Orphans' Treasurer.[54]

Clearly, the Orphans' Treasury effectively acted as a bank, with merchants, in particular, making ample use of the available capital. Rich orphans benefited, though never as much as those whose funds were administered by a guardian, because instead of 10 to 12 per cent, these funds *continued* to collect an annual interest of 15 to 20 per cent on the cash they loaned out.[55]

The End of the Orphan's Minority

Legally, minority ended with the onset of physical maturity.[56] Once physically mature (*baligh*), one could represent him/herself in court independently, without his or her guardian. Now responsible for his/her own actions, the orphan no longer needed to be supervised by guardians. However, before orphans were allowed to manage their inherited property, they needed to provide proof of their mental ability. While a young man or woman could be legally accepted as *baligh* upon reaching the age of fifteen,[57] the mental maturity (*rushd*) had to be determined in court and required the testimony of two trustworthy men.[58] In other words, it was only after a fatherless minor had successfully proved he or she had become mentally mature (*rashid*) that they were considered as having completed their period as an orphan.

The many cases in the court records generally show that guardians were ready to release the assets of orphans once they had reached the age of twenty or more.[59] Regularly, procedure was initiated by the orphans themselves, who claimed before the *qadi* that they had become *rashid*s and now asked the court to end the guardianship and to transfer their assets. The guardian then denied this allegation, and demanded they provide proof for their claim. The orphan would then bring two witnesses to testify that they had, indeed, become mentally mature, and only then did the court acknowledge the end of their minority and give them full control of their inherited assets.[60]

Such cases were brought before the court by both men and women and were dealt with similarly. Significantly, most cases brought by orphaned women were brought before the court after their marriage had been consummated.[61] Once the *rushd* was proved, the guardian was asked to transfer the funds to the concerned *rashida*. In cases of very large funds, some guardians delivered the full accounts of the fund to the court so as to avert future allegations concerning the fund.[62]

Conclusion

Since an orphan's material and other needs traditionally were immediately taken care of by members of their family or the local community, Muslim society at least until the arrival in mid-nineteenth century of Christian missionary societies, did not have, nor did not need, private or public institutions in which to shelter orphans. When a child's father died, the full responsibility for under-aged children (*wilaya*) passed on to the guardian, who was nominated by the *qadi*.

During the nineteenth century, and unlike Christian missionary orphanages and strict adherence to Islamic jurisprudence in the Ottoman Empire, *Shari'ah* law dominated, as in the pre-modern period, which encouraged Muslim society to ensure the rights of orphans and prevent them from being discriminated against vis-a-vis other children. *Shari'ah* provided the essential bases for the orphan's material rights. As with other topics that belong to the social history of pre-modern Muslim societies, the *Shari'ah* court records are very helpful in gaining a deeper insight into the ways and customs of its propertied members, although less so for its poorer members. Orphans appear in the court records frequently, not because they are orphans, but because of the legal procedures that stipulated how their property ought to be dealt with and administered. Since guardianship could be a source of profit and remuneration, wealthy orphans were eagerly sought by guardians. Generally speaking, the *Shari'ah* and the courts invested huge efforts in guaranteeing the maintenance of the property of these orphans, thus smoothing their way into society. Thus, it is no surprise that we encounter orphans of wealthy parents enjoying the inherited wealth and social status of their fathers. The challenge remains of discovering how orphans in general, particularly those who were poor, were able to manage their daily lives, raised as they were by other poor relatives or at times by complete strangers. However, the institutionalisation of state-run orphanages in Middle Eastern countries only began at the turn of the twentieth century.

Notes

1. The court records (*sijill*, in Arabic) of the *Shari'ah* (Islamic Law) include information covering almost all aspects of life. The *Shari'ah* court was the main institution for adjudicating civil and criminal disputes, and an office for registering deeds and contracts. Thus, the *sijill* includes registers of credit, property rights, sales or real estate and houses, commercial dealings, marriage contracts, divorce, child custody, inheritance, appointments to public offices, charitable endowments and so on. Many of the *sijill* documents deal with cases related to children in different judicial situations. These documents tell us much about social practices of society concerning daily life of children. In this chapter I have chosen the court records from the Nablus and Jerusalem courts, primarily of the nineteenth century, which dealt with orphans, but, of course, other subjects related to children can be studied based on this important local source.
2. NCR 23, pp. 276–7 (1300/1882).
3. Maksudyan, *Orphans and Distitute Children in the Late Ottoman Empire*, p. 78. See in particular Chapter 3, pp. 78–115.
4. Mansur, *Ta'rih al-Nasira*, p. 87.
5. Tucker, 'Muftis and Matrimony', pp. 283–94.
6. Al-Astrushni, *Ahkam al-Sighar*, p. 343; Al-Ramli, *al-Fatawa al-Khayriyya*, vol. 2, pp. 217, 221.
7. Al-Astrushni, *Ahkam al-Sighar*, p. 343.
8. See, for example, NCR 23, p. 51 (1299/1882).
9. NCR 23, pp. 276–7 (1300/1882).
10. O'Shaughnessy and Manila, 'The Qur'anic View', pp. 35, 37.
11. Shacht, '*Yatim*', p. 1160; Sabiq, *Fiqh al-Sunnah*, vol. 3, p. 570; al-Rif'i, *al-Wilaya 'Ala al-Mal*, pp. 51, 264. A similar procedure was enacted by the Jewish community of medieval Cairo, see: Goitien, *A Mediterranean Society*, vol. 3, pp. 292–312.
12. Calder, 'Khums in Imami Shi'i', pp. 39, 45.
13. Mahamid, *al-Tatuwwurat fi Nidham al-Hukum*, pp. 149–52; Stillman, 'Charity and Social Service', p. 112; Amin (1980), *al-Awqaf*, pp. 261–73; Goitein, *A Mediterranean Society*, p. 304.
14. Ibshirli and al-Tamimi, *Awqaf wa-Amlak al-Muslimin fi Filastin*, pp. 26, 38; al-'Asali, *Ma'ahid al-'Ilm fi Bayt al-Maqdis*, p. 249.
15. Peri, '*Waqf* and Ottoman Welfare Policy', pp. 1167–86.
16. Huart, '*Imaret*', p. 475.
17. *Mausu'at al-Hadith al-Sharif*, al-Bukhari, p. 4892; *Mausu'at al-Hadith al-Sharif*, al-Termidhi, p. 1841.
18. Al-Astrushni, *Ahkam al-Sighar*, pp. 340–77.

19. Qur'an, *al-Nisa'*: 6.
20. Sonbol, 'Adoption in Islamic Society', p. 57.
21. NCR 23, p. 94 (1299/1882). For other examples, see: p. 10 (1299/1882); JCR 122, p. 31 (1308/1890); JCR 53, pp. 205 (1306/1889); and hundreds of similar documents in the court records.
22. Qur'an, *al-Isra'*: 34.
23. Qur'an, *al-Baqara*: 220.
24. Ali, *A Manual of Hadith*, p. 218; see also, *Mausu'at al-Hadith al-Sharif*, al-Termidhi, p. 580.
25. Al-Astrushni, *Ahkam al-Sighar*, pp. 195–201, 243–57, 361–6.
26. Al-Ramli, *al-Fatawa al-Khayriyya*, vol. 2, p. 224.
27. Al-Astrushni, *Ahkam al-Sighar*, pp. 202, 204, 239; al-Sarkhasi, *Kitab al-Mabsut*, vol. 22, pp. 20, 186–7.
28. Al-Astrushni, *Ahkam al-Sighar*, vol. 2, p. 367.
29. NCR 1, p. 293 (1068/1658); NCR 24, p. 26 (1065/1655); NCR 24, p. 211 (1067/1657).
30. Qur'an, *al-Nisa'*: 6.
31. Al-Ramli, *al-Fatawa al-Khayriyya*, vol. 2, p. 218.
32. NCR 25, p. 90 (1301/1884); NCR 24, p. 220 (1300/1883); NCR 23, p. 199 (1300/1882); JCR 51, p. 512 (1300/1883); JCR 53, p. 33 (1301/1884).
33. NCR 25, p. 338 (1302/1885).
34. NCR 24, p. 220 (1300/1883).
35. Al-Ramli, *al-Fatawa al-Khayriyya*, vol. 2, p. 218; Al-Astrushni, *Ahkam al-Sighar*, p. 363.
36. Al-Astrushni, *Ahkam al-Sighar*, pp. 363–4.
37. NCR 30, p. 13 (1309/1892).
38. For examples, see: NCR 1, p. 293 (1068/1658); NCR 44, p. 104 (1330/1912); NCR 30, p. 267 (1310/1893); JCR 43, p. 419 (1222/1807); and many similar cases.
39. NCR 38, p. 22 (1316/1898); NCR 32, p. 13 (1312/1894); NCR 30, p. 86 (1310/1892).
40. NCR 23, p. 335 (1296/1879).
41. NCR 23, p. 82 (1299/1882).
42. NCR 26, p. 215 (1303/1886); NCR 44, p. 361 (1330/1912); NCR 30, p. 239 (1311/1893).
43. Yazbak, 'The Municipality of a Muslim Town', pp. 19–22.
44. Ibid., p. 20.
45. Nawfal, *al-Dustur*, vol. 1, p. 103.
46. See, for example: NCR 20, p. 398 (1297/1880), p. 385 (1300/1882).
47. Nawfal, *al-Dustur*, vol. 1, p. 104.
48. Ibid., p. 106.
49. Ibid., p. 108.
50. NCR 29, p. 117 (1308/1891).
51. NCR 44, p. 296 (1330/1912).

52. NCR 35, p. 269 (1317/1899).
53. The NCR (*sijillat*) contain hundreds of such lending cases.
54. NCR 33, p. 85 (1314/1896).
55. NCR 23, p. 286 (1300/1882).
56. Giladi, 'Saghir', p. 821.
57. Ibid., p. 821.
58. Al-Ramli, *al-Fatawa al-Khayriyya*, vol. 2, p. 144; al-Mabsut, vol. 24, p. 161.
59. NCR 33, p. 325 (1300/1882).
60. NCR 23, p. 357 (1300/1882).
61. Ibid., p. 357.
62. NCR 25, p. 90 (1301/1884).

Bibliography

Archival Sources
Nablus Court Records (*Sijill*) (NCR): 1 (1068/1658); 2 (1065–7/1655–7); 23 (1296–1300/1879–82); 24 (1300/1882–3); 25 (1301–2/1884–5); 26 (1303/1886); 29 (1308/1891); 30 (1309–11/1892–3); 33 (1314/1896); 35 (1317/1899); 44 (1330/1912)
Jerusalem Court Records (*Sijill*) (JCR): 53 (1306/1889); 122 (1308/1890–1)

Secondary Sources
Al-Albani, Muhammad Nasir al-Din, *Sahih Sunan al-Tirmidhi*, 2 vols (al-Riyad: Maktab al-Tarbiya al-'Arabi li-Duwal al-Khalij, 1988).
Amin, Muhammad M., *Al-Awqaf wa-al-Hayat al-Ijtima'iyya fi Misr, 1250–1517 A.D.* (Cairo: Dar al-Nahda, 1980).
As'ad, Mansur, *Tarikh al-Nasira min Aqdam Azmaniha Ila Ayamina al-Hadira* (Cairo: Matba'at al-Hilal, 1924).
Al-'Asali, Kamil Jamil, *Ma'ahid al-'Ilm fi Bayt al-Maqdis* (Amman: Jordanian University of Amman, 1981).
Al-Astrushni, Muhammad Bin Mahmoud Bin Husayn, *Ahkam al-Sighar* (Beirut: al-'Ilmiyya, 1997).
Calder, Norman, 'Khums in Imami Shi'i Jurisprudence, from the Tenth to the Sixteenth Century A.D.', *Bulletin of the School of Oriental and African Studies*, 45 (1982), pp. 39–47.
Giladi, Avner, 'Saghir', *EI²*, vol. 8 (2004), pp. 826–8.
Goitien, S. D., *A Mediterranean Society: The Jewish Community of the Arab World as Portrayed in the Documents of the Cairo Geniza*, 4 vols (Berkeley: University of California Press, 1967).
Huart, Claude, 'Imaret', *EI¹*, vol. 2 (2002), pp. 475–7.
Ibshirli, Muhammad and al-Tamimi Muhammad (1982), *Awqf wa-Amlak al-Muslimin fi Filastin* (Istanbul: Markaz al-Abhath, 1982).
Mahamid, Hatim, *al-Tatuwwurat fi Nidham al-Hukum wa-al-Idarah fi Masr al-Fatimiyya* (Jerusalem: Asil, 2001).

Maksudyan, Nazan, *Orphans and Destitute Children in the Late Ottoman Empire* (Syracuse: Syracuse University Press, 2014).
Mausu'at al-Hadith al-Sharif, CD, 2nd edn (al-Riad: Global Islamic Software Company, 1991–7).
Nawfal, Ni'mat allah Nawfal (trans.), *Al-Dustur*, 2 vols (Beirut: al-Matba'a al-Adabiyya, 1301/1883).
O'Shaughnessy, Thomas J. O., and S. J. Manila, 'The Qur'anic View of Youth and Old Age', *Zeitschrift der Deutschen Morgenländischen Gesellschaft*, 141/1 (1991), pp. 33–51.
Peri, Oded, 'Waqf and Ottoman Welfare Policy: The Poor Kitchen of Haseki Sultan in Eighteenth-Century Jerusalem', *Journal of the Economic and Social History of the Orient*, 35 (1992), pp. 167–86.
Al-Qaramani, Muhammad Bin Yusuf, *Sahih al-Bukhari bi-Sharh al-Qaramani*, 24 vols (Cairo: al-Matba'a al-Misriyya, 1937).
Qur'an, trans. N. J. Dawood (London: Penguin Books, 1990).
Al-Ramli, Khayr al-Din, *Al-Fatawa al-Khayriyya fi Naf' al-Bariyya*, 2 vols (Istanbul, 1311/1893).
Al-Rif'i, 'Abd al-Salam, *Al-Wilaya 'Ala al-Mal fi al-Shari'a al-Islamiyya wa-Tatbiqatiha fi al-Madhhab al-Maliki* (al-Dar al-Bayda: Ifriqiya al-Sharq, 1996).
Sabiq, Al-Sayyid, *Fiqh al-Sunnah*, 4 vols (Beirut: al-Kitab al-'Arabi, 1971).
Al-Sarakhisi, Shams al-Din, *Kitab al-Mabsut*, 24 vols (Beirut: Dar al-Ma'rifa, 1978).
Shacht, Joseph, 'Yatim', in *EI²*, 2nd edn, vol. 12 (Leiden: Brill, 2002), pp. 1160–2.
Sonbol, Amira El-Azhary, 'Adoption in Islamic Society: A Historical Survey', in Elizabeth W. Fernea (ed.), *Children in the Muslim Middle East* (Austin: University of Texas Press, 1995), pp. 45–67.
Stillman, Norman A., 'Charity and Social Service in Medieval Islam', *Societias*, 5 (1975), pp. 105–16.
Tucker, Judith E., 'Muftis and Matrimony: Islamic Law and Gender in Ottoman Syria and Palestine', *Islamic Law and Society*, 1/3 (1994), pp. 283–300.
Yazbak, Mahmoud, 'The Municipality of a Muslim Town: Nablus 1868–1914', *Archiv Orientální*, 67/3 (1999), pp. 339–60.

PART IV
CHILDREN'S BODIES

Chapter 10

Body Politics and the *Devşirme*s in the Early Modern Ottoman Empire: The Conscripted Children of Herzegovina[1]

Gülay Yılmaz

Dimitri, the son of Radasin, was conscripted from Polimiye, Mileşeva, Herzegovina (Hersek) in 1493–4. He was fair-skinned, had hazel-blue eyes and arched eyebrows. He was approximately fourteen years old. Gorgi was another fourteen-year-old enlisted from Polimiye. He was the son of Obrav, had dark skin, black eyes and frowning eyebrows. Twenty-four others were taken away from the same small town, and 115 in total from the wider Herzegovina region in that year.[2] A little more than a century later, in 1604, in another levy from the Herzegovina region, 141 boys were taken. Among them, Yusuf, the son of İbrahim and Fatima, who was fifteen years old. He was short, blond, with blue eyes and had scars on his forehead. İbrahim, the son of Üveyş and Emine, was a brown-haired eighteen-year-old boy of medium height, with light blue eyes. He had a long scar on his face.[3] These are all descriptions of enlisted boys recorded in the registers of *devşirme* officers during the two levies from Herzegovina in 1493–4 and 1604. For centuries, the Ottomans levied children of their Christian population, converted them to Islam, taught them Turkish, educated them and eventually placed them in administrative and military posts under what is called the *devşirme* system.

Why were the physical traits of the boys recorded during conscriptions? How is this data in the levy registers [*eşkal* (lit. description) *defter*s] to be read as part of the children's history? What do the registers tell us regarding the control of children's bodies? This chapter will deal with these questions in an attempt to introduce a new approach to a historiographical debate on the status of the boys conscripted as *devşirme*s. In this chapter, I move my analysis to the treatment of the *devşirme* bodies by the state and the corporeal experiences of the children throughout the conscription process, away from the legal interpretations of the *devşirme* status, which focus on whether those levied were slaves or not according to Islamic law.

I do that by tracing what I define as the body politics behind the *devşirme* system imposed by the state and which applied both at the moment of the enlistment and afterwards. I will argue that there was a consciously developed policy towards selecting the *proper* bodies and controlling those bodies throughout the *devşirme* process, both of which should be read as methods of enslavement. I will also argue that the definition of a *proper* body was not static, but subject to change according to the state's needs or according to what regional resources offered. The chapter is based on an analysis of sample groups of levied boys from two different recruitment events (1493–4 and 1604) in Herzegovina, and a comparison between the two, questioning whether there were any differences in the selection criteria applied in this period.

In the literature dealing with the *devşirme*, the childhood stage of the levied masses is largely ignored. The study of the *devşirme*, however, is not complete without incorporating the history of the children into the narrative. Many historians have highlighted the positive features of the system by stressing the opportunities it provided for upward mobility, interpreting it as an imperial magnet for those who wanted to have better options in life for themselves or for their children.[4] The system's merit lay in its ability to raise an individual to the highest ranks in Ottoman politics and society, independent of their origins.[5] The fact, however, that the system was not voluntary but operated through enslavement is less widely addressed. As such, the acquiescence of the levied boys in proving their merit is questionable.

Unfortunately, on the issue of whether the *devşirme* was enslavement or not, the existing literature focuses mainly on examining the legal status of the *devşirme* children in Ottoman society. It concentrates less on the living conditions of the children or the actual process of transition they were subjected to, which arguably could be considered as a form of premodern enslavement.[6] Thanks to Ehud Toledano's attempts to define the forms of slavery in Ottoman society, the view of the *devşirme* as enslavement has become more prominent in discussions. Toledano argues that the *devşirme* has to be treated as part of the discussion on Ottoman slavery,[7] since the levied people serving the sultan (*devşirme kul*s) were 'supposed to substitute their loyalty to their parents for loyalty to their sovereign',[8] and were then attached to the sultan's housefolk (*kapı halkı*). He asserts that Ottoman slavery should be interpreted through a continuum model, where the notions of patronage and attachment replace the master–slave paradigm.[9] This approach shows that the military–administrative body of the Ottoman Empire, the *kul*s, was able to enjoy some privileges, since they were incorporated into their patron's social and political environment.[10] There is still, however, a continuing historiographical debate on the status of the *devşirme*s, with some scholars pointing out the enslaved loyalties expected from these people,[11] and with some highlighting the privileges they enjoyed as proof of their 'servant' status.[12] There is no space in this chapter to delve into these discussions; however, I will briefly contribute to the debate by arguing that the complexity and variation of the definition of slavery and slave institutions during medieval times and the early modern era should be carefully elaborated if trying to understand the *devşirme* as a slave institution.

In this chapter, I am looking for a new approach to historical discourse and concentrate more on the body politics exercised over the levied boys. This approach helps to reveal the world of those boys who started their lives as Christian commoners and ended up as possessions of the sultan, whom they had to serve under a newly defined identity. The chapter examines this transformation by concentrating particularly on the control of the *devşirme* bodies by the authorities.

Some Thoughts on the Relationship between the **Devşirme** *Body and the Ottoman Authorities*

Foucault's definition of biopolitics, developed in the West from the seventeenth century onwards, led many researchers to question the role of power relations through different treatments of the body. In his 1976 essay 'Right of Death and Power of Life', Foucault gave a new meaning to the term. He described the power of the sovereigns of ancient regimes over their subjects as the 'power of life and death', which gave the sovereign 'a right to seizure of things, time, bodies, and ultimately life itself'.[13] From the seventeenth century onwards, there had been a shift from the right of death into, what Foucault defined as, a life-administering power. There were two dimensions to the new mechanisms of power: one was the disciplining of the body, the 'anatomo-politics of the human body', which was embodied in institutions such as schools and the army; and the second mechanism followed the first in establishing regulatory controls. This was the administration of bodies, such as births and mortality, the level of health and life expectancy, and the economic observation of bodies, which he called 'a bio-politics of the population'.[14]

Prior to the development of this all-encompassing, exhaustive, modern notion of biopower politics, as defined by Foucault, states attempted to control and discipline the bodies they possessed. Here, I am not suggesting that the power over *devşirme* bodies was a form of biopolitics in an exact Foucauldian sense, but rather that the use of Foucault's insights regarding his definition can help in presenting the ways in which *devşirme* bodies were treated, controlled and possessed by the Ottoman state before the biopolitics of the modern state developed. The Ottoman state saw as its inalienable right the ability to transform the identities of levied children through surveillance and control, through its capacity as the main power-holder and initiator of an unequal relationship with children of Christian families living under Ottoman rule (*zımmi*). This control very much reflected control of the body itself, since the state, in this logic, *owned* the bodies of the levied, possessing the ultimate authority over how and where they would be used as resources.

State Surveillance and Levy Registers

Pre-modern states controlled the movements of individual bodies. The identification practices were very limited compared to modern applications of surveillance; however, it was still necessary for the state to know who people were and thus kept records of their physical appearance.[15] This tendency, in the case of the Ottoman state, manifested itself above all in the practice of recording the features of *devşirme*s. Similar to slave-owners, who registered the purchase of a new slave in the *qadi* courts, the state kept registers of the boys as they were levied.

Keeping records of features of a body reflects the power relation between masters and slaves. It is seen very frequently in different cultures and periods, especially in the practice of recording the descriptions of slaves' faces and hands, which was widespread in the early modern Mediterranean and was equally prominent in both Christian and Muslim slave trade practices. Valentin Groebner mentions a unique register from the Florentine archives listing the detailed descriptions of the bodies of female slaves purchased during the period 1366–97, alongside their age and name. The level of detail is exemplified in the case of a female slave named Marta, who was 'around eighteen years of age, of Tatar origin, a little under medium height with olive skin [. . .] [with] a scar on the right side of the forehead, a black tooth, some pockmarks in the face, a scar on the right index finger, and a pierced left ear'.[16] The similarities between this description and those mentioned at the beginning of this chapter for the *devşirme* levies cannot be ignored. Research on Spanish sources also reveals a similar tendency to record the physical characteristics of slaves, which was very common in the Iberian Peninsula.[17] Alessandro Stella gives various examples of such records from Barcelona, Seville, Madrid and Valance dating from the sixteenth to the eighteenth centuries, interpreting this practice as the 'animalisation' of humans. He argues that people were treated as if they were merchandise, furniture or even animals, such as cows, sheep or horses, which led to the debasing and humiliation of the slaves.[18] Also, slave traders of the Barbary Coast selected slaves according to their age and strength, therefore 'examining their teeth, arms and legs, making them walk, jump and leap about with blows of a stick'.[19] Davis references a striking painting by Pierre Dan depicting the examination of slaves in the Algiers slave market (*badestan*) in 1684, showing the dehumanising effect of the process.[20] Similarly, in the Ottoman sources, as Toledano notes, slaves' faces, predominantly their eyes, hair and teeth, received special examination. The health, nutrition, cleanliness and, for females, beauty of the slaves were judged through these features and recorded in the sources.[21]

The registers of the levied boys served the same purpose of surveillance and control of the newly recruited bodies, while also acting as an indication of the power exercised over the *devşirme* levies. These registers begin by listing boys by geographical area, according to the district (*liva*), subdistrict (*kaza*) and then village (*karye*) from where they were selected. The type of information included in these registers varied according to the period during which they were kept. The most complete information registered in these sources included the new Muslim name given to the boy, the original Christian name, the names of the father and mother and the boy's physical description. Not all registers, however, contained the same information. It depended to a certain extent on the geographical area, but also showed significant variation through time. The comparison of the two data sets from Herzegovina in 1493–4 and in 1604 reflects this change.

Herzegovina became a district (*sancak/liva*) of the Ottoman Empire shortly after it was conquered. The first register that I examined was a levy that took place almost twenty years after its conquest. In 1493–4, 115 children were levied from the region. The description of the boys in this register contained few details. Only the names of the child and his father, the colour of his eyes and eyebrows and his age were noted down. The officers recorded details of the appearance of the children responding simply to a need to identify them. This register was found in the archives along with other sets of registers that contain levies from the years 1494–5 and 1498–9. These lists of child levies may potentially be excerpts of a master levy register, rather than being complete registers of each and every year in themselves. The registers of different years are not systematic or consistent. For example, only the levies from Albanian Alexandria (İskenderiye), Vize, Elbasan (İlbasan) and Herzegovina (Hersek) provide information on the patronymic, physical characteristics and the age of the children. The ones from Euboea (Ağrıboz), Albanian Belgrade (Belgrad) and Vlore (Avlonya) only give the name of the parents and the age of the children, lacking information on the physical characteristics of the levies, whereas those from Trikala (Tırhala) and Kyustendil (Köstendil) record the name of the parents and the physical characteristics of the children, but not their age. The physical descriptions of the children are not necessarily recorded in the registers of the late fifteenth and early sixteenth centuries, and if recorded they provide a very general overview of their appearance.

Later on, the scribes of the 1603–4 levy were much more meticulous in recording the appearances of the levied boys. The levy was undertaken in different localities: Rumelia, Bosnia and Herzegovina, Avlonya (a province corresponding to most of today's Albania, the centre of which was Vlore) and Anatolia (levies from around Bursa). In these four regions, different groups of officers were responsible for levying the boys. Even though the scribes for these four regions were different, they were consistent in providing the same type of information on the boys. These records can be viewed almost as pre-modern mugshots of the levied boys, as a more detailed identification process was pursued. The officers recorded the original name of the levies, the names of their father and mother, their newly given Muslim name and their physical characteristics. The colour of their eyes and/or the shape of their eyebrows, their height and their age were among the immediate characteristics registered.

In addition, any kind of distinguishing mark on their faces, heads or hands became the legal paradigm of identification. Birthmarks (*nişan*), scars (*yare*), signs (*alamet*) or marks due to disease, such as chicken pox or plague, were noted down whenever necessary, and the location of the scars was given in detail.[22] This gives a sense that the officers were more eager to identify the levied boys during the early seventeenth century, as compared to the late fifteenth century.

The exact reasons for this shift are not known, but one can speculate on some possibilities. Improvements in the keeping of registers (*defters*) could be a factor. Additionally, state officials might have felt the need to control the levy process more closely, which may have resulted in directives to scribes to provide more detailed descriptions of the boys. This need for control might have come about due to the rapid expansion of the Ottoman territories and the increase in the number of regions subject to the child levy. The rise in the age of recruited boys, which made defection easier if desired, could have played a role in this tendency to increase surveillance. Whatever the reason behind this change, however, we derive more detailed information on the appearance of the levied boys during the early seventeenth century.

Definitions of Ideal *Candidates and* Proper *Bodies: Regulations and Practice*

The main source historians use to detect what the Ottoman state looked for in a suitable candidate for *devşirme* recruitment is the *Kavanin-i Yeniçeriyan* (the *Regulations for Janissaries*). This anonymous work was written by an old janissary, who was levied as a *devşirme* before entering the army ranks. It was written in 1606 as a present to Ahmed I (r. 1603–17). The *Regulations* aimed to highlight the tradition and rules surrounding the levying of boys, the functioning of the janissary army and to warn the sultan against new practices. The text provides information on what an official should look for in a child before choosing him as a levy. The eligibility criteria include physical, ethnic and sociological characteristics, drawing a picture for us of what was generally accepted as the *ideal* candidate, at least in theory.

The text which describes the boys reflects the existing stereotypes and prejudices of Ottoman society about looks. In the required category, it underlined the necessity of choosing strong, clever and good-looking children. It also warned the authorities about which boys not to select. For example, boys with strong social and economic ties, such as married boys, those with artisanal skills, those living in towns (in contrast to those in rural areas) or even those who had visited Istanbul and returned were not to be taken.[23] This stress on 'unattachment' in the *Regulations* was clearly intended to enable a stronger 'attachment' (*intisab*) to the new environment into which the levies would be introduced. The fewer ties they had back home or in the capital, the more likely that they would become better adjusted to the new socio-economic environment they would be introduced to following the conscription. Here, Toledano's argument that slavery in Ottoman society was a continuum of bondage at various levels, where a slave was absorbed into the owner's social group, should be emphasised.[24] Based on the traits of the *ideal* candidate, it can be argued that the choice of who would be levied was strongly tied to who was more susceptible to this kind of relationship.

The fact that those who had been to Istanbul were not desirable candidates is quite interesting in respect to the above-mentioned concept of bondage. The author of the *Regulations* defines these types of boys as ones who know a lot of people and who would be vigilant (*çok yüz görmüş ve bi haya olur*). This could be read as boys with developed social networking skills and, more importantly, with an already established social network in the capital. As such, the implication is that they would be harder to control for the authorities. Another factor might be that such boys would not be so easily inducted into the new social environment following the levy. Calling them vigilant (*bi-haya*) hints at the difficulty in controlling them, since they might already have established a support system, which would allow them to resist the requirements of being a *devşirme*.

No clear definition exists for those who were perceived as harder to assimilate into the system. Nevertheless, the repetition of certain negative traits associated with a given ethnicity, or even with particular physical characteristics, can offer some conclusions. The negative connotations can be seen not only as a result of prejudice against certain communities and appearances, but also as a way of stressing what types of boys were undesirable. From this perspective, the most frequent undesirable personal traits were those of troublemaking, obstinacy and stubbornness. These characteristics, however, were not spelled out explicitly, but were most often associated with bodily traits. This tradition of learning about a person's character by looking at his/her physiognomy was not unique to the selection of the *devşirme*s. There existed a genre of manuals of physiognomy (*kıyafetname*), which was considered a subdiscipline of medicine, and which described in great detail how character contributed in the shaping of the body's external appearance. Therefore, these manuals argued, by looking at a person's appearance, certain traits of their character could be readily understood.[25] Dror Ze'evi, in his meticulous study on *kıyafetnames*, delineates the sexual and asexual characteristics of men and women as described in four texts. He also mentions that these manuals of physiognomy were used when levying boys in the *devşirme*, or by palace officials when buying slave girls for the *harem*, adding that it was hard to tell how far the descriptions in the manuals were adhered to.[26]

Keeping this tradition in mind, the *Regulations for Janissaries* mentions that cross-eyed boys would be stubborn (*mu'annid*), beardless ones would be troublemakers (*fitne vü fesad*) and bald ones would be garrulous (*fuzul* and *geveze-hor*).[27] The ideal candidates should be of medium height. The author demonstrates the prejudice that short ones would be obstinate (*fitne*), whereas tall ones would be foolish (*ahmak*).[28] All these assumptions regarding physical characteristics were prejudices. Since the physical descriptions in the registers touch upon limited features, it cannot be ascertained whether the officers levied bald, beardless or cross-eyed boys, to which these negative connotations were attributed. It can be argued, however, that there was an inclination towards levying tall and medium-height boys in the register. Yet, short boys were recruited to a certain extent as well. Thus, in this instance, height prejudices were sidelined. Here, our focus is not only on physical features such as being cross-eyed, bald, short or tall, but also on the associations behind those

Body Politics and the Devşirmes

features. It is clear that the authorities were not keen on boys who would be stubborn, rebellious or troublesome, but the association of these traits with particular physical features was not necessarily relevant.

The inclination not to allow obstinate boys into the system is apparent also in ethnic stereotyping. The author reiterates the belief that those from Trabzon exhibited negative character traits; therefore, they were not accepted into the *devşirme* system until the reign of Selim I (r. 1512–20). They were defined as evil-doers (*şerir*) and troublemakers (*fitneye ve fesada ba'is*).[29] The *Regulations* describes the unfortunate outcome of Selim I's levying from Trabzon, despite the warnings of the authorities. It is alleged in the text that this group of levies within the janissary army opposed the sultan when he wanted to spend the winter in the region after defeating Shah Ismail, at which time he harboured plans to organise a campaign against Egypt. The janissaries from Trabzon, the author argues, resisted the sultan's decision in the belief that the army would not survive the winter in the region due to food shortages. While they stood against him, he explains, the rest of the soldiers did not have any energy to resist them, because of the famine. It is unclear how the author knew that those who resisted the sultan included only recruitments from Trabzon, but there was similar ethnic stereotyping against other groups, such as the Gypsies, who were considered unreliable, and the Jews, who were thought to be unfit for warfare.[30]

Another ethnicity that was strictly forbidden from being *devşirme* was the Turks. The *Regulations* characterises them as cruel (*bi-rahm*) and lacking in religious sensibility (*din ü diyaneti az*).[31] The Turkish stereotype in the *Regulations* is of one who would be capable of using his privileges as a *devşirme* to oppress his own people. It is known, however, that Christian levies were also used as officials representing the sultan's authority in their lands of origin, and they also must have had the opportunity to oppress their countrymen. However, the stereotypical interpretation was more about not taking Muslims as *devşirme*. In the same vein, Kurds, Gurcus and Persians were felt to be equally undesirable. Cutting the religious ties of the boys was key in this assimilation project, and if the boys were Muslims already the assimilation would not have been successful. The only exception to this conversion element was the Muslim boys from Bosnia, which will be considered in the following pages.

In terms of desirability, boys who already had a certain level of upbringing and education were preferred. Good candidates were expected to pursue their education further. The *Regulations* clarify that orphans should not be levied, since they would lack a proper background and education and might act greedily. The same argument was made for shepherds (*sığırtmaç* and *çoban*s) and the sons of village wardens (*köy kethüdası*).[32] It is also noted that boys from good Christian families, and the sons of grandees (*ekabir*) and priests were among the most preferred candidates. The emphasis on education was crucial in the levying system. Lowry has shown that many Ottoman statesmen were levied from prominent families of the Balkans, taken directly to palace schools, assimilated and trained to become members of the Ottoman elite.[33] Ottoman governance saw these candidates as ideal and frequently entrusted them with positions of importance back home. They were supported by the state, as well as the prestige of their original families as rulers of their homelands. Speaking the language of the region, of course, was also a big advantage. The sons of priests were considered ideal candidates during the early seventeenth century. Whenever they were recruited, the scribe would note specifically in the margins that the boy was the son of a priest.

Naturally, in describing the ideal candidate, the *Regulations* provides guidelines that could only be followed to a certain extent. The levy registers investigated in this study show that the officers strictly followed some of these criteria, and not others. The levy process, in practice, was influenced by two factors: first, the conditions in the regions where the conscriptions were made; and second, the changing needs of the state. For example, while the *Regulations* are clear that shepherds' sons should not be levied, there is an instance in the sources where people from a village called Bursa visited the Bursa court to file against the levy officers who had levied some children of the village, despite their status as shepherds of state land (*hass*). The villagers insisted that the village needed children who would continue this occupation.[34]

The comparison of the two levies from the Herzegovina region in 1493–4 and 1604 proves that what a region might offer changed over time. The traits of the boys are shown to be quite different between the levies. In the earliest register, the ages of the boys varied between twelve and fifteen.[35] Their average age was 13.6 (Graph 10.1). The vast majority of the levies were hazel-eyed (Graph 10.2). The most common skin type was fair (40 per cent), followed by brown (36.5 per cent); and taking the blond and fair children together, it can be concluded that more than half of them were light-skinned (Graph 10.3).

In 1604, the levy officers in Herzegovina recruited a group of boys with different physical traits from the earlier period. The levies were picked from among the age groups of fifteen to twenty,[36] and the average age was increased to 16.7 (Graph 10.4), compared to 13.6 in the late fifteenth century (Graph 10.7). The general appearance of the Herzegovina levies was as follows: black and brown eye colours formed a higher percentage compared

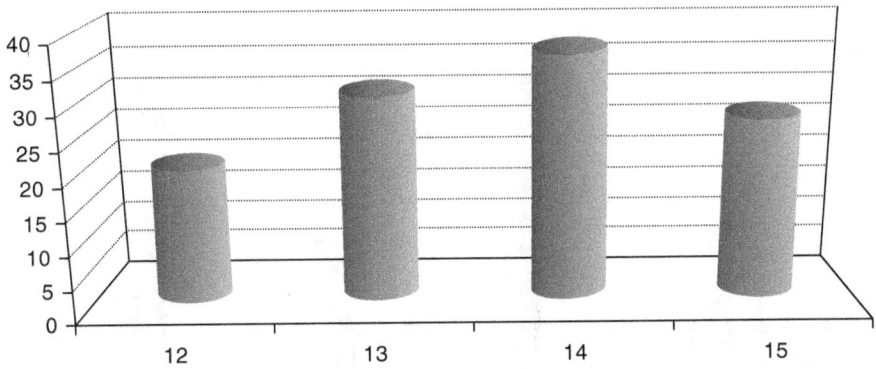

Graph 10.1 The ages of the boys conscripted from Herzegovina in 1493–4.
Source BOA, D.M.d. 36805 (899/1493–4).

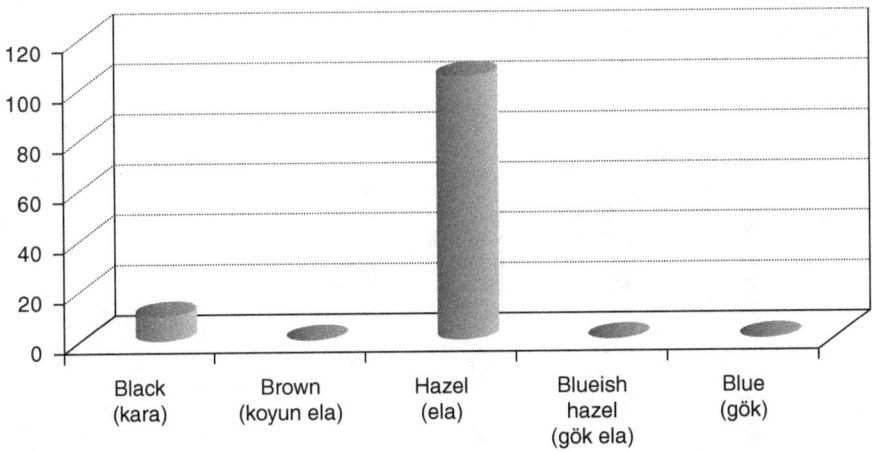

Graph 10.2 The eye colours of the boys conscripted from Herzegovina in 1493–4.
Source BOA, D.M.d. 36805 (899/1493–4).

to blue or blueish colours. However, blue (23 per cent) and blueish hazel (15 per cent) were new colours recorded by the scribes, compared to the former register.[37] Most were brown haired (38.5 per cent), and some (28.5 per cent) had even darker complexions (Graphs 10.5 and 10.6). It should be underlined that the way to describe boys physically also changed over time. In 1493–4, eye colour and skin tones were used as identifiers, whereas in 1604 eyebrow colours replaced skin tones. Last but not least, the entire batch of the 1493–4 levy consisted of Christian children, whereas in 1604, there were only fifteen Christian boys among a batch of 141, and the rest were Muslim. This was unique to Bosnia and Herzegovina (Graph 10.8).

The comparison shows that the characteristics of the boys selected

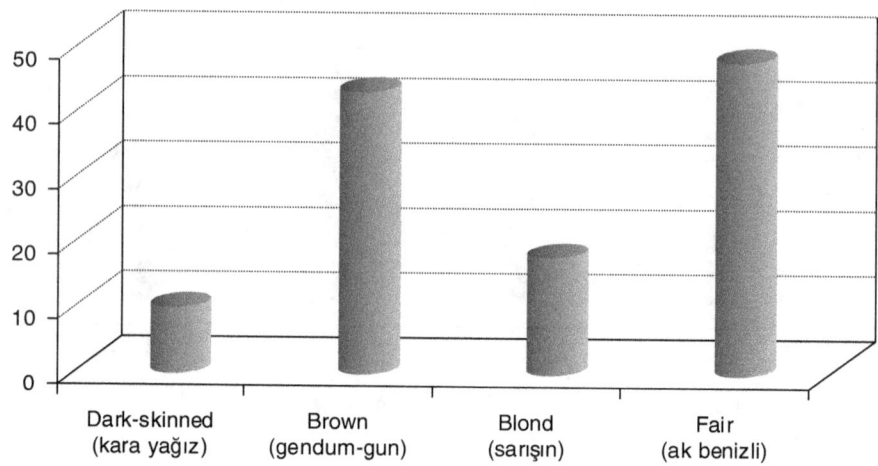

Graph 10.3 The colouration of the boys conscripted from Herzegovina in 1493–4.
Source BOA, D.M.d. 36805 (899/1493–4).

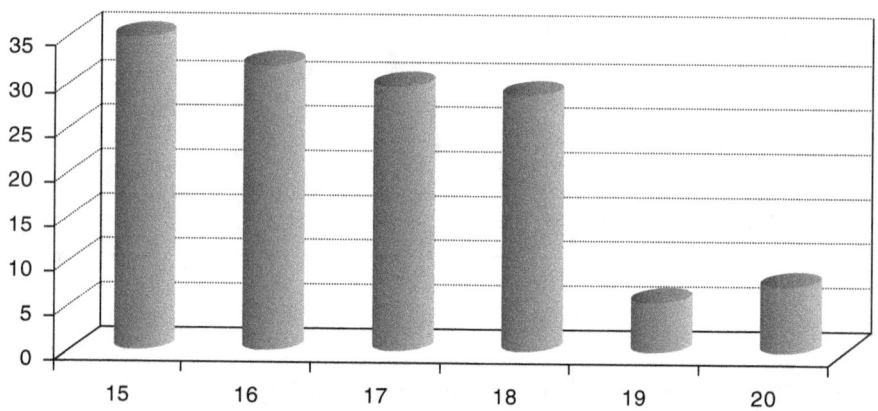

Graph 10.4 The ages of the boys conscripted from Herzegovina in 1604.
Source BOA, MAD 7600 (1012/1604).

from the same region changed through time. In 1493–4, thirteen-year-old Christian children with a mostly light complexion were conscripted, while in 1604 preference was largely for Muslim, brown-haired sixteen-year-old boys. Therefore, it is clear that the *Regulations* were not strictly adhered to. According to what, then, did the system operate?

At the local level, it is seen that the complexion and religion of the local population changed within approximately four generations. In the 1493–4 register, the entire batch of levies was Christian, whereas in 1604 it was predominantly Muslim. The number of Muslims seems to have

Body Politics and the Devşirmes

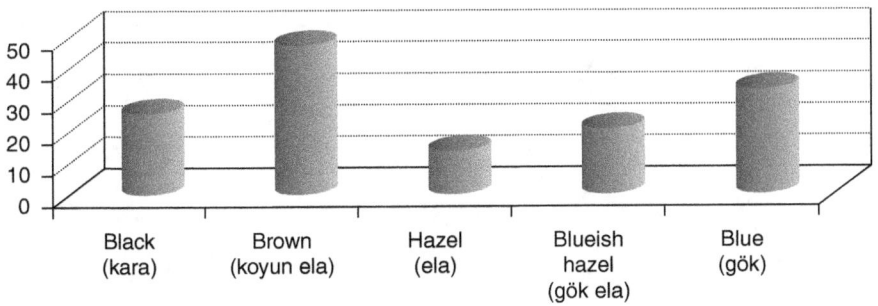

Graph 10.5 The eye colours of the boys conscripted from Herzegovina in 1604.
Source BOA, MAD 7600 (1012/1604).

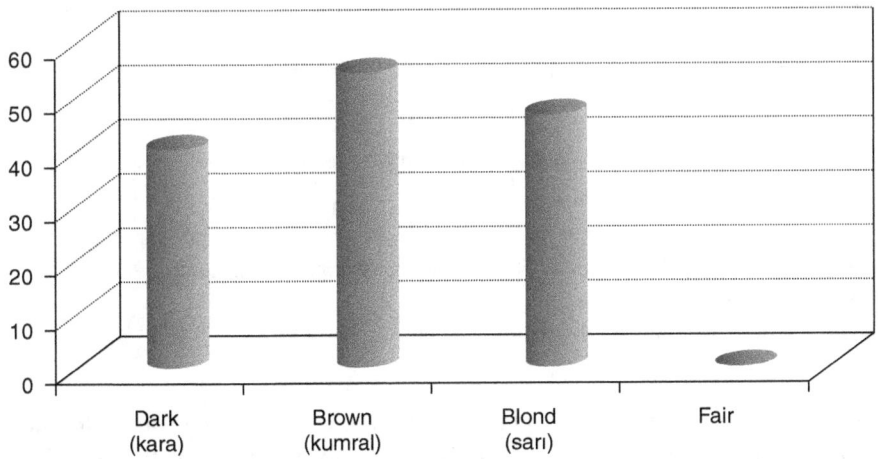

Graph 10.6 The colouration of the boys conscripted from Herzegovina in 1604.
Source BOA, MAD 7600 (1012/1604).

increased in the region, which could be due to immigration or conversions. It is not likely that Turkish–Muslim immigrant groups would be levied, since this was forbidden and, as a rule, it was strictly followed in the Balkans. A decree sent to the governor (*beglerbeg*) of Bosnia warned him against sparing the boys who spoke Turkish and Turkified (*Türkleşmiş*) while recruiting the circumcised ones in the region.[38] The enlistments were among the sons of the Bosnian families who had converted to Islam (*potur oğlans*), but not the Turks.

An often reiterated argument in the literature regarding the reasons behind levying the Bosnian Muslim boys (*potur oğlans*) is based on the *Regulations*.[39] In this document, it is argued that Bosnian Muslims could

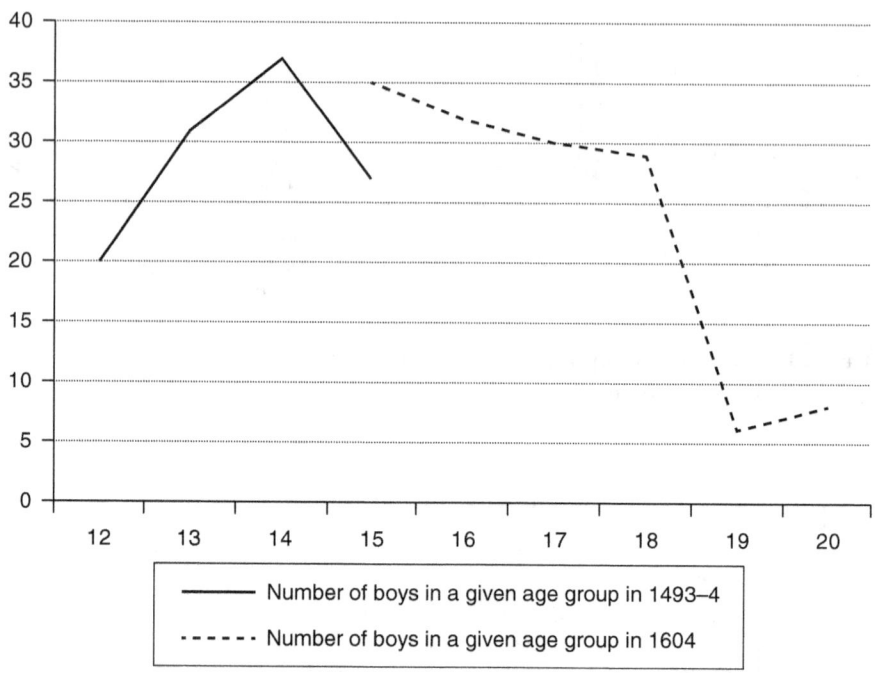

Graph 10.7 Comparison of the ages of the boys conscripted from Herzegovina in 1493–4 and 1604.

Source BOA, D.M.d. 36805 (899/1493–4) and MAD 7600 (1012/1604).

be levied thanks to special permission given to the locals by Mehmed II (r. 1451–81) at their request. This argument accepts that the Bosnians converted *en masse* to Islam and asked for the right to give away boys, despite the change of religion. The register of 1493–4, which took place twenty years after the conquest, shows that the boys were selected entirely from Christian families. This information indicates that a mass conversion did not take place right after the conquest, in contrast to what is accepted in the literature. Koyuncu offers a detailed analysis of this Islamisation theory and shows that the conversion did not happen in one event, but that it was a slow and gradual process.[40] Without a mass conversion, there could not be any petition to the sultan requesting to supply children as part of the *devşirme*. Crucially, this indicates that participation in the levy process on the Bosnians' side was not always voluntary. On the contrary, there were several decrees sent to the authorities in the region declaring that those who resisted giving their children away, whether Christian or Muslim, would be punished, which implies that Muslim families also tried to escape the levy.[41]

If there was no mass conversion and no official request to the state

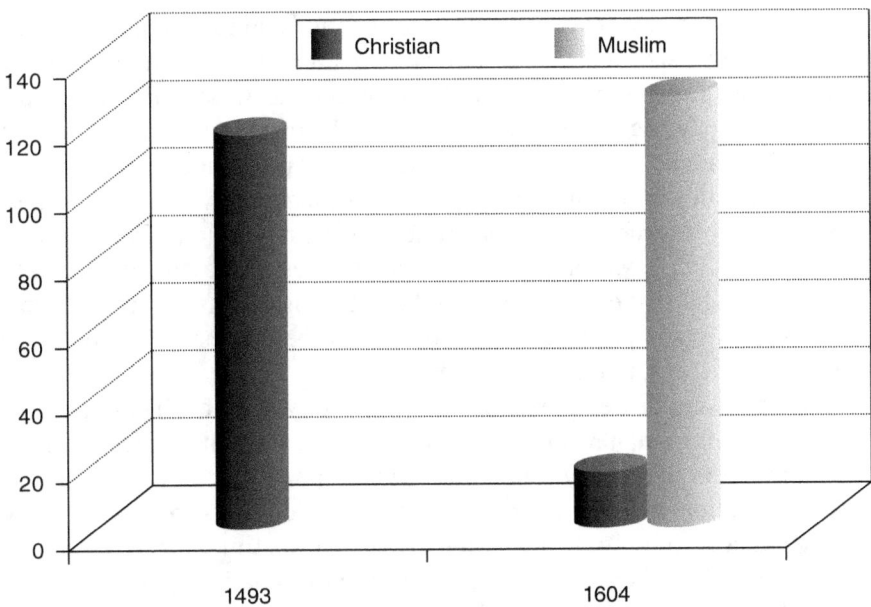

Graph 10.8 Comparison of the religions of the conscripted boys from Herzegovina in 1493–4 and 1604.

Source BOA, D.M.d. 36805 (899/1493–4) and MAD 7600 (1012/1604).

in favour of levying, then when and why did the authorities decide to recruit boys from among the Muslim Bosnians? Unfortunately, the exact beginning of this practice is not known. The actual reasons are concealed by the argument of the common petition and the special permission given by Mehmed II in the *Regulations for Janissaries*. The author of the *Regulations* was possibly aware that Muslims should not be levied, and therefore there must be a reasonable explanation to support such a decision. It is likely that the *devşirme* officers originally enlisted Christian boys after the conquest and conversion to Islam took place gradually in the region. With the acceleration of the Islamisation process from the end of the fifteenth century onwards, the authorities proved reluctant to forego this rich resource and continued to collect boys from among converted locals.[42] The *Regulations* were overlooked for the sake of continuing to operate the system.

In the literature, it is stressed that the levies from this region were bigger in stature, handsomer and more able than others.[43] It is argued that since these boys were better looking, many were kept for palace service. Indeed, my examination of the physical traits of boys from the Bosnia and Herzegovina region in 1603–4 has revealed that, compared to the boys from other regions, most were blond with blue eyes and had fewer marks on their faces, which was seen as a sign of beauty. Although there might be many other reasons for continuing to levy from among the Muslim Bosnians, this stress on looks brings us back to the issue of the body politics as one of the important dimensions of the *devşirme* system. The authorities adhered to a certain politics in defining the *proper* or *required* body and levied those displaying the desirable traits, sometimes despite regulations. In the case of the Bosnians, the boys continued to be enlisted despite having converted to Islam, which had, in effect, rendered their levying against the regulations. Moreover, this was probably not performed at the request of the locals; to the contrary, it was, at times, involuntary.

The state authorities pursued conscious body politics. They more or less knew their human resource base and had at least a rough idea of where to deploy them upon levy. They searched for particular characteristics in suitable candidates. Not only did they know which traits to look for, they also acted according to the changing criteria of the time. From the state's perspective, the criteria for selection changed dramatically from the late fifteenth to the early seventeenth centuries, and this had predominantly to do with the needs of the army, as reflected in the ages of the enlisted children. Despite the fact that there was no specific change in the regulations regarding the desirable age of the children, the officers targeted boys from entirely different age groups in the 1493–4 and 1604 samples from Herzegovina (Graph 10.7). The target group moved from adolescences (thirteen- to fifteen-year-olds) to youth (fifteen- to twenty-year-olds).

This was not unique to the Herzegovina region. In the 1603–4 levy, the average age of approximately 2,600 levied boys was sixteen-and-a-half. Almost 40 per cent of the boys were aged eighteen to twenty years old. It seems that by the early seventeenth century levying from among this age group was already widely accepted. In several decrees, state officers specifically requested boys aged between fifteen and twenty.[44] As the preferred age of the boys increased, this impacted heavily on the entire meaning of the *devşirme* system, which had been designed to recruit youngsters with a view to assimilation through training and acculturation into Ottoman society. The levies were predominantly trained to be janissaries, with the most successful and capable among them given a formal education, with the view to their becoming administrators. As a result of major changes in war techniques and the wide usage of firearms at the end of the sixteenth century, a janissary coming from the *devşirme* system, having trained as a professional soldier using traditional weapons, became redundant.[45] The body politics were accordingly modified. Older boys who could be trained faster to use the new weaponry were now preferred.[46]

As can be seen in the case of Herzegovina, the state consciously applied a meticulous body politics to select proper bodies for conscription. The preferences shifted in parallel with the change in the human landscape of the regions of levy, and with a growing change in the state's needs and priorities. The state's preferences for certain physical traits superseded the rule of not levying Muslims, or of not levying and converting boys older than fifteen years.

Alienation through Controlling the Body: Circumcision

The control of the body started with that moment in a *devşirme*'s life, when his entire life and identity was drastically changed, and he became a possession of the state. This could be tragic for a child. The moment that the state exercised this power, it signalled the initialisation of enslavement for them. This power over the body first manifested itself when the officers physically examined the selected boys, recording all their characteristics, converting them to Islam, giving them new Muslim names and dressing them in red garb (an early modern *uniform* in a sense) in order to transfer them to Istanbul. From this moment onwards, they belonged to the state.

Surveillance was initially one of the primary reasons for keeping records of physical characteristics. The state needed the boys to be identifiable so that they could track them. The officers controlled them so that they would not be able to run away, be kidnapped or exchanged. This concern also manifested in the tactics used when transferring the boys to the capital, such as not camping in the same area for more than three nights in a row and not asking for food from the locals as they camped.

The boys levied from their hometowns completed a difficult journey to the capital. There are a lot of gaps in our knowledge regarding the early experiences of *devşirme* life, as there are no relevant extant sources. Where were they first brought? How did they feel seeing the silhouette of Istanbul embellished with palaces and mosque complexes? Were they first taken to the janissary barracks? As batches of boys passed through the city to their destinations, what were their emotions towards the crowds gazing at them? It is probable that these boys did not know much about the new religion and language into which they were being inducted. One thing they surely must have felt, however, was that they were entering into something new and that they had relinquished control to something bigger and more powerful than themselves.

Upon reaching Istanbul, the boys were distributed to 976 deported non-Muslims residing in fourteen neighbourhoods in the city. Hosting the new arrivals, in order to give them rest after the long journey, was part of these non-Muslims' duties.[47] This could have provided some relief from the shock the Christian boys experienced, before they were placed in their new posts with their newly introduced identities. The control over their bodies may have started with the selection and recording processes, but did not end there. After changing their names to Muslim ones, the most remarkable moment of their transformation was the circumcision (*sünnet*). This was probably performed in Istanbul, but the exact time might have varied for each boy. Circumcision was the most important manifestation of being possessed and transformed by the state. It was a direct intervention on the body of the possessed.

Şehinşahname of Lokman narrates the circumcision festival of Sultan Murad III's son Prince Mehmed in 1582. The account illustrates the festival with thirty-five miniatures, one of them depicting the circumcision of the levied boys. In the miniature, the boys are shown to be circumcised together with Muslim children, being defined in the manuscript as new Muslims (*nev-müslimun*).[48] The emblematic nature of the circumcision ceremony of the *devşirme*s on the way to becoming new Muslims was also an important marker of the full possession of their bodies by the state.

With this life-changing experience, the boys were placed in different posts. Some were hired out to Turkish families in Anatolia or Rumelia in order to learn Turkish and Islamic practices.[49] Their exploitation of these boys as agricultural labourers should also not be overlooked. Heavy physical labour was an element of their new lives, since it was seen as part of their training, assuring strength and endurance. Similarly, the ones who stayed in Istanbul were used in multiple ways, ranging from skilled artisans to unqualified labourers. Their body and abilities were beneficial resources that were exploited in the best-suited areas in a manner strictly decided by the authorities. A select few were placed in the palaces to receive formal education on the way to becoming administrators. These were subjected to a stricter bodily discipline. The royal modes of behaviour, such as walking slowly, kissing the hands of their superiors and reverencing by holding their heads down with their hands crossed before them were all internalised by the boys. Their behaviours and bodies were under the control of their teachers, who monitored them closely.

Conclusion

The Ottoman state developed body politics for determining ideal candidates for the levy. Besides regulations, the authorities also made their decisions according to their available options. In other words, they were cognisant of the conditions of the region they were in and conscripted

Body Politics and the Devşirmes

Figure 10.1 Circumcision ceremony of Muslim and *Devşirme* boys together, 1582.

Source *Şehinşahname*, vol. 2, fol. 81a. Topkapı Palace Museum, B.200. Courtesy of the Directorate of National Palaces.

boys accordingly. Another factor that affected body politics was the state's needs. What type of duties these bodies would be used for probably affected the criteria for levy candidates. The authorities deliberately developed body politics in selecting which boys to levy and did not hesitate to change their policies according to the emerging needs of the state, such as those on the battlefield. In this regard, the *devşirme* process was not static, but rather a flexible one.

The possession and control of the boys' bodies began during the selection process and continued throughout their training. Setting criteria for body traits, recording their physical characteristics into levy registers, using them as surveillance precautions in addition to dressing them in the same type of garment during transportation, circumcising them, monitoring their body acts and assigning them duties according to their bodily performance were parts of the enslavement and possession of their body by the state. Although we have no information on how these children may have felt, examining the *devşirme* institution helps us to reflect upon at least one of the possible ways a Christian child experienced living under Ottoman rule.

Notes

1. This study is part of a research project (The Devşirme System and the Levied-Children of the Ottoman Empire (1460–1650), no. 115K354) funded by the *Scientific and Technological Research Council of Turkey (TÜBİTAK)*.
2. BOA, D.M.d. 36805 (899/1493–4). The entire batch is composed of 147 boys, however, the last thirty-two of them were recruited from the district of Akçahisar, from the towns of Mat and Yukarı Debre (corresponding to today's Northern Macedonia and Albania).
3. BOA, MAD 7600 (1012/1603–4).
4. Uzunçarşılı, *Kapıkulu Ocakları*; İnalcık, *The Ottoman Empire: The Classical Age 1300–1600*.
5. The argument that the system was based on merit should also be open to discussion, since it is known that households were formed through an 'attachment network' (*intisab ağı*), which valued loyalty more than merit.
6. Palmer, 'The Origins of the Janissaries', pp. 448–81; Wittek, '*Devşirme* and Shari'a'; Menage, 'Notes and Communications: Sidelights on the Devshirme from Idris and Sa'uddin'; Özcan, 'Devşirme', p. 256; Karamuk, 'Devşirmelerin Hukuki Durumları Üzerine', pp. 555–72.
7. Toledano, 'The Concept of Slavery', pp. 173–5.
8. Toledano, 'Enslavement in the Ottoman Empire in the Early Modern Period', p. 37.
9. Toledano, *As if Silent and Absent*, pp. 24–5.

10. Toledano, 'The Concept of Slavery', p. 167; Yılmaz, 'Becoming a Devşirme', pp. 127–8.
11. Papoulia, *Ursprung und Wisen der "Knabenlese"*; Vryonis, 'Isidore Glabas and the Turkish Devşirme'; Vryonis, 'Seljuk Gulams and Ottoman Devshirmes', pp. 224–52; Peirce, *Morality Tales*, p. 315; Zilfi, *Women and Slavery in the Late Ottoman Empire*, pp. 100–4.
12. The *devşirme* system is not seen as a form of slavery in the collective memory of today's Turkish society. Özcan's article is a good reflection of this view. Özcan, 'Devşirme'. Yet, there are more sophisticated attempts to explain the complex status of *devşirme* in Ottoman society: Faroqhi, *Slavery in the Ottoman World: A Literature Survey*, pp. 35–7. Kunt declares the slave status of the *devşirme*s, but stresses the fact that they were not the only source of manpower for the Ottoman military and administrative body. Kunt, *The Sultan's Servants*, pp. 32–3; Beydilli stresses that the enslaved children turned into *kul*s after their *çıkma* (promoted to administrative and military positions, lit. *kapıya çıkma* – entering from the gate), which is quite interesting since he is offering a model of transition from slavery to servitude, Beydilli, *Yeniçeriler ve Bir Yeniçerinin Hatıratı*, p. 10.
13. Foucault, 'Right of Death and Power of Life', p. 136.
14. Ibid., p. 139.
15. Groebner, *Who Are You?*
16. Ibid., p. 108.
17. Stella, ' "Herrado en el rostro con una S y un sclavo" ', pp. 147–63; Groebner, *Who Are You?*, p. 109.
18. Stella, ' "Herrado en el rostro con una S y un sclavo" ', pp. 148–9.
19. Davis, *Christian Slaves, Muslim Masters*, p. 62.
20. Ibid., p. 61.
21. Toledano, 'The Slave's Body in Ottoman Society', p. 68.
22. 'Such as a mark on the right side of his head and on his right wrist' (*başının sağ yanında ve sağ bileğinde*), 'marks of chicken pox on his face and a mark on his right hand' (*yüzünde çiçek alameti ve sağ elinde yaresi*).
23. *Kavanin-i Yeniçeriyan*, p. 139.
24. Toledano, 'The Concept of Slavery', p. 167.
25. Ze'evi, *Producing Desire*, pp. 26–7.
26. Ibid., pp. 26–30. La Rue also gives striking examples from a medieval Arab manual for slave owners, where body traits are treated as revealing a slave's character. For example, soft hair was an indication of cowardice, and a small-sized head was an indication of a weak brain that could result in stubbornness and quick temper. The manual also discusses eyes, eyebrows, ears, nose, lips, cheeks, gums, face and the neck. See La Rue, 'The Egyptian Slave Trade in Sudan', p. 75.
27. *Kavanin-i Yeniçeriyan*, p. 138.
28. Ibid.
29. Ibid., pp. 141–2.

30. Wittek, 'Devşirme and Shari'a', p. 278.
31. Kavanin-i Yeniçeriyan, p. 138.
32. Ibid.
33. Lowry, *The Nature of the Early Ottoman State*, pp. 118–22.
34. BCR, A 155, no. 1131 (1012/1603).
35. Many chapters in this book show various age ranges of adolescent boys.
36. See Telci's Chapter 2 in this volume for a discussion of the age twenty marking the end of bachelor (*mücerred*) status in young adolescents who were not married and lived under the roof of their father's house. After twenty, they were considered as fiscally responsible.
37. What is perceived as a certain colour might have changed over time. For example, the difference between hazel (*ela*), blueish hazel (*gök ela*) and blue (*gök*) might be different in different regions, and the perceptions of these colour might have varied over time.
38. Uzunçarşılı, *Kapıkulu Ocakları*, vol. 1, pp. 108–9.
39. Uzunçarşılı, *Osmanlı Tarihi*, vol. 1, pp. 84–5, 551, 554; Akgündüz, *İslam Hukukunda Kölelik-Cariyelik Müessesesi ve Osmanlı'da Harem*, pp. 46–7; Özcan, *Devşirme*, p. 255; Albayrak, *Bogomilizm ve Bosna Kilisesi*, p. 273; Özdemir, *Osmanlı Devleti'nde Devşirme Sistemi*, pp. 110, 122; Yıldız, *Osmanlı Devlet Teşkilatında Bostancı Ocağı*, pp. 7, 15.
40. Koyuncu, 'Kavanin-i Yeniçeriyân and the Recruitment of Bosnian Muslim Boys as Devşirme Reconsidered', pp. 296–7.
41. BOA, MD 35, no. 49 (986/1578); BOA, MD 22, no. 590 (981/1573); BOA, MD 5, no. 220 (973/1565).
42. Koyuncu, pp. 302–3.
43. Ibid., p. 300.
44. BCR, A 155, no. 1128 (1012/1603).
45. For a detailed explanation of this shift, see Yılmaz, 'Change in Manpower in the Early Modern Janissary Army', pp. 181–8.
46. The change in the composition of the janissary army was way more drastic. Muslim commoners were enlisted as new soldiers: İnalcık, 'Military and Fiscal Transformation in the Ottoman Empire (1600–1700)', pp. 288–97. Ágoston, *Guns for the Sultan: Military Power and the Weapons Industry in the Ottoman Empire*, p. 26.
47. *Kanunname*, no. 1734, pp. 51b–52a.
48. *Şehinşahname*, vol. 2, fol. 81a.
49. *Kavanin-i Yeniçeriyan*, p. 137.

Bibliography

Archival sources
Cumhurbaşkanlığı Devlet Arşivleri (BOA)
Bab-ı Defteri Müteferrik Defterler (D.M.d.) 36805 (899/1493–4).
Maliyeden Müdevver (MAD) 7600 (1012/1603–4).

Bab-ı Asafi Divan-ı Hümayun Mühimme Kalemi (MD) 35, no. 49 (986/1578); 22, no. 590 (981/1573); 5, no. 220 (973/1565).
İstanbul Müftülüğü Şer'iyye Sicilleri Arşivi (Archives of Istanbul Religious Courts)
Bursa Court Records (BCR) A 155 (1012/1603).
Atıf Efendi Library
Kanunname, no. 1734, fol. 51b–52a.
Topkapı Sarayı Müzesi
Şehinşahname, vol. 2, B. 200.

Published primary sources
Anonymous, *Kavanin-i Yeniçeriyan*, in Ahmet Akgündüz (ed.), *Osmanlı Kanunnameleri ve Hukuki Tahlilleri, I. Ahmet Devri Kanunnameleri*, vol. 9 (Istanbul: Fey Vakfı Yayınları, 1990).

Secondary sources
Ágoston, Gábor, *Guns for the Sultan: Military Power and the Weapons Industry in the Ottoman Empire* (New York: Cambridge University Press, 2005).
Akgündüz, Ahmet, *İslam Hukukunda Kölelik-Cariyelik Müessesesi ve Osmanlı'da Harem* (Istanbul: Osmanlı Araştırmaları Vakfı, 1995).
Albayrak, Kadir, *Bogomilizm ve Bosna Kilisesi* (Istanbul: Emre Yayınları, 2005).
Beydilli, Kemal, *Yeniçeriler ve Bir Yeniçerinin Hatıratı* (Istanbul: Yitik Hazine Yayınları, 2013).
Davis, Robert C., *Christian Slaves, Muslim Masters: White Slavery in the Mediterranean, the Barbary Coast, and Italy, 1500–1800* (Basingstoke and New York: Palgrave Macmillan, 2003).
Faroqhi, Suraiya, *Slavery in the Ottoman World: A Literature Survey*, Otto Spies Memorial Lecture (Berlin: EB-Verlag, 2017).
Foucault, Michele, *The History of Sexuality*, vol. 1 (New York: Pantheon Books, 1978).
Groebner, Valentin, *Who Are You? Identification, Deception and Surveillance in Early Modern Europe* (New York: Zone Books, 2007).
İnalcık, Halil, 'Military and Fiscal Transformation in the Ottoman Empire (1600–1700)', *Archivum Ottomanicum*, 6 (1980), pp. 283–339.
_____, *The Ottoman Empire: The Classical Age 1300–1600* (London: Phoenix Press, 2000).
Karamuk, Gümeç, 'Devşirmelerin Hukuki Durumları Üzerine', in Mehmet Öz and Oktay Özel (eds), *Söğüt'ten İstanbul'a Osmanlı Devleti'nin Kuruluşu Üzerine Tartışmalar* (Ankara: İmge Kitabevi, 2000), pp. 555–72.
Koyuncu, Aşkın, 'Kavanin-i Yeniçeriyân and the Recruitment of Bosnian Muslim Boys as Devşirme Reconsidered', in Srđan Rudić and Selim Aslantaş (eds), *State and Society in the Balkans Before and After Establishment of Ottoman Rule* (Belgrade: The Institute of History Belgrade, 2017), pp. 283–319.

Kunt, Metin, *The Sultan's Servants: The Transformation of Ottoman Provincial Government, 1550–1650* (New York: Columbia University Press, 1983).

La Rue, George Michael, 'The Brief Life of 'Ali the Orphan of Kordofan: The Egyptian Slave Trade in Sudan, 1820–35', in Gwyn Campbell, Suzanne Miers, and Joseph C. Miller (eds), *Children in Slavery Through the Ages* (Athens, OH: Ohio University Press, 2009), pp. 71–87.

Lowry, Heath, *The Nature of the Early Ottoman State* (New York: State University of New York Press, 2003).

Menage, V. L., 'Notes and Communications: Sidelights on the Devshirme from Idris and Sa'uddin', *Bulletin of the School of Oriental African Studies*, 18/1 (1956), pp. 181–3.

Özcan, Abdulkadir, 'Devşirme', *İslam Ansiklopedisi*, vol. 9 (Ankara: Turkiye Diyanet Vakfı, 1988), pp. 254–7.

Özdemir, Serdar, *Osmanlı Devleti'nde Devşirme Sistemi* (Istanbul: Rağbet Yayınları, 2008).

Palmer, J. A. B., 'The Origins of the Janissaries', *John Rylands Library Bulletin*, 35/2 (1953), pp. 448–81.

Papoulia, Basilike D., *Ursprung und Wisen der "Knabenlese" im osmanishen Reich* (Munich: Verlag R. Oldenburg, 1963).

Peirce, Leslie, *Morality Tales: Law and Gender in the Ottoman Court of Aintab* (Berkeley, CA: University of California Press, 2003).

Stella, Alessandro, 'Herrado en el rostro con una S y un sclavo': L'homme-animal dans l'Espagne des XV-XVIIe siècle', in Henri Bersc (ed.), *Figures de l'esclave au Moyen Age et dans le monde modern* (Paris: L'Harmattan, 1996), pp. 147–63.

Toledano, Ehud, *As if Silent and Absent* (New Haven: Yale University Press, 2007).

———, 'The Concept of Slavery in Ottoman and Other Muslim Societies: Dichotomy or Continuum', in Miura Toru and John Edward Philips (eds), *Slave Elites in the Middle East and Africa: A Comparative Study* (London and New York: Kegan Paul International, 2000), pp. 159–76.

———, 'Enslavement in the Ottoman Empire in the Early Modern Period', in David Eltis and Stanley L. Engerman (eds), *The Cambridge World History of Slavery* (Cambridge: Cambridge University Press, 2011), pp. 25–47.

———, 'The Slave's Body in Ottoman Society', in Thomas Wiedeman and Jane Gardner (eds), *Representing the Body of the Slave* (Portland: Frank Cass, 2002), pp. 57–74.

Uzunçarşılı, Ismail H., *Osmanlı Devlet Teşkilatında Kapıkulu Ocakları*, 2 vols (Ankara: Türk Tarih Kurumu Basımevi, 1943).

———, *Osmanlı Tarihi*, vol. 2, 5th edn (Ankara: Türk Tarih Kurumu Basımevi, 1988).

Vryonis, Speros, 'Isidore Glabas and the Turkish Devşirme', *Speculum*, 31 (1956), pp. 433–43.

_____, 'Seljuk Gulams and Ottoman Devshirmes', *Der Islam*, 41 (1965), pp. 224–52.
Wittek, Paul, 'Devşirme and Sharia', *Bulletin of the School of Oriental African Studies*, 17/2 (1955), pp. 271–8.
Yıldız, Murat, *Bahçıvanlıktan Saray Muhafızlığına: Bostancı Ocağı* (Istanbul: Yitik Hazine Yayınları, 2011).
Yılmaz, Gülay, 'Becoming a Devşirme: The Training of Conscripted Children in the Ottoman Empire', in Gwyn Campbell, Suzanne Miers, and Joseph C. Miller (eds), *Children in Slavery Through the Ages* (Athens, OH: Ohio University Press, 2009), pp. 119–35.
_____, 'Change in Manpower in the Early Modern Janissary Army and its Impact on the Devshirme System', *Rivista di Studi Militari*, 6 (2017), pp. 181–8.
Ze'evi, Dror, *Producing Desire: Changing Sexual Discourse in the Ottoman Middle East 1500–1900* (Berkeley: University of California Press, 2006).
Zilfi, Madeline C., *Women and Slavery in the Late Ottoman Empire: The Design of Difference* (New York: Cambridge University Press, 2010).

Chapter 11

Pastimes for the Child Breadwinners: The Sanitisation and Recreation Facilities of the Hereke Factory Campus[1]

Didem Yavuz Velipaşaoğlu

During the nineteenth century, child labour in the Ottoman Empire was not well recorded, documented or charted, however, the history of children during the period is mostly covered. In the case of one particular Ottoman textile factory, the Hereke Imperial Factory, it is hidden in the construction records of dormitories, in the number of migrant families employed at the factory and in the oral history of those workers.

Located to the east of Istanbul on the waterfront of İzmid Bay on the Sea of Marmara, the Hereke factory was established in 1842[2] as a broadcloth plant founded by the Ottoman entrepreneur Hovhannes Dadyan (1799–1869),[3] who played a key role in applying new mechanical techniques to textile production in the Ottoman Empire during the nineteenth century. The factory was renamed the Imperial Factory in 1845 and became one of the major exemplars of a series of modernisation projects in the late Ottoman Empire, producing textiles and carpets to address the needs of local and international markets.[4] A self-sustained habitat, the plant had its own school, mosque, bathhouse, communal vegetable gardens, vineyard and shops.

This chapter elaborates the conditions children and workers were exposed to in their work in the Hereke Imperial Factory. The wage-earning workers at the factory, mostly children but also some single adults, dwelt in high-density multistoried cellular dormitories. The chapter focuses on the excluded voices of the Orthodox Greek, Armenian and Muslim orphans and other children who were conscripted into service at the factory. It aims to shed light on the different spatial conditions of these child workers through an examination of their accommodation at the factory campus, particularly their living standards, the regulation of their sanitary conditions and their recreational landscape. I show how, paralleling growing concerns about insanitary conditions in industrial cities in the nineteenth century, the state's efforts to sanitise the living conditions of the workers at the Hereke Imperial Factory merged with the philanthropic approaches of the Ottoman sultans in the second half of the nineteenth century and the early twentieth century. I argue that the result of these circumstances/ changes was the creation of new social, moral and healthcare infrastructure at the factory, including sanitary and recreational facilities. Aside from their role in the charitable programme of the sultans, such facilities and the practices associated with them also played an important role in new labour-management practices and in the disciplining and regulation of children's bodies. The regulation of the body led to better living arrangements and a work environment where children could socialise and get recreational pleasure. During the industrial era, children were often subject to unsanitary working conditions and unhealthy living conditions. However, at the Hereke factory campus, the working and living conditions were better; the facilities built around the Hereke Imperial Factory offered a chance for positive experiences in the working and living space for the children.

The nineteenth century witnessed the industrialisation of the Ottoman Empire. The state established a number of factories, including a fez factory, the İslimye broadcloth factory, the Zeytinburnu ironworks, the Bakırköy print works, the Yeşilköy agricultural college, the İzmid broadcloth factory, the Balıkesir textile factory, the Bursa silk factory, the Samakov iron foundry and the Hereke textile factory.[5] In the earliest documentation, belonging to the time period between 1842 and 1845 in which the İzmid Imperial Factory was under construction, the Hereke Imperial Factory was not classified by the state as an imperial investment, but as a branch of the İzmid broadcloth factory.

Until 1845, the factory operated as a privately owned enterprise.[6] The factory started to manufacture silk cloths from this date on, and in 1891, two buildings were constructed for a carpet workshop.[7] A broadcloth factory was later added to the factory in 1903.[8] Under the Republic of Turkey, the factory was transferred to the Turkish Industry and Metal Bank (Sanayi ve Maadin Bankası), founded in 1925. The factory was later transferred to Sümerbank, a state economic enterprise, in 1933 by Mustafa Kemal Atatürk as a modernisation project of early Republican Turkey.

An Overview on Child Labour Literature

There is a small but growing body of literature on child labour in the Ottoman Empire. Three recent studies shed light on children's working and housing issues. Yahya Araz looks at child labour prior to the second half of the nineteenth century. First, he focuses on child apprentices who worked in large cities. Araz talks about guild traditions, apprenticeship conventions and contracts between masters and apprentices. Focusing on the reforms of nineteenth century, he shows how children played a key role in the conveying of vocational information to new generations in the guild systems.[9] He also discusses how Anatolian girls were used in domestic services in Istanbul. As an example of charity, these girls were employed in household services at a cheaper rate than female child slaves (*cariyes*).[10]

Nazan Maksudyan examines foster-daughter labour within the blurring borders of charity and abuse at the hands of the upper classes and the state in the nineteenth-century Ottoman Empire. According to Maksudyan, the declining use of slaves in homes in the second half of the eighteenth century must be considered in relation to the increase of child adoption. They were often nursed, reared and 'rented' for service in the households of others, where they were often sexually exploited. Maksudyan also successfully shows that foster-daughters employed strategies of resistance, therefore she presents these girls as actors who took control of their own lives by making their voices heard in many diverse ways, such as escape, official complaint and suicide.[11]

Erdem Kabadayı investigates forced labour through the lens of the child workforce. He points out that military conscription resulted in a new and hybrid form of forced labour for some of the military recruits at state factories in the nineteenth century. He determines that in the case of the Ottomans, forced-labour practices illustrate the changing nature of the social contract between the ruled and the ruler during the nineteenth century and provide insight into other forms of employment by the state or in the service of the state. Kabadayı's work is important in showing the transformation from the traditional and archaic form of forced labour, corvée, to a new form of forced labour.[12]

In these studies, the major focus of child labour in nineteenth-century Ottoman Empire has been on domestic labour rather than on child labour in the public sphere, such as the case of the Hereke factory.

Child and Youth Labour at the Hereke Factory

Employment practices at the Hereke factory changed over time. In the early years of the factory, from its foundation in 1842 to 1855, its workforce comprised mostly slave children (*cariye* and *gulam*) and conscripted youths, both male and female. In later years, the factory transitioned to a workforce employed by consent. When it could no longer conscript child labourers, it began to invite children, mostly young girls, to work at the factory, and also to employ orphans.

In the second half of the nineteenth century, poor male children in the Ottoman Empire worked mostly in the mining industry, while female children were employed predominately in the textile industry. In the latter case, it was mechanisation programmes carried out by the state and by the private sector that created room for children and women to be employed as low-cost labour during the period.[13] The distribution of children in the workforce of the Empire depended on gender. Different types of work were clearly segregated by gender in this period, with jobs requiring physical strength assigned to males and those involving less intensive sorts of manual labour to females.

The vocational education of the poor and orphan children was managed in a similar way to the system of vocational orphanages (*ıslahhane*s), where current administrative expenses were covered by donations, along with the revenues of the landed estates of the orphanages.[14] The first vocational school, named a vocational orphanage, was launched in 1863 for orphans and destitute children in Niš.[15] A common statute for prospective vocational orphanages (*Vilayat Islahhaneleri Nizamnamesi*) was based on the one prepared by Governor Midhad Pasha for *ıslahhane*s in the Danube province. This regulation, which was sent to other provinces on 21 June 1867, ordered the establishment of an *ıslahhane* for vagrant orphans and destitute children in each province.[16] This idea of offering vocational education to children in the Ottoman Empire can be traced back decades earlier. In the 1830s, Sadık Rıfat Pasha (1807–57) reported on his observations of European practices while he was working as an ambassador in Vienna between 1836 and 1838.[17] The booklet he wrote, in which he introduced an ethical framework for children, claimed that children could become morally superior by making good use of their time through ingenuity and art, rather than wasting their time with idleness and games with no purpose (*faidesiz oyunlar*). A child, according to Sadık Rıfat Pasha, should go to school every day and should engage with ingenuity, art, trade and crafts for the public welfare.[18]

In fact, the imperial policy of the second half of the nineteenth century was oriented towards the creation of an industrial network that would demonstrate the Empire's independence in industrial power and that would shape modern Ottoman civilisation. The first prototypes of trade and industrial schools in the Ottoman Empire emerged during the *Tanzimat* reform period as part of an imperial modernisation process and later evolved into full-time schools after a special decree was issued to regulate technical education. In the late nineteenth century, the students of these schools, mostly orphans and poor children, increased in number, and so were assigned their own buildings and other technical facilities. After the circulation of the Imperial order, many industrial orphanages were opened simultaneously for destitute and orphan children in the provinces. These included Bursa (province of Hüdavendigar), Sivas, Aleppo, Kastamonu, Izmir, Kandiye (in Crete), Salonica and Diyarbekir. By 1899, there were thirty-four vocational orphanages operating, including in the provinces of Mamuretülaziz, Adana, Konya, Jerusalem, Kosova, Monastir and Janina.[19]

This was also true for the Hereke Imperial Factory, whose workforce consisted mostly of young girls, though it also included some single adults and families. The children employed at the factory, often orphans, were offered housing on the factory grounds in exchange for work. Across this industrial network, the trade (industrial) schools encouraged modernisation and the establishment of factories, and thus provided many qualified staff for the workshops at the Hereke Imperial Factory.

This philanthropic aspect to the factory's employment of children is apparent in the factory's early years. In 1845, when fire ravaged the Samatya district of Istanbul, the factory's founder, Hovhannes Dadyan, brought in a number of orphans to live and work at the Hereke factory, and he did the same at his factory in Zeytinburnu.[20] Over the following years, however, this philanthropic approach – housing in exchange for work – was replaced by the use of forced labour at the factory. The archives of the Imperial Treasury provide evidence of slaves working at the factory in 1846 and 1847. The documents record the food, drink and clothing expenses for twenty-four male and female child slaves, who were identified respectively with the words male slave (*gulam*) and female slave (*cariye*).[21] In 1849, the twenty-four child slaves remain on the payroll sheets.[22] The number of child slaves decreased to nineteen in the records from 1852, and these nineteen slaves were still working in the factory for a monthly salary in 1853.[23]

A document from 1855 shows that thirty Greek girls were requisitioned from among the inhabitants of Karasi for 'use' as weavers at the Hereke Imperial Factory. The girls were to be chosen on the basis of their skills and receive vocational training after being chosen.[24] The recruitment of non-Muslims as forced labourers in state factories shows that non-Muslims' religious and communal institutions played a central role in forced-labour conscription from among the Empire's Christian subjects.[25] The factory guaranteed the families that they would receive some of their daughters' wages and that the girls' honour and religion would be protected by the factory. The girls received vocational training, according to the document, which also emphasises that the factory foundation should not be perceived as a frightening place.[26] The method of employment in the factory carries the traces of forced labour. The children did not have full consent in their employment, but their work had a monetary value. To Kabadayı, these forms of unfree labour, and especially their manifestation in state enterprises, demonstrate a specific and coercive social contract between the ruled and the ruler.[27] In the case of the Ottomans, forced-labour practices illustrate the changing nature of this contract during the nineteenth century and provide insight into other forms of employment by the state or in the service of the state.

New reforms were introduced with the aim of abolishing corvée, a traditional and longstanding form of unfree labour in the Ottoman Empire in the second half of the nineteenth century.[28] However, the conscription of children to work in the workshops of the Hereke factory demonstrates that forms of forced labour continued, even though those forcibly conscripted earned a wage in the factory.[29] Up until the banning of forced labour, a process that began with the enactment of the first mining regulations in 1861, compulsory work and corvée labour were in widespread use throughout the Empire. The 1930 Compulsory Work Convention (No. 29) defined forced or corvée labour as: '[A]ll work or service which is exacted from any person under the menace of any penalty and for which the said person has not offered himself voluntarily'.[30] As can be understood from this definition, compulsory work carries many of the characteristics of slavery.[31] As a form of slavery, the forced labourers in the factory were mostly non-Muslims. After the fire of 1878, the factory stopped production for five years.[32]

When the factory was reopened, a Monsieur Martel from Lyon was appointed as the factory manager. Martel carried out an initial investigation of the factory, following which he drew up a project (*layiha*) for its operation. He proposed reorganising the factory's workforce, with different groups of female youths assigned to work particular machines. In his 1885 reports, Martel laid out the projected requirements for the factory's female workforce (*kadınlar ve genç kızlar*): looms (*eblimiye* [?] *destgahı*), warping mills (*çözgü dolabı*) and bobbin holders (*masura destgahı*).[33]

In addition, women and girls from Christian and Muslim neighbourhoods close to the factory campus were also summoned to work in the carpet section by the factory administration, which was opened in 1891.[34] In 1902, the factory went once more in search of Ottoman girls who had a grasp of weaving techniques. The interior ministry (*dahiliye nezareti*) sought to find girls in Ankara province, and specifically those from the towns of Kırşehir and Isparta.[35] The girls offered work in the factory were mostly selected from these towns, where rug weaving was a well-developed practice that many households engaged in to earn income. However, the governor was unable to find any weaving girls from Kırşehir,[36] which resulted in a labour shortage. Therefore, the factory began employing poor children and orphans again in the early 1900s, especially after a broadcloth section was added to the plant site in 1903.[37] An article in *Servet-i Fünun* published on 12 July 1906 stated that there were 2,000 workers employed at the factory at that time, including both adults and children. However, increasing domestic and international demand for Hereke products[38] and the sultan's desire to strengthen the Ottoman textile industry to compete with European products led the state to double the size of the workforce. As part of this expansion, many poor children and orphans (*nice etfal-i fukara ve yetime*) were to be hired.[39] By the 1910s, the factory had three carpet-weaving workshops employing 2,400 girls.[40]

Body Regulations

The children working at the Hereke factory were divided into a day shift and a night shift, and all of them worked six days a week.[41] The day shift on the Hereke campus began with the ringing of the morning bell, after which they would have a breakfast of soup. According to one contemporary observer, the workers worked from eleven o'clock in the morning to eleven o'clock in the evening, with a one-hour break for lunch.[42] The knotters on the carpet line worked eleven hours per day, except the youngest girls, who were allowed to stop when they got tired.[43] The female workers ranged from four to fifteen years of age, and worked under the supervision of older women.[44] The female workers dressed in uniform smock frocks.[45] They could take a vacation with one month's pay during the spring. This payment was calculated as the average of their wages for one month.[46] The child labourers worked for low wages,[47] ranging from three to ten *qurush*, while the salaried masters earned between 400 and 600 *qurush* monthly. The workers also received free meals and some additional pocket money.[48] For those who had families outside the factory, the families would send meals to their working daughters by boat, and the girls would send back money to their families. The girls would often convert their money into pieces of gold and wear them as a necklace. Since the majority of the workforce at the factory was Christian, there was no work on Sundays. Groups of 200 to 300 girls would play the barrel organ (*laterna*) and dance,[49] while others would go on outings to the waterfront or to the orchard gardens with their overseers.

Over the years, the administration of the factory was to take charge of

Pastimes for the Child Breadwinners

Figure 11.1 Workers at the Hereke factory with a Gördes-style carpet in the background.
Source Istanbul Rare Works Library, 90453–34, 1892.

all responsibilities of the girls up to their marriage. The girls would work in the factory for fifteen years, after which they could retire. When one of them was to be engaged, the father-in-law and mother-in-law would come to the plant site, and they would be given away in marriage. When they got married, the administration of the factory gifted them silk fabrics and they retired.[50] The factory controlled children's bodies independently of their mothers and fathers and changed their bodies into a source of local labour up to their adulthood. Their post-marriage adulthood was also guaranteed through the system of a retirement fund (*tekaüd sandığı*), founded in 1895.[51]

By the 1890s, the factory began to produce carpets in 'monumental' proportions (see Figure 11.1).[52] Children worked in large groups in routine jobs, and their bodies became a site for the demonstration of mass management. Although carpet making is a pre-industrial craft tradition, the Hereke products were depicted as industrial artistic products by Europeans during the Paris Exposition of 1900, where Hereke products were on display.[53] But what, exactly, was 'industrial' about them? The answer to this question is related to the disciplined way the factory operated. In the case of the Hereke factory, it was the bodies of the labourers, children, orphans and masters that were industrialised. The knotters worked in large groups in routine jobs, and their bodies were manipulated and regulated for craft production. Although the knotters did not work on mechanised looms, the process of the production was industrial. New forms of social organisation and control turned workers into veritable automatons or machines. By controlling children's bodies, they were collectively transformed, in effect, into vast carpet looms.

However, evidence also shows that women found ways to retain and exercise power within this new industrial order by taking up roles teaching others the practice of weaving and new weaving methods. Female masters were even awarded for their teaching skills. In 1896, for example, several female teachers were awarded industrial medals by the sultan for teaching their students how to make a *kaliçe*, a sort of small rug.[54] In 1905, another sixteen teachers at the rug-weaving workshop were awarded the same honour.[55]

Accommodation

An investigation into barracks-inspired dormitories (*koğuş*) such as the one at the Hereke site provides us with a way to better understand the labour relations in this period. From the second half of the eighteenth century onwards, the model of the barracks-inspired structure spread to manufacturing workshops, factories, schools, prisons and asylums in a series of concerted attempts to create 'ideal citizens' or vassals.[56] Military barracks and factories became laboratories of standardisation for the creation of soldier–citizens and industrial proletarians. The outsiders of industrial production, such as vagrants, beggars, prostitutes and criminals, were disciplined in workhouses and houses of correction in London, Amsterdam, north Germany and the Baltic as early as the sixteenth century. For example, a workhouse, named Tuchthuis, was opened in Amsterdam in 1596, gathering together vagrants, beggars and criminals, along with children and young people whose expenses were met by their families, in order to teach them manufacturing.[57]

Similar dwellings in the Hereke factory campus, especially the ones for children, played a key role in the transition of the Ottoman workforce from forced labour to free labour. A dormitory for single workers was constructed on the waterfront after the foundation of the factory (see Figure 11.2).[58]

In 1847, sixteen dormitories were erected inside the commercial building at the factory.[59] At that time, there were eight single-room residences for European masters and thirty rooms for the accommodation of unmarried Ottoman workers.[60] After the addition of the *kemhahane* (building for the production of *kemha*, a form of silk cloth) in 1848, new houses for workers and officials were added to the campus, as was a new dormitory for the girls involved in spinning silk yarn.[61] In 1850, one new dormitory was constructed inside the village and another across from the coffeehouse.[62]

By this time, dormitories were already part of factory life. However, there was still an acute housing shortage for the workers. The new, barracks-inspired dormitories were a solution that allowed the factory to

Figure 11.2 The dormitories for the single workers at the waterfront, and the row houses for the technical staff behind the dormitories.

Source Istanbul Rare Works Library, 90453–004, 1890.

accommodate its worker population. After the addition of a carpet section in 1891, women from the nearby Christian and Muslim neighbourhoods commuted daily and weekly to Hereke.[63] In 1893, the rug-weaving workshop (*kaliçehane*) was expanded. At that time, the repairs records demonstrate that there was a dormitory for Greek Orthodox girls, along with a dormitory for unmarried people (*bekar koğuşu*), at the factory campus. With the expansion of the workshop, the construction of rooms for the increasing number of unmarried workers (*günden güne çoğalan amele için odalar inşası*) became more pressing.[64] In 1898, a new dormitory was added after the foundation of the rug-weaving workshop.[65] In 1899, another dormitory was constructed.[66] Dormitories were mostly occupied by young girls and were strictly separated from the dormitories of the male workers.[67]

In the 1890s, the dormitories were overcrowded and unhygienic. The correspondence between the administration and the imperial treasury demonstrates that with the construction of new workshops on the site in 1898, the number of workers increased, with the number of male workers approaching 600, while the number of female workers increased to around 1,000. The workers dwelt in multistorey high-density cellular dormitories. The existing dormitories were inadequate to house all the workers, and they were already overcrowded, with each room occupied by twenty workers. Inevitably, this situation fostered epidemics; contagious diseases spread among the workers.[68]

Shortly afterwards, by the first decade of the 1900s, the administration of the factory envisioned a new structure. For the dormitories, this was one in which sanitation was a key concern. With the new typology, the number of people in each dormitory would be decreased; each dormitory housed forty girls, and each group of forty girls had a foster-mother responsible for cooking and cleaning. Separate dormitories for workers with families allowed them to stay in accommodation with a bedroom, sitting room and kitchen.[69] The construction of a new dormitory with annexes including wet areas, such as kitchens and toilets, was also envisioned in 1903.[70]

At the Hereke factory, the 'ideal worker' was created by the regulation of the crowd; the workforce, composed of mostly children, was created through the standardisation of everyday life practices in the dormitories. The children and single workers woke up at a certain hour in their rooms with a sea view. They retrieved their belongings from their individual cabinets and changed into their uniforms in their communal bedrooms. They ate breakfast prepared by their foster-mothers in the dining hall. They worked for a certain period; they knotted and weaved together all day on the looms (see Figure 11.3) and gathered in the lunchroom or else in the coffee shop during the lunch hour. They dined together, and at night they slept together, with separate dormitories for the Greek Orthodox and Muslim girls.[71] And the next morning, the same routine began again.

Hospital

Only in 1898, did the administration of the factory request that the imperial treasury construct a hospital on the plant site, since contagious diseases spread among the workers because of the overcrowded conditions of the dormitories.[72] The administration of the factory asked that a hospital be built on the factory campus, as had been done at imperial factories such as the İzmid broadcloth factory and the fez factory.[73] The hospital initially had twenty beds. Later, this number increased to fifty.[74]

The hospital opened on 13 February 1899.[75] The opening of hospitals for the working poor was a part of the modern social welfare programme of the Hamidian regime, and institutions of public health and social relief became widespread during the Hamidian period. The factory's hospital

Pastimes for the Child Breadwinners

Figure 11.3 Girls on the carpet loom.
Source Zsigmond Fejes, July 1914, Gróf Esterházy Károly Museum, 70.63.60.

was opened just after the launch of the Hamidiye Children's Hospital (*Hamidiye Etfal Hastane-i Alisi*) in 1899. Additionally, many hospitals for the poor (*gureba hastaneleri*) opened in the provinces across the Empire during the nineteenth century; this trend accelerated during the reign of Abdülhamid II.[76] The Ottoman Empire also participated in various international health congresses.[77]

The accelerated state intervention in sanitary matters shows that the state had serious concerns about public health threats. Cholera became a major disease during the nineteenth century. For instance, in Istanbul, the first epidemic happened in 1831, and this was followed by epidemics in 1847, 1865 and 1893–5. Cholera outbreaks led to quarantines in the provinces, which had a negative effect on commercial life. Malaria was also a concern, specifically in rice-growing regions, such as Iraq, eastern Anatolia, Maraş, the Black Sea coast and Thessaloniki.[78] Other cities, especially those near swamps or on important transit routes, were also threatened by various diseases. Baghdad, for example, suffered epidemics of cholera, plague, typhoid, dysentery, variola and pox.[79]

The Ottomans worked to address the threat of disease in a number of ways. In addition to building hospitals, they also instituted measures regulating the sale of different types of fruits and vegetables and the filtering of drinking water.[80] At Hereke, the factory administration was concerned that contagious diseases might spread rapidly among the factory children staying in the dormitories. In addition, epidemics were caused by the production techniques of the factory. The use of chemicals during the dyeing process, especially after the adoption of European dyeing techniques in 1895, and the dumping of chemicals into the Ulupınar stream near the factory campus both caused health problems in the area of the factory.[81] After the construction of the dyeing plant at the broadcloth factory in 1903, cholera also became widespread on the factory campus. Since the dyeing plant had an open drainage system and little in the way of adequate sanitation, cholera spread easily through the campus in 1911. In 1912, a new sewage system with a 150m span was constructed.[82]

A hospital on the factory campus was necessary to improve the efficiency of the workforce, to create a healthy workforce through health facilities and finally to improve public hygiene. In addition, these children had been entrusted to the factory by their families. Therefore, the factory administration and the state were responsible for the health and quality of life of the little breadwinners.

Gardens, Revenue-generating Lands and Regenerating the Bodies

In 1906, a reporter for the *Servet-i Fünun*, during his trip to the Hereke Imperial Factory, described the picturesque landscape he found there in these words:

> The landscape surrounding the factory consists of mulberry gardens, orchards, vegetable gardens ... In the woods, a farmer is working. The son of a fisherman is playing in the sea. A country girl is singing.[83]

By the same token, a photograph taken around 1880 by Guillaume Berggren, a Swedish photographer, demonstrates that the factory campus was surrounded with gardens and a graveyard (see Figure 11.4). The waterfront was occupied by dormitories and shops. A self-sustained habitat, the Hereke factory campus had its own mulberry gardens, communal vegetable gardens, vineyards, olive grove and shops. The factory campus also had its own social infrastructure, including a school, mosque, bathhouse and lunchroom. The factory campus was designed to meet the needs of the workers and officials employed there. The entirety of this

Figure 11.4 Hereke Imperial Factory.
Source Istanbul Rare Works Library, 90490–0005, Guillaume Berggren, c. 1880.

picturesque, self-sustained habitat was owned by the imperial treasury, and the factory grounds and the economic activities that took place on them were part of a rental system and programme of nationalisation developed by the state.

In becoming a modern state, during the nineteenth century, the Ottoman state centralised its policies of land taxation. At the Hereke factory campus, the land, including its gardens and shops, was part of a rental agreement (*akaret-i seniyye*) that gave the central state total control over its revenues.

The description of the report for the *Servet-i Fünun* and the photograph which was taken by Guillaume Berggren show the development of the Hereke factory and its facilities during the nineteenth century. In 1845, aside from the factory itself, the grounds contained little more than a bakery.[84] By 1874, the facilities of the factory campus had increased in number, including a baked-goods vendor, a coffeehouse, a tobacco shop (*duhancı*), a lunchroom, a windmill, a bathhouse, a barbershop and a sweets shop (*halva*). Furthermore, during those years, new lands and orchards were added to the property of the imperial estates.[85]

From 1874, there was also an increase in rental incomes, since the factory had begun taking in new revenues, such as taxes from jetties

Didem Yavuz Velipaşaoğlu

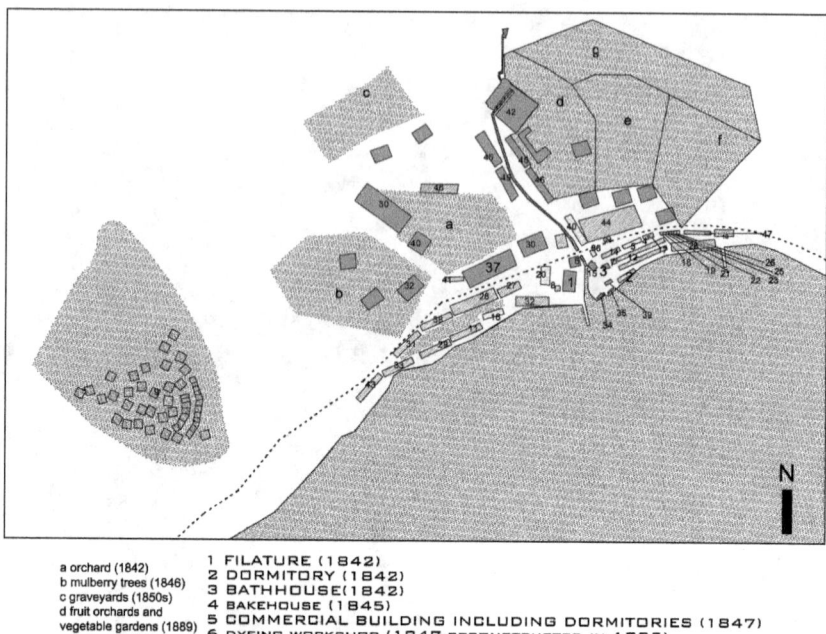

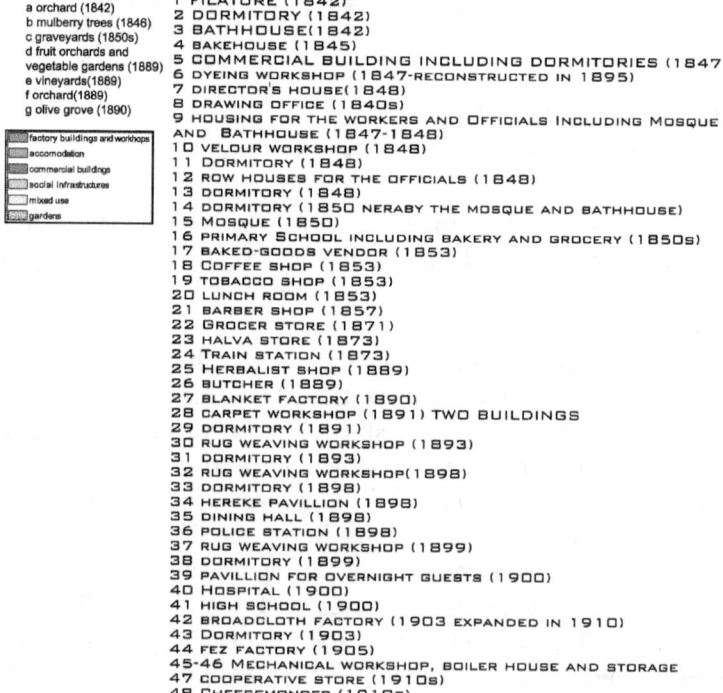

a orchard (1842)
b mulberry trees (1846)
c graveyards (1850s)
d fruit orchards and vegetable gardens (1889)
e vineyards(1889)
f orchard(1889)
g olive grove (1890)

- factory buildings and workshops
- accomodation
- commercial buildings
- social infrastructures
- mixed use
- gardens

1 FILATURE (1842)
2 DORMITORY (1842)
3 BATHHOUSE(1842)
4 BAKEHOUSE (1845)
5 COMMERCIAL BUILDING INCLUDING DORMITORIES (1847)
6 DYEING WORKSHOP (1847-RECONSTRUCTED IN 1895)
7 DIRECTOR'S HOUSE(1848)
8 DRAWING OFFICE (1840s)
9 HOUSING FOR THE WORKERS AND OFFICIALS INCLUDING MOSQUE AND BATHHOUSE (1847-1848)
10 VELOUR WORKSHOP (1848)
11 DORMITORY (1848)
12 ROW HOUSES FOR THE OFFICIALS (1848)
13 DORMITORY (1848)
14 DORMITORY (1850 NERABY THE MOSQUE AND BATHHOUSE)
15 MOSQUE (1850)
16 PRIMARY SCHOOL INCLUDING BAKERY AND GROCERY (1850s)
17 BAKED-GOODS VENDOR (1853)
18 COFFEE SHOP (1853)
19 TOBACCO SHOP (1853)
20 LUNCH ROOM (1853)
21 BARBER SHOP (1857)
22 GROCER STORE (1871)
23 HALVA STORE (1873)
24 TRAIN STATION (1873)
25 HERBALIST SHOP (1889)
26 BUTCHER (1889)
27 BLANKET FACTORY (1890)
28 CARPET WORKSHOP (1891) TWO BUILDINGS
29 DORMITORY (1891)
30 RUG WEAVING WORKSHOP (1893)
31 DORMITORY (1893)
32 RUG WEAVING WORKSHOP(1898)
33 DORMITORY (1898)
34 HEREKE PAVILLION (1898)
35 DINING HALL (1898)
36 POLICE STATION (1898)
37 RUG WEAVING WORKSHOP (1899)
38 DORMITORY (1899)
39 PAVILLION FOR OVERNIGHT GUESTS (1900)
40 HOSPITAL (1900)
41 HIGH SCHOOL (1900)
42 BROADCLOTH FACTORY (1903 EXPANDED IN 1910)
43 DORMITORY (1903)
44 FEZ FACTORY (1905)
45-46 MECHANICAL WORKSHOP, BOILER HOUSE AND STORAGE
47 COOPERATIVE STORE (1910s)
48 CHEESEMONGER (1910s)

Figure 11.5 Hypothetical plan showing the functions of the buildings.

Note The site plan of 1986 is taken from the Municipality of İzmid: the descriptions are from the archival documents, oral history and excursions to the site.

Source Image prepared by the author according to the Ottoman Military Academy (*Erkan-ı Harbiye*) map of 1915, taken from IRCICA Library (H772_001).

Pastimes for the Child Breadwinners

Figure 11.6 Young girls having lunch in the gardens of the factory campus, c. 1900.
Source Nazım Demirtaş Personal Archive.

and rental income from orchards, gardens and shops, along with profits from the sale of the output of the olive and walnut trees and the leaves of the mulberry trees.[86] The revenue list also included other shops.[87] In the 1890s, the revenue-generating lands expanded once again in tandem with the construction of carpet lines and new land registrations. In late 1880s and early 1890s, there were newly added gardens and shops.[88]

Once dormitories were added, the social gathering units expanded. The commercial buildings were located near the workers' dormitories and the officials' row houses. They were also close to the waterfront and the factory buildings, such as the main carpet workshop, where most of the workers spent their days. At the centre of the factory campus there were social infrastructures, such as a hospital, mosque, bathhouse and lunchroom (Figure 11.6). The planning principle of the factory campus was to situate the social infrastructures at the core of the factory campus, allowing easy access from both the factories and the dormitories. In everyday life practices, the multiethnic and multireligious workers composed of mostly children and officials of every age met in these spaces, chatted, had lunch, had a bath, drank coffee and shopped together. They worked and spent time together. At nights they slept in their respective dormitories and houses, which were separated strictly according to their religion.

Pastimes of the Children

Once the dormitories were added to the factory campus, places for socialisation and recreation began to expand. The gardens were not only a source of revenue for the imperial treasury or reserve areas to meet the needs of the factory workers, but also a place for recreation for the workers and officials. A photograph taken around 1900 shows young Muslim and non-Muslim girls, workers at the factory, having lunch in the gardens of the factory campus (see Figure 11.6). The roadside of the garden is decorated with flowers. The gardens served as a public space for workers of every age group. According to the 1906 account of the reporter for the *Servet-i Fünun*, some parts of the gardens were separated by curtains for the recreation of women. The waterfront was decorated with flowers and fountains.[89] These facilities also became a leisure space for the children working in the factory. In this way, the factory turned into a friendlier place for them. The gardens were social gathering places for the multiethnic workers and officials of every age. For instance, some concerts were held in the gardens of the factory. In 1910, a music society consisting of 250 railway men from Austria gave a concert at the Hereke factory campus on behalf of the Red Crescent.[90] The young workers of the Hereke factory dedicated their time outside of work to communal pastimes. The creation of such a picturesque and pastoral landscape on an industrial campus was a deliberate attempt to return sanity to the densely populated environment of the workhouses and dormitories, and leisure time spent there played a key role in the lives of the child breadwinners in terms of socialising and creating a life independent from their families.

Conclusion

Standardisation first became common practice with the emergence of mass society, when industrialisation brought about the development of technical standards and vice versa.[91] At the Hereke plant, the wage-earning workers were mostly children and unmarried adults. The bodies of the children and youths were standardised in cellular dormitories called *koğuş*, regulated on the rug looms, managed on the vast carpet looms, relaxed in the dormitories, rehabilitated in the hospital and recreated in the gardens.

When new production lines were added to the factory campus, new dormitories were constructed. When new dormitories were constructed, new lands were purchased to turn into gardens, which were incorporated into the grounds according to the land codes and organising schema of the imperial treasury. The regimentation of the workforce enabled the production of vast carpets in monumental sizes. The Ottoman experience of sanitising a textile factory – the Hereke Imperial Factory – merged with the sultan's philanthropic approaches to managing labour in the second half of nineteenth century and the early twentieth century. The 'ideal workers' were repaid with recreational facilities and social and healthcare institutions. The self-sustaining work environment provided the children a chance to socialise, and lunchtime picnics, holiday dances and evening concerts on the campus all fostered the friendships that developed among them. The young workers dedicated their free time to pastimes, and these pastimes were generally enjoyed as communal activities. At the same time, this environment also increased their sense of belonging to the workplace, and the establishment of recreational facilities led children to identify with the factory. Even though there was a closer control of the child labourers through industrialisation, the work environment provided was full of education, health and recreational facilities. 'The wasted time children spent in idleness and games with no purpose', an expression Sadık Rıfat Pasha used in his booklet *Risale-i Ahlak*, was replaced by defined leisure times centred on recreational facilities designed to provide a reprieve from the children's working hours in this industrial environment. The children became dedicated actors of 'public welfare', another expression from the booklet *Risale-i Ahlak*, with their disciplined bodies engaged with 'ingenuity, art, trade, and crafts'.

Notes

1. This chapter was partially produced from my PhD dissertation, Didem Yavuz, 'Crafting an Empire: Hereke Factory Campus (1842–1914)', PhD dissertation, NJIT–Rutgers State University of New Jersey, 2018.
2. 'Kuruluşundan Cumhuriyet'e Kadar Hereke Fabrikası' (1983), Hayri Tokay Documents, Edhem Eldem Personal Archive.
3. Between 1820 and 1822, Hovhannes Dadyan was the director of the paper mill in Beykoz. He acted as a director of the weaving factory in Eyüp between the years 1826 and 1829 and became the chargeman (*barutçubaşı*) in the Azadlı gunpowder factory in 1842. He established a tannery in Beykoz, as well as the İzmid broadcloth factory, the Hereke cloth factory and the Zeytinburnu ironworks. He invented machines for a spinning factory in Eyüp and for the armoury and also constructed an 18m-long iron bridge in Çırağan Palace in 1845. Pamukciyan, *Biyografilerle Ermeniler*, pp. 195–8.
4. For details on the expansion of the factory, see: Buluş, 'Osmanlı Tekstil

Sanayi Hereke Fabrikası'; Sezgin, 'Atölyeden Fabrikaya Geçiş Modeli Olarak Hereke Fabrika-i Hümayunu ve Endüstri Mirasımız Olarak Taşıdığı Değer', pp. 214–31; Küçükerman, *The Rugs and Textiles of Hereke*; Kaya, 'Hereke Fabrika-i Hümayunu Tarihçesi', pp. 10–21; Utkaner and Aydın Oral, 'Hereke Fabrika-i Hümayunu'nun Mimari Analizi ve Koruma Önerileri', pp. 46–51.
5. Buluş, 'Osmanlı Tekstil Sanayi Hereke Fabrikası', p. 102.
6. BOA, HH. HRK. 35/42 (1313/1895).
7. Ibid.
8. BOA, HH.THR. 315/28 (1321/1904).
9. Araz, 'Yoksulluk ve Çocuk Emeği', pp. 142–55.
10. For further discussion on domestic child labour, see Araz's Chapter 8 in this volume. Araz, 'Tebenni ve İcar-ı Sagir: Hayır İşlemek ve Eve Hizmetçi Almak', pp. 155–76.
11. Maksudyan, 'Foster-Daughter or Servant, Charity or Abuse', pp. 488–512.
12. Kabadayı, 'Working for the State in a Factory in Istanbul'. See also, Kabadayı, 'Working in a Fez Factory in Istanbul in the Late Nineteenth Century', pp. 69–91.
13. Quataert, *Miners and the State in the Ottoman Empire*, pp. 90–1; Quataert, 'Manufacturing in the Nineteenth Century', p. 93; Araz, 'Yoksulluk ve Çocuk Emeği', pp. 143–4.
14. Maksudyan's article discusses the connection between these rental agreements and the vocational orphanages. Maksudyan, 'Orphans, Cities and the State', pp. 493–511.
15. Semiz and Kuş, 'Osmanlıda Mesleki Teknik Eğitim', pp. 272–95.
16. Maksudyan, 'Orphans, Cities and the State', pp. 493–511.
17. Mehmed Sadık Rıfat Paşa, 'Merhumun Viyana'da İbtidaki Sefaretinde Avrupa Ahvaline Dair Yazdığı Risale', pp. 1–12. Sadık Rıfat Paşa was appointed Viennese ambassador in 1836 for two years. See Semiz, 'Sadık Rıfat Paşa (1807–1857) Hayatı ve Görüşleri', pp. 135–44.
18. Mehmed Sadık Rıfat Paşa, *Risale-i ahlak*, pp. 2–23.
19. Maksudyan, 'Hearing the Voiceless – Seeing the Invisible', pp. 200–81. According to Maksudyan, the opening of factories and the resulting need for unskilled and cheap labour tied the orphans and orphanages to the industrial production in a very curious way.
20. Yıldırım, *A History of Healthcare in Istanbul*, p. 180.
21. Buluş, 'Osmanlı Tekstil Sanayi Hereke Fabrikası', p. 315.
22. Ibid.
23. Ibid., p. 318.
24. BOA, MKT.UM. 209/56 (1272/1855).
25. Kabadayı, 'Working for the State in a Factory in Istanbul', p. 9.
26. BOA, A.MKT.UM. 209/56 (1272/1855).
27. Kabadayı, 'Working for the State in a Factory in Istanbul', pp. 8–9.
28. Ibid.

29. Özdemir, 'Türkiye'de "Zorunlu Çalışma" Uygulamaları', pp. 181–213.
30. International Labour Organization, 'Forced Labour', p. 9; also in Özdemir, 'Türkiye'de "Zorunlu Çalışma" Uygulamaları', p. 182. The terms 'corvée' and 'forced work', though frequently confused, have an important distinction. Corvée is to force a person or a community to work without recompense, whereas forced labour is work for which a small wage is paid. See Özdemir, 'Türkiye'de "Zorunlu Çalışma" Uygulamaları', p. 183.
31. Ibid., p. 182.
32. Buluş, 'Osmanlı Tekstil Sanayi Hereke Fabrikası', pp. 140–3.
33. BOA, Y.MTV. 15/7 (1301/1884).
34. BOA, HH.HRK. 35/42 (1313/1895).
35. BOA, DH.MKT. 621/12 (1320/1902).
36. Ibid.
37. Anonymous, 'Hereke Fabrika-i Hümayunu Ziyaret', p. 219; Kemalettin Apak, *Türkiye'de Devlet Sanayi ve Maadin İşletmeleri*, p. 178.
38. By the 1890s, Hereke products had become a symbol of national consumption, as well as an insignia of the Oriental art industry in Europe and the United States of America. Its products were on sale in shops in various parts of Istanbul, including on Doğru Yol in Beyoğlu, in the Grand Bazaar and on Zabıta Street. See BOA Y.MTV. 79/40 (1310/1893); BOA, HH.HRK. 35/42 (1313/1895); BOA, HH.THR. 277/24 (1312/1895). The reputation of the products of Hereke Imperial Factory were known outside the Empire. In 1908, two stores were reportedly opened in Washington, DC and New York, since the American elite greatly appreciated the factory's products. BOA, Y.MTV. 311/192 (1326/1908).
39. Anonymous, 'Hereke Fabrika-i Hümayunu Ziyaret', pp. 216–19.
40. CAM, Bithynia-İzmid-Hereke, B110, p. 12 (1964). The Orthodox Greeks left the factory after Greek commanders began operations in Eskişehir in 1922.
41. CAM, Bithynia-İzmid-Hereke, B110, p. 12 (1964).
42. Lorenz, 'Die frauenfrage im Osmanischen Reiche', pp. 161–2.
43. Quataert, 'The Age of Reforms, 1812–1914', p. 918.
44. Lorenz, 'Die frauenfrage im Osmanischen Reiche', pp. 161–2.
45. BOA, HH.THR. 293/27 (1318/1901)
46. Lorenz, 'Die frauenfrage im Osmanischen Reiche', pp. 161–2.
47. Quataert, 'The Age of Reforms', p. 918.
48. Lorenz, 'Die frauenfrage im Osmanischen Reiche', pp. 161–2.
49. CAM, Bithynia-İzmid-Hereke, B110, p. 12 (1964).
50. Ibid.
51. 'Kuruluşundan Cumhuriyete Kadar Hereke Fabrikası' (1983), Hayri Tokay Documents, Edhem Eldem Personal Archive.
52. Küçükerman, *The Rugs and Textiles of Hereke*, p. 74.
53. According to an issue of *L'Illustration* published on 11 August 1900, Hereke products became an exemplar of the Oriental art industry during the Paris

Exposition of 1900. See '1900 Paris Sergisindeki Resmi Osmanlı Pavyonu', p. 5.
54. BOA, İ. TAL. 401/39 (1324/1906).
55. BOA, İ.TAL. 365/46 (1323/1905).
56. Weber, *Wirtschaft und gesellschaft*, p. 684; Yıldız, 'Ondokuzuncu Yüzyılın İki "Standardizasyon Ütopyası"', pp. 118–35.
57. Ibid.
58. BOA, HH.HRK. 35/42 (1313/1895).
59. BOA, HH.d. 65/9 (1263/1847); BOA, HH.d. 256/5a (1263/1847). Also in Buluş, 'Osmanlı Tekstil Sanayi Hereke Fabrikası', p. 132.
60. Topal, Erdemir and Kırlı, 'Tanzimat Dönemi Sanayileşme Hareketinin Türkiye'de İşletmecilik Anlayışının Oluşumuna Etkileri Hereke Fabrikası ve Nizamnamesi', pp. 37–64.
61. BOA, HH.HRK. 64/36 (1316/1898); BOA, HH.HRK. 35/42 (1313/1895).
62. BOA, HH.HRK. 35/42 (1313/1895).
63. Ibid.
64. BOA, Y.MTV. 79/40 (1310/1893).
65. BOA, HH.THR. 1241/71 (1316/1898).
66. BOA, HH.d. 31625 (1316/1899).
67. BOA, HH.HRK. 35/42 (1313/1895); BOA, HH.THR. 305/30 (1320/1903).
68. BOA, HH.THR. 293/14 (1316/1898); BOA, HH.THR. 293/16 (1316/1898).
69. CAM, Bithynia-İzmid-Hereke, B110, p. 12 (1964).
70. BOA, HH.THR. 315/28 (1321/1904).
71. Quataert, 'The Age of Reforms', p. 918.
72. BOA, HH.THR. 293/14 (1316/1898); BOA, HH.THR. 293/16 (1316/1898).
73. Ibid.
74. 'Kuruluşundan Cumhuriyet'e Kadar Hereke Fabrikası' (1983), Hayri Tokay Documents, Edhem Eldem Personal Archive.
75. BOA, HH.THR. 293/19 (1316/1899).
76. Özbek, *Osmanlı İmparatorluğunda Sosyal Devlet*, pp. 195–6.
77. Yıldırım, *14. Yüzyıldan Cumhuriyet'e Hastalıklar Hastaneler Kurumlar*.
78. Graiten, 'Pilavdan Dönen İmparatorluk: Meclis-i Mebusan'da Sıtma ve Çeltik Tartışmaları', p. 99.
79. Kurt, 'Osmanlı Doğu Sınırında Kamu Sağlığı ve Siyaset: 19. Yüzyıl Bağdad'ında Hastaneler', pp. 151–2.
80. For further information, see Yıldırım, *14. Yüzyıldan Cumhuriyet'e Hastalıklar Hastaneler Kurumlar*.
81. BOA, HH.HRK. 35/42 (1313/1895); BOA, HH.THR. 277/24 (1312/1895).
82. BOA, HH.THR. 283/20 (1330/1912).
83. 'Hereke Fabrika-i Hümayunu Ziyaret', *Servet-i Fünun*, 794 (29 June 1322/12 July 1906), p. 218.
84. BOA, HH.HRK. 35/42 (1313/1895).
85. BOA, HH.d. 155/1a (1262/1846); BOA, HH.d. 65/26 (1290/1873); cited in Buluş, 'Osmanlı Tekstil Sanayi Hereke Fabrikası', pp. 126–7, 137–8.

86. Buluş, 'Osmanlı Tekstil Sanayi Hereke Fabrikası', p. 138.
87. Ibid.
88. BOA, HH.HRK. 27/19 (1307/1890); BOA, HH.HRK. 28/37 (1308/1891); BOA, HH.HRK. 28/37 (1308/1891).
89. Anonymous, 'Hereke Fabrika-i Hümayunu Ziyaret', p. 218.
90. BOA, BEO. 3743/280656 (1328/1910).
91. Yıldız, 'Ondokuzuncu Yüzyılın İki "Standardizasyon Ütopyası"', pp. 118–35.

Bibliography

Archival Sources
Cumhurbaşkanlığı Devlet Arşivleri (Presidency Ottoman Archives) (BOA)
Hazine-i Hassa Nezareti Hereke Fabrikası İdaresi (HH.HRK.) 35/42 (1313/1895); 27/19 (1307/1890); 28/37 (1308/1891); 64/36 (1316/1898).
Hazine-i Hassa Nezareti Tahrirat Kalemi (HH.THR.) 315/28 (1321/1904); 277/24 (1312/1895); 293/27 (1318/1901); 305/30 (1320/1903); 293/1 (1315/1897); 315/28 (1321/1904); 293/14 (1316/1898); 293/16 (1316/1898); 293/19 (1316/1899); 1241/71 (1316/1898); 277/24 (1312/1895); 283/20 (1330/1912); 277/24 (1312/1895).
Hazine-i Hassa Defterleri (HH.d.) 65/9 (1263/1847); 256/5a (1263/1847); 31625 (1316/1899); 155/1a (1262/1846); 65/26 (1290/1873).
Sadaret Mektubi Kalemi Umum Vilayat Evrakı (A.MKT.UM.) 209/56 (1272/1855).
Yıldız Mütenevvi Maruzat Evrakı (Y.MTV.) 15/7 (1301/1884); 79/40 (1310/1893); 311/192 (1326/1908); 79/40 (1310/1893).
Dahiliye Nezareti Mektubi Kalemi (DH.MKT.) 621/12 (1320/1902).
Hariciye Nezareti Mektubi Kalemi Evrakı (HR.MKT.) 88/81 (1271/1854); 85/24 (1270/1854).
İrade Taltifat (İ.TAL.) 401/39 (1324/1906); 365/46 (1323/1905).
Babıali Evrak Odası Evrakı (BEO.) 3743/280656 (1328/1910).

Primary Sources
Anonymous, 'Hereke Fabrika-i Hümayunu Ziyaret', *Servet-i Fünun*, 794 (1322/1906), pp. 216–19.
Anonymous, '1900 Paris Sergisindeki Resmi Osmanlı Pavyonu', trans. Zeynep Menemencioğlu, *Tarih ve Toplum*, no. 8 (August 1984), p. 5.
Centre for Asia Minor Studies (CAM), Athens: Bithynia-İzmid-Hereke, B110, p. 12, 1964. (Oral history by Dimitrios Lokmanidis, the grocer of the Hereke Imperial Factory, who migrated from Hereke to Greece in 1921. This oral history was recorded by Babis Nikiforidis from CAM in 1964 in Volos.)
Edhem Eldem Personal Archive: 'Kuruluşundan Cumhuriyet'e Kadar Hereke Fabrikası' (1983), Hayri Tokay Documents.
Gróf Esterházy Károly Museum, Pápa Zsigmond Fejes, 1914, 70.63.60.

Istanbul Rare Works Library, Istanbul: Guillaume Berggren, c. 1880, 90490–0005; 1892, 90453–34; 1890, 90453–004.

Mehmed Sadık Rıfat Paşa, *Risale-i Ahlak* (Istanbul: m.y., 1288/1371), pp. 2–23.

———, 'Merhumun Viyana'da İbtidaki Sefaretinde Avrupa Ahvaline Dair Yazdığı Risale', in *Müntebat-ı Asar-ı Rıfat Paşa* (Istanbul: Tatyos Divitciyan Matbaası 1290/1873), pp. 1–12.

Nazım Demirtaş Personal Archive: c. 1900.

Secondary Sources

Apak, Kemalettin, *Türkiye'de Devlet Sanayi ve Maadin İşletmeleri* (İzmit: Selüloz Basımevi, 1952).

Araz, Yahya, *16. Yüzyıldan 19. Yüzyıl Başlarına Osmanlı Toplumunda Çocuk Olmak* (Istanbul: Kitap Yayınevi, 2013).

Bullock, Nicholas, and James Read, *The Movement for Housing Reform in Germany and France, 1840-1914* (Cambridge: Cambridge University Press, 2010).

Buluş, Abdülkadir, 'Osmanlı Tekstil Sanayi Hereke Fabrikası', PhD dissertation, Istanbul University, 2000.

Georgeon, François, *Sultan Abdülhamid*, trans. Ali Berktay (Istanbul: İletişim Publication, 2006).

Gözel, Oya, 'The Implementation of the Ottoman Land Code of 1858 in the Eastern Anatolia', unpublished MA thesis, Middle Eastern Technical University, 2007.

Graiten, Chris, 'Pilavdan Dönen İmparatorluk: Meclis-i Mebusan'da Sıtma ve Çeltik Tartışmaları', in Burcu Kurt and İsmail Yaşayanlar (eds), *Osmanlı'dan Cumhuriyet'e Salgın Hastalıklar ve Kamu Sağlığı* (Istanbul: Tarih Vakfı Yurt Yayınları, 2017), pp. 97–118.

Heywood, Colin, *A History of Childhood: Children and Childhood in the West from Medieval to Modern Times* (Cambridge: Polity Press, 2001).

İslamoğlu, Huricihan, 'Property as a Contested Domain: A Re-evaluation of the Ottoman Land Code of 1858', in Roger Owen (ed.), *New Perspectives on Property and Land in the Middle East* (Cambridge, MA: Harvard University Press, 2001), pp. 3–42.

Kabadayı, Erdem, 'Working for the State in a Factory in Istanbul: The Role of Factory Workers' Ethno-Religious and Gender Characteristics in State-Subject Interaction in the Late Ottoman Empire', PhD dissertation, Munich University, 2008.

———, 'Working in a Fez Factory in Istanbul in the Late Nineteenth Century: Division of Labour and Networks of Migration formed along Ethno-Religious Lines', *International Review of Social History*, 54 (2009), pp. 69–90.

Kaya, Mehmet Kenan, 'Hereke Fabrika-i Hümayunu Tarihçesi', in Mehmet Kenan Kaya, Yaşar Yılmaz, Sara Boynak, and Vahide Gezgör (eds), *Milli Saraylar Koleksiyonunda Hereke Dokumaları ve Halıları* (Istanbul: Milli Saraylar Daire Başkanlığı Press, 1999), pp. 10–21.

Küçükerman, Önder, *The Rugs and Textiles of Hereke: A Documentary Account of the History of Hereke Court Workshop to Model Factory*, trans. M. E. Quigley-Pınar (Istanbul: Sümerbank, 1987).

Kurt, Burcu, 'Osmanlı Doğu Sınırında Kamu Sağlığı ve Siyaset: 19. Yüzyıl Bağdad'ında Hastaneler', in Burcu Kurt and İsmail Yaşayanlar (eds), *Osmanlı'dan Cumhuriyet'e Salgın Hastalıklar ve Kamu Sağlığı* (Istanbul: Tarih Vakfı Yurt Yayınları, 2017), pp. 143–69.

Lorenz, Charlotte, 'Die frauenfrage im Osmanischen Reiche mit besonderer berücksichtigung der arbeitenden klasse', *Die Welt des Islams*, 6/3–4 (31 December 1918), pp. 72–214.

Maksudyan, Nazan, 'Foster-Daughter or Servant, Charity or Abuse: *Beslemes* in the Late Ottoman Empire', *Journal of Historical Sociology*, 21/4 (December 2008), pp. 488–512.

———, 'Hearing the Voiceless – Seeing the Invisible: Orphans and Destitute Children as Actors of Social, Economic, and Political History in the late Ottoman Empire', PhD dissertation, Sabancı University, 2008.

———, 'Orphans, Cities and the State: Vocational Orphanages (*Islahhanes*) and Reform in the Late Ottoman Urban Space', *International Journal of Middle East Studies* 43 (2011), pp. 493–511.

Ökçün, Gündüz, *Osmanlı Sanayii: 1913–1915 İstatistikleri* (Istanbul: Hil Press, 1984).

Özbek, Nadir, *Osmanlı İmparatorluğunda Sosyal Devlet: Siyaset, İktidar ve Meşrutiyet 1876–1914* (Istanbul: İletişim Publications, 2002).

Özdemir, Süleyman, 'Türkiye'de "Zorunlu Çalışma" Uygulamaları', *Sosyal Siyaset Konferansları Dergisi*, 41–2 (1998), pp. 181–213.

Pamukciyan, Kevork, *Biyografilerle Ermeniler* (Istanbul: Aras Yayıncılık, 2003).

Prout, Alan, and Allison James, 'A New Paradigm for the Sociology of Childhood? Provenance, Province and Problems', in Alan Prout and Allison James (eds), *Constructing and Reconstructing Childhood: Contemporary Issues in the Sociological Study of Childhood* (London: The Falmer Press, 1990), pp. 7-33.

Quataert, Donald, 'Manufacturing in the Nineteenth Century', in Donald Quataert (ed.), *Manufacturing in the Ottoman Empire and Turkey, 1500–1950* (Albany, NY: State University of New York Press, 1994), pp. 87–123.

———, 'The Age of Reforms, 1812-1914', in Halil İnalcık and Donald Quataret (eds), *An Economic and Social History of the Ottoman Empire: 1600–1914* (Cambridge: Cambridge University Press, 1997), pp. 759–945.

———, *Miners and the State in the Ottoman Empire: The Zonguldak Coalfield, 1822–1920* (New York: Berghahn Books, 2006).

Semiz, Yaşar, 'Sadık Rıfat Paşa (1807–1857) Hayatı ve Görüşleri', *SU Türkiyat Araştırmaları Dergisi*, 1 (1994), pp. 135–44.

Semiz, Yaşar, and Recai Kuş, 'Osmanlıda Mesleki Teknik Eğitim: İstanbul Sanayi Mektebi (1869-1930)', *SU Türkiyat Araştırmaları Dergisi*, 15 (2004), pp. 275–95.

Sezgin, Candan, 'Atölyeden Fabrikaya Geçiş Modeli Olarak Hereke Fabrika-i Hümayunu ve Endüstri Mirasımız Olarak Taşıdığı Değer', in Kemal Kahraman and Ilona Baytar (eds), *Sultan Abdülmecid ve Dönemi (1823–1861)* (Istanbul: Milli Saraylar Press, 2015), pp. 214–31.

Terzi, Arzu, *Hazine-i Hassa Nezareti* (Ankara: Türk Tarih Kurumu, 2000).

Topal, Mehmet, Erkan Erdemir, and Engin Kırlı, 'Tanzimat Dönemi Sanayileşme Hareketinin Türkiye'de İşletmecilik Anlayışının Oluşumuna Etkileri Hereke Fabrikası ve Nizamnamesi', *SDU Faculty of Arts and Sciences Journal of Social Sciences*, 25 (May 2012), pp. 37–64.

Utkaner, Yusuf, and Özlem Aydın Oral, 'Hereke Fabrika-i Hümayunu'nun Mimari Analizi ve Koruma Önerileri', *Mimarlık*, 350 (November–December 2009), pp. 46–51.

Weber, Max, *Wirtschaft und Gesellschaft* (Tübingen: Mohr Siebeck, 1980).

Yıldırım, Nuran, *A History of Healthcare in Istanbul: Health Organizations, Epidemics, Infections and Disease Control, Preventive Health Institutions, Hospitals, Medical Education* (Istanbul: Istanbul University and Istanbul 2010 European Capital of Culture, 2010).

——, *14. Yüzyıldan Cumhuriyet'e Hastalıklar Hastaneler Kurumlar* (Istanbul: Tarih Vakfı Yurt Publication, 2014).

Yıldız, Gültekin, 'Ondokuzuncu Yüzyılın İki "Standardizasyon Ütopyası": Kışla ve Hücre Tipi Hapishane', *Türkiye Günlüğü*, 112 (2012), pp. 118–35.

Chapter 12

Beating is Heaven-sent: Corporal Punishment of Children in the Late Ottoman and Early Republican Era

Nazan Çiçek

Chris Goddard, the prolific writer on the thorny issue of child abuse, flatly yet succinctly contends in the opening of his book *Child Abuse and Child Protection* that:

> To the casual reader of history with an interest in children and childhood, two impressions are soon gained; firstly children do not feature prominently in historical texts; and, secondly, it is clear that where they are referred to, children have frequently suffered at the hands of adults.[1]

In that regard, Ottoman and Turkish Muslim children are no exceptions. Accordingly, in this study, which is based on a series of memoirs, biographies, autobiographies and oral history works, I by no means claim to unveil an unknown facet of childhood as perceived and practised in the late Ottoman and early Republican era in Turkey, yet I revisit and elaborate on a phenomenon that has not been esteemed worthy of much academic interest, due to its pervasive nature. Sadly, it has been taken for granted that in those times corporal punishment was an essential and extensively exerted component of social and cultural repertoire that ruled the childrearing as well as educational processes, and almost no childhood experience escaped encounters with corporal punishment in varying degrees and forms. Looking back at their childhood, all adults whose memoirs and reminiscences are referred to in this work confess or imply that incidents of corporal punishment left indelible marks on their psyche and contributed to their life choices. My narration is placed within the theoretical framework that considers the children's bodies 'as a site of disciplinary and regulatory regimes'.[2] Mostly drawing on Foucauldian discussions of biopolitics, discipline and modernity, as well as the revisions they have received, I argue in this study that the continuing support for corporal punishment of children in modern times represents an anachronism. Foucault identifies 'the transition from the public spectacle of theatrical torture' at the end of the eighteenth century to 'the use of power through surveillance and confinement' as a threshold of modernity.[3] What distinguishes modern times from pre-modern times, in other words, is 'the transfer from the liturgy of punishment of the body to the control of the mind' and the regulation of the body through the disciplinary gaze.[4]

Accordingly, as biopolitics gained ground and the ordering of the spatial and temporal lives of individuals through modern state institutions became the norm, in a gradual yet irrevocable process bodily punishments such as flogging, beating, whipping and lashing were legally abolished and lost their status as legitimate and licit methods. Therefore, corporal punishment has been considered a yardstick of civilisation for a society, and its employment has worked as a litmus test to distinguish modernity from pre-modernity, enlightened and progressive from barbaric and backward cultures. Seen through the prism of this line of thought corporal punishment of children appears as an utmost example of a pre-modern practice that somehow survived in modern existence where inflicting bodily pain as punishment has supposedly long fallen from grace. Yet scholars, such as Guy Geltner, convincingly argues that:

> The [modern times'] alleged birthing of the prison hardly announced the death of the rod and that far from an aberration of modernity, recourse to corporal punishment only expanded since the late eighteenth century, along with slavery, colonialism, penal incarceration, advanced science and medicine, and the nation-state.[5]

At least for a large subgroup of people who Geltner regards as socially 'otherised' people including children, corporal punishment never disappeared from penal theory, policy or practice. As Anthony Graziano and Karen Namaste remark, with the exception of war, self-defence and police law enforcement, 'no human interactions other than adult-child interactions carry social supports for the unilateral use of physical punishment by one party to another'.[6] Corporal punishment of children, in other words, appears as the most modern of 'pre-modern' notions and practices of our times that persistently resists the Foucauldian notion of the modernity threshold. The majority of 'modern' parents and educators appear unwilling to abandon the mental architecture of the old pre-modern regime regarding physically hurting children for disciplinary purposes. Employing Shilling's notion of 'the body as socially and biologically unfinished at birth',[7] I assert that the practice of corporal punishment on children epitomises the biological and social processes that simultaneously construct, shape and change children's bodies and address society's aspiration to create docile bodies throughout human history. Ironically, research shows that corporal punishment fails to produce the desired results in the long run and that transiently obedient child bodies constructed under physical force strike back as adults using violence towards either others or themselves.[8]

All in all, corporal punishment as a manifestation of adult domination and control over the body of the child is directly linked with the perception of the child as a 'property' or 'possession'. As 'embryonic' beings, children are considered subordinate and not quite human, a notion which I believe prompts the otherisation process that legitimises the employment of pre-modern disciplinary techniques in modern times. 'As projects belonging to their parents and compelled to attend institutions such as churches and schools, children may be disciplined, punished and tamed "for their own good and the good of others"';[9] indeed, the unquestioned assault of children may stem from disrespectful attitudes toward children that emanate from images of the child as 'a genderless object, less than a subject, not human and not a person'.[10]

By using numerous accounts culled from memoirs and oral history works, I contend that beating children was a diehard, socially and culturally highly esteemed child-raising practice in the Turkish-speaking Muslim community. It was never legally banned as a parenting technique, and in the case of bastinado (*falaka*, foot whipping) it strongly and successfully resisted the legal ban in school settings. Because the transformation of a value or a notion that rooted deep in the cultural make-up and *habitus* of a society cannot be easily and rapidly achieved through legal changes, and because child-rearing practices are highly resistant to change,[11] beating children for disciplinary and educational purposes maintained its tenacious status. It was not the practice of corporal punishment *per se*, but the severity of its application that became increasingly subject to criticism throughout decades and possibly had an effect on the collective cognitive map of the general public. The merits of corporal punishment in moulding children into responsible, submissive and normatively successful adults were never genuinely disputed in society other than in small circles of pedagogues.[12] Yet again the 'modern' child-rearing models that condemned bodily punishment and were championed by a handful of child professionals and intellectuals did not find their way into the homes and schools where the screams of children who were systematically physically punished echoed for generations. This study shall capture those screams, or rather the much silenced recollections of them, as they were relayed by their owners in their later life.[13]

Corporal Punishment as 'Ordinary' and 'Child-rearing Violence'

Literature on childhood firmly suggests the concept of childhood is ever changing. As a social construction and 'distinct from biological immaturity, childhood is neither a natural nor biological feature of human groups but appears as a specific structural and cultural component of many societies'.[14] It is reinvented or rediscovered as well as restructured by each society over time in accordance with the prevailing world views supporting those societies.[15]

There has been no consensus among scholars as to when children began to be regarded as a *sui generis* category ontologically different from adults, which in turn has led to the emergence of the concept of childhood as a social construct, rather than a mere stage in the biological life cycle. Similarly, the existent literature does not provide clear-cut answers about whether the entry of childhood into human history caused an increase or decrease in the crudity and frequency of physical punishment that children had to suffer. However, from Lloyd De Mause to Linda Pollock,[16] many childhood historians suggest that as a rule, children have been constantly and systematically abused, although there always have been some indulgent parents in every historical period.

As De Mause put it: '[C]entury after century of battered children grew up and in turn battered their own children'.[17] Definitions of corporal punishment have changed over time and are politically and historically constructed. In more recent times a tendency to separate the term 'corporal punishment' from the term 'physical abuse' has gained ground with a view to accentuate the former's supposed 'acceptability' and relative 'harmlessness'. Due to corporal punishment's broad manifestations and community approval even in an 'age of child' and in ostensibly child-centred societies, some scholars have suggested distinguishing it from the category of child abuse and placing it under the rubric of 'sub-abusive violence', which includes 'appropriate' and 'well-meaning' disciplinary responses from parents, caregivers and instructors.[18]

Some scholars have been inclined to downplay the magnitude and abusiveness of corporal punishment exercised on children by referring to it as 'child-rearing violence',[19] 'ordinary violence'[20] and 'normal violence'.[21] Some scholars, however, do not concur in such differentiation and maintain that the term and practice of corporal punishment is part and parcel of physical abuse exerted on children. Today, 'corporal punishment is defined generally as the use of physical force with the intention of causing a child to experience pain so as to punish or correct their behaviour'.[22] Although corporal punishment is mostly associated with spanking and hitting children with a hand or with an object, it nevertheless is not restricted to forms of hitting. It takes several forms, some of which may occur consecutively or concurrently in a particular incident of corporal punishment. Children are kicked, shaken, thrown, choked, scratched, bitten, burned, scalded, dragged by the arm or hair, locked up, tied up, their mouths washed out with soap or taped shut, meals withheld, hair pulled and even forced to engage in dangerous behaviours ranging from ingesting noxious substances to remaining in a fixed position for a long period of time.[23] Corporal punishment and its privileged status seems to be directly linked to the parents' and educators' demands of obedience from children, as well as to the notion that children are not complete and proper humans and are in constant need of regulation, control and discipline. Regulating children's bodies in home and school settings in order to create socially conforming/normalised individuals stands at the crux of the corporal punishment.

The Late Ottoman and Early Republican Turkish Case

Research shows that punitive child-rearing practices are in a positive correlation with authoritarianism.[24] The degree and frequency with which children are exposed to corporal punishment largely depends on how inherent and approved of violence towards children and other subordinates is in that particular culture and society. It also varies in accordance with the level of obedience and individual autonomy that parents and other caregivers expect from children, which, in turn, inform and influence the prevailing disciplinary methods. Although there is no data set compiled circa the collapse of the Ottoman Empire and the formation of the Republic as to the parental expectations of obedience, the findings of the first Turkish Value of Children (VOC) study conducted in 1982 provides insights into the basic values and norms that must have dominated the child-rearing practices in the late nineteenth and early twentieth century. In the first Turkish VOC study, parents 'emphasized obedience as the most and independence and self-esteem as the least anticipated features needed by a child'.[25] Both in the late Ottoman and early Republican era, the Turkish-speaking Muslim community seemed rather oblivious to the 'modern' notion of romanticised childhood, as well as child-centred parenting, that required treating children in accordance with their *sui generis* qualities and 'tolerating their childishness'. The majority of parents across all economic and educational backgrounds thought they were turning the naturally 'uncivilised' little people in their charge into proper adults through the best available and conventionally approved method: beating and fear of beating. The theory of 'disciplinary intimacy', which Richard H. Brodhead asserts constructed a model through a strategic relocation of authority relations in the realm of emotion and a conscious intensification of the emotional bond between the authority figure and its charge, strongly tied with the emergence of nineteenth-century middle-class domesticity in the Western world (America) from the 1830s onwards,[26] does not seem to have made a pervasive appearance in Turkey. Two examples from affluent upper-class Ottoman families display that being born with a silver spoon in the mouth did not spare children from tasting the bitterness of parental harshness, since the social order and acculturation system they lived in required all parents to follow the same patriarchal authoritarian disciplinary regimen when they saw fit. Ali Ekrem Bolayır (1867–1937), son of the famous poet and politician Namık Kemal, describes violent scenes where he was both witness to, and a victim of, corporal punishment. He writes that: 'Once, I myself was beaten ruthlessly and I believe I had deserved it. It was so harsh that I can still feel the pain'.[27]

Similarly, another child from a prosperous, upper-echelon family, Halide Nusret Zorlutuna (1901–84), recalls how she discovered that beating could befall any child at any time: 'I remember the first time I was beaten by my mother as a vivid nightmare. I was shocked because I did not know beating could happen to me as well.'[28]

The regime change in 1923, with all its rejection of the Ottoman past, does not seem to have brought about any substantial transformation in the construction of child–parent relationships, except for in a minority of well-educated family units that embraced the new middle-class paradigm professing 'discipline through love'. The famous Sertel household appears as one of those exceptional physical violence-free sites where Yıldız Sertel, daughter of Turkish intellectuals and journalists Zekeriya and Sabiha Sertel, born in 1923 in New York, recalls that she was never corporally punished: 'My mother had learned about pedagogical theories and principles of John Dewey when she lived in America. Beating was absolutely forbidden. She believed that childrearing had to be based on love and knowledge.'[29]

Children born to less intellectual and less Westernised parents were not as fortunate as Yıldız Sertel. Huriye Özgüler, born in 1916 in Ankara and interviewed for the *Cumhuriyette Çocuktular* oral history project, explains how the cultural repertoire of the early Republican ruling elites failed to penetrate the majority of houses:

> On one occasion my mother threatened to beat me. I protested saying that because the Republican regime was in power, she was no longer allowed to

beat me. Her response was: 'The Republic is outside of the home, it does not reign in the home, there is no Republic in this house'. Then she spanked me.[30]

Behiç Duygulu (1933–85), the writer and publisher, born in the western part of Turkey of humble origins, graphically narrates how he took his own share of corporal punishment as a child at the hands of his easily enraged father.[31] Likewise, the memoirs of the famous sculptor Mehmed Aksoy (b. 1939) hints that beating children was not a peculiarity of socially shunned dysfunctional adults; on the contrary, generous and socially well-respected people also honoured the saying 'spare the rod and spoil the child':

> [My father who was a court clerk] was a very charitable person. He would help anyone in trouble. Acted like law adviser to the whole town. But when it came to us, he would not tolerate even a simple minor misdeed. I was being beaten every day. You would not call this love, would you?[32]

Süleyman Yılmaz, born in 1915 in central-eastern region of Turkey (Yozgat), and interviewed in an oral history work, confesses that 'he did not love his father since his father was constantly violent towards him throughout his childhood'.[33] However, not many who were battered as children go so far as to question their parents' (or parental figures') love for them. As Geltner opines: '[I]t is undeniable that non-public disciplinary action, including the use of corporal punishment, offers a political education and helps shape new generations' ideas of licit and illicit violence, hierarchies, and desired power relations in the world around them'.[34] Children may internalise and normalise beating, perceiving it 'as a parental right and unquestionably accept it as such simultaneously associating love and care with the infliction of pain'.[35]

Ziya Hatun, born in Antolia in 1912 (Ünye) and also interviewed in the same oral history project, reveals that his father hit him horribly innumerable times, despite his mother's protests. Yet he adds: 'Because I was his only son, I suppose he wanted me to become a good person.'[36] Likewise, Melih Keçecioğlu, born in 1923 in Istanbul, remembers how his bad-tempered teacher beat students every hour:

> He struck us on the head. He has been dead long. God bless him. I do not wish him ill, I do not want him to be punished in the next world just because he beat us. But I can say that he killed our enthusiasm for school.[37]

In fact, there seems to be a strong current, an unmistakable tendency, among the owners of these recollections to cast their beating experience in an affirmative light. They are mostly at pains to emphasise that as naughty children they deserved the corporal punishment they received.[38] The painter Fikret Otyam (b. 1926) is another good example:

> I loved my father so much in spite of the fact that he used to clobber me on a regular basis. My childhood was replete with those infamous beatings which were justifiable in the face of my endless misdeeds.[39]

In some accounts the protagonists do not condemn the beating as an act in itself, but they object to being beaten unjustly. The famous Ottoman novelist Mehmed Rauf (1875–1931), for instance, displays this attitude in heart-rending terms:

> I had never been hit before, even once, and now I was being beaten with bastinado in front of the whole school assembly. I was such a docile, well-behaved child and even the most unruly and wildest of my friends had not been beaten this harshly. Due to an unfair accusation I was tortured as if I was the ringleader of thugs, the naughtiest of the naughty children.[40]

Others, while not applauding corporal punishment *per se*, nevertheless think that they owe their motivation in achieving life's goals to the beatings they received in their childhood. Ahmed Mithad Efendi (1844–1912), another famous Ottoman writer and statesman who taught pedagogy in *Darü'l Fünun*, confesses that he would not have become a prominent public figure had it not been for the strong stimulus caused by the beatings to get rid of the misery, poverty and ignorance he had lived in:

> I cannot believe how much beating I put up with as a child. In my apprenticeship I was constantly beaten by my master and his wife. I was also beaten regularly in my own house that I simply lost track. Had I not suffered terribly I would not have felt the urge for escape. That is why I think of my master with gratitude. He consciously or unconsciously taught me the most important lesson of my life. Each slap whipped up an ever stronger desire in my soul to become successful in life. I managed to mount the steep road of enlightenment thanks to the beatings that crushed me.[41]

Similarly, the legendary Minister of Education of early Republican Turkey, Hasan Ali Yücel (1897–1961), agrees that his life would probably have turned out completely different if he had not been beaten by his father:

> So powerful were the slaps that I was seeing stars. My face was swollen. I was sick for three days and could not go to school. Looking back at that beating almost half a century later, I can tell that if I had not been exposed to it god only knows what sort of a person I would have become. Would I be still alive, would I be the person as I am now?[42]

Nevertheless, the same Yücel also bitterly complains about the beatings that occurred at his neighbourhood Quranic school, hinting that he did not see any reasonable grounds for hitting children for academic and training purposes:

> My heart was filled with rebellious feelings towards the *hodja* [*hoca*] who was slapping the pupil at each mispronounced word in reading. The fear I had felt in the beginning was now replaced with hatred and grudge towards a cruel oppressor.[43]

Beating at School and the Bastinado as Ottoman–Turkish Children's 'Favourite' Nightmare

In the Ottoman and Turkish case, bastinado, a particular practice designed to immobilise and beat children in school settings, was the most feared item in the large repertoire of hitting forms. In bastinado beatings children were forced to the ground with their legs up, their feet were squeezed in a fixed position and then hit with a whip, cane or lash. Because there was no chance of flight during beating, which completely diminished the child's agency, and because it was usually exercised in front of school peers as a ceremonial performance that profoundly bruised the child's honour and dignity, bastinado came to represent the ultimate demonic nature of the prevailing school system in the eyes of its victims. What Richard H. Brodhead asserts in explaining the role of whipping in constructing slavery as a system in the American case[44] also applies to bastinado beatings and gives insights into understanding the role it played. Through the bodily enacted and bodily received nature of its disciplinary transaction and the perfect asymmetry of power expressed in its practice, bastinado beating emblematised the whole structure of relations between children and adults in authority in the Muslim Ottoman–Turkish context. It was, albeit with more violent properties, the Ottoman–Turkish counterpart of the paddle (or cane) in Western schools. Although the practice of bastinado has long ceased to exist in Turkey, paddling or caning as a disciplinary institution in Western school settings seems to have survived into the late twentieth century, and in the North American case into the twenty-first century. The horrors of bastinado were depicted numerous times in literary style, the most famous of which being Ömer Seyfeddin's short story *Falaka*. What has been reported as harmful effects of paddling (or caning) in Western scholarly research, ranging from 'bruises, cuts, hematomas, nerve and muscle damage to mental and emotional trauma',[45] could perhaps also be extended to, and deemed valid for, bastinado.

In fact, some of these harmful effects seem to have been recognised by the Ottoman decision-makers as early as the start of the *Tanzimat* period (1839–76). Judging from the content and tenor of the *Regulation to be Submitted to Teachers of Sıbyan Schools about the Methods to be Employed in the Process of Teaching, Instruction and Discipline of Children* of 1847, it can be clearly inferred that modernising Ottoman ruling elites saw bastinado as an archaic practice that had no place in modern pedagogy. Although the Regulation did not completely abolish corporal punishment, use of bastinado at schools was banned on the grounds that it had no place in *Shari'ah*. Instead of using bastinado:

> The teacher would punish the lazy or misbehaving children by frowning, scolding with words that are not hurtful to their pride, keeping them standing, using them in menial jobs, clipping their ear without causing injury, and when the permission from child's parents obtained, hitting or softly beating them with fragile sticks such as vine stem or jasmine stem without touching their critical body parts.[46]

The Regulation definitely looked good on paper, contributing to the new image of the reforming Ottoman Empire. Yet an ingrained practice such as bastinado was not to be uprooted by a mere legal document. Research demonstrates 'that legality alone does not determine use or non-use of corporal punishment'; and that 'state law acts as a moderator variable in determining attitudes toward corporal punishment'.[47] Removing corporal punishment from schools will not be achieved effectively through a top-down approach of applying state or international law to local schools, unless a change of attitudes about it at the community level is generated.[48] In the Ottoman case, without the accumulation of any grassroots support and demand from the public, abolishment of bastinado largely failed to provide the desired effects. According to an inspection report written by the Director of Education in Bursa at the request of the Ministry of Education in 1889: 'The school buildings were indescribably squalid. Teachers' words were unintelligible. Screams of children suffering under bastinado and the sound of whipping accompanied this scene'.[49]

Corporal punishment in school settings was obviously loathed by the progressive educational community. From the beginning of *Tanzimat* onwards, many Ottoman intellectuals who took an interest in pedagogy and reflected upon restructuring the Ottoman educational system invariably condemned the ongoing practice of rote learning and bastinado disciplining. Münif Paşa (1830–1910), statesman and writer, three times Minister of Education, wrote in his article in 1862 '*Ehemmiyet-i Terbiye-i Sıbyan*' (The Importance of Children's Education) that: 'It is terribly wrong of us to implement beating in our schools. Beating suits the donkey, not the child'.[50] In the same vein, Selim Sabit Efendi, the famous pedagogue who introduced a new method (*usul-i cedid*) into the

Ottoman educational system in the 1870s[51] and the author of *Rehnüma-yı Muallimin* (Teacher's Guide) of 1874, suggested that teachers of *sıbyan* schools should be female. Male teachers, especially unmarried, young and inexperienced ones, should not be preferred for these schools, because they were more likely to beat a child for no apparent reason.[52] He also excluded corporal punishment from the list of punishments that teachers could employ. Teachers should punish the child after anger has subsided, not immediately after the offence.[53]

When the goal was to turn the inherently wild and ignorant child into an obedient being who would observe and reproduce the normative values of the society, then teachers were expected to contribute to the task and act as the substitute for the parents. School was simply an extension of home or its tutelary adjunct located in the public domain where corporal punishment was exerted in front of a larger audience. In Hasan Ali Yücel's words: '[T]there was no difference between home and school in terms of freedom, or rather the lack of it. In those times fear ruled our lives'.[54] The blurred borders between home and school in the late Ottoman times with respect to the regulation of children's bodies through corporal punishment manifests itself in many memoir accounts in which children were taken to the school teacher for a beating, due to some offences that occurred at home or in the street. Ahmed Rasim (1864–1932) reminisces in his short memoir titled *Falaka*:

> Our teacher had a reputation for disciplining children harshly. Occasionally some strangers would show up at the school gate with a child. Those children who were said to have been disobedient towards their parents were brought to be beaten with bastinado. The teacher accepted these demands and flogged children who were not in fact his charges.[55]

In some cases, parents informed the school about their own badly behaved children, creating a sufficiently 'justified' case for a bastinado beating. Ahmed Rasim also tells how he was exposed to a gruesome beating after his own mother reported him.[56] What was uttered to the teacher when enrolling the child in school, namely, 'flesh is yours and bone is mine', worked as a sort of authorisation endowing the teacher with the right to act as *parens patriae* over the child's body.[57] For parents, teachers appeared as more effective and less sentimental versions of themselves in child education. Melahat Gözek, born in 1925 in the eastern part of Anatolia and interviewed for an oral history project, tells how her mother delegated her parental status to the teacher at the beginning of her school career: '"From now on", my mother said, "your teacher will become your mother and your father. If you show your teacher respect, he/she would neither beat you nor scold you"'.[58]

As Çiğdem Kağıtçıbaşı remarks, 'individuals are part of the culture of relatedness in the Turkish context', which refers to 'contexts and relational patterns identified by relations between connected, expanding and therefore partially overlapping selves with diffuse boundaries'.[59] In other words, children were not regarded as individual units but as parts of their societal groups, and their discipline concerned the whole community they belonged to. Hence the disappointment of many children documented in memoirs when they saw their parents heartily approve of the violent teaching and disciplining practices at school. The Ottoman statesman and writer Ebubekir Hazım Tepeyran (1864–1947), who ascended to the Interior Ministry in the late Ottoman times, bitterly observes how disillusioned and surprised he became in the face of his mother's reaction:

> At the end of my first school day I was convinced that after telling my mother what I saw that day she would be devastated and not even consider sending me there again. Yet her response was in the vein of the following: 'My dear child, I too was taught by the same teacher. I was punished regularly and in most cases without any fault of my own. Never forget that where your mentor hits you blooms a rose'.[60]

Memoirs testify to the widespread practice of hitting and beating and the occasional use of bastinado well into the early Republican era. Childhood recollections of different Muslim–Turkish people cutting across time and social strata overlap vis-à-vis corporal punishment and thus demonstrate that it was endemic in educational practices. When it comes to beating at school, stories from famous figures such as Ziya Pasha the Young Ottoman (1825–80),[61] Zekeriya Sertel (1890–1980)[62] or Halide Edib Adıvar (1884–1964[63] bear a striking resemblance to the stories of the 'common' men and women born and educated in Turkey in the first half of the twentieth century. Teachers in some of those accounts appear as sadistic individuals who derive pleasure from persecuting defenceless children. Ömer Faruk Numanzade (1872–1937) recounts how as a student in *Darüşşafaka* (1883–91) he was fiercely struck on one occasion fifty times so that his body was temporarily paralysed.[64] Aziz Nesin (1915–95), a famous Turkish novelist, recalls less violent yet equally unforgettable experiences in the same school at the start of the Republic. After the corporal punishment he was exposed to, he claims he was unable to hold a spoon at dinner.[65] Ebubekir Hazım Tepeyran vividly describes how the classroom served as a 'torture chamber':

> Two hours into my first school day I got to see those torture instruments in operation. The long stick hit the head of a weak and sickly girl like a thunderbolt. A boy who was caught drawing a picture on a green piece of paper that

looked like a human figure quickly became the victim of the bastinado. There was also this girl who could not pronounce some words. The teacher stuck a pencil in her nostrils and caused a profuse nosebleed.[66]

The novelist Hüseyin Rahmi Gürpınar (1864–1944), utilising his satirical style, eloquently hints that bastinado was almost inescapable for a schooled Ottoman–Turkish child:

> For us, the *hodja* was the head bogeyman. Bastinado made regular appearance. Once I had my own share of drama. Not learning a hymn properly led to my punishment. That week my parents transferred me to another school. The only difference in my new school was the quality of the material the bastinado was made from. It was silver-plated. No matter how luxurious the bastinado is, the pain you go through is not diminished in the least.[67]

While bastinado continued to put fear in children's hearts, there were significant signs that the use of corporal punishment in schools was becoming an anathema among intellectuals in the late Ottoman era. The influential youth magazine *Talebe Defteri* (Student's Notebook) (1913–19), founded and directed by Ahmed Halid (Yaşaroğlu) (1891–1951), who would later become the first school inspector of the Turkish Republic, evidences the extent of disapproval and condemnation corporal punishment received from the intelligentsia circa the collapse of the Empire. İsmail Hakkı Baltacıoğlu (1886–1978), a prominent pedagogue whose work and ideas would have profound impact on the construction of the Republic's educational policies, was a regular contributor to *Talebe Defteri*. Numerous articles appeared in the volumes of the magazine, each urging teachers and school administrations to abandon the practice of physical punishment. In a piece titled Heaven-sent (*Cennetten Çıkma*) an anonymous author, after reminiscing about their own painful childhood memories tainted by corporal punishment, asked historians and linguists to question the meaning of 'beating is heaven-sent'. Did the saying mean beating children was legitimised in Islamic thought and tradition and hence truly acceptable or did it mean that beating was kicked out of heaven and hence totally abhorred and prohibited?[68] Decades later, writing in the 1930s, Baltacıoğlu would unrelentingly reiterate that the still ongoing practice of corporal punishment as a disciplinary and academic measure did not befit the modern times and had to stop:

> Even in the era of despotism (alluding to the imperial era) beating was seen as an assault that lied heavily on one's conscience. How can beating possibly be allowed in our Republican regime which surely consists of justice and equality? The essential moral importance generated by the problem of beating is about how it attacks some values and violates the dignity and honour of

human beings. How can such an act be allowed in a society that believes in the freedom of morality, equality between sexes, value of children and dignity and integrity of human beings?[69]

While the founding cadres of the Republic embarked on a project of wholly replacing the former Ottoman–Islamic regulations of body, home and social and public space, childhood was rediscovered. The value of the child was re-established in accordance with the expectations of the new regime, and the issue of corporal punishment became charged with a new symbolic meaning. As the modernising decision-makers and pro-regime intelligentsia worked their way into constructing the modern conception of the child, reconstituting the image of the child as the personification of the Turkish nation and the nation-state, and formulating their vision of modern childhood, they not only romanticised the child, but also often stigmatised the 'other' – namely, non-modern interpretations of childhood and treatment of children that were invariably represented by the Eastern and, by implication, Ottoman and Islamic forms of conduct with children. In the Republican discursive cosmos, the child served as a metaphor or a potent vehicle which carried the spontaneity, joy, purity and naturalness of the Turkish Revolution and had notably positive connotations. Such a perception had no room for battered children. Corporal punishment in the newly organised modern national schools was considered an anachronism belonging to the 'disgraceful' Ottoman school system where the future of the nation had been systematically 'slaughtered'.[70]

It was clear that children were to be given a new agency, although it would mostly be limited to the symbolic realm and pragmatically exploited and utilised by the ruling cadres. Writing in 1929 Nafi Atuf (Kansu), teacher, inspector and the publisher of *Muallim Mecmuası* (Teacher's Magazine), who also acted as the general secretary of CHP (People's Republican Party), signalled what would become the official pedagogical approach informing the educational policies of the Republic:

> The ideal form of school discipline is designed in a way that ensures forestalling the perpetration of an offence or mistake instead of punishing the offender after whatever misdeed was already committed. Any sort of disciplinary idea adopted for the school system is directly related to how properly the characteristics and developmental stages of childhood are understood. The ideas and mores of children are fashioned under the influence of their social environments. Unlike the clergy of old times who saw children as creatures with demonic tendencies we today no longer see children as a box of malice. Neither do we see children, as some philosophers did in the past, as pure angels full of goodness. We today tend to regard children as human beings who grow and develop and interact with the influences of their social environment. Therefore,

we do not consider our students as criminals who should be punished through the use of instruments that cause pain.[71]

A year later in another publication he openly dismissed the Ottoman understanding of child education as 'categorically against the grain of the natural constitution of the child'.[72] Given the newly discovered value of children, as well as the embracing of highly psychologised and scientifically constructed Western pedagogy by the young regime, no more recommendations to employ corporal punishment in the classroom would be issued by Republican educational authorities.

Unfortunately, what really happened in classrooms did not always conform to the recommendations and expectations of the Ministry of Education. Introducing and imposing a new matrix of disciplinary thought purged of the evils of bodily correction was no simple task. Memoirs and oral history works show that despite the Republican founding elite's dream about recreating the institution of school as an oasis in the desert that would not replicate but transform the society, the process of change was slow and fragmentary, and school often still reflected the authoritarian and hierarchical values of the world outside. Testimonies provide abundant examples indicating that teachers and school administrations that strictly followed the non-coercive and more child-centred teaching methods were in a minority. Children who had been born and started school in Ottoman times and then continued their education in Republican schools emphasise in their accounts that, in spite of other profound changes ranging from the curriculum to the physical conditions of school buildings, the practice of corporal punishment remained largely unchanged. Ali Erbaş, born in 1913 in Çorum (northern Anatolian), states:

> In the Ottoman neighbourhood school the *hodja* had a long stick to hit our head from where he was seated. After the Republic, the *hodja* was replaced by teachers who did not own a stick. Yet, they too hit us, usually on our hands with a wooden ruler.[73]

Conclusion

Children, like many other groups of people who throughout history have not been considered 'civilised enough' and therefore otherised, dominated and suppressed by 'superior groups', remain victims of 'primordial violence'[74] in the form of legal corporal punishment. In the Western world and the modern era, while physical violence, especially that performed in public, has gradually been replaced with more humane punishment for privileged social groups, a range of subordinate groups who have been denied any meaningful position in power relations, such as women, colonised people, slaves, serfs, convicts and domestic servants, have had to wait longer to be rid of legal whipping, flogging and other similar punitive measures.[75]

Today children in many parts of the Western world, however, still lack equal footing. In condemning the corporal punishment of children when launching the 'Raise your hand against smacking!' campaign, Thomas Hammarberg, then Commissioner for Human Rights for the Council of Europe, expressed his astonishment that as late as mid-2000s, 'children have had to wait until last to be given equal legal protection from deliberate assaults—a protection the rest of us take for granted'. 'It is extraordinary', Hammarberg remarked, 'that children, whose developmental state and small size is acknowledged to make them particularly vulnerable to physical and psychological injury, should be singled out for less protection from assaults on their fragile bodies, minds and dignity'.[76]

It is the case that in the Ottoman Empire the conceptualisation of crime and punishment over the nineteenth century underwent a considerable shift. 'With the exception of execution for very serious offences, such as premeditated homicide, banditry, rebellion, and treason, lawmakers eventually discontinued all forms of corporal punishment and the use of torture'.[77] After the foundation of the Republic, Turkish decision-makers adopted the main formative legal texts, including the Criminal Code, from the West and persistently claimed the existence of an ontological break between the young Turkish nation-state and the Ottoman Empire. The official publications of *Himaye-i Etfal/Çocuk Esirgeme Kurumu* (Children's Protection Society) and *Gürbüz Türk Çocuğu* (Robust Turkish Child, later The Child, 1926–35; 1936–48) relentlessly explained to Turkish children that they were tremendously fortunate to be born under the child-loving Republican regime. Resorting to endless comparisons between the 'ominous' old times and the 'auspicious' new times, those magazines, along with numerous other similar ones, depicted the gruesome scenes from the classrooms of the Ottoman schools. Ottoman *hodja*s were portrayed as 'satan like creatures whose only talent was using bastinado', and the classrooms in Ottoman schools were likened to 'hell'.[78] Yet, as we have seen in this study, children in 'heaven-like schools' of the early Republic also had their share of corporal punishment.

Child abuse is a socially constructed phenomenon, its perception, definition and impact adjust continually as cultural values change over time. In today's Turkey, some of the recollections referred to in this text would probably prompt intervention from either authorities or the public on behalf of the abused child. As another one of the interviewees in *Cumhuriyette*

Çocuktular remarks: '[C]hildren in Turkey are no longer treated as the way they did in olden times. They are caressed and well looked after. There is not much kicking or slapping';[79] an observation shared by many others. Nevertheless, children continue to be subjected to changing levels of corporal punishment everywhere in the world. As Bernadette Saunders and Chris Goddard point out: '[A]ttitudes of caring and concern towards children appear to co-exist comfortably with attitudes of indifference and even disdain towards them'.[80]

It seems that as long as children continue to be perceived as incomplete, the property of their parents whose bodies are in need of constant correction and reform and as long as their image 'as weak, ignorant, irrational, incompetent, unrestrained and uncivilised'[81] beings impedes concerns about their treatment and well-being, corporal punishment may remain modern and never become truly a part of ancient history.

Notes

1. Goddard, *Child Abuse and Child Protection*, p. 7.
2. Prout, 'Childhood Bodies', p. 9.
3. Foucault, *Discipline and Punish*.
4. Simpson, 'Regulation and Resistance', p. 62.
5. Geltner, *Flogging Others*, p. 10.
6. Graziano and Namaste, 'Parental Use of Physical Punishment', p. 450.
7. Shilling, *The Body and Social Theory*.
8. Hyman et al., 'Psychological and Physical Abuse', pp. 243–67; Turner and Finkelhor, 'Corporal Punishment as a Stressor', pp. 155–66; Muller et al., 'The Intergenerational Transmission of Corporal Punishment', pp. 1323–35; Straus and Mouradian, 'Impulsive Corporal Punishment', pp. 353–74; DuRant et al., 'Factors Associated with the Use of Violence', pp. 612–17; Strauss and Yodanis, 'Corporal Punishment in Adolescence', pp. 825–41.
9. Saunders and Goddard, *Physical Punishment in Childhood*, p. 18
10. Saunders and Goddard, 'The Textual Abuse of Childhood', p. 457; Smart et al., *The Changing Experience of Childhood*, p. 8.
11. Kağıtçıbaşı, *Family and Human Development*.
12. Perhaps the reason why the efforts of the modernist Ottoman and Turkish pedagogues did not attract much public attention and gain grassroots support was because neither the late Ottoman nor the early Republican Turkish society had conditions conducive to linking the corporal punishment of children to a bigger social cause of which public beating and corporal punishment were emblematic, such as serfdom in Tzarist Russia or slavery in the United States. See Eklof, 'Worlds in Conflict', p. 792; Brodhead, 'Sparing the Rod', p. 68.
13. The oral history works that I rely on throughout this chapter are Tan et al., *Cumhuriyette Çocuktular* and Cem, *İmkânsız Hayatlar*.

14. Prout and James, 'A New Paradigm for the Sociology of Childhood?', p. 8.
15. Ambert, 'An International Perspective on Parenting', pp. 529–43; Kessen, *Psychological Development from Infancy*; Hendrick, *Childhood and English Society*.
16. Pollock, *Forgotten Children*.
17. De Mause, *The History of Childhood*, p. 41.
18. Graziano, 'Why We Should Study Sub-Abusive Violence Against Children', pp. 412–19; Graziano et al., 'Sub-Abusing Violence in Child-Rearing', pp. 845–8.
19. Hemenway et al., 'Child Rearing Violence', pp. 1011–20.
20. Straus, 'Ordinary Violence', pp. 213–34.
21. Gelles and Cornell, *Intimate Violence in Families*, p. 21.
22. Gershoff and Bitensky, 'The Case Against Corporal Punishment of Children', pp. 231–7.
23. Hyman, 'Corporal Punishment, Psychological Maltreatment', pp. 113–30; Nilsson, *Global Initiative Handbook*, p. 3; Human Rights Watch and ACLU, *Impairing Education*.
24. Bogacky et al., 'Reducing School Violence', pp. 367–86.
25. Kağıtçıbaşı, *The Changing Value of Children in Turkey*, p. 65.
26. Brodhead, 'Sparing the Rod', p. 71.
27. Özgül, *Ali Ekrem Bolayırın Hatıraları*, pp. 38–9.
28. Zorlutuna, *Bir Devrin Romanı*, p. 14.
29. Sertel, *Ardımdaki Yıllar*, p. 22.
30. Tan et al., *Cumhuriyette Çocuktular*, p. 223.
31. Seyda, *Çocukluk Yılları*, p. 114.
32. Engin, *Heykel Oburu*, p. 29.
33. Tan et al., *Cumhuriyette Çocuktular*, p. 420.
34. Geltner, *Flogging Others*, p. 79.
35. Saunders and Goddard, *Physical Punishment in Childhood*, p. 110.
36. Tan et al., *Cumhuriyette Çocuktular*, p. 441.
37. Ibid., p. 325.
38. The findings of Straus et al. show that 'spanking teaches the morality of violence' and that 'the more a child was spanked, the greater probability that he or she will approve of violence later in life'. See Straus et al., *The Primordial Violence*, p. 3.
39. Seyda, *Çocukluk Yılları*, p. 213.
40. Tarım, *Mehmet Rauf'un Anıları*, pp. 25, 31.
41. Yardım, *Tanzimat'tan Günümüze Edebiyatçılarımızın Çocukluk Hatıraları*, pp. 18–19.
42. Yücel, *Geçtiğim Günlerden*, p. 102.
43. Ibid., pp. 69–70.
44. Brodhead, 'Sparing the Rod', pp. 67–8.
45. Gershoff et al., *Corporal Punishment in U.S. Public Schools*, p. 39.
46. 'Etfalin Talim ve Tedris ve Terbiyelerini ne Veçhile İcra Eylemeleri Lazım

Geleceğine Dair Sıbyan Mekatibi Haceleri (Öğretmen) Efendilere İta Olunacak Talimat', quoted in Akyüz, *Türk Eğitim Tarihi*, p. 141.
47. Bogacky et al., 'Reducing School Violence', p. 378.
48. Imbrogno, 'Corporal Punishment in America's Public Schools', pp. 125–47.
49. Akyüz, *Türk Eğitim Tarihi*, p. 199.
50. Ibid., p. 226.
51. Somel, *Osmanlı'da Eğitimin Modernleşmesi*, p. 217.
52. Akyüz, *Türk Eğitim Tarihi*, p. 178.
53. Sakaoğlu, *Osmanlı'dan Günümüze Eğitim Tarihi*, p. 305.
54. Yücel, *Geçtiğim Günlerden*, p. 104.
55. Ahmet Rasim, *Falaka*, pp. 111–12. For a similar example that occurred in a state-run boarding school in Republican times, see Tan et al., *Cumhuriyette Çocuktular*, p. 347.
56. Ahmet Rasim, *Gecelerim*, pp. 27–9.
57. Geltner emphasises that 'disciplinary action in domains such as the home and the school and in religious and vocational institutions both reflects and extends mechanisms, procedures and power structures in the world outside'. See Geltner, *Flogging Others*, p. 78. In this sense, it is not surprising to see that what Gibson says about Victorian English fathers also applied to Ottoman and Turkish Muslim parents: 'If Victorian fathers were prepared to beat their own children, it followed that they would be prepared to have them whipped at school'. See Gibson, *The English Vice*, p. 64.
58. Tan et al., *Cumhuriyette Çocuktular*, p. 320.
59. Kağıtçıbaşı, *Family and Human Development*, p. 65.
60. Tepeyran, *Hatıralar*, pp. 6–9.
61. Koçu and Akbay, *Halil İbrahim Aşçıdede*, pp. 20–1.
62. Sertel, *Hatırladıklarım*, p. 17.
63. Adıvar, *Mor Salkımlı Ev*, p. 53.
64. Numanzade, *Kafkasya'dan İstanbul'a Hatıralar*, pp. 38–40.
65. Nesin, *Böyle Gelmiş Böyle Gitmez*, pp. 75–8. Hayri Cem's *İmkânsız Hayatlar* contains numerous interviews, as well as his own memoirs, most containing incidences of corporal punishment. All those accounts spanning from the early 1920s to the 1970s corroborate the testimonies of the other oral history work I have referred to throughout this text: beating did not vanish at schools when the Ottoman Empire ceased to exist. See Cem, *İmkânsız Hayatlar*.
66. Tepeyran, *Hatıralar*, pp. 3–6.
67. Gürpınar, *Eti Senin Kemiği Benim*, pp. 4–5 and 10–11.
68. Atakan, *A Teacher*, pp. 124–5.
69. Baltacıoğlu, *Terbiye*, p. 121.
70. One of the most important organisers of the national resistance movement in Anatolia Kâzım Karabekir (1882–1948) published a school play in a children's magazine, *Yeni Yol* (1923–6), circa the foundation of the Republic. In the play titled 'Hâlâ Bu Mektep' [Still this Same Old School], the protagonist, a district governor in late Ottoman times, visits a school in his area and regrets

to see that bastinado is still in operation. He then suggests adopting the educational methods practised in advanced countries. See Kazım Karabekir, 'Hâlâ Bu Mektep', *Yeni Yol*, 23, p. 304, quoted in Esmer, 'Cumhuriyet Döneminin İlk Yıllarında', pp. 54–5. Republican founding elites seem to have been misled about conditions in advanced countries – namely, the Western world – where corporal punishment at schools had been very common, approved of and deep-rooted indeed.

71. Nafi Atuf, 'Mektep Cezaları', p. 167.
72. Nafi Atuf, 'Türkiye Maarifi Hakkında', p. 30.
73. Tan et al., *Cumhuriyette Çocuktular*, p. 124.
74. Straus et al., *The Primordial Violence*, p. 3.
75. Briggs et al., *Crime and Punishment in England*.
76. Hammarberg, 'Children and Corporal Punishment', quoted in Gershoff et al., *Corporal Punishment in U.S. Public Schools*, pp. 70–1.
77. Schull, 'Criminal Codes', p. 162.
78. Alabaş, 'Cumhuriyet Dönemi Çocuk Dergilerinin', pp. 75, 77, 116–17, 146–7.
79. Tan et al., *Cumhuriyette Çocuktular*, p. 308.
80. Saunders and Goddard, 'The Textual Abuse', p. 443.
81. Scarre, *Children, Parents and Politics*, p. x.

Bibliography

Primary Sources

Adıvar, Halide Edip, *Mor Salkımlı Ev* (Istanbul: Atlas Kitabevi, 1992).

Ahmet Rasim, *Falaka* (Istanbul: Arba Yayınları, 1987).

_____, *Gecelerim* (Istanbul: ArbaYayınları, 1987).

Baltacıoğlu, İsmail Hakkı, *Terbiye* (Istanbul: Suhulet Kütüphanesi, 1932).

Cem, İsmail Hayri, *İmkânsız Hayatlar: Darüşşafakalıların Anıları* (Istanbul: Kalkedon, 2010).

Gürpınar, Hüseyin Rahmi, *Eti Senin Kemiği Benim* (Istanbul: Gürpınar Yayınları, 1963).

Human Rights Watch and ACLU (2009), 'Impairing Education: Corporal Punishment of Students with Disabilities in U.S. Public Schools', available at: <https://www.hrw.org/report/2009/08/10/impairing-education/corporal-punishment-students-disabilities-us-public-schools> (last accessed 10 February 2018).

Koçu, Reşat Ekrem, and Mehmet Ali Akbay (eds), *Halil İbrahim Aşçıdede, Hatıralar* (Istanbul: Istanbul Ansiklopedisi ve Neşriyat, 1960).

Nafi Atuf, 'Mektep Cezaları', *Terbiye*, 19 (1929), pp. 167–8.

_____, *Türkiye Maarifi Hakkında Bir Deneme* (Istanbul: Muallim Ahmet Halit Kitaphanesi, 1930).

Nesin, Aziz, *Böyle Gelmiş Böyle Gitmez, Yol*, vol. 1 (Istanbul: Tekin Yayınevi, 1977).

Numanzade, Ömer Faruk, *Kafkasya'dan İstanbul'a Hatıralar* (Izmir: Akademi Kitabevi, 2000).
Ömer Seyfeddin, *Falaka* (Istanbul: Alba, 1987).
Özgül, Metin Kayahan (ed.), *Ali Ekrem Bolayırın Hatıraları* (Ankara: Kültür Bakanlığı Yayımlar Dairesi Başkanlığı, 1991).
Sertel, Yıldız, *Ardımdaki Yıllar* (Istanbul: Milliyet Yayınları, 1990).
Sertel, Zekeriya, *Hatırladıklarım* (Istanbul: Remzi Kitabevi, 2000).
Seyda, Mehmet (ed.), *Çocukluk Yılları* (Ankara: TDK Yayınları, 1980).
Tan, Mine Göğüş, and Özlem Şahin, Mustafa Sever, and Aksu Bora, *Cumhuriyette Çocuktular*, 2nd edn (Istanbul: Boğaziçi Üniversitesi Yayınları, 2007).
Tarım, Rahim (ed.), *Mehmet Rauf'un Anıları* (Istanbul: ÖzgürYayınları, 2001).
Tepeyran, Ebubekir Hazım, *Hatıralar* (Istanbul: Pera Turizm ve Ticaret, 1998).
Yardım, M. Nuri (ed.), *Tanzimat'tan Günümüze Edebiyatçılarımızın Çocukluk Hatıraları* (Istanbul: Timaş, 1998).
Yücel, Hasan Ali, *Geçtiğim Günlerden* (Istanbul: İletişim Yayınları, 1990).
Zorlutuna, Halide Nusret, *Bir Devrin Romanı*, 2nd edn (Ankara: Kültür ve Turizm Bakanlığı Yayınları, 1986).

Secondary Sources
Akyüz, Yahya, *Türk Eğitim Tarihi, Başlangıçtan 1997'ye* (Istanbul: Kültür Üniversitesi Yayınları, 1997).
Alabaş, Ramazan, 'Cumhuriyet Dönemi Çocuk Dergilerinin Eğitim ve Tarih Anlayışı Açısından İncelenmesi (1923–1950)', unpublished PhD dissertation, Ankara University, 2014.
Ambert, Anne-Marie, 'An International Perspective on Parenting: Social Change and Social Constructs', *Journal of Marriage and Family*, 56 (1994), pp. 529–43.
Atakan, Atacan, *A Teacher, Agitator and Guide: Talebe Defteri and Formation of an Ideal Child (1913–1919)* (Istanbul: Libra, 2016).
Bogacky, David F., Deborah Armstrong, and Kenneth J. Weiss, 'Reducing School Violence: The Corporal Punishment Scale and its Relationship to Authoritarianism and Pupil-Control Ideology', *The Journal of Psychiatry and Law*, 33 (2005), pp. 367–86.
Briggs, John, Christopher Harrison, Angus McInnes, and David Wilson, *Crime and Punishment in England: An Introductory History* (London: UCL Press, 1996).
Brodhead, Richard H., 'Sparing the Rod: Discipline and Fiction in Antebellum America', *Representations*, 21 (1988), pp. 67–96.
De Mause, Lloyd (ed.), *The History of Childhood* (London: Souvenir Press, 1976).
DuRant, Robert H., Chris Cadenhead, Robert A. Pendergrast, Greg Slavens, and Charles W. Linder, 'Factors Associated with the Use of Violence among Urban Black Adolescents', *American Journal of Public Health*, 84/4 (1994), pp. 612–17.

Eklof, Ben, 'Worlds in Conflict: Patriarchal Authority, Discipline and the Russian Schools, 1861–1914', *Slavic Review*, 50/4 (1991), pp. 792–806.

Engin, Aydın (ed.), *Heykel Oburu Mehmet Aksoy Kitabı* (Istanbul: İş Bankası Kültür Yayınları, 2002).

Esmer, Seyhan Kübra, 'Cumhuriyet Döneminin İlk Yıllarında (1923–1928) Yayımlanan Çocuk Dergilerindeki Tahkiyeli Metinlerin Çocuklara Değer Aktarımı Açısından Değerlendirilmesi', unpublished MA thesis, Gazi University, 2007.

Foucault, Michel, *Discipline and Punish: The Birth of the Prison* (London: Penguin, 1977).

Gelles, Richard, and Claire Pedrick Cornell, *Intimate Violence in Families* (Beverly Hills: Sage, 1990).

Geltner, Guy, *Flogging Others: Corporal Punishment and Cultural Identity from Antiquity to the Present* (Amsterdam: Amsterdam University Press, 2014).

Gershoff, Elizabeth T., and Susan H. Bitensky, 'The Case Against Corporal Punishment of Children: Converging Evidence from Social Science Research and International Human Rights Law and Implications for U.S. Public Policy', *Psychology, Public Policy and Law*, 13 (2007), pp. 231–7.

Gershoff, Elizabeth T., Kelly M. Purtell, and Igor Holas, *Corporal Punishment in U.S. Public Schools, Legal Precedents, Current Practices and Future Policy* (New York: Springer, 2015).

Gibson, Ian, *The English Vice: Beating, Sex and Shame in Victorian England and After* (London: Duckworth, 1978).

Goddard, Chris, *Child Abuse and Child Protection: A Guide for Health, Education and Welfare Workers* (South Melbourne: Churchill Livingstone, 1996).

Graziano, Anthony M., 'Why We Should Study Sub-Abusive Violence Against Children', *Journal of Interpersonal Violence*, 9 (1994), pp. 412–19.

Graziano, Anthony M., and Karen A. Namaste, 'Parental Use of Physical Punishment in Child Discipline: A Survey of 679 College Students', *Journal of Interpersonal Violence*, 5 (1990), pp. 449–63.

Graziano Anthony M., Jessica Hamblen, and Wendy A. Plante, 'Sub-Abusive Violence in Child-Rearing in Middle-Class American Families', *Pediatrics*, 98/4 (1996), pp. 845–8.

Hammarberg, Thomas, *Children and Corporal Punishment: The Right not to be Hit, also a Children's Right*, Issue Paper, No: 2006/I (Strasbourg: Council of Europe, 2006).

Hemenway, D., S. Solnick, and J. Carter, 'Child Rearing Violence', *Child Abuse & Neglect*, 18 (1994), pp. 1011–20.

Hendrick, Harry, *Childhood and English Society, 1880–1990* (Cambridge: Cambridge University Press, 1997).

Hyman, Irwin A., 'Corporal Punishment, Psychological Maltreatment, Violence and Punitiveness in America: Research, Advocacy, and Public Policy', *Applied and Preventive Psychology*, 4 (1995), pp. 113–30.

Hyman, Irwin A., Wendy Zelikoff, and Jacqueline Clarke, 'Psychological and Physical Abuse in the Schools: A Paradigm for Understanding Post-Traumatic Stress Disorder in Children and Youth', *Journal of Traumatic Stress*, 1/2 (1988), pp. 243–67.

Imbrogno, A. R., 'Corporal Punishment in America's Public Schools and the U.N. Convention on the Rights of the Child: A Case for Non-Ratification', *The Journal of Law and Education*, 29 (2000), pp. 125–47.

Kağıtçıbaşı, Çiğdem, *The Changing Value of Children in Turkey* (Honolulu, HI: East–West Center, 1982).

_____, *Family and Human Development Across Cultures: Theory and Applications*, 2nd edn (New Jersey: Lawrence Erlbaum Associates, 1996).

Kessen, William, *Psychological Development from Infancy: Image to Intention* (New York and London: Wiley, 1979).

Muller, Robert T., John E. Hunter, and Gary Stollak, 'The Intergenerational Transmission of Corporal Punishment: A Comparison of Social Learning and Temperament Models', *Child Abuse & Neglect*, 19/11 (1995), pp. 1323–35.

Nilsson, Mali, *Global Initiative Handbook: Hitting People is Wrong – and Children are People Too* (Sweden: Save the Children, 2003).

Pollock, Linda, *Forgotten Children: Parent-Child Relations from 1500 to 1900* (Cambridge: Cambridge University Press, 1983).

Prout, Alan, 'Childhood Bodies: Construction, Agency and Hybridity', in Alan Prout (ed.), *The Body, Childhood and Society* (London: Palgrave Macmillan, 2000), pp. 1–18.

Prout, Alan, and Allison James, 'A New Paradigm for the Sociology of Childhood? Provenance, Promise and Problems', in Alan Prout and Allison James (eds), *Constructing and Reconstructing Childhood* (London: Routledge, 1990), pp. 7–33.

Sakaoğlu, Necdet, *Osmanlı'dan Günümüze Eğitim Tarihi* (Istanbul: İstanbul Bilgi Üniversitesi Yayınları, 2003).

Saunders, Bernadette J., and Chris Goddard, 'The Textual Abuse of Childhood in the English-Speaking World: The Contribution of Language to the Denial of Children's Rights', *Childhood*, 8 (2001), pp. 443–62.

_____, *Physical Punishment in Childhood: The Rights of the Child* (Chichester: Wiley-Blackwell, 2010).

Scarre, Geoffrey (ed.), *Children, Parents and Politics* (Cambridge: Cambridge University Press, 1989).

Schull, Kent F., 'Criminal Codes, Crime and the Transformation of Punishment in the Late Ottoman Empire', in Kent F. Schull, M. Safa Saraçoğlu, and Robert Zens (eds), *Law and Legality in the Ottoman Empire and Republic of Turkey* (Bloomington, IN: Indiana University Press, 2016), pp. 156–78.

Shilling, Chris, *The Body and Social Theory* (London: Sage, 1993).

Simpson, Brenda, 'Regulation and Resistance: Children's Embodiment during the Primary-Secondary School Transition', in Alan Prout (ed.), *The Body, Childhood and Society* (London: Palgrave Macmillan, 2000), pp. 60–88.

Smart, Carol, Bren Neale, and Amanda Wade, *The Changing Experience of Childhood: Families and Divorce* (Cambridge: Polity Press, 2001).

Somel, Selçuk Akşin, *Osmanlı'da Eğitimin Modernleşmesi (1839–1908), İslamlaşma, Otokrasi ve Disiplin* (Istanbul: İletişim Yayınları, 2010).

Straus, Murray A., 'Ordinary Violence, Child Abuse and Wife Beating: What Do They Have in Common?', in David Finkelhor, Richard Gelles, Gerald Hotaling, and Murray Straus (eds), *The Dark Side of Families* (Beverly Hills: Sage, 1983), pp. 213–34.

Straus, Murray A., and Vera E. Mouradian, 'Impulsive Corporal Punishment by Mothers and Antisocial Behaviour and Impulsiveness of Children', *Behavioral Sciences and the Law*, 16 (1998), pp. 353–74.

Straus, Murray A., and Carrie L. Yodanis, 'Corporal Punishment in Adolescence and Physical Assault on Spouses in Later Life: What Accounts for the Link?', *Journal of Marriage and the Family*, 58 (1996), pp. 825–41.

Straus, Murray A., Emily M. Douglas, and Rose Ann Medeiros, *The Primordial Violence: Spanking Children, Psychological Development, Violence, and Crime* (New York: Routledge, 2014).

Turner, Heather A., and David Finkelhor, 'Corporal Punishment as a Stressor Among Youth', *Journal of Marriage and the Family*, 58 (1996), pp. 155–66.

PART V
CHILDREN AND EDUCATION

Chapter 13

Childhood and Education in Ottoman Bosnia during the Early Modern Period (Mid-fifteenth to Late Eighteenth Century)

Elma Korić

The organisation of the education process in early modern Bosnia was unique to the Ottoman state and relied on education in the Islamic world before the founding of the Ottoman state. Prior to the arrival of the Ottomans, in the medieval Bosnian Kingdom, the focal points of education and cultural life were the rulers' courts, the monasteries of the Franciscans, the Orthodox monasteries, the houses of the Bosnian Church and larger town settlements.[1] As well as these focal points, in the apprentice contracts for young men and girls from medieval Bosnia in Dubrovnik, there were often clauses that obliged the masters to supply a good upbringing, including knowledge of customs, reading and writing.[2]

During the early modern period, from the mid-fifteenth to the end of the eighteenth centuries, the territory of present Bosnia and Herzegovina was under Ottoman rule. Urban settlements in the province of Bosnia were developed through the construction of endowment facilities (*waqf*), as was the case in other regions of the Ottoman Empire.[3] The entire system of objects of religious, educational and general cultural character was established in that period. As in other regions of the Ottoman Empire, primary education took place in mosques and institutions of elementary education attached to them. In the archival sources of Ottoman origin, these primary educational institutions are mentioned under titles such as the house of knowledge (*bayt al-'ilm*), the house of teaching (*bayt al-ta'lim*), the primary school (*maktab*) or the house of the teacher (*mu'allimhane*). Institutions of higher education were called *madrasa*s.

The construction of educational facilities, financial support for education through the salaries of school personnel (*muderris, mu'allim*) and their deputies (*muste'id, halifa*), student scholarships, the purchase of necessary textbooks, meals and clothes for the students and so on was realised from the funds of the *waqf*. In the province of Bosnia, educational institutions were established mainly through donations to the *waqf* from members of the Ottoman elite of Bosnian origin. In some of these facilities, such as the Ghazi Husrev Beg *madrasa* in Sarajevo established in 1537, Mohammad Beg *madrasa* in Mostar established in 1557 and Behram Beg *madrasa* in Tuzla established in 1626, teenagers are still being educated today. In addition to the above-mentioned educational institutions in the province of Bosnia, knowledge was acquired through some special institutions, related to Sufi orders such as hospices (*zaviya*), and dervish monasteries (*tekke* or *khankah*).

Most of the archival sources of the Ottoman administration in this period offer very little information that would help to reconstruct the lives of people from the margins of society – that is to say, common people, especially women and children. In literature there is only basic information regarding childhood and education in the Ottoman Empire, but there is even less information about children that lived in Ottoman Bosnia. Several Bosnian–Herzegovinian scholars provided basic information about the education of Muslim children in Bosnia during the Ottoman rule and afterwards, but they focused mainly on the institutions, rather than on the impact of the educational process and the lives of children.[4] Information on non-Muslim children is completely absent in the sources studied.

In order to paint a picture of the educational life of children in early modern Ottoman Bosnia based on the data in Ottoman documents, the present chapter focuses on the attitude towards the childhood of Muslim children and youth in Ottoman Bosnia through their education in primary schools and institutions of higher education (*maktab*s and *madrasa*s). The chapter focuses on Ottoman endowment deeds (*waqfiyya*s) for the foundations established by local administrators, their wives and sisters, and other wealthy local people.

Primary schools (maktabs)

Qur'an verses in which men and women were motivated to learn and educate themselves were cited in the texts of *waqfiyya*s as a primary motive for a benefactor to support education by founding educational institutions and funding teaching.[5] The most frequently mentioned words (Hadith) of the Prophet Mohammad cited in *waqfiyya*s are those in which he reminds people that life is transient, but that a person can leave a trace of his existence if he leaves knowledge that others will benefit from and which will be used by generations to come; if he gives a donation from his property to help the wider community; and especially if he raises his offspring in a good way.[6] These words apply equally to women and men and serve as a motive for learning, teaching, educating and raising children, as well as for charitable activities. Some benefactors combined all of these objectives and founded *waqf*s, making certain, however, that the *waqf*s would also cater for their own descendants.[7]

And, indeed, throughout the entire Ottoman Empire, religious educational institutions for primary education were established mostly within the frames of the *waqf* facilities. They were located in the mosques or in separate buildings. In the Ottoman province of Bosnia during the early modern period, primary education of Muslim children was also carried out in these institutions. In various sources of Ottoman origin, these primary schools are most commonly mentioned as *maktab* or *mu'allimhane*. They were endowed by individuals, and almost every town and village in the province of Bosnia had its own school. According to Evliya Chelebi, in Sarajevo around 1660, there was 'a school beside every mosque. To every hardworking and diligent pupil, clothes are given by the *waqf*'.[8] According to the data from the archival documents, there were around 100 mosques in Sarajevo in 1660, perhaps not quite as many as Chelebi suggests.[9]

In the Ottoman education system, there were no classes, and the children mastered the material sitting in a circle around the teacher. This way of teaching, with pupils of different ages all together in one class, was crucial for the formation of the school building, because only one room was used. In these schools, children from the age of six or seven began acquiring a basic knowledge of Islam and morality and learned to read and write. The teacher, as well as his assistant, had special roles in teaching. They were chosen according to strict norms based on *waqfiyya* that everyone had to adhere to. They had to respect the curriculum and were supervised by a person chosen by the benefactor himself.[10] The teacher (*mu'allim* or *havace*) was usually the preacher (*imam*) of the mosque, and he had a deputy or assistant (*halifa*). There were many schools whose *waqfiyya*s were not preserved, and we know about their existence based on details from other Ottoman sources. Some of the sources include data such as the name of the founder of the school, the amount of money paid to teachers and their assistants and sometimes the sources of the finances used. Although the data in these sources are very useful in many ways, they do not offer any other information related to the specifics of education and upbringing of children in these educational institutions.

The oldest document on the existence of primary schools in the territory of present Bosnia and Herzegovina is the *waqfiyya* of the Bosnian governor Ayas Beg from the year 1477. He left funds for the work of the teacher in the primary school, referred to as 'the house of the teacher', which he built in Sarajevo, close to his mosque. He also left funds for repairing and maintaining the school building.[11] Among the first known schools in Sarajevo was the one within the Hajj Muslihuddin mosque, near the Isa Beg hospice.[12] In the *waqfiyya* of Isa Beg from the year 1462, the benefactor stated that every day in his public kitchen (*imaret*) in Sarajevo, a soup of meat and wheat should be prepared for guests, as well as for the employees of the hospice. A part of that meal should be given 'to the poor orphans who live in that town'.[13] And although not explicitly stated, it can be assumed that the 'poor' children who were educated in the above mentioned *maktab* were also fed there. Based on the text of the *waqfiyya* of Mustafa Beg, the son of Iskender Pasha, written between 1517 and 1518, it is evident that he decided to build a school beside his mosque in Sarajevo in order 'to teach the children of the poor the Holy Qur'an'.[14]

From Ottoman sources it is clear that, apart from high-ranked officials and their relatives, support for education was provided by businessmen and people who were engaged in other occupations through the planning of funds within their own *waqf*s. They founded smaller *waqf*s, established primary schools and left funds for their work, for the salaries of teachers, for scholarships, as well as for necessary repairs and other school needs.[15] Some wealthy Muslims who performed the duties of pilgrimage also founded *waqf*s and supported the work of schools.[16] Teachers themselves, as well as members of their families, were also sponsors of education.[17]

In the texts of the *waqfiyyas*, as well as information on how to fund the work of the school and its employees, there are also descriptions of the school buildings, the criteria for selecting teaching staff and their duties, as well as the methodology of teaching and which textbooks should be used. In this respect, the *waqfiyya* of Keyvan Kethuda from the year 1554 is very illustrative. Alongside his mosque in Mostar, this benefactor had also founded

> a school, beautiful and neat, in which the children were to be taught the sublime Qur'an, a Glorious Book that distinguishes truth from falsehood. He left it for the children of the poor and the poor children, whoever they were.[18]

According to Muslim scholars such as al-Isfahani and al-Ghazali, the first among many duties of the teacher is 'to be sympathetic to students and treat them as his own children'.[19] Ibn Khaldun's conclusion was similar: 'Thus a teacher must not be too severe towards his pupil, nor a father towards his son, in educating them . . .'.[20]

In that sense, some benefactors, among them Keyvan Kethuda, determined what qualities the teacher in the school should possess and what precisely his duties were:

The given school should have a teacher who knows the methods of teaching, who is reliable, devout, cheerful and physically healthy. He should educate the children of Muslims in this school; teach them the teachings of the Holy Qur'an and good behaviour (*edeb*).

In order to make the educational process more effective, the benefactor determined that the teacher should also have an assistant 'who is trustworthy as a man', whose duty was to repeat with the children a particular lesson, as well as to practice earlier ones with them.[21] The same benefactor, along with his mosque in the town of Gabela, founded a 'beautiful and neat school for the educating of poor children in virtues and the Holy Qur'an'. The basic prerequisites for selecting the teacher, as well as his assistant, were similar: teachers should be

> mild in nature, know the significance of Allah's words . . . they should teach the children of the Muslims and guide them according to a Holy Book . . . treat them as fathers treat their own children, not making the difference between them in teaching and educating.[22]

Also in Mostar, Hajj Muhammad Beg built a mosque before 1570 and along with it a 'building for teaching Muslim children the Qur'an'.[23] This benefactor also demanded that the teacher should possess certain qualities: '[T]o be honest, devout and a married man, to know the rules of the teachings of the Qur'an and its orthography'.[24]

Among the *waqf* facilities that were built by Mustafa Pasha in the village of Rudo in 1555, his *waqfiyya* emphasises the description of 'a school that takes away the hearts . . .'. This school was built for

> . . . the children of the believers and children of those who believe in the unity of God, as well as their teachers who teach them the Holy Qur'an and provide training for them in order to understand and interpret the Qur'an as the source of the truth about the difference between good and evil.

The benefactor also set down precise conditions for choosing the teacher, who should be an educated man, with a pleasant voice and devout. The teacher should have two assistants.[25] Before 1582, Sinan Beg founded a mosque in Čajniće and established a school next to his mosque. The criteria for selecting the teacher were that he must be

> morally honest, valid and truthful, who knows *Shari'ah* rules, who knows the rules of reading the Qur'an, who possesses beautiful qualities. He should educate children and teach them the Qur'an's teachings, according to their capabilities, and also grammar, syntax and language. He should not make any difference in teaching and instruction and should take care of them as if they were his own children. During the education process, he should not be absent

without a legitimate justification, and he should be a true guardian in the process of raising them, as a merciful father, he should make great effort and have genuine concern.

His assistant should also be a man 'who possesses the same mentioned commendable qualities ... a pure soul, truthful, who will explain the lessons to the children in order for them to better understand'.[26] The teachers themselves sometimes developed new methods of teaching and made the newly learned language more accessible and fun for the children. In order to bring pupils closer to Arab letters, a teacher from the town of Kulen Vakuf compared the letters to things from their surroundings, familiar to them. For example, the letter 'elif' is compared to 'a stick', the letter 'jim' with 'a sickle that has a point in the stomach', the letter 'ri' with a 'hook that is used for getting cherries form the tree', the letter 'ze' with 'Zelić's sword' (Zelić was a policeman at that time and had a sword) and 'lam-elif' as '[s]cissors of Huso Lezić' (Lezić was a famous tailor).[27]

Therefore, one can say that among the benefactors there was a great awareness of the importance of choosing capable teachers in the educational process. Not only the teacher's professional qualifications, but also his moral virtues were considered. In addition, the aesthetic characteristics of the spaces and buildings in which the children were educated were also taken into account.

We can assume that some teachers actually met the above-mentioned criteria and were gentle and loving towards children. This resulted in creating a bond between tutors and their students. Among the documents found in the Ghazi Husrev Beg Library, there is also a petition (*arzuhal*) from the children of Prusac (Akhisar) to the Sultan, because their teacher, Davud Sipahi, was arrested and imprisoned in the Travnik fortress. The children said that they missed his classes and asked for his release.[28] We do not know exactly how the case ended, but it shows the strong connection between the teacher and pupils, to the extent that they petitioned to save him. The connection and closeness between teacher and pupil is also evidenced in a biography written by the intellectual Ibrahim (d. 1725), a professor of Arabic language in the Mohammad Beg *madrasa* in Mostar. He wrote of Shaikh Yuyo, proudly and gratefully, and pointed out that he was his 'teacher and professor, and that he had an attitude towards him like father to his son'.[29]

In a song in the Ottoman language, written by an unnamed poet at the beginning of the seventeenth century, a man from Sarajevo, who had moved to Constantinople, after a while met one of his fellow citizens, and during a conversation with him, felt a longing for his old homeland and thus sang these verses. He sang of his fellow citizens and, among others, his professor Abdul Celil Efendi, a prominent professor of Ghazi Husrev Beg *madrasa*, and his other professor, Pari Efendi, 'who lectures grammar and Arabic syntax every morning'. Also, he asked in verse: 'Are the schools still full of innocent children? Do they learn a lesson each day with the teacher's assistants?'.[30] This song also points to the emotional bond between the children and their teachers. But we do not know if the relationship between teachers and students was always a pleasant one or if the wishes of the *waqf*, in terms of the way in which teachers should behave towards children, were always respected. In one *waqfiyya* it was stated that the assistant was obliged to ensure that the children were not restless during classes, but the way this was to be achieved was not specified.[31] We are not familiar with Ottoman sources which provide information on a more rigorous teacher-to-child relationship.[32]

However, the fact that the practice of corporal punishment for disobedience was applied is testified in Bosnian–Herzegovinian tradition by what was said by parents to teachers: 'Your flesh, my bones'.[33] This phrase essentially gave parental permission for the teacher to apply mild corporal punishment as needed. Molla Mustafa Basheski notes sadly that a ten-year-old boy in Sarajevo in 1793, who used to help his blind father, was beaten by his teacher so hard that he died. Everyone in the town was horrified.[34]

In some *waqfiyya*s, it is pointed out that the supervision of the work of the officials in the mosque and school was to be performed by a specially paid officer. His duty was to encourage them to perform their duties and keep records of absences.[35] In addition, some benefactors paid special attention to those who performed the duties of doormen in the *waqf* facilities, especially in the *madrasa*s.[36]

There was an interest not only in building schools and financing the educational process, but also in other needs of the school-age children. A high-ranking officer, the chief court eunuch (*darüssaade ağası*) Mustafa Agha, along with his mosque and other facilities built a primary school for Muslim children in Jajce (Yayçe-i Yenicesi), his birthplace in northern Bosnia. For the maintenance of these facilities, he had left a large number of gold coins. He allocated resources for changing the rugs in the mosque and in the 'beautiful school' every year. He also decided that every year the clothes for all the children in the school (up to eighty of them) should be bought (white shirts and trousers made from a very expensive and durable material called *çuha*, a colourful belt and a small hat). These presents should be given to them during the month of Ramadan, on the holy Night of Destiny (*Leylet-ul Qadr*).[37] *Çuha* was a very expensive and highly valued material priced around fifty *akçes* per ell (*arşin*). In that period in the Sarajevo market a big ox was worth around 130 *akçes*. Therefore, it could be said that every child received a gift equivalent to the value of a big ox, which was highly significant at the time.[38] Another benefactor, the chief white eunuch (*babüssaade ağası*) Mustafa Agha, built a mosque and *maktab* in his hometown of Ljubinje. For every poor child and orphan in the *maktab* he left a sum of money in order to buy them a new shirt at the end of the month of Ramadan, 'so that their hearts would not suffer when they found themselves among the people in the days of Bayram'.[39] These examples show that the benefactors were even chief eunuchs at the Ottoman court in Istanbul, and therefore high up in the Ottoman administrative echelons, and they were sensitive to the needs of small children, especially orphans.

The earlier mentioned Kejvan Kethuda left two *akçes* to be given each day for the needs of children in his school in Mostar

> ... so that the teacher could acquire seasonal fruit for children. And, if there were no fruits, then fine sweets should be purchased. Fruits should be given to children attending school every Thursday afternoon. If there is anything left, it should be given to the poor children and adults. Neither the teacher nor the assistant should take it home.[40]

An integral part of another *waqfiyya* is a list of the items that the benefactor left. Among other things, for the mosque in Mostar he left 'two small tables for the Holy Qur'an' and 'two Holy Qur'an, in smaller size, for the *maktab*'.[41] This points to the benefactor's awareness that the children were not 'little men' and that they had different needs and abilities from adults. The tables and copies of the Holy Qur'an that were used by the children were to be smaller in size and more suitable for children to use. For the physical development of the children, he supplied them with vitamins in the form of fresh fruit and some sweets also. These things could also be used as a motivation for learning or reward for good behaviour.

Some teachers travelled in order to teach children. Basheski was absent from Sarajevo for eight months from 2 July 1781 to 1 March 1782. During that time, he taught children in the school in a village near Sarajevo. A few years earlier, in 1779, another teacher from Sarajevo, Molla Shakir, also went to a village for a year, taking the place of the *imam* in a mosque and teacher in the village school.[42]

School children and their teachers participated in the occasional public event. There are records in the literature that in Mostar in the middle of the nineteenth century, there was an old tradition regarding a ceremonial procession which was held during the departure of the pilgrims to the *Hajj* in Mecca. At the ceremony, the main participants were school children who went from their *maktab*s in a procession through the city to a gathering place. The eldest among them was at the head of the parade and loudly recited the text of a prayer that was specific for Mostar and only delivered during these festivities. Other children followed him saying 'Ameen'. In the same way, they were welcomed to the *hajji*'s house and received bread, sweets and some money.[43]

Girls and Education

Although small children usually learned together in *maktab*s, more often girls from the upper classes were educated in their own homes by their mothers. In most of the rich noble houses a medieval Bosnian script – the 'bosančica' – was preserved until the beginning of the last century, because mothers had given it to their female children for centuries.[44] The Bosnian version of the Turkish and Persian variants of the Arabic script and books in the Bosnian language, written in Arabic (bos. *alhamijado*), were also widespread.[45]

Based on the data in Ottoman archival and other sources, such as Ottoman tax registers and land cadastre (*tapu tahrir defter*s) and *waqfiyya*s, the role of women in the educational process was mostly connected to their position in providing financial support for education. Through the institution of the *waqf*, women invested in the education of children by establishing schools or by financing existing ones. The financial support for the work of the school was given by wealthy women, primarily by the wives of high-ranking Ottoman administrators. One of them was Shahdidar, the wife of the local Ottoman governor (*sancakbey*) in Bosnia, Ghazi Husrev Beg, who provided money for building a mosque in Sarajevo and entrusted 3,000 *akçe*s for building a *maktab* in its courtyard. Her motive was to establish a place where underage children from underprivileged families could gain support and an Islamic education. The teacher was required to be 'trustworthy, devout, to have a cheerful face while educating the children and teaching them the Qur'an'. The same criteria were required from the assistant.[46] In some cases, where they did not personally establish schools, some women left funds for those already in existence. Hajj Ibrahim Agha built a mosque and school, and his wife, Aisha Hatun, left a remarkable amount of 100,000 *akçe*s in order to support the work of those facilities.[47] The wife of Huseyn Beg, Shemsa, sister of the great vizier Mehmed Pasha Sokollu, left 80,000 silver *akçe*s for her *waqf* and, among other things, planned to repair two *maktab*s. Before 1604, Fatima

Hatun left 17,000 *akçes* for the needs of a *maktab* in Sarajevo. The money was intended for the *imam*, probably for additional activity and teaching children. A note in the Ottoman tax register of Bosnia from 1604 stated that the school had been damaged by fire.[48] It can be assumed that Fatima Hatun was aware of this and that she donated her money for the revitalisation of the demolished school for the improvement of working conditions in it and also for the salaries of teaching staff.[49]

Similar practices prevailed in later centuries. The mosque and *maktab* of the wife of the tax farmer *cum* governor (*voyvoda*) Sinan, established in Sarajevo, were destroyed in the fire caused by the Habsburg military troops of Eugene of Savoy in 1697. Later, it was re-established, and it still exists today.[50] After the building collapsed in the fire, on the opposite side of the same street, a certain Hanifa built the new school building, which served its purpose until 1908.[51] Aisha, the daughter of Hajj Ahmed in Mostar, determined in her *waqfiyya* that part of her *waqf* funds should be spent on supporting 'the poor students in the *madrasa* of Muhammad Beg and for heating every room of this *madrasa* in the winter'.[52]

Until the end of the early modern period there are very few documents that show that there were separate schools for girls with female teachers. However, Basheski mentioned several teachers in Sarajevo during the eighteenth century (such as Osman Hoca, Mumin Hoca and Emir Ahmed) who taught female pupils and gave lectures to women.[53] It is assumed that in some *maktab*s, where conditions existed, young girls were educated by female teachers (*mu'allima*). A female teacher named Dudi Bula built a mosque in Sarajevo between 1528 and 1540 and an entire town block was named after it for centuries (*Mahalle-i Dudi Bula*).[54] In house *maktab*s, female teachers held private classes for the children of a family, their siblings or other relatives.[55] For example, Mula Hamsha, the daughter of Mulalić Avdija, was a female teacher in the house *maktab* of a wealthy Sabura family in Sarajevo. The testimony to the importance of that duty is the fact that it was carved on her gravestone.[56]

The first documented girls' school with a female teacher in Sarajevo was opened in 1784, when the benefactor Mehmed Razi Velihodžić rebuilt his house as a school for girls. The documentation states that, for education purposes, a good woman should be chosen, capable of being a female teacher to female pupils in the neighbourhood, with a daily salary of ten *akçes*. In addition to good behaviour, she was supposed to teach young women how to read and recite the Qur'an, the foundations of faith, and regulations on ablutions, fasting, prayer and so on. The documentation went on to say that the female teacher should reside in the actual building.[57]

However, there is evidence indicating that even before the establishment of this school, some women were being educated in this way. A certain Emine, the daughter of Mustafa Chelebi, on 20 December 1764 in the town of Sarajevo, transcribed the entire text of the Holy Qur'an.[58] Some women appear as supervisors of a *waqf*, so it is assumed that they had to be educated to a certain level in order to perform their duties.[59] At the same time, in his *Chronicle*, Basheski wrote that during the war period of 1788–91, he had to write personal letters for women in Sarajevo to their husbands in the battlefields.[60] It therefore must be assumed that those women were not literate; they did not know the Ottoman Turkish language, if correspondence was carried out in that language. However, that does not mean that they were completely uneducated. Many other forms of informal education existed. For example, within the Sufi community, people were educated orally, so there could be many 'illiterate' people who were at the same time very knowledgeable.[61] In that sense, in Bosnia some women acted as teachers within the framework of the *tekke* (residence of the members of the *sufi* orders). These women were not only characterised by a high degree of spirituality, but some of them had also been engaged in formal education. For example, one Hajj Bacı Kadun founded a *madrasa* in the town of Tuzla.[62] In eighteenth-century Sarajevo, Basheski mentioned the wife of Recep Dede as a 'famous teacher' (*bacı hoca kadın, meşhure*).[63]

Madrasa

After finishing primary school, depending on the social position of their parents, students could go to work or be involved in trade or in craft, or continue their education in the *madrasa*. According to research by M. Bećirbegović, in the province of Bosnia there were 110 *madrasa*, built mostly as a part of *waqf* facilities.[64] Benefactors decided what subjects should be taught in the *madrasa*s, they left funds for education and other student needs (books, food, firewood) and accordingly set certain conditions regarding the students, as well as the qualifications and duties of teachers.

One of the most important benefactors of Sarajevo, Ghazi Husrev Beg, left a *waqfiyya* for establishing the *madrasa*, in which he specified the methods of its functioning. He devoted special attention to the programme and the subjects to be studied in it, the duties and the qualities necessary in the professors (educated, virtuous, perfect and prudent men, who had mastered spiritual and traditional science), the schedule of lectures and leisure time (a lecture could be missed only with an apology accepted by *Shari'ah* law, and students could leave lectures only with permission). Husrev Beg determined the salary of the professor (*muderris*) to be fifty *akçe*s per day, the assistant student (*muste'id*) four *akçe*s and for each student two *akçe*s of scholarships. All those who lived in the *madrasa* building, students and teaching staff, as well as the doorman, had the right to a free daily meal (wheat and meat soup and bread) that was prepared daily in the nearby Husrev Beg *imaret*.[65]

Before 1569, Hajj Mehmed Beg built a mosque in the town of Foča and established a boarding school type *madrasa*. The benefactor set the conditions for selecting students: '[H]onest and capable students to stay in it and not bad and incompetent ones'. For the maintenance of the *madrasa* he left a sum of 320,400 silver *akçe*s.[66]

Hajj Mohammad Beg left 100,000 silver *akçe*s intended for the education process in the *madrasa* that he built near his mosque in Mostar. Among other things, twenty *akçe*s daily were intended for the 'maintenance of teaching', while eight *akçe*s were intended for '*madrasa* students who live in four rooms in the *madrasa*'.[67] The same benefactor stated that the professor could hire someone from the local population to be a tutor for the pupils. The content of the lectures in this *madrasa* was not strictly limited to students. The lectures were open access, because the professor was obliged to teach 'all and anyone who comes to listen to useful subjects, and listeners should not be sent away from the door of the *madrasa*'.[68]

Prior to the foundation of the Atik *madrasa* in Banja Luka, the pupils were educated in private homes and other buildings that were not officially called schools.[69] Later on, Evliya Chelebi, who travelled to Banja Luka in the middle of the seventeenth century, mentions also the famous Ferhad Pasha *madrasa*.[70]

In his *waqfiyya* from 1642, Mustafa (Mustay) Beg decided that in his *madrasa* in Livno, all previously established subjects, as well as logic, mystical philosophy and other traditional and rational sciences, were to be studied.[71] In the inscription on the Simzade Abdulkerim *madrasa* in Sarajevo, among the subjects to be taught in the *madrasa*, geometry was listed.[72] The programme in some of the *madrasa*s was expanded so that in the eighteenth century, elements of astronomy and the use of the astrolabe were taught.[73] In the second half of the eighteenth century, in his *Chronicle* Basheski mentioned only a few astronomers in Sarajevo, Ibrahim Muzaferi and Mehmed Razi Velihodžić, as true specialists of practical astronomy. About Hoca Mola Mahmud, who was a librarian at Osman Shehdi's library and also a teacher, he wrote: 'He was especially capable of astronomy, so it can be freely said that he is the other Ptolemy'.[74]

Books and Transcribing Activities

Some benefactors were aware of the importance of having literature available as part of the educational process, and therefore, along with the *maktab*s and *madrasa*s, they also founded libraries. Ghazi Husrev Beg founded a library in Sarajevo that still exists.[75] In the Ghazi Husrev Beg library there are large numbers of manuscripts from disciplines such as medicine, veterinary medicine and pharmacology in the Arabic, Turkish and Persian languages.[76] Shaikh Muslihuddin pointed out that for the needs of students in the *madrasa* in Banja Luka, he donated 120 books and determined the conditions under which these books should be used, and that they should not be sold after his death.[77] The benefactor Mustafa Agha also upgraded a number of books that were placed in his mosque, and were taken care of by a special officer (librarian) who had a daily salary of two *akçe*s.[78] For his library, next to his *madrasa* in Travnik, Ibrahim Pasha donated ninety-eight volumes and five more books from various disciplines: exegesis *(tafsir)*, Hadith, grammar and syntax of Arabic language, stylistics, law, rhetoric and logic.[79] The library of Mehmed Razi Velihodžić contained 199 titles from various disciplines, among them *Shari'ah* law, history, geography, astronomy and mathematics.[80]

However, it was not always possible to obtain several copies of books, and so the transcribing of books was increased in the province of Bosnia. Due to the lack of basic manuals for their own needs, students of each *madrasa* had to transcribe the textbooks of the school curriculum determined by the founder. As scribes, students were designated as *softa* (from Persian *suhte*) and rarely as an Arabic student *(talib)*.[81] Textbooks used in everyday teaching were often transcribed in courtrooms, *maktab*s and *madrasa*s.[82]

Realising that students needed textbooks for particular subjects, some teachers became authors. Ismail Abdulkemal from Travnik, who was a teacher of the Arabic language, wrote a manual and grammar of the Arabic language in 1643.[83] In 1669 Osman Shugli wrote a commentary on the work in Arabic in the form of questions and answers. The explanations were in Turkish, but sometimes he inserted whole sentences in the Bosnian language (he called it *Bosna dilince, Bosnaca* or *Boşnakça*).[84]

Since the main languages of the intellectual world of the Ottoman Empire – Arabic, Persian and Turkish – were foreign for Muslim children in Bosnia, they first had to master these languages in order to access the teaching of the basis of religion. For the purpose of understanding textbooks, the existing dictionaries of the Arabic language were transcribed, but also new ones were created. Among the authors of the dictionaries was

Muhammad ibn Ahmed Nerkesi (d. 1635), who wrote an Arabic–Turkish dictionary for beginners called Children's rosary (*Subha-i sibyan*).[85] The first Bosnian–Turkish dictionary, entitled *Makbul-i 'Arif* (Affirmed Intellectual), was written by Muhammad Hevai Uskufi Bosnevi in 1631.[86]

During the eighteenth century, Muhamed Razi Velihodžić (1722–86) was the first among Muslim intellectuals who asked for the teaching of religious education in schools to be in the Bosnian language, instead of partially in Turkish and Arabic.[87] Other local intellectuals also sought to bring educational topics closer to children in primary schools, writing customised manuals in the Bosnian language. Abdulvehab Ilhami (d. 1821) wrote a short book entitled *'Ilm-i hal* (Catechism) for children, about the most basic Islamic regulations and duties.[88]

Sometimes teachers themselves translated books in order to help students in the learning process, but also to make them more accessible to the wider reading audience. The above-mentioned Shaikh Musafi translated his work from Arabic to Ottoman Turkish, because, as he stated, 'in Bosnia, especially in Banja Luka, in the area, not many people know Arabic'. Later, he added: '[T]here are also not many of them who know Turkish'. In the introduction to the work, he discussed how he began translating at the request of the students in his *madrasa*.[89]

Conclusion

In the territory of Ottoman Bosnia during the early modern period, the education of Muslim children and youth took place in *maktab*s and *madrasa*s, official education facilities within or attached to mosques. Non-Muslim children acquired their education in their own religious facilities. During the considered time period, there were more than 110 *madrasa*s, while *maktab*s existed in almost every town and village.

As well as in the rest of the Ottoman state, *maktab*s in Ottoman Bosnia most often existed within the mosques, as a part of the *waqf* of prominent individuals, but often the benefactors built, maintained and repaired separated facilities, while *madrasa*s were always separate buildings. The salaries of the teaching staff, teachers, professors and their assistants, as well as the supervisors, guardians and gatekeepers, were also paid from the *waqf* funds. These funds were used to repair buildings, pay for scholarships, supply food and purchase books, seasonal fruit, firewood and blankets for cold days. It was assumed that very young boys and girls would be educated together, while in the next phase, the girls continued their education separately, in private homes, and much later in special girls' schools. It seems that girls from the upper classes were educated in their own homes by their mothers and private teachers. In most of the rich noble houses a medieval Bosnian script – the 'bosančica' – was preserved until the beginning of the twentieth century, because mothers had always handed it down to their daughters.

Women as teachers, and generally educated women, rarely appeared in Ottoman documents, and if they did, mostly under the name *mu'allima*. The first girls' school with a female teacher in Sarajevo was opened in 1784. Some women acted as teachers within the framework of the *tekke* (residence of the members of the *sufi* orders or dervish monasteries). These women were not only characterised by a high degree of spirituality, but some of them were also engaged in formal education, such as Hajj Bacı Kadun, who founded a *madrasa* in the town of Tuzla.

Among the benefactors there was a strong awareness of the importance of choosing capable teachers as part of the educational process. Not only the teacher's professional qualifications, but also their moral virtues were considered. In addition, the aesthetic characteristics of the spaces and buildings in which the children were educated were also taken into account. Benefactors showed an interest not only in building schools and financing the educational process, but also in the other needs of school-age children. They were mostly aware of the fact that the children were not 'miniature adults' and that they had different needs and abilities from adults.

Since the general languages of the intellectual world of the Ottoman Empire – Arabic, Persian and Turkish – were foreign for Muslim children in the province of Bosnia, they first had to master the basics of those languages in order to access the religious teaching. For the purpose of understanding the textbooks, the existing dictionaries of the Arabic language were transcribed, but also new ones were created. However, since multiple copies of books and manuals were not available, students of the *madrasa* had to transcribe the textbooks of the school curriculum. This is one of the reasons why transcription expanded in the province of Bosnia.

Notes

1. Kovačević-Kojić, *Gradska naselja*; Anđelić, *Doba srednjovjekovne Bosanske države*; Kurtović, *Iz historije odgoja i obrazovanja*.
2. Kurtović, *Iz historije odgoja i obrazovanja*, pp. 185–93.
3. İhsanoğlu, *Ottoman Educational Institutions*, pp. 361–512.
4. Ćurić, *Muslimansko školstvo*; Bećirbegović, *Prosvjetni objekti*, pp. 223–364; Kasumović, *Školstvo i obrazovanje*.
5. 'Read in the name of your Lord', Qur'an, *Al-'Alaq*: 1.
6. *Sahihu-l Muslim*, p. 429.

7. From the funds of the *waqf* of a certain Hadjj Hajdar, the son of Abdullah, the *muʻallim*s were to be chosen among the benefactor's descendants and had a daily allowance. *Opširni popis Bosanskog sandžaka iz 1604*, p. 499.
8. Čelebi, *Putopis*, p. 110.
9. Based on his research, Kasumović reports seventy-nine *maktab*s and *muʻallimhane*s in Sarajevo. Kasumović, *Školstvo i obrazovanje*, pp. 107–9.
10. Ćurić, *Muslimansko školstvo*; Bećirbegović, *Prosvjetni objekti*; Kasumović, *Školstvo i obrazovanje*, pp. 88–9.
11. *Vakufname*, p. 30.
12. *Opširni popis Bosanskog sandžaka iz 1604*, p. 489.
13. *Vakufname*, p. 15.
14. Ibid., p. 35.
15. For example, before 1604 in Sarajevo, material support for education was left by the fermented millet drink seller (*bozacı*) Hadži Hasan, the pulley-maker (*çekrekçi*) Muslihuddin and the jeweller (*kuyumcu*) Mehmed.
16. Several *hajji*s in Sarajevo before 1604 left money for the educational purposes of children: Hajj Ejnebegi, Hajj Murad, Hajj Ali, Hajj Idris and so on.
17. Havace Kemal founded a mosque (*masjid*) with a school in Sarajevo, and his daughters Nefisa and Hanifa also left money for his *waqf*. Havace Durak built a mosque before 1528 and a few decades later, his son, Mehmed Chelebi, left 10,000 *akçe*s, from which the teacher in his father's *maktab* was paid and funds were allocated for repairing the *maktab* building.
18. *Vakufname*, p. 84.
19. Mohamed, *The Duties of the Teacher*, pp. 186–206.
20. Giladi, *Concepts of Childhood*, p. 125.
21. *Vakufname*, pp. 87–8.
22. Ibid., pp. 113, 119.
23. Ibid., p. 161.
24. Ibid., pp. 165–7.
25. Ibid., pp. 103–8.
26. Ibid., pp. 193–216.
27. Kasumović, *Školstvo i obrazovanje*, p. 87.
28. Gadžo-Kasumović, *Diplomatički dokumenti*, p. 19.
29. Mušić, *Ibrahim Opijač*, p. 51.
30. Mušić, *Jedna turska pjesma*, p. 584.
31. BOA, TSMA.d. 6965, f. 11a–14a. 1606.
32. About variations of corporal punishment that were used in many educational settings, see Lamdan's Chapter 14 and Çiçek's Chapter 12 in this volume.
33. Alibašić, *Vjersko obrazovanje*, pp. 11–34.
34. Bašeskija, *Ljetopis*, p. 309. The *Chronicle* of Molla Mustafa Basheski, where he wrote every day and reported on historically important events in the history of Sarajevo and Bosnia in the second half of the eighteenth century, is written in Ottoman–Turkish language, including some words and sentences in the Bosnian language. It covers several decades, at the end of the eight-

eenth century and early nineteenth century, and has great cultural significance for the history of Ottoman Bosnia.

35. Bašeskija, *Ljetopis*, p. 117.
36. Ibid., p. 65.
37. Ibid., pp. 252, 254–5.
38. Husić, *Novčani vakufi*, p. 53.
39. BOA, TSMA.d. 6965, f. 14a. 1606.
40. *Vakufname*, p. 88.
41. Ibid., p. 126.
42. Filan, *Iz svakodnevice*, p. 123.
43. Hasandedić, *Muslimanska društva*, p. 198.
44. Hadžijahić, *Građa o posljednjim ostacima bosančice*, pp. 101–11.
45. Ždralović, *Bosansko-hercegovački prepisivači*, p. 205.
46. *Vakufname*, p. 76.
47. *Opširni popis Bosanskog sandžaka iz 1604*, p. 93.
48. Ibid., p. 81.
49. Nevbiha Hatun in Sarajevo left 12,000 *akçe* for the teacher in the school, while Hafsa Hatun left 4,000 *akçe* for the masjid and *muʿallimhana* (school) of Hajj Idris, also in Sarajevo. Čar-Drnda, *Društveni i pravni položaj*, pp. 124–53.
50. Zlatar, *Zlatno doba*, pp. 58–9.
51. Traljić, *Sarajevski grad Vratnik*, p. 51.
52. Nametak, *Vakufnama Aiše*, pp. 363–4.
53. Filan, *Sarajevo u Bašeskijino doba*, p. 167.
54. Zlatar, *Zlatno doba*, p. 55.
55. Kasumović, *Školstvo i obrazovanje*, p. 146.
56. Mujezinović, *Islamska epigrafika Bosne i Hercegovine*, p. 320.
57. Mujezinović, *Biblioteka Mehmed-razi Velihodžića*, p. 67.
58. Ždralović, *Bosansko-hercegovački prepisivači*, p. 193; Dervišević, *18th Century Qurʾan*.
59. Čar-Drnda, *Društveni i pravni položaj*, pp. 124–53; Filan, *Žena i institucija vakufa*, pp. 117–43.
60. Bašeskija, *Ljetopis*, p. 268.
61. Hanna, *Literacy Among Artisans*.
62. Hadžijahić, *Badžijanije*, p. 128.
63. Filan, *Sarajevo u Bašeskijino doba*, p. 168.
64. Bećirbegović, *Prosvjetni objekti*; Kasumović, *Školstvo i obrazovanje*.
65. *Vakufname*, pp. 64–5.
66. Ibid., pp. 152–3.
67. Ibid., p. 170.
68. Ibid., p. 171.
69. Paić-Vukić and Al-Dujaily, *Zbornik Muslihuddina Kninjanina*, p. 142.
70. Čelebi, *Putopis*, p. 214; Bejtić, *Banjaluka*, p. 99.
71. Bećirbegović, *Prosvjetni objekti*, p. 278.

72. Ibid.
73. Kasumović, *Školstvo i obrazovanje*, p. 98.
74. Bašeskija, *Ljetopis*, p. 187.
75. *Vakufname*, p. 63.
76. Dobrača, *Orijentalni medicinski rukopisi*, pp. 57–76.
77. Ždralović, *Bosansko-hercegovački prepisivači*, p. 49.
78. *Vakufname*, p. 256.
79. Ždralović, *Bosansko-hercegovački prepisivači*, p. 60.
80. For a complete list, see Mujezinović, *Biblioteka Mehmed-razi Velihodžića*, pp. 70–82.
81. For example, Hussein, a student in the Mohammad Beg *madrasa* in Mostar in 1760, transcribed three manuscripts from the Arabic language. Ždralović, *Bosansko-hercegovački prepisivači*, p. 106.
82. As places of transcription, *madrasa*s in Sarajevo, Mostar, Travnik, Banja Luka, Maglaj, Prusac (Akhisar), Foča, Livno, Novi Pazar, Stolac, Tešanj, Tuzla, Užice and Donji Vakuf are mentioned.
83. Mušić, *En-nemliyye*, pp. 39–54.
84. Popara, *Nekoliko novih podataka*, pp. 24–5.
85. Ibid., p. 23.
86. Filan, *Turska leksika*; Kalajdžija, *O nekim leksikološkim aspektima*.
87. Huković, *Napori za uvođenje narodnog jezika*, p. 245.
88. Dobrača, *Tuhfetul Musallin*, p. 50.
89. Paić-Vukić and Al-Dujaily, *Zbornik Muslihuddina Kninjanina*, p. 148.

Bibliography

Archival Sources

Nametak, Fehim, 'Vakufnama Aiše, kćeri hadži Ahmeda iz Mostara', *Prilozi za orijentalnu filologiju*, vol. 44–5 (1996), pp. 363–4.

Opširni popis Bosanskog sandžaka iz 1604. godine, vol. 1, 1/2, 2 and 3 (Sarajevo: Bošnjački Institut Zürich Odjel Sarajevo and Orijentalni Institute, 2000).

The Archive of Topkapı Palace Museum (TSMA.d.) 6965, 1606.

Vakufname iz Bosne i Hercegovine (XV i XVI vijek) (Sarajevo: Orijentalni Institut, 1985).

Primary Sources

Bašeskija, Mula Mustafa Ševki, *Ljetopis (1746–1804)*, trans. Mehmed Mujezinović (Sarajevo: Sarajevo Publishing, 1997).

Čelebi, Evlija, *Putopis-odlomci o jugoslovenskim zemljama*, trans. Hazim Šabanović (Sarajevo: Veselin Masleša, 1979).

Sahihu-l Muslim, trans. Muhamed Mrahorović, Mustafa Prljača, Nurko Karaman, Jusuf Karaman, and Aida Mujezin (Sarajevo: El-Kalem, 2004).

Secondary Sources

Alibašić, Ahmet, 'Vjersko obrazovanje u javnim školama u BiH: Ka modelu koji podržava suživot i uzajamno razumijevanje', in Ahmet Alibašić, Sabina Ćudić, Zlatiborka Popov-Momčinović, Amina Mulabdić, and Emina Abrahamsdotter (eds), *Religija i školovanje u otvorenom društvu: Preispitivanje modela religijskog obrazovanja u Bosni i Hercegovini* (Sarajevo: Fond Otvoreno Društvo, 2009), pp. 11–34.

Anđelić, Pavao, 'Doba srednjovjekovne bosanske države', *Kulturna istorija Bosne i Hercegovine od najstarijih vremena do pada ovih zemalja pod osmansku vlast* (Sarajevo: Veselin Masleša, 1984).

Bećirbegović, Madžida, 'Prosvjetni objekti islamske arhitekture u Bosni i Hercegovini', *Prilozi za Orijentalnu Filologiju*, 20–21 (1974), pp. 223–364.

Bejtić, Alija, 'Banjaluka pod turskom vladavinom', *Naše starine*, 1 (1953), pp. 91–115.

――――, 'Pjesnik Sabit Alauddin Užičanin kao sarajevski kadija i bosanski mula', *Anali Gazi Husrev Begove Biblioteke*, 2–3 (1974), pp. 3–20.

Čar-Drnda, Hatidža, 'Društveni i pravni položaj žene muslimanke u osmanskoj Bosni', *Znakovi Vremena*, 10 (2007), pp. 124–53.

Ćurić, Hajrudin, *Muslimansko školstvo u Bosni i Hercegovini do 1918* (Sarajevo: Veselin Masleša, 1983).

Derviševic, Haris, '18th Century Qur'an Transcribed by a Woman', *Islamic Art Magazine*, 1 June 2017, available at: <http://islamicartsmagazine.com/magazine/view/18th_century_quran_transcribed_by_a_woman/> (last accessed February 2018).

Dobrača, Kasim, 'Tuhfetul Musallin ve Zubdetul-Haši'in od Abdul-Vehaba Žepčevije Ilhamije', *Anali Gazi Husrev Begove Biblioteke*, 2–3 (1974), pp. 41–69.

――――, 'Orijentalni medicinski rukopisi u Gazi Husrev Begovoj biblioteci', *Anali Gazi Husrev Begove Biblioteke*, 7–8 (1982), pp. 57–76.

Filan, Kerima, 'Turska leksika u rječniku Makbuli Arif Muhameda Hevaija Uskufija', *Anali Gazi Husrev Begove Biblioteke*, 23–4 (2005), pp. 205–17.

――――, 'Iz svakodnevnice osmanskog Sarajeva: Druženja i razonode', *Anali Gazi Husrev Begove Biblioteke*, 31 (2010), pp. 113–38.

――――, 'Žena i institucija vakufa u osmanskoj Bosni', in *Zbornik radova Vakufi u Bosni i Hercegovini*, ed. Nedim Begović (Sarajevo: Vakufska direkcija, 2013), pp. 117–43.

――――, *Sarajevo u Bašeskijino doba* (Sarajevo: Connectum, 2014).

Gadžo-Kasumović, Azra, 'Diplomatički dokumenti: arzuhali, mahzari, arzovi, ilami i sahha bujuruldije', *Anali Gazi Husrev Begove Biblioteke*, 31 (2010), pp. 5–44.

Giladi, Avner, 'Concepts of Childhood and Attitudes Towards Children in Medieval Islam', *Journal of Economic and Social History of the Orient*, 32/2 (1989), pp. 121–52.

Gölen, Zafer, 'Tanzimat Döneminde Bosna Hersek'te Eğitim', *Prilozi za Orijentalnu Filologiju*, 52–3 (2004), pp. 213–66.

Hadžijahić, Muhamed, 'Badžijanije u Sarajevu i Bosni: Prilog historiji duhovnosti u nas', *Anali Gazi Husrev Begove Biblioteke*, 7–8 (1982), pp. 109–33.

———, 'Građa o posljednjim ostacima bosančice u nas', *Anali Gazi Husrev Begove Biblioteke*, 11–12 (1985), pp. 101–11.

Handžić, Adem, 'O formiranju nekih gradskih naselja u Bosni u XVI stoljeću (uloga države i vakufa)', *Prilozi za Orijentalnu Filologiju*, 25 (1977), pp. 133–69.

Handžić, Mehmed, 'Dva popisa sarajevskih mekteba', *El-Hidaje*, 6 (1942–3), pp. 119–23.

Hanna, Nelly, 'Literacy Among Artisans and Tradesmen in Ottoman Cairo', in Christine Woodhead (ed.), *The Ottoman World* (London and New York: Routledge, 2012), pp. 319–31.

Hasandedić, Hivzija, 'Hercegovački vakufi i vakifi', *Anali Gazi Husrev Begove Biblioteke*, 9–10 (1983), pp. 29–73.

———, 'Muslimanska društva u Mostaru', *Anali Gazi Husrev Begove Biblioteke*, 19–20 (2001), pp. 197–213.

Huković, Muhamed, 'Napori za uvođenje narodnog jezika u početne vjerske škole muslimana', *Anali Gazi Husrev Begove Biblioteke*, 17–18 (1996), pp. 241–51.

Husić, Aladin, 'Novčani vakufi u Bosni u drugoj polovini 16. Stoljeća', *Anali Gazi Husrev Begove Biblioteke*, 32 (2011), pp. 35–59.

İhsanoğlu, Ekmelettin, 'Ottoman Educational and Scholarly-Scientific Institutions', in Ekmelettin Ihsanoğlu (ed.), *History of the Ottoman State and Society and Civilisation*, vol. 2 (Istanbul: IRCICA, 2002), pp. 361–512.

Kalajdžija, Alen, 'O nekim leksikološkim aspektima proučavanja Makbuli-arifa', *Bosanskohercegovački slavistički kongres I: Zbornik radova*, 1 (2012), pp. 99–107.

Kasumović, Ismet, *Školstvo i obrazovanje u Bosanskom ejaletu za vrijeme osmanske uprave* (Mostar: Islamski Kulturni Centar, 1999).

Kovačević-Kojić, Desanka, *Gradska naselja srednovjekovne bosanske države* (Sarajevo: Veselin Masleša, 1978).

Kurtović, Esad, 'Iz historije odgoja i obrazovanja u Dubrovniku i dubrovačkom zaleđu (Učenje dobrih običaja, manira i pismenosti)', *Radovi Filozofskog fakulteta u Sarajevu*, vol. 2 (Historija, Historija umjetnosti, Arheologija) (2012), pp. 185–93.

Mohamed, Yasien, 'The Duties of the Teacher: Al Isfahani's Dhari'a as a Source of Inspiration for al-Ghazali's Mizan al-'Amal'', in Georges Tamer (ed.), *Islam and Rationality: The Impact of al-Ghazâlî*, vol. 1 (Leiden: Brill, 2015), pp. 186–206.

Mujezinović, Mehmed, 'Biblioteka Mehmed-razi Velihodžića, šejha i muderisa Gazi Husrev Begova hanikaha u Sarajevu', *Anali Gazi Husrev Begove Biblioteke*, 5–6 (1978), pp. 55–64.

_____, *Islamska epigrafika Bosne i Hercegovine*, vol. 1 (Sarajevo: Sarajevo Publishing, 1998).
Mulaomerović, Jasminko, 'Astronomija u djelima bosanskohercegovačkih autora 18. Stoljeća', *Radio Sarajevo – Treći program*, 36 (1982), pp. 423–32.
Mušić, Omer, 'Jedna turska pjesma o Sarajevu iz 17. Vijeka', *Prilozi za Orijentalnu Filologiju*, 3–4 (1953), pp. 575–87.
_____, 'En-nemliyye fi 'izhari-l-qawa'idi s-sarfiyye we n-nahwiyye', *Prilozi za Orijentalnu Filologiju*, 6–7 (1958), pp. 39–54.
_____, 'Ibrahim Opijač Mostarac', *Prilozi za Orijentalnu Filologiju*, 10–11 (1960–1), pp. 31–53.
Paić-Vukić, Tatjana, and Linda Al-Dujaily, 'Pedagoški i moralno-didaktički zbornik Muslihuddina Kninjanina iz 1609. godine: Rukopisi arapskog izvornika i osmanskog prijevoda', *Zbornik*, 33 (2015), pp. 133–62.
Popara, Haso, 'Nekoliko novih podataka o Visočaninu Osman ef. Šugliji sinu Ahmedovu', *Anali Gazi Husrev Begove Biblioteke*, 32 (2011), pp. 7–34.
_____, 'Šejh Muslihuddin Kninjanin: Prilog izučavanju kulturne historije Banje Luke', *Prilozi za Orijentalnu Filologiju*, 63 (2014), pp. 232–60.
Trako, Salih, 'Šerhi Wasiyyetname-i Bergiwi sa prevodom na srpskohrvatskom jeziku', *Anali Gazi Husrev Begove Biblioteke*, 5–6 (1978), pp. 117–26.
Traljić, Seid M., *Sarajevski grad Vratnik* (Sarajevo: Štamparija Bosanska pošta, 1937).
Ždralović, Muhamed, *Bosansko-hercegovački prepisivači djela u arabičkim rukopisima*, vols 1 and 2 (Sarajevo: Svjetlost, 1988).
Zlatar, Behija, *Zlatno doba Sarajeva* (Sarajevo: Svjetlost, 1996).
_____, *Gazi Husrev Beg* (Sarajevo: Orijentalni Institut, 2010).

Chapter 14

Children's Education in Ottoman Jewish Society (Sixteenth to Eighteenth Centuries)

Ruth Lamdan

Judaism, like Islam, is a faith based on a set of laws, one that instructs its believers on their proper daily conduct. Providing schooling from a young age is the key to socialisation, and a considerable part of children's education includes teaching behaviour according to Jewish law (*halakha*) – that is, Jewish legal norms – observance of the commandments and recital of individual and public prayers. Indeed, over the generations, traditional age-appropriate education has been used to ensure that people practice a Jewish lifestyle, beginning using teachers of the very young (*melamdim*) in early education and school settings for young children (*Talmud Torah*) through to higher school (*yeshiva*) settings for older students.

For this reason, it is surprising that the research on children in Jewish society is so sparse compared to research on childhood in the non-Jewish world, possibly because sources on this subject are few and scattered. The little that has been published refers mostly to early periods in history and to the Ashkenazi Jewish society of medieval Europe.[1] Until recent years, very little has been written about childhood in Ottoman Jewish society.[2]

The period from the early sixteenth to the mid-eighteenth century was an era of transition and of considerable change in Jewish society and family because of the significant migration of Jews from the Iberian Peninsula, and to a lesser degree from European countries and North Africa, to the Ottoman Empire. Sephardic (Spanish-originating) customs were adopted over the years by most Jewish communities throughout the Empire, and by the end of the process, through assimilation, a Jewish–Ottoman society was formed, with most of its leaders and sages originating from Spain. Most Jewish males received a basic education within the community and knew or understood at least two languages: a local language and a Jewish language. Over the years speakers of Ladino, the language of the Spanish and Portuguese migrants, became dominant, and it was necessary to publish and translate books into this language, which was understood by most. Much has been written about the cultural and moral changes that occurred following the arrival of the Spanish exiles (1492) in the territory of the Ottoman Empire, but there has only been scant reference to early basic education.[3]

The main sources of information from which the current chapter draws were also written and devised by Spanish Jewish sages and spiritual authorities. The available sources include sermons, books of ethics and extensive legal literature (*responsa*) by contemporary adjudicators (*poskim*), all in Hebrew. Sermons and homilies, as pedagogic means, indicate, among other subjects, the expected conduct of boys and youths, while ethical advisory literature (*musar* books) provides recommendations for young people and instructions for their parents on matters of child education. *Responsa* volumes encompass legal discussions, and children are only mentioned in cases of legal problems, such as unwanted child marriage, guardianship and inheritance rights. But the stories that underlie the legal (*halakhic*) discussions in such matters attest to children's rights and to the relationships between family members and guardians in issues pertaining to children. This information contributes to broadening the scope of research on young children's education in different Jewish communities in the Ottoman space and can lead to a better understanding of how the Jewish religious obligation to educate children was practiced. It also highlights the complexity of pre-modern Ottoman society. The Empire was a multicultural and multicommunal entity that maintained a range of educational institutions and took a variety of approaches towards children in which religion was the main determinant. A closer look at Jewish communal educational institutions provides new insights into specific Jewish concepts of childhood in pre-modern times. By using these rarely researched sources, this chapter concentrates on the education and upbringing of five- to thirteen-year-olds, the structure of Jewish educational institutions and educational theories, and the responsibility of society and the family for their schooling in Jewish communities in the Ottoman Empire. The Jewish communities were autonomous with respect to education, and were not influenced by Ottoman rules or traditions.[4] Nevertheless, an analysis of the Jewish sources reveals similarities in perceptions of childhood between the Jewish community and Ottoman society at large, such as a patriarchal and gendered approach towards education.

Early Education

The sources available to us describe some sort of school system as existing in Jewish society from a very early stage. The sages of the *Mishna* and *Talmud*[5] acknowledged the concept whereby every man has an obligation to study Holy Scriptures (Torah). According to a tradition cited in the name of Rav in the third century AD (Babylon):

> A certain man is remembered for the good, and his name is Yehoshua ben Gamla. If not for him the Torah would have been forgotten from the Jewish people. [Because] at first those [boys] who had a father – the father would teach them ... Our forefathers instituted a regulation decreeing that teachers would be employed [only] in Jerusalem. High Priest Yehoshua ben Gamla came and prescribed that teachers be appointed in every country and in every city, and children were brought to study at the age of six or seven.[6]

Hence, as early as the first century, during Yehoshua ben Gamla's term of office, something that resembled a 'compulsory schooling law' was prescribed, placing the responsibility for the schooling of all Jewish children on the entire community, and it is the gradual nature of this description that lends it historical credibility.[7]

Many Jewish sages in the Ottoman Empire referred to the significance of early education. Mothers were instructed not to sing meaningless lullabies to their babies, rather only songs that told of good deeds and of reward and punishment. They were to tell them about the existence of the Creator, teach them select verses from the prayers, train them to say the blessings before eating and to answer amen when appropriate. The mother was charged with these things, as most of the day it was she who was at home with the infant.[8]

Imparting traditions at a very young age was stressed in private homes as well as in synagogues.[9] Jewish children needed to be familiar with the prayers, with the orders of the synagogue – the centre of community life – and with the basic religious values of Jewish society, so that they could become socialised in it as adults. R. Jacob Khuli (Jerusalem 1689 – Istanbul 1732) recommended that children be brought to the synagogue and taught to answer amen in the proper places, but not played with or permitted to run around and 'play games'.[10] At a young age it was necessary to instill in them good ethics, humility and modesty.[11] It was important to explain to the children the significance of observing the commandments in general, and in particular to stress the precept of honouring one's father and mother, which was a proven remedy for reaching old age, in the spirit of the verse: 'Honor thy father and mother that thy days may be long' (Ex. 20:12).[12]

From the moment the child learned to talk, the father was obliged to teach his son, and in the absence of a father, the grandfather was responsible for the child's schooling. This is a precept discussed by Maimonides and many other adjudicators, and a summary is provided in Rabbi Yosef Caro's legal code, the *Shulhan Arukh*, written in the sixteenth century.[13] In addition to instilling values, at an early age the child could first be taught the alphabet and the vocalisation marks, according to his ability and skills, and even parts of the weekly portion. Thus, when reaching the age of five, he would already be able to commence reading the Torah.[14]

The Talmud Torah

The preparations made at a young age have one purpose: to bring the child to the Torah study stage, which was, and still is, the essence and the first stage in the formal studies of all Jewish males. The *Mishna* says: 'Five years old to learn the Torah, ten years old to learn the *Mishna*; thirteen years old to obey the commandments (*mitzvoth*); fifteen years old to learn the Talmud' (Avot 5:21); and, indeed, most boys from the age of five or six received minimal schooling at an institution called Torah School for the Young (*Talmud Torah le-Ketanim*).

The *Talmud Torah* was intended only for boys, and its purpose was to impart a basic education and fundamental Jewish values not only to the sons of the rich, but also to poor children and orphans. The public *Talmud Torah* constituted a foundation of every community, and in fact it is not possible to think of a Jewish community with no study facilities for children. 'Who can live in a place that has no Torah study society?', wrote R. Hayim Benveniste (1603–73).[15]

It was agreed by all educators that at a young age a child is like a blank page; he has yet to sin, is not occupied with worldly matters and his heart and thoughts are pure and ready to absorb. R. Shemuel di Uceda of Safed (d. c. 1604) stressed that the seedling, when still young, could be grown to produce a straight rather than a crooked trunk, but once it grew crooked, it was hard to fix.[16] Nonetheless, the dominant rule in Jewish education was: 'Train up a child in the way he should go' (Prov. 22:6). R. Yehoshua Benveniste of Istanbul (c. 1590–1665) recommended that the child's physical state and mental capacity be taken into consideration, while verifying that he was capable of coping with formal studies.[17]

The basic education included learning prayers and the weekly portion with commentary or translation, and most of the boys were, at minimum, proficient in Hebrew reading, and by the age of thirteen could read from the Torah traditionally and take part in the synagogue's activities.[18]

R. Yaakov Faraji of Alexandria (d. 1759), when asked about young boys who were called up to read from the Torah in the synagogue, spoke about the techniques he employed as a teacher:

> When I taught boys, when the boy reached the age of *bar mitzvah* (thirteen), if he was capable of reciting a sermon – I would arrange for him an appropriate sermon, and if he was not capable of reciting a sermon – I would make sure that he could recite the weekly portion, and [he] would say it in public instead of a [*bar mitzva*] sermon . . . [and] I had another custom, that I would teach these boys [once again] to read the weekly portion when they reached the age of fifteen or sixteen . . . as the material you study in your youth remains with you; and all the cantors among us, who read from the Torah and do not miss a thing, I taught them all when they were young . . . and I do not praise a good voice . . . I only attribute importance to how the letters and words and vowels are uttered and to the different cantillation notes as given at Sinai and conveyed to us.[19]

From the 1520s in Jerusalem we know of a *melamed* called R. Yosef Midrash, of whom the immigrant R. Israel Ashkenazi related in a letter sent to Italy: 'He teaches all the young boys of Jerusalem the verses and the laws . . . and those who cannot afford to pay are taught free of charge, and he is the most loyal person'.[20] Ashkenazi reported on his three sons: Baruch, the eldest, was occupied with commerce; Shelomo, the second, was beginning his studies at *yeshiva*; and the youngest son, Yitzhak, was doing well in his studies, had a good mind and could already translate every verse in the weekly portion by heart, and the father meant to start teaching him Talmud.

The school was usually located within the synagogue or in its vicinity and was managed as a charity by a community agency, called Torah Study Confraternity (*Hevrat Talmud Torah*), whose managers employed a teacher and arranged his employment terms, and if possible provided the children with a daily meal and clothing for the needy. The financial funds for maintaining the facility were usually provided by internal community taxes, charity collections, donations and bequests, and sometimes through the dedication of property or capital to cover its expenses and to pay the teachers' salary. The importance of schooling for the young is evident from the fact that rich people often donated to facilities for Torah study on the condition that the donation went to young children, rather than *yeshiva* students.[21] The managers of the *Talmud Torah* invested the capital and increased its revenues by lending money at interest and other investments.[22] The forming of such societies was characteristic of communities from the Iberian Peninsula, and one of the customs that Spanish Jews brought with them to the Ottoman Empire was the levy of the *gabella* (a type of indirect tax on meat and wine), whose returns were used for Torah study and which constituted an important economic source for maintaining Torah institutions in all communities throughout the Empire.[23]

An agreement reached in the community of Chios, Greece, indicates the educational and financial arrangements made in a Jewish Ottoman community. It said:

> We, the holy community of Chios, have made a regulation under warning of strict excommunication to maintain the arrangement of a *Talmud Torah*, as follows: Since ... the infants have no arrangement and they roam around as a flock with no shepherd ... we roused ourselves and found the strength and arranged the students, may God keep them, in grades such that they shall pass from grade to grade and increase the Torah and glorify it; and in order to support the teachers ... to pay them their salary so that they should perform their work faithfully, we ... have volunteered ... to give *tamid* [a regular tax] every month. And we appointed two people, notables, to oversee collecting all the regular taxes and donations, with God's help.[24]

In this specific case, regretfully, those who signed it fell into discord and approached several sages to help them resolve their problems.[25]

Although studies depended at times on the availability of teachers and the necessary funds to employ them, as well as on the awareness and goodwill of the parents, in any case everything was done to award at least a basic Jewish education, and *Talmud Torah* schools were found in each Jewish community in the Empire. R. Moshe Basola, who visited Damascus in early 1522, stated that although the city had 500 Jewish families, there was no *yeshiva* for advanced studies, but it did have primary instruction, with each teacher responsible for thirty or forty students. It appears that in the early sixteenth century, exiles from Spain and from other places had not yet arrived in Damascus, and the Jewish community was nearly all local and Arabic-speaking (*Musta'arab*s), and its members, aside from a select few, did not excel in Torah study. Subsequently, sages from Safed, Aleppo and other places settled in Damascus, and the level of education and schooling rose.[26]

In the mid-seventeenth century, over 100 children studied at a central *Talmud Torah* in Jerusalem. The students were divided among the desks (classes) of some ten teachers. The *Talmud Torah* was utilised by members of all congregations, and its maintenance and the teachers' salaries were part of the community's regular expenditures. The wages of a teacher in Jerusalem consisted of eight *qurush* a week, but the community, which was heavily in debt, found it hard to cover this expense and its other public commitments. Its leaders tried to raise funds wherever possible, and sent desperate delegates to communities in the diaspora in the hope that they would increase their support of Jerusalem's Jews, and particularly of the

Talmud Torah, 'which has insufficient books and is incapable of paying the teachers' salaries'.[27] The letters of the delegates and the documents of the *Shari'ah* court in Jerusalem show that in such a situation the Sephardic community leaders were compelled to apply for additional loans and even to use as collateral the very rooms in which the children were taught.[28]

Involvement of Fathers in their Children's Studies

When possible, fathers took part in choosing the teachers and the curriculum of the *Talmud Torah*. A deed of association between several fathers and a teacher in 1611 said that, in return for the tuition determined, the tutor assumed responsibility under strict oath to teach the children for an entire year 'diligently, with a full heart and mind, guilelessly', and agreed to take on no more than six students. Later, he increased the number of students, to the chagrin of the fathers.[29] In one city there was a rumour that a teacher had engaged in a forbidden relationship with a certain young woman. Several fathers thought that he might have a bad influence on their children and decided by a majority vote to end his employment, thinking that they would find a better teacher. Others, however, did not believe the rumour and said that the teacher was an excellent one and that their children learned well. They said that once he left, the boys became idle and went downhill. In this case, R. Shemuel de Medina thought that proof of the teacher's aberration should be brought before he was laid off, rather than relying on rumours.[30] In Jerusalem, a group of scholars who had young sons made a commitment in a deed from 1754 that if one of them passed, his friends would take responsibility for educating his sons and make sure that they took the right path.[31] In Salonica, a teacher told of a father, apparently one of the Spanish exiles, who arranged for the education of his son, born out of wedlock:

> How when he was in Fez, teaching boys to write, R. Yaakov brought him this boy who was young at the time and asked him to teach him to write and he would pay him, and he taught him. Then R. Yaakov returned to him another time and said that he would like the boy to live with him and sleep in his house, and he would add to his wages . . .[32]

In general, a father was instructed to educate his son with pleasantness and tolerance, as detailed in The Book of Morals (*Sefer Ha-Musar*):

> How? When he is young before he begins to speak he should teach him to recite 'Moses commanded the Torah to us' (*Deut.* 33:4), and so on, and the first verse of the *Shema* [Hear!][33], and when he grows he should add to this, and once he recognizes the letters he should buy him books and employ a *melamed* for him.

And if this is too difficult for the child he should tempt him with things that the little ones like and yearn for, such as honey and nuts . . . and say to him: This is for you so that you should go to school and learn; and when he grows further and has had enough of these things . . . he shall say to him: Go to school and I'll buy you a nice belt and nice shoes, and when he grows further he shall say to him: I'll give you money so that you shall learn the blessing after meals and prayers, and he should buy him *tzitzit* [fringes] . . . and *tefillin* [phylacteries][34] . . . thus educating him to fulfill the commandments.[35]

Similarly, Rachel Sussman, an Ashkenazi grandmother from Jerusalem, sent letters to her son, who had moved to Cairo with his family, and among other things advised him to treat his son, who seems to have been rebellious and naughty, patiently and softly and to tempt him with small gifts and kind words.[36]

Affluent families would hire a private tutor for their children, and they studied at home and were not sent to the community *Talmud Torah*.[37] This was the case, for example, in the home of R. David ben Zimra (Radbaz, 1480–1573) in Egypt.[38] But not many could afford a private tutor. Educated fathers devoted some of their time to teaching their sons, and many sons mentioned this in their writings as adults.[39]

Talmud Torah Hagadol *in Salonica – 'An Unparalleled Torah Study Society'*[40]

The Great *Talmud Torah* (*Talmud Torah Hagadol*) of Salonica, which operated for some 400 years, was one of its kind and is commended in many sources. Although much has been written about it, it is worthy of mention, albeit concisely.

Salonica was known as a city of Torah and study, due to its many scholars and thanks to the *Talmud Torah* Confraternity established in it not long after the Spanish exiles arrived. The various congregations organised themselves in this unique fraternity and jointly established a facility shared by all, where education, teaching and study activities for children and youth were carried out according to age and level, including a synagogue and a *yeshiva*. This organisation became the centre of Jewish life in the city, and to it were appended a hospital, a guest house for guests passing through, a workshop for processing wool and manufacturing clothes and, from the late seventeenth century, also a printing house. The institution followed set rules and was managed by select community elders who were responsible for revenues and expenditures, appointing teachers and aides and so on.[41] It was maintained through the donations of rich members of the community, estates and inheritances, as well as by elaborate collections and product presentations held once a year. These were also utilised as an opportunity to distribute sets of clothing to all the students and teachers.[42] The exemption from tuition and allowances awarded to students encouraged poor parents to send their children to school. Throughout the sixteenth and seventeenth centuries, more than 1,000 students and 200 teachers studied and taught at this acclaimed institution, and its praise was voiced by all, as related by R. Shemuel de Medina: 'We are all aware of the high praise granted to the sanctified *Talmud Torah* society in this city of Salonica, may God preserve it, amen, with its quantity and quality that are not to be surpassed in the Jewish diaspora'.[43]

Educational Methods

Schooling methods ranged from light to heavy. Educators normally agree that people differ; there is no one technique that is appropriate for everyone and for every age. R. Shem Tov ibn Shem Tov, a sermoniser who based his words on those of Aristotle, said:

> As there is a specific way to instruct a young boy, and another for a young man, and yet another for an older man ... [and] there are different ethical courses for a person when a boy or a young man or an old man ... and thus the middle [way] is the most commendable and worthy of following.[44]

He saw a great deal of benefit in providing references to sources such as the *Mishna*'s tractate Fathers (*Avot*), which includes many sayings dealing with desirable courses of conduct.

Setting a personal example, sermons, and homilies on ethical matters were all considered ways of educating members of the public, including women and children. Public sermons occupied a major role in community life and were given frequently at synagogues and at special events, and the older *yeshiva* students would practice giving sermons in public as preparation for their role as future community rabbis and teachers.[45]

In their sermons the preachers (*darshanim*) endeavoured to attract a large following by using unusual interpretations, parables and tales. Moshe, son of R. Yosef di Trani (Maharit), talked of his father with great admiration and described how

> ... he would speak [in public] in poetic phrases and riddles and the value of virtues, sermons for Sabbaths and festivals and the first day of the month, and moral reproaches for those who leave the way of Torah, and these would bring forth tears from the eyes of men and women.[46]

Many preachers compared the relationship between the People of Israel and God to that of a father and son. For example, R. Shelomo Halevi compared God to a father who led his son along a road and when the son grew tired, he lifted him up on his shoulders.[47]

One notable educational means shared by members of all faiths in Jerusalem and described by many travellers who visited the city was that in order to teach children to respect their parents, they would be taken to the Absalom Monument (Yad Avshalom) to throw stones at it and curse Absalom, the son who rebelled against his father, King David. R. Meshulam of Volterra, who arrived in Jerusalem in 1481, related: 'All who pass Absalom's monument, even the Muslims, throw a stone on his grave, because he rebelled against his father, and on the side, there is a very great heap of stones, and every year the heap is removed'.[48] The French monk Jean Boucher, who visited Jerusalem in 1611–12, related that:

> The Turks, the Moors [Arabs], the Jews, and the Eastern Christians, who take their sons to the Valley of Jehoshaphat, stand to this very day near this accursed building, throw stones at it, instruct their sons to do the same, and yell out: Here is the wicked man, the cruel hangman, who declared war on his father![49]

In the mid-seventeeth century, Jerusalem was in turmoil because of the affair of a Jewish boy who converted to Islam and fled to Cairo. According to a Christian source, the affair began when a father beat his son as punishment, causing the boy to convert, followed by his younger eight-year-old brother.[50] The Hebrew sources do not mention that the boy was beaten, but a similar incident that occurred in the mid-eighteenth century also documents the beating of a minor by his father, and this child's flight to a Muslim elder to receive his patronage and convert. In this case, the father was warned to refrain from beating his son unjustifiably.[51] These few descriptions cannot be taken as an indication that beatings were a customary method of punishment in Jewish society, but it appears that when 'lighter' means or threats were of no avail, fathers and educators opted for corporal punishment, and the general opinion was that beating one's son or student was for his benefit and that children should not be excessively indulged.[52]

Adolescence

The stage of adolescence, as it is known to us today, did not exist in the Middle Ages. The transition from childhood to adulthood was rapid and was usually not marked by any transition ceremony. Jewish children – both boys and girls – were considered adults in all respects once they reached puberty, and usually married at a young age.[53] Nonetheless, there is a stage in the life of teenage boys when they tend to behave wildly, show disrespect for adults and go against their parents, 'because the nature of the young man is to desire the opposite of the old, and thus the young perceives the advice of the old as silliness'.[54]

Miriam Frenkel's studies on youth in the Geniza period during the eleventh to thirteenth centuries show that adolescence was perceived as a risky age, when the young were given to many temptations, and the educational aim of parents and teachers was to prevent them from being attracted to behaviour perceived as negative. Frenkel describes the wild lifestyle of groups of young Jews under Islamic rule.[55] Weinstein details how the rebelliousness of Jewish teens in sixteenth–seventeenth century Italy was handled and how they were restrained.[56] Fruma Zachs' studies on education in nineteenth-century Muslim society also stress that one of the aims when educating boys was to suppress their desires.[57] Adolescent boys appear to resemble each other across different periods and places. This is undoubtedly also true of young Jews throughout the Ottoman Empire, and the sages devote attention to the education of adolescents and particularly to their sexual experiences. R. Shelomo Halevi stressed that from early adolescence the child should be warned to distance himself from physical desires.[58] In Jerusalem a regulation was instated forbidding teens from wandering the streets alone at night, even for purposes of Torah study, and in Safed boys, as well as girls, were married off at a very young age to prevent them from sexual temptations.[59]

In certain cases, fathers even appealed to *Shari'ah* courts to gain control of their sons. In 1578 there was the incident of Yaakov ben Yosef, an incalcitrant youth who rebelled against his father and wished to marry against the father's will. The boy gave the *qadi* his word 'that from this day on he would not act against his father's will or any of his commands and prohibitions, would apply himself to reading and writing, and would not rebel against his father'. In 1583, five years later, the boy was ordered to leave his father's household 'because he does not obey him'.[60] A case discussed by R. Israel Yaakov Algazi tells of a father who made a commitment to support his son at the expense of his business so that the son could devote himself to his studies, but later on they had a falling out, the son was rude to his father, and the father sought to terminate his support.[61] These cases and others, as well as the affair mentioned above of the boy who converted, may indicate a certain decline in the dominant role that fathers occupied in the life of their sons.

Working Boys

Despite all the efforts, the education that children received at most local institutions was very basic. Many acquired only three or four years of schooling, and when reaching the age of thirteen were required to help support the family. Only a small number continued to a higher *yeshiva*, the educational institute for advanced studies. Accordingly, R. Jacob Khuli recommended that fathers teach their sons a trade and not only Torah.[62] In the best scenario, boys acquired a profession by working as apprentices with their father.[63] Some were sent to train with merchants or artisans, sometimes away from home. Children, and particularly orphans, would live with their beneficiaries or tutors, and sometimes served as their servants.[64] In one case we hear of a young boy who arranged for an apprenticeship with a Jewish physician, and then had a disagreement with him and converted.[65]

A deed from the early seventeenth century set down the relationship between a craftsman and his apprentice, whereby the craftsman was obliged 'to do with him good company, and to teach him the mentioned trade as customary . . . and to give him food and drink and the robes and shoes he needs'.[66]

In the latter half of the seventeenth century, the physician R. Refael Mordekhai Malki, who resided in Jerusalem, offered several wise proposals on matters of education. About the education of orphans, he wrote:

> . . . [A]nd if the minor shall remain an orphan from both father and mother, they [the community] should supervise him . . . and they should have righteous women who are widows and elders who shall raise the orphans when these have no relatives, and guide them to worthy conduct . . . He who so wishes, they shall teach him Torah, and if [he prefers] a trade – a trade . . . [and] the guardian shall do his best to teach the orphan a trade from which [will come] his livelihood.[67]

A question sent to R. Yom Tov Zahalon (Safed, 1558–1638) also indicates the significance of learning a trade, particularly in the case of orphans, so that in the future they would be able to support themselves. It tells of Reuven, whose father died, and who had a younger brother:

> Reuven supported and fed his brother and raised him with longing [with love] and employed teachers who taught him Torah and translation of the Torah from a foreign language and the laws of ritual slaughtering and taught him a trade. In this way, he raised his brother until he could [support] himself.[68]

Girls' Education

According to Jewish law, a father is not obliged to teach his daughter, and women are not obliged to study Torah. Women do not take part in synagogue activities, and in traditional Jewish society they do not appear to have needed any educational framework.[69] Indeed, until the early nineteenth century, there is very little information on the formal education of girls in the geographical area under discussion, and it may be assumed that – but for learning some prayers and blessings – their education varied according to the family's economic, social and schooling status.[70] There are no sources attesting to organised school settings for girls, and the words of R. David ben Zimra that 'most women cannot write'[71] seem to reflect current circumstances, certainly among the lower classes and the lower-middle social class. Women who were literate were considered the exception.[72]

In several *halakhic* discussions on matters of guardianship, all the adjudicators agreed that it is in the girls' interest to remain in the custody of their mother or grandmother, in order to learn from them 'the craft of women and the modesty of womens ways'.[73] Feminine crafts, such as sewing, embroidery and cooking were the main fields of study that girls were taught as preparation for their marriage to be carried out as early as possible. However, the involvement of women in economic life and the variety of occupations and crafts performed by adult women attest to their having received some early training.[74]

As for orphan girls, both guardians and the sages thought that the best way of ensuring their future and protecting their modesty was to marry them off early.[75] Funds called Bridal Fund (*hakhnasat kala*) or orphan girls societies (*hevrot yetomot*) were established in the various communities and were intended to raise a minimal dowry for orphans and poor girls.[76] Many missives were sent from Jerusalem to diaspora congregations in order to seek donations for this purpose, and letters of recommendation were borne by relatives and poor fathers who travelled to collect money for their daughters' dowries.[77]

Conclusion

The sources on the education of children in Ottoman Jewish society, from the period between the sixteenth to the eighteenth centuries, indicate the great significance attributed to the basic schooling of boys, and first and foremost to the study of Torah and familiarisation with religious precepts and prayers, which was similar to the preference of schooling boys in pre-modern Ottoman society in general. The literature, consisting of *Responsa*, books of ethics and public sermons, preached religious values such as being God fearing and observing the commandments, as well as modesty and moderation, but emphasised, in particular, the significance of studying per se as a distinct value.

Fathers were very much involved in choosing the teachers and in their children's curriculum, and as much as possible a boy's education was adapted to his age and abilities. This patriarchal and religious education endowed the primary role to the father, as was customary in pre-modern Ottoman Muslim communities. In general, it may be said that almost all boys from the age of five or six studied at a public *Talmud Torah* or with a private tutor for several years at least, learned the values, customs and precepts of Jewish society, and acquired a basic knowledge of reading and writing. Familiarity with the precepts of rabbinic laws and ethics and of reading the Torah was necessary for the continued existence of Jewish congregations and for the socialisation and cohesiveness of their members, and from this derived the significance of children's education.

Notes

1. See Kottek, 'On Children and Childhood'; Bar Ilan, 'The Status of "Childhood"'; Kraemer, 'Images of Childhood'. On Ashkenazi society, see Gartner, 'Celebrating Bar Mitzva'; Baumgarten, *Mothers and Children*; Goldin, 'Jewish Children'; Goldin, *Uniqueness*; Ta-Shema, 'The Earliest Literary Sources'; Kanarfogel, *Jewish Education*; Marcus, *Rituals*. On Western Sephardic society, see Lieberman, 'Childhood and Family'. On Italian Jewry, see Rivlin, *Mutual Responsibility*; Weinstein, 'Between Liberty and Control'. On Geniza society, see Goitein, *Jewish Education*; Frenkel, 'Adolescence'; Frenkel, 'The Roaring Waves'. On North-African society, see Bashan, *Parents and Children*.
2. Rozen, *A History*, pp. 179–91; Rozen, 'Of Orphans'; Lamdan, *A Separate People*, pp. 24–57; Lamdan, 'Mothers and Children'; Lamdan, 'Mothers and Children in Ottoman Jewish Society'; Ben-Naeh, *Jews in the Realm*, pp. 251–7; Ben-Naeh, 'Marriages'; Lehmann, *Ladino Rabbinic*, pp. 28–30; Meyuhas Ginio, 'Meam Loez', pp. 163–7.
3. De Medina, *Orah Hayim*, no. 35; Levi, *The Sephardim*; Beinart, *The Sephardi Legacy*; Barnai, 'The Jews of the Ottoman Empire'; Benbassa and Rodrigue, *Sephardi Jewry*; Rodrigue, *Ottoman and Turkish Jewry*, pp. iv–xv; Rozen, *A History* (mainly pp. 45–61, 87–98); Lehmann, *Ladino Rabbinic* (mainly pp. 15–24, 36); Hacker, 'The Intellectual Activity'; Hacker, 'The Sephardim'; Hacker, 'Authors', pp. 20, 29; Ben-Naeh, *Jews in the Realm*; Ben-Naeh, 'Urban Encounters'.
4. Yousif, 'Islam', p. 37.
5. Mishna (c. 200 CE) and Babilonian Talmud (c. 500 CE, hereafter BT) are the central texts of Rabbinic Judaism and the primary sources of Jewish religious law and Jewish theology.
6. BT, *Baba Batra*, 21a. Also, BT, *Shabbat*, 119b; Caro, *Shulhan Arukh*, *Yoreh De'ah*, Laws of Talmud Torah, no. 245, 7.

7. Bar Ilan, 'The Status of "Childhood" '.
8. Ha-Cohen, *Shevet Musar*, p. 194 (Lamdan, 'Mothers and Children in Ottoman Jewish Society', pp. 78–9); Pinto, *Kessef Mezokak*, p. 189a. Cf. Zachs, 'Growing Consciousness', mainly pp. 117–21; see Zachs' Chapter 15 in this volume; Zachs, 'The Private World'.
9. Halevi, *Divrei Shelomo*, p. 191b. Goldin, *Uniqueness*, pp. 113–15.
10. Khuli, *Me'am Lo'ez*, p. 46 (cited by Meyuhas Ginio, 'Meam Loez', pp. 166–7; Meyuhas Ginio, 'Everyday Life', p. 141). In Ashkenazi communities, children were also brought to the synagogue as an educational means, though sometimes their presence interrupted the prayers, and their parents were asked to leave. See Baumgarten, *Mothers and Children*, p. 160; Goldin, 'Jewish Children', pp. 114–17; Goldin, *Uniqueness*, pp. 111–13. In Western Sephardic society, though, there were restrictions on the presence of young children in the synagogue. See Lieberman, 'Childhood and Family', pp. 152–3.
11. R. Eliya Ha-Cohen from Izmir (1645–1729) emphasised that a man must not kiss and hug his wife, and certainly not have sexual relations with her, in front of his children, even if they were babies in a crib (Ha-Cohen, *Shevet Musar*, p. 127; Meyuhas Ginio, 'Everyday Life', p. 138).
12. Benveniste, *Sefer Orekh Yamim*, pp. 4–6 (Ha-Cohen, *Shevet Musar*, Chapter 17). See also Bar Ilan, 'The Status of "Childhood" ', pp. 30–1; Safran, *Studies in the History of Jewish Education*, pp. 442–57; Frenkel, 'Education', pp. 116–17.
13. Maimonides, *Mishneh Torah*, Laws of Talmud Torah, Chapter 1, nos. 1–4, 6; Caro, *Shulhan Arukh, Yoreh De'ah*, Laws of Talmud Torah, no. 245, 1–9. On the educational obligations of a grandfather, see Trani Moshe, vol. 1, no. 164. See also Safran, *Studies in the History of Jewish Education*, pp. 127–8; Bornstein-Makovetzky, 'Rabbi Shelomo Barukh', p. 191.
14. Uceda, *Midrash*, 5:23; Ha-Cohen, *Shevet Musar*, p. 127; Rivlin, 'On the History', p. 82.
15. Benveniste Hayim, *Responsa, Yoreh De'ah*, p. 220 (pp. 163a–b); BT, *Baba Batra*, 21a; De Medina, *Orah Hayim*, no. 20; Perahya, *Perah*, vol. 1, no. 109; Khalatz, *Sefer ha-Musar*, Chapter 7, p. 179.
16. Uceda, *Midrash*, p. 30b. See also p. 24; Halevi, *Divrei Shelomo*, Sermon for the Eighth Day of Passover 1572, p. 126b; Pinto, *Kessef Mezokak*, pp. 77a, 213a, 231a; Benveniste, *Sefer Beit Israel*, Sermon 21, p. 310. Cf. Giladi, *Children of Islam*, pp. 50–4.
17. Benveniste, *Oznei Yehoshua*, pp. 48b–49a. See also Maimonides, Laws of Talmud Torah, Chapter 2, no. 2; Caro, *Shulhan Arukh, Yoreh De'ah*, Laws of Talmud Torah, no. 245, 8 ('. . . and if he is thin he should complete at least six years').
18. On studying in Ottoman Sephardic society: Lehmann, *Ladino Rabbinic*, pp. 28–9; Hacker, 'The Intellectual Activity', pp. 107–8; Hacker, 'Authors', p. 21; Bornstein-Makovetzky, 'The Community', pp. 212–13, 178, 180;

Bornstein-Makovetzky, *A City of Sages*, pp. 125–8; Rozen, 'The Life Cycle', pp. 110–11; Ben-Naeh, 'Education', pp. 73–5. Cf. Giladi, *Children of Islam*, pp. 54–7.

19. Halevi, *Ginat Veradim*, *Orah Hayyim*, rule 2, no. 23 (cited by Havlin, 'Intellectual Creativity', pp. 286–7). This description, by a Rabbi who operated in Egypt in the second half of the seventeenth century, is apparently the first and only one to mention the term 'bar mitzvah' in the writings of Ottoman Rabbis. The custom of holding a family celebration to mark reaching the age of thirteen is an Ashkenazi custom from late Medieval times that spread to congregations in Italy and the Ottoman Empire at a later stage. See: Gartner, 'Celebrating Bar Mitzva'; Marcus, *Rituals*, pp. 118–27; Marcus, *The Jewish Life Cycle*, pp. 82–116; Ta Shema, 'The Earliest Literary Sources', especially pp. 151–4; Regev, *Oral*, pp. 184–5; Gilat, *Studies in the Development*.

20. David, 'The Letter', pp. 114, 116–17. Rabbi Moshe Basola, who visited Jerusalem in the early 1520s, also mentioned this *melamed* who was blind and taught children at his home (David, *Basola*, p. 84). On the education of the children of an Ashkenazi family that migrated to Egypt it was related: the youngest is learning with a *ma'alma* (female teacher!), the second with a *melamed* at the *Talmud Torah* and the third is working as a servant in a rich man's house (Turniansky, 'A Correspondence', pp. 166–7, 191).

21. Estrosa, nos. 6, 20; Ben Zimra, vol. 4, no. 252 (vol. 8, no. 323); De Medina, *Yoreh De'ah*, nos. 158, 167 (cf. no. 174); Benveniste Hayim, *Responsa, Yoreh De'ah*, nos. 220, 221; Trani, vol. 1, no. 75; Bassan, *Responsa*, no. 82; Qalai, *Mishpetei Shemuel*, no. 36; Molho and Amarijlio, 'A Collection', 2nd regulation, p. 36; Hacker, 'The Intellectual Activity', pp. 106–7; Ben-Naeh, *Jews in the Realm*, p. 253.

22. On the organisation in Istanbul, see Ben Hayim, *Responsa*, no. 84. Also, the case described by Bornstein-Makovetzky, 'Rabbi Shelomo Barukh', pp. 192–3. Ben-Naeh, 'Jewish Confraternities', pp. 284–5, 312–13; Ben-Naeh, *Jews in the Realm*, pp. 251–3, 312.

23. For references, see Geller, 'The Economic Basis'; Ben-Naeh, 'Jewish Confraternities', pp. 302–10; Amarillio, *Kerem Shelomo*, no. 84.

24. Zahalon, *New Responsa*, no. 35. Cf. agreement in Kastoria (Perahya, *Perah*, vol. 1, no. 5).

25. Shabetai, *Torat Hayim*, vol. 3, nos. 29–30; Ben Hasson, *Beit Shelomo*, no. 17, pp. 37a–b; Halevi, *Ein Mishpat*, *Yoreh De'ah*, no. 4. Cf. Mizrahi, *Responsa*, no. 12. About a *melamed* for the children of Tirea (Anatolia), see Benveniste Hayim, *Responsa, Hoshen Mishpat*, vol. 1, no. 220.

26. David, *In Zion*, p. 87. On the community of Damascus in the sixteenth century, see Arad, '"A Clearly Distinnguished Community"'; Arad, 'R. Josef ibn Sayah'; Hacker, 'Authors', p. 37.

27. Rozen, *The Jewish Community*, Letter 109, pp. 512–13. See Letter 34, pp. 424–5, and pp. 94, 175, 182, 197 for further references. Among the poor people who asked for an exemption from poll tax in 1691 were three teachers

of young children (Cohen-Pikali, *17th Century*, vol. 1, doc. 181, pp. 238–40, and ref. 10 there).
28. Cohen-Pikali, *17th Century*, vol. 1, doc. 47, p. 71; vol. 2, doc. 645, pp. 743–6; doc. 654, pp. 760–1; doc. 676, p. 792.
29. Melamed, *Mishpat Tzedek*, vol. 1, no. 38, p. 128a. See also Mizrahi, *Responsa*, no. 12.
30. De Medina, *Yoreh De'ah*, no. 141. See also no. 210.
31. Algazi, *Shemah Yaakov*, Addendum, pp. 6–7.
32. Edrabi, *Sefer Divrei*, no. 82.
33. Basic statement of the Jewish faith, declaring God's unity: 'Hear, O Israel, the Lord is our God, the Lord is one', recited in the morning and evening services.
34. *Tsitsit*: four-cornered fringed undergarment worn by observant Jewish males. *Tefillin*: scriptural passages bound in two small quadrangular leather boxes, worn by Jewish males from the age of thirteen for the weekly morning service.
35. Khalatz, *Sefer ha-Musar*, Chapter 7, p. 179.
36. Turniansky, 'A Correspondence', p. 197. See also pp. 166–7.
37. Algazi, *Responsa*, no. 61; Hacker, 'Intellectual Activity', p. 107.
38. Rabbi Itzhak Aqrish tells of his ten years as a teacher for Radbaz grandchildren and great-grandchildren (Assaf, *A Source-Book*, p. 532).
39. For example: Albelda, *Reshit Da'at*, p. 10a; Yosef Trani, *Responsa*, Introduction; Melamed, *Mishpat Tzedek*, vol. 1, Introduction; Benveniste, *Oznei Yehoshua*, Introducion; Najara, *Miqve Israel*, Introduction, p. 127; no. 21 p. 393 (see also p. 388, ref. 1); Bornstein-Makovetzky, *A City of Sages*, p. 126.
40. Perahya, *Perah*, vol. 1, no. 110.
41. Some references: Amarillio, 'The Great Talmud'; Molho and Amarijlio, 'A Collection'; Rozen, 'Individual and Community', pp. 243–5; Hacker, 'The Intellectual Activity', pp. 108–9; Ben-Naeh, 'Jewish Confraternities', pp. 312–14; Ben-Naeh, *Jews in the Realm*, pp. 256–7.
42. Yaron Ben-Naeh suggests that this was an imitation of the customary Ottoman ceremony of distributing clothes to the *yeniçeri*s, the Sultan's infantry soldiers ('Jewish Confraternities', p. 313, ref. 152). De Medina, *Hoshen Mishpat*, no. 372; Molho and Amarijlio, 'A Collection'; Benveniste, *Sefer Beit Israel*, Sermon 21, p. 39a.
43. De Medina, *Yoreh De'ah*, no. 158. See also nos. 167, 174; Edrabi, *Sefer Divrei*, no. 223; Perahya, *Perah*, vol. 1, no. 110. According to one source, it had 5,000 students (Urfali, *Imanuel*, p. 268).
44. Shem Tov, *Commentary*, 2:1 (p. 89); 3:12 (pp. 108–9); Regev, 'Introduction', pp. 51–2 (cf. Aristotle, *Ethics*, Book 2, Chapter 2). See also Galiko, *Commentary*, p. 133b.
45. Regev, *Oral*; Hacker, 'The Sephardi Sermon', pp. 112–20; Havlin, 'Intellectual Creativity', pp. 297–8; Ben-Naeh, *Jews in the Realm*, pp. 298–

300; Dan, *Hebrew Ethical*; Pachter, 'The Land of Israel'; Gilat, *Studies*, pp. 350–59. Also: Halevi, *Divrei Shelomo*, Sermon for the Eighth Day of Passover 1572, p. 126b; Melamed, *Mishpat Tzedek*, vol. 1(b), no. 78.
46. Yosef Trani, *Responsa*, on the second page of the Introduction.
47. Halevi, *Divrei Shelomo*, p. 247a. For other images, see Ibid., pp. 290b, 135a; Koriel, *Sermons*, p. 217; Pinto, *Kessef Mezokak*, p. 135b.
48. Adler, 'Rabbi Meshullam', p. 192.
49. Boucher, *Le Bouquet*, p. 342. For the biblical story of the rebellious son, Absalom, see 2 Samuel, Chapters 13–18 (note 18: 17–18).
50. Rozen, 'The Incident'; Rozen, *The Jewish Community*, pp. 51–4; Cohen-Pikali, *17th Century*, vol. 1, doc. 257, pp. 338–40. On children who converted to Islam, see Cohen-Pikali, *17th Century*, vol. 1, pp. 335–50, and Bassan, *Responsa*, nos. 70, 115. On their legal status, see Bornstein-Makovetzky, 'The Legal Status' and 'Jewish Converts'. In the sixteenth century, a sultanate decree was issued, forbidding the conversion of children to Islam by means of false witnesses for extortion (Cohen-Pikali, *16th Century*, doc. 154, p. 156).
51. Cohen-Pikali, *18th Century*, doc. 228, pp. 268–9; docs 222–3, p. 265. A conversion ceremony is described in Cohen-Pikali, *16th Century*, doc. 118, p. 130.
52. Caro, *Shulhan Arukh, Yoreh De'ah*, Laws of Talmud Torah, no. 245 (10), says: 'The *melamed* shall not strike him in the manner of an enemy . . . neither with a whip nor a stick, but only with a small strap'. See also Benveniste, *Sefer Orekh Yamim*, pp. 3, 6; Algazi, *Ahavat Olam*, p. 9b; Halevi, *Divrei Shelomo*, Sermon for the Eighth Day of Passover 1572, p. 126b; Sermon for the portion *Ki Tavoh*, p. 290a; Khalatz, *Sefer ha-Musar*, Chapter 7, pp. 175–6; Najara, *Miqve Israel*, no. 21, p. 392; Frenkel, 'Education', pp. 116–17. Cf. Zachs, 'Growing Consciousness', pp. 124–5; Giladi, *Children of Islam*, pp. 62–5. See Çiçek's Chapter 12 in this volume for further discussion on corporal punishment.
53. In Jewish *halakha*, the term 'minor' refers to a girl younger than twelve years and a day. Girls aged twelve-and-a-half were legally considered adults. Between these two ages, a girl was considered a *na'arah* (a young female teenager). Boys were considered adults from the age of thirteen. On the age of marriage in Jewish society, see Lamdan, 'Child Marriage'; Lamdan, *A Separate People*, pp. 46–57; Ben-Naeh, 'Marriages'; Rozen, 'The Life Cycle', pp. 112, 118–20; Rozen, *A History*, p. 187; Rozen, 'Of Orphans', pp. 152–4; Bornstein-Makovetzky, *A City of Sages*, pp. 230–2; Bornstein-Makovetzky, 'Patterns', pp. 324–5; Bashan, *Parents and Children*, pp. 18–23. On the age of marriage in Muslim society, see Motzki, 'Child Marriage', esp. pp. 136–9.
54. Khalatz, *Sefer ha-Musar*, Chapter 5, p. 151. See also a father's report from Cairo on his son, 'who does not listen to anyone' (Turniansky, 'A Correspondence', p. 191); Galiko, *Commentary*, pp. 133a–b.
55. Frenkel, 'Adolescence'; Frenkel, 'The Roaring Waves'.

56. Weinstein, 'Between Liberty and Control'.
57. Zachs, 'Growing Consciousness', p. 120.
58. Halevi, *Divrei Shelomo*, p. 267b.
59. Badhab, 'Regulations of the Community', p. 52a; Falaji, *Sefer*, no. 56, p. 44a; Hallamish, 'On the Text', no. 31, p. 92; Schechter, *Studies*, p. 298, no. 12; Elyashar, *Sefer*, pp. 41a–b.
60. Cohen-Pikali, *16th Century*, doc. 403, p. 355; doc. 407, p. 358.
61. Algazi, *Responsa*, no. 10. About 'youthful deeds', see Caro, *Avkat Rokhel*, no. 121; Pinto, *Kessef Mezokak*, p. 44b.
62. Meyuhas Ginio, '*Meam Loez*', pp. 165–7; Ben-Naeh, 'Education', p. 243; Lehmann, *Ladino Rabbinic*, p. 29; Yosef Trani, *Responsa*, vol. 1, no. 75. See also Halevi, *Divrei Shelomo*, 247a.
63. For instance: Gavizon, *Responsa*, vol. 1, no. 28.
64. Zahalon, *Responsa*, no. 254; Zahalon, *New Responsa*, no. 21; Halevi, *Zekan Aharon*, no. 88; Benveniste Hayim, *Hoshen Mishpat*, 1, no. 83; Ben Haviv, *Responsa*, no. 117. Bornstein-Makovetzky, 'The Jewish Family', pp. 330–1.
65. Bassan, *Responsa*, no. 115.
66. Lamdan, *Sefer Tikkun Soferim*, no. 76, p. 193. Cf. to a contract for three years, made by a father on behalf of his son (Assaf, *A Source-Book*, pp. 513–14).
67. Rivlin, *Selections*, p. 30. See also Rozen, *Jewish Identity*, pp. 153–4.
68. Zahalon, *New Responsa*, no. 25. See also Bornstein-Makovetzky, 'The Jewish Family', pp. 330–1.
69. Simon, 'Jewish Female Education', pp. 127–32; Schwarzwald, 'The Status'; Ben-Naeh, *Jews in the Realm*, p. 252; Meyuhas Ginio, 'The Burden'.
70. In this respect, a girl's education was very similar in Islam, where girls from the upper classes could learn at home with a private teacher. See Zachs' Chapter 15 in this volume. See also Rozen, 'The Family at War', pp. 411–12.
71. Ben Zimra, *Responsa*, vol. 2, no. 801.
72. Lamdan, *A Separate People*, pp. 110–14; Schwarzwald, 'The Status', pp. 5–6, 9; Rozen, *A History*, p. 187; Rivlin, 'On the History', p. 83; Bornstein-Makovetzky, *A City of Sages*, pp. 242–5; Frenkel, 'Education', p. 17. Cf. Giladi, *Children of Islam*, p. 51 and note 39 on p. 139. On the education of girls in Ashkenaz, see Turniansky, 'Girls'.
73. Moshe Trani, vol. 2, no. 62. Also: Ben Zimra, *Responsa*, vol. 1, no. 360; Zahalon, *New Responsa*, no. 16; Pinto, *Nivhar mi-Kesef, Even Ha-Ezer*, no. 76; Qalai, *Mishpetei Shemuel*, no. 90; Lehmann, *Ladino Rabbinic*, pp. 131–4; Lamdan, 'Mothers and Children', pp. 81–7. Cf. Zachs, 'Growing Consciousness', pp. 117–18.
74. Lamdan, 'Jewish Women'; Hofmeester, 'Jewish Ethics'; Rivlin, 'On the History', pp. 84–5; Bornstein-Makovetzky, *A City of Sages*, pp. 247–8; Ben-Naeh, *Jews in the Realm*, pp. 368–9.
75. Lamdan, *A Separate People*, pp. 53–4; Rozen, 'Of Orphans', pp. 163–5. The case described is from the early nineteenth century, but as Rozen concludes

it appears that the Istanbul Jewish community looked much the same in the nineteenth century as it had at the start of the Ottoman era (p. 172).
76. Ben-Naeh, 'Jewish Confraternities', p. 315 (see notes on this page).
77. Rozen, *The Jewish Community*, p. 174; Lamdan, *A Separate People*, pp. 24–6; Rivlin, *Selections*, p. 29.

Bibliography

Primary Sources (Hebrew)
(note: first edition is indicated in square brackets.)
Albelda, Moshe, *Reshit Daʻat* (Venice, 1583).
Algazi, Nissim Shelomo, *Ahavat Olam*, Sermons (Istanbul, 1642).
Algazi, Yaakov Israel, *Responsa* (Jerusalem, 1977).
_____, *Shemah Yaakov*, Sermons [Livorno, 1783] (Nahariya, 1990).
Amarillio, Shelomo, *Kerem Shelomo*, Responsa (Salonica, 1719).
Bassan, Yehiel, *Responsa* (Venice, 1737).
Ben Hasson, Shelomo, *Beit Shelomo*, Responsa (Salonica, 1720).
Ben Haviv, Levi (Ralbah), *Responsa* [Lemberg] (Jerusalem, 1975).
Ben Hayim, Eliyahu (Ranah), *Mayyim Amuqim*, Responsa, vol. 2 (Venice, 1657).
_____, *Responsa* (Istanbul, 1610).
Benveniste, Hayim, *Ba'ei Hayyei*, Responsa, 4 vols (Salonica, 1788–91).
Benveniste, Israel, *Sefer Beit Israel*, Sermons (Istanbul, 1678).
Benveniste Shemuel, *Sefer Orekh Yamim* [Istanbul, 1560] (Jerusalem, 1996).
Benveniste Yehoshua, *Oznei Yehoshua*, Sermons (Istanbul, 1677).
Ben Zimra, David (Radbaz), *Responsa*, 8 vols (7 vols, Warsaw, 1882; vol. 8, BneiBeraq, 1975).
Boucher, Jean, *Le Bouquet sacre ou le voyage de la Terre Sainte* (Roven: J. B. Besongne, [1610] (1643) (in French).
BT, *Babylonian Talmud* (traditional editions).
Caro, Yossef, *Avkat Rokhel*, Responsa (Salonica, 1791).
_____, *Shulhan Arukh* [Venice, 1565] (traditional reprints).
De Medina, Shemuel (Rashdam), *Responsa* [Salonica, 1862] (New York, 1959).
Edrabi, Itzhak, *Sefer Divrei Rivot*, Responsa (Venice, 1587).
Elyashar, Yaakov Shaul, *Sefer Hatakanot* (Jerusalem, 1883).
Estrosa, Daniel, *Magen Gibborim*, Responsa (Salonica, 1754).
Falaji, Hayim, *Sefer Arzot ha-Hayim* (Jerusalem, 1872).
Galiko, Elisha, *Commentary on the Book of Koheleth* (Venice, 1578).
Gavizon, Meir, *Responsa*, 2 vols, ed. Eliav Shochetman (Jerusalem, 1985).
Ha-Cohen, Eliya, *Shevet Musar* [Istanbul, 1712] (Jerusalem: Or Hasefer, 1978).
Halevi, Avraham ben Mordechai, *Ginat Veradim*, Responsa (Istanbul, 1716).
Halevi, Avraham ben Yossef, *Ein Mishpat* (Salonica, 1897).
Halevi, Eliyahu, *Zekan Aharon*, Responsa (Istanbul, 1734).
Halevi, Shelomo, *Divrei Shelomo*, Sermons (Venice, 1596).
Khalatz Yehuda, *Sefer ha-Musar* [Istanbul, 1537] (Jerusalem, 1973).

Khuli, Yaakov, *Me'am Lo'ez* [Istanbul, 1730, in Ladino] (trans. Samuel Yerushalmi, Jerusalem: Or Hadash, 1967).
Koriel, Israel di-, *Sermons and Homilies*, ed. Shaul Regev (Jerusalem: Yad Harav Nissim, 1992).
Maimonaides, Moshe ben Maimon (Rambam), *Mishneh Torah* (traditional editions).
Melamed, Meir, *Mishpat Tzedek*, Responsa, 3 vols (Salonica, 1615).
Mizrahi, Eliyahu, *Responsa* (Jerusalem, 1938).
Najara, Israel, *Miqve Israel*, Sermons, ed. Shaul Regev (Ramat-Gan, 2004).
Perahya, Aharon, *Perah Mateh Aharon*, Responsa (Amsterdam, 1703).
Pinto, Yoshiyahu, *Kessef Mezokak*, Sermons (Venice, 1628).
_____, *Nivhar mi-Kesef*, Responsa (Aleppo, 1869).
Qalai Shemuel, *Mishpetei Shemuel*, Responsa (Venice, 1600).
Shabetai, Hayim, *Torat Hayim*, Responsa, 3 vols (Salonica, 1713–22).
Shem Tov ben Yossef ibn Shem Tov, *Commentary on Tractate Avot* (with Introduction by J. S. Spigel), [1980] (Petah-Tiqua, IS: 2011).
Trani, Moshe (Mabit), *Responsa* (Lvov, 1861).
Trani, Yosef (Maharit), *Responsa* [Venice, 1645] (Lemberg, 1861).
Uceda (Uzida), Shemuel di, *Midrash Shemuel on Tractate Avot* (Venice, 1585).
Zahalon, Yom Tov, *New Responsa* (Jerusalem, 1980–1).
_____, *Responsa* (Jerusalem, 1968).

Secondary Sources
Adler, Elkan Nathan (ed.), 'Rabbi Meshullam ben Menahem of Volterra', in *Jewish Travellers in the Middle Ages* (New York: Dover Publications, 2014), pp. 156–208.
Amarillio, Abraham, 'The Great Talmud Torah of Salonica', *Sefunot*, 13 (1971), pp. 273–308 (Hebrew).
Arad, Dotan, '"A Clearly Distinguished Community": The Musta'ribs in Damascus in the 16th Century', in Yaron Harel (ed.), *Syrian Jewry, History, Culture and Identity* (Tel Aviv: Bar-Ilan University Press, 2015), pp. 95–130 (Hebrew).
_____, 'R. Joseph ibn Sayah: A Profile of a 16th Century Musta'rib Sage', in Joseph Hacker (ed.), *Shalem, Studies in the History of the Jews*, vol. 8 (2008), pp. 134–248 (Hebrew).
Assaf, Simcha, *A Source-Book for the History of Jewish Education*, vol. 2, New Edition, Shmuel Glick (ed. and ann.) (New York and Jerusalem: The Jewish Theological Seminary of America, 2001) (Hebrew).
Badhab, Isaac, 'Regulations of the Community of Jerusalem', *Ha-Yerushalmi*, vol. 2 (Jerusalem: Ma'arav Press, 1930) (Hebrew).
Bar Ilan, Meir, 'The Status of "Childhood" in the Biblical and Talmudic Society', *Beit Mikra: Journal for the Study of the Bible and its World*, 40/1 (1994), pp. 19–32 (Hebrew).
Barnai, Yaakov, 'The Jews of the Ottoman Empire in the 17th–18th Centuries',

in H. Beinart (ed.), *Moreshet Sepharad: The Sephardi Legacy* (Jerusalem: Magnes Press, 1992), pp. 479–502 (Hebrew).

Bashan, Eliezer, *Parents and Children as Reflected in the Literature of North African Rabbis* (Tel-Aviv: Hakibbutz Hameuchad, 2005) (Hebrew).

Baumgarten, Elisheva, *Mothers and Children: Jewish Family Life in Medieval Europe* (Princeton, NJ: Princeton University Press, 2004).

Beinart, Haim (ed.), *The Sephardi Legacy* (Jerusalem: Magnes Press, 1992) (Hebrew).

Benbassa, Esther, and Aron Rodrigue, *Sephardi Jewry: A History of the Judeo-Spanish Community, 14th–20th Centuries* (Berkeley, CA: University of California Press, 2000).

Ben-Naeh, Yaron, 'Education' and 'Life Cycle', in Yaron ben-Naeh (ed.), *Turkey* (Jerusalem: Ben-Zvi Institute, 2009), pp. 74–6; 237–48 (Hebrew).

_____, 'Jewish Confraternities in the Ottoman Empire in the 17th and 18th Centuries', *Zion, A Quarterly for Research in Jewish History*, 63 (1998), pp. 277–318 (Hebrew).

_____, *Jews in the Realm of the Sultans* (Tubingen: Mohr Siebeck, 2008).

_____, 'Marriages of Minors among Jews in the Ottoman Empire', *Zmanim: A Historical Quarterly*, 102 (2008), pp. 38–45 (Hebrew).

_____, 'Urban Encounters: The Muslim-Jewish Case in the Ottoman Empire', in Eyal Ginio and Elie Podeh (eds), *The Ottoman Middle East: Studies in Honor of Amnon Cohen* (Leiden and Boston: Brill, 2014), pp. 177–97.

Bornstein-Makovetsky, Leah, *A City of Sages and Merchants: The Community of Aleppo during the Years 1492–1800* (Ariel: University Center Ariel, 2012) (Hebrew).

_____, 'The Community and its Institutions', in Jacob M. Landau (ed.), *The Jews in Ottoman Egypt* (Jerusalem: Misgav Yerushalaim, 1988), pp. 129–216 (Hebrew).

_____, 'Jewish Converts to Islam and Christianity in the Ottoman Empire in the 16th to 18th Centuries', in Michel Abitbol, Yom-Tov Assis, and Galit Hasan-Rokem (eds), *Hispano-Jewish Civilization after 1492* (Jerusalem: Misgav Yerushalayim, 1997), pp. 3–29 (Hebrew).

_____, 'The Jewish Family in Istanbul in the 18th and 19th Centuries as an Economic Unit', in Israel Bartal and Isaiah Gafni (eds), *Sexuality and the Family in History* (Jerusalem: Zalman Shazar Center, 1998), pp. 305–33 (Hebrew).

_____, 'The Legal Status in Jewish and Ottoman Law of Jewish Children, One of Whose Parents Converted to Christianity or Islam in the Ottoman Empire in the 16th–19th Centuries', *International Journal of the Jurisprudence of the Family*, 5 (2014), pp. 169–8.

_____, 'Patterns of the Jewish Family: Characteristics of the Jewish Family in the Communities of Morea and Epirus in the 16th Century', in Daniel Panzac (ed.), *Histoire economique et sociale de L' Empire ottoman et de la Turquie* (Paris: Peeters, 1995), pp. 323–9.

_____, 'Rabbi Shelomo Barukh', *Moreshet Israel*, 14 (2017), pp. 171–95 (Hebrew).
Cohen, Amnon, and Elisheva Simon-Pikali, *Jews in the Moslem Religious Court* (in the 16th Century) (Jerusalem: Yad Izhak Ben-Zvi, 1993) (Hebrew).
_____, *Jews in the Moslem Religious Court* (in the 17th Century), 2 vols (Jerusalem: Yad Izhak Ben-Zvi, 2010) (Hebrew).
Cohen, Amnon, Elisheva ben-Shimon-Pikali, and Ovadia Salama, *Jews in the Moslem Religious Court* (in the 18th Century) (Jerusalem: Yad Izhak Ben-Zvi, 1996) (Hebrew).
Dan, Joseph, *Hebrew Ethical and Homiletical Literature* (Jerusalem: Keter Publishing House, 1975) (Hebrew).
David, Abraham, *In Zion and Jerusalem: The Itinerary of Rabbi Moses Basola* (Jerusalem: Bar Ilan University, 1999).
_____, 'The Letter of R. Israel Ashkenazi of Jerusalem to R. Abraham of Perugia', *Alei Sefer*, 16 (1990), pp. 95–122 (Hebrew).
Frenkel Miriam, 'Adolescence in Medieval Jewish Society under Islam', in D. J. Lasker and H. ben-Shammai (eds), *Alei Asor, Proceedings of the 10th Conference of the Society for Judeo-Arabic Studies* (Beer-Sheva: Ben Gurion University, 2008), pp. 203–23 (Hebrew).
_____, 'Education', in Norman A. Stillman (ed.), *Encyclopedia of Jews in the Islamic World*, vol. 2 (Leiden: Brill, 2010), pp. 116–19.
_____, '"The Roaring Waves of Youth", Adolescence and Adolescents in Jewish Medieval Society under Islam', *Zmanim: A Historical Quarterly*, 102 (2008), pp. 8–19 (Hebrew).
Gartner, Yaakov, 'Celebrating Bar Mitzva: The Background and Emergence of the Custom', in Joseph Hacker, Moshe Halbertal, Avraham Reiner, Moshe Idel, Ephraim Kanarfogel, and Elchanan Reiner (eds), *Ta Shma, Studies in Judaica in Memory of Israel M. Ta-Shma* (Alon Shevut: Tevunot Press, 2011), pp. 235–56 (Hebrew).
Geller, Jacob, 'The Economic Basis of the Yeshivot in the Ottoman Empire', in H. Z. Hirschberg and E. Bashan, *East and Maghreb* (Ramat Gan: Bar Ilan University, 1974), pp. 167–221 (Hebrew).
Giladi, Avner, *Children of Islam: Concepts of Childhood in Medieval Muslim Society* (Oxford: Macmillan in association with St Antony's College, 1992).
Gilat, Yitzhak D., *Studies in the Development of the Halakha* (Tel Aviv: Bar-Ilan University Press, 1992) (Hebrew).
Goitein, Shelomo D., *Jewish Education in Muslim Countreis, Based on Records from the Cairo Geniza* (Jerusalem: Ben Zvi Institute, 1962) (Hebrew).
Goldin, Simha, 'Jewish Children and Christian Missionizing', in Israel Bartal and Isaiah Gafni (eds), *Sexuality and the Family in History* (Jerusalem: Zalman Shazar Center, 1998), pp. 97–118 (Hebrew).
_____, *"Uniqueness and Togetherness", The Enigma of the Survival of the Jews in the Middle Ages* (Tel Aviv: Hakibbutz Hameuchad, 1997) (Hebrew).
Hacker, Joseph, 'Authors, Readers and Printers of Sixteenth Century Hebrew

Books in the Ottoman Empire', in Peggy K. Pearlstein (ed.), *Perspectives on the Hebraic Book* (Washington, DC: Library of Congress, 2012), pp. 17–63.

———, 'The Intellectual Activity of the Jews of the Ottoman Empire during the 16th and 17th Centuries', in Isadore Twersky and Bernard Septimus (eds), *Jewish Thought in the Seventeenth Century* (Cambridge, MA, and London: Harvard University Press, 1987), pp. 95–135.

———, 'The Sephardi Sermon in the 16th Century – Between Literature and Historical Source', *Pe'amim, Studies in Oriental Jewry*, 26 (1986), pp. 108–27 (Hebrew).

———, 'The Sephardim in the Ottoman Empire in the 16th Century: Community and Society', in H. Beinart (ed.), *Moreshet Sepharad: The Sephardi Legacy* (Jerusalem: Magnes Press, 1992), pp. 460–78 (Hebrew).

Hallamish, Moshe, 'On the Text of Behavioral Mannerisms of the Sages of Safed', *Alei Sefer*, 14 (1987), pp. 89–97 (Hebrew).

Havlin, Shlomo Zalman, 'Intellectual Creativity', in Jacob M. Landau (ed.), *The Jews in Ottoman Egypt* (Jerusalem: Misgav Yerushalaim, 1988), pp. 245–310 (Hebrew).

Hofmeester, Karin, 'Jewish Ethics and Women's Work in the Late Medieval and Early Modern Arab-Islamic World', *International Review of Social History*, 56 (2011), no. S19, pp. 141–64.

Kanarfogel, Ephraim, *Jewish Education and Society in the High Middle Ages* (Detroit, MI: Wayne State University Press, 1992).

Kottek, Samuel, 'On Children and Childhood in Ancient Jewish Sources', *Koroth*, 9/5–6 (1987), pp. 452–71 (Hebrew).

Kraemer, David, 'Images of Childhood and Adolescence in Talmudic Literature', in David Kraemer (ed.), *The Jewish Family, Metaphor and Memory* (New York and Oxford: Oxford University Press, 1989), pp. 65–80.

Lamdan, Ruth, 'Child Marriage in Jewish Society in the Eastern Mediterranean during the Sixteenth Century', *Mediterranean Historical Review*, 11 (1996), pp. 37–59.

———, 'Jewish Women as Providers in the Generations Following the Expulsion from Spain', *Nashim, A Journal of Jewish Women and Gender Studies*, 13 (2007), pp. 49–67.

———, 'Mothers and Children in Ottoman Jewish Society as Reflected in Hebrew Sources of the 16th to 18th Centuries', in Marjorie Lehman, Jane L. Kanarek, and Simon J. Bronner (eds), *Mothers in the Jewish Cultural Imagination* (Liverpool: The Littman Library of Jewish Civilization with Liverpool University Press, 2017), pp. 77–101.

———, 'Mothers and Children as Seen by 16th Century Rabbis in the Ottoman Empire', in Julia R. Lieberman (ed.), *Sephardi Family Life in the Early Modern Diaspora* (Waltham, MA: Brandeis University Press, 2011), pp. 70–98.

———, *Sefer Tikkun Soferim of Rabbi Itzhak Tzabah, Copied in Jerusalem in the Year 1635 by Yehudah Mor'ali* (Tel Aviv: Tel Aviv University, 2009) (Hebrew).

_____, *A Separate People: Jewish Women in Palestine, Syria and Egypt in the Sixteenth Century* (Leiden and Boston: Brill, 2000).

Lehmann, Matthias B., *Ladino Rabbinic Litarature and Ottoman Sephardic Culture* (Bloomington, IN: Indiana University Press, 2005).

Levi, Avigdor, *The Sephardim in the Ottoman Empire* (Princeton, NJ: The Darwin Press, 1992).

Lieberman, Julia R., 'Childhood and Family among the Western Sephardim in the Seventeenth Century', in Julia R. Lieberman (ed.), *Sephardi Family Life in the Early Modern Diaspora* (Waltham, MA: Brandeis University Press, 2011), pp. 129–76.

Marcus, Ivan G., *The Jewish Life Cycle* (Seattle and London: University of Washington Press, 2004).

_____, *Rituals of Childhood, Jewish Acculturation in Medieval Europe* (New Haven and London: Yale University Press, 1984).

Meyuhas Ginio, '"The Burden of a Daughter" as Expressed in Two Educational Books, *Meam Loez* and *Peleh Yoetz*', in E. Papo, H. Weiss, Y. Bentolila, and Y. Harari (eds), *Dameta Le Tamar, Studies in Honor of Tamar Alexander* (El Prezente, 8–9, part 2, May 2015), pp. 357–74 (Hebrew).

_____, 'Everyday Life in the Sephardic Community of Jerusalem According to the *Meam Loez* of Rabbi Jacob Kuli', *Studia Rosenthaliana*, 35 (2001), pp. 133–42.

_____, '*Meam Loez* (1730): Daily Life of Sephardic Families in Jerusalem', in Miriam Eliav-Feldon and Yitzhak Hen (eds), *Women, Children and the Elderly, Essays in Honour of Shulamit Shahar* (Jerusalem: Zalman Shazar Center, 2001), pp. 139–71 (Hebrew).

Molho, I. R., and A. Amarijlio, 'A Collecion of Communal Regulations in Ladino from Salonica', *Sefunot*, vol. 2 (1958), pp. 26–60 (Hebrew).

Motzki, Harold, 'Child Marriage in 17th Century Palestine', in M. K. Masud, B. Messick, and D. S. Powers (eds), *Islamic Legal Interpretation* (Cambridge, MA: Harvard University Press, 1996), pp. 129–40.

Pachter, Mordechai, 'The Land of Israel in the Homiletic Literature of Sixteenth Century Safed', in Moshe Hallamish and Aviezer Ravitzky (eds), *The Land of Israel in Medieval Jewish Thought* (Jerusalem: Yad Izhak Ben-Zvi, 1991), pp. 290–319 (Hebrew).

Regev, Shaul, 'Introduction to Miqve Israel', in *Miqve Israel, R. Israel Najara* [Sermons], ed. Shaul Regev (Ramat-Gan, 2004), pp. 9–119 (Hebrew).

_____, *Oral and Written Sermons in the Middle Ages* (Jerusalem: Rubin Mass, 2010) (Hebrew).

Rivlin (Ardos), Bracha, *Mutual Responsibility in the Italian Ghetto* (Jerusalem: Magnes Press, 1991) (Hebrew).

_____, 'On the History of the Jewish Family in Greece in the 16th–17th Centuries', in Michel Abitbol, Yom-Tov Assis, and Galit Hasan-Rokem (eds), *Hispano-Jewish Civilization after 1492* (Jerusalem: Misgav Yerushalayim, 1997), pp. 79–104 (Hebrew).

Rivlin, Eliezer (ed.), *Selections from Rabbi Refael Mordekhai Malki's Commentary on the Torah* (Jerusalem: Solomon Publishing House, 1923) (Hebrew).

Rodrigue, Aron (ed.), *Ottoman and Turkish Jewry: Community and Leadership* (Bloomington: Indiana University Press, 1992).

Rozen, Minna, 'The Family at War: Istanbul Jewry 1914–1923', in Minna Rozen, *Studies in the History of Istanbul Jewry 1453–1923, A Journey through Civilizations* (Turnhout: Brepols Publications, 2015), pp. 409–32.

_____, *A History of the Jewish Community in Istanbul: The Formative Years 1453–1566* (Leiden and Boston: Brill, 2002).

_____, 'The Incident of the Converted Boy: A Chapter in the History of the Jews in 17th Century Jerusalem', *Cathedra*, 14, pp. 65–80 (Hebrew).

_____, 'Individual and Community in the Jewish Society of the Ottoman Empire: Salonica in the 16th Century', in A. Levi (ed.), *The Jews of the Ottoman Empire* (Princeton, NJ: Darwin Press, 1994), pp. 215–73.

_____, *The Jewish Community of Jerusalem in the 17th Century* (Tel Aviv: Tel Aviv University, 1984) (Hebrew).

_____, *Jewish Identity and Society in the 17th Century, Reflections on the Life and Work of Refael Mordekhai Malki* (Tübingen: J. C. B. Mohr, 1992).

_____, 'The Life Cycle and the Significance of Old Age during the Ottoman Period', in D. Porat, A. Shapira, and M. Rozen (eds), *Daniel Carpi Jubilee Volume* (Tel Aviv: Tel Aviv University, 1996), pp. 109–75.

_____, 'Of Orphans, Marriage and Money: Mating Patterns of Istanbul's Jews in the Early 19th Century', in Eyal Ginio and Elie Podeh (eds), *The Ottoman Middle East: Studies in Honor of Amnon Cohen* (Leiden–Boston: Brill 2014), pp. 149–75.

Safran, Joseph, *Studies in the History of Jewish Education*, vol. 1 (Jerusalem: Mossad Harav Kook, 1983–6) (Hebrew).

Schechter, Solomon, *Studies in Judaism, Second Series* (Philadelphia: Jewish Publication Society of America, 1908).

Schwarzwald (Rodrigue), Ora, 'The Status of 16th Century Jewish Women in the Ottoman Empire', *Women in Judaism: A Multidisciplinary e-Journal*, 14/1 (2017), available at: <http://www.womeninjudaism.org> (last accessed 1 September 2019).

Simon, Rachel, 'Jewish Female Education in the Ottoman Empire 1840–1914', in A. Levi (ed.), *Jews, Turks, Ottomans, A Shared History* (Syracuse: Syracuse University Press, 2002), pp. 127–52.

Ta-Shema, Israel, 'The Earliest Literary Sources for the Bar-Mitzva Ritual and Festivity', *Tarbiz, A Quarterly for Jewish Studies*, 68/4 (1999), pp. 587–98 (Hebrew).

Turniansky, Chava, 'A Correspondence in Yiddish from Jerusalem, Dating from the 1560s', in Joseph Hacker (ed.), *Shalem, Studies in the History of the Jews in Eretz-Israel*, vol. 4, pp. 149–210 (Hebrew).

_____, 'Girls and Young Women in Yiddish Literature of the Early Modern Era', *Massekhet*, 12 (2016), pp. 65–84 (Hebrew).

Urfali, Moises (trans. and ed.), *Imanuel Aboab's Nomologia o Discursos Legales* (Jerusalem: Ben-Zvi Institute, 1997).

Weinstein, Roni, 'Between Liberty and Control: Jewish Juveniles in Early Modern Italy', *Zmanim: A Historical Quarterly*, 102 (2008), pp. 30–3 (Hebrew).

Yousif, Ahmad, 'Islam, Minorities and Religious Freedom: A Challenge to Modern Theory Pluralism', *Journal of Muslim Minority Affairs*, 20/1 (2000), pp. 29–41, available at: <http://dx.doi.org/10.1080/13602000050008889> (last accessed 1 September 2019).

Zachs, Fruma, 'Growing Consciousness of the Child in Ottoman Syria in the 19th Century: Modes of Parenting and Education in the Middle Class', in E. Ginio and E. Podeh (eds), *The Ottoman Middle East, Studies in Honor of Amnon Cohen* (Leiden and Boston: Brill, 2014), pp. 113–28.

———, 'The Private World of Women and Children: Lullabies and Nursery Rhymes in 19th Century Greater Syria', in Hoda Mahmoudi and Steven Mintz (eds), *Children and Youth in an Interconnected World: Multidisciplinary Perspective* (London: Routledge, 2019), pp. 77–99.

Chapter 15

Women as Educators towards the End of the *Nahda* Period: Labiba Hashim and Children's Upbringing

Fruma Zachs

> There is no alternative, since nature bestowed upon her [woman] this right and provided her with this delicate closed-eye creature so that she can transform him into a real human being. Moreover, she enables him to give birth to a nation...[1]

Introduction: Men's View of Women's and Girls' Education in the **Nahda**

The rapid economic changes, the process of modernisation and cultural encounters in the nineteenth century between the Ottoman Empire and the West influenced both Ottoman and Arab societies. Both underwent a process of redefining themselves as modern. Fuelled by the rise of patriotism and proto-nationalism among the Arab and Ottoman upper and middle classes, the nature of family was revisited. From the *Tanzimat* period onward, Ottoman intellectuals saw women as the gatekeepers of the household and the mothers of the future generation. Ottoman children became the heralds of the future of the Ottoman Empire. This attitude toward women and children developed more intensively after the Young Turk Revolution in 1908 that triggered significant changes in the Ottoman public discourse, political agendas and the organisation of daily life with respect to gender. Ottoman women, taking advantage of the new venues and opportunities provided by the revolution, played a vital role in creating and implementing these new attitudes and practices. As of 1908 and up to the demise of Empire, the *woman question* and the education of children became an increasing part of the political agenda. Hence, the dramatic military conflicts and political developments leading to the fall of the Empire and the emergence of a nation-state were crucial in the shaping of women's and children's lives.[2]

This changing attitude toward women and children was experienced in the Empire's centre as well as in middle-class urban settings in the Arab lands[3] more or less at the same time and in similar contexts/topics. This chapter illustrates the changes in perception of the importance of women's and children's education, especially through Arab women's writings from the mid-nineteenth century to the 1920s that demonstrate this upheaval.

In Arab societies children tend to be seen as the crucial generational link in the family unit and the key to its continuation: they bind the present to the past and the future. During the nineteenth century, as in the case of the Ottoman Empire, the centrality of children to family and society gradually took shape in Arab society. This period, which became known as the *nahda* (the awakening of Arab language and culture), was characterised by massive social and economic changes,[4] as well as by gender role transformation[5] and the impact of missionary educational activities. There was a concomitant awareness of the importance of children's education (for both boys and girls) in the regions of Greater Syria and Egypt.[6]

The need to forge a modern civil society redefined the place of women and, hence, children in it, in the sense that children were now considered to determine not only their families' future, but also that of society. Arab intellectuals of the time tended to see the family, and not the individual, as the basic socio-political unit and viewed marriage, the marital relationship and children's education as vital building blocks of modern society. This family-centred attitude, in particular concerning the place of women and children in society, was partly influenced by the discourse on domesticity taking place at that time in Europe and America.[7] This also led to a change in the notion that 'child-rearing' was not only a 'duty', but was an active process of 'child education'.

From the mid- to the late nineteenth century, debates on children's upbringing and women's education were part of the discourse on the *woman question*, among the Arab middle and upper classes.[8] This topic dominated the Syrian and Egyptian press, and was debated in articles, commentary and letters to the media that emphasised the important work of women in raising and educating their children and their role in the home. Child-rearing was seen as a profession that women should learn and aspire to. Therefore, the idea of women turning into the primary educator became inseparably bound to the concept of children's history during the nineteenth century.[9] Redefining and strengthening the role of women in raising and educating the children of the nation not only revolutionised the position of women in Arab society, but also altered the experiences of children in the *nahda* period and targeted them as a focus of societal interest and concern.

Labiba Hashim and Children's Upbringing

Although the debate on children's upbringing and women's education took an increasingly modern and rational attitude towards children and women, in both Ottoman and Arab societies, it nevertheless reflected a particular Arab gender schema.[10] The first generation of male intellectuals of the *nahda* and those that followed all expressed the need to incorporate changes supporting social progress as regards the status of women and by extension children's education by women without altering the traditional/patriarchal hierarchy. Leading figures, such as the Egyptian Rifa'a Rafi' al-Tahtawi (1801–73) and the Syrian–Lebanese Butrus al-Bustani (1819–83) and later Salim al-Bustani (1848–84) and Farah Antun (1874–1922), saw women as the key players in advancing society, since they were entrusted with the education of the next generation, who would shape the future of the family, society and homeland.

As early as 1849, for instance, al-Bustani promoted women's education in a lecture entitled *Khitab fi Ta'lim al-Nisa'* (A Lecture on the Education of Women).[11] He presented women as educators, not only naturally through motherhood, but primarily through attention to child-rearing as a valuable field of knowledge that women must acquire. Al-Bustani argued that civilised women should be taught religion because it was their right, privilege and duty; they should be taught their native tongue so that they could express themselves correctly; they should learn to write so that they could communicate their views and feelings to those whom their voices could not reach; and they should know how to read so as to remember their duties, both secular and religious, which they tended to forget when taught orally. Women should be instructed in child-rearing, he maintained, since bringing up children was not an instinct, but was learned from experience and observation. They should also learn home economics, serving, cooking and care of the sick, as well as geography, arithmetic and history. In other words, al-Bustani called for a restricted, structured Arab education, in which women learned selected areas of knowledge that would directly impact on the betterment of their children. This also kept women from explicitly challenging men in the public realm or exposing them to Western culture as a whole.

Somewhat later, in 1872, the Egyptian al-Tahtawi wrote *al-Murshid al-Amin lil-Banat wal-Banin* (A Guide for Girls and Boys),[12] a textbook for use in the newly established schools of Egypt, in response to an 1837 ordinance issued by the Ministry of Schools (*Diwan al-Madaris*), in which al-Tahtawi was a central figure. One chapter is devoted to the argument that it is preferable not to discriminate between teaching boys and girls, and claims that girls' education has an enormous impact on marital happiness and education, and that good manners on the mother's part determines how children are raised. His key point was that Egyptian girls and boys need a comprehensive and enlightened education that includes European sciences and methods, as well as traditional ones. He took the position that girls' education does not go against religious principles and that the benefits derived from girls' education outweighs its disadvantages. Al-Bustani and Tahtawi, like later intellectuals writing at the end of the nineteenth and the beginning of the twentieth centuries, such as Qasim Amin (1863–1908), saw a direct connection between women's education and their children's success, and by extension the enhancement of family, society and homeland.[13]

This perception did, indeed, alter the more traditional role of the mother. In the classic Arab view, mothering was a temporary activity undertaken for the good of the child, but also for the benefit of the patrilineal family. Mothering was mainly defined as maternal warmth and careful attention to the welfare of the child. The mother was the child's nurturer, protector and something of an instructor, mostly on the basis of her own experience, since women were more often than not uneducated. Women, for example, taught their daughters sewing and cooking within the home and in the private sphere, told stories and sang nursery rhymes, but dealt less with their education or, for that matter, with their sons' education.

The visionaries of the *nahda* not only championed women's/mothers' educational role, but also expected them to become role models for both girls and boys as a way of integrating them into the new and rapidly changing society. This new perspective on parenthood, and especially the difference in terms regarding mothers' roles, did not challenge the Islamic/religious or Arab view of the marriage contract, which was to maintain harmony. In that era, a marital relationship was complementary and not one of equality. Hence, patriarchy was still exercised, and authority, guidance and discipline continued to be viewed as the father's exclusive province. However, these attitudes did ascribe more agency to women, which also turned them into new role models, in particular for their daughters, who aspired to greater access to education and a more active role in their future families. This new attitude also helped progressively influence children's experience and changed their perception of women in general and their mothers in particular.

Throughout the nineteenth century, children's education became a heated topic in the public sphere, among the local bourgeoisie as well as the upper classes in Greater Syria and Egypt. The growing notion of the need for women's education[14] evolved into a major concern among male educators and eventually among women educators, who started to voice their own ideas about children's education toward the end of the century.

Beth Baron points out that women writers of this time '... strove to restructure family roles and relations, placing the couple at the centre of the family, shifting some authority from the husband to the wife, and turning more attention to childhood'.[15]

This chapter extends Baron's observations through a case study of Labiba Hashim, a Syrian immigrant to Egypt, and shows that although men educators were in favour of children's education because it impacted on the family, society and nation, women educators broadened the scope of children's education in general and girls' education in particular to assist them (and themselves) in becoming not only educated mothers, but also educated women. Children's education allowed women to transform attitudes toward themselves and resituate their place and their children's place in the patriarchal family and society. Moreover, the changing attitude of mothers toward their children eventually influenced the way children perceived themselves.

Debating Girls' Education in Egypt[16]

As early as the 1880s, Syrian Christian women were writing about women's and children's education in journals such as *al-Hilal* and *al-Muqtataf* and arguing that girls' education should include both scholarly subjects and practical skills in home economics and crafts. At the same time they also insisted that women should have the same education as men.[17] Istir Wakid from Antioch, referred to by the Beiruti newspaper *Lisan al-Hal* as an 'educated woman' (*adiba*), wrote a series of articles in 1891 entitled 'The Mother at Home' (*al-Umm fil-Bayt*). In these articles, also read by an Egyptian audience, she advised women on how to raise their children, especially girls between the ages of eight and ten. Wakid blamed the school system for not doing enough to teach girls how to educate their children.[18] She also elaborated on the correct way to discipline children (while criticising the harsh methods used in schools) and advised women to punish their children only after gently explaining why in a rational and didactic way. Wakid felt that children learned right and wrong by realising the ramifications of their acts, rather than through physical punishment.[19] Corporal punishment was customary in Arab/Muslim society. Fathers administered punishment as part of their patriarchal role,[20] and the head of the household or the teacher in the *kuttab* had the right to beat pupils.

Other educated women, such as Hind Nawfal (1860–1920), a Syrian immigrant to Egypt, and the founder of the first women's newspaper in Cairo, *al-Fatat*, also discussed changes in children's education. Nawfal instructed her readers on how to educate themselves and their children for the sake of the homeland – clearly an echo of the mantra of male intellectuals – but she also tried to broaden the scope of women's education. In 1894, she published an article which presented a list of almost thirty, mainly French, books by women authors writing on children's education that Arab women should read to educate themselves and their daughters. The list was designed to educate them morally and modestly, and to teach them conduct and how to raise their children.[21] This list in fact contained a concealed message: broaden your education, see the accomplishments of other women and try to educate your daughters in this way. Nawfal thus appealed to her female audience to write and influence children's education, which would eventually influence them and their future,[22] something that the Egyptian educational system was unable to achieve throughout most of the nineteenth and the beginning of the twentieth century. In Egypt, until the nineteenth century, women's education was based on religion and was pursued for its own sake by the upper class. Girls from the upper class usually studied at home. Women of humbler origins were educated at the traditional Qur'anic school (*kuttab*). Their curriculum usually included the Qur'an and Hadith and, in some cases, poetry, mathematics and Arabic. Most girls were taught to read but not to write and learned needlework and embroidery from their female relatives.

As noted by Mona Russell, in the nineteenth century, girls' education was influenced by government schools, foreign/minority schools and the British occupation. During the reign of Muhammad 'Ali (1769–1849) local governments made several attempts to start schools for girls.[23] The first primary school for girls, *al-Siyufia*, was founded in 1873 by Khedive Isma'il (1863–79) and admitted girls from both the lower and upper classes. Its curriculum was comparable to European schools of the time, although it had an Egyptian flavour that included reading, writing, religion, Arabic Turkish, French, arithmetic, history, geography, natural history, drawing, geometry, childcare, cooking, home economics, needle work and music. The needlework and home economics classes were more likely to appeal to the lower classes, since they provided income-producing skills, whereas upper-class girls would be more interested in languages, music and art. A second government primary school for girls, the 'Abbas School', was founded in 1895, and catered exclusively to lower class girls.

The Egyptian government in general was slow to respond to the increasing demands for girls' education, prompted by the conviction that women's ignorance was a fundamental problem in society that could shift the balance in the nationalist struggle against the British occupation. Nevertheless, there was a slow trend away from home tutoring to an institutionalisation of girls' education at the turn of the twentieth century, although one of the major obstacles was the lack of female teachers. As a result, many girls and boys were enrolled in missionary[24] and foreign/minority schools. These schools taught girls writing, arithmetic and needlework and mainly emphasised home economics. Advanced students studied geography, home economics, French and art.

When the British occupied Egypt in 1882, they limited access to education by increasing fees. Female education was not a high priority for the British.[25] Lord Cromer, the Consul General of Egypt from 1883–1907, instigated a 'two tiered' class system. One stream was aimed at promoting literacy among the lower classes and was directed toward the network of *kuttab* and native elementary schools, whose curriculum was restricted to reading, writing, arithmetic and religious studies. The second stream provided education for small groups of upper-class students to meet the requirements for government service jobs and was oriented towards positions such as midwifery, nursing and teaching.[26]

The Egyptian University (later the University of Cairo) opened its doors in 1908, with a female enrolment of only three. In 1909, Huda Sha'arawi (1879–1947) was one of the organisers of a special lecture series at the university for women, and invited the French feminist Marguerite Clément to speak. This series was so successful that it became a regular Friday afternoon event held in the women's section when the rest of the university was not in session. Speakers talked about the importance of girls' education, women's rights, health and hygiene.[27] The audience was composed of the upper classes, such as princesses, wives of *bey*s and pashas and Christian notables. The lectures were in French, and the message of greater educational opportunities for women and the importance of women to the home, family and nation was emphasised. By 1911 more facilities were made available to women, and the programme expanded to include lectures in Arabic on subjects such as history, education and home economics. Labiba Hashim was one of these women lecturers.

Recasting the Patriarchal Family through Children's Education: Hashim's Concepts/Philosophy/Vision

Labiba Madi al-Hashim (1882–1952), a pioneer of the *nahda* period, was a distinguished educator, novelist, journalist, playwright and translator. She was born in Beirut and studied at the *Sisters of Love (Rahibat al-Mahabba)* and the English missionary schools and later at the Syrian Protestant College.[28] Jurji Niqula Baz, a leading intellectual and journalist of that era, described her as 'an example for the women of her time'.[29] According to Baz, she was nicknamed 'Madame de Staël' for her political, literary and cultural activities.³⁰ Although she was only eight when she immigrated to Egypt, she depicted her life as divided between Syria and Egypt, the two locations where she had an impact on women's and children's issues.

In 1900 Hashim moved with her family to Cairo, like many Syrian/Lebanese families who sought a more liberal, political and cultural environment. In Cairo, she frequented the literary salon of Warda al-Yaziji (1838–1924), the sister of Ibrahim al-Yaziji, and was rapidly integrated into Cairene circles. She was multitalented and fluent in English, French and Persian. She apparently wrote, as of 1896, for the *nahda* newspapers. She published a number of articles on the situation of women in *Anis al-Jalis*, a journal for women, which was founded in Alexandria in 1898. In 1899 she started writing for *al-Diya'* and continued to do so until 1906.[31] From 1906 until 1939 she published her own journal, *The Eastern Young Woman* (*Fatat al-Sharq*), in Egypt, which was one of the first women's periodicals in the Arab world that rapidly became a leading journal for women in Egypt and Greater Syria. *Fatat al-Sharq* was well-known for its columns on famous women and for its aphorisms.[32] She distributed the journal for free to girls' schools in Egypt, Syria and Lebanon to encourage them to read and write poetry, articles and editorials.

Like several other educated Arab and Ottoman women of her time, Hashim was interested in the education of women and children, and she gave these topics considerable space in her journal. In 1909, she sent a long letter to the Ottoman Parliament (*Majlis al-Nuwwab al-'Uthmani*) outlining her vision for Arab female education and demanding changes in the curriculum from the new Sultan Mehmed V Reshad (1844–1918).[33] Specifically, she stipulated that there should be more funds provided for girls' schools in Syria and Lebanon.

In October 1918, the Ottoman Empire was defeated, and an Arab government was set up in Damascus under the leadership of King Faysal. Hashim supported King Faysal, the new ruler of Syria, who declared himself an advocate of women's rights. In turn, Faysal appointed her Inspector of Education at the Ministry of Education, and she worked with the minister and scholar Sati al-Husri. Hashim was one of the first women to hold a government post in Syria, which was dominated at the time by an all-male bureaucracy. After the battle of Maysalun, the fall of King Faysal's government and the entry of the invading French forces, Hashim moved to Chile with her husband and founded a newspaper called *al-Sharq wal-Gharb* (The East and the West). She returned to Egypt in 1923 and continued publishing *Fatat al-Sharq* until the eve of World War II.[34]

In 1911, in recognition of her promotion of children's and women's education, the Egyptian University invited Hashim to lecture several times in the women's section. In 1912 Hashim published a book titled *A Book on Child Upbringing* (*Kitab fil Tarbiya*),[35] which included ten of the lectures she delivered there to middle-class and elite women. In these lectures Hashim presented her philosophy/concepts and gave advice on how mothers should treat and educate their young children (*tufula*), whom she called 'the future generation' (*jil al-mustaqbal*), and she also referred to schooling. She reflected on some of the notions that prevailed in her time concerning girls' education, but emphasised her own ideas on children's education in general and girls' education in particular. The book attracted the interest of intellectuals and readers of her journal, some of whom commented on its importance and suggested it should be studied in every school in Egypt.[36]

As Egypt was drawn into the world economy in the nineteenth century, the Egyptian economy increasingly turned towards wage labourers. A working class emerged from the beginning of the twentieth century. After World War I, the industrial boom led to the creation of an indigenous middle class. These processes tended to channel women into service occupations, where they spent longer hours outside the home, which threatened gender roles.[37] The growing numbers of women in the workforce made balancing home and work more difficult. This sparked a debate in the press on the role of men and women, where women writers articulated what Baron terms a 'new domestic ideology', in which male members of the family were expected to earn an income and support female members of the family, who in turn provided what were now seen as household services.[38] In proposing this domestic ideology, women such as Hashim were not trying to return to traditional Islamic gender roles, but rather to redefine the role of mothers and children in the family. Their claim was that child-rearing was no longer a job to be delegated to servants or relatives. Now mothers were directed to spend more time with their children and supervise their health and development. Some women supported these ideas, but others, including upper-middle and upper-class women, viewed domestic labour as below them.

In her book Hashim made a series of recommendations to improve institutionalised education and the upbringing of children in elementary and high schools and called for education to be an academic subject at the Egyptian University. She wanted children's education to be governed by a formal programme taught in a special 'department' (*far' khass*) at the Egyptian University where women would study (but also teach) the principles of children's education (especially topics such as young children's health and values). She believed that the graduates would influence young women students (*fatayat*) and prepare their pupils for future motherhood.³⁹ She also lobbied for an increase in the number of girl pupils in schools.⁴⁰

Hashim felt that children's education in schools in Egypt was lacking, and she often wrote editorials in her publications about the need for educated teachers and rigorous training.⁴¹ She complained that the teachers were not qualified. Hashim noted that although more girls were enrolled in the *kuttab*, only a few became teachers, and she argued that this was detrimental to Egyptian society and would affect the family in the long run, since young men would not be able to find an educated wife and would marry foreign girls instead.⁴²

She introduced a scientific approach to children's education which she termed 'the science of children's education' (*fann tarbiyat al-awlad*). For example, her journal included a 'Questions and Answers' section on children with responses from physicians. She specifically targeted middle- and upper-class women, and called upon them to take a larger part in rearing their children and to depend less on nannies from the lower classes, whom she felt were ignorant and unaware of their duties. She was also opposed to hiring European women as nursemaids, since they usually came from the lower classes, knew little about child-rearing and held contempt for Eastern peoples.⁴³

Her book is divided into three sections, each of which covered a topic she considered crucial to child-rearing. The first, Upbringing (*Tarbiya*), discusses ways to nurture and guide children to maturity, through tenderness, firmness, obedience and love. The process of *Tarbiya* covers the child's whole period of development: infancy (*al-tufuliyya*), youth (*sabwa*) and education in terms of self-acquired knowledge (*tarbiyat al-mir' nafsihi bi-nafsihi*), as well as learning from others.⁴⁴

The second section, entitled *The Physical* (*Badaniyya*), deals with the child's body, hygiene and health from infancy onward. Hashim argued that maternal ignorance was responsible for the high rates of infant mortality in Egypt.⁴⁵ She referred to contemporary research linking germs and disease. She called on women to use soap, and she took a stand against traditional habits, such as rubbing the newborn baby's body with oil and salt to protect the skin, which only damages it.⁴⁶

She dealt with health in detail. She vouched for the importance of breastfeeding, but also talked about substitutes and recommended cow's milk diluted with water. She stressed that milk should be clean and should be bought from merchants who came to the house with their cow and not from the market where milk was often diluted with contaminated water. She pointed out that milk must be boiled.⁴⁷ She discussed how to dress a child, wash children's clothes and clean and air children's rooms,⁴⁸ and urged mothers to see a doctor when children were sick and to give them medicine. She discussed activities that stimulate mind and body, including games and exercise.[49]

The third section, entitled *Character Development (Adabiyya)*, examines how a child could become a refined, disciplined, cultured adult and acquire a sound basis for moral and social behaviour. Hashim also encouraged parents to let their children develop their inner world before going to school. In this way she emphasised, to some extent, the child's individuality.[50] She believed that education was the prime way to influence children and a source of (self) discipline and felt that a good education was superior to beating and spanking, but supported positive punishment (*'iqab tabi'i*), suggesting, for example, that if a child did not put away his games and the mother, as punishment, did not allow him to play, he would not do it again.[51] Muslim thinkers of the time tended to believe that alongside the notion of children's purity and innocence, the child was an ignorant creature, full of desires with a weak and vulnerable spirit. This image and the concept behind it – namely, that childhood was no more than a 'passage' leading to the 'parlour' of adulthood – justified extensive, sometimes excessive use of corporal punishment by parents and teachers to correct undesirable traits.[52]

Hashim argued that there are two approaches to people's natural traits. The first approach is that a person (*al-makhluq*) is created either good or evil, regardless of external influences, whereas the second claims that a person is born with the ability to become either good or evil. She considered that every individual has a good and an evil facet. In some, the good traits are dominant, while in others evil triumphs, which raises the question of how a person becomes good or evil. In her opinion the outcome was determined by self-esteem (literally, self-love) (*hubb al-dhat*), which existed in everyone.[53] Since all people are different, how does one maintain this self-love? Hashim gave the example of the thief and the physician. Both have self-love, and thus both care about themselves. One achieves this by helping others and the other by hurting others; but the latter is, admittedly, responding to his inner needs. In fact, by stealing he believes he is protecting himself. Hashim claimed that education imprints traits in children and orients them towards goodness. In her view this did not imply that education is a panacea that can prevent people from becoming evil; rather, it can help in most cases.

Like the male intellectuals of the *nahda*, Hashim aimed to formulate a modern, rational and scientific attitude towards children's education which contrasted with education based on bad habits and superstitions that were common, especially among mothers from poor families. Nevertheless, she also felt that children's education depended primarily on adults learning to understand their children. She encouraged parents to treat their children with sensitivity and tenderness (while also expecting obedience), and she asked teachers and parents to respect the children and to work towards fostering their self-esteem. She saw the child as a sensitive whole and called on adults to respect each child's individuality and feelings. She told mothers to treat their children with mercifulness and to reward them for doing well.[54]

In her articles and short stories[55] in her journal, Hashim was one of the first to stress the need to educate children on how to express emotions appropriately and how to deal with pain, such as losing one of their close relatives.[56] In 1912 she published a short story called *The Little Orphan Girl* (*al-Yatima al-Saghira*), which describes the day that a four-year-old lost her mother and how she confronted her loss. After her mother's death, she was sent to her aunt, but sometime later returned home to find that her father had married another woman. The new wife and her children had the father's entire attention, and the little girl was forgotten. This was a unique plot, since in most short stories and novels of that time children were not usually part of the storyline and certainly not the proponent or the leading figure. Here, the story is narrated through the eyes of the motherless girl. Although Hashim criticised excessive outpourings of grief among Easterners, she emphasised the fact that mothers should educate their children to accept pain as part of the inevitable. She counselled that mothers should teach their children sensitivity so that they could deal with the pain in silence and with patience. She described her own experiences as a six-year-old when her younger brother died and related how, as a result of her grief, she contracted a stomach ailment that almost killed her.

Hashim therefore saw both boys and girls as the main focus of the family. Like other intellectuals of her time, she tended mainly to see the family, and not the individual, as the basic socio-political unit of society and the nation. Nevertheless, she innovated by insisting that the family activities should mainly revolve around children and their upbringing. She believed that both parents should understand that their behaviour could eventually influence their children and made it clear that children imitate whatever they see or hear from their parents. One of her lectures at the Egyptian University opened with this anecdote:

> One of them, while out walking, saw a boy who was hurling stones and curses at his brothers and friends and became interested in his stupid, reckless behaviour. He approached the boy and asked him his name. The boy replied, 'the devil', 'And what is your father's name?' 'The devil' he replied. 'And your mother's name?' 'devil'. So he asked 'how is this possible?' The boy replied:

'I hear my father call my mother "devil" and her calling him "devil" and both of them call me "oh devil" '.[57]

While this anecdote still targets how parents should educate their children, and although Hashim emphasised that parents are the source of the family, the focus is also on the child itself and the way in which parents should treat children. It underscores the importance of mutual respect between parents, but more importantly parents' recognition/respect of their children's needs. Her subtext suggests that children's education should be more sensitive to children's emotions. She called for children to be treated as active listeners with minds of their own, thus boosting children's confidence in themselves and fostering individualism and self-monitoring.

Echoing the call of male intellectuals of her time, Hashim demanded better education for girls (as the women of the future); however, she envisioned the mother as the main educator of her children (especially before they went to school). In this way she extended the mother's role in the family and thus women's core curriculum of education, although she called on both parents to be knowledgeable and to be involved in their children's education.[58] For example, she called for girls to be educated beyond embroidery, playing the piano or learning a foreign language, since this kind of education would not benefit their children.[59] She termed her homeland the 'country of mothers' (*madinat al-ummahat*), since they educated their sons to have the virtues of manhood (*sifat al-rujula*).[60] She stressed, as did other intellectuals, that mothers were the ones who raised the men of the future, but they also raised the mothers of the future. She recognised that her research and attitude mainly dealt with mothers/women, even though both parents wanted the best for their children. However, since the father had to provide the income, it was the mother who raised her children alone most of the time, and thus the father should give her full latitude (*huriyya mutlaqa*)[61] in their upbringing.

Echoing *Mrs. Beeton's Book of Household Management*,[62] she believed, like al-Bustani and other intellectuals, that girls should be taught more than the simple principles (*al-mabadi' al-basita*) of home economics and home management. She recommended teaching girls the history of civilisation (*ta'rikh al-tamaddun*) and the cultures of advanced nations in order to understand men's way of thinking. She encouraged teaching girls about famous women, along with the biographies of famous men. They should learn geography, mathematics, sciences, such as chemistry, natural history and to understand how technologies work. Girls, in her mind, should also be taught art and music, to appreciate the beauty of nature and develop their taste.[63] To enhance their sense of taste, in her journal, *Fatat*

Figure 15.1 'The fashion'.
Source 'Al-Azya'', *Fatat al-Sharq*, 7/9 (June 1913), p. 364.

al-Sharq, Hashim regularly published children's fashion (for both boys and girls), alongside women's fashion, encouraging parents' awareness of children's appearance as well. Hashim's attitude was typical of opinions in articles in Ottoman women's journals such as *Hanımlara Mahsus Gazete* (Newspaper for Ladies), which was published in Istanbul from 1895 to 1908.[64]

As seen in Figures 15.1 and 15.2, the journal *Fatat al-Sharq* reproduced European images. The article provided explanations that emphasised Hashim's awareness of the child's welfare from an early age: she insisted that comfort and simple design should not be neglected, and that girls should wear subdued colours for modesty.

Although Hashim talked about girls' appearance, her main purpose was to transform them into educated women who were self-aware. She made it clear that she did not want to transform girls into philosophers or to be the equal of religious men in their knowledge, but she urged them to study these topics to an extent that would benefit the family and the nation.[65]

Figure 15.2 'Fashions of the month'.
Source 'Azya' Hadha al-Shahr', *Fatat al-Sharq*, 8/3 (December 1913), p. 120.

Hashim regularly published a column entitled 'The Mother and the Men of the Future: Between Mother and Child'. This helpful hints column was written as a series of conversations that drew on her own exchanges with her five-year-old son.[66] In these talks, the mother satisfies the child's curiosity about questions on science or technology, including questions such as why the wind blows or how a tramway works. The main goal of this column was to depict the figure of an educated mother in her women readers' imagination. She probably hoped that her female readers would use these explanations with their own children. These popular science conversations were open and simple and could be illustrated without specialised terms, complicated instruments or apparatuses, so that women could experiment with their own children. In this way, Hashim engaged with a form of educational practice that utilised the format of the mentor–younger learner typical of many women's didactic texts in Europe.[67] The image was not only of a woman/mother telling stories to her children or singing lullabies, but of a mother who educated her children and was capable of answering their complicated questions in simple language.[68] This perception, which was promoted by Ottoman women such as Halide Edib (1884–1964),[69] not only helped to change the traditional role of the mother, which had been mainly defined as maternal warmth and careful attention to the welfare of the child, but it also changed the perception of children and childhood.[70] These educational texts, by explaining scientific activities and principles, also promoted science as a form of public enlightenment.

The by-product of this process of extending girls' education beyond what was suggested by male intellectuals was that women educators such as Hashim eventually hoped these girls would turn into the educated women of the future. Hence, one of the most important outcomes of defining the changing place of women as educators was also the expansion of girls' education. In general, this redefinition of children (both boys and girls) helped to transform the local society, through its children, into a modern one. These new perceptions of children and childhood further enhanced the role of women as educators.[71] Although male intellectuals of the nineteenth century, and later educated women, emphasised the importance of children in society, they also criticised the patriarchal status quo. Thus, the debate regarding children became one of the vehicles by which to transform not only the history of children and childhood, but ultimately society itself.

Conclusion

In Muslim and Ottoman societies the main purpose of education was to ensure the future of the believer (or the child) in the next world.[72] Traditionally, the head of the household or the teacher in the *kuttab* was the main educator. During the Arab *nahda*, the *Tanzimat* period and more comprehensively from 1908, children's education was discussed extensively in the Arabic/Ottoman press, lectures and in books. This topic, which had mostly been the fief of men of religion, ethics and philosophy, became a central issue in the public sphere. Not only men but also women put forward their opinions and interpretations and attempted to readjust themselves to the modern family and times. When women wrote about teaching or upbringing, they adopted a form of what Mary Hilton terms *praxis*.⁷³ In this way their ideas became part of experience in the public imagination, thus connecting abstract concepts with lived reality alongside men educators and helped to shape children's education from a young age. Women such as Labiba Hashim were at the forefront and published their philosophy of children's education. Her writing served as a way to carefully link women's ideas with those of male writers. In so doing she popularised new notions concerning children and their position in the family that were acceptable to both genders. She articulated a new type of duties and experiences for women. Through their writing on the education of children, women such as Hashim constructed and defended a woman's aspirations in the face of omnipresent patriarchy. They championed female intellectual life and called for educating the female mind. 'Concomitantly, they underlined in their various ways the vital importance of the educated female experience in relation to the proper education of the young'.⁷⁴ They all were in favour of reformulating female authority from within, and continuously reclaimed large parts of children's educational territory as a rational but also sensitive move, thus transforming relations within the family and resituating themselves and their children in their family and society. Their efforts also shifted the child from the margins to the centre of the family and the centre of cultural life.

Notes

1. Hashim, 'al-Mar'a wal-Ta'lim', p. 15.
2. In the post-Second Constitutional period women's writings differed from texts in previous periods. During this period, economic and political topics appeared alongside more traditional subjects, such as housekeeping, childcare and fashion. After the Young Turk Revolution in 1908, many more women's newspapers were launched. The increasing recognition of the importance of girls' education and literacy furthered the acknowledgement of women's and children's roles in Ottoman society. On the redefinition of the role of women and children in Ottoman society, see Zeren Enis, *Everyday Lives of Ottoman Muslim Women*; Frierson, 'Women in Ottoman Intellectual History'; Atamaz-Hazar, 'The Hands that Rock the Cradle will Rise'; Aygül, 'Change in the Status of Turkish Women during the Ottoman Modernization', pp. 24–60; Fortna, 'Bonbons and Bayonets', pp. 173–88.
3. Ottoman intellectuals debated issues related to women and children earlier than in the Arab provinces.
4. On the impact of the global market and capitalist development on Middle Eastern women, see Meriwether, 'Women and Economic Change', pp. 65–83; Thompson, *Colonial Citizens*, pp. 34–6; Khater, '"House" to "Goddess of the House"', pp. 325–48.

5. See, for more details, Hanssen and Weiss (eds), *Arabic Thought beyond the Liberal Age*; Abou Hodeib, *A Taste for Home*.
6. Zachs and Halevi, 'From *Difa'al-Nisa'* to *Mas'alat al-Nisa'* in Greater Syria', pp. 615–33; Cole, 'Feminism, Class, and Islam in Turn of the Century Egypt', pp. 387–407.
7. For more details, see Zachs, 'Growing Consciousness', pp. 113–28.
8. Baron makes it clear in the introduction that her work deals with elite women and their involvement in Egyptian nationalism at a time when elite women dominated nationalist politics. She indicates that the politics of lower-class women deserves to be studied in its own right and should cover the post-1952 period, since these women only began to engage in this process later. Baron, *Egypt as a Woman: Nationalism, Gender and Politics*, p. 3. This chapter mainly discusses the end of the nineteenth century and the beginning of the twentieth century when elite and middle-class women dominated the domestic discourse, which was addressed primarily to their own class. Nevertheless, these women hoped that their ideas would eventually percolate to the lower classes.
9. On the response to this process within Egyptian society, see Ibrahim, *Child Custody in Islamic Law*. This book criticises the new family ideology and the increasing role of women in it. Ibrahim argues against the idea of connecting women and children's experiences.
10. For more details, see also Booth, 'Woman in Islam', pp. 171–201; Tucker, *Women in Nineteenth Century Egypt*.
11. Al-Bustani, 'Khitab fi Ta'lim al-Nisa'', pp. 45–53.
12. See al-Tahtawi, *Tahrir al-Mar'a al-Muslima*.
13. Russell, *Creating the New Egyptian Women*, pp. 1–2.
14. The growing discourse on children's and women's education in the second half of the nineteenth century and the growing number of missionary schools in the Ottoman Empire eventually brought about the promulgation of the Education Regulation (*Maarif Nizamnamesi*) of 1869. For more details, see Fortna, *Imperial Classroom*, pp. 99–117; Deguilhem, 'A Revolution in Learning?', pp. 285–95.
15. Baron, *The Women's Awakening in Egypt*, p. 146.
16. This background to girls' education in Egypt draws on Russell, *Consumerism, Creating the New Egyptian Women*, especially Chapters 6 and 7; Russell, 'Competing, Overlapping, and Contradictory Agendas', pp. 50–60; and Baron, *The Women's Awakening in Egypt*.
17. Ilyan, 'The Rights of Women and the Necessity of their Education', pp. 358–60; Tanus, 'Women's Education and Their Upbringing', pp. 234–5; the growing attitude toward the need for the education of girls was evident throughout the Ottoman Empire. See Yıldız, 'Knowledgeable Ottoman Girls', pp. 143–55; on this issue in the later period, see Hauser et al. (eds), *Entangled Education*.
18. Wakid, 'al-Umm fil-Bayt', no. 1377, p. 4.

19. Wakid, 'al-Umm fil-Bayt', no. 1328, p. 3; Wakid, 'al-Umm fi al-Bayt', no. 1326, p. 3; Wakid, 'Sultat al-Umm', no. 1329, p. 3.
20. Giladi, 'Concepts of Childhood', pp. 125–6.
21. Nawfal, '*Fa'ida Adabiyya*', pp. 446–8.
22. For more details, see Zachs, 'Growing Consciousness', pp. 113–28.
23. Yousef, 'Reassessing Egypt's Dual System of Education under Isma'il', pp. 109–30.
24. Baron, *The Women's Awakening in Egypt*, pp. 104–5, 131.
25. Cochran, *Education in Egypt*, pp. 10–11.
26. Baron, *The Women's Awakening in Egypt*, pp. 126–7.
27. Ibid., pp. 123–4.
28. Al-Qiyadi, *Isham al-Katiba al-'Arabiyya*, p. 58.
29. Baz, *al-Nisa'iyat*, p. 44.
30. Ibid.
31. Ibid., p. 45.
32. Elsadda, 'Egypt', pp. 107–8.
33. This letter could not be located in the archives.
34. Baron, *Egypt as a Woman*; Zachs, 'Challenging the Ideal'.
35. Hashim, *Kitab fil Tarbiya*; see on this book, Baron, *The Women's Awakening in Egypt*, pp. 162–3.
36. Mirziyan, 'Kitab fil-Tarbiya', p. 226; 'Abd al-Sahid, 'Muqtatafat', pp. 270–1.
37. For more detail, see Elsadda, 'Gendered Citizenship', pp. 1–28.
38. Baron, *The Women's Awakening in Egypt*, pp. 144–5.
39. Hashim, *Kitab fil-Tarbiya*, pp. 4, 9–11.
40. Hashim, 'Mashru'at Nizarat al-Ma'arif', pp. 99–103.
41. Hashim, *Kitab fil-Tarbiya*, pp. 72–6.
42. Hashim, 'Mashru'at Nizarat al-Ma'arif', pp. 99–103; Hashim, 'al-Hukuma al-Misriyya', pp. 131–3.
43. Hashim, *Kitab fil-Tarbiya*, pp. 51–2.
44. Ibid., p. 11.
45. For more on child mortality, see Baron, *The Women's Awakening in Egypt*, p. 160.
46. Hashim, *Kitab fil-Tarbiya*, pp. 24–5.
47. Ibid., pp. 29–30.
48. Ibid.
49. Ibid., pp. 39–52.
50. Ibid., p. 67.
51. Ibid., pp. 14, 61–2.
52. Giladi, *Children of Islam*, pp. 117–18.
53. Rousseau believed self-esteem (*amour de soi*) was tainted by society and thus turned into pride and evil behaviour, but this could be remedied by 'good' institutions.
54. Hashim, *Kitab fil-Tarbiya*, pp. 57–9.

55. Hashim, 'al-Yatima al-Saghira', pp. 197–200.
56. Hashim, 'Tarbiyat al-'Awatif', pp. 188–9.
57. Hashim, *Kitab fil-Tarbiya*, pp. 11–12.
58. Although Hashim argued that every man should learn a profession that corresponded to his own class in society, all girls from all classes should be educated and know how to raise children. Hashim, *Kitab fil-Tarbiya*, pp. 80–2.
59. Ibid., p. 9.
60. Ibid., p. 24.
61. Ibid., p. 60.
62. Beeton, *Mrs. Beeton's Book of Household Management*. Far more than just a cookbook, Beeton's book was a *vade mecum* for the newlywed woman to keep house with confidence – what kitchen equipment to buy, how to clean the house, what servants to have, what to look for in hiring them, how to raise children and cure their diseases and much more.
63. Hashim, *Kitab fil-Tarbiya*, pp. 114–20.
64. As in the case of Hashim's journal, the goals of *Hanımlara Mahsus Gazete* were to turn women into good mothers, good wives, but also good Muslims. The journal published articles on topics similar to those of Hashim's journal, such as home management, childcare, family life, fashion, health and women's education. For more details, see Zeren Enis, *Everyday Lives of Ottoman Muslim Women*, pp. 371–91; Atamaz-Hazar, 'The Hands that Rock the Cradle will Rise', pp. 79–80.
65. Atamaz-Hazar, 'The Hands that Rock the Cradle will Rise', pp. 81–6.
66. For example, see Hashim, 'al-Umm wa-Rijal al-Mustaqbal', pp. 136–41, 174–8.
67. Hilton, *Women and the Shaping of the Nation's Young*, pp. 128–30.
68. See, for example, Hashim, 'Bayna Umm wa-waladiha', pp. 379–82; Hashim, 'al-Kahraba'iyya, Bayna Umm Wa-waladiha', pp. 5–10, 18–19.
69. For more details, see Atamaz-Hazar, 'The Hands that Rock the Cradle will Rise', p. 119.
70. Tucker, 'The Fullness of Affection', pp. 232–52.
71. This was also apparent in the Ottoman case. While most male Ottoman intellectuals focused on the role of education in creating the 'ideal woman' and consequently the 'ideal society', many women considered it a basic right which enabled them to exist as independent individuals and to participate actively in social and economic life. For more details, see Aynur, 'In Pursuit of the Ottoman Women's Movement'.
72. Giladi, *Children of Islam*, p. 51.
73. Hilton, *Women and the Shaping of the Nation's Young*, pp. 228–9.
74. Ibid., p. 230.

Bibliography

Primary Sources

'Abd al-Sahid, Aulifya, 'Muqtatafat', *Fatat al-Sharq*, 7/6 (15 April 1913), pp. 270–1.

Baz, Jurji N., *Al-Nisa'iyat: Kitab Adabi Akhlaki Ijtima'i* (Beirut: al-Matba'a al-'Abasiyya, 1919).

Beeton, Isabella, *Mrs Beeton's Book of Household Management* (London: S. O. Beeton Publishing, 1861).

Al-Bustani, Butrus, 'Khitab fi Ta'lim al-Nisa'', *al-Jam'iyya al-Suriyya lil-'Ulum wal-Funun 1847–1852*, ed. Yusuf Qizma al-Khuri (Beirut: Dar al-Hamra lil-Taba'a wal-Nashr, 1900), pp. 45–53.

Hashim, Labiba, 'Al-Hukuma al-Misriyya wa-Ta'lim al-Banat', *Fatat al-Sharq*, 7/4 (15 January 1913), pp. 131–3.

———, *Kitab fil Tarbiya* (Cairo: Matba'at al-Ma'arif, 1912).

———, 'Al-Mar'a wal-Ta'lim', *Fatat al-Sharq*, 7/1 (15 October 1912), pp. 12–28.

———, 'Mashru'at Nizarat al-Ma'arif', *Fatat al-Sharq*, 7/2 (15 December 1912), pp. 99–103.

———, 'Tarbiyat al-'Awatif', *Fatat al-Sharq*, 7/5 (15 February 1912), pp. 188–9.

———, 'Al-Umm wa-Rijal al-Mustaqbal – Bayna Umm wa-Waladiha', *Fatat al-Sharq*, 7/4 and 7/5 (15 January and February 1913), pp. 136–41, 174–8.

———, 'Al-Yatima al-Saghira', *Fatat al-Sharq*, 7/5 (15 February 1912), pp. 197–200.

Ilyan, Maryam Jurji, 'The Rights of Women and the Necessity of their Education', *al-Muqtataf*, 7/8 (1884), pp. 358–60.

Mirziyan, Budur, 'Kitab fil-Tarbiya', *Fatat al-Sharq*, 7/6 (15 March 1913), p. 226.

Nawfal, Hind, 'Fa'ida Adabiyya', *al-Fatat*, 1/10 (1894), pp. 446–8.

Al-Tahtawi, Rifa'a Rafi', *Tahrir al-Mar'a al-Muslima: Kitab al-Murshid al-Amin fi Tarbiyat al-Banat wal-Banin*, ed. Yahya al-Shaykh (Beirut: Dar al-Buraq, 2000).

Tanus, Salma, 'Women's Education and Their Upbringing', *al-Muqtataf*, 8/4 (1884), pp. 234–5.

Wakid, Istir, 'Sultat al-Umm', *Lisan al-Hal*, no. 1329 (1891), p. 3.

———, 'Al-Umm fil-Bayt', *Lisan al-Hal*, no. 1326 (1891), p. 3.

———, 'Al-Umm fil-Bayt', *Lisan al-Hal*, no. 1328 (1891), p. 3.

———, 'Al-Umm fil-Bayt', *Lisan al-Hal*, no. 1377 (1891), p. 4.

Secondary Sources

Abou Hodeib, Toufoul, *A Taste for Home: The Modern Middle Class in Ottoman Beirut* (Stanford: Stanford University Press, 2017).

Atamaz-Hazar, Serpil, 'The Hands that Rock the Cradle will Rise: Women,

Gender, and Revolution in Ottoman Turkey, 1908–1918', PhD dissertation, the University of Arizona, 2010.

Aygül, Ceren, 'Change in the Status of Turkish Women during the Ottoman Modernization and Self-Evaluation of Women in Kadınlar Dünyasi of 1913', MA thesis, Middle East Technical University, 2016.

Baron, Beth, *Egypt as a Woman: Nationalism, Gender and Politics* (Berkeley: University of California Press, 2005).

———, *The Women's Awakening in Egypt: Culture, Society, and the Press* (New Haven: Yale University Press, 1994).

Booth, Marilyn, 'Woman in Islam: Men and the "Women's Press" in Turn-of-the-20th-Century Egypt', *International Journal of Middle East Studies*, 33/2 (2001), pp. 171–201.

Cochran, Judith, *Education in Egypt* (London: Croom Helm, 1986).

Cole, Juan Ricardo, 'Feminism, Class, and Islam in Turn of the Century Egypt', *International Journal of Middle East Studies*, 13/4 (1981), pp. 387–407.

Deguilhem, Randi, 'A Revolution in Learning? The Islamic Contribution to the Ottoman State Schools: Examples from the Syrian Provinces', in Ali Çaksu (ed.), *Proceedings of the International Congress on Learning and Education in the Ottoman World* (Istanbul: IRCICA, 2001), pp. 285–95.

Demirdirek, Aynur, 'In Pursuit of the Ottoman Women's Movement', in Zehra F. Arat (ed.), *Deconstructing Images of 'The Turkish Woman'* (New York: St. Martin's Press, 1998), pp. 65–81.

Elsadda, Hoda, 'Egypt', in Radwa Ashour, Ferial J. Ghazoul and Hasna Reda-Mekdashi (eds), *Arab Women Writers – A Critical Reference Guide 1873–1999*, trans. Mandy McClure (Cairo and New York: The American University in Cairo Press, 2008), pp. 107–8.

———, 'Gendered Citizenship: Discourses on Domesticity in the Second Half of the Nineteenth Century', *Hawwa*, 4/1 (2006), pp. 1–28.

Fortna, Benjamin C., 'Bonbons and Bayonets: Mixed Messages of Childhood in the Late Ottoman Empire and the Early Turkish Republic', in Benjamin C. Fortna (ed.), *Childhood in the Late Ottoman Empire and After* (Leiden and Boston: Brill, 2016), pp. 173–88.

———, *Imperial Classroom: Islam, the State, and Education in the Late Ottoman Empire* (Oxford: Oxford University Press, 2002).

Frierson, Elizabeth B., 'Women in Ottoman Intellectual History', in Elisabeth Özdalga (ed.), *Late Ottoman Society: The Intellectual Legacy* (London: Routledge Curzon, 2005), pp. 135–61.

Giladi, Avner, *Children of Islam: Concepts of Childhood in Medieval Muslim Society* (London: Macmillan, in association with St Antony's College, 1992).

———, 'Concepts of Childhood and Attitudes towards Children in Medieval Islam: A Preliminary Study with Special Reference to Reaction to Infant and Child Morality', *Journal of the Economic and Social History of the Orient*, 32/2 (1989), pp. 125–6.

Hanssen, Jens, and Max Weiss (eds), *Arabic Thought beyond the Liberal Age:*

Towards an Intellectual History of the Nahda (Cambridge: Cambridge University Press, 2016).
Hauser, Julia, Christian B. Lindner, and Esther Moller (eds), *Entangled Education: Foreign and Local Schools in Ottoman Syria and Mandate Lebanon* (19–20th centuries), (Beirut: Ergon Verlag Würzburg in Kommission, 2016).
Hilton, Mary, *Women and the Shaping of the Nation's Young: Education and the Public Doctrine in Britain, 1750–1850* (Hampshire: Ashgate, 2007).
Ibrahim, Ahmed Fekry, *Child Custody in Islamic Law: Theory and Practice in Egypt since the Sixteenth Century* (Cambridge, MA: Cambridge University Press, 2018).
Khater, Akram Fouad, '"House" to "Goddess of the House": Gender, Class, and Silk in 19th Century Mount Lebanon', *International Journal of Middle East Studies*, 28/3 (1996), pp. 325–48.
Meriwether, Margaret L., 'Women and Economic Change in Nineteenth-Century Syria – The Case of Aleppo', in Judith E. Tucker (ed.), *Arab Women: Old Boundaries, New Frontiers* (Bloomington and Indianapolis: Indiana University Press, 1993), pp. 65–83.
Al-Qiyadi, Sharifa, *Isham al-Katiba al-'Arabiyya fi 'Asr al-Nahda hatta 1914* (Malta: Sharikat Elga, 1999).
Russell, Mona L., 'Competing, Overlapping, and Contradictory Agendas: Egyptian Education under British Occupation, 1882–1922', *Comparative Studies of South Asia, Africa and the Middle East*, 21 (2001), pp. 50–60.
_____, *Creating the New Egyptian Women: Consumerism, Education, and National Identity: 1863–1922* (New York: Palgrave, 2004).
Thompson, Elizabeth, *Colonial Citizens: Republican Rights, Paternal Privilege, and Gender in French Syria and Lebanon* (New York: Columbia University Press, 2000).
Tucker, Judith E., *Women in Nineteenth Century Egypt* (Cambridge, MA: Cambridge University Press, 1985).
Yıldız, Hülya, 'Knowledgeable Ottoman Girls: Ottoman Women's Education in the Nineteenth Century', in Julia C. Paulk (ed.), *Dominant Culture and the Education of Women* (Newcastle: CSP, 2008), pp. 143–55.
Yousef, Hoda A., 'Reassessing Egypt's Dual System of Education under Isma'il: Growing *'Ilm* and Shifting Ground in Egypt's First Educational Journal, *Rawdat al-Madaris*, 1870–77', *International Journal of Middle East Studies*, 40 (2008), pp. 109–30.
Zachs, Fruma, 'Challenging the Ideal: al-Diya' as Labiba Hashim's Stepping Stone', in Börte Sagaster, Theoharis Stavridis, and Michalis N. Michael (eds), *Past and Present of the Press in the Middle East: Festschrift for Professor Martin Strohmeier* (Bamburg: University of Bamburg Press, 2017), pp. 219–36.
_____, 'Growing Consciousness of the Child in Ottoman Syria in the 19th Century: New Modes of Parenting and Education in the Middle Class', in Eli Podeh and Eyal Ginio (eds), *Researching Ottoman History: Studies in Honour of Amnon Cohen* (Leiden: Brill, 2013), pp. 113–30.

Zachs, Fruma, and Sharon Halevi, 'From *Difa' al-Nisa'* to *Mas'alat al-Nisa'* in Greater Syria: Readers and Writers Debate Women and their Rights, 1858–1900', *International Journal of Middle East Studies*, 41/4 (2009), pp. 615–33.

Zeren Enis, Ayşe, *Everyday Lives of Ottoman Muslim Women: Hanımlara Mahsus Gazete (Newspaper for Ladies) (1895–1908)* (Istanbul: Libra Kitapçılık ve Yayıncılık, 2013).

Glossary

Note: This glossary focuses on children and childhood related terms.

baligh	physically mature boy/girl
bar mitzvah	a coming of age ritual for Jewish boys who reach the age of thirteen
bayt al-ta'lim	house of teaching
beslemes	foster daughters
buluğ	puberty
cariye	female (child or adult) slave
çocuk hizmetçi	girls working as domestic labourers
çora	male child slave captured during slaving raids, usually those aged between seven up to maturity
darüleytam	orphanage
devke	young female slave from seven up to the age when they could have sexual relations
devşirme	child levy
dogma	male or female child slaves who were born to slave mothers and slave fathers in seventeenth-century Crimea. Slaves were recorded as *dogma* from birth until six or seven years of age
dogma–çora	male slaves born in Crimea, but no longer infants
emred, şabb-ı emred, oğlan	beardless youth, young boy
ergenlik	puberty
evlatlık	foster child
falaka	bastinado, foot whipping

Glossary

fesh-i icar	wage contract
gulam	male (child or adult) slave
harcırah/masarıf-ı rahiyye	travel expenses for the person accompanying girls who were sent to Istanbul for domestic labour
havace	teacher
hoca/hodja	Muslim schoolmaster
ıskat-ı cenin	abortion or miscarriage
ıslahhanes	reformatories, vocational orphanages
icar	labour hiring
icar-ı sagir/e	hiring of child labour
'iqab tabi'i	'positive' punishment
kafil	guardian or sponsor
kebir	older child, mature (lit. large)
kız	girl, daughter
koğuş	barracks-inspired dormitories for female labourers
kuttab	Qur'anic school
madrasa	school (primary or higher education)
maktab	primary school
masum	a breastfed infant aged up to three years old (lit. innocent)
melamdim	teachers of the very young in the Jewish community
mu'allim	teacher
mu'allimhane	teacher's house
muderris	teacher
murahık/a	novices on the verge of puberty, between the ages of nine and fifteen and still not having shown the physical signs of puberty
mücerred	unmarried young male still living under his father's roof, adolescents
mücerredlik	adolescence
müderris	instructor in a madrasa
mümeyyiz/e	child who reached puberty
na-reşide	someone who is not physically and mentally mature
nafaqa	alimony
Nizarit Amwal al-Aytam	administration of Orphans' Funds that was established in 1851; the supervision of

Glossary

	orphans' assets moved from the *Shari'ah* courts to this administration
oğlan, oğul	son, adolescent boy
oğlancık, uşak	refers to the tender ages of childhood
potur oğlan	the sons of the Bosnian families who had converted to Islam
rashid/reşid	mentally mature
rushd	maturity
sabi	infant
sabwa	youth
sagir	minor child, juvenile
sıbyan mektebi	elementary schools
sicill/sijill	Islamic court records
Sunduq al-Aytam	Orphans' Treasury
sünnet	circumcision
Talmud Torah le-ketanim	Torah elementary school for very young Jewish boys, which also operated under the Ottoman rule
tarbiya	upbringing
tufuliyya	infancy
wasiyy mukhtar	chosen legal guardian
wilayat al-mal	guardianship over the property
wilayat al-nafs	guardianship over persons
yamak	auxiliary troop (lit. assistant)
yaya	foot soldier
yaya-müsellem	peasant militia system to gather an army
yeshiva	Jewish boy school following elementary school, which also operated under the Ottoman rule
yetim/yatim	orphan

Notes on Contributors

Yahya Araz is an Associate Professor of Education at Dokuz Eylül University (Izmir). He lectures on Ottoman History with an emphasis on the early modern period. He is particularly interested in the history of children and childhood in the Ottoman Empire and is the author of *Osmanlı Toplumunda Çocuk Olmak: 16. Yüzyıldan 19. Yüzyıl Başlarına* (2013, republished 2017). Other topics he has written about include non-Muslims, women and slavery. His latest book is *Osmanlı Istanbul'unda Çocuk Emeği* (Kitap Yayınevi, 2020).

Nazan Çiçek completed her PhD at the History Department of the School of Oriental and African Studies at the University of London in 2006. Her dissertation has been published under the title *The Young Ottomans: Turkish Critics of the Eastern Question in the Late Nineteenth Century*. She was awarded a postdoctoral fellowship by the British Academy and Economic and Social Research Council (ESRC) in 2008–9 for her project entitled 'How "Childish" were Ottoman/Turkish Children? Childhood as a Social Construction in the 19th-Century Ottoman Empire and the Early Republican Era?'. She has published articles on the political, social, cultural and intellectual history of the Ottoman Empire and Turkish Republic in several journals, including *Middle Eastern Studies* and *Études Balkaniques*. She currently teaches at Ankara University in the Faculty of Political Sciences.

Eleni Gara is a member of the Department of Social Anthropology and History at the University of the Aegean (Mytilene). She is the co-author of *Christians and Muslims in the Ottoman Empire* (with Yorgos Tzedopoulos, 2015, in Greek) and co-editor of *Popular Protest and Political Participation in the Ottoman Empire* (with M. Erdem Kabadayı and Christoph K. Neumann, 2011). Her other publications include articles and book chapters on the administration of justice, communal organisation, protest, revolt and rebellion, and history writing.

Colin Heywood is Emeritus Professor of Modern French History at the University of Nottingham. His research on childhood has led to publications including *Childhood in Nineteenth-Century France* (1988) and *Growing Up in Modern France* (2007). He has also written two more general works on the subject, *A History of Childhood: Children and Childhood in the West from Medieval to Modern Times* (2018) and *Childhood in Modern Europe* (2018).

Leyla Kayhan Elbirlik is an Assistant Professor at Özyeğin University. She holds a PhD from Harvard University and specialises in Ottoman History, Middle Eastern and Islamic History, the History of the Family, the History of Childhood and Parenting, and Women and Gender Studies. Her most recent publications include 'Reflections of Modernity in the Eighteenth Century: The Specialization of the Davud Paşa Court in Marriage-Related Disputes', *Archivum Ottomanicum*; 'Dialogue Beyond Margins: Patronage of Chief Eunuchs in the late 16th Century Ottoman Court', *Sanat Tarihi Yıllığı*; 'The Chivalric Ethos and Reflections of Masculinity in Early Anatolian Frontier Culture', *Journal of Turkish Literature* (Winter 2012). She has also co-edited, with M. Baha Tanman, a book titled *The Balat Ilyas Bey Complex: History, Architecture, Restoration* in 2011. Kayhan-Elbirlik is currently a collaborator in PLOTINA (promoting gender balance and inclusion in research, innovation and training), an EU Horizon 2020 project.

İrfan Kokdaş is an Assistant Professor of History at Izmir Katip Çelebi University specialising in the early modern economic transition in the Ottoman world. He was awarded his doctoral degree (dissertation titled 'When the Countryside is Free: Urban Politics, Local Autonomy and the Changing Social Structure in Ottoman Salonika, 1740–1820') at Binghamton University, New York. He has published several articles on the socio-economic history of the Ottoman Balkans and Western Anatolia (such as 'Land Ownership, Tax Farming and the Social Structure of Local Credit Markets in the Ottoman Balkans, 1685–1855' in *Financial History Review* and a forthcoming chapter, 'Sheep, Cotton, Wheat and Commerce: Changes and Continuities in the Demo-economic System of Çiftliks in Western Anatolia During the 1745–1845 Period').

Notes on Contributors

Elma Korić obtained her MSc diploma in History in 2006, and her PhD in History from the University of Sarajevo in 2012. Since 2000 she has been at the Oriental Institute in Sarajevo. The scope of her research is the history of Bosnia and Herzegovina during the early modern period and under the Ottoman administration. She has published a monograph titled *Životni put prvog beglerbega Bosne: Ferhad-paša Sokolović (530–1590)*, posebna izdanja XLIV, Oriental Institute of Sarajevo, Sarajevo, 2015, papers in both Bosnian and English and has participated in many academic conferences.

Ruth Lamdan was a lecturer for many years in the Department of Jewish History at Tel-Aviv University on subjects concerning Mediterranean Jewish society, especially in the Ottoman Empire following the expulsion of the Jews from Spain (1492). She published many articles and encyclopaedic entries in Hebrew and English, as well as two books: *A Separate People – Jewish Women in Palestine, Syria and Egypt in the 16th Century* (2000) and *Sefer Tikkun Soferim of Rabbi Itzhak Tzabah* (2009). The latter is an edited collection of 100 Hebrew legal bills from 1635. Currently, she is a Research Member in the Goldstein-Goren Diaspora Research Centre at Tel-Aviv University.

Nicoleta Roman is a researcher at the 'Nicolae Iorga' Institute of History in Bucharest under the auspices of the Romanian Academy. Her areas of expertise are social and cultural history; women, family and childhood history; micro-history and the history of pre-modern and modern Romania. Following on from her PhD dissertation on women in nineteenth-century Wallachia, she developed an interest in two related subjects: childhood history and welfare systems. Her main publications include *Orphans and Abandoned Children in European History: Sixteenth to Twentieth Centuries* (2017) (as editor); '*Deznădăjduită muiere n-au fost ca mine*'; *Femei, onoare și păcat în Valahia secolului al XIX-lea* (Women, Honour and Sin in 19th century, 2016) (as author); and *Copilăria Românească între familie și societate (secolele XVII–XX)* (Romanian Childhood between Family and Society (17th–20th centuries), 2015) (as editor). She has published extensively in academic journals such as *The History of the Family*, *Popolazione e Storia* and *Annales de Démographie Historique*.

Cahit Telci is a Professor of History at Izmir Katip Çelebi University. He obtained his PhD from Ege University, with a thesis entitled 'XV–XVI. Yüzyıllarda Ayasuluğ Kazası'. His research focuses on the early modern Ottoman world, utilising a broad range of Ottoman archival sources. He has published extensively on such topics as confiscation (*müsadere*), endowments and the nature of cadastral surveys of the fifteenth and sixteenth centuries. He is the author of 'Halil Beğ Defteri: Fetihten Sonra Aydın Sancağının İlk Mufassal Tahrir Defteri 1425–1430' and 'Ücra Yerde ve Deniz Kenarında İhtiyatlu Mahalde Bir Şehir Ayasuluğ'.

Didem Yavuz Velipaşaoğlu obtained her master's degree from the Architectural Design Program of Istanbul Bilgi University in 2008. As a Fulbright Scholar, she received her PhD from the joint programme at New Jersey Institute of Technology and Rutgers University with a dissertation titled 'Crafting an Empire: Hereke Factory Campus (1842–1914)'. She has lectured at Izmir University of Economics, taking classes on Architectural Design Studios and Art and Architectural History. Her publications include 'Weaving for War and Peace: Hereke Factory Campus (1912–1918)', *Cihannüma*, 2018; 'Casa del Fascio: Tortular ve Maskeler' (*Casa del Fascio, the Residues and the Masks*), *Betonart*, 2009; 'Mimarlık–Sanat Birlikteliğinde 1950–70 Aralığı' (*Art and Architecture Association in between 50s to 70s*), *Mimarlık*, 2008.

Fırat Yaşa is a member of the History Department at Düzce University (Turkey). He received his PhD in Ottoman History from Sakarya University in 2017. His main interests encompass the early modern Ottoman Empire and Crimean Khanate (1500–1700), focusing on subjects such as violence, fear, emotions, death, loyalty and social statuses. Slaves' private life and their expectations are also included in his academic studies. Some of the articles he has published include 'Desperation, Hopelessness, and Suicide: An Initial Consideration of Self-Murder by Slaves in Seventeenth-Century Crimean Society', *Turkish Historical Review*; 'Did Kirazuy Have to Divorce Her Non-Muslim Husband?: A Controversial Case of Apostasy and Conversion to Islam in the Bahçesaray Court', *Al-Qalam*. He has also edited a volume with Yağcı Zübeyde Güneş entitled *Slavery in the Ottoman Empire: Trade, Captivity and Daily Life* (2017).

Mahmoud Yazbak is a Professor of Middle Eastern History at the University of Haifa, teaching Palestinian History. He headed the department of Middle Eastern and Islamic Studies at the university, as well as the MISAI (Middle Eastern and Islamic Studies Association in Israel). He is the author of *Haifa in the Late Ottoman Period, 1864–1914: A Muslim Town in Transition* (1998); and of *The City of Oranges, Jaffa 1700–1840, Civilization and Society* (2019); and edited, with Yifaat Weiss, *Haifa Before & After 1948, Narratives of a Mixed City* (2011). He publishes frequently on social history and issues concerning modern Palestinian society.

Gülay Yılmaz is an Associate Professor at the Department of History, Akdeniz University. She completed her PhD at McGill University in 2011. While writing her dissertation on the social and economic roles of the janissaries in seventeenth-century Istanbul, she won a Canadian Government SSHRC doctoral fellowship and an RCAC residential fellowship at Koç University. Yılmaz was a 2018–19 Fulbright Visiting Scholar at CMES, Harvard University, studying the early modern *devşirme* system in the Ottoman Empire. She has published several articles and book chapters on the recruitment process of *devşirme*s and its impact on local politics, the janissary involvement on the urban culture and economy of seventeenth-century Istanbul and early modern popular protests in Istanbul.

Fruma Zachs is a Professor of History in the department of Middle Eastern and Islamic Studies at the University of Haifa, where she completed her PhD. Her postdoctoral studies were at St Antony's College (Oxford). She is the author of *The Making of a Syrian Identity – Intellectuals and Merchants in Nineteenth-Century Beirut* (2005) and co-author of *Gendering Culture in Greater Syria: Intellectuals and Ideology in the Late Ottoman Period* (2015). She is also co-editor of *Ottoman Reform and Muslim Regeneration* (2005). Zachs specialises in the *nahda* period (Arab Awakening) in Greater Syria and Egypt. Her research focuses on intellectual, social, cultural and gender perspectives and the history of children and childhood in late Ottoman Syria. She has published many articles on these topics in leading journals.

Index

Note: page numbers in **bold** refer to figures and those in *italic* refer to tables

abandonment, 13, 32, 38–9, 200
'Abbas School, 368
'Abd al-Hadi (family), 223, 224
abortion, 111–12
Absalom Monument (Jerusalem), 345
abuse, 197–8
   of girls in domestic service, 205–6, 208–9
   see also corporal punishment
adabiyya, 373
adolescence and adolescents, 6, 33, 157
   Jews and Judaism, 345–6
   in Ottoman registers, 66–7
   in peasant militia registers, 67–9, 71
   rebelliousness, 345–6
   as a separate category to childhood, 9–12, 58
Adrianople, Treaty of, 153
adulthood/adult(s) *see* fatherhood; motherhood; parents/parental relations
Aegean, 15, 88, 90
Africa, 33, 44, 185, 336
age, 57
   and adolescence, 66–7
   categories, 8, 9, 11, 15, 58, 62, 71, 105, 178
   child levies, 244, 248, *249*, *252*, 254
   of discernment, 9, 16, 33, 155, 157
   of juvenile delinquents, 11, 13, 152, 155–7, 159, 162, 165–6
   at marriage, 11, 23n, 24n, 33–4, 112, 345, 346
   of majority, 33
   in peasant militia registers, 63–6, *64*, 67–72
   of sexual maturity, 11, 33, 178, 180
agency, 2, 3, 91, 302, 366
agent(s), 1, 2, 5, 17, 86, 91
Akçakızanlık, 58
Aksoy, Mehmet, 295
Albania, 7, 77, 243–4
alcohol, 160–3
Alexandria (İskenderiye), 243, 370
alhamijado, 323
Amin, Qasim, 366
Anatolia, 197, 202, 211
   migration of girls to Istanbul, 201–6
   poverty, 198–201
Anderson, Michael, 36, 130
Andrews, Walter, 138
Ankara, 201, 202
Antun, Farah, 365
apprenticeship *see* labour
Araz, Yahya, 8, 17, 20–1n, 42, 143, 196–219, 265–6
Ariès, Philippe, 4, 9, 12, 36, 130–1, 137
   Centuries of Childhood: A Social History of Family Life, 2
   L'Enfant et la vie amiliale sous l'ancien régime, 31
Arıkan, Muzaffer, 61, 62

Index

Aristotle, 141
Armenians, 8, 45, 86, 90, 111, 189, 264
army *see* conscription of children
Ashkenazi, R. Israel, 340
Asia, 31, 33, 44
askeri, 104, 106, 113, 114
Athens, 15, 77, 79–82, 87, 88, 92
Atuf, Nafı, 302–3
Augustine, Saint, 34
Austrian Empire, 153, 158
autobiography *see* Skouzes, Panayis, autobiography
avant-gardes, demographic, 122
Avicenna, 141
Avlonya (Vlore), 244
Aydemir, Şevket Süreyya, 45
Aydın, 58, 59, 63, *64*, 66, 67, 69

baccalauréat (examination), 46
badaniyya, 372
Bakhchysarai, 189
Balkans, 5, 104
  socio-economic status and demographic transformation, 113–21
Baltacıoğlu, İsmail Hakkı, 301–2
Banja Luka, 326, 327, 328
Barbu Ştirbey, 156
Barkley, Henry C., 198–9
Baron, Beth, 367, 371, 380n
Basheski, Molla Mustafa, 321, 322, 324, 325, 326, 330–1n
Basil, Saint, 155
bastinado, 43, 84, 291, 296, 297–303
Bayezid II, Sultan, 58
Baz, Jurji Niqula, 369–70
Behar, Cem, 5, 35, 103–4
Behcetü'l-Fetava, 136, 146n, 147n
Beirut, 367, 369
Belgrade (Belgrad), 243
Benveniste, Hayim, 339
Berlin, Treaty of, 153
Besim Ömer (Akalın), 111
beslemes, 38, 211
beşe, 114
Biga, 59, 63, *64*, 65, 70
biopolitics, 241–2, 289, 290
birth control, 103, 110
Black Sea, 181, 182, 275

body politics, 239–40
  ages and colouration, 248–50, **249**, **250**, **251**, **252**, 253–4
  controlling the body: circumcision, 255–6, **257**
  devşirme ideal candidates and proper bodies, 245–55, **249**, **250**, **251**, **252**, **253**
  regulation of children's bodies, 265, 270–2
  relationship between the *devşirme* body and Ottoman authorities, 241–2
  religion, 249, 251–3, **253**
  state surveillance and levy registers, 242–4
  see also corporal punishment
Bolayır, Ali Ekrem, 294
Bolu, 59, 68, 131
Book of Morals, 342–3
bosančica (Bosnian script), 323, 329
Bosnia, 7, 154, 251, 325–6
  books and transcribing activities, 327–8
  education in the early modern period, 315–35
  girls' education, 323–5
  *madrasa*s, 325–6
  primary schools (*maktab*s), 316–23
Bosnia and Herzegovena *see* Bosnia; Herzegovina (Hersek)
Bouvier, Jeanne, 40–1, 42–3
boys/boyhood
  Jewish boys and education, 339–42
  rebelliousness, 345–6
  slaves, 178
  working Jewish boys, 346–7
  see also Skouzes, Panayis, autobiography; sons
Bozkurt, Fatih, 106
Britain, 205, 207
Brodhead, Richard H., 294, 297
brokers, 202
Bucharest, 154, 163
Bukovina, 152–3
Bulgaria, 34, 111, 112, 121, 155
buluğ, 9, 23n, 73n
Bursa, 198, 200, 244, 248, 265, 268, 298
al-Bustani, Butrus, 365, 366, 375

Index

cadastral surveys (*tahrir defteri*), 57, 69
caning *see* corporal punishment
Caragea Laws (1818) *see* Romania
cariye, 144, 178, 182–3, 188, 268
Caro, Yosef, 339
Carol I of Hohenzollern-Sigmaringen, 153
Catholics, 33, 34, 86, 90
Cennetten Çıkma, 301
Chalkis, 87, 88, 89, 90, 91
Charron, Pierre, 37
Chernomen (Çirmen), 58, 59
child labour *see* labour
child marriage *see* marriage
child-rearing, 130–1, 364–7, 371
    division in parental roles and parental love, 134–40
    fatherly advice to sons, 140–5
    hygiene and health, 372–3
    Vehbi's *Lütfiyye*, 133–45
    see also corporal punishment
child slave *see* slavery
childhood and children
    childhood as an age of deficiency, 91
    children and family life, 36–9
    children as a burden, 32
    comparative perspectives, 31–54
    conceptions of childhood, 31–2, 292, 302
    cultural attitudes towards, 6–7
    duality between childhood and children, 3–4
    extent of childhood, 32–4
    modern notion of, 18, 293
    nature of the child, 34–5
    notions of childhood as historical constructs, 83
    research on, 2–3
    as a separate category to adolescence, 9–12
    see also demographic roots of childhood; *sagir* child
China, 31–2
Chios, 153, 341
Christianity/Christians, 32, 33, 34, 153, 221, 270
    in Athens, 88–90, 94n
    and child conscription, 251–3, **253**, 256
    forced labour, 268–9

chronicles, 183, 325, 326, 330–1n
circumcision, 255–6, **257**
civil laws, 157
civil servants, 82, 196–7, 202, 204
cizye (poll tax), 83–4
colonial regimes, 40, 44
Committee of Union and Progress (CUP), 11–12
conscription of children, 6, 11, 12, 15, 17, 239–63
    ages and colouration, 248–50, **249**, **250**, **251**, **252**, 253–4
    attachment, 245
    body politics, 239–40
    controlling the body: circumcision, 255–6, **257**
    as enslavement, 240–1, 245, 259n
    ideal candidates and proper bodies, 245–55, **249**, **250**, **251**, **253**
    relationship between the *devşirme* body and Ottoman authorities, 241–2
    religion, 249, 251–3, **253**
    state surveillance and levy registers, 242–4
    see also peasant militia
Constantinople, 153, 223, 320; *see also* Istanbul
Cook, M. A., 66
corporal punishment, 13, 18, 37–8, 43, 45, 84, 92, 157, 289–312, 345, 367, 373
    abolition of, 290, 291
    authoritarianism, 293, 294
    caning, 297
    and control over children's bodies, 290–1
    disciplinary intimacy theory, 294
    forms of, 293
    memories of, 294–7
    as ordinary and child-rearing violence, 292–3
    school beatings, 297–303, 321
    Turkish Value of Children (VOC) study, 293
countrymen, 201–2, 203, 206, 211, 247
courts, 11
    records, 4, 16–17, 105, 106, 155, 198, 206

Index

courts *(cont.)*
   and orphans, 223, 225-6, 230-1
   and slavery, 180, 181, 183, 184-7, 188
   see also Shari'ah court records
craftsmen, 85, 86, 92, 347
Crimea, 12
   changes in slave status, 186-9
   child slavery, 177-95
   cultural belonging and children, 182-3
   Shari'ah court records, 179-84, 186, 187-8, 190n
   slave raids, 180-1, 182
   slaves as sexual objects, 180, 184-6
   social realities and children, 180-2
   violence and child slaves, 183-4, 186
Crimean Tatars, 181, 183, 189-90, 242
Crimean War (1853-6), 153
Criminal Code of Romania 1852, 11, 16
criminal liability, 4; *see also* juvenile delinquents
Criminal Register (1852), 162
criminality
   juvenile criminality *see* juvenile delinquents
   Romanian sources, 154-5
cultural awareness, 177, 182-3
Cuno, Kenneth, 121
custody, 4, 9, 14, 16, 23n, 136
Cuza Alexandru Ioan, 156

Çankırı, 201
Çelebi (Chelebi), Evliya, 184, 185, 317, 326
Çiçek, Nazan, 13, 18, 37, 289-312
çift
   çift-hane, 57
   tam çift, 57
Çocuk Esirgeme Kurumu, 304
çora (child slaves), 178, 179, 183, 186, 187, 188, 189

Dadyan, Hovhannes, 264, 268, 281n
Danubian Principalities of Moldavia *see* Moldavia
darüleytam (orphanage) *see* orphanages and orphans
Darwazah (family), 221
daughters, 9-10, 106, 136-7, 202-3, 204, 210, 347

David, Geza, 57
Dean, John, 79, 93n
dellal, 202, 205
Demidov, Anatol, 160
demographic roots of childhood, 103-28
   demographic trends and wealth, 107, *108, 109*
   expectant couples and wealth, 107, 110-11
   methodological problems and sources, 105-6
   probate inventories, 105-6, 107, 110-11, 122-3n
   socio-economic dynamics and demographic structures, 111-13
   socio-economic status and demographic transformation in the Balkans, 113-21, *115, 116*
   status and numbers of surviving children, 114-17, *115, 116*
   tendency of the wealthy to have fewer children, 120-2
   titles, use of, 113-14, *115, 116*, 124n
derdest defters, 65
Devellioğlu, Ferit, 70
devke (child slaves), 178, 179
   and sexuality, 184-6
devşirme system, 6, 7, 12, 17, 239-63
   ages and colouration, 248-50, **249, 250, 251, 252,** 253-4
   attachment, 245
   controlling the body: circumcision, 255-6, **257**
   as enslavement, 240-1, 245, 259n
   ideal candidates and proper bodies, 245-55, **249, 250, 251, 252, 253**
   relationship between the *devşirme* body and Ottoman authorities, 241-2
   religion, 249, 251-3, **253**
   state surveillance and levy registers, 242-4
Dickens, Charles, 39
discernment, age of, 9, 16, 33, 155, 157
diseases, 274, 275-6, 372
divorce, 16, 136-7
dogma (child slaves), 178, 179, 182-3, 186, 187, 189

Index

Doğru, Halime, 61
domestic service, 17, 38–9, 196–219, 266
  abuse, 205–6, 208–9
  becoming settled in Istanbul, 211–12
  contracts, 207, 210
  families hiring out children, 200, 201, 202–3, 204
  intermediaries, 201–2, 205–6
  living and working in Istanbul, 206–11
  migration of girls to Istanbul, 201–6, 211
  probation period, 207
  relations with host families, 209–11
  running away, 205, 208, 209
  social morality problems, 204–6
  wages and fees, 202, 204, 207, 210, 212
dormitories, 42, 272–4, **273**, 279–80
Douglas, Kate, 81
Dörtdivan, 201, 202
Duben, Alan, 5, 35, 103–4
Duygulu, Behiç, 295

education, 4, 5, 6–7, 13, 18, 82, 137, 177
  archival sources and literature on, 316
  books and transcribing activities, 327–8
  in Bosnia, early modern period, 315–35
  and ceremonial events, 322–3
  early Jewish education, 338–9
  emotional bonds between teachers and pupils, 320–1
  fathers' involvement, 342–3, 349
  funding for, 315–16, 318, 321–2, 323–4, 328, 340–1
  girls' education, 7, 19, 43, 45–6, 323–5, 328–9, 347–8
  girls' education in Egypt, 367–9
  girls' education, men's view of in the *nahda* period, 363–7
  Greater Syria, 19, 364, 366, 370
  al-Hashim's concepts, philosophy and vision for girls' education, 369–78
  in Jewish society, sixteenth to eighteenth centuries, 336–62
  *madrasa*s, 182, 190–1n, 315, 316, 325–6, 328
  methods, 43, 45, 317, 320, 344–5
  Ottoman Public Education Regulations, 1869, 7, 45

  Ottomanism, 44, 45
  primary and secondary education, 43–6
  primary schools (*maktab*s), 182, 315, 316–23, 323–4, 328, 368
  religious education, 12, 43, 45, 180, 317
  state policy, 44, 45
  Talmud Torah, 338, 339–42, 349
  Talmud Torah Hagadol, Salonica, 343–4
  teachers, 43, 82, 84, 272, 295, 298–9, 300, 318–21, 323, 324, 325–6, 329, 338, 340, 341–2, 372
  women's role in, 323–4, 329, 338, 363–86
Edwards, Jonathan, 34
Efendi, Ahmet Mithad, 296
Efendi, Ebussuud, 71
Efendi, Selim Sabit, 298–9
ego documents, 2, 5
Egypt, 154, 364, 365, 366, 370
  economy, 371
  girls' education, 367–9
  al-Hashim's views on education in Egypt, 369–78
Egyptian University, 369, 370–1
Elbasan (İlbasan), 243
Elbirlik, Leyla Kayhan, 16, 129–50
Elifoğlu, Eugenie, 62
emanetçi, 202, 205
Emecen, Feridun, 68
Émile see Rousseau, Jean-Jacques
emotions, 2–3, 8, 294
  bonds between teachers and pupils, 320–1
  child-rearing manuals, 130–1
  division in parental roles and parental love, 134, 135–40
  emotionology, 134, 146n
  expression of, 374
  fatherly advice to sons, 140–5
  of slaves, 181–2
  ties to parents, 12–13, 15–16, 80, 129–50, 210–11
  Vebhi's *Lütfiyye*, 133–45
employment *see* labour
emred, şabb-ı emred (beardless youth), 9, 22–3n, 67
endowment deeds, 18, 316

Index

Enlightenment, 35
enslavement *see* slavery
Erbaş, Ali, 303
ergen/ergenlik, 9; *see also* adolescence and adolescents
eşkal defteri, 239
Euboea (Eğriboz), 77, 82, 87, 88, 91, 243
Evered, Emine, 45

factories *see* labour
falaka see bastinado
families, 3, 4, 5, 364
  child-rearing manuals, 130–1
  children and family life, 36–9
  division in parental roles and parental love, 134, 135–40
  emotional ties between children and parents, 12–13, 15–16, 36–8, 80, 129–50
  family ideology, 121–2
  family planning practices, 103
  fatherly advice to sons, 140–5
  murder in the family, reasons for, 159–65
  recasting the patriarchal family through education, 369–78
  tendency for fewer children, 103–4
  Vehbi's *Lütfiyye*, 133–45
famines, 198–9, 200–1
Faraji, Yaakov, 340
farming, 33, 40–1, 46, 67, 159
  soldier/militia farms, 60–1, 62–3, 66, 70
fashion, 376, **376**, **377**
Fatat al-Sharq, 370, 375–6, **376**, **377**
fatherhood, 12, 16, 345, 346
  advice to sons, 140–5
  child maintenance costs, 136
  children envisioned in the father's image, 137–8
  death of a father, 221–2
  involvement in education, 342–3, 349
  Jewish fathers, 339
  murder of fathers by sons, 161–4; *see also* parricide
  pride and love, 138–40
  primary care-takers, 137
  relationship with sons, 133–45
fatwas, 129–30, 136, 137, 225

fertility, 5, 16, 46, 103, 104, 111–12
  and status, 113, 120–1
flogging *see* corporal punishment
folk songs, 177, 178, 181, 200
forced labour *see* labour; slavery
Fortna, Benjamin, 35, 46
  Childhood in the Late Ottoman Empire and After, 4–5
fostering, 38–9, 211, 266
Foucault, Michel, 241–2, 289–90
free labour *see* labour
French Penal Code (1810), 152, 156–7, 165
Frenkel, Miriam, 346

Gara, Eleni, 13, 15, 33, 77–99
Gelibolu (Gallipoli), 59
Geltner, Guy, 290, 295
gender
  and labour, 267
  segregation, 89–90, 91, 134, 142–3
Gennep, Arnold Van, 33
Gerede, 201, 204
Germany, 37, 44, 272
Al-Ghazali, 32, 318
Ghazi Husrev Beg, 325–6, 327
Giladi, Avner, *Children of Islam: Concepts of Childhood in Medieval Muslim Society*, 4
Ginio, Eyal, 5
girls
  body regulations at the Hereke factory, 265, 270–2
  domestic service, 17, 38–9, 196–219
  education, 7, 9, 43, 45–6, 323–5, 328–9, 347–8
  education in Egypt, 367–9
  education, men's view of in the *nahda* period, 363–7
  al-Hashim's concepts, philosophy and vision for girls' education, 369–78
  at the Hereke factory, 267, 268–70, **275**, **279**
  migration of girls to Istanbul, 201–6
  slaves, 178
Goddard, Chris, 289, 305
Golescu, Iordache, 159
Gosse, Edmund, 38

Index

Gökçe, Turan, 68
Gözek, Melahat, 299
Graziano, Anthony, 290
Greece
   Greek Revolution (1821), 15, 77
   Greek War of Independence (1821–30), 82
   Revolution of the 3rd of September 1843, 82
Greek Orthodox Church, 82, 83, 90
Grier, Beverly, 40
The Guide to the Law (1652), 155, 156, 157
gulam, 268
Gürbüz Türk Çocuğu, 304
Gürpınar, Hüseyin Rahmi, 301

Ha-Cohen, Eliya, 350n
Hacı Ali Haseki, 77, 80–1, 82, 85, 88–9, 90, 92
Hadith, 141, 222, 316
hafız, 114
Hajj Bacı Kadun, 325, 329
Hajnal, John, 33–4
halakhic sources, 337, 348
Hamid, 59, 61, 68
Hamidiye Etfal Hastane-i Alisi, 275
hammam (public baths) *see* public baths
Hammarberg, Thomas, 304
Hanımlara Mahsus Gazete, 205, 376, 382n
al-Hashim, Labiba Madi, 19, 367, 379
   concepts, philosophy and vision, 369–78
   Fatat al-Sharq, 370, 375–6, **376**, **377**
   The Little Orphan Girl, 374
Hatun, Ziya, 295
Hereke Hospital *see* hospitals
Hereke Imperial Factory *see* labour
Herzegovina (Hersek), 17
   conscripted children, 239–63
Heywood, Colin, 14–15, 31–54, 135–6
Himaye-i Etfal, 304
hoca, 114, 297
hospitals, 272–4
Hsiung, Ping-chen, 31–2
Humphries, Jane, 40
Hüdavendigar, 59, 60, 63, *64*
Hydra, 84, 86, 88, 91, 92

ıskat-ı cenin, 112
ıslahhanes, 39, 267
ıtkname/itakname, 187
icar, 202
   fesh-i icar, 207
   icar-ı sagir/e, 198
infant
   infant mortality, 38, 65, 111, 372
   infanticide, 159, 166–7n
   masum, 70
   sabi, 70
inscriptions, 12–13
Al-Isfahani, 318
Islam, 32, 34, 45, 90, 142, 239, 251–2 253, 254, 255, 345
   Islamic law, 8, 10, 33, 83, 89, 136
   and orphans, 221–3
   see also Muslims; Qur'an
Istanbul, 5, 6, 8, 17, 34, 38, 44, 103
   cemeteries, 12–13
   censuses, 11
   coffee houses, 203
   domestic service, 196–219
   families hiring out children, 200, 201, 202–3
   girls becoming settled in Istanbul, 211–12
   living and working in in domestic service in Istanbul, 206–11
   migration of girls to, 201–6, 211
Ivanova, Svetlana, 113
Izmir, 86, 87, 91, 92
Îndreptarea Legii *see Guide to the Law* (1652)

Jajce (Yayçe), 321–2
James, Allison, 2
janissaries, 6, 11, 17, 113, 114, 124n
   attachment, 245
   regulations for, 245–8, 250, 251–2, 253
Japan, 32, 36, 41–2, 44, 46
Jerusalem, 221, 222–3, 229, 338, 340, 341–3, 345, 346, 348
Jesus Christ, 34
Jews and Judaism, 7, 10–11, 18–19, 32, 33, 34
   Absalom Monument (Jerusalem), 345
   adolescence and adolescents, 345–6

Index

Jews and Judaism *(cont.)*
  bar mitzva, 340, 351n
  early education, 338–9
  education, sixteenth to eighteenth centuries, 336–62
  educational methods, 344–5
  fathers' involvement in education, 342–3, 349
  girls' education, 347–8
  Jewish law, 336, 338
  orphans, 347, 348
  sources on education, 336, 337
  Talmud Torah, 338, 339–42, 349
  Talmud Toraḥ Hagadol, Salonica, 343–4
  teachers, 338
  working boys, 346–7
juvenile delinquents, 11, 13, 16, 152
  classification of crimes, 156
  death sentences, 155–6
  law on criminality, 155–8, 165–6
  law on degrees of culpability, 155
  lists of Romanian minors condemned in 1853, 158–9, *158*
  murder in the family, reasons for, 159–65
  non-responsibility of minors, 157
  Romanian sources, 154–5
  supervision of, 156–7, 161, 164–5

Kabadayı, Erdem, 266, 269
kafil (guardian or sponsor), 222, 223–8
Kağıtçıbaşı, Çiğdem, 300
Karahisar, 58, 59, 60–1, 63, *64*, 65, 69, 111
Kardzhali riots, 105
Karesi, 59
Kaş, 58
Kastamonu, 208, 210, 215n, 268
katırcı, 205
Kavanin-i Yeniçeriyan, 245
kazak 182, 186
Kazım Karabekir, 307–8n
kebir child, 105
Keçecioğlu, Melih, 295
kemha, 272
Kenya, 44
kethuda, 114

Kethuda, Keyvan, 318–19, 322
Khuli, Jacob, 338
kız, 9–10
Kızılca, 58
Kitab fil Tarbiya, 371
*kocabaşı*s, 82
Kocaeli, 59
Kokdaş, İrfan, 8, 16, 35, 103–28
Kołodziejzyk, Dariusz, 181
Korić, Elma, 18, 43, 315–35
Koyuncu, Aşkın, 252
Krausman Ben-Amos, Ilana, 10, 71
kuttab, 367, 368, 369, 372, 378
Kütahya, 59, 63, *64*, 69–70
Kyustendil (Köstendil), 244

labour
  accommodation at the Hereke factory, 272–4, **273**, 279–80
  agriculture and handicraft trades, 40–1
  apprenticeship, 8, 12, 42, 85, 86–8, 89, 266, 347
  body regulations, 265, 270–2
  child and youth labour at the Hereke Factory, 266–70, **271**
  child labour, 7–8, 10, 12, 18, 86–8
  child labour literature, overview on, 265–6
  corvée, 8, 269
  in factories, 41–2
  forced labour, 8, 42, 266, 268–9
  foster-daughter labour, 266
  free labour, 196, 272
  gardens and land at the Hereke factory, 276–80, **277**, **278**, **279**, 281
  hospital at the Hereke factory, 274–6
  in industry, 41–3
  pastimes for children at the Hereke factory, **279**, 280
  sanitisation and recreation facilities, Hereke factory, 18, 264–88
  vocational education and training, 267–8
  wage labourers, 371
  wages, 202, 204, 207, 210, 212, 270, 326, 341–2
  working Jewish boys, 346–7
  see also domestic service; slavery
Lamdan, Ruth, 18–19, 336–62

Index

law
  Byzantine, 83, 155
  Eastern Roman *see* law, Byzantine
  Hanafi school, 83, 89, 136
  Islamic, 8, 10, 33
  Jewish, 336, 338
  Romanian *see* Romania
Lefebvre, Henri, 129
Legiuirea Caragea (Caragea Laws) *see* Romania
Lejeune, Philippe, 79
levy *see* conscription of children
liability *see* juvenile delinquents
libraries, 327
literacy, 43, 44, 369
Livi-Bacci, Massimo, 122
Lütfiyye see Vehbi, Sünbülzade
Lütfullah (son of Vehbi) *see* Vehbi, Sünbülzade
lycée, 44–5, 46

*madrasa*s, 182, 190–1n, 315, 316, 325–6, 328
magazines, 18, 35, 301, 302, 304
Mağmumi, Şerafeddin, 199
majority (legal), 83, 84
Makbul-i 'Arif, 328
Maksudyan, Nazan, 4, 19n, 21n, 22n, 25n, 38, 47n, 48n, 145n, 213n, 215n, 232n, 266, 282n
*maktab*s, 182, 315, 316–23, 323–4, 328
Malki, Refael Mordekhai, 347
Malthus/Malthusian, 104
marriage, 144, 271, 364, 366
  age at marriage, 11, 23n, 24n, 33–4, 112, 345, 346
  child marriage, 4, 10, 11, 14, 23n, 24n
  polygyny, 24n, 113
  remarriage, 112–13, 136
Martel, Monsieur, 269
masum, 70, 71
Mause, Lloyd De, 292
Mechling, Jay, 130
Mehmed II, Sultan, 58, 65, 251–2, 253
Meiji regime, 44, 46
melamed, 340, 342
memoirs, 2, 15, 18, 80, 81, 92, 289, 291, 295, 299, 300, 303

memory, 81
  autobiographical memory, 78–9
mensuhat registers, 61
Menteşe, 59
Meriwether, Margaret, 37
middle classes, 9, 45–6, 47, 122, 294, 363, 364, 371
Midhad Pasha, Governor, 267
migration, 197–8, 200
  of girls to Istanbul, 201–6, 211
Mikriyannis, Yannis, 81, 82
military *see* conscription of children
militia farms *see* farming
militia registers *see* peasant militia
Mislea, 157
modernisation and modernity, 5, 6, 7, 21–2n, 290
Moldavia, 153, 154, 178
monasteries, 86, 90, 92, 156, 157, 315, 316
  Snagov monastery, 162, 164
monks, 82, 91
mortality rates, 117, 120; *see also* infant mortality
Mostar, 316, 318, 319, 322–3, 326
motherhood, 16, 36, 135–6, 338, 366
  abuse of mothers, by sons, 160
  al-Hashim's concepts, philosophy and vision for girls' education, 369–78
  remarriage, 136
Mrs Beeton's Book of Household Management, 375, 382n
mu'allimhane, 315, 317
Muallim Mecmuası, 302
*mufassal defter*s, 67
Muhammad 'Ali, 368
muleteers, 202
murabaha, 224
musar books, 19, 337
Muslims, 33, 247
  and child conscription, 249, 251–3, **253**, 256
  and Christians, 88–90
  education, 43
  family size, 36
  marriage, 113
  orphans, 17, 220–35

mücerred, 33, 66
müderris, 133
mükatebe, 187
müzayaka, 200

Nabi (poet), 133, 143
Nablus, 112
  Muslim orphans, 220–35
  Shari'ah court records, 220–1, 223–4, 225–6, 227–8, 232n
nafaqa, 221, 227
Nafi Atuf (Kansu), 302
nahda period, 363–86
  girls' education in Egypt, 367–9
  al-Hashim's concepts, philosophy and vision for girls' education, 369–78
  men's view of women's and girls' education, 363–7
Namaste, Karen, 290
narration/narrative, 78–9
nasihatname, 133, 143
nationalism, 4, 5, 7, 363
Nawfal, Hind, 367–8
Naxos, 153
Neisser, Ulric, 78–9, 93n
Nesin, Aziz, 300
newborn, 37, 372
newspapers, 17, 18, 35, 196, 205, 367, 370, 376
Norway, 36
Numanzade, Ömer Faruk, 300

oğlan, 9–10
oğlancık, 9
Old Testament, 32
Olsen, Stephanie, *Childhood, Youth and Emotions in Modern History*, 3–4
Onur, Bekir, 4
Organic Regulations (1831) *see* Romania
orphanages and orphans, 4, 13, 17, 38–9, 39, 264, 270
  Administration of Orphans' Funds, 228–9
  bringing up orphans, 220–1
  establishment of orphanages, 221
  Islam and orphans, 221–3
  Jewish orphans, 347, 348
  kafil (guardians), 222, 223–8
  Muslim orphans, 220–35
  orphans' minority, end of, 230–1
  Orphans' Treasury, 229–30
  Ottoman reforms, 228–30
  poor orphans, 228
  property of orphans, 223–7, 229
  schools for orphans, 222–3
  vocational orphanages, 267–8
Orta Congar, 184
Otho, King of Greece, 82
Ottoman Empire, 1–2, 6, 34, 153
Ottoman Penal Code 1840, 157
Ottoman Penal Code 1858, 11, 16
Otyam, Fikret, 295–6
Özgüler, Huriye, 294–5
Özünlü, Emine, 65

paddling (caning) *see* corporal punishment
Palestine, Muslim orphans, 220–35
parents/parental relations, 374–5
  child rearing manuals, 130–1
  children's respect for parents, 143
  division in parental roles, 134
  division in parental roles and parental love, 135–8
  emotional bonds with children, 129–50
  fatherly advice to sons, 140–5
  Vehbi's *Lütfiyye*, 133–45
  youth and violence towards parents, 151–73
parricide, 16, 152, 155, 159, 162, 166
Pasha, Münif, 298
Pasha, Sadık Rıfat, 267
pastimes, 141–2, 143, **279**, 280
paternal authority, 83, 84, 91
patriarchy, 12–14, 366
  recasting the patriarchal family through education, 369–78
peasant militia, 57–76
  adolescence in Ottoman registers, 66–7
  adolescents in peasant militia registers, 67–9, 71
  children's ages, 57–8, 61–6, *64*, 70–1
  handicapped children, 62
  minors in peasant militia registers, 68–70
  peasant-militia system and its registers, 59–61

Index

record-keeping practices, 58–9, 59–61, 62–3, 65–6, 69–71
Peirce, Leslie, 34
penal codes, 11, 16, 156–7, 159
penalty/penalties, 155, 156–7, 269
   death sentences, 155–6
   see also corporal punishment
Phanariotes, 153
physical
   characteristics, 246–7
   health, 18, 35, 103, 241, 243, 265, 276, 319, 371, 372
   maturity, 230
piyade defters, 68
Plato, 141
poetry, 132
Polish-Lithuanian Commonwealth, 181
Pollock, Linda, 292
polygyny *see* marriage
potur oğlan, 251
poverty, 38–9, 84–5, 88, 92, 207, 223, 296
   in Anatolia, 198–201
   and infant mortality, 111
prisons, 39, 85, 158–9
probate inventories *see* demographic roots of childhood
Prophet, the, 89, 143, 222, 223, 225, 316–17
Prout, Alan, 2
Prussia, 44, 46
puberty, 9–10, 16, 32, 33, 71, 105
   and punishment, 157
public baths, 10, 89–90, 91, 185
Pulevskii, Savva Dmitrievich, 34

qadi, 131, 133, 220–1, 222, 223, 224, 226–8, 229
Qaysariyya, 220, 227
Quataert, Donald, 8, 36
Qur'an, 43, 45, 141, 222, 224–5, 226, 316, 318, 319, 325

Ragusa, 153
rashid, 220, 222, 230–1
Rasim, Ahmet, 299
Rauf, Mehmed, 296
rebellion, 10–11

recreation *see* pastimes
reformatories, 4, 6, 13
religious education *see* education
Richter, Jean Paul, 35
Roman, Nicoleta, 11, 16, 151–73
Romania
   Caragea Laws (1818), 155–6
   Criminal Code 1852, 11, 16, 152, 156, 157
   Criminal Register and Its Procedures (1852), 161
   juvenile delinquents, 152
   law on criminality, 155–8, 165–6
   lists of minors condemned in 1853, 158–9, *158*
   murder in the family, reasons for, 159–65
   non-responsibility of minors, 157
   Organic Regulations (1831), 153, 154, 156
   Penal Code (1865), 159
   sources on delinquency and criminality, 154–5
   Wallachia, province of, 152–4
Rousseau, Jean-Jacques, 138
   Émile or On Education, 35, 37, 134–5, 139
Rubin, Avi, 158
Rumelia, 197
rural areas, 159, 200; *see also* farming
Rus/Urus, 189
Ruse (Rusçuk), 16, 35, 104, 105
   demographic trends and wealth, 107, *108*, *109*
   expectant couples and wealth, 107, 110–11
   socio-economic dynamics and demographic structures, 111–13
   socio-economic status and demographic transformation, 113–21, *115*, *116*, *118*, *119*
Russell, Mona, 368
Russian Empire, 34, 153–4, 156, 158

sabi, 9
Safranbolu, 17, 211
sagir child/children, 9, 63, 65, 71, 105
   in peasant militia registers, 68–70

Index

Salonica, 342, 343–4
sanitary conditions *see* labour
Sarajevo, 316, 317, 319, 321, 324–5, 325–6, 327
Saruhan, 59, 69
Saunders, Bernadette, 305
schools, 7, 37, 82, 180, 190–1n
  corporal punishment, 82, 84, 295, 296–7, 297–303, 321
  emotional bonds between teachers and pupils, 320–1
  *madrasa*s, 182, 190–1n, 315, 316, 325–6, 328
  for orphans, 222–3
  primary and secondary education, 43–6
  primary schools (*maktab*s), 182, 190–1n, 315, 316–23, 323–4, 328, 368
  Qur'an schools, 43, 45
  regulations, 298
  sibyan schools, 298, 299
  see also Jews and Judaism
Schull, Kent, 4, 11, 157, 158
self-esteem, 373, 374
Sephardi/Sephardim, 336
Sertel, Yıldız, 294
Servet-i-Fünun, 270, 276, 277, 280
sex
  sexual desire, 89–90
  slaves as sexual objects, 180, 184–6
Seyfeddin, Ömer, 297
Shari'ah, 11, 17, 33, 135
  law, 9, 16
  and Muslim orphans, 220–35
Shari'ah courts and records, 129–30, 135–7, 136, 178, 221, 229, 232n, 338, 340, 341–2, 345, 346
  Crimea, 179, 180, 181–2, 183, 184, 186, 187–8, 190n
  Davudpaşa, 136
  Nablus, 220–1, 223–4, 225–6, 227–8
  Ordu, 17, 209
  Sofia, 105, 106
  Ruse, 105, 106, 112–13
  Vidin, 105, 106, 112, 114
Shilling, Chris, 290
Shorter, Edward, 36–7, 130–1
sicill/sijill, 220, 223, 229, 232n

Sirko, Ivan, 183
Skouzes, Panayis, autobiography, 10, 15, 33, 77–99
  childhood autobiography as a subgenre, 81
  Christianity and Muslims, 88–90
  conception of childhood as an age of deficiency, 91
  definition of autobiography, 79, 80
  description of a hard life, 84–6
  education, 82, 84
  from memory to life narrative, 78–9
  poverty, 84–6
  as a record of a personal and collective past, 80–3
  semi-adult status, 83–4
  target audience, 80–1
  working life, 86–8, 89
slavery, 3, 6, 7, 8, 12, 177–95, 196, 268
  ages of child slaves, 178
  changes in slave status, 186–9
  cultural backgrounds, 177
  cultural belonging and children, 182–3
  emotions, 181–2
  escapes, 177–8, 183
  freed slaves, 187–8
  inborn slaves, 16–17, 179, 189
  manumission contracts, 187
  religion, 178–9
  slave prices, 181, 197
  slaves as sexual objects, 180, 184–6
  social realities and children, 180–2
  suicide, 178, 180
  violence and child slaves, 183–4, 186
  see also conscription of children
Snagov monastery *see* monasteries
social cohesion, 18
social control, 18
Sofia, 16, 35, 104, 105, 107, 110–11
  demographic trends and wealth, 107, *108, 109*
  socio-economic dynamics and demographic structures, 111–13
  socio-economic status and demographic transformation, 113–21, *115, 116, 118*
soldiers *see* conscription of children; farming

Index

Sonbol, Amira El Azhary, 4
sons, 133–45
  abuse of mother, 160
  envisioned in the father's image, 137–8
  fatherly advice, 140–5
  fatherly love, 138–40
  murder of fathers by sons, 161–4
Spain, 44, 46, 336, 341
standardisation, 60, 272, 274, 280
status
  and fertility, 113, 120–1
  and numbers of surviving children, 114–17, *115*, *116*
  socio-economic status and demographic transformation, 113–21, *115*, *116*, *118*, *119*
Stearns, Carol, 134
Stearns, Peter, 134
Stone, Lawrence, 36–7
Sultanönü, 59, 63, *64*, 68
Sururi (poet), 132, 133
Sussman, George, 37
Süleyman, Avanzade, 121
Süleyman I, Sultan, 58, 65, 69, 71
Sümerbank, 265
sünnet see circumcision

şabb-ı emred (beardless youth), 9
Şerif, Ahmed, 199

Al-Tahtawi, Rif'a Rafi', 365–6
Talebe Defteri, 301
Talmud Torah see Jews and Judaism
Talmud Torah Hagadol see Jews and Judaism
Tanzimat period, 35, 46, 159, 199, 204, 221, 267, 290–9, 363
tarbiya, 372
Tekirdağ (Eastern Thrace), 59
Telci, Cahit, 15, 33, 57–76
Tepeyran, Ebubekir, Hazım, 300–1
Tezcan, Hülya, 4
timar, 59, 60, 61, 65
Tinos, 86
titles, 113–14, *115*, *116*, 124n
Todorova, Maria, 104, 112, 120, 121
Toledano, Ehud, 240, 245
Torah *see* Jews and Judaism

traditions, 32, 43, 88, 152, 157, 165, 245, 246, 301, 321, 322–3, 338
Transylvania, 153
trauma, 81
Travnik, 320, 327
Trikala (Tırhala), 244
trustees, 202
Tucker, Judith, 112
tufula, 371
tufuliyya, 372
Tunis, 154
Turkish Value of Children (VOC) study, 293
Tuzla, 316

Ukraine, 177, 178, 181, 183
ulema, 43, 131
upbringing *see* child-rearing
Usta, Mehmed, 88, 89, 91

Vatin, Nicolas, 12–13
Vehbi, Sünbülzade
  advice to Lütfullah (son), 140–5
  attire, views on, 142–3
  children envisioned in the father's image, 137–8
  on family life and a functional household, 143–4
  'ideal' child (1700–1800), 129–50
  life and career, 131–3
  Lütfiyye, 16, 131, 133–45
  marriage, views on, 144
  parental love and divided roles, 135–40
  pastimes and interests, views on, 141–2, 143
  on respect for parents, 143
  study of sciences, views on, 140–1
Velihodžić, Mehmed Razi, 324, 326, 327
Velipaşaoğlu, Didem Yavuz, 18, 264–88
Velyčko, Samijlo, 183
Vidin, 16, 35, 104, 105, 124n
  demographic trends and wealth, 107, *108*, *109*
  expectant couples and wealth, 107, 110–11
  socio-economic dynamics and demographic structures, 111–13

Vidin *(cont.)*
  socio-economic status and demographic transformation, 113–21, *115*, *116*, *118*, *119*
violence, 8, 16, 37
  and child slaves, 183–4
  classification of crimes, 156
  death sentences, 155–6
  law on degrees of culpability, 155
  law on juvenile criminality, 155–8
  murder in the family, reasons for, 159–65
  Romanian criminality sources, 154–5
  youth and violence towards parents, 151–73
  see also corporal punishment
virgins, 9, 186
vocational training *see* labour

wages, 202, 204, 207, 210, 212, 270, 326, 341–2
Wakid, Istir, 367
Wallachia, 16, 178
  age of criminality, 157
  classification of crimes, 156
  criminality sources, 154–5
  death sentences, 155–6
  law on criminality, 155–8, 165–6
  law on degrees of culpability, 155
  murder in the family, reasons for, 159–65
  as a province, 152–4
  Romanian criminality sources, 154–5
  violence towards parents, 151–73
*waqf*s, 315–16, 317, 318, 319, 323, 325, 328
wasiyy (guardian), 220–1, 222
wealth, 16, 32, 104
  and demographic trends, 107, *108*, *109*
  distribution by social groups, 117, *118*, *119*
  expectant couples and wealth, 107, 110–11
  and infant mortality, 111
  and numbers of surviving children, 114, *115*, *116*
  socio-economic dynamics and demographic structures, 111–13
  and tendency for fewer children, 120–2
Weinstein, Roni, 345–6
Western values/Westernisation, 5
wet nursing, 37, 372
women, 8, 10, 19, 144
  changing attitudes to, 363–4
  domestic ideology, 371
  girls' education, men's view of in the *nahda* period, 363–7
  al-Hashim's concepts, philosophy and vision for girls' education, 369–78
  and male servants, 89–90
  place in society, 143
  role in education, 323–4, 329, 338, 363–86
  woman question discourse, 364
Wordsworth, William, 35
workhouses, 39

Yabanabad, 201
yamak, 58, 68
Yaşa, Fırat, 12, 16–17, 177–95
yatim/yetim see orphans
*yaya-sancak*s, 59
Yazbak, Mahmoud, 17, 220–35
yeniçeri see janissaries
Yılmaz, Fikret, 62, 68
Yılmaz, Gülay, 1–30, 239–63
Yılmaz, Süleyman, 295
young men/girls, violence towards parents, 151–73
Yöntem, Ali Canip, 132
Yücel, Hasan Ali, 296–7, 299

Zachs, Fruma, 1–30, 346, 363–86
Zağra Yenicesi (Nova Zagora), 58
zakat, 222, 225, 228
Ze'evi, Dror, 246
Zimbabwe, 40
Zorlatuna, Halide Nusret, 294

EU representative:
Easy Access System Europe
Mustamäe tee 50, 10621 Tallinn, Estonia
Gpsr.requests@easproject.com

www.ingramcontent.com/pod-product-compliance
Lightning Source LLC
Chambersburg PA
CBHW061703300426
44115CB00014B/2544